Introduction to Information Retrieval

Introduction to Information Retrieval is the first textbook with a coherent treatment of classical and web information retrieval, including web search and the related areas of text classification and text clustering. Written from a computer science perspective, it gives an up-to-date treatment of all aspects of the design and implementation of systems for gathering, indexing, and searching documents and of methods for evaluating systems, along with an introduction to the use of machine learning methods on text collections.

Designed as the primary text for a graduate or advanced undergraduate course in information retrieval, the book will also interest researchers and professionals. A complete set of lecture slides and exercises that accompany the book are available on the web.

Christopher D. Manning is Associate Professor of Computer Science and Linguistics at Stanford University.

Prabhakar Raghavan is Head of Yahoo! Research and a Consulting Professor of Computer Science at Stanford University.

Hinrich Schütze is Chair of Theoretical Computational Linguistics at the Institute for Natural Language Processing, University of Stuttgart.

Introduction to Information Retrieval

Christopher D. Manning
Stanford University

Prabhakar Raghavan
Yahoo! Research

Hinrich Schütze
University of Stuttgart

CAMBRIDGE
UNIVERSITY PRESS

CAMBRIDGE UNIVERSITY PRESS
Cambridge, New York, Melbourne, Madrid, Cape Town, Singapore, São Paulo, Delhi

Cambridge University Press
32 Avenue of the Americas, New York, NY 10013-2473, USA

www.cambridge.org
Information on this title: www.cambridge.org/9780521865715

First published 2008
Reprinted 2008, 2009

Printed in the United States of America

A catalog record for this publication is available from the British Library.

Library of Congress Cataloging in Publication Data

Manning, Christopher D.
Introduction to information retrieval / Christopher D. Manning, Prabhakar
Raghavan, Hinrich Schütze.
    p. cm.
Includes bibliographical references and index.
ISBN 978-0-521-86571-5 (hardback)
1. Text processing (Computer science)   2. Information retrieval.   3. Document
clustering.   4. Semantic Web.   I. Raghavan, Prabhakar.   II. Schütze, Hinrich.
III. Title.
QA76.9.T48M26   2008
025.04 – dc22   2008001257

ISBN 978-0-521-86571-5 hardback

Contents

Table of Notation

df_t	108	The document frequency of term t (the total number of documents in the collection the term appears in)
H	91	Entropy
H_M	93	Mth harmonic number
$I(X; Y)$	252	Mutual information of random variables X and Y
idf_t	108	Inverse document frequency of term t
J	237	Number of classes
k	267	Top k items from a set, e.g., k nearest neighbors in kNN, top k retrieved documents, top k selected features from the vocabulary V
k	50	Sequence of k characters
K	326	Number of clusters
L_d	214	Length of document d (in tokens)
L_a	242	Length of the test document (or application document) in tokens
L_{ave}	64	Average length of a document (in tokens)
M	4	Size of the vocabulary ($|V|$)
M_a	242	Size of the vocabulary of the test document (or application document)
M_{ave}	71	Average size of the vocabulary in a document in the collection
M_d	218	Language model for document d
N	4	Number of documents in the retrieval or training collection
N_c	240	Number of documents in class c
$N(\omega)$	275	Number of times the event ω occurred
$O(\cdot)$	10	A bound on the complexity of an algorithm
$O(\cdot)$	203	The odds of an event
P	142	Precision
$P(\cdot)$	202	Probability
P	425	Transition probability matrix
q	55	A query
R	143	Recall
s_i	53	A string
s_i	103	Boolean values for zone scoring
$\mathrm{sim}(d_1, d_2)$	111	Similarity score for documents d_1, d_2
T	40	Total number of tokens in the document collection
T_{ct}	240	Number of occurrences of word t in documents of class c
t	4	Index of the tth term in the vocabulary V
t	56	A term in the vocabulary
$\mathrm{tf}_{t,d}$	107	The term frequency of term t in document d (the total number of occurrences of t in d)

U_t	246	Random variable taking values 0 (term t is present) and 1 (t is not present)
V	190	Vocabulary of terms $\{t_1, \ldots, t_M\}$ in a collection (a.k.a. the lexicon)
$\vec{v}(d)$	111	Length-normalized document vector
$\vec{V}(d)$	110	Vector of document d, not length normalized
$\mathrm{wf}_{t,d}$	115	Weight of term t in document d
w	103	A weight, for example, for zones or terms
$\vec{w}^\mathsf{T}\vec{x} = b$	269	Hyperplane; $\vec{w}$ is the normal vector of the hyperplane and w_i component i of $\vec{w}$
$\vec{x}$	204	Term incidence vector $\vec{x} = (x_1, \ldots, x_M)$; more generally: document feature representation
X	246	Random variable taking values in V, the vocabulary (e.g., at a given position k in a document)
$\mathbb{X}$	237	Document space in text classification
$|A|$	56	Set cardinality: the number of members of set A
$|S|$	370	Determinant of the square matrix S
$|s_i|$	53	Length in characters of string s_i
$|\vec{x}|$	128	Length of vector $\vec{x}$
$|\vec{x} - \vec{y}|$	121	Euclidean distance of $\vec{x}$ and $\vec{y}$ (which is the length of $(\vec{x} - \vec{y})$)

Preface

As recently as the 1990s, studies showed that most people preferred getting information from other people rather than from information retrieval (IR) systems. Of course, in that time period, most people also used human travel agents to book their travel. However, during the last decade, relentless optimization of information retrieval effectiveness has driven web search engines to new quality levels at which most people are satisfied most of the time, and web search has become a standard and often preferred source of information finding. For example, the 2004 Pew Internet Survey (Fallows 2004) found that "92% of Internet users say the Internet is a good place to go for getting everyday information." To the surprise of many, the field of information retrieval has moved from being a primarily academic discipline to being the basis underlying most people's preferred means of information access. This book presents the scientific underpinnings of this field, at a level accessible to graduate students as well as advanced undergraduates.

Information retrieval did not begin with the Web. In response to various challenges of providing information access, the field of IR evolved to give principled approaches to searching various forms of content. The field began with scientific publications and library records but soon spread to other forms of content, particularly those of information professionals, such as journalists, lawyers, and doctors. Much of the scientific research on IR has occurred in these contexts, and much of the continued practice of IR deals with providing access to unstructured information in various corporate and governmental domains, and this work forms much of the foundation of our book.

Nevertheless, in recent years, a principal driver of innovation has been the World Wide Web, unleashing publication at the scale of tens of millions of content creators. This explosion of published information would be moot if the information could not be found, annotated, and analyzed so that each user can quickly find information that is both relevant and comprehensive for their needs. By the late 1990s, many people felt that continuing to index the whole Web would rapidly become impossible, due to the Web's

exponential growth in size. But major scientific innovations, superb engineering, the rapidly declining price of computer hardware, and the rise of
a commercial underpinning for web search have all conspired to power today's major search engines, which are able to provide high-quality results
within subsecond response times for hundreds of millions of searches a day
over billions of web pages.

Book organization and course development

This book is the result of a series of courses we have taught at Stanford University and at the University of Stuttgart, in a range of durations including
a single quarter, one semester, and two quarters. These courses were aimed
at early stage graduate students in computer science, but we have also had
enrollment from upper-class computer science undergraduates, as well as
students from law, medical informatics, statistics, linguistics, and various engineering disciplines. The key design principle for this book, therefore, was
to cover what we believe to be important in a one-term graduate course on
IR. An additional principle is to build each chapter around material that we
believe can be covered in a single lecture of 75 to 90 minutes.

The first eight chapters of the book are devoted to the basics of information
retrieval and in particular the heart of search engines; we consider this material to be core to any course on information retrieval. Chapter 1 introduces
inverted indexes and shows how simple Boolean queries can be processed
using such indexes. Chapter 2 builds on this introduction by detailing the
manner in which documents are preprocessed before indexing and by discussing how inverted indexes are augmented in various ways for functionality and speed. Chapter 3 discusses search structures for dictionaries and
how to process queries that have spelling errors and other imprecise matches
to the vocabulary in the document collection being searched. Chapter 4 describes a number of algorithms for constructing the inverted index from a
text collection with particular attention to highly scalable and distributed algorithms that can be applied to very large collections. Chapter 5 covers techniques for compressing dictionaries and inverted indexes. These techniques
are critical for achieving subsecond response times to user queries in large
search engines. The indexes and queries considered in Chapters 1 through 5
only deal with *Boolean retrieval*, in which a document either matches a query
or does not. A desire to measure the *extent* to which a document matches a
query, or the score of a document for a query, motivates the development of
term weighting and the computation of scores in Chapters 6 and 7, leading
to the idea of a list of documents that are rank-ordered for a query. Chapter 8
focuses on the evaluation of an information retrieval system based on the
relevance of the documents it retrieves, allowing us to compare the relative

performances of different systems on benchmark document collections and queries.

Chapters 9 through 21 build on the foundation of the first eight chapters to cover a variety of more advanced topics. Chapter 9 discusses methods by which retrieval can be enhanced through the use of techniques like relevance feedback and query expansion, which aim at increasing the likelihood of retrieving relevant documents. Chapter 10 considers IR from documents that are structured with markup languages like XML and HTML. We treat structured retrieval by reducing it to the vector space scoring methods developed in Chapter 6. Chapters 11 and 12 invoke probability theory to compute scores for documents on queries. Chapter 11 develops traditional probabilistic IR, which provides a framework for computing the probability of relevance of a document, given a set of query terms. This probability may then be used as a score in ranking. Chapter 12 illustrates an alternative, wherein, for each document in a collection, we build a language model from which one can estimate a probability that the language model generates a given query. This probability is another quantity with which we can rank-order documents.

Chapters 13 through 18 give a treatment of various forms of machine learning and numerical methods in information retrieval. Chapters 13 through 15 treat the problem of classifying documents into a set of known categories, given a set of documents along with the classes they belong to. Chapter 13 motivates statistical classification as one of the key technologies needed for a successful search engine; introduces Naive Bayes, a conceptually simple and efficient text classification method; and outlines the standard methodology for evaluating text classifiers. Chapter 14 employs the vector space model from Chapter 6 and introduces two classification methods, Rocchio and k nearest neighbor (kNN), that operate on document vectors. It also presents the bias-variance tradeoff as an important characterization of learning problems that provides criteria for selecting an appropriate method for a text classification problem. Chapter 15 introduces support vector machines, which many researchers currently view as the most effective text classification method. We also develop connections in this chapter between the problem of classification and seemingly disparate topics such as the induction of scoring functions from a set of training examples.

Chapters 16, 17, and 18 consider the problem of inducing clusters of related documents from a collection. In Chapter 16, we first give an overview of a number of important applications of clustering in IR. We then describe two flat clustering algorithms: the K-means algorithm, an efficient and widely used document clustering method, and the expectation-maximization algorithm, which is computationally more expensive, but also more flexible. Chapter 17 motivates the need for hierarchically structured clusterings (instead of flat clusterings) in many applications in IR and introduces a number of clustering algorithms that produce a hierarchy of clusters. The chapter also addresses the difficult problem of automatically computing labels for clusters. Chapter 18 develops methods from linear algebra that constitute an extension of clustering and also offer intriguing prospects for algebraic methods in IR, which have been pursued in the approach of latent semantic indexing.

Chapters 19 through 21 treat the problem of web search. We give in Chapter 19 a summary of the basic challenges in web search, together with a set of techniques that are pervasive in web information retrieval. Next, Chapter 20 describes the architecture and requirements of a basic web crawler. Finally, Chapter 21 considers the power of link analysis in web search, using in the process several methods from linear algebra and advanced probability theory.

This book is not comprehensive in covering all topics related to IR. We have put aside a number of topics, which we deemed outside the scope of what we wished to cover in an introduction to IR class. Nevertheless, for people interested in these topics, we provide the following pointers to mainly textbook coverage:

Cross-language IR Grossman and Frieder 2004, ch. 4, and Oard and Dorr 1996.

Image and multimedia IR Grossman and Frieder 2004, ch. 4; Baeza-Yates and Ribeiro-Neto 1999, ch. 6; Baeza-Yates and Ribeiro-Neto 1999, ch. 11; Baeza-Yates and Ribeiro-Neto 1999, ch. 12; del Bimbo 1999; Lew 2001; and Smeulders et al. 2000.

Speech retrieval Coden et al. 2002.

Music retrieval Downie 2006 and http://www.ismir.net/.

User interfaces for IR Baeza-Yates and Ribeiro-Neto 1999, ch. 10.

Parallel and peer-to-peer IR Grossman and Frieder 2004, ch. 7; Baeza-Yates and Ribeiro-Neto 1999, ch. 9; and Aberer 2001.

Digital libraries Baeza-Yates and Ribeiro-Neto 1999, ch. 15, and Lesk 2004.

Information science perspective Korfhage 1997; Meadow et al. 1999; and Ingwersen and Järvelin 2005.

Logic-based approaches to IR van Rijsbergen 1989.

Natural language processing techniques Manning and Schütze 1999; Jurafsky and Martin 2008; and Lewis and Jones 1996.

Prerequisites

Introductory courses in data structures and algorithms, in linear algebra, and in probability theory suffice as prerequisites for all twenty-one chapters. We now give more detail for the benefit of readers and instructors who wish to tailor their reading to some of the chapters.

Chapters 1 through 5 assume as prerequisite a basic course in algorithms and data structures. Chapters 6 and 7 require, in addition, a knowledge of basic linear algebra, including vectors and dot products. No additional prerequisites are assumed until Chapter 11, for which a basic course in probability theory is required; Section 11.1 gives a quick review of the concepts necessary in Chapters 11, 12, and 13. Chapter 15 assumes that the reader is familiar with the notion of nonlinear optimization, although the chapter may be read without detailed knowledge of algorithms for nonlinear optimization. Chapter 18 demands a first course in linear algebra, including familiarity with the notions of matrix rank and eigenvectors; a brief review is given in Section 18.1. The knowledge of eigenvalues and eigenvectors is also necessary in Chapter 21.

Book layout

Worked examples in the text appear with a pencil sign next to them in the left margin. Advanced or difficult material appears in sections or subsections indicated with scissors in the margin. Exercises are marked in the margin with a question mark. The level of difficulty of exercises is indicated as easy [⋆], medium [⋆⋆], or difficult [⋆ ⋆ ⋆].

Acknowledgments

The authors thank Cambridge University Press for allowing us to make the draft book available online, which facilitated much of the feedback we have received while writing the book. We also thank Lauren Cowles, who has been an outstanding editor, providing several rounds of comments on each chapter; on matters of style, organization, and coverage; as well as detailed comments on the subject matter of the book. To the extent that we have achieved our goals in writing this book, she deserves an important part of the credit.

We are very grateful to the many people who have given us comments, suggestions, and corrections based on draft versions of this book. We thank for providing various corrections and comments: Cheryl Aasheim, Björn Andrist, Josh Attenberg, Luc Bélanger, Tom Breuel, Daniel Burckhardt, Georg Buscher, Fazli Can, Dinquan Chen, Ernest Davis, Pedro Domingos, Miklós Erdélyi, Rodrigo Panchiniak Fernandes, Paolo Ferragina, Norbert Fuhr, Vignesh Ganapathy, Elmer Garduno, Xiubo Geng, David Gondek, Sergio Govoni, Corinna Habets, Ben Handy, Donna Harman, Benjamin Haskell, Thomas Hühn, Deepak Jain, Ralf Jankowitsch, Dinakar Jayarajan, Vinay Kakade, Mei Kobayashi, Marek Kowalkiewicz, Wessel Kraaij, Rick Lafleur, Florian Laws, Hang Li, Juha Makkonen, David Mann, Ennio Masi, Frank McCown, Paul McNamee, Sven Meyer zu Eissen, Alexander Murzaku,

Gonzalo Navarro, Scott Olsson, Daniel Paiva, Tao Qin, Megha Ragha-van, Karthik Raghunathan, Ghulam Raza, Michal Rosen-Zvi, Klaus Rothenhäusler, Kenyu L. Runner, Alexander Salamanca, Grigory Sapunov, Tobias Scheffer, Nico Schlaefer, Evgeny Shadchnev, Ian Soboroff, Benno Stein, Marcin Sydow, Andrew Turner, Jason Utt, Huey Vo, Travis Wade, Mike Walsh, Changliang Wang, Renjing Wang, Thomas Zeume, and Dell Zhang.

Many people gave us detailed feedback on individual chapters, either at our request or through their own initiative. For this, we're particularly grateful to James Allan, Omar Alonso, Ismail Sengor Altingovde, Vo Ngoc Anh, Roi Blanco, Eric Breck, Eric Brown, Mark Carman, Carlos Castillo, Junghoo Cho, Aron Culotta, Doug Cutting, Meghana Deodhar, Susan Du-mais, Johannes Fürnkranz, Andreas Heß, Djoerd Hiemstra, David Hull, Thorsten Joachims, Siddharth Jonathan J. B., Jaap Kamps, Mounia Lalmas, Amy Langville, Nicholas Lester, Dave Lewis, Stephen Liu, Daniel Lowd, Yosi Mass, Jeff Michels, Alessandro Moschitti, Amir Najmi, Marc Najork, Giorgio Maria Di Nunzio, Paul Ogilvie, Priyank Patel, Jan Pedersen, Kathryn Ped-ings, Vassilis Plachouras, Daniel Ramage, Stefan Riezler, Michael Schiehlen, Helmut Schmid, Falk Nicolas Scholer, Sabine Schulte im Walde, Fabrizio Sebastiani, Sarabjeet Singh, Valentin I. Spitkovsky, Alexander Strehl, John Tait, Shivakumar Vaithyanathan, Ellen Voorhees, Gerhard Weikum, Dawid Weiss, Yiming Yang, Yisong Yue, Jian Zhang, and Justin Zobel.

And finally there were a few reviewers who absolutely stood out in terms of the quality and quantity of comments that they provided. We thank them for their significant impact on the content and structure of the book. We ex-press our gratitude to Pavel Berkhin, Stefan Büttcher, Jamie Callan, Byron Dom, Torsten Suel, and Andrew Trotman.

Parts of the initial drafts of Chapters 13, 14, and 15 were based on slides that were generously provided by Ray Mooney. Although the material has gone through extensive revisions, we gratefully acknowledge Ray's contri-bution to the three chapters in general and to the description of the time complexities of text classification algorithms in particular.

The above is unfortunately an incomplete list; we are still in the process of incorporating feedback we have received. And, like all opinionated authors, we did not always heed the advice that was so freely given. The published versions of the chapters remain solely the responsibility of the authors.

The authors thank Stanford University and the University of Stuttgart for providing a stimulating academic environment for discussing ideas and the opportunity to teach courses from which this book arose and in which its contents were refined. CM thanks his family for the many hours they've let him spend working on this book and hopes he'll have a bit more free time on weekends next year. PR thanks his family for their patient support through the writing of this book and is also grateful to Yahoo! Inc. for providing a fertile environment in which to work on this book. HS would like to thank his parents, family, and friends for their support while writing this book.

Web and contact information

This book has a companion website at http://informationretrieval.org. As well as links to some more general resources, it is our intention to maintain on this website a set of slides for each chapter that may be used for the corresponding lecture. We gladly welcome further feedback, corrections, and suggestions on the book, which may be sent to all the authors at informationretrieval@yahoogroups.com.

1 *Boolean retrieval*

The meaning of the term *information retrieval* (IR) can be very broad. Just getting a credit card out of your wallet so that you can type in the card number is a form of information retrieval. However, as an academic field of study, *information retrieval* might be defined thus:

INFORMATION
RETRIEVAL

> Information retrieval (IR) is finding material (usually documents) of an unstructured nature (usually text) that satisfies an information need from within large collections (usually stored on computers).

As defined in this way, information retrieval used to be an activity that only a few people engaged in: reference librarians, paralegals, and similar professional searchers. Now the world has changed, and hundreds of millions of people engage in information retrieval every day when they use a web search engine or search their email.[1] Information retrieval is fast becoming the dominant form of information access, overtaking traditional database-style searching (the sort that is going on when a clerk says to you: "I'm sorry, I can only look up your order if you can give me your order ID").

Information retrieval can also cover other kinds of data and information problems beyond that specified in the core definition above. The term "unstructured data" refers to data that does not have clear, semantically overt, easy-for-a-computer structure. It is the opposite of structured data, the canonical example of which is a relational database, of the sort companies usually use to maintain product inventories and personnel records. In reality, almost no data are truly "unstructured." This is definitely true of all text data if you count the latent linguistic structure of human languages. But even accepting that the intended notion of structure is overt structure, most text has structure, such as headings, paragraphs, and footnotes, which is commonly represented in documents by explicit markup (such as the coding underlying web pages). Information retrieval is also used to facilitate "semistructured"

---

[1] In modern parlance, the word "search" has tended to replace "(information) retrieval"; the term "search" is quite ambiguous, but in context we use the two synonymously.

search such as finding a document where the title contains Java and the body contains threading.

The field of IR also covers supporting users in browsing or filtering document collections or further processing a set of retrieved documents. Given a set of documents, clustering is the task of coming up with a good grouping of the documents based on their contents. It is similar to arranging books on a bookshelf according to their topic. Given a set of topics, standing information needs, or other categories (such as suitability of texts for different age groups), classification is the task of deciding which class(es), if any, each of a set of documents belongs to. It is often approached by first manually classifying some documents and then hoping to be able to classify new documents automatically.

Information retrieval systems can also be distinguished by the scale at which they operate, and it is useful to distinguish three prominent scales. In *web search*, the system has to provide search over billions of documents stored on millions of computers. Distinctive issues are needing to gather documents for indexing, being able to build systems that work efficiently at this enormous scale, and handling particular aspects of the web, such as the exploitation of hypertext and not being fooled by site providers manipulating page content in an attempt to boost their search engine rankings, given the commercial importance of the web. We focus on all these issues in Chapters 19–21. At the other extreme is *personal information retrieval*. In the last few years, consumer operating systems have integrated information retrieval (such as Apple's Mac OS X Spotlight or Windows Vista's Instant Search). Email programs usually not only provide search but also text classification: they at least provide a spam (junk mail) filter, and commonly also provide either manual or automatic means for classifying mail so that it can be placed directly into particular folders. Distinctive issues here include handling the broad range of document types on a typical personal computer, and making the search system maintenance free and sufficiently lightweight in terms of startup, processing, and disk space usage that it can run on one machine without annoying its owner. In between is the space of *enterprise, institutional,* and *domain-specific search*, where retrieval might be provided for collections such as a corporation's internal documents, a database of patents, or research articles on biochemistry. In this case, the documents are typically stored on centralized file systems and one or a handful of dedicated machines provide search over the collection. This book contains techniques of value over this whole spectrum, but our coverage of some aspects of parallel and distributed search in web-scale search systems is comparatively light owing to the relatively small published literature on the details of such systems. However, outside of a handful of web search companies, a software developer is most likely to encounter the personal search and enterprise scenarios.

In this chapter, we begin with a very simple example of an IR problem, and introduce the idea of a term-document matrix (Section 1.1) and the central inverted index data structure (Section 1.2). We then examine the Boolean retrieval model and how Boolean queries are processed (Sections 1.3 and 1.4).

1.1 An example information retrieval problem

A fat book that many people own is *Shakespeare's Collected Works*. Suppose you wanted to determine which plays of Shakespeare contain the words Brutus AND Caesar AND NOT Calpurnia. One way to do that is to start at the beginning and to read through all the text, noting for each play whether it contains Brutus and Caesar and excluding it from consideration if it contains Calpurnia. The simplest form of document retrieval is for a computer to do this sort of linear scan through documents. This process is commonly GREP referred to as *grepping* through text, after the Unix command grep, which performs this process. Grepping through text can be a very effective process, especially given the speed of modern computers, and often allows useful possibilities for wildcard pattern matching through the use of regular expressions. With modern computers, for simple querying of modest collections (the size of *Shakespeare's Collected Works* is a bit under one million words of text in total), you really need nothing more.

But for many purposes, you do need more:

1. To process large document collections quickly. The amount of online data has grown at least as quickly as the speed of computers, and we would now like to be able to search collections that total in the order of billions to trillions of words.
2. To allow more flexible matching operations. For example, it is impractical to perform the query Romans NEAR countrymen with grep, where NEAR might be defined as "within 5 words" or "within the same sentence."
3. To allow ranked retrieval. In many cases, you want the best answer to an information need among many documents that contain certain words.

INDEX   The way to avoid linearly scanning the texts for each query is to *index* the documents in advance. Let us stick with *Shakespeare's Collected Works*, and use it to introduce the basics of the Boolean retrieval model. Suppose we record for each document – here a play of Shakespeare's – whether it contains each word out of all the words Shakespeare used (Shakespeare used about 32,000 INCIDENCE different words). The result is a binary term-document *incidence matrix*, as in MATRIX Figure 1.1. *Terms* are the indexed units (further discussed in Section 2.2); they TERM are usually words, and for the moment you can think of them as words, but the information retrieval literature normally speaks of terms because some of them, such as perhaps I-9 or Hong Kong are not usually thought of as words. Now, depending on whether we look at the matrix rows or columns, we can

	Antony and Cleopatra	Julius Caesar	The Tempest	Hamlet	Othello	Macbeth	...
Antony	1	1	0	0	0	1	
Brutus	1	1	0	1	0	0	
Caesar	1	1	0	1	1	1	
Calpurnia	0	1	0	0	0	0	
Cleopatra	1	0	0	0	0	0	
mercy	1	0	1	1	1	1	
worser	1	0	1	1	1	0	
...							

Figure 1.1 A term-document incidence matrix. Matrix element (t, d) is 1 if the play in column d contains the word in row t, and is 0 otherwise.

have a vector for each term, which shows the documents it appears in, or a vector for each document, showing the terms that occur in it.[2]

To answer the query Brutus AND Caesar AND NOT Calpurnia, we take the vectors for Brutus, Caesar and Calpurnia, complement the last, and then do a bitwise AND:

110100 AND 110111 AND 101111 = 100100

The answers for this query are thus *Antony and Cleopatra* and *Hamlet* (Figure 1.2).

The *Boolean retrieval model* is a model for information retrieval in which we BOOLEAN can pose any query which is in the form of a Boolean expression of terms, RETRIEVAL that is, in which terms are combined with the operators AND, OR, and NOT. MODEL The model views each document as just a set of words.

Let us now consider a more realistic scenario, simultaneously using the opportunity to introduce some terminology and notation. Suppose we have DOCUMENT $N = 1$ million documents. By *documents* we mean whatever units we have decided to build a retrieval system over. They might be individual memos or chapters of a book (see Section 2.1.2 (page 20) for further discussion). We refer to the group of documents over which we perform retrieval as the (doc-COLLECTION ument) *collection*. It is sometimes also referred to as a *corpus* (a *body* of texts). CORPUS Suppose each document is about 1,000 words long (2–3 book pages). If we assume an average of 6 bytes per word including spaces and punctuation, then this is a document collection about 6 gigabytes (GB) in size. Typically, there might be about $M = 500,000$ distinct terms in these documents. There is nothing special about the numbers we have chosen, and they might vary by an order of magnitude or more, but they give us some idea of the dimensions of the kinds of problems we need to handle. We will discuss and model these size assumptions in Section 5.1 (page 79).

AD HOC Our goal is to develop a system to address the *ad hoc retrieval* task. This is RETRIEVAL the most standard IR task. In it, a system aims to provide documents from

[2] Formally, we take the transpose of the matrix to be able to get the terms as column vectors.

Antony and Cleopatra, Act III, Scene ii
Agrippa [Aside to Domitius Enobarbus]:   Why, Enobarbus,
When Antony found Julius Caesar dead,
He cried almost to roaring; and he wept
When at Philippi he found Brutus slain.

Hamlet, Act III, Scene ii
Lord Polonius: I did enact Julius Caesar: I was killed i' the
Capitol; Brutus killed me.

Figure 1.2 Results from Shakespeare for the query Brutus AND Caesar AND NOT Calpurnia.

within the collection that are relevant to an arbitrary user information need, communicated to the system by means of a one-off, user-initiated query. An INFORMATION *information need* is the topic about which the user desires to know more, and NEED is differentiated from a *query*, which is what the user conveys to the com-QUERY puter in an attempt to communicate the information need. A document is RELEVANCE *relevant* if it is one that the user perceives as containing information of value with respect to their personal information need. Our example above was rather artificial in that the information need was defined in terms of particular words, whereas, usually a user is interested in a topic like "pipeline leaks" and would like to find relevant documents regardless of whether they precisely use those words or express the concept with other words such as EFFECTIVENESS pipeline rupture. To assess the *effectiveness* of an IR system (the quality of its search results), a user usually wants to know two key statistics about the system's returned results for a query:

PRECISION   *Precision*: What fraction of the returned results are relevant to the information need?

RECALL   *Recall*: What fraction of the relevant documents in the collection were returned by the system?

Detailed discussion of relevance and evaluation measures including precision and recall is found in Chapter 8.

We now cannot build a term-document matrix in a naive way. A 500K × 1M matrix has half-a-trillion 0's and 1's – too many to fit in a computer's memory. But the crucial observation is that the matrix is extremely sparse, that is, it has few nonzero entries. Because each document is 1,000 words long, the matrix has no more than one billion 1's, so a minimum of 99.8% of the cells are zero. A much better representation is to record only the things that do occur, that is, the 1 positions.

This idea is central to the first major concept in information retrieval, INVERTED the *inverted index*. The name is actually redundant: an index always maps INDEX back from terms to the parts of a document where they occur. Nevertheless, *inverted index*, or sometimes *inverted file*, has become the standard term in

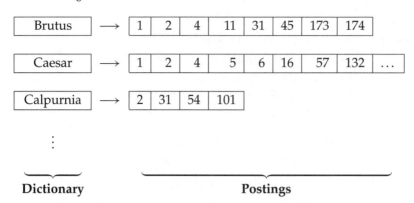

Dictionary   **Postings**

Figure 1.3 The two parts of an inverted index. The dictionary is commonly kept in memory, with pointers to each postings list, which is stored on disk.

IR.[3] The basic idea of an inverted index is shown in Figure 1.3. We keep a
DICTIONARY   *dictionary* of terms (sometimes also referred to as a *vocabulary* or *lexicon*; in
VOCABULARY   this book, we use *dictionary* for the data structure and *vocabulary* for the set of
LEXICON   terms). Then, for each term, we have a list that records which documents the
term occurs in. Each item in the list – which records that a term appeared in
a document (and, later, often, the positions in the document) – is convention-
POSTING   ally called a *posting*.[4] The list is then called a *postings list* (or inverted list),
POSTINGS LIST and all the postings lists taken together are referred to as the *postings*. The
POSTINGS   dictionary in Figure 1.3 has been sorted alphabetically and each postings list
is sorted by document ID. We see why this is useful in Section 1.3; later, we
also consider alternatives to doing this (Section 7.1.5).

1.2 A first take at building an inverted index

To gain the speed benefits of indexing at retrieval time, we have to build the
index in advance. The major steps in this are:

1. Collect the documents to be indexed:

   | Friends, Romans, countrymen. | So let it be with Caesar | ...

2. Tokenize the text, turning each document into a list of tokens:

   | Friends | Romans | countrymen | So | ...

---

[3] Some IR researchers prefer the term inverted file, but expressions like index construction and index compression are much more common than inverted file construction and inverted file compression. For consistency, we use (inverted) index throughout this book.

[4] In a (nonpositional) inverted index, a posting is just a document ID, but it is inherently associated with a term, via the postings list it is placed on; sometimes we will also talk of a (term, docID) pair as a posting.

3. Do linguistic preprocessing, producing a list of normalized tokens, which are the indexing terms:

| friend | roman | countryman | so | ...

4. Index the documents that each term occurs in by creating an inverted index, consisting of a dictionary and postings.

We define and discuss the earlier stages of processing, that is, steps 1–3, in Section 2.2. Until then you can think of *tokens* and *normalized tokens* as also loosely equivalent to *words*. Here, we assume that the first three steps have already been done, and we examine building a basic inverted index by sort-based indexing.

Within a document collection, we assume that each document has a unique serial number, known as the document identifier (*docID*). During index construction, we can simply assign successive integers to each new document when it is first encountered. The input to indexing is a list of normalized tokens for each document, which we can equally think of as a list of pairs of term and docID, as in Figure 1.4. The core indexing step is *sorting* this list so that the terms are alphabetical, giving us the representation in the middle column of Figure 1.4. Multiple occurrences of the same term from the same document are then merged.[5] Instances of the same term are then grouped, and the result is split into a *dictionary* and *postings*, as shown in the right column of Figure 1.4. Because a term generally occurs in a number of documents, this data organization already reduces the storage requirements of the index. The dictionary also records some statistics, such as the number of documents which contain each term (the *document frequency*, which is here also the length of each postings list). This information is not vital for a basic Boolean search engine, but it allows us to improve the efficiency of the search engine at query time, and it is a statistic later used in many ranked retrieval models. The postings are secondarily sorted by docID. This provides the basis for efficient query processing. This inverted index structure is essentially without rival as the most efficient structure for supporting ad hoc text search.

In the resulting index, we pay for storage of both the dictionary and the postings lists. The latter are much larger, but the dictionary is commonly kept in memory, and postings lists are normally kept on disk, so the size of each is important. In Chapter 5, we examine how each can be optimized for storage and access efficiency. What data structure should be used for a postings list? A fixed length array would be wasteful; some words occur in many documents, and others in very few. For an in-memory postings list, two good alternatives are singly linked lists or variable length arrays. *Singly linked lists* allow cheap insertion of documents into postings lists (following updates, such as when recrawling the web for updated documents), and naturally extend

DOCID

SORTING

DOCUMENT FREQUENCY

---

[5] Unix users can note that these steps are similar to use of the `sort` and then `uniq` commands.

Doc 1

I did enact Julius Caesar: I was
killed i' the Capitol; Brutus killed
me.

Doc 2

So let it be with Caesar. The noble
Brutus hath told you Caesar was
ambitious:

term	docID
I	1
did	1
enact	1
julius	1
caesar	1
I	1
was	1
killed	1
i'	1
the	1
capitol	1
brutus	1
killed	1
me	1
so	2
let	2
it	2
be	2
with	2
caesar	2
the	2
noble	2
brutus	2
hath	2
told	2
you	2
caesar	2
was	2
ambitious	2

$\Longrightarrow$

term	docID
ambitious	2
be	2
brutus	1
brutus	2
capitol	1
caesar	1
caesar	2
caesar	2
did	1
enact	1
hath	1
I	1
I	1
i'	1
it	2
julius	1
killed	1
killed	1
let	2
me	1
noble	2
so	2
the	1
the	2
told	2
you	2
was	1
was	2
with	2

$\Longrightarrow$

term	doc. freq.	$\rightarrow$	postings lists
ambitious	1	$\rightarrow$	2
be	1	$\rightarrow$	2
brutus	2	$\rightarrow$	1 $\rightarrow$ 2
capitol	1	$\rightarrow$	1
caesar	2	$\rightarrow$	1 $\rightarrow$ 2
did	1	$\rightarrow$	1
enact	1	$\rightarrow$	1
hath	1	$\rightarrow$	2
I	1	$\rightarrow$	1
i'	1	$\rightarrow$	1
it	1	$\rightarrow$	2
julius	1	$\rightarrow$	1
killed	1	$\rightarrow$	1
let	1	$\rightarrow$	2
me	1	$\rightarrow$	1
noble	1	$\rightarrow$	2
so	1	$\rightarrow$	2
the	2	$\rightarrow$	1 $\rightarrow$ 2
told	1	$\rightarrow$	2
you	1	$\rightarrow$	2
was	2	$\rightarrow$	1 $\rightarrow$ 2
with	1	$\rightarrow$	2

Figure 1.4 Building an index by sorting and grouping. The sequence of terms in each document, tagged by their documentID (*left*) is sorted alphabetically (*middle*). Instances of the same term are then grouped by word and then by documentID. The terms and documentIDs are then separated out (*right*). The dictionary stores the terms, and has a pointer to the postings list for each term. It commonly also stores other summary information such as, here, the document frequency of each term. We use this information for improving query time efficiency and, later, for weighting in ranked retrieval models. Each postings list stores the list of documents in which a term occurs, and may store other information such as the term frequency (the frequency of each term in each document) or the position(s) of the term in each document.

to more advanced indexing strategies such as skip lists (Section 2.3), which require additional pointers. *Variable length arrays* win in space requirements by avoiding the overhead for pointers and in time requirements because their use of contiguous memory increases speed on modern processors with memory caches. Extra pointers can in practice be encoded into the lists as offsets. If updates are relatively infrequent, variable length arrays are more compact and faster to traverse. We can also use a hybrid scheme, with a linked list of fixed length arrays for each term. When postings lists are stored on disk, they are stored (perhaps compressed) as a contiguous run of postings without explicit pointers (as in Figure 1.3), so as to minimize the size of the postings list and the number of disk seeks to read a postings list into memory.

? **Exercise 1.1** [⋆] Draw the inverted index that would be built for the following document collection. (See Figure 1.3 for an example.)

Doc 1   new home sales top forecasts
Doc 2   home sales rise in july
Doc 3   increase in home sales in july
Doc 4   july new home sales rise

Exercise 1.2 [⋆] Consider these documents:

Doc 1   breakthrough drug for schizophrenia
Doc 2   new schizophrenia drug
Doc 3   new approach for treatment of schizophrenia
Doc 4   new hopes for schizophrenia patients

a. Draw the term-document incidence matrix for this document collection.

b. Draw the inverted index representation for this collection, as in Figure 1.3 (page 6).

Exercise 1.3 [⋆] For the document collection shown in Exercise 1.2, what are the returned results for these queries?

a. schizophrenia AND drug

b. for AND NOT (drug OR approach)

1.3 Processing Boolean queries

SIMPLE How do we process a query using an inverted index and the basic Boolean
CONJUNCTIVE retrieval model? Consider processing the *simple conjunctive query*:
QUERIES

(1.1)   Brutus AND Calpurnia

over the inverted index partially shown in Figure 1.3 (page 6). We:

1. Locate Brutus in the dictionary.
2. Retrieve its postings.
3. Locate Calpurnia in the dictionary.

Brutus $\longrightarrow$ $\boxed{1}\to\boxed{2}\to\boxed{4}\to\boxed{11}\to\boxed{31}\to\boxed{45}\to\boxed{173}\to\boxed{174}$

Calpurnia $\longrightarrow$ $\boxed{2}\to\boxed{31}\to\boxed{54}\to\boxed{101}$

Intersection $\implies$ $\boxed{2}\to\boxed{31}$

Figure 1.5 Intersecting the postings lists for Brutus and Calpurnia from Figure 1.3.

4. Retrieve its postings.

5. Intersect the two postings lists, as shown in Figure 1.5.

POSTINGS LIST   The *intersection* operation is the crucial one: We need to efficiently intersect
INTERSECTION   postings lists so as to be able to quickly find documents that contain both
POSTINGS   terms. (This operation is sometimes referred to as *merging* postings lists, this
MERGE   slightly counterintuitive name reflects using the term *merge algorithm* for a
general family of algorithms that combine multiple sorted lists by inter-
leaved advancing of pointers through each; here we are merging the lists
with a logical AND operation.)

There is a simple and effective method of intersecting postings lists using
the merge algorithm (see Figure 1.6): We maintain pointers into both lists and
walk through the two postings lists simultaneously, in time linear in the total number of postings entries. At each step, we compare the docID pointed
to by both pointers. If they are the same, we put that docID in the results
list, and advance both pointers. Otherwise we advance the pointer pointing
to the smaller docID. If the lengths of the postings lists are x and y, the intersection takes $O(x + y)$ operations. Formally, the complexity of querying
is $\Theta(N)$, where N is the number of documents in the collection.[6] Our indexing methods gain us just a constant, not a difference in Θ time complexity
compared with a linear scan, but in practice the constant is huge. To use this
algorithm, it is crucial that postings be sorted by a single global ordering.
Using a numeric sort by docID is one simple way to achieve this.

We can extend the intersection operation to process more complicated
queries like:

(1.2)   (Brutus OR Caesar) AND NOT Calpurnia

QUERY   *Query optimization* is the process of selecting how to organize the work of an-
OPTIMIZATION   swering a query so that the least total amount of work needs to be done by
the system. A major element of this for Boolean queries is the order in which
postings lists are accessed. What is the best order for query processing? Consider a query that is an AND of t terms, for instance:

(1.3)   Brutus AND Caesar AND Calpurnia

---

[6] The notation $\Theta(\cdot)$ is used to express an asymptotically tight bound on the complexity of
an algorithm. Informally, this is often written as $O(\cdot)$, but this notation really expresses an
asymptotic upper bound, which need not be tight (Cormen et al. 1990).

INTERSECT(p_1, p_2)
```
 1  answer ← ⟨ ⟩
 2  while p₁ ≠ NIL and p₂ ≠ NIL
 3  do if docID(p₁) = docID(p₂)
 4      then ADD(answer, docID(p₁))
 5          p₁ ← next(p₁)
 6          p₂ ← next(p₂)
 7      else if docID(p₁) < docID(p₂)
 8              then p₁ ← next(p₁)
 9              else  p₂ ← next(p₂)
10  return answer
```

Figure 1.6   Algorithm for the intersection of two postings lists p_1 and p_2.

For each of the t terms, we need to get its postings, then AND them together. The standard heuristic is to process terms in order of increasing document frequency; if we start by intersecting the two smallest postings lists, then all intermediate results must be no bigger than the smallest postings list, and we are therefore likely to do the least amount of total work. So, for the postings lists in Figure 1.3 (page 6), we execute the above query as:

(1.4)   (Calpurnia AND Brutus) AND Caesar

This is a first justification for keeping the frequency of terms in the dictionary; it allows us to make this ordering decision based on in-memory data before accessing any postings list.

Consider now the optimization of more general queries, such as:

(1.5)   (madding OR crowd) AND (ignoble OR strife) AND (killed OR slain)

As before, we get the frequencies for all terms, and we can then (conservatively) estimate the size of each OR by the sum of the frequencies of its disjuncts. We can then process the query in increasing order of the size of each disjunctive term.

For arbitrary Boolean queries, we have to evaluate and temporarily store the answers for intermediate expressions in a complex expression. However, in many circumstances, either because of the nature of the query language, or just because this is the most common type of query that users submit, a query is purely conjunctive. In this case, rather than viewing merging postings lists as a function with two inputs and a distinct output, it is more efficient to intersect each retrieved postings list with the current intermediate result in memory, where we initialize the intermediate result by loading the postings list of the least frequent term. This algorithm is shown in Figure 1.7. The intersection operation is then asymmetric: The intermediate results list is in memory while the list it is being intersected with is being read from disk. Moreover, the intermediate results list is always at least as short as the other list, and in many cases it is orders of magnitude shorter. The postings

INTERSECT($\langle t_1, \ldots, t_n \rangle$)
1   *terms* ← SORTBYINCREASINGFREQUENCY($\langle t_1, \ldots, t_n \rangle$)
2   *result* ← *postings*(*first*(*terms*))
3   *terms* ← *rest*(*terms*)
4   **while** *terms* ≠ NIL and *result* ≠ NIL
5   **do** *result* ← INTERSECT(*result*, *postings*(*first*(*terms*)))
6   *terms* ← *rest*(*terms*)
7   **return** *result*

Figure 1.7 Algorithm for conjunctive queries that returns the set of documents containing each term in the input list of terms.

intersection can still be done by the algorithm in Figure 1.6, but when the difference between the list lengths is very large, opportunities to use alternative techniques open up. The intersection can be calculated in place by destructively modifying or marking invalid items in the intermediate results list. Or the intersection can be done as a sequence of binary searches in the long postings lists for each posting in the intermediate results list. Another possibility is to store the long postings list as a hashtable, so that membership of an intermediate result item can be calculated in constant rather than linear or log time. However, such alternative techniques are difficult to combine with postings list compression of the sort discussed in Chapter 5. Moreover, standard postings list intersection operations remain necessary when both terms of a query are very common.

Exercise 1.4 [⋆] For the queries below, can we still run through the intersection in time $O(x + y)$, where x and y are the lengths of the postings lists for Brutus and Caesar? If not, what can we achieve?
   a. Brutus AND NOT Caesar
   b. Brutus OR NOT Caesar

Exercise 1.5 [⋆] Extend the postings merge algorithm to arbitrary Boolean query formulas. What is its time complexity? For instance, consider:
   c. (Brutus OR Caesar) AND NOT (Antony OR Cleopatra)
Can we always merge in linear time? Linear in what? Can we do better than this?

Exercise 1.6 [⋆⋆] We can use distributive laws for AND and OR to rewrite queries.
   a. Show how to rewrite the query in Exercise 1.5 into disjunctive normal form using the distributive laws.
   b. Would the resulting query be more or less efficiently evaluated than the original form of this query?
   c. Is this result true in general or does it depend on the words and the contents of the document collection?

Exercise 1.7 [⋆] Recommend a query processing order for

   d. (tangerine OR trees) AND (marmalade OR skies) AND (kaleidoscope OR eyes)

given the following postings list sizes:

Term	Postings size
eyes	213312
kaleidoscope	87009
marmalade	107913
skies	271658
tangerine	46653
trees	316812

Exercise 1.8 [⋆] If the query is:

   e. friends AND romans AND (NOT countrymen)

how could we use the frequency of countrymen in evaluating the best query evaluation order? In particular, propose a way of handling negation in determining the order of query processing.

Exercise 1.9 [⋆⋆] For a conjunctive query, is processing postings lists in order of size guaranteed to be optimal? Explain why it is, or give an example where it is not.

Exercise 1.10 [⋆⋆] Write out a postings merge algorithm, in the style of Figure 1.6 (page 11), for an x OR y query.

Exercise 1.11 [⋆⋆] How should the Boolean query x AND NOT y be handled? Why is naive evaluation of this query normally very expensive? Write out a postings merge algorithm that evaluates this query efficiently.

1.4 The extended Boolean model versus ranked retrieval

RANKED
RETRIEVAL
MODELS
The Boolean retrieval model contrasts with *ranked retrieval models* such as the vector space model (Section 6.3), in which users largely use *free text queries*, that is, just typing one or more words rather than using a precise language
FREE TEXT
QUERIES
with operators for building up query expressions, and the system decides which documents best satisfy the query. Despite decades of academic research on the advantages of ranked retrieval, systems implementing the Boolean retrieval model were the main or only search option provided by large commercial information providers for three decades until the early 1990s (approximately the date of arrival of the World Wide Web). However, these systems did not have just the basic Boolean operations (AND, OR, and NOT) that have been presented so far. A strict Boolean expression over terms with an unordered results set is too limited for many of the information needs that people have, and these systems implemented extended Boolean retrieval models by incorporating additional operators such as term proximity

PROXIMITY operators. A *proximity operator* is a way of specifying that two terms in a
OPERATOR query must occur close to each other in a document, where closeness may
be measured by limiting the allowed number of intervening words or by
reference to a structural unit such as a sentence or paragraph.

 Example 1.1: Commercial Boolean searching: Westlaw. Westlaw (http://
www.westlaw.com/) is the largest commercial legal search service (in terms
of the number of paying subscribers), with over half a million subscribers
performing millions of searches a day over tens of terabytes of text data.
The service was started in 1975. In 2005, Boolean search (called *Terms and
Connectors* by Westlaw) was still the default, and used by a large percentage of users, although ranked free text querying (called *Natural Language*
by Westlaw) was added in 1992. Here are some example Boolean queries
on Westlaw:

Information need: Information on the legal theories involved in preventing
the disclosure of trade secrets by employees formerly employed by a competing company.
Query: "trade secret" /s disclos! /s prevent /s employe!

Information need: Requirements for disabled people to be able to access a
workplace.
Query: disab! /p access! /s work-site work-place (employment /3 place)

Information need: Cases about a host's responsibility for drunk guests.
Query: host! /p (responsib! liab!) /p (intoxicat! drunk!) /p guest

Note the long, precise queries and the use of proximity operators, both
uncommon in web search. Submitted queries average about ten words in
length. Unlike web search conventions, a space between words represents
disjunction (the tightest binding operator), & is AND and /s, /p, and /*k*
ask for matches in the same sentence, same paragraph or within *k* words
respectively. Double quotes give a *phrase search* (consecutive words); see
Section 2.4 (page 36). The exclamation mark (!) gives a trailing wildcard
query (see Section 3.2, page 48); thus liab! matches all words starting with
liab. Additionally work-site matches any of *worksite*, *work-site* or *work site*;
see Section 2.2.1. Typical expert queries are usually carefully defined and
incrementally developed until they obtain what look to be good results to
the user.

Many users, particularly professionals, prefer Boolean query models.
Boolean queries are precise: A document either matches the query or it
does not. This offers the user greater control and transparency over what
is retrieved. And some domains, such as legal materials, allow an effective means of document ranking within a Boolean model: Westlaw returns documents in reverse chronological order, which is in practice quite

effective. In 2007, the majority of law librarians still seem to recommend terms and connectors for high recall searches, and the majority of legal users think they are getting greater control by using them. However, this does not mean that Boolean queries are more effective for professional searchers. Indeed, experimenting on a Westlaw subcollection, Turtle (1994) found that free text queries produced better results than Boolean queries prepared by Westlaw's own reference librarians for the majority of the information needs in his experiments. A general problem with Boolean search is that using AND operators tends to produce high precision but low recall searches, while using OR operators gives low precision but high recall searches, and it is difficult or impossible to find a satisfactory middle ground.

In this chapter, we have looked at the structure and construction of a basic inverted index, comprising a dictionary and postings lists. We introduced the Boolean retrieval model, and examined how to do efficient retrieval via linear time merges and simple query optimization. In Chapters 2–7, we consider in detail richer query models and the sort of augmented index structures that are needed to handle them efficiently. Here we just mention a few of the main additional things we would like to be able to do.

1. We would like to better determine the set of terms in the dictionary and to provide retrieval that is tolerant to spelling mistakes and inconsistent choice of words.
2. It is often useful to search for compounds or phrases that denote a concept such as "operating system." As the Westlaw examples show, we might also wish to do proximity queries such as Gates NEAR Microsoft. To answer such queries, the index has to be augmented to capture the proximities of terms in documents.
3. A Boolean model only records term presence or absence, but often we would like to accumulate evidence, giving more weight to documents that have a term several times as opposed to ones that contain it only once. To TERM be able to do this we need *term frequency* information (the number of times FREQUENCY a term occurs in a document) in postings lists.
4. Boolean queries just retrieve a set of matching documents, but commonly we wish to have an effective method to order (or *rank*) the returned results. This requires having a mechanism for determining a document score which encapsulates how good a match a document is for a query.

With these additional ideas, we will have seen most of the basic technology that supports ad hoc searching over unstructured information. Ad hoc searching over documents has recently conquered the world, powering not only web search engines but the kind of unstructured search that lies behind the large eCommerce web sites. Although the main web search engines differ by emphasizing free text querying, most of the basic issues and technologies of indexing and querying remain the same, as we will see in later chapters. Moreover, over time, web search engines have added at least partial implementations of some of the most popular operators from extended Boolean models: phrase search is especially popular and most have a very partial implementation of Boolean operators. Nevertheless, although these options are liked by expert searchers, they are little used by most people and are not the main focus in work on trying to improve web search engine performance.

? **Exercise 1.12** [$\star$] Write a query using Westlaw syntax that would find any of the words professor, teacher, or lecturer in the same sentence as a form of the verb explain.

Exercise 1.13 [$\star$] Try using the Boolean search features on a couple of major web search engines. For instance, choose a word, such as burglar, and submit the queries (i) burglar, (ii) burglar AND burglar, and (iii) burglar OR burglar. Look at the estimated number of results and top hits. Do they make sense in terms of Boolean logic? Often they haven't for major search engines. Can you make sense of what is going on? What about if you try different words? For example, query for (i) knight, (ii) conquer, and then (iii) knight OR conquer. What bound should the number of results from the first two queries place on the third query? Is this bound observed?

1.5 References and further reading

The practical pursuit of computerized information retrieval began in the late 1940s (Cleverdon 1991; Liddy 2005). A great increase in the production of scientific literature, much in the form of less formal technical reports rather than traditional journal articles, coupled with the availability of computers, led to interest in automatic document retrieval. However, in those days, document retrieval was always based on author, title, and keywords; full-text search came much later.

The article by Bush (1945) provided lasting inspiration for the new field:

Consider a future device for individual use, which is a sort of mechanized private file and library. It needs a name, and, to coin one at random, 'memex' will do. A memex is a device in which an individual stores all his books, records, and communications, and which is mechanized so that it may be consulted with exceeding speed and flexibility. It is an enlarged intimate supplement to his memory.

The term *information retrieval* was coined by Calvin Mooers in 1948/1950 (Mooers 1950).

In 1958, much newspaper attention was paid to demonstrations at a conference (see Taube and Wooster 1958) of IBM "auto-indexing" machines, based primarily on the work of H. P. Luhn. Commercial interest quickly gravitated toward Boolean retrieval systems, but the early years saw a heady debate over various disparate technologies for retrieval systems. For example, Mooers (1961) dissented:

> It is a common fallacy, underwritten at this date by the investment of several million dollars in a variety of retrieval hardware, that the algebra of George Boole (1847) is the appropriate formalism for retrieval system design. This view is as widely and uncritically accepted as it is wrong.

The observation of AND versus OR giving you opposite extremes in a precision/recall tradeoff, but not the middle ground comes from (Lee and Fox 1988).

The book (Witten et al. 1999) is the standard reference for an in-depth comparison of the space and time efficiency of the inverted index versus other possible data structures; a more succinct and up-to-date presentation appears in Zobel and Moffat (2006). We further discuss several approaches in Chapter 5.

REGULAR   Friedl (2006) covers the practical usage of *regular expressions* for searching. EXPRESSIONS The underlying computer science appears in (Hopcroft et al. 2000).

2 The term vocabulary and postings lists

Recall the major steps in inverted index construction:

1. Collect the documents to be indexed.
2. Tokenize the text.
3. Do linguistic preprocessing of tokens.
4. Index the documents that each term occurs in.

In this chapter, we first briefly mention how the basic unit of a document can be defined and how the character sequence that it comprises is determined (Section 2.1). We then examine in detail some of the substantive linguistic issues of tokenization and linguistic preprocessing, which determine the vocabulary of terms that a system uses (Section 2.2). *Tokenization* is the process of chopping character streams into tokens; linguistic preprocessing then deals with building equivalence classes of tokens, which are the set of terms that are indexed. Indexing itself is covered in Chapters 1 and 4. Then we return to the implementation of postings lists. In Section 2.3, we examine an extended postings list data structure that supports faster querying, and Section 2.4 covers building postings data structures suitable for handling phrase and proximity queries, of the sort that commonly appear in both extended Boolean models and on the web.

2.1 Document delineation and character sequence decoding

2.1.1 Obtaining the character sequence in a document

Digital documents that are the input to an indexing process are typically bytes in a file or on a web server. The first step of processing is to convert this byte sequence into a linear sequence of characters. For the case of plain English text in ASCII encoding, this is trivial. But often things get much more complex. The sequence of characters may be encoded by one of various single-byte or multibyte encoding schemes, such as Unicode UTF-8,

كِتابٌ ⇐ ` ب ا ت ` ك

un b ā t i k

/kitābun/ *'a book'*

Figure 2.1 An example of a vocalized Modern Standard Arabic word. The writing is from right to left and letters undergo complex mutations as they are combined. The representation of short vowels (here, /i/ and /u/) and the final /n/ (nunation) departs from strict linearity by being represented as diacritics above and below letters. Nevertheless, the represented text is still clearly a linear ordering of characters representing sounds. Full vocalization, as here, normally appears only in the Koran and children's books. Day-to-day text is unvocalized (short vowels are not represented, but the letter for ā would still appear) or partially vocalized, with short vowels inserted in places where the writer perceives ambiguities. These choices add further complexities to indexing.

or various national or vendor-specific standards. We need to determine the correct encoding. This can be regarded as a machine learning classification problem, as discussed in Chapter 13,[1] but is often handled by heuristic methods, user selection, or using provided document metadata. Once the encoding is determined, we decode the byte sequence to a character sequence. We might save the choice of encoding because it gives some evidence about what language the document is written in.

The characters may have to be decoded out of some binary representation like Microsoft Word DOC files and/or a compressed format such as zip files. Again, we must determine the document format, and then an appropriate decoder has to be used. Even for plain text documents, additional decoding may need to be done. In XML documents (Section 10.1, page 180), character entities, such as &, need to be decoded to give the correct character, namely, & for &. Finally, the textual part of the document may need to be extracted out of other material that will not be processed. This might be the desired handling for XML files, if the markup is going to be ignored; we would almost certainly want to do this with postscript or PDF files. We do not deal further with these issues in this book, and assume henceforth that our documents are a list of characters. Commercial products usually need to support a broad range of document types and encodings, because users want things to just work with their data as is. Often, they just think of documents as text inside applications and are not even aware of how it is encoded on disk. This problem is usually solved by licensing a software library that handles decoding document formats and character encodings.

The idea that text is a linear sequence of characters is also called into question by some writing systems, such as Arabic, where text takes on some two-dimensional and mixed-order characteristics, as shown in Figures 2.1 and 2.2. But, despite some complicated writing system conventions, there is an underlying sequence of sounds being represented and hence an

---

[1] A classifier is a function that takes objects of some sort and assigns them to one of a number of distinct classes. Usually classification is done by machine learning methods such as probabilistic models, but it can also be done by hand-written rules.

استقلت الجزائر في سنة 1962 بعد 132 عاما من الاحتلال الفرنسي.

$\leftarrow \rightarrow \quad \leftarrow \rightarrow$ $\leftarrow$ START

'Algeria achieved its independence in 1962 after 132 years of French occupation.'

Figure 2.2 The conceptual linear order of characters is not necessarily the order that you see on the page. In languages that are written right to left, such as Hebrew and Arabic, it is quite common to also have left-to-right text interspersed, such as numbers and dollar amounts. With modern Unicode representation concepts, the order of characters in files matches the conceptual order, and the reversal of displayed characters is handled by the rendering system, but this may not be true for documents in older encodings.

essentially linear structure remains. This is what is represented in the digital representation of Arabic, as shown in Figure 2.1.

2.1.2 *Choosing a document unit*

DOCUMENT UNIT   The next phase is to determine what the *document unit* for indexing is. Thus far, we have assumed that documents are fixed units for the purposes of indexing. For example, we take each file in a folder as a document. But there are many cases in which you might want to do something different. A traditional Unix (mbox-format) email file stores a sequence of email messages (an email folder) in one file, but you might wish to regard each email message as a separate document. Many email messages now contain attached documents, and you might then want to regard the email message and each contained attachment as separate documents. If an email message has an attached zip file, you might want to decode the zip file and regard each file it contains as a separate document. Going in the opposite direction, various pieces of web software (such as latex2html) take things that you might regard as a single document (e.g., a Powerpoint file or a LATEX document) and split them into separate HTML pages for each slide or subsection, stored as separate files. In these cases, you might want to combine multiple files into a single document.

INDEXING GRANULARITY   More generally, for very long documents, the issue of *indexing granularity* arises. For a collection of books, it would usually be a bad idea to index an entire book as a document. A search for Chinese toys might bring up a book that mentions China in the first chapter and toys in the last chapter, but this does not make it relevant to the query. Instead, we may well wish to index each chapter or paragraph as a mini-document. Matches are then more likely to be relevant, and because the documents are smaller it will be much easier for the user to find the relevant passages in the document. But why stop there? We could treat individual sentences as mini-documents. It becomes clear that there is a precision/recall tradeoff here. If the units get too small, we are likely to miss important passages because terms were distributed over several mini-documents, whereas if units are too large we tend to get spurious matches and the relevant information is hard for the user to find.

The problems with large document units can be alleviated by use of explicit or implicit proximity search (Sections 2.4.2 and 7.2.2), and the trade-offs in resulting system performance that we are hinting at are discussed in Chapter 8. The issue of index granularity, and in particular a need to simultaneously index documents at multiple levels of granularity, appears prominently in XML retrieval, and is taken up again in Chapter 10. An information retrieval (IR) system should be designed to offer choices of granularity. For this choice to be made well, the person who is deploying the system must have a good understanding of the document collection, the users, and their likely information needs and usage patterns. For now, we assume that a suitable size document unit has been chosen, together with an appropriate way of dividing or aggregating files, if needed.

2.2 Determining the vocabulary of terms

2.2.1 Tokenization

Given a character sequence and a defined document unit, tokenization is the task of chopping it up into pieces, called *tokens*, perhaps at the same time throwing away certain characters, such as punctuation. Here is an example of tokenization:

Input: Friends, Romans, Countrymen, lend me your ears;

Output: | Friends | Romans | Countrymen | lend | me | your | ears |

These tokens are often loosely referred to as terms or words, but it is some-
TOKEN times important to make a type/token distinction. A *token* is an instance of a sequence of characters in some particular document that are grouped to-
TYPE gether as a useful semantic unit for processing. A *type* is the class of all tokens
TERM containing the same character sequence. A *term* is a (perhaps normalized) type that is included in the IR system's dictionary. The set of index terms could be entirely distinct from the tokens, for instance, they could be semantic identifiers in a taxonomy, but in practice in modern IR systems they are strongly related to the tokens in the document. However, rather than being exactly the tokens that appear in the document, they are usually derived from them by various normalization processes which are discussed in Section 2.2.3.[2] For example, if the document to be indexed is *to sleep perchance to dream*, then there are five tokens, but only four types (because there are two instances of *to*). However, if *to* is omitted from the index (as a stop word; see

---

[2] That is, as defined here, tokens that are not indexed (stop words) are not terms, and if multiple tokens are collapsed together via normalization, they are indexed as one term, under the normalized form. However, we later relax this definition when discussing classification and clustering in Chapters 13–18, where there is no index. In these chapters, we drop the requirement of inclusion in the dictionary. A *term* means a normalized word.

Section 2.2.2 (page 25)), then there are only three terms: *sleep, perchance,* and *dream.*

The major question of the tokenization phase is what are the correct tokens to use? In this example, it looks fairly trivial: you chop on whitespace and throw away punctuation characters. This is a starting point, but even for English there are a number of tricky cases. For example, what do you do about the various uses of the apostrophe for possession and contractions?

Mr. O'Neill thinks that the boys' stories about Chile's capital aren't amusing.

For *O'Neill,* which of the following is the desired tokenization?

And for *aren't,* is it:

A simple strategy is to just split on all nonalphanumeric characters, but although $\boxed{\text{o}}\,\boxed{\text{neill}}$ looks okay, $\boxed{\text{aren}}\,\boxed{\text{t}}$ looks intuitively bad. For all of them, the choices determine which Boolean queries match. A query of neill AND capital matches in three cases but not the other two. In how many cases would a query of o'neill AND capital match? If no preprocessing of a query is done, then it would match in only one of the five cases. For either Boolean or free text queries, you always want to do the exact same tokenization of document and query words, generally by processing queries with the same tokenizer. This guarantees that a sequence of characters in a text will always match the same sequence typed in a query.[3]

LANGUAGE
IDENTIFICATION
These issues of tokenization are language specific. It thus requires the language of the document to be known. *Language identification* based on classifiers that use short character subsequences as features is highly effective; most languages have distinctive signature patterns (see page 43 for references).

---

[3] For the free text case, this is straightforward. The Boolean case is more complex; this tokenization may produce multiple terms from one query word. This can be handled by combining the terms with an AND or as a phrase query (see Section 2.4, page 36). It is harder for a system to handle the opposite case, where the user enters as two terms something that was tokenized together in the document processing.

For most languages, and for particular domains within them, there are unusual specific tokens that we wish to recognize as terms, such as the programming languages C++ and C#, aircraft names like B-52, or a television show name such as M*A*S*H – which is sufficiently integrated into popular culture that you find usages such as *M*A*S*H-style hospitals*. Computer technology has introduced new types of character sequences that a tokenizer should probably tokenize as a single token, including email addresses (jblack@mail.yahoo.com), web URLs (http://stuff.big.com/new/specials.html), numeric IP addresses (142.32.48.231), package tracking numbers (1Z9999W99845399981), and more. One possible solution is to omit from indexing tokens such as monetary amounts, numbers, and URLs, because their presence greatly expands the size of the vocabulary. However, this comes at a high cost in restricting what people can search for. For instance, people might want to search in a bug database for the line number where an error occurs. Items such as the date of an email, which have a clear semantic type, are often indexed separately as document metadata (see Section 6.1, page 101).

HYPHENS   In English, *hyphenation* is used for various purposes ranging from splitting up vowels in words (*co-education*) to joining nouns as names (*Hewlett-Packard*) to a copyediting device to show word grouping (*the hold-him-back-and-drag-him-away maneuver*). It is easy to feel that the first example should be regarded as one token (and is indeed more commonly written as just *coeducation*), the last should be separated into words, and that the middle case is unclear. Handling hyphens automatically can thus be complex: it can either be handled as a classification problem, or more commonly by some heuristic rules, such as allowing short hyphenated prefixes on words, but not longer hyphenated forms.

Conceptually, splitting on white space can also split what should be regarded as a single token. This occurs most commonly with names (*San Francisco, Los Angeles*) but also with borrowed foreign phrases (*au fait*) and compounds that are sometimes written as a single word and sometimes space separated (such as *white space* vs. *whitespace*). Other cases with internal spaces that we might wish to regard as a single token include phone numbers [(800) 234-2333] and dates (Mar 11, 1983). Splitting tokens on spaces can cause bad retrieval results, for example, if a search for York University mainly returns documents containing *New York University*. The problems of hyphens and nonseparating whitespace can even interact. Advertisements for air fares frequently contain items like *San Francisco-Los Angeles*, where simply doing whitespace splitting would give unfortunate results. In such cases, issues of tokenization interact with handling phrase queries (which we discuss in Section 2.4 (page 36)), particularly if we would like queries for all of *lowercase, lower-case* and *lower case* to return the same results. The last two can be handled by splitting on hyphens and using a phrase index. Getting the first case right would depend on knowing that it is sometimes written as two words

莎拉波娃现在居住在美国东南部的佛罗里达。今年 4 月
9 日，莎拉波娃在美国第一大城市纽约度过了 1 8 岁生
日。生日派对上，莎拉波娃露出了甜美的微笑。

Figure 2.3 The standard unsegmented form of Chinese text using the simplified characters of
mainland China. There is no whitespace between words, not even between sentences – the apparent space after the Chinese period (。) is just a typographical illusion caused by placing the
character on the left side of its square box. The first sentence is just words in Chinese characters with no spaces between them. The second and third sentences include Arabic numerals and
punctuation breaking up the Chinese characters.

and also indexing it in this way. One effective strategy in practice, which is
used by some Boolean retrieval systems such as Westlaw and Lexis-Nexis
(Example 1.1), is to encourage users to enter hyphens wherever they may be
possible, and whenever there is a hyphenated form, the system will generalize the query to cover all three of the one word, hyphenated, and two word
forms, so that a query for over-eager will search for over-eager OR "over eager"
OR overeager. However, this strategy depends on user training; if you query
using either of the other two forms, you get no generalization.

Each new language presents some new issues. For instance, French has
a variant use of the apostrophe for a reduced definite article "the" before
a word beginning with a vowel (e.g., *l'ensemble*) and has some uses of the
hyphen with postposed clitic pronouns in imperatives and questions (e.g.,
donne-moi – "give me"). Getting the first case correct affects the correct indexing of a fair percentage of nouns and adjectives: you would want documents mentioning both *l'ensemble* and *un ensemble* to be indexed under *ensemble*. Other languages make the problem harder in new ways. German
COMPOUNDS   writes *compound nouns* without spaces (e.g., *Computerlinguistik* – "computational linguistics"; *Lebensversicherungsgesellschaftsangestellter* – "life insurance
company employee"). Retrieval systems for German greatly benefit from the
COMPOUND   use of a *compound splitter* module, which is usually implemented by seeing if
SPLITTER   a word can be subdivided into multiple words that appear in a vocabulary.
This phenomenon reaches its limit case with major East Asian Languages
(e.g., Chinese, Japanese, Korean, and Thai), where text is written without any
spaces between words. An example is shown in Figure 2.3. One approach
WORD   here is to perform *word segmentation* as prior linguistic processing. Methods
SEGMENTATION   of word segmentation vary from having a large vocabulary and taking the
longest vocabulary match with some heuristics for unknown words to the
use of machine learning sequence models, such as hidden Markov models
or conditional random fields, trained over hand-segmented words (see the
references in Section 2.5). Because there are multiple possible segmentations
of character sequences (Figure 2.4), all such methods make mistakes sometimes, and so you are never guaranteed a consistent unique tokenization. The
other approach is to abandon word-based indexing and to do all indexing
via just short subsequences of characters (character *k*-grams), regardless of

和尚

Figure 2.4 Ambiguities in Chinese word segmentation. The two characters can be treated as one word meaning "monk" or as a sequence of two words meaning "and" and "still."

whether particular sequences cross word boundaries or not. Three reasons why this approach is appealing are that an individual Chinese character is more like a syllable than a letter and usually has some semantic content, that most words are short (the commonest length is two characters), and that, given the lack of standardization of word breaking in the writing system, it is not always clear where word boundaries should be placed anyway. Even in English, some cases of where to put word boundaries are just orthographic conventions – think of *notwithstanding* versus *not to mention* or *into* versus *on to* – but people are educated to write the words with consistent use of spaces.

2.2.2 Dropping common terms: stop words

Sometimes, some extremely common words that would appear to be of little value in helping select documents matching a user need are excluded from STOP WORDS the vocabulary entirely. These words are called *stop words*. The general strat- COLLECTION egy for determining a stop list is to sort the terms by *collection frequency* (the FREQUENCY total number of times each term appears in the document collection), and then to take the most frequent terms, often hand-filtered for their semantic STOP LIST content relative to the domain of the documents being indexed, as a *stop list*, the members of which are then discarded during indexing. An example of a stop list is shown in Figure 2.5. Using a stop list significantly reduces the number of postings that a system has to store; we present some statistics on this in Chapter 5 (see Table 5.1, page 80). And a lot of the time not indexing stop words does little harm: keyword searches with terms like the and by don't seem very useful. However, this is not true for phrase searches. The phrase query "President of the United States," which contains two stop words, is more precise than President AND "United States." The meaning of flights to London is likely to be lost if the word to is stopped out. A search for Vannevar Bush's article *As we may think* will be difficult if the first three words are stopped out, and the system searches simply for documents containing the word think. Some special query types are disproportionately affected. Some song titles and well-known pieces of verse consist entirely of words that are commonly on stop lists (*To be or not to be, Let It Be, I don't want to be, . . .*).

a	an	and	are	as	at	be	by	for	from
has	he	in	is	it	its	of	on	that	the
to	was	were	will	with					

Figure 2.5 A stop list of twenty-five semantically nonselective words that are common in Reuters-RCV1.

The general trend in IR systems over time has been from standard use of quite large stop lists (200–300 terms) to very small stop lists (7–12 terms) to no stop list whatsoever. Web search engines generally do not use stop lists. Some of the design of modern IR systems has focused precisely on how we can exploit the statistics of language so as to be able to cope with common words in better ways. We show in Section 5.3 (page 87) how good compression techniques greatly reduce the cost of storing the postings for common words. Section 6.2.1 (page 108) then discusses how standard term weighting leads to very common words having little impact on document rankings. Finally, Section 7.1.5 (page 129) shows how an IR system with impact-sorted indexes can terminate scanning a postings list early when weights get small, and hence common words do not cause a large additional processing cost for the average query, even though postings lists for stop words are very long. So for most modern IR systems, the additional cost of including stop words is not that high – either in terms of index size or in terms of query processing time.

2.2.3 *Normalization (equivalence classing of terms)*

Having broken up our documents (and also our query) into tokens, the easy case is if tokens in the query just match tokens in the token list of the document. However, there are many cases when two character sequences are not quite the same but you would like a match to occur. For instance, if you search for *USA*, you might hope to also match documents containing *U.S.A.*

TOKEN   *Token normalization* is the process of canonicalizing tokens so that matches
NORMALIZATION occur despite superficial differences in the character sequences of the to-
EQUIVALENCE kens.[4] The most standard way to normalize is to implicitly create *equivalence*
CLASSES   *classes*, which are normally named after one member of the set. For instance,
if the tokens *anti-discriminatory* and *antidiscriminatory* are both mapped onto the term antidiscriminatory, in both the document text and queries, then searches for one term will retrieve documents that contain either.

The advantage of just using mapping rules that remove characters like hyphens is that the equivalence classing to be done is implicit, rather than being fully calculated in advance: the terms that happen to become identical as the result of these rules are the equivalence classes. It is only easy to write rules of this sort that remove characters. Because the equivalence classes are implicit, it is not obvious when you might want to add characters. For instance, it would be hard to know to turn *antidiscriminatory* into *anti-discriminatory*.

An alternative to creating equivalence classes is to maintain relations between unnormalized tokens. This method can be extended to hand-constructed lists of synonyms such as *car* and *automobile*, a topic we discuss further in Chapter 9. These term relationships can be achieved in two

---

[4] It is also often referred to as *term normalization*, but we prefer to reserve the name *term* for the output of the normalization process.

Query term	Terms in documents that should be matched
Windows	Windows
windows	Windows, windows, window
window	window, windows

Figure 2.6 An example of how asymmetric expansion of query terms can usefully model users' expectations.

ways. The usual way is to index unnormalized tokens and to maintain a query expansion list of multiple vocabulary entries to consider for a certain query term. A query term is then effectively a disjunction of several postings lists. The alternative is to perform the expansion during index construction. When the document contains automobile, we index it under car as well (and, usually, also vice versa). Use of either of these methods is considerably less efficient than equivalence classing, because there are more postings to store and merge. The first method adds a query expansion dictionary and requires more processing at query time, whereas the second method requires more space for storing postings. Traditionally, expanding the space required for the postings lists was seen as more disadvantageous, but with modern storage costs, the increased flexibility that comes from distinct postings lists is appealing.

These approaches are more flexible than equivalence classes because the expansion lists can overlap while not being identical. This means there can be an asymmetry in expansion. An example of how such an asymmetry can be exploited is shown in Figure 2.6: if the user enters windows, we wish to allow matches with the capitalized *Windows* operating system, but this is not plausible if the user enters window, even though it is plausible for this query to also match lowercase *windows*.

The best amount of equivalence classing or query expansion to do is a fairly open question. Doing some definitely seems a good idea. But doing a lot can easily have unexpected consequences of broadening queries in unintended ways. For instance, equivalence-classing *U.S.A.* and *USA* to the latter by deleting periods from tokens might at first seem very reasonable, given the prevalent pattern of optional use of periods in acronyms. However, if I put in as my query term *C.A.T.*, I might be rather upset if it matches every appearance of the word *cat* in documents.[5]

Below we present some of the forms of normalization that are commonly employed and how they are implemented. In many cases they seem helpful, but they can also do harm. In fact, you can worry about many details of equivalence classing, but it often turns out that providing processing is done consistently to the query and to documents, the fine details may not have much aggregate effect on performance.

---

[5] At the time we wrote this chapter (August 2005), this was actually the case on Google: the top result for the query *C.A.T.* was a site about cats, the Cat Fanciers Web Site www.fanciers.com/.

Accents and diacritics. Diacritics on characters in English have a fairly marginal status, and we might well want *cliché* and *cliche* to match, or *naive* and *naïve*. This can be done by normalizing tokens to remove diacritics. In many other languages, diacritics are a regular part of the writing system and distinguish different sounds. Occasionally words are distinguished only by their accents. For instance, in Spanish, *peña* is "a cliff," whereas *pena* is "sorrow." Nevertheless, the important question is usually not prescriptive or linguistic, but is a question of how users are likely to write queries for these words. In many cases, users enter queries for words without diacritics, whether for reasons of speed, laziness, limited software, or habits born of the days when it was hard to use non-ASCII text on many computer systems. In these cases, it might be best to equate all words to a form without diacritics.

CASE-FOLDING **Capitalization/case-folding.** A common strategy is to do *case-folding* by reducing all letters to lower case. Often this is a good idea: it allows instances of *Automobile* at the beginning of a sentence to match with a query of *automobile*. It also helps on a web search engine when most of your users type in *ferrari* when they are interested in a *Ferrari* car. On the other hand, such case folding can equate words that might better be kept apart. Many proper nouns are derived from common nouns and so are distinguished only by case, including companies (*General Motors*, *The Associated Press*), government organizations (*the Fed* vs. *fed*) and person names (*Bush*, *Black*). We already mentioned an example of unintended query expansion with acronyms, which involved not only acronym normalization (*C.A.T.* → *CAT*) but also case-folding (*CAT* → *cat*).

For English, an alternative to making every token lowercase is to just make some tokens lowercase. The simplest heuristic is to convert to lowercase words at the beginning of a sentence and all words occurring in a title that is all uppercase or in which most or all words are capitalized. These words are usually ordinary words that have been capitalized. Midsentence capitalized words are left as capitalized (which is usually correct). This mostly avoids case-folding in cases where distinctions should be kept apart. The same task can be done more accurately by a machine learning sequence model that uses more features to make the decision of when to case-fold. This is known TRUECASING as *truecasing*. However, trying to get capitalization right in this way probably doesn't help if your users usually use lowercase regardless of the correct case of words. Thus, lowercasing everything often remains the most practical solution.

Other issues in English. Other possible normalizations are quite idiosyncratic and particular to English. For instance, you might wish to equate *ne'er* and *never* or the British spelling *colour* and the American spelling *color*. Dates,

ノーベル平和賞を受賞したワンガリ・マータイさんが名誉会長を務め
るＭＯＴＴＡＩＮＡＩキャンペーンの一環として、毎日新聞社とマガ
ジンハウスは「私の、もったいない」を募集します。皆様が日ごろ
「もったいない」と感じて実践していることや、それにまつわるエピ
ソードを８００字以内の文章にまとめ、簡単な写真、イラスト、図
などを添えて１０月２０日までにお送りください。大賞受賞者には、
５０万円相当の旅行券とエコ製品２点の副賞が贈られます。

Figure 2.7 Japanese makes use of multiple intermingled writing systems and, like Chinese, does not segment words. This text is mainly Chinese characters with the hiragana syllabary for inflectional endings and function words. The part in latin letters is actually a Japanese expression, but has been taken up as the name of an environmental campaign by 2004 Nobel Peace Prize winner Wangari Maathai. His name is written using the katakana syllabary in the middle of the first line. The first four characters of the final line express a monetary amount that we would want to match with ¥500,000 (500,000 Japanese yen).

times, and similar items come in multiple formats, presenting additional challenges. You might wish to collapse together *3/12/91* and *Mar. 12, 1991*. However, correct processing here is complicated by the fact that in the United States, *3/12/91* is *Mar. 12, 1991*, whereas in Europe it is *3 Dec. 1991*.

Other languages. English has maintained a dominant position on the WWW; approximately 60% of web pages are in English (Gerrand 2007). But that still leaves 40% of the web, and the non-English portion might be expected to grow over time, because less than one third of Internet users and less than 10% of the world's population primarily speak English. And there are signs of change: Sifry (2007) reports that only about one third of blog posts are in English.

Other languages again present distinctive issues in equivalence classing. The French word for *the* has distinctive forms based not only on the gender (masculine or feminine) and number of the following noun, but also depending on whether the following word begins with a vowel: *le, la, l', les*. We may well wish to equivalence class these various forms of *the*. German has a convention whereby vowels with an umlaut can be rendered instead as a two-vowel digraph. We would want to treat *Schütze* and *Schuetze* as equivalent.

Japanese is a well-known difficult writing system, as illustrated in Figure 2.7. Modern Japanese is standardly an intermingling of multiple alphabets, principally Chinese characters, two syllabaries (hiragana and katakana), and Western characters (Latin letters, Arabic numerals, and various symbols). Although there are strong conventions and standardization through the education system over the choice of writing system, in many cases the same word can be written with multiple writing systems. For example, a word may be written in katakana for empasis (somewhat like italics). Or a word may sometimes be written in hiragana and sometimes in Chinese characters. Successful retrieval thus requires complex equivalence classing across the writing systems. In particular, an end user might commonly present a query entirely in hiragana, because it is easier to type, just as Western end users commonly use all lowercase letters.

Document collections being indexed can include documents from many different languages. Or a single document can easily contain text from multiple languages. For instance, a French email might quote clauses from a contract document written in English. Most commonly, the language is detected and language-particular tokenization and normalization rules are applied at a predetermined granularity, such as whole documents or individual paragraphs, but this still does not correctly deal with cases where language changes occur for brief quotations. When document collections contain multiple languages, a single index may have to contain terms of several languages. One option is to run a language identification classifier on documents and then to tag terms in the vocabulary for their language. Or this tagging can simply be omitted, because it is relatively rare for the exact same character sequence to be a word in different languages.

When dealing with foreign or complex words, particularly foreign names, the spelling may be unclear or there may be variant transliteration standards giving different spellings (e.g., *Chebyshev* and *Tchebycheff* or *Beijing* and *Peking*). One way of dealing with this is to use heuristics to equivalence class or expand terms with phonetic equivalents. The traditional and best known such algorithm is the Soundex algorithm, which we cover in Section 3.4 (page 58).

2.2.4 *Stemming and lemmatization*

For grammatical reasons, documents are going to use different forms of a word, such as *organize*, *organizes*, and *organizing*. Additionally, there are families of derivationally related words with similar meanings, such as *democracy*, *democratic*, and *democratization*. In many situations, it seems as if it would be useful for a search for one of these words to return documents that contain another word in the set.

The goal of both stemming and lemmatization is to reduce inflectional forms and sometimes derivationally related forms of a word to a common base form. For instance:

am, are, is $\Rightarrow$ be
car, cars, car's, cars' $\Rightarrow$ car

The result of this mapping of text will be something like:

the boy's cars are different colors $\Rightarrow$
the boy car be differ color

STEMMING   However, the two words differ in their flavor. *Stemming* usually refers to a crude heuristic process that chops off the ends of words in the hope of achieving this goal correctly most of the time, and often includes the re-

LEMMATIZATION moval of derivational affixes. *Lemmatization* usually refers to doing things properly with the use of a vocabulary and morphological analysis of words, normally aiming to remove inflectional endings only and to return the base

LEMMA or dictionary form of a word, which is known as the *lemma*. If confronted with the token *saw*, stemming might return just *s*, whereas lemmatization would attempt to return either *see* or *saw*, depending on whether the use of the token was as a verb or a noun. The two may also differ in that stemming most commonly collapses derivationally related words, whereas lemmatization commonly only collapses the different inflectional forms of a lemma. Linguistic processing for stemming or lemmatization is often done by an additional plug-in component to the indexing process, and a number of such components exist, both commercial and open source.

The most common algorithm for stemming English, and one that has re-

PORTER peatedly been shown to be empirically very effective, is *Porter's algorithm*

STEMMER (Porter 1980). The entire algorithm is too long and intricate to present here, but we indicate its general nature. Porter's algorithm consists of five phases of word reductions, applied sequentially. Within each phase, there are various conventions to select rules, such as selecting the rule from each rule group that applies to the longest suffix. In the first phase, this convention is used with the following rule group:

(2.1) **Rule** **Example**

SSES	→	SS	caresses	→	caress
IES	→	I	ponies	→	poni
SS	→	SS	caress	→	caress
S	→		cats	→	cat

Many of the later rules use a concept of the *measure* of a word, which loosely checks the number of syllables to see whether a word is long enough that it is reasonable to regard the matching portion of a rule as a suffix rather than as part of the stem of a word. For example, the rule:

$(m > 1)$ EMENT →

would map *replacement* to *replac*, but not *cement* to *c*. The official site for the Porter Stemmer is:

www.tartarus.org/˜martin/PorterStemmer/

Other stemmers exist, including the older, one-pass Lovins stemmer (Lovins 1968), and newer entrants like the Paice/Husk stemmer (Paice 1990); see:

www.cs.waikato.ac.nz/˜eibe/stemmers/
www.comp.lancs.ac.uk/computing/research/stemming/

Sample text: Such an analysis can reveal features that are not easily visible from the variations in the individual genes and can lead to a picture of expression that is more biologically transparent and accessible to interpretation

Lovins stemmer: such an analys can reve featur that ar not eas vis from th vari in th individu gen and can lead to a pictur of expres that is mor biolog transpar and acces to interpres

Porter stemmer: such an analysi can reveal featur that ar not easili visibl from the variat in the individu gene and can lead to a pictur of express that is more biolog transpar and access to interpret

Paice stemmer: such an analys can rev feat that are not easy vis from the vary in the individ gen and can lead to a pict of express that is mor biolog transp and access to interpret

Figure 2.8   A comparison of three stemming algorithms on a sample text.

Figure 2.8 presents an informal comparison of the different behaviors of these stemmers. Stemmers use language-specific rules, but they require less knowledge than a lemmatizer, which needs a complete vocabulary and morphological analysis to accurately lemmatize words. Particular domains may also require special stemming rules. However, the exact stemmed form does not matter, only the equivalence classes it forms.

LEMMATIZER   Rather than using a stemmer, you can use a *lemmatizer*, a tool from Natural Language Processing, that does full morphological analysis to accurately identify the lemma for each word. Doing full morphological analysis produces at most very modest benefits for retrieval. It is hard to say more, because either form of normalization tends not to improve English information retrieval performance in aggregate – at least not by very much. Although it helps a lot for some queries, it equally hurts performance a lot for others. Stemming increases recall while harming precision. As an example of what can go wrong, note that the Porter stemmer stems all of the following words:

operate operating operates operation operative operatives operational

to *oper*. However, because *operate* in its various forms is a common verb, we would expect to lose considerable precision on queries such as the following with Porter stemming:

operational AND research
operating AND system
operative AND dentistry

For a case like this, moving to using a lemmatizer does not completely fix the problem because particular inflectional forms are used in particular collocations: a sentence with the words *operate* and *system* is not a good match for the query operating AND system. Getting better value from term normalization depends more on pragmatic issues of word use than on formal issues of linguistic morphology.

The situation is different for languages with much more morphology (such as Spanish, German, and Finnish). Results in the European CLEF evaluations have repeatedly shown quite large gains from the use of stemmers (and compound splitting for languages like German); see the references in Section 2.5.

?

Exercise 2.1 [⋆] Are the following statements true or false?

    a. In a Boolean retrieval system, stemming never lowers precision.

    b. In a Boolean retrieval system, stemming never lowers recall.

    c. Stemming increases the size of the vocabulary.

    d. Stemming should be invoked at indexing time, but not while processing a query.

Exercise 2.2 [⋆] Suggest what normalized form should be used for these words (including the word itself as a possibility):

    a. 'Cos

    b. Shi'ite

    c. cont'd

    d. Hawai'i

    e. O'Rourke

Exercise 2.3 [⋆] The following pairs of words are stemmed to the same form by the Porter stemmer. Which pairs, would you argue, should not be conflated? Give your reasoning.

    a. abandon/abandonment

    b. absorbency/absorbent

    c. marketing/markets

    d. university/universe

    e. volume/volumes

Exercise 2.4 [⋆] For the Porter stemmer rule group shown in (2.1):

    a. What is the purpose of including an identity rule such as SS → SS?

    b. Applying just this rule group, what will the following words be stemmed to?

        circus   canaries   boss

    c. What rule should be added to correctly stem *pony*?

    d. The stemming for *ponies* and *pony* might seem strange. Does it have a deleterious effect on retrieval? Why or why not?

2.3 Faster postings list intersection via skip pointers

In the remainder of this chapter, we discuss extensions to postings list data structures and ways to increase the efficiency of using postings lists. Recall the basic postings list intersection operation from Section 1.3 (page 9): we walk through the two postings lists simultaneously, in time linear in the total number of postings entries. If the list lengths are *m* and *n*, the intersection

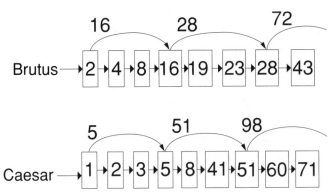

Figure 2.9 Postings lists with skip pointers. The postings intersection can use a skip pointer when the end point is still less than the item on the other list.

takes $O(m + n)$ operations. Can we do better than this? That is, empirically, can we usually process postings list intersection in sublinear time? We can, if the index isn't changing too fast.

SKIP LIST   One way to do this is to use a *skip list* by augmenting postings lists with skip pointers (at indexing time), as shown in Figure 2.9. Skip pointers are effectively shortcuts that allow us to avoid processing parts of the postings list that will not figure in the search results. The two questions are then where to place skip pointers and how to do efficient merging using skip pointers.

Consider first efficient merging, with Figure 2.9 as an example. Suppose we've stepped through the lists in the figure until we have matched 8 on each list and moved it to the results list. We advance both pointers, giving us 16 on the upper list and 41 on the lower list. The smallest item is then the element 16 on the top list. Rather than simply advancing the upper pointer, we first check the skip list pointer and note that 28 is also less than 41. Hence we can follow the skip list pointer, and then we advance the upper pointer to 28. We thus avoid stepping to 19 and 23 on the upper list. A number of variant versions of postings list intersection with skip pointers is possible depending on when exactly you check the skip pointer. One version is shown in Figure 2.10. Skip pointers will only be available for the original postings lists. For an intermediate result in a complex query, the call *hasSkip(p)* will always return false. Finally, note that the presence of skip pointers only helps for AND queries, not for OR queries.

Where do we place skips? There is a tradeoff. More skips means shorter skip spans, and that we are more likely to skip. But it also means lots of comparisons to skip pointers, and lots of space storing skip pointers. Fewer skips means few pointer comparisons, but then long skip spans, which means that there will be fewer opportunities to skip. A simple heuristic for placing skips, which has been found to work well in practice, is that for a postings list of length P, use $\sqrt{P}$ evenly spaced skip pointers. This heuristic can be improved upon; it ignores any details of the distribution of query terms.

INTERSECTWITHSKIPS(p_1, p_2)

```
1   answer ← ⟨ ⟩
2   while p₁ ≠ NIL and p₂ ≠ NIL
3   do if docID(p₁) = docID(p₂)
4       then ADD(answer, docID(p₁))
5            p₁ ← next(p₁)
6            p₂ ← next(p₂)
7       else if docID(p₁) < docID(p₂)
8            then if hasSkip(p₁) and (docID(skip(p₁)) ≤ docID(p₂))
9                 then while hasSkip(p₁) and (docID(skip(p₁)) ≤ docID(p₂))
10                     do p₁ ← skip(p₁)
11                else p₁ ← next(p₁)
12           else if hasSkip(p₂) and (docID(skip(p₂)) ≤ docID(p₁))
13                then while hasSkip(p₂) and (docID(skip(p₂)) ≤ docID(p₁))
14                     do p₂ ← skip(p₂)
15                else p₂ ← next(p₂)
16  return answer
```

Figure 2.10 Postings lists intersection with skip pointers.

Building effective skip pointers is easy if an index is relatively static; it is harder if a postings list keeps changing because of updates. A malicious deletion strategy can render skip lists ineffective.

Choosing the optimal encoding for an inverted index is an ever-changing game for the system builder, because it is strongly dependent on underlying computer technologies and their relative speeds and sizes. Traditionally, CPUs were slow, and so highly compressed techniques were not optimal. Now CPUs are fast and disk is slow, so reducing disk postings list size dominates. However, if you're running a search engine with everything in memory, then the equation changes again. We discuss the impact of hardware parameters on index construction time in Section 4.1 (page 62) and the impact of index size on system speed in Chapter 5.

?

Exercise 2.5 [⋆] Why are skip pointers not useful for queries of the form x OR y?

Exercise 2.6 [⋆] We have a two-word query. For one term the postings list consists of the following 16 entries:

[4,6,10,12,14,16,18,20,22,32,47,81,120,122,157,180]

and for the other it is the one entry postings list:

[47].

Work out how many comparisons would be done to intersect the two postings lists with the following two strategies. Briefly justify your answers:

a. Using standard postings lists

b. Using postings lists stored with skip pointers, with the suggested skip length of $\sqrt{P}$.

Exercise 2.7 [⋆] Consider a postings intersection between this postings list, with skip pointers:

3 5 9 15 24 39 60 68 75 81 84 89 92 96 97 100 115

and the following intermediate result postings list (which hence has no skip pointers):

3 5 89 95 97 99 100 101

Trace through the postings intersection algorithm in Figure 2.10.

a. How often is a skip pointer followed (i.e., p_1 is advanced to $skip(p_1)$)?

b. How many postings comparisons will be made by this algorithm while intersecting the two lists?

c. How many postings comparisons would be made if the postings lists are intersected without the use of skip pointers?

2.4 Positional postings and phrase queries

Many complex or technical concepts and many organization and product names are multiword compounds or phrases. We would like to be able to pose a query such as Stanford University by treating it as a phrase so that a sentence in a document like *The inventor Stanford Ovshinsky never went to university* is not a match. Most recent search engines support a double quotes syntax ("stanford university") for *phrase queries*, which has proven to be very easily understood and successfully used by users. As many as 10% of web queries are phrase queries, and many more are implicit phrase queries (such as person names), entered without use of double quotes. To be able to support such queries, it is no longer sufficient for postings lists to be simply lists of documents that contain individual terms. In this section, we consider two approaches to supporting phrase queries and their combination. A search engine should not only support phrase queries, but implement them efficiently. A related but distinct concept is term proximity weighting, where a document is preferred to the extent that the query terms appear close to each other in the text. This technique is covered in Section 7.2.2 (page 132) in the context of ranked retrieval.

PHRASE
QUERIES

2.4.1 Biword indexes

One approach to handling phrases is to consider every pair of consecutive terms in a document as a phrase. For example, the text *Friends, Romans, Countrymen* would generate the *biwords*:

BIWORD INDEX

> friends romans
> romans countrymen

In this model, we treat each of these biwords as a vocabulary term. Being able to process two-word phrase queries is immediate. Longer phrases can be processed by breaking them down. The query stanford university palo alto can be broken into the Boolean query on biwords:

"stanford university" AND "university palo" AND "palo alto"

This query could be expected to work fairly well in practice, but there can and will be occasional false positives. Without examining the documents, we cannot verify that the documents matching the above Boolean query do actually contain the original four-word phrase.

Among possible queries, nouns and noun phrases have a special status in describing the concepts people are interested in searching for. But related nouns can often be divided from each other by various function words, in phrases such as *the abolition of slavery* or *renegotiation of the constitution*. These needs can be incorporated into the biword indexing model in the following way. First, we tokenize the text and perform part-of-speech tagging.[6] We can then group terms into nouns, including proper nouns, (N) and function words, including articles and prepositions, (X), among other classes. Now deem any string of terms of the form NX*N to be an extended biword. Each such extended biword is made a term in the vocabulary. For example:

renegotiation of the constitution
N   X   X   N

To process a query using such an extended biword index, we need to also parse it into Ns and Xs, and then segment the query into extended biwords, which can be looked up in the index.

This algorithm does not always work in an intuitively optimal manner when parsing longer queries into Boolean queries. Using the above algorithm, the query

cost overruns on a power plant

is parsed into

"cost overruns" AND "overruns power" AND "power plant"

whereas it might seem a better query to omit the middle biword. Better results can be obtained by using more precise part-of-speech patterns that define which extended biwords should be indexed.

The concept of a biword index can be extended to longer sequences of words, and if the index includes variable length word sequences, it is generally referred to as a *phrase index*. Indeed, searches for a single term are not naturally handled in a biword index (you would need to scan the dictionary for all biwords containing the term), and so we also need to have

PHRASE INDEX

---

[6] Part-of-speech taggers classify words as nouns, verbs, and so on – or, in practice, often as finer grained classes like "plural proper noun." Many fairly accurate (c. 96% per-tag accuracy) part-of-speech taggers now exist, usually trained by machine learning methods on hand-tagged text. See, for instance, Manning and Schütze (1999, ch. 10).

to, 993427:

  ⟨ 1, 6: ⟨7, 18, 33, 72, 86, 231⟩;
    2, 5: ⟨1, 17, 74, 222, 255⟩;
    4, 5: ⟨8, 16, 190, 429, 433⟩;
    5, 2: ⟨363, 367⟩;
    7, 3: ⟨13, 23, 191⟩; ...⟩

be, 178239:

  ⟨ 1, 2: ⟨17, 25⟩;
    4, 5: ⟨17, 191, 291, 430, 434⟩;
    5, 3: ⟨14, 19, 101⟩; ...⟩

Figure 2.11 Positional index example. The word *to* has a document frequency 993,477, and occurs six times in document 1 at positions 7, 18, 33, and so on.

an index of single-word terms. Although there is always a chance of false-positive matches, the chance of a false-positive match on indexed phrases of length three or more becomes very small indeed. But on the other hand, storing longer phrases has the potential to greatly expand the vocabulary size. Maintaining exhaustive phrase indexes for phrases of length greater than two is a daunting prospect, and even use of an exhaustive biword dictionary greatly expands the size of the vocabulary. However, toward the end of this section, we discuss the utility of the strategy of using a partial phrase index in a compound indexing scheme.

2.4.2 Positional indexes

For the reasons given, a biword index is not the standard solution. Rather, POSITIONAL a *positional index* is most commonly employed. Here, for each term in the INDEX vocabulary, we store postings of the form docID: ⟨position1, position2, ...⟩, as shown in Figure 2.11, where each position is a token index in the document. Each posting will also usually record the term frequency, for reasons discussed in Chapter 6.

To process a phrase query, you still need to access the inverted index entries for each distinct term. As before, you start with the least frequent term and then work to further restrict the list of possible candidates. In the merge operation, the same general technique is used as before, but rather than simply checking that both terms are in a document, you also need to check that their positions of appearance in the document are compatible with the phrase query being evaluated. This requires working out offsets between the words.

 Example 2.1: Satisfying phrase queries. Suppose the postings lists for *to* and *be* are as in Figure 2.11, and the query is "to be or not to be." The postings lists to access are: *to*, *be*, *or*, *not*. We examine intersecting the postings lists for *to* and *be*. We first look for documents that contain both terms. Then,

POSITIONAL INTERSECT(p_1, p_2, k)

```
 1  answer ← ⟨ ⟩
 2  while p₁ ≠ NIL and p₂ ≠ NIL
 3  do if docID(p₁) = docID(p₂)
 4      then l ← ⟨ ⟩
 5          pp₁ ← positions(p₁)
 6          pp₂ ← positions(p₂)
 7          while pp₁ ≠ NIL
 8          do while pp₂ ≠ NIL
 9              do if |pos(pp₁) − pos(pp₂)| ≤ k
10                  then ADD(l, pos(pp₂))
11                  else if pos(pp₂) > pos(pp₁)
12                          then break
13              pp₂ ← next(pp₂)
14          while l ≠ ⟨ ⟩ and |l[0] − pos(pp₁)| > k
15          do DELETE(l[0])
16          for each ps ∈ l
17          do ADD(answer, ⟨docID(p₁), pos(pp₁), ps⟩)
18          pp₁ ← next(pp₁)
19      p₁ ← next(p₁)
20      p₂ ← next(p₂)
21      else if docID(p₁) < docID(p₂)
22              then p₁ ← next(p₁)
23              else p₂ ← next(p₂)
24  return answer
```

Figure 2.12 An algorithm for proximity intersection of postings lists p_1 and p_2. The algorithm finds places where the two terms appear within k words of each other and returns a list of triples giving docID and the term position in p_1 and p_2.

we look for places in the lists where there is an occurrence of *be* with a token index one higher than a position of *to*, and then we look for another occurrence of each word with token index four higher than the first occurrence. In the above lists, the pattern of occurrences that is a possible match is:

to: ⟨...; 4:⟨...,429,433⟩; ...⟩
be: ⟨...; 4:⟨...,430,434⟩; ...⟩

The same general method is applied for within k word proximity searches, of the sort we saw in Example 1.1 (page 14):

employment /3 place

Here, /k means "within k words of (on either side)." Clearly, positional indexes can be used for such queries; biword indexes cannot. We show in Figure 2.12 an algorithm for satisfying within k word proximity searches; it is further discussed in Exercise 2.12.

Positional index size. Adopting a positional index expands required postings storage significantly, even if we compress position values/offsets as we discuss in Section 5.3 (page 87). Indeed, moving to a positional index also changes the asymptotic complexity of a postings intersection operation, because the number of items to check is now bounded not by the number of documents but by the total number of tokens in the document collection T. That is, the complexity of a Boolean query is $\Theta(T)$ rather than $\Theta(N)$. However, most applications have little choice but to accept this, because most users now expect to have the functionality of phrase and proximity searches.

Let's examine the space implications of having a positional index. A posting now needs an entry for each occurrence of a term. The index size thus depends on the average document size. The average web page has fewer than 1,000 terms, but documents like SEC stock filings, books, and even some epic poems easily reach 100,000 terms. Consider a term with frequency 1 in 1,000 terms on average. The result is that large documents cause an increase of two orders of magnitude in the space required to store the postings list:

Document size	Expected postings	Expected entries in positional posting
1,000	1	1
100,000	1	100

Although the exact numbers depend on the type of documents and the language being indexed, some rough rules of thumb are to expect a positional index to be two to four times as large as a nonpositional index, and to expect a compressed positional index to be about one third to one half the size of the raw text (after removal of markup, etc.) of the original uncompressed documents. Specific numbers for an example collection are given in Table 5.1 (page 80) and Table 5.6 (page 95).

2.4.3 Combination schemes

The strategies of biword indexes and positional indexes can be fruitfully combined. If users commonly query on particular phrases, such as Michael Jackson, it is quite inefficient to keep merging positional postings lists. A combination strategy uses a phrase index, or just a biword index, for certain queries and uses a positional index for other phrase queries. Good queries to include in the phrase index are ones known to be common based on recent querying behavior. But this is not the only criterion: the most expensive phrase queries to evaluate are ones where the individual words are common but the desired phrase is comparatively rare. Adding *Britney Spears* as a phrase index entry may only give a speedup factor to that query of about three, because most documents that mention either word are valid results, whereas adding *The Who* as a phrase index entry may speed up that query by a factor of 1,000. Hence, having the latter is more desirable, even if it is a relatively less common query.

NEXT WORD INDEX Williams et al. (2004) evaluate an even more sophisticated scheme that uses indexes of both these sorts as well as a partial next word index as a halfway house between the first two strategies. For each term, a *next word index* records terms that follow it in a document. They conclude that such a strategy allows a typical mixture of web phrase queries to be completed in one quarter of the time taken by use of a positional index alone, while taking up 26% more space than use of a positional index alone.

Exercise 2.8 [⋆] Assume a biword index. Give an example of a document that will be returned for a query of New York University but is actually a false positive that should not be returned.

Exercise 2.9 [⋆] Shown below is a portion of a positional index in the format: term: doc1: ⟨position1, position2, . . . ⟩; doc2: ⟨position1, position2, . . . ⟩; etc.

angels: 2: ⟨36,174,252,651⟩; 4: ⟨12,22,102,432⟩; 7: ⟨17⟩;
fools: 2: ⟨1,17,74,222⟩; 4: ⟨8,78,108,458⟩; 7: ⟨3,13,23,193⟩;
fear: 2: ⟨87,704,722,901⟩; 4: ⟨13,43,113,433⟩; 7: ⟨18,328,528⟩;
in: 2: ⟨3,37,76,444,851⟩; 4: ⟨10,20,110,470,500⟩; 7: ⟨5,15,25,195⟩;
rush: 2: ⟨2,66,194,321,702⟩; 4: ⟨9,69,149,429,569⟩; 7: ⟨4,14,404⟩;
to: 2: ⟨47,86,234,999⟩; 4: ⟨14,24,774,944⟩; 7: ⟨199,319,599,709⟩;
tread: 2: ⟨57,94,333⟩; 4: ⟨15,35,155⟩; 7: ⟨20,320⟩;
where: 2: ⟨67,124,393,1001⟩; 4: ⟨11,41,101,421,431⟩; 7: ⟨16,36,736⟩;

Which document(s) if any match each of the following queries, where each expression within quotes is a phrase query?
a. "fools rush in"
b. "fools rush in" AND "angels fear to tread"

Exercise 2.10 [⋆] Consider the following fragment of a positional index with the format:

word: document: ⟨position, position, . . .⟩; document: ⟨position, . . .⟩
. . .
Gates: 1: ⟨3⟩; 2: ⟨6⟩; 3: ⟨2,17⟩; 4: ⟨1⟩;
IBM: 4: ⟨3⟩; 7: ⟨14⟩;
Microsoft: 1: ⟨1⟩; 2: ⟨1,21⟩; 3: ⟨3⟩; 5: ⟨16,22,51⟩;

The /k operator, word1 /k word2 finds occurrences of word1 within k words of word2 (on either side), where k is a positive integer argument. Thus $k = 1$ demands that word1 be adjacent to word2.

a. Describe the set of documents that satisfy the query Gates /2 Microsoft.

b. Describe each set of values for k for which the query Gates /k Microsoft returns a different set of documents as the answer.

Exercise 2.11 [★★] Consider the general procedure for merging two positional postings lists for a given document, to determine the document positions where a document satisfies a /k clause (in general, there can be multiple positions at which each term occurs in a single document). We begin with a pointer to the position of occurrence of each term and move each pointer along the list of occurrences in the document, checking as we do so whether we have a hit for /k. Each move of either pointer counts as a step. Let L denote the total number of occurrences of the two terms in the document. What is the big-O complexity of the merge procedure, if we wish to have postings including positions in the result?

Exercise 2.12 [★★] Consider the adaptation of the basic algorithm for intersection of two postings lists (Figure 1.6, page 11) to the one in Figure 2.12 (page 39), which handles proximity queries. A naive algorithm for this operation could be $O(PL_{max}^2)$, where P is the sum of the lengths of the postings lists (i.e., the sum of document frequencies) and L_{max} is the maximum length of a document (in tokens).

a. Go through this algorithm carefully and explain how it works.

b. What is the complexity of this algorithm? Justify your answer carefully.

c. For certain queries and data distributions, would another algorithm be more efficient? What complexity does it have?

Exercise 2.13 [★★] Suppose we wish to use a postings intersection procedure to determine simply the list of documents that satisfy a /k clause, rather than returning the list of positions, as in Figure 2.12 (page 39). For simplicity, assume $k \geq 2$. Let L denote the total number of occurrences of the two terms in the document collection (i.e., the sum of their collection frequencies). Which of the following is true? Justify your answer.

a. The merge can be accomplished in a number of steps linear in L and independent of k, and we can ensure that each pointer moves only to the right.

b. The merge can be accomplished in a number of steps linear in L and independent of k, but a pointer may be forced to move nonmonotonically (i.e., to sometimes back up).

c. The merge can require kL steps in some cases.

Exercise 2.14 [★★] How could an IR system combine use of a positional index and use of stop words? What is the potential problem, and how could it be handled?

2.5 References and further reading

EAST ASIAN LANGUAGES   Exhaustive discussion of the character-level processing of East Asian languages can be found in Lunde (1998). Character bigram indexes are perhaps the most standard approach to indexing Chinese, although some systems use word segmentation. Due to differences in the language and writing system, word segmentation is most usual for Japanese (Luk and Kwok 2002; Kishida et al. 2005). The structure of a character k-gram index over unsegmented text differs from that in Section 3.2.2 (page 50): there the k-gram dictionary points to postings lists of entries in the regular dictionary, whereas here it points directly to document postings lists. For further discussion of Chinese word segmentation, see (Sproat et al. 1996; Sproat and Emerson 2003; Tseng et al. 2005; and Gao et al. 2005).

Lita et al. (2003) present a method for truecasing. Natural language processing work on computational morphology is presented in (Sproat 1992; Beesley and Karttunen 2003).

Language identification was perhaps first explored in cryptography; for example, Konheim (1981) presents a character-level k-gram language identification algorithm. Although other methods such as looking for particular distinctive function words and letter combinations have been used, with the advent of widespread digital text, many people have explored the character n-gram technique, and found it to be highly successful (Beesley 1998; Cavnar and Trenkle 1994; Dunning 1994). Written language identification is regarded as a fairly easy problem, whereas spoken language identification remains more difficult; see Hughes et al. (2006) for a recent survey.

Experiments on and discussion of the positive and negative impact of stemming in English can be found in the following works: Salton (1989), Harman (1991), Krovetz (1995), and Hull (1996). Hollink et al. (2004) provide detailed results for the effectiveness of language-specific methods on eight European languages. In terms of percent change in mean average precision (see page 147) over a baseline system, diacritic removal gains up to 23% (being especially helpful for Finnish, French, and Swedish). Stemming helped markedly for Finnish (30% improvement) and Spanish (10% improvement), but for most languages, including English, the gain from stemming was in the range 0–5%, and results from a lemmatizer were poorer still. Compound splitting gained 25% for Swedish and 15% for German, but only 4% for Dutch. Rather than language-particular methods, indexing character k-grams (as we suggested for Chinese) could often give as good or better results: using within-word character four-grams rather than words gave gains of 37% in Finnish, 27% in Swedish, and 20% in German, while even being slightly positive for other languages, such as Dutch, Spanish, and English. Tomlinson (2003) presents broadly similar results. Bar-Ilan and Gutman (2005) suggest that, at the time of their study (2003), the major commercial web search engines suffered from lacking decent language-particular processing; for example, a query on www.google.fr for l'électricité did not separate off the article *l'* but only matched pages with precisely this string of article+noun.

SKIP LIST   The classic presentation of skip pointers for IR can be found in Moffat and Zobel (1996). Extended techniques are discussed in Boldi and Vigna (2005). The main paper in the algorithms literature is Pugh (1990), which uses multilevel skip pointers to give expected $O(\log P)$ list access (the same expected efficiency as using a tree data structure) with less implementational complexity. In practice, the effectiveness of using skip pointers depends on various system parameters. Moffat and Zobel (1996) report conjunctive queries running about five times faster with the use of skip pointers, but Bahle et al. (2002, p. 217) report that, with modern CPUs, using skip lists instead slows down search because it expands the size of the postings list (i.e., disk I/O dominates performance). In contrast, Strohman and Croft (2007) again show good performance gains from skipping, in a system architecture designed to optimize for the large memory spaces and multiple cores of recent CPUs.

Johnson et al. (2006) report that 11.7% of all queries in two 2002 web query logs contained phrase queries, although Kammenhuber et al. (2006) report only 3% phrase queries for a different data set. Silverstein et al. (1999) note that many queries without explicit phrase operators are actually implicit phrase searches.

3 Dictionaries and tolerant retrieval

In Chapters 1 and 2, we developed the ideas underlying inverted indexes for handling Boolean and proximity queries. Here, we develop techniques that are robust to typographical errors in the query, as well as alternative spellings. In Section 3.1, we develop data structures that help the search for terms in the vocabulary in an inverted index. In Section 3.2, we study the idea of a *wildcard query*: a query such as *a*e*i*o*u*, which seeks documents containing any term that includes all the five vowels in sequence. The * symbol indicates any (possibly empty) string of characters. Users pose such queries to a search engine when they are uncertain about how to spell a query term, or seek documents containing variants of a query term; for instance, the query automat* seeks documents containing any of the terms automatic, automation, and automated.

WILDCARD QUERY

We then turn to other forms of imprecisely posed queries, focusing on spelling errors in Section 3.3. Users make spelling errors either by accident, or because the term they are searching for (e.g., Herman) has no unambiguous spelling in the collection. We detail a number of techniques for correcting spelling errors in queries, one term at a time as well as for an entire string of query terms. Finally, in Section 3.4 we study a method for seeking vocabulary terms that are phonetically close to the query term(s). This can be especially useful in cases like the Herman example, where the user may not know how a proper name is spelled in documents in the collection.

Because we develop many variants of inverted indexes in this chapter, we sometimes use the phrase *standard inverted index* to mean the inverted index developed in Chapters 1 and 2, in which each vocabulary term has a postings list with the documents in the collection.

3.1 Search structures for dictionaries

Given an inverted index and a query, our first task is to determine whether each query term exists in the vocabulary and, if so, identify the pointer to the corresponding postings. This vocabulary lookup operation uses a classical data structure called the *dictionary* and has two broad classes of solutions: hashing and search trees. In the literature of data structures, the entries in the vocabulary (in our case, terms) are often referred to as *keys*. The choice of solution (hashing or search trees) is governed by a number of questions: (1) How many keys are we likely to have? (2) Is the number likely to remain static, or change a lot – and in the case of changes, are we likely to only have new keys inserted, or to also have some keys in the dictionary be deleted? (3) What are the relative frequencies with which various keys will be accessed?

Hashing has been used for dictionary lookup in some search engines. Each vocabulary term (key) is hashed into an integer over a large enough space that hash collisions are unlikely; collisions are resolved by auxiliary structures that can demand care to maintain.[1] At query time, we hash each query term separately and, following a pointer to the corresponding postings, taking into account any logic for resolving hash collisions. There is no easy way to find minor variants of a query term (such as the accented and unaccented versions of a word like resume), because these could be hashed to very different integers. In particular, we cannot seek (for instance) all terms beginning with the prefix automat, an operation that we require in Section 3.2. Finally, in a setting (such as the Web), where the size of the vocabulary keeps growing, a hash function designed for current needs may not suffice in a few years' time.

Search trees overcome many of these issues – for instance, they permit us to enumerate all vocabulary terms beginning with automat. The best-known BINARY TREE search tree is the *binary tree*, in which each internal node has two children. The search for a term begins at the root of the tree. Each internal node (including the root) represents a binary test, based on whose outcome the search proceeds to one of the two subtrees below that node. Figure 3.1 gives an example of a binary search tree used for a dictionary. Efficient search (with a number of comparisons that is $O(\log M)$) hinges on the tree being balanced: the numbers of terms under the two subtrees of any node are either equal or differ by 1. The principal issue here is that of rebalancing; as terms are inserted into or deleted from the binary search tree, it needs to be rebalanced so that the balance property is maintained.

To mitigate rebalancing, one approach is to allow the number of subtrees under an internal node to vary in a fixed interval. A search tree commonly B-TREE used for a dictionary is the *B-tree* – a search tree in which every internal node has a number of children in the interval $[a,b]$, where a and b are appropriate positive integers; Figure 3.2 shows an example with $a = 2$ and $b = 4$. Each branch under an internal node again represents a test for a range of character sequences, as in the binary tree example of Figure 3.1. A B-tree may

---

[1] So-called perfect hash functions are designed to preclude collisions, but are rather more complicated both to implement and to compute.

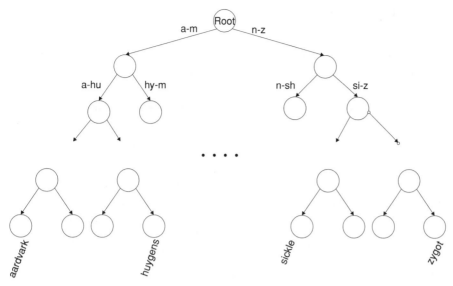

Figure 3.1 A binary search tree. In this example, the branch at the root partitions vocabulary terms into two subtrees, those whose first letter is between a and m, and the rest.

be viewed as "collapsing" multiple levels of the binary tree into one; this is especially advantageous when some of the dictionary is disk resident, in which case this collapsing serves the function of prefetching imminent binary tests. In such cases, the integers a and b are determined by the sizes of disk blocks. Section 3.5 contains pointers to further background on search trees and B-trees.

It should be noted that, unlike hashing, search trees demand that the characters used in the document collection have a prescribed ordering; for instance, the 26 letters of the English alphabet are always listed in the specific order A through Z. Some Asian languages such as Chinese do not always have a unique ordering, although by now all languages (including Chinese and Japanese) have adopted a standard ordering system for their character sets.

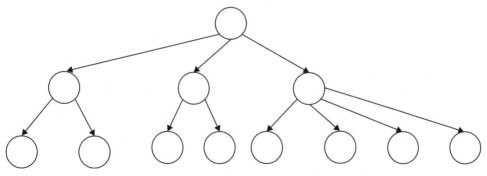

Figure 3.2 A B-tree. In this example every internal node has between 2 and 4 children.

3.2 Wildcard queries

Wildcard queries are used in any of the following situations: (1) the user is uncertain of the spelling of a query term (e.g., Sydney vs. Sidney, which leads to the wildcard query S*dney); (2) the user is aware of multiple variants of spelling a term and (consciously) seeks documents containing any of the variants (e.g., color vs. colour); (3) the user seeks documents containing variants of a term that would be caught by stemming, but is unsure whether the search engine performs stemming (e.g., judicial vs. judiciary, leading to the wildcard query judicia*); or (4) the user is uncertain of the correct rendition of a foreign word or phrase (e.g., the query Universit* Stuttgart).

WILDCARD   A query such as mon* is known as a *trailing wildcard query*, because the *
QUERY   symbol occurs only once, at the end of the search string. A search tree on the dictionary is a convenient way of handling trailing wildcard queries: we walk down the tree following the symbols m, o, and n in turn, at which point we can enumerate the set W of terms in the dictionary with the prefix mon. Finally, we use $|W|$ lookups on the standard inverted index to retrieve all documents containing any term in W.

But what about wildcard queries in which the * symbol is not constrained to be at the end of the search string? Before handling this general case, we mention a slight generalization of trailing wildcard queries. First, consider *leading wildcard queries*, or queries of the form *mon. Consider a *reverse B-tree* on the dictionary – one in which each root-to-leaf path of the B-tree corresponds to a term in the dictionary written *backwards:* thus, the term lemon would, in the B-tree, be represented by the path root-n-o-m-e-l. A walk down the reverse B-tree then enumerates all terms R in the vocabulary with a given postfix.

In fact, using a regular B-tree together with a reverse B-tree, we can handle an even more general case: wildcard queries in which there is a single * symbol, such as se*mon. To do this, we use the regular B-tree to enumerate the set W of dictionary terms beginning with the prefix se and a non-empty suffix, then the reverse B-tree to enumerate the set R of terms ending with the suffix mon. Next, we take the intersection $W \cap R$ of these two sets, to arrive at the set of terms that begin with the prefix se and end with the suffix mon. We scan and filter out any terms that match the prefix as well as the suffix because these two strings overlap (for instance, the query ba*ba would result in the term ba being in $W \cap R$; this would be filtered out). Finally, we use the standard inverted index to retrieve all documents containing any terms in this intersection. We can thus handle wildcard queries that contain a single * symbol using two B-trees, the normal B-tree and a reverse B-tree.

3.2.1 General wildcard queries

We now study two techniques for handling general wildcard queries. Both techniques share a common strategy: express the given wildcard query q_w as

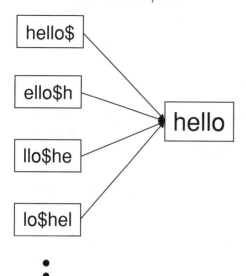

Figure 3.3 A portion of a permuterm index.

a Boolean query Q on a specially constructed index, such that the answer to Q is a superset of the set of vocabulary terms matching q_w. Then, we check each term in the answer to Q against q_w, discarding those vocabulary terms that do not match q_w. At this point, we have the vocabulary terms matching q_w and can resort to the standard inverted index.

Permuterm indexes

PERMUTERM   Our first special index for general wildcard queries is the *permuterm index*, a
INDEX   form of inverted index. First, we introduce a special symbol $ into our character set, to mark the end of a term. Thus, the term hello is shown here as the augmented term hello$. Next, we construct a permuterm index, in which the various rotations of each term (augmented with $) all link to the original vocabulary term. Figure 3.3 gives an example of such a permuterm index entry for the term hello.

We refer to the set of rotated terms in the permuterm index as the *permuterm vocabulary*.

How does this index help us with wildcard queries? Consider the wildcard query m*n. The key is to *rotate* such a wildcard query so that the * symbol appears at the end of the string; thus, the rotated wildcard query becomes n$m*. Next, we look up this string in the permuterm index, where seeking n$m* (via a search tree) leads to rotations of (among others) the terms man and moron.

Now that the permuterm index enables us to identify the original vocabulary terms matching a wildcard query, we look up these terms in the standard inverted index to retrieve matching documents. We can thus handle any wildcard query with a single * symbol. But what about a query such as fi*mo*er? In this case, we first enumerate the terms in the dictionary that are in the permuterm index of er$fi*. Not all such dictionary terms have the string

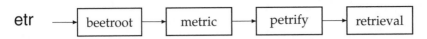

Figure 3.4 Example of a postings list in a 3-gram index. Here the 3-gram etr is illustrated. Matching vocabulary terms are lexicographically ordered in the postings.

mo in the middle – we filter these out by exhaustive enumeration, checking each candidate to see if it contains mo. In this example, the term fishmonger would survive this filtering but filibuster would not. We then run the surviving terms through the standard inverted index for document retrieval. One disadvantage of the permuterm index is that its dictionary becomes quite large, including as it does all rotations of each term.

Notice the close interplay between the B-tree and the permuterm index above. Indeed, it suggests that the structure should perhaps be viewed as a permuterm B-tree. However, we follow traditional terminology here in describing the permuterm index as distinct from the B-tree that allows us to select the rotations with a given prefix.

3.2.2 *k-Gram indexes for wildcard queries*

Whereas the permuterm index is simple, it can lead to a considerable blowup from the number of rotations per term; for a dictionary of English terms, this can represent an almost tenfold space increase. We now present a second technique, known as the k-gram index, for processing wildcard queries. We also use k-gram indexes in Section 3.3.4. A *k-gram* is a sequence of k characters. Thus cas, ast and stl are all 3-grams occurring in the term castle. We use a special character $ to denote the beginning or end of a term, so the full set of 3-grams generated for castle is: $ca, cas, ast, stl, tle, le$.

k-GRAM INDEX   In a *k-gram index*, the dictionary contains all k-grams that occur in any term in the vocabulary. Each postings list points from a k-gram to all vocabulary terms containing that k-gram. For instance, the 3-gram etr would point to vocabulary terms such as metric and retrieval. An example is given in Figure 3.4.

How does such an index help us with wildcard queries? Consider the wildcard query re*ve. We are seeking documents containing any term that begins with re and ends with ve. Accordingly, we run the Boolean query $re AND ve$. This is looked up in the 3-gram index and yields a list of matching terms such as relive, remove, and retrieve. Each of these matching terms is then looked up in the standard inverted index to yield documents matching the query.

There is, however, a difficulty with the use of k-gram indexes that demands one further step of processing. Consider using the 3-gram index described for the query red*. Following the process described, we first issue the Boolean query $re AND red to the 3-gram index. This leads to a match on terms such as retired, which contain the conjunction of the two 3-grams $re and red, yet do not match the original wildcard query red*.

To cope with this, we introduce a *postfiltering* step, in which the terms enumerated by the Boolean query on the 3-gram index are checked individually against the original query red*. This is a simple string-matching operation and weeds out terms such as retired that do not match the original query. Terms that survive are then searched in the standard inverted index as usual.

We have seen that a wildcard query can result in multiple terms being enumerated, each of which becomes a single-term query on the standard inverted index. Search engines do allow the combination of wildcard queries using Boolean operators, for example, re*d AND fe*ri. What are the appropriate semantics for such a query? Because each wildcard query turns into a disjunction of single-term queries, the appropriate interpretation of this example is that we have a conjunction of disjunctions: we seek all documents that contain any term matching re*d *and* any term matching fe*ri.

Even without Boolean combinations of wildcard queries, the processing of a wildcard query can be quite expensive, because of the added lookup in the special index, filtering, and finally the standard inverted index. A search engine may support such rich functionality, but most commonly, the capability is hidden behind an interface (say an "Advanced Query" interface) that most users never use. Exposing such functionality in the search interface often encourages users to invoke it even when they do not require it (say, by typing a prefix of their query followed by a *), increasing the processing load on the search engine.

?

Exercise 3.1 In the permuterm index, each permuterm vocabulary term points to the original vocabulary term(s) from which it was derived. How many original vocabulary terms can there be in the postings list of a permuterm vocabulary term?

Exercise 3.2 Write down the entries in the permuterm index dictionary that are generated by the term mama.

Exercise 3.3 If you wanted to search for s*ng in a permuterm wildcard index, what key(s) would one do the lookup on?

Exercise 3.4 Refer to Figure 3.4; it is pointed out in the caption that the vocabulary terms in the postings are lexicographically ordered. Why is this ordering useful?

Exercise 3.5 Consider again the query fi*mo*er from Section 3.2.1. What Boolean query on a bigram index would be generated for this query? Can you think of a term that matches the permuterm query in Section 3.2.1, but does not satisfy this Boolean query?

Exercise 3.6 Give an example of a sentence that falsely matches the wildcard query mon*h if the search were to simply use a conjunction of bigrams.

3.3 Spelling correction

We next look at the problem of correcting spelling errors in queries. For instance, we may wish to retrieve documents containing the term carrot when the user types the query carot. Google reports (www.google.com/jobs/britney. html) that the following are all treated as misspellings of the query britney spears: britian spears, britney's spears, brandy spears, and prittany spears. We look at two steps to solving this problem: the first based on *edit distance* and the second based on *k-gram overlap*. Before getting into the algorithmic details of these methods, we first review how search engines provide spell correction as part of a user experience.

3.3.1 *Implementing spelling correction*

There are two basic principles underlying most spelling correction algorithms.

1. Of various alternative correct spellings for a misspelled query, choose the "nearest" one. This demands that we have a notion of nearness or proximity between a pair of queries. We develop these proximity measures in Section 3.3.3.

2. When two correctly spelled queries are tied (or nearly tied), select the one that is more common. For instance, grunt and grant both seem equally plausible as corrections for grnt. Then, the algorithm should choose the more common of grunt and grant as the correction. The simplest notion of more common is to consider the number of occurrences of the term in the collection; thus if grunt occurs more often than grant, it is the chosen correction. A different notion of more common is employed in many search engines, especially on the web. The idea is to use the correction that is most common among queries typed in by other users. The idea here is that if grunt is typed as a query more often than grant, then it is more likely that the user who typed grnt intended to type the query grunt.

Beginning in Section 3.3.3, we describe notions of proximity between queries, as well as their efficient computation. Spelling correction algorithms build on these computations of proximity; their functionality is then exposed to users in one of several ways:

1. On the query carot always retrieve documents containing carot as well as any "spell-corrected" version of carot, including carrot and tarot.
2. As in (1) above, but only when the query term carot is not in the dictionary.
3. As in (1) above, but only when the original query returned fewer than a preset number of documents (say fewer than five documents).

4. When the original query returns fewer than a preset number of documents, the search interface presents a *spelling suggestion* to the end user: this suggestion consists of the spell-corrected query term(s). Thus, the search engine might respond to the user: "Did you mean carrot?"

3.3.2 *Forms of spelling correction*

We focus on two specific forms of spelling correction that we refer to as *isolated-term* correction and *context-sensitive* correction. In isolated-term correction, we attempt to correct a single query term at a time – even when we have a multiple-term query. The carot example demonstrates this type of correction. Such isolated-term correction fails to detect, for instance, that the query flew form Heathrow contains a misspelling of the term from – because each term in the query is correctly spelled in isolation.

We begin by examining two techniques for addressing isolated-term correction: edit distance and k-gram overlap. We then proceed to context-sensitive correction.

3.3.3 *Edit distance*

EDIT DISTANCE Given two character strings s_1 and s_2, the *edit distance* between them is the minimum number of *edit operations* required to transform s_1 into s_2. Most commonly, the edit operations allowed for this purpose are (i) insert a character into a string, (ii) delete a character from a string, and (iii) replace a character of a string by another character; for these operations, edit distance
LEVENSHTEIN is sometimes known as *Levenshtein distance*. For example, the edit distance
DISTANCE between cat and dog is three. In fact, the notion of edit distance can be generalized to allowing different weights for different kinds of edit operations; for instance, a higher weight may be placed on replacing the character s by the character p, than on replacing it by the character a (the latter being closer to s on the keyboard). Setting weights in this way – depending on the likelihood of letters substituting for each other – is very effective in practice (see Section 3.4 for the separate issue of phonetic similarity). However, the remainder of our treatment here focus on the case in which all edit operations have the same weight.

It is well-known how to compute the (weighted) edit distance between two strings in time $O(|s_1| \times |s_2|)$, where $|s_i|$ denotes the length of a string s_i. The idea is to use the dynamic programming algorithm in Figure 3.5, where the characters in s_1 and s_2 are given in array form. The algorithm fills the (integer) entries in a matrix m whose two dimensions equal the lengths of the two strings whose edit distances is being computed; the (i, j) entry of the matrix holds (after the algorithm is executed) the edit distance between

EDITDISTANCE(s_1, s_2)
```
 1  int m[|s1|, |s2|] = 0
 2  for i ← 1 to |s1|
 3  do m[i, 0] = i
 4  for j ← 1 to |s2|
 5  do m[0, j] = j
 6  for i ← 1 to |s1|
 7  do for j ← 1 to |s2|
 8      do m[i, j] = min{m[i − 1, j − 1] + if (s1[i] = s2[j]) then 0 else 1 fi,
 9                       m[i − 1, j] + 1,
10                       m[i, j − 1] + 1}
11  return m[|s1|, |s2|]
```

Figure 3.5 Dynamic programming algorithm for computing the edit distance between strings s_1 and s_2.

the strings consisting of the first i characters of s_1 and the first j characters of s_2. The central dynamic programming step is depicted in lines 8–10 of Figure 3.5, where the three quantities whose minimum is taken correspond to substituting a character in s_1, inserting a character in s_1, and inserting a character in s_2.

Figure 3.6 shows an example Levenshtein distance computation of Figure 3.5. The typical cell $[i, j]$ has four entries formatted as a 2×2 cell. The lower right entry in each cell is the min of the other three, corresponding to the main dynamic programming step in Figure 3.5. The other three entries are the three entries $m[i − 1, j − 1] + 0$ or 1 depending on whether $s_1[i] = s_2[j]$, $m[i − 1, j] + 1$ and $m[i, j − 1] + 1$. The cells with numbers in italics depict the path by which we determine the Levenshtein distance.

			f		a		s		t	
		0	1	1	2	2	3	3	4	4
c		1	*1*	2	2	3	3	4	4	5
		1	2	*1*	2	2	3	3	4	4
a		2	2	2	*1*	3	3	4	4	5
		2	3	2	3	*1*	2	2	3	3
t		3	3	3	3	2	2	3	*2*	4
		3	4	3	4	2	3	*2*	3	2
s		4	4	4	4	3	*2*	3	3	3
		4	5	4	5	3	4	*2*	3	*3*

Figure 3.6 Example Levenshtein distance computation. The 2×2 cell in the $[i, j]$ entry of the table shows the three numbers whose minimum yields the fourth. The cells in italics determine the edit distance in this example.

The spelling correction problem however demands more than computing edit distance: given a set V of strings (corresponding to terms in the vocabulary) and a query string q, we seek the string(s) in V of least edit distance from q. We may view this as a decoding problem, in which the codewords (the strings in V) are prescribed in advance. The obvious way of doing this is to compute the edit distance from q to each string in V, before selecting the string(s) of minimum edit distance. This exhaustive search is inordinately expensive. Accordingly, a number of heuristics are used in practice to efficiently retrieve vocabulary terms likely to have low edit distance to the query term(s).

The simplest such heuristic is to restrict the search to dictionary terms beginning with the same letter as the query string; the hope is that spelling errors do not occur in the first character of the query. A more sophisticated variant of this heuristic is to use a version of the permuterm index, in which we omit the end-of-word symbol $. Consider the set of all rotations of the query string q. For each rotation r from this set, we traverse the B-tree into the permuterm index, thereby retrieving all dictionary terms that have a rotation beginning with r. For instance, if q is mase and we consider the rotation $r =$ sema, we would retrieve dictionary terms such as semantic and semaphore, which do not have a small edit distance to q. Unfortunately, we would miss more pertinent dictionary terms such as mare and mane. To address this, we refine this rotation scheme: for each rotation, we omit a suffix of ℓ characters before performing the B-tree traversal. This ensures that each term in the set R of terms retrieved from the dictionary includes a "long" substring in common with q. The value of ℓ could depend on the length of q. Alternatively, we may set it to a fixed constant such as 2.

3.3.4 k-Gram indexes for spelling correction

To further limit the set of vocabulary terms for which we compute edit distances to the query term, we now show how to invoke the k-gram index of Section 3.2.2 (page 50) to assist with retrieving vocabulary terms with low edit distance to the query q. Once we retrieve such terms, we can then find the ones of least edit distance from q.

In fact, we use the k-gram index to retrieve vocabulary terms that have many k-grams in common with the query. We argue that, for reasonable definitions of "many k-grams in common," the retrieval process is essentially that of a single scan through the postings for the k-grams in the query string q.

The 2-gram (or *bigram*) index in Figure 3.7 shows (a portion of) the postings for the three bigrams in the query bord. Suppose we wanted to retrieve vocabulary terms that contained at least two of these three bigrams. A single scan of the postings (much as in Chapter 1) would let us enumerate all such

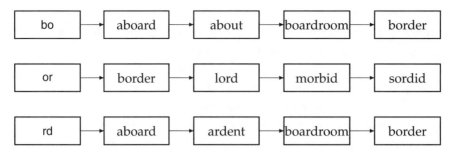

Figure 3.7 Matching at least two of the three 2-grams in the query bord.

terms; in the example of Figure 3.7, we would enumerate aboard, boardroom, and border.

This straightforward application of the linear scan intersection of postings immediately reveals the shortcoming of simply requiring matched vocabulary terms to contain a fixed number of k-grams from the query q: terms like boardroom, an implausible "correction" of bord, get enumerated. Consequently, we require more nuanced measures of the overlap in k-grams between a vocabulary term and q. The linear scan intersection can be adapted JACCARD when the measure of overlap is the *Jaccard coefficient* for measuring the over-COEFFICIENT lap between two sets A and B, defined to be $|A \cap B|/|A \cup B|$. The two sets we consider are the set of k-grams in the query q, and the set of k-grams in a vocabulary term. As the scan proceeds, we proceed from one vocabulary term t to the next, computing on the fly the Jaccard coefficient between q and t. If the coefficient exceeds a preset threshold, we add t to the output; if not, we move on to the next term in the postings. To compute the Jaccard coefficient, we need the set of k-grams in q and t.

Because we are scanning the postings for all k-grams in q, we immediately have these k-grams on hand. What about the k-grams of t? In principle, we could enumerate these on the fly from t. In practice, this is not only slow but potentially infeasible; in all likelihood, the postings entries themselves do not contain the complete string t but rather some encoding of t. The crucial observation is that to compute the Jaccard coefficient, we only need the length of the string t. To see this, recall the example of Figure 3.7 and consider the point when the postings scan for query $q =$ bord reaches term $t =$ boardroom. We know that two bigrams match. If the postings stored the (precomputed) number of bigrams in boardroom (namely, 8), we have all the information we require to compute the Jaccard coefficient to be $2/(8 + 3 - 2)$; the numerator is obtained from the number of postings hits (2, from bo and rd); the denominator is the sum of the number of bigrams in bord and boardroom, less the number of postings hits.

We could replace the Jaccard coefficient by other measures that allow efficient on the fly computation during postings scans. How do we use these for spelling correction? One method that has some empirical support is to first use the k-gram index to enumerate a set of candidate vocabulary terms that are potential corrections of q. We then compute the edit distance from q to each term in this set, selecting terms from the set with small edit distance to q.

3.3.5 Context-sensitive spelling correction

Isolated-term correction would fail to correct typographical errors such as flew form Heathrow, where all three query terms are correctly spelled. When a phrase such as this retrieves few documents, a search engine may like to offer the corrected query flew from Heathrow. The simplest way to do this is to enumerate corrections of each of the three query terms (using the methods leading up to Section 3.3.4) even though each query term is correctly spelled, then try substitutions of each correction in the phrase. For the example flew form Heathrow, we enumerate such phrases as fled form Heathrow and flew fore Heathrow. For each such substitute phrase, the search engine runs the query and determines the number of matching results.

This enumeration can be expensive if we find many corrections of the individual terms; we could encounter a large number of combinations of alternatives. Several heuristics are used to trim this space. In this example, as we expand the alternatives for flew and form, we retain only the most frequent combinations in the collection or in the query logs, which contain previous queries by users. For instance, we would retain flew from as an alternative to try and extend to a three-term corrected query, but perhaps not fled fore or flea form. In this example, the biword fled fore is likely to be rare compared with the biword flew from. Then, we only attempt to extend the list of top biwords (such as flew from), to corrections of Heathrow. As an alternative to using the biword statistics in the collection, we may use the logs of queries issued by users; these could of course include queries with spelling errors.

?

Exercise 3.7 If $|s_i|$ denotes the length of string s_i, show that the edit distance between s_1 and s_2 is never more than $\max\{|s_1|, |s_2|\}$.

Exercise 3.8 Compute the edit distance between paris and alice. Write down the 5×5 array of distances between all prefixes as computed by the algorithm in Figure 3.5.

Exercise 3.9 Write pseudocode showing the details of computing on the fly the Jaccard coefficient while scanning the postings of the k-gram index, as mentioned on page 56.

Exercise 3.10 Compute the Jaccard coefficients between the query bord and each of the terms in Figure 3.7 that contain the bigram or.

Exercise 3.11 Consider the four-term query catched in the rye and suppose that each of the query terms has five alternative terms suggested by isolated-term correction. How many possible corrected phrases must we consider if we do not trim the space of corrected phrases, but instead try all six variants for each of the terms?

Exercise 3.12 For each of the prefixes of the query – catched, catched in, and catched in the – we have a number of substitute prefixes arising from each term and its alternatives. Suppose that we were to retain only the top ten of these substitute prefixes, as measured by its number of occurrences in the collection. We eliminate the rest from consideration for extension to longer prefixes: thus, if batched in is not one of the ten most common two-term queries in the collection, we do not consider any extension of batched in as possibly leading to a correction of catched in the rye. How many of the possible substitute prefixes are we eliminating at each phase?

Exercise 3.13 Are we guaranteed that retaining and extending only the ten commonest substitute prefixes of catched in will lead to one of the ten commonest substitute prefixes of catched in the?

3.4 Phonetic correction

Our final technique for tolerant retrieval has to do with *phonetic* correction: misspellings that arise because the user types a query that sounds like the target term. Such algorithms are especially applicable to searches on the names of people. The main idea here is to generate, for each term, a "phonetic hash" so that similar-sounding terms hash to the same value. The idea owes its origins to work in international police departments from the early 20th century, seeking to match names for wanted criminals despite the names being spelled differently in different countries. It is mainly used to correct phonetic misspellings in proper nouns.

SOUNDEX Algorithms for such phonetic hashing are commonly collectively known
ALGORITHMS as *soundex algorithms*. However, there is an original soundex algorithm, with various variants, built on the following scheme:

1. Turn every term to be indexed into a four-character reduced form. Build an inverted index from these reduced forms to the original terms; call this the soundex index.
2. Do the same with query terms.
3. When the query calls for a soundex match, search this soundex index.

The variations in different soundex algorithms have to do with the conversion of terms to four-character forms. A commonly used conversion results in a four-character code, with the first character being a letter of the alphabet and the other three being digits between 0 and 9.

1. Retain the first letter of the term.
2. Change all occurrences of the following letters to '0' (zero): A, E, I, O, U, H, W, and Y.

3. Change letters to digits as follows:

   B, F, P, V to 1.

   C, G, J, K, Q, S, X, Z to 2.

   D, T to 3.

   L to 4.

   M, N to 5.

   R to 6.

4. Repeatedly remove one out of each pair of consecutive identical digits.

5. Remove all zeros from the resulting string. Pad the resulting string with trailing zeros and return the first four positions, which will consist of a letter followed by three digits.

For an example of a soundex map, Hermann maps to H655. Given a query (say herman), we compute its soundex code and then retrieve all vocabulary terms matching this soundex code from the soundex index, before running the resulting query on the standard inverted index.

This algorithm rests on a few observations: (1) vowels are viewed as interchangeable, in transcribing names; (2) consonants with similar sounds (e.g., D and T) are put in equivalence classes. This leads to related names often having the same soundex codes. Although these rules work for many cases, especially European languages, such rules tend to be writing-system dependent. For example, Chinese names can be written in Wade-Giles or Pinyin transcription. Although soundex works for some of the differences in the two transcriptions – for instance, mapping both Wade-Giles hs and Pinyin x to 2 – it fails in other cases – for example, Wade-Giles j and Pinyin r are mapped differently.

?

Exercise 3.14 Find two differently spelled proper nouns whose soundex codes are the same.

Exercise 3.15 Find two phonetically similar proper nouns whose soundex codes are different.

3.5 References and further reading

Knuth (1997) is a comprehensive source for information on search trees, including B-trees and their use in searching through dictionaries.

Garfield (1976) gives one of the first complete descriptions of the permuterm index. Ferragina and Venturini (2007) give an approach to addressing the space blowup in permuterm indexes.

One of the earliest formal treatments of spelling correction was due to Damerau (1964). The notion of edit distance that we have used is due to Levenshtein (1965) and the algorithm in Figure 3.5 is due to Wagner and Fischer (1974). Peterson (1980) and Kukich (1992) developed variants of methods based on edit distances, culminating in a detailed empirical study of several methods by Zobel and Dart (1995), which shows that k-gram indexing is very effective for finding candidate matches, but should be combined with a more fine-grained technique such as edit distance to determine the most likely misspellings. Gusfield (1997) is a standard reference on string algorithms such as edit distance.

Probabilistic models ("noisy channel" models) for spelling correction were pioneered by Kernighan et al. (1990) and further developed by Brill and Moore (2000) and Toutanova and Moore (2002). In these models, the misspelled query is viewed as a probabilistic corruption of a correct query. They have a similar mathematical basis to the language model methods presented in Chapter 12, and also provide ways of incorporating phonetic similarity, closeness on the keyboard, and data from the actual spelling mistakes of users. Many would regard them as the state-of-the-art approach. Cucerzan and Brill (2004) show how this work can be extended to learning spelling correction models based on query reformulations in search engine logs.

The soundex algorithm is attributed to Margaret K. Odell and Robert C. Russelli (from U.S. patents granted in 1918 and 1922); the version described here draws on Bourne and Ford (1961). Zobel and Dart (1996) evaluate various phonetic matching algorithms, finding that a variant of the soundex algorithm performs poorly for general spelling correction, but that other algorithms based on the phonetic similarity of term pronunciations perform well.

4 *Index construction*

In this chapter, we look at how to construct an inverted index. We call this
INDEXING process *index construction* or *indexing*; the process or machine that performs it
INDEXER the *indexer*. The design of indexing algorithms is governed by hardware constraints. We therefore begin this chapter with a review of the basics of computer hardware that are relevant for indexing. We then introduce blocked sort-based indexing (Section 4.2), an efficient single-machine algorithm designed for static collections that can be viewed as a more scalable version of the basic sort-based indexing algorithm we introduced in Chapter 1. Section 4.3 describes single-pass in-memory indexing, an algorithm that has even better scaling properties because it does not hold the vocabulary in memory. For very large collections like the web, indexing has to be distributed over computer clusters with hundreds or thousands of machines. We discuss this in Section 4.4. Collections with frequent changes require *dynamic indexing* introduced in Section 4.5 so that changes in the collection are immediately reflected in the index. Finally, we cover some complicating issues that can arise in indexing – such as security and indexes for ranked retrieval – in Section 4.6.

Index construction interacts with several topics covered in other chapters. The indexer needs raw text, but documents are encoded in many ways (see Chapter 2). Indexers compress and decompress intermediate files and the final index (see Chapter 5). In web search, documents are not on a local file system, but have to be spidered or crawled (see Chapter 20). In enterprise search, most documents are encapsulated in varied content management systems, email applications, and databases. We give some examples in Section 4.7. Although most of these applications can be accessed via http, native Application Programming Interfaces (APIs) are usually more efficient. The reader should be aware that building the subsystem that feeds raw text to the indexing process can in itself be a challenging problem.

Table 4.1 Typical system parameters in 2007. The seek time is the time needed to position the disk head in a new position. The transfer time per byte is the rate of transfer from disk to memory when the head is in the right position.

Symbol	Statistic	Value
s	average seek time	$5 \text{ ms} = 5 \times 10^{-3}$ s
b	transfer time per byte	$0.02 \, \mu s = 2 \times 10^{-8}$ s
	processor's clock rate	10^9 s^{-1}
p	lowlevel operation	
	(e.g., compare & swap a word)	$0.01 \, \mu s = 10^{-8}$ s
	size of main memory	several GB
	size of disk space	1 TB or more

4.1 Hardware basics

When building an information retrieval (IR) system, many decisions are based on the characteristics of the computer hardware on which the system runs. We therefore begin this chapter with a brief review of computer hardware. Performance characteristics typical of systems in 2007 are shown in Table 4.1. A list of hardware basics that we need in this book to motivate IR system design follows.

CACHING

- Access to data in memory is much faster than access to data on disk. It takes a few clock cycles (perhaps 5×10^{-9} seconds) to access a byte in memory, but much longer to transfer it from disk (about 2×10^{-8} seconds). Consequently, we want to keep as much data as possible in memory, especially those data that we need to access frequently. We call the technique of keeping frequently used disk data in main memory *caching*.

SEEK TIME

- When doing a disk read or write, it takes a while for the disk head to move to the part of the disk where the data are located. This time is called the *seek time* and it averages 5 ms for typical disks. No data are being transferred during the seek. To maximize data transfer rates, chunks of data that will be read together should therefore be stored contiguously on disk. For example, using the numbers in Table 4.1 it may take as little as 0.2 seconds to transfer 10 megabytes (MB) from disk to memory if it is stored as one chunk, but up to $0.2 + 100 \times (5 \times 10^{-3}) = 0.7$ seconds if it is stored in 100 noncontiguous chunks because we need to move the disk head up to 100 times.

BUFFER

- Operating systems generally read and write entire blocks. Thus, reading a single byte from disk can take as much time as reading the entire block. Block sizes of 8, 16, 32, and 64 kilobytes (KB) are common. We call the part of main memory where a block being read or written is stored a *buffer*.

- Data transfers from disk to memory are handled by the system bus, not by the processor. This means that the processor is available to process data during disk I/O. We can exploit this fact to speed up data transfers by storing compressed data on disk. Assuming an efficient decompression algorithm, the total time of reading and then decompressing compressed data is usually less than reading uncompressed data.

- Servers used in IR systems typically have several gigabytes (GB) of main memory, sometimes tens of GB. Available disk space is several orders of magnitude larger.

4.2 Blocked sort-based indexing

The basic steps in constructing a nonpositional index are depicted in Figure 1.4 (page 8). We first make a pass through the collection assembling all term–docID pairs. We then sort the pairs with the term as the dominant key and docID as the secondary key. Finally, we organize the docIDs for each term into a postings list and compute statistics like term and document frequency. For small collections, all this can be done in memory. In this chapter, we describe methods for large collections that require the use of secondary storage.

TERMID   To make index construction more efficient, we represent terms as termIDs (instead of strings as we did in Figure 1.4), where each *termID* is a unique serial number. We can build the mapping from terms to termIDs on the fly while we are processing the collection; or, in a two-pass approach, we compile the vocabulary in the first pass and construct the inverted index in the second pass. The index construction algorithms described in this chapter all do a single pass through the data. Section 4.7 gives references to multipass algorithms that are preferable in certain applications, for example, when disk space is scarce.

REUTERS-   We work with the *Reuters-RCV1* collection as our model collection in this
RCV1   chapter, a collection with roughly 1 GB of text. It consists of about 800,000 documents that were sent over the Reuters newswire during a 1-year period between August 20, 1996, and August 19, 1997. A typical document is shown in Figure 4.1, but note that we ignore multimedia information like images in this book and are only concerned with text. Reuters-RCV1 covers a wide range of international topics, including politics, business, sports, and (as in this example) science. Some key statistics of the collection are shown in Table 4.2.

Reuters-RCV1 has 100 million tokens. Collecting all termID–docID pairs of the collection using 4 bytes each for termID and docID therefore requires 0.8 GB of storage. Typical collections today are often one or two orders of magnitude larger than Reuters-RCV1. You can easily see how such collections overwhelm even large computers if we try to sort their termID–docID pairs in memory. If the size of the intermediate files during index construction is within a small factor of available memory, then the compression techniques introduced in Chapter 5 can help; however, the postings file of many large collections cannot fit into memory even after compression.

REUTERS 🔴

You are here: Home > News > Science > Article

Go to a Section: U.S.   International   Business   Markets   Politics   Entertainment   Technology   Sports   Oddly Enough

Extreme conditions create rare Antarctic clouds

Tue Aug 1, 2006 3:20am ET

Email This Article | Print This Article | Reprints

[-] Text [+]

SYDNEY (Reuters) - Rare, mother-of-pearl colored clouds caused by extreme weather conditions above Antarctica are a possible indication of global warming, Australian scientists said on Tuesday.

Known as nacreous clouds, the spectacular formations showing delicate wisps of colors were photographed in the sky over an Australian meteorological base at Mawson Station on July 25.

Figure 4.1   Document from the Reuters newswire.

EXTERNAL
SORTING
ALGORITHM

With main memory insufficient, we need to use an *external sorting algorithm*, that is, one that uses disk. For acceptable speed, the central requirement of such an algorithm is that it minimize the number of random disk seeks during sorting – sequential disk reads are far faster than seeks as we explained in Section 4.1. One solution is the *blocked sort-based indexing algorithm* or *BSBI* in Figure 4.2. BSBI (i) segments the collection into parts of equal size, (ii) sorts the termID–docID pairs of each part in memory, (iii) stores intermediate sorted results on disk, and (iv) merges all intermediate results into the final index.

BLOCKED
SORT-BASED
INDEXING
ALGORITHM

The algorithm parses documents into termID–docID pairs and accumulates the pairs in memory until a block of a fixed size is full (PARSENEXTBLOCK in Figure 4.2). We choose the block size to fit comfortably into memory to permit a fast in-memory sort. The block is then inverted and written to disk. *Inversion* involves two steps. First, we sort the termID–docID pairs. Next, we collect all termID–docID pairs with the same termID into a postings list, where a *posting* is simply a docID. The result, an inverted index for the block we have just read, is then written to disk. Applying this to Reuters-RCV1 and

INVERSION

POSTING

Table 4.2   Collection statistics for Reuters-RCV1. Values are rounded for the computations in this book. The unrounded values are: 806,791 documents, 222 tokens per document, 391,523 (distinct) terms, 6.04 bytes per token with spaces and punctuation, 4.5 bytes per token without spaces and punctuation, 7.5 bytes per term, and 96,969,056 tokens. The numbers in this table correspond to the third line ("case folding") in Table 5.1 (page 80).

Symbol	Statistic	Value
N	documents	800,000
L_{ave}	avg. # tokens per document	200
M	terms	400,000
	avg. # bytes per token (incl. spaces/punct.)	6
	avg. # bytes per token (without spaces/punct.)	4.5
	avg. # bytes per term	7.5
T	tokens	100,000,000

BSBINDEXCONSTRUCTION()
1 $n \leftarrow 0$
2 **while** (all documents have not been processed)
3 **do** $n \leftarrow n + 1$
4      $block \leftarrow$ PARSENEXTBLOCK()
5   BSBI-INVERT(*block*)
6   WRITEBLOCKTODISK(*block*, f_n)
7 MERGEBLOCKS($f_1, \ldots, f_n; f_{\text{merged}}$)

Figure 4.2 Blocked sort-based indexing. The algorithm stores inverted blocks in files $f_1, \ldots, f_n$ and the merged index in f_{merged}.

assuming we can fit 10 million termID–docID pairs into memory, we end up with ten blocks, each an inverted index of one part of the collection.

In the final step, the algorithm simultaneously merges the ten blocks into one large merged index. An example with two blocks is shown in Figure 4.3, where we use d_i to denote the ith document of the collection. To do the merging, we open all block files simultaneously, and maintain small read buffers for the ten blocks we are reading and a write buffer for the final merged index we are writing. In each iteration, we select the lowest termID that has not been processed yet using a priority queue or a similar data structure. All postings lists for this termID are read and merged, and the merged list is written back to disk. Each read buffer is refilled from its file when necessary.

How expensive is BSBI? Its time complexity is $\Theta(T \log T)$ because the step with the highest time complexity is sorting and T is an upper bound for the number of items we must sort (i.e., the number of termID–docID pairs). But the actual indexing time is usually dominated by the time it takes to parse

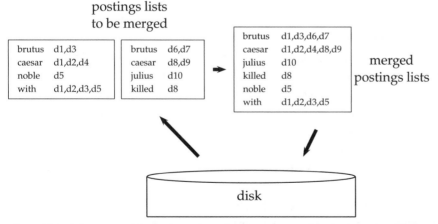

Figure 4.3 Merging in blocked sort-based indexing. Two blocks ("postings lists to be merged") are loaded from disk into memory, merged in memory ("merged postings lists") and written back to disk. We show terms instead of termIDs for better readability.

the documents (PARSENEXTBLOCK) and to do the final merge (MERGEBLOCKS). Exercise 4.6 asks you to compute the total index construction time for RCV1 that includes these steps as well as inverting the blocks and writing them to disk.

Notice that Reuters-RCV1 is not particularly large in an age when 1 or more GB of memory are standard on personal computers. With appropriate compression (Chapter 5), we could have created an inverted index for RCV1 in memory on a not overly beefy server. The techniques we have described are needed, however, for collections that are several orders of magnitude larger.

? **Exercise 4.1** If we need $T \log_2 T$ comparisons (where T is the number of termID–docID pairs) and two disk seeks for each comparison, how much time would index construction for Reuters-RCV1 take if we used disk instead of memory for storage and an unoptimized sorting algorithm (i.e., not an external sorting algorithm)? Use the system parameters in Table 4.1.

Exercise 4.2 [⋆] How would you create the dictionary in blocked sort-based indexing on the fly to avoid an extra pass through the data?

4.3 Single-pass in-memory indexing

Blocked sort-based indexing has excellent scaling properties, but it needs a data structure for mapping terms to termIDs. For very large collections, this data structure does not fit into memory. A more scalable alternative is SINGLE-PASS *single-pass in-memory indexing* or *SPIMI*. SPIMI uses terms instead of termIDs, IN-MEMORY writes each block's dictionary to disk, and then starts a new dictionary for the INDEXING next block. SPIMI can index collections of any size as long as there is enough disk space available.

The SPIMI algorithm is shown in Figure 4.4. The part of the algorithm that parses documents and turns them into a stream of term–docID pairs, which we call *tokens* here, has been omitted. SPIMI-INVERT is called repeatedly on the token stream until the entire collection has been processed.

Tokens are processed one by one (line 4). When a term occurs for the first time, it is added to the dictionary (best implemented as a hash), and a new postings list is created (line 6). The call in line 7 returns this postings list for subsequent occurrences of the term.

A difference between BSBI and SPIMI is that SPIMI adds a posting directly to its postings list (line 10). Instead of first collecting all termID–docID pairs and then sorting them (as we did in BSBI), each postings list is dynamic (i.e., its size is adjusted as it grows) and it is immediately available to collect postings. This has two advantages: It is faster because there is no sorting

SPImI-Invert(*token_stream*)
 1   *output_file* = NewFile()
 2   *dictionary* = NewHash()
 3   **while** (free memory available)
 4   **do** *token* ← *next(token_stream)*
 5   **if** *term(token)* ∉ *dictionary*
 6   **then** *postings_list* = AddToDictionary(*dictionary, term(token)*)
 7   **else** *postings_list* = GetPostingsList(*dictionary, term(token)*)
 8   **if** *full(postings_list)*
 9   **then** *postings_list* = DoublePostingsList(*dictionary, term(token)*)
10   AddToPostingsList(*postings_list, docI D(token)*)
11   *sorted_terms* ← SortTerms(*dictionary*)
12   WriteBlockToDisk(*sorted_terms, dictionary, output_file*)
13   **return** *output_file*

Figure 4.4 Inversion of a block in single-pass in-memory indexing.

required, and it saves memory because we keep track of the term a postings
list belongs to, so the termIDs of postings need not be stored. As a result, the
blocks that individual calls of SPIMI-Invert can process are much larger and
the index construction process as a whole is more efficient.

Because we do not know how large the postings list of a term will be when
we first encounter it, we allocate space for a short postings list initially and
double the space each time it is full (lines 8–9). This means that some memory is wasted, which counteracts the memory savings from the omission of
termIDs in intermediate data structures. However, the overall memory requirements for the dynamically constructed index of a block in SPIMI are
still lower than in BSBI.

When memory has been exhausted, we write the index of the block (which
consists of the dictionary and the postings lists) to disk (line 12). We have to
sort the terms (line 11) before doing this because we want to write postings
lists in lexicographic order to facilitate the final merging step. If each block's
postings lists were written in unsorted order, merging blocks could not be
accomplished by a simple linear scan through each block.

Each call of SPIMI-Invert writes a block to disk, just as in BSBI. The last
step of SPIMI (corresponding to line 7 in Figure 4.2; not shown in Figure 4.4)
is then to merge the blocks into the final inverted index.

In addition to constructing a new dictionary structure for each block and
eliminating the expensive sorting step, SPIMI has a third important component: compression. Both the postings and the dictionary terms can be stored
compactly on disk if we employ compression. Compression increases the efficiency of the algorithm further because we can process even larger blocks,
and because the individual blocks require less space on disk. We refer readers
to the literature for this aspect of the algorithm (Section 4.7).

The time complexity of SPIMI is $\Theta(T)$ because no sorting of tokens is required and all operations are at most linear in the size of the collection.

4.4 Distributed indexing

Collections are often so large that we cannot perform index construction efficiently on a single machine. This is particularly true of the World Wide Web for which we need large computer *clusters*[1] to construct any reasonably sized web index. Web search engines, therefore, use *distributed indexing* algorithms for index construction. The result of the construction process is a distributed index that is partitioned across several machines – either according to term or according to document. In this section, we describe distributed indexing for a term-partitioned index. Most large search engines prefer a Document-partitioned index (which can be easily generated from a term-partitioned index). We discuss this topic further in Section 20.3 (page 415).

MapReduce The distributed index construction method we describe in this section is an application of *MapReduce*, a general architecture for distributed computing. MapReduce is designed for large computer clusters. The point of a cluster is to solve large computing problems on cheap commodity machines or *nodes* that are built from standard parts (processor, memory, disk) as opposed to on a supercomputer with specialized hardware. Although hundreds or thousands of machines are available in such clusters, individual machines can fail at any time. One requirement for robust distributed indexing is, therefore, that we divide the work up into chunks that we can easily assign and –

MASTER NODE in case of failure – reassign. A *master node* directs the process of assigning and reassigning tasks to individual worker nodes.

The map and reduce phases of MapReduce split up the computing job into chunks that standard machines can process in a short time. The various steps of MapReduce are shown in Figure 4.5 and an example on a collection consisting of two documents is shown in Figure 4.6. First, the input data, in

SPLITS our case a collection of web pages, are split into *n splits* where the size of the split is chosen to ensure that the work can be distributed evenly (chunks should not be too large) and efficiently (the total number of chunks we need to manage should not be too large); 16 or 64 MB are good sizes in distributed indexing. Splits are not preassigned to machines, but are instead assigned by the master node on an ongoing basis: As a machine finishes processing one split, it is assigned the next one. If a machine dies or becomes a laggard due to hardware problems, the split it is working on is simply reassigned to another machine.

In general, MapReduce breaks a large computing problem into smaller

KEY-VALUE parts by recasting it in terms of manipulation of *key-value pairs*. For index-
PAIRS ing, a key-value pair has the form (termID,docID). In distributed indexing, the mapping from terms to termIDs is also distributed and therefore more

---

[1] A cluster in this chapter is a group of tightly coupled computers that work together closely. This sense of the word is different from the use of cluster as a group of documents that are semantically similar in Chapters 16–18.

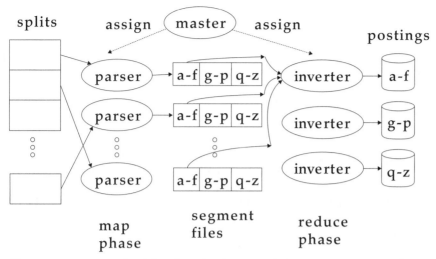

Figure 4.5 An example of distributed indexing with MapReduce. Adapted from Dean and Ghemawat (2004).

complex than in single-machine indexing. A simple solution is to maintain
a (perhaps precomputed) mapping for frequent terms that is copied to all
nodes and to use terms directly (instead of termIDs) for infrequent terms.
We do not address this problem here and assume that all nodes share a consistent term → termID mapping.

MAP PHASE   The *map phase* of MapReduce consists of mapping splits of the input data
to key-value pairs. This is the same parsing task we also encountered in BSBI
and SPIMI, and we therefore call the machines that execute the map phase
PARSER   *parsers*. Each parser writes its output to local intermediate files, the *segment*
SEGMENT FILE   *files* (shown as a-f | g-p | q-z in Figure 4.5).
REDUCE PHASE   For the *reduce phase*, we want all values for a given key to be stored close
together, so that they can be read and processed quickly. This is achieved by
partitioning the keys into j term partitions and having the parsers write key-
value pairs for each term partition into a separate segment file. In Figure 4.5,
the term partitions are according to first letter: a–f, g–p, q–z, and $j = 3$. (We
chose these key ranges for ease of exposition. In general, key ranges need not
correspond to contiguous terms or termIDs.) The term partitions are defined
by the person who operates the indexing system (Exercise 4.10). The parsers
then write corresponding segment files, one for each term partition. Each
term partition thus corresponds to r segments files, where r is the number
of parsers. For instance, Figure 4.5 shows three a–f segment files of the a–f
partition, corresponding to the three parsers shown in the figure.

Collecting all values (here: docIDs) for a given key (here: termID) into one
INVERTER   list is the task of the *inverters* in the reduce phase. The master assigns each
term partition to a different inverter – and, as in the case of parsers, reas-
signs term partitions in case of failing or slow inverters. Each term partition

Schema of map and reduce functions
map: input $\rightarrow$ list(k, v)
reduce: $(k,$list$(v))$ $\rightarrow$ output

Instantiation of the schema for index construction
map: web collection $\rightarrow$ list(termID, docID)
reduce: $(\langle$termID$_1$, list(docID)$\rangle$, $\langle$termID$_2$, list(docID)$\rangle$, ...) $\rightarrow$ (postings_list$_1$, postings_list$_2$, ...)

Example for index construction
map: d_2 : C died. d_1 : C came, C c'ed. $\rightarrow$ $(\langle$C, $d_2\rangle$, $\langle$died,$d_2\rangle$, $\langle$C,$d_1\rangle$, $\langle$came,$d_1\rangle$, $\langle$C,$d_1\rangle$, $\langle$c'ed,$d_1\rangle)$
reduce: $(\langle$C,$(d_2,d_1,d_1)\rangle$,$\langle$died,$(d_2)\rangle$,$\langle$came,$(d_1)\rangle$,$\langle$c'ed,$(d_1)\rangle)$ $\rightarrow$ $(\langle$C,$(d_1$:2,d_2:1)$\rangle$,$\langle$died,$(d_2$:1)$\rangle$,$\langle$came,$(d_1$:1)$\rangle$,$\langle$c'ed,$(d_1$:1)$\rangle)$

Figure 4.6 Map and reduce functions in MapReduce. In general, the map function produces a list of key-value pairs. All values for a key are collected into one list in the reduce phase. This list is then processed further. The instantiations of the two functions and an example are shown for index construction. Because the map phase processes documents in a distributed fashion, termID–docID pairs need not be ordered correctly initially as in this example. The example shows terms instead of termIDs for better readability. We abbreviate Caesar as C and conquered as c'ed.

(corresponding to r segment files, one on each parser) is processed by one inverter. We assume here that segment files are of a size that a single machine can handle (Exercise 4.9). Finally, the list of values is sorted for each key and written to the final sorted postings list ("postings" in the figure). (Note that postings in Figure 4.6 include term frequencies, whereas each posting in the other sections of this chapter is simply a docID without term frequency information.) The data flow is shown for a–f in Figure 4.5. This completes the construction of the inverted index.

Parsers and inverters are not separate sets of machines. The master identifies idle machines and assigns tasks to them. The same machine can be a parser in the map phase and an inverter in the reduce phase. And there are often other jobs that run in parallel with index construction, so in between being a parser and an inverter a machine might do some crawling or another unrelated task.

To minimize write times before inverters reduce the data, each parser writes its segment files to its *local disk*. In the reduce phase, the master communicates to an inverter the locations of the relevant segment files (e.g., of the r segment files of the a–f partition). Each segment file only requires one sequential read because all data relevant to a particular inverter were written to a single segment file by the parser. This setup minimizes the amount of network traffic needed during indexing.

Figure 4.6 shows the general schema of the MapReduce functions. Input and output are often lists of key-value pairs themselves, so that several MapReduce jobs can run in sequence. In fact, this was the design of the Google indexing system in 2004. What we describe in this section corresponds to only one of five to ten MapReduce operations in that indexing system. Another MapReduce operation transforms the term-partitioned index we just created into a document-partitioned one.

MapReduce offers a robust and conceptually simple framework for implementing index construction in a distributed environment. By providing a semiautomatic method for splitting index construction into smaller tasks, it can scale to almost arbitrarily large collections, given computer clusters of sufficient size.

? **Exercise 4.3** For $n = 15$ splits, $r = 10$ segments, and $j = 3$ term partitions, how long would distributed index creation take for Reuters-RCV1 in a MapReduce architecture? Base your assumptions about cluster machines on Table 4.1.

4.5 Dynamic indexing

Thus far, we have assumed that the document collection is static. This is fine for collections that change infrequently or never (e.g., the Bible or Shakespeare). But most collections are modified frequently with documents being added, deleted, and updated. This means that new terms need to be added to the dictionary, and postings lists need to be updated for existing terms.

The simplest way to achieve this is to periodically reconstruct the index from scratch. This is a good solution if the number of changes over time is small and a delay in making new documents searchable is acceptable – and if enough resources are available to construct a new index while the old one is still available for querying.

If there is a requirement that new documents be included quickly, one solution is to maintain two indexes: a large main index and a small *auxiliary index* that stores new documents. The auxiliary index is kept in memory. Searches are run across both indexes and results merged. Deletions are stored in an invalidation bit vector. We can then filter out deleted documents before returning the search result. Documents are updated by deleting and reinserting them.

AUXILIARY INDEX

Each time the auxiliary index becomes too large, we merge it into the main index. The cost of this merging operation depends on how we store the index in the file system. If we store each postings list as a separate file, then the merge simply consists of extending each postings list of the main index by the corresponding postings list of the auxiliary index. In this scheme, the reason for keeping the auxiliary index is to reduce the number of disk seeks required over time. Updating each document separately requires up to M_{ave} disk seeks, where M_{ave} is the average size of the vocabulary of documents in the collection. With an auxiliary index, we only put additional load on the disk when we merge auxiliary and main indexes.

Unfortunately, the one-file-per-postings-list scheme is infeasible because most file systems cannot efficiently handle very large numbers of files. The

LMERGEADDTOKEN(*indexes*, Z_0, *token*)

```
1   Z_0 ← MERGE(Z_0, {token})
2   if |Z_0| = n
3     then for i ← 0 to ∞
4         do if I_i ∈ indexes
5             then Z_{i+1} ← MERGE(I_i, Z_i)
6                 (Z_{i+1} is a temporary index on disk.)
7                 indexes ← indexes − {I_i}
8             else I_i ← Z_i   (Z_i becomes the permanent index I_i.)
9                 indexes ← indexes ∪ {I_i}
10                BREAK
11            Z_0 ← ∅
```

LOGARITHMICMERGE()

```
1   Z_0 ← ∅   (Z_0 is the in-memory index.)
2   indexes ← ∅
3   while true
4   do LMERGEADDTOKEN(indexes, Z_0, GETNEXTTOKEN())
```

Figure 4.7 Logarithmic merging. Each token (termID,docID) is initially added to in-memory index Z_0 by LMERGEADDTOKEN. LOGARITHMICMERGE initializes Z_0 and *indexes*.

simplest alternative is to store the index as one large file, that is, as a concatenation of all postings lists. In reality, we often choose a compromise between the two extremes (Section 4.7). To simplify the discussion, we choose the simple option of storing the index as one large file here.

In this scheme, we process each posting $\lfloor T/n \rfloor$ times because we touch it during each of $\lfloor T/n \rfloor$ merges where n is the size of the auxiliary index and T the total number of postings. Thus, the overall time complexity is $\Theta(T^2/n)$. (We neglect the representation of terms here and consider only the docIDs. For the purpose of time complexity, a postings list is simply a list of docIDs.)

We can do better than $\Theta(T^2/n)$ by introducing $\log_2(T/n)$ indexes I_0, I_1, $I_2, \ldots$ of size $2^0 \times n, 2^1 \times n, 2^2 \times n \ldots$. Postings percolate up this sequence of LOGARITHMIC indexes and are processed only once on each level. This scheme is called *loga-* MERGING *rithmic merging* (Figure 4.7). As before, up to n postings are accumulated in an in-memory auxiliary index, which we call Z_0. When the limit n is reached, the $2^0 \times n$ postings in Z_0 are transferred to a new index I_0 that is created on disk. The next time Z_0 is full, it is merged with I_0 to create an index Z_1 of size $2^1 \times n$. Then Z_1 is either stored as I_1 (if there isn't already an I_1) or merged with I_1 into Z_2 (if I_1 exists); and so on. We service search requests by querying in-memory Z_0 and all currently valid indexes I_i on disk and merging the results. Readers familiar with the binomial heap data structure[2] will recognize its similarity with the structure of the inverted indexes in logarithmic merging.

[2] See, for example, (Cormen et al. 1990, Chapter 19).

Overall index construction time is $\Theta(T \log(T/n))$ because each posting is processed only once on each of the $\log(T/n)$ levels. We trade this efficiency gain for a slow down of query processing; we now need to merge results from $\log(T/n)$ indexes as opposed to just two (the main and auxiliary indexes). As in the auxiliary index scheme, we still need to merge very large indexes occasionally (which slows down the search system during the merge), but this happens less frequently and the indexes involved in a merge on average are smaller.

Having multiple indexes complicates the maintenance of collection-wide statistics. For example, it affects the spelling correction algorithm in Section 3.3 (page 52) that selects the corrected alternative with the most hits. With multiple indexes and an invalidation bit vector, the correct number of hits for a term is no longer a simple lookup. In fact, all aspects of an IR system – index maintenance, query processing, distribution, and so on – are more complex in logarithmic merging.

Because of this complexity of dynamic indexing, some large search engines adopt a reconstruction-from-scratch strategy. They do not construct indexes dynamically. Instead, a new index is built from scratch periodically. Query processing is then switched from the new index and the old index is deleted.

Exercise 4.4 For $n = 2$ and $1 \leq T \leq 30$, perform a step-by-step simulation of the algorithm in Figure 4.7. Create a table that shows, for each point in time at which $T = 2 * k$ tokens have been processed ($1 \leq k \leq 15$), which of the three indexes $I_0, \dots, I_3$ are in use. The first three lines of the table are given below.

	I_3	I_2	I_1	I_0
2	0	0	0	0
4	0	0	0	1
6	0	0	1	0

4.6 Other types of indexes

This chapter only describes construction of nonpositional indexes. Except for the much larger data volume we need to accommodate, the main difference for positional indexes is that (termID, docID, (position1, position2, ...)) triples, instead of (termID, docID) pairs have to be processed and that tokens and postings contain positional information in addition to docIDs. With this change, the algorithms discussed here can all be applied to positional indexes.

In the indexes we have considered so far, postings lists are ordered with respect to docID. As we see in Chapter 5, this is advantageous for compression – instead of docIDs we can compress smaller *gaps* between IDs, thus

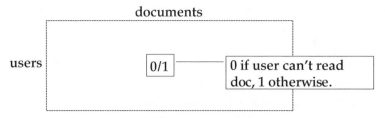

Figure 4.8 A user-document matrix for access control lists. Element (i, j) is 1 if user i has access to document j and 0 otherwise. During query processing, a user's access postings list is intersected with the results list returned by the text part of the index.

reducing space requirements for the index. However, this structure for the
RANKED   index is not optimal when we build *ranked* (Chapters 6 and 7) – as opposed
RETRIEVAL   to Boolean – *retrieval systems*. In ranked retrieval, postings are often ordered
SYSTEMS   according to weight or impact, with the highest-weighted postings occurring
first. With this organization, scanning of long postings lists during query processing can usually be terminated early when weights have become so small that any further documents can be predicted to be of low similarity to the query (see Chapter 6). In a docID-sorted index, new documents are always inserted at the end of postings lists. In an impact-sorted index (Section 7.1.5, page 129), the insertion can occur anywhere, thus complicating the update of the inverted index.

SECURITY   *Security* is an important consideration for retrieval systems in corporations. A low-level employee should not be able to find the salary roster of the corporation, but authorized managers need to be able to search for it. Users' results lists must not contain documents they are barred from opening; the very existence of a document can be sensitive information.

ACCESS   User authorization is often mediated through *access control lists* or ACLs.
CONTROL LISTS   ACLs can be dealt with in an information retrieval system by representing each document as the set of users that can access them (Figure 4.8) and then inverting the resulting user-document matrix. The inverted ACL index has, for each user, a "postings list" of documents they can access – the user's access list. Search results are then intersected with this list. However, such an index is difficult to maintain when access permissions change – we discussed these difficulties in the context of incremental indexing for regular postings lists in Section 4.5. It also requires the processing of very long postings lists for users with access to large document subsets. User membership is therefore often verified by retrieving access information directly from the file system at query time – even though this slows down retrieval.

We discussed indexes for storing and retrieving terms (as opposed to documents) in Chapter 3.

? **Exercise 4.5** Can spelling correction compromise document-level security? Consider the case where a spelling correction is based on documents to which the user does not have access.

Table 4.3 The five steps in constructing an index for Reuters-RCV1 in blocked sort-based indexing. Line numbers refer to Figure 4.2.

	Step	Time
1	reading of collection (line 4)	
2	10 initial sorts of 10^7 records each (line 5)	
3	writing of 10 blocks (line 6)	
4	total disk transfer time for merging (line 7)	
5	time of actual merging (line 7)	
	total	

? **Exercise 4.6** Total index construction time in blocked sort-based indexing is broken down in Table 4.3. Fill out the time column of the table for Reuters-RCV1 assuming a system with the parameters given in Table 4.1.

Exercise 4.7 Repeat Exercise 4.6 for the larger collection in Table 4.4. Choose a block size that is realistic for current technology (remember that a block should easily fit into main memory). How many blocks do you need?

Exercise 4.8 Assume that we have a collection of modest size whose index can be constructed with the simple in-memory indexing algorithm in Figure 1.4 (page 8). For this collection, compare memory, disk and time requirements of the simple algorithm in Figure 1.4 and blocked sort-based indexing.

Exercise 4.9 Assume that machines in MapReduce have 100 GB of disk space each. Assume further that the postings list of the term the has a size of 200 GB. Then the MapReduce algorithm as described cannot be run to construct the index. How would you modify MapReduce so that it can handle this case?

Exercise 4.10 For optimal load balancing, the inverters in MapReduce must get segmented postings files of similar sizes. For a new collection, the distribution of key-value pairs may not be known in advance. How would you solve this problem?

Exercise 4.11 Apply MapReduce to the problem of counting how often each term occurs in a set of files. Specify map and reduce operations for this task. Write down an example along the lines of Figure 4.6.

Table 4.4 Collection statistics for a large collection.

Symbol	Statistic	Value
N	# documents	1,000,000,000
L_{ave}	# tokens per document	1000
M	# distinct terms	44,000,000

Exercise 4.12 We claimed (on page 73) that an auxiliary index can impair the quality of collection statistics. An example is the term weighting method idf, which is defined as $\log(N/\mathrm{df}_i)$ where N is the total number of documents and df_i is the number of documents that term i occurs in (Section 6.2.1, page 108). Show that even a small auxiliary index can cause significant error in idf when it is computed on the main index only. Consider a rare term that suddenly occurs frequently (e.g., Flossie as in Tropical Storm Flossie).

4.7 References and further reading

Witten et al. (1999, Chapter 5) present an extensive treatment of the subject of index construction and additional indexing algorithms with different trade-offs of memory, disk space, and time. In general, blocked sort-based indexing does well on all three counts. However, if conserving memory or disk space is the main criterion, then other algorithms may be a better choice. See Witten et al. (1999), Tables 5.4 and 5.5; BSBI is closest to "sort-based multi-way merge," but the two algorithms differ in dictionary structure and use of compression.

Moffat and Bell (1995) show how to construct an index "in situ," that is, with disk space usage close to what is needed for the final index and with a minimum of additional temporary files (cf. also Harman and Candela (1990)). They give Lesk (1988) and Somogyi (1990) credit for being among the first to employ sorting for index construction.

The SPIMI method in Section 4.3 is from (Heinz and Zobel 2003). We have simplified several aspects of the algorithm, including compression and the fact that each term's data structure also contains, in addition to the postings list, its document frequency and house keeping information. We recommend Heinz and Zobel (2003) and Zobel and Moffat (2006) as up-do-date, in-depth treatments of index construction. Other algorithms with good scaling properties with respect to vocabulary size require several passes through the data, e.g., FAST-INV (Fox and Lee 1991, Harman et al. 1992).

The MapReduce architecture was introduced by Dean and Ghemawat (2004). An open source implementation of MapReduce is available at http://lucene.apache.org/hadoop/. Ribeiro-Neto et al. (1999) and Melnik et al. (2001) describe other approaches to distributed indexing. Introductory chapters on distributed IR are (Baeza-Yates and Ribeiro-Neto 1999, Chapter 9) and (Grossman and Frieder 2004, Chapter 8). See also Callan (2000).

Lester et al. (2005) and Büttcher and Clarke (2005a) analyze the properties of logarithmic merging and compare it with other construction methods. One of the first uses of this method was in Lucene (http://lucene.apache.org). Other dynamic indexing methods are discussed by Büttcher et al. (2006) and Lester et al. (2006). The latter paper also discusses the strategy of replacing the old index by one built from scratch.

Heinz et al. (2002) compare data structures for accumulating the vocabulary in memory. Büttcher and Clarke (2005b) discuss security models for a common inverted index for multiple users. A detailed characterization of the Reuters-RCV1 collection can be found in (Lewis et al. 2004). NIST distributes the collection (see http://trec.nist.gov/data/reuters/reuters.html).

Garcia-Molina et al. (1999, Chapter 2) review computer hardware relevant to system design in depth.

An effective indexer for enterprise search needs to be able to communicate efficiently with a number of applications that hold text data in corporations, including Microsoft Outlook, IBM's Lotus software, databases like Oracle and MySQL, content management systems like Open Text, and enterprise resource planning software like SAP.

5 *Index compression*

Chapter 1 introduced the dictionary and the inverted index as the central data structures in information retrieval (IR). In this chapter, we employ a number of compression techniques for dictionary and inverted index that are essential for efficient IR systems.

One benefit of compression is immediately clear. We need less disk space. As we will see, compression ratios of 1:4 are easy to achieve, potentially cutting the cost of storing the index by 75%.

There are two more subtle benefits of compression. The first is increased use of caching. Search systems use some parts of the dictionary and the index much more than others. For example, if we cache the postings list of a frequently used query term t, then the computations necessary for responding to the one-term query t can be entirely done in memory. With compression, we can fit a lot more information into main memory. Instead of having to expend a disk seek when processing a query with t, we instead access its postings list in memory and decompress it. As we will see below, there are simple and efficient decompression methods, so that the penalty of having to decompress the postings list is small. As a result, we are able to decrease the response time of the IR system substantially. Because memory is a more expensive resource than disk space, increased speed owing to caching – rather than decreased space requirements – is often the prime motivator for compression.

The second more subtle advantage of compression is faster transfer of data from disk to memory. Efficient decompression algorithms run so fast on modern hardware that the total time of transferring a compressed chunk of data from disk and then decompressing it is usually less than transferring the same chunk of data in uncompressed form. For instance, we can reduce input/output (I/O) time by loading a much smaller compressed postings list, even when you add on the cost of decompression. So, in most cases, the retrieval system runs faster on compressed postings lists than on uncompressed postings lists.

If the main goal of compression is to conserve disk space, then the speed of compression algorithms is of no concern. But for improved cache utilization and faster disk-to-memory transfer, decompression speeds must be high. The compression algorithms we discuss in this chapter are highly efficient and can therefore serve all three purposes of index compression.

POSTING   In this chapter, we define a *posting* as a docID in a postings list. For example, the postings list (6; 20, 45, 100), where 6 is the termID of the list's term, contains three postings. As discussed in Section 2.4.2 (page 38), postings in most search systems also contain frequency and position information; but we will only consider simple docID postings here. See Section 5.4 for references on compressing frequencies and positions.

This chapter first gives a statistical characterization of the distribution of the entities we want to compress – terms and postings in large collections (Section 5.1). We then look at compression of the dictionary, using the dictionary-as-a-string method and blocked storage (Section 5.2). Section 5.3 describes two techniques for compressing the postings file, variable byte encoding and γ encoding.

5.1 Statistical properties of terms in information retrieval

As in the last chapter, we use Reuters-RCV1 as our model collection (see Table 4.2, page 64). We give some term and postings statistics for the collection in Table 5.1. "Δ%" indicates the reduction in size from the previous line. "T%" is the cumulative reduction from unfiltered.

The table shows the number of terms for different levels of preprocessing (column 2). The number of terms is the main factor in determining the size of the dictionary. The number of nonpositional postings (column 3) is an indicator of the expected size of the nonpositional index of the collection. The expected size of a positional index is related to the number of positions it must encode (column 4).

In general, the statistics in Table 5.1 show that preprocessing affects the size of the dictionary and the number of nonpositional postings greatly. Stemming and case folding reduce the number of (distinct) terms by 17% each and the number of nonpositional postings by 4% and 3%, respectively. The

RULE OF 30   treatment of the most frequent words is also important. The *rule of 30* states that the 30 most common words account for 30% of the tokens in written text (31% in the table). Eliminating the 150 most common words from indexing (as stop words; cf. Section 2.2.2, page 25) cuts 25% to 30% of the nonpositional postings. But, although a stop list of 150 words reduces the number of postings by a quarter or more, this size reduction does not carry over to the size of the compressed index. As we will see later in this chapter,

Table 5.1 The effect of preprocessing on the number of terms, nonpositional postings, and tokens for Reuters-RCV1. "Δ%" indicates the reduction in size from the previous line, except that "30 stop words" and "150 stop words" both use "case folding" as their reference line. "T%" is the cumulative ("total") reduction from unfiltered. We performed stemming with the Porter stemmer (Chapter 2, page 31).

	(distinct) terms			nonpositional postings			tokens (= number of position entries in postings)		
	number	Δ%	T%	number	Δ%	T%	number	Δ%	T%
unfiltered	484,494			109,971,179			197,879,290		
no numbers	473,723	−2	−2	100,680,242	−8	−8	179,158,204	−9	−9
case folding	391,523	−17	−19	96,969,056	−3	−12	179,158,204	−0	−9
30 stop words	391,493	−0	−19	83,390,443	−14	−24	121,857,825	−31	−38
150 stop words	391,373	−0	−19	67,001,847	−30	−39	94,516,599	−47	−52
stemming	322,383	−17	−33	63,812,300	−4	−42	94,516,599	−0	−52

the postings lists of frequent words require only a few bits per posting after compression.

The deltas in the table are in a range typical of large collections. Note, however, that the percentage reductions can be very different for some text collections. For example, for a collection of web pages with a high proportion of French text, a lemmatizer for French reduces vocabulary size much more than the Porter stemmer does for an English-only collection because French is a morphologically richer language than English.

LOSSLESS   The compression techniques we describe in the remainder of this chap-
LOSSY   ter are *lossless*, that is, all information is preserved. Better compression ratios
COMPRESSION   can be achieved with *lossy compression*, which discards some information. Case folding, stemming, and stop word elimination are forms of lossy compression. Similarly, the vector space model (Chapter 6) and dimensionality reduction techniques like latent semantic indexing (Chapter 18) create compact representations from which we cannot fully restore the original collection. Lossy compression makes sense when the "lost" information is unlikely ever to be used by the search system. For example, web search is characterized by a large number of documents, short queries, and users who only look at the first few pages of results. As a consequence, we can discard postings of documents that would only be used for hits far down the list. Thus, there are retrieval scenarios where lossy methods can be used for compression without any reduction in effectiveness.

Before introducing techniques for compressing the dictionary, we want to estimate the number of distinct terms M in a collection. It is sometimes said that languages have a vocabulary of a certain size. The second edition of the *Oxford English Dictionary* (OED) defines more than 600,000 words. But the vocabulary of most large collections is much larger than the OED. The OED does not include most names of people, locations, products, or scientific entities like genes. These names need to be included in the inverted index, so our users can search for them.

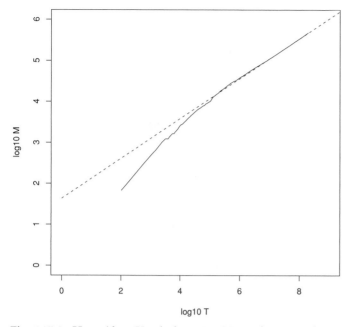

Figure 5.1 Heaps' law. Vocabulary size M as a function of collection size T (number of tokens) for Reuters-RCV1. For these data, the dashed line $\log_{10} M = 0.49 * \log_{10} T + 1.64$ is the best least-squares fit. Thus, $k = 10^{1.64} \approx 44$ and $b = 0.49$.

5.1.1 Heaps' law: Estimating the number of terms

HEAPS' LAW A better way of getting a handle on M is *Heaps' law*, which estimates vocabulary size as a function of collection size:

(5.1) $$M = kT^b$$

where T is the number of tokens in the collection. Typical values for the parameters k and b are: $30 \leq k \leq 100$ and $b \approx 0.5$. The motivation for Heaps' law is that the simplest possible relationship between collection size and vocabulary size is linear in log–log space and the assumption of linearity is usually born out in practice as shown in Figure 5.1 for Reuters-RCV1. In this case, the fit is excellent for $T > 10^5 = 100{,}000$, for the parameter values $b = 0.49$ and $k = 44$. For example, for the first 1,000,020 tokens Heaps' law predicts 38,323 terms:

$$44 \times 1{,}000{,}020^{0.49} \approx 38{,}323.$$

The actual number is 38,365 terms, very close to the prediction.

The parameter k is quite variable because vocabulary growth depends a lot on the nature of the collection and how it is processed. Case-folding and stemming reduce the growth rate of the vocabulary, whereas including numbers and spelling errors increase it. Regardless of the values of the parameters for a particular collection, Heaps' law suggests that (i) the dictionary size continues to increase with more documents in the collection, rather than a maximum vocabulary size being reached, and (ii) the size of the dictionary is quite large for large collections. These two hypotheses have been empirically shown to be true of large text collections (Section 5.4). So dictionary compression is important for an effective information retrieval system.

5.1.2 Zipf's law: Modeling the distribution of terms

We also want to understand how terms are distributed across documents. This helps us to characterize the properties of the algorithms for compressing postings lists in Section 5.3.

ZIPF'S LAW   A commonly used model of the distribution of terms in a collection is *Zipf's law*. It states that, if t_1 is the most common term in the collection, t_2 is the next most common, and so on, then the collection frequency cf_i of the ith most common term is proportional to $1/i$:

$$(5.2) \qquad\qquad cf_i \propto \frac{1}{i}.$$

So if the most frequent term occurs cf_1 times, then the second most frequent term has half as many occurrences, the third most frequent term a third as many occurrences, and so on. The intuition is that frequency decreases very rapidly with rank. Equation (5.2) is one of the simplest ways of formalizing such a rapid decrease and it has been found to be a reasonably good model.

Equivalently, we can write Zipf's law as $cf_i = ci^k$ or as $\log cf_i = \log c + k \log i$ where $k = -1$ and c is a constant to be defined in Section 5.3.2. It is POWER LAW   therefore a *power law* with exponent $k = -1$. See Chapter 19, page 389, for another power law, a law characterizing the distribution of links on web pages.

The log–log graph in Figure 5.2 plots the collection frequency of a term as a function of its rank for Reuters-RCV1. A line with slope –1, corresponding to the Zipf function $\log cf_i = \log c - \log i$, is also shown. The fit of the data to the law is not particularly good, but good enough to serve as a model for term distributions in our calculations in Section 5.3.

? **Exercise 5.1** [⋆] Assuming one machine word per posting, what is the size of the uncompressed (nonpositional) index for different tokenizations based on Table 5.1? How do these numbers compare with Table 5.6?

5.2 Dictionary compression

This section presents a series of dictionary data structures that achieve increasingly higher compression ratios. The dictionary is small compared with the postings file as suggested by Table 5.1. So why compress it if it is responsible for only a small percentage of the overall space requirements of the IR system?

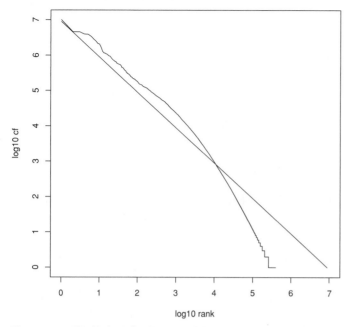

Figure 5.2 Zipf's law for Reuters-RCV1. Frequency is plotted as a function of frequency rank for the terms in the collection. The line is the distribution predicted by Zipf's law (weighted least-squares fit; intercept is 6.95).

One of the primary factors in determining the response time of an IR system is the number of disk seeks necessary to process a query. If parts of the dictionary are on disk, then many more disk seeks are necessary in query evaluation. Thus, the main goal of compressing the dictionary is to fit it in main memory, or at least a large portion of it, to support high query throughput. Although dictionaries of very large collections fit into the memory of a standard desktop machine, this is not true of many other application scenarios. For example, an enterprise search server for a large corporation may have to index a multiterabyte collection with a comparatively large vocabulary because of the presence of documents in many different languages. We also want to be able to design search systems for limited hardware such as mobile phones and onboard computers. Other reasons for wanting to conserve memory are fast startup time and having to share resources with other applications. The search system on your PC must get along with the memory-hogging word processing suite you are using at the same time.

5.2.1 Dictionary as a string

The simplest data structure for the dictionary is to sort the vocabulary lexicographically and store it in an array of fixed-width entries as shown in Figure 5.3. We allocate 20 bytes for the term itself (because few terms have more than twenty characters in English), 4 bytes for its document frequency,

term	document frequency	pointer to postings list
a	656,265	$\longrightarrow$
aachen	65	$\longrightarrow$
...	...	...
zulu	221	$\longrightarrow$

space needed: 20 bytes   4 bytes   4 bytes

Figure 5.3 Storing the dictionary as an array of fixed-width entries.

and 4 bytes for the pointer to its postings list. Four-byte pointers resolve a 4 gigabytes (GB) address space. For large collections like the web, we need to allocate more bytes per pointer. We look up terms in the array by binary search. For Reuters-RCV1, we need $M \times (20 + 4 + 4) = 400,000 \times 28 = 11.2$ megabytes (MB) for storing the dictionary in this scheme.

Using fixed-width entries for terms is clearly wasteful. The average length of a term in English is about eight characters (Table 4.2, page 64), so on average we are wasting twelve characters in the fixed-width scheme. Also, we have no way of storing terms with more than twenty characters like hydrochlorofluorocarbons and supercalifragilisticexpialidocious. We can overcome these shortcomings by storing the dictionary terms as one long string of characters, as shown in Figure 5.4. The pointer to the next term is also used to demarcate the end of the current term. As before, we locate terms in the data structure by way of binary search in the (now smaller) table. This scheme

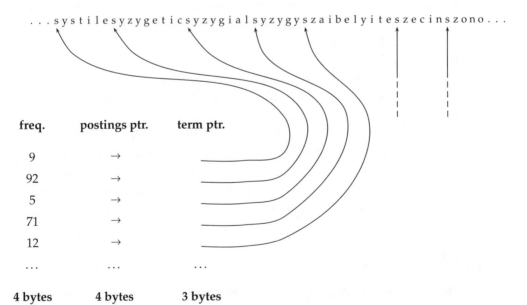

Figure 5.4 Dictionary-as-a-string storage. Pointers mark the end of the preceding term and the beginning of the next. For example, the first three terms in this example are systile, syzygetic, and syzygial.

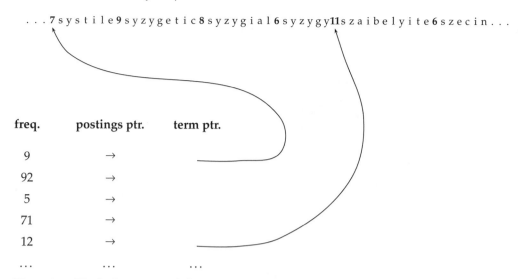

...**7**s y s t i l e**9**s y z y g e t i c**8**s y z y g i a l**6**s y z y g y**11**s z a i b e l y i t e**6**s z e c i n...

freq.	postings ptr.	term ptr.
9	→	
92	→	
5	→	
71	→	
12	→	
...	...	...

Figure 5.5 Blocked storage with four terms per block. The first block consists of systile, syzygetic, syzygial, and syzygy with lengths of seven, nine, eight, and six characters, respectively. Each term is preceded by a byte encoding its length that indicates how many bytes to skip to reach subsequent terms.

saves us 60% compared to fixed-width storage – 12 bytes on average of the 20 bytes we allocated for terms before. However, we now also need to store term pointers. The term pointers resolve $400{,}000 \times 8 = 3.2 \times 10^6$ positions, so they need to be $\log_2 3.2 \times 10^6 \approx 22$ bits or 3 bytes long.

In this new scheme, we need $400{,}000 \times (4 + 4 + 3 + 8) = 7.6$ MB for the Reuters-RCV1 dictionary: 4 bytes each for frequency and postings pointer, 3 bytes for the term pointer, and 8 bytes on average for the term. So we have reduced the space requirements by one third from 11.2 to 7.6 MB.

5.2.2 Blocked storage

We can further compress the dictionary by grouping terms in the string into blocks of size k and keeping a term pointer only for the first term of each block (Figure 5.5). We store the length of the term in the string as an additional byte at the beginning of the term. We thus eliminate $k - 1$ term pointers, but need an additional k bytes for storing the length of each term. For $k = 4$, we save $(k - 1) \times 3 = 9$ bytes for term pointers, but need an additional $k = 4$ bytes for term lengths. So the total space requirements for the dictionary of Reuters-RCV1 are reduced by 5 bytes per four-term block, or a total of $400{,}000 \times 1/4 \times 5 = 0.5$ MB, bringing us down to 7.1 MB.

By increasing the block size k, we get better compression. However, there is a tradeoff between compression and the speed of term lookup. For the eight-term dictionary in Figure 5.6, steps in binary search are shown as double lines and steps in list search as simple lines. We search for terms in the uncompressed dictionary by binary search (a). In the compressed dictionary, we first

(a)

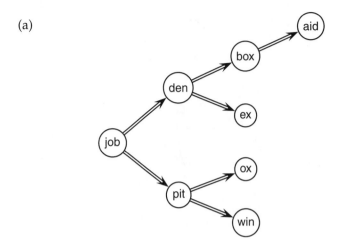

(b)

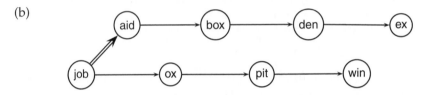

Figure 5.6 Search of the uncompressed dictionary (a) and a dictionary compressed by blocking with $k = 4$ (b).

locate the term's block by binary search and then its position within the list by linear search through the block (b). Searching the uncompressed dictionary in (a) takes on average $(0 + 1 + 2 + 3 + 2 + 1 + 2 + 2)/8 \approx 1.6$ steps, assuming each term is equally likely to come up in a query. For example, finding the two terms, aid and box, takes three and two steps, respectively. With blocks of size $k = 4$ in (b), we need $(0 + 1 + 2 + 3 + 4 + 1 + 2 + 3)/8 = 2$ steps on average, $\approx 25\%$ more. For example, finding den takes one binary search step and two steps through the block. By increasing k, we can get the size of the compressed dictionary arbitrarily close to the minimum of $400{,}000 \times (4 + 4 + 1 + 8) = 6.8$ MB, but term lookup becomes prohibitively slow for large values of k.

One source of redundancy in the dictionary we have not exploited yet is the fact that consecutive entries in an alphabetically sorted list share com-
FRONT CODING mon prefixes. This observation leads to *front coding* (Figure 5.7). A common prefix is identified for a subsequence of the term list and then referred to with a special character. In the case of Reuters, front coding saves another 1.2 MB, as we found in an experiment.

Other schemes with even greater compression rely on minimal perfect hashing, that is, a hash function that maps M terms onto $[1, \ldots, M]$ without collisions. However, we cannot adapt perfect hashes incrementally because each new term causes a collision and therefore requires the creation of a new

One block in blocked compression ($k = 4$) ...

8 a u t o m a t a **8** a u t o m a t e **9** a u t o m a t i c **10** a u t o m a t i o n

$\Downarrow$

... further compressed with front coding.

8 a u t o m a t * a **1** ◇ e **2** ◇ i c **3** ◇ i o n

Figure 5.7 Front coding. A sequence of terms with identical prefix ("automat") is encoded by marking the end of the prefix with * and replacing it with ◇ in subsequent terms. As before, the first byte of each entry encodes the number of characters.

perfect hash function. Therefore, they cannot be used in a dynamic environment.

Even with the best compression scheme, it may not be feasible to store the entire dictionary in main memory for very large text collections and for hardware with limited memory. If we have to partition the dictionary onto pages that are stored on disk, then we can index the first term of each page using a B-tree. For processing most queries, the search system has to go to disk anyway to fetch the postings. One additional seek for retrieving the term's dictionary page from disk is a significant, but tolerable increase in the time it takes to process a query.

Table 5.2 summarizes the compression achieved by the four dictionary data structures.

? **Exercise 5.2** Estimate the space usage of the Reuters-RCV1 dictionary with blocks of size $k = 8$ and $k = 16$ in blocked dictionary storage.

Exercise 5.3 Estimate the time needed for term lookup in the compressed dictionary of Reuters-RCV1 with block sizes of $k = 4$ (Figure 5.6, b), $k = 8$, and $k = 16$. What is the slowdown compared with $k = 1$ (Figure 5.6, a)?

5.3 Postings file compression

Recall from Table 4.2 (page 64) that Reuters-RCV1 has 800,000 documents, 200 tokens per document, six characters per token, and 100,000,000 postings where we define a posting in this chapter as a docID in a postings list, that is, excluding frequency and position information. These numbers

Table 5.2 Dictionary compression for Reuters-RCV1.

data structure	size in MB
dictionary, fixed-width	11.2
dictionary, term pointers into string	7.6
~, with blocking, $k = 4$	7.1
~, with blocking & front coding	5.9

Table 5.3 Encoding gaps instead of document IDs. For example, we store gaps 107, 5, 43, ..., instead of docIDs 283154, 283159, 283202, ... for computer. The first docID is left unchanged (only shown for arachnocentric).

	encoding	postings list							
the	docIDs	...		283042		283043	283044		283045 ...
	gaps				1		1	1	...
computer	docIDs	...		283047		283154	283159		283202 ...
	gaps				107		5	43	...
arachnocentric	docIDs	252000		500100					
	gaps	252000	248100						

correspond to line 3 ("case folding") in Table 5.1. Document identifiers are $\log_2 800{,}000 \approx 20$ bits long. Thus, the size of the collection is about $800{,}000 \times 200 \times 6$ bytes $= 960$ MB and the size of the uncompressed postings file is $100{,}000{,}000 \times 20/8 = 250$ MB.

To devise a more efficient representation of the postings file, one that uses fewer than 20 bits per document, we observe that the postings for frequent terms are close together. Imagine going through the documents of a collection one by one and looking for a frequent term like computer. We will find a document containing computer, then we skip a few documents that do not contain it, then there is again a document with the term and so on (see Table 5.3). The key idea is that the *gaps* between postings are short, requiring a lot less space than 20 bits to store. In fact, gaps for the most frequent terms such as the and for are mostly equal to 1. But the gaps for a rare term that occurs only once or twice in a collection (e.g., arachnocentric in Table 5.3) have the same order of magnitude as the docIDs and need 20 bits. For an economical representation of this distribution of gaps, we need a *variable encoding* method that uses fewer bits for short gaps.

To encode small numbers in less space than large numbers, we look at two types of methods: bytewise compression and bitwise compression. As the names suggest, these methods attempt to encode gaps with the minimum number of bytes and bits, respectively.

5.3.1 Variable byte codes

VARIABLE BYTE   *Variable byte (VB) encoding* uses an integral number of bytes to encode a gap.
ENCODING   The last 7 bits of a byte are "payload" and encode part of the gap. The first

Table 5.4 VB encoding. Gaps are encoded using an integral number of bytes. The first bit, the continuation bit, of each byte indicates whether the code ends with this byte (1) or not (0).

docIDs	824		829	215406
gaps			5	214577
VB code	00000110 10111000		10000101	00001101 00001100 10110001

VBEncodeNumber(n)
1 bytes ← ⟨⟩
2 while true
3 do Prepend(bytes, n mod 128)
4   if n < 128
5   then Break
6   n ← n div 128
7 bytes[Length(bytes)] += 128
8 return bytes

VBEncode(numbers)
1 bytestream ← ⟨⟩
2 for each n ∈ numbers
3 do bytes ← VBEncodeNumber(n)
4   bytestream ← Extend(bytestream, bytes)
5 return bytestream

VBDecode(bytestream)
1 numbers ← ⟨⟩
2 n ← 0
3 for i ← 1 to Length(bytestream)
4 do if bytestream[i] < 128
5   then n ← 128 × n + bytestream[i]
6   else n ← 128 × n + (bytestream[i] − 128)
7   Append(numbers, n)
8   n ← 0
9 return numbers

Figure 5.8 VB encoding and decoding. The functions div and mod compute integer division and remainder after integer division, respectively. Prepend adds an element to the beginning of a list, for example, Prepend(⟨1, 2⟩, 3) = ⟨3, 1, 2⟩. Extend extends a list, for example, Extend(⟨1, 2⟩, ⟨3, 4⟩) = ⟨1, 2, 3, 4⟩.

CONTINUATION bit of the byte is a *continuation bit*. It is set to 1 for the last byte of the encoded
BIT gap and to 0 otherwise. To decode a variable byte code, we read a sequence of bytes with continuation bit 0 terminated by a byte with continuation bit 1. We then extract and concatenate the 7-bit parts. Figure 5.8 gives pseudocode for VB encoding and decoding and Table 5.4 an example of a VB-encoded postings list.[1]

With VB compression, the size of the compressed index for Reuters-RCV1 is 116 MB as we verified in an experiment. This is a more than 50% reduction of the size of the uncompressed index (see Table 5.6).

---

[1] Note that the origin is 0 in the table. Because we never need to encode a docID or a gap of 0, in practice the origin is usually 1, so that 10000000 encodes 1, 10000101 encodes 6 (not 5 as in the table), and so on.

Table 5.5 Some examples of unary and γ codes. Unary codes are only shown for the smaller numbers. Commas in γ codes are for readability only and are not part of the actual codes.

number	unary code	length	offset	γ code
0	0			
1	10	0		0
2	110	10	0	10,0
3	1110	10	1	10,1
4	11110	110	00	110,00
9	1111111110	1110	001	1110,001
13		1110	101	1110,101
24		11110	1000	11110,1000
511		111111110	11111111	111111110,11111111
1025		11111111110	0000000001	11111111110,0000000001

The idea of VB encoding can also be applied to larger or smaller units than NIBBLE bytes: 32-bit words, 16-bit words, and 4-bit words or *nibbles*. Larger words further decrease the amount of bit manipulation necessary at the cost of less effective (or no) compression. Word sizes smaller than bytes get even better compression ratios at the cost of more bit manipulation. In general, bytes offer a good compromise between compression ratio and speed of decompression.

For most IR systems variable byte codes offer an excellent tradeoff between time and space. They are also simple to implement – most of the alternatives referred to in Section 5.4 are more complex. But if disk space is a scarce resource, we can achieve better compression ratios by using bit-level encodings, in particular two closely related encodings: γ codes, which we will turn to next, and δ codes (Exercise 5.9).

5.3.2 γ codes

VB codes use an adaptive number of *bytes* depending on the size of the gap. Bit-level codes adapt the length of the code on the finer grained *bit* level. The UNARY CODE simplest bit-level code is *unary code*. The unary code of n is a string of n 1s followed by a 0 (see the first two columns of Table 5.5). Obviously, this is not a very efficient code, but it will come in handy in a moment.

How efficient can a code be in principle? Assuming the 2^n gaps G with $1 \leq G \leq 2^n$ are all equally likely, the optimal encoding uses n bits for each G. So some gaps ($G = 2^n$ in this case) cannot be encoded with fewer than $\log_2 G$ bits. Our goal is to get as close to this lower bound as possible.

γ ENCODING   A method that is within a factor of optimal is γ *encoding*. γ codes implement variable-length encoding by splitting the representation of a gap G into a pair of *length* and *offset*. *Offset* is G in binary, but with the leading 1

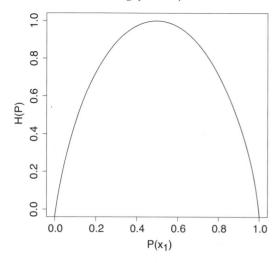

Figure 5.9 Entropy $H(P)$ as a function of $P(x_1)$ for a sample space with two outcomes x_1 and x_2.

removed.[2] For example, for 13 (binary 1101) *offset* is 101. *Length* encodes the length of *offset* in unary code. For 13, the length of *offset* is 3 bits, which is 1110 in unary. The γ code of 13 is therefore 1110101, the concatenation of length 1110 and offset 101. The right hand column of Table 5.5 gives additional examples of γ codes.

A γ code is decoded by first reading the unary code up to the 0 that terminates it, for example, the four bits 1110 when decoding 1110101. Now we know how long the offset is: 3 bits. The offset 101 can then be read correctly and the 1 that was chopped off in encoding is prepended: $101 \rightarrow 1101 = 13$.

The length of *offset* is $\lfloor \log_2 G \rfloor$ bits and the length of *length* is $\lfloor \log_2 G \rfloor + 1$ bits, so the length of the entire code is $2 \times \lfloor \log_2 G \rfloor + 1$ bits. γ codes are always of odd length and they are within a factor of 2 of what we claimed to be the optimal encoding length $\log_2 G$. We derived this optimum from the assumption that the 2^n gaps between 1 and 2^n are equiprobable. But this need not be the case. In general, we do not know the probability distribution over gaps a priori.

The characteristic of a discrete probability distribution[3] P that determines its coding properties (including whether a code is optimal) is its *entropy* $H(P)$, which is defined as follows:

ENTROPY

$$H(P) = -\sum_{x \in X} P(x) \log_2 P(x)$$

where X is the set of all possible numbers we need to be able to encode (and therefore $\sum_{x \in X} P(x) = 1.0$). Entropy is a measure of uncertainty as shown

---

[2] We assume here that G has no leading 0s. If there are any, they are removed before deleting the leading 1.

[3] Readers who want to review basic concepts of probability theory may want to consult Rice (2006) or Ross (2006). Note that we are interested in probability distributions over integers (gaps, frequencies, etc.), but that the coding properties of a probability distribution are independent of whether the outcomes are integers or something else.

in Figure 5.9 for a probability distribution P over two possible outcomes, namely, $X = \{x_1, x_2\}$. Entropy is maximized ($H(P) = 1$) for $P(x_1) = P(x_2) = 0.5$ when uncertainty about which x_i will appear next is largest; and minimized ($H(P) = 0$) for $P(x_1) = 1$, $P(x_2) = 0$ and for $P(x_1) = 0$, $P(x_2) = 1$ when there is absolute certainty.

It can be shown that the lower bound for the expected length $E(L)$ of a code L is $H(P)$ if certain conditions hold (see the references). It can further be shown that for $1 < H(P) < \infty$, γ encoding is within a factor of 3 of this optimal encoding, approaching 2 for large $H(P)$:

$$\frac{E(L_\gamma)}{H(P)} \leq 2 + \frac{1}{H(P)} \leq 3.$$

What is remarkable about this result is that it holds for any probability distribution P. So without knowing anything about the properties of the distribution of gaps, we can apply γ codes and be certain that they are within a factor of ≈ 2 of the optimal code for distributions of large entropy. A code like γ code with the property of being within a factor of optimal for an arbitrary UNIVERSAL distribution P is called *universal*.
CODE

In addition to universality, γ codes have two other properties that are use-PREFIX FREE ful for index compression. First, they are *prefix free*, namely, no γ code is the prefix of another. This means that there is always a unique decoding of a sequence of γ codes – and we do not need delimiters between them, which would decrease the efficiency of the code. The second property is that γ codes PARAMETER are *parameter free*. For many other efficient codes, we have to fit the parame-FREE ters of a model (e.g., the binomial distribution) to the distribution of gaps in the index. This complicates the implementation of compression and decompression. For instance, the parameters need to be stored and retrieved. And in dynamic indexing, the distribution of gaps can change, so that the original parameters are no longer appropriate. These problems are avoided with a parameter-free code.

How much compression of the inverted index do γ codes achieve? To answer this question we use Zipf's law, the term distribution model introduced in Section 5.1.2. According to Zipf's law, the collection frequency cf_i is proportional to the inverse of the rank i, that is, there is a constant c' such that:

(5.3)
$$\text{cf}_i = \frac{c'}{i}.$$

We can choose a different constant c such that the fractions c/i are relative frequencies and sum to 1 (that is, $c/i = \text{cf}_i/T$):

(5.4)
$$1 = \sum_{i=1}^{M} \frac{c}{i} = c \sum_{i=1}^{M} \frac{1}{i} = c\, H_M$$

(5.5)
$$c = \frac{1}{H_M}$$

	N documents
Lc most frequent terms	N gaps of 1 each
Lc next most frequent terms	N/2 gaps of 2 each
Lc next most frequent terms	N/3 gaps of 3 each
...	...

Figure 5.10 Stratification of terms for estimating the size of a γ encoded inverted index.

where M is the number of distinct terms and H_M is the Mth harmonic number.[4] Reuters-RCV1 has $M = 400{,}000$ distinct terms and $H_M \approx \ln M$, so we have

$$c = \frac{1}{H_M} \approx \frac{1}{\ln M} = \frac{1}{\ln 400{,}000} \approx \frac{1}{13}.$$

Thus the ith term has a relative frequency of roughly $1/(13i)$, and the expected average number of occurrences of term i in a document of length L is:

$$L \frac{c}{i} \approx \frac{200 \times \frac{1}{13}}{i} \approx \frac{15}{i}$$

where we interpret the relative frequency as a term occurrence probability. Recall that 200 is the average number of tokens per document in Reuters-RCV1 (Table 4.2).

Now we have derived term statistics that characterize the distribution of terms in the collection and, by extension, the distribution of gaps in the postings lists. From these statistics, we can calculate the space requirements for an inverted index compressed with γ encoding. We first stratify the vocabulary into blocks of size $Lc = 15$. On average, term i occurs $15/i$ times per document. So the average number of occurrences $\overline{f}$ per document is $1 \le \overline{f}$ for terms in the first block, corresponding to a total number of N gaps per term. The average is $\frac{1}{2} \le \overline{f} < 1$ for terms in the second block, corresponding to $N/2$ gaps per term, and $\frac{1}{3} \le \overline{f} < \frac{1}{2}$ for terms in the third block, corresponding to $N/3$ gaps per term, and so on. (We take the lower bound because it simplifies subsequent calculations. As we will see, the final estimate is too pessimistic, even with this assumption.) We will make the somewhat unrealistic assumption that all gaps for a given term have the same size as shown in Figure 5.10.

---

[4] Note that, unfortunately, the conventional symbol for both entropy and harmonic number is H. Context should make clear which is meant in this chapter.

Assuming such a uniform distribution of gaps, we then have gaps of size 1 in block 1, gaps of size 2 in block 2, and so on.

Encoding the N/j gaps of size j with γ codes, the number of bits needed for the postings list of a term in the jth block (corresponding to one row in the figure) is:

$$bits\text{-}per\text{-}row = \frac{N}{j} \times (2 \times \lfloor \log_2 j \rfloor + 1)$$

$$\approx \frac{2N \log_2 j}{j}.$$

To encode the entire block, we need $(Lc) \cdot (2N \log_2 j)/j$ bits. There are $M/(Lc)$ blocks, so the postings file as a whole will take up:

(5.6)
$$\sum_{j=1}^{\frac{M}{Lc}} \frac{2NLc \log_2 j}{j}.$$

For Reuters-RCV1, $\frac{M}{Lc} \approx 400{,}000/15 \approx 27{,}000$ and

(5.7)
$$\sum_{j=1}^{27{,}000} \frac{2 \times 10^6 \times 15 \log_2 j}{j} \approx 224 \text{ MB}.$$

So the postings file of the compressed inverted index for our 960 MB collection has a size of 224 MB, one fourth the size of the original collection.

When we run γ compression on Reuters-RCV1, the actual size of the compressed index is even lower: 101 MB, a bit more than one tenth of the size of the collection. The reason for the discrepancy between predicted and actual value is that (i) Zipf's law is not a very good approximation of the actual distribution of term frequencies for Reuters-RCV1 and (ii) gaps are not uniform. The Zipf model predicts an index size of 251 MB for the unrounded numbers from Table 4.2. If term frequencies are generated from the Zipf model and a compressed index is created for these artificial terms, then the compressed size is 254 MB. So to the extent that the assumptions about the distribution of term frequencies are accurate, the predictions of the model are correct.

Table 5.6 summarizes the compression techniques covered in this chapter. The term incidence matrix (Figure 1.1, page 4) for Reuters-RCV1 has size $400{,}000 \times 800{,}000 = 40 \times 8 \times 10^9$ bits or 40 GB.

γ codes achieve great compression ratios – about 15% better than variable byte codes for Reuters-RCV1. But they are expensive to decode. This is because many bit-level operations – shifts and masks – are necessary to decode a sequence of γ codes as the boundaries between codes will usually be somewhere in the middle of a machine word. As a result, query processing is more expensive for γ codes than for variable byte codes. Whether we choose variable byte or γ encoding depends on the characteristics of an application, for example, on the relative weights we give to conserving disk space versus maximizing query response time.

Table 5.6 Index and dictionary compression for Reuters-RCV1. The compression ratio depends on the proportion of actual text in the collection. Reuters-RCV1 contains a large amount of XML markup. Using the two best compression schemes, γ encoding and blocking with front coding, the ratio compressed index to collection size is therefore especially small for Reuters-RCV1: $(101 + 5.9)/3600 \approx 0.03$.

data structure	size in MB
dictionary, fixed-width	11.2
dictionary, term pointers into string	7.6
$\sim$, with blocking, $k = 4$	7.1
$\sim$, with blocking & front coding	5.9
collection (text, xml markup etc)	3600.0
collection (text)	960.0
term incidence matrix	40,000.0
postings, uncompressed (32-bit words)	400.0
postings, uncompressed (20 bits)	250.0
postings, variable byte encoded	116.0
postings, γ encoded	101.0

The compression ratio for the index in Table 5.6 is about 25%: 400 MB (uncompressed, each posting stored as a 32-bit word) versus 101 MB (γ) and 116 MB (VB). This shows that both γ and VB codes meet the objectives we stated in the beginning of the chapter. Index compression substantially improves time and space efficiency of indexes by reducing the amount of disk space needed, increasing the amount of information that can be kept in the cache, and speeding up data transfers from disk to memory.

?

Exercise 5.4 [⋆] Compute variable byte codes for the numbers in Tables 5.3 and 5.5.

Exercise 5.5 [⋆] Compute variable byte and γ codes for the postings list $\langle 777, 17743, 294068, 31251336 \rangle$. Use gaps instead of docIDs where possible. Write binary codes in 8-bit blocks.

Exercise 5.6 Consider the postings list $\langle 4, 10, 11, 12, 15, 62, 63, 265, 268, 270, 400 \rangle$ with a corresponding list of gaps $\langle 4, 6, 1, 1, 3, 47, 1, 202, 3, 2, 130 \rangle$. Assume that the length of the postings list is stored separately, so the system knows when a postings list is complete. Using variable byte encoding: (i) What is the largest gap you can encode in 1 byte? (ii) What is the largest gap you can encode in 2 bytes? (iii) How many bytes will the above postings list require under this encoding? (Count only space for encoding the sequence of numbers.)

Exercise 5.7

A little trick is to notice that a gap cannot be of length 0 and that the stuff left to encode after shifting cannot be 0. Based on these observations: (i) Suggest a modification to variable byte encoding that allows you to encode slightly larger gaps in the same amount of space. (ii) What is the largest gap you can encode in 1 byte? (iii) What is the largest gap you can encode in 2 bytes? (iv) How many bytes will the postings list in Exercise 5.6 require under this encoding? (Count only space for encoding the sequence of numbers.)

Exercise 5.8 [⋆] From the following sequence of γ-coded gaps, reconstruct first the gap sequence and then the postings sequence: 1110001110101011111101101111011.

Exercise 5.9 γ codes are relatively inefficient for large numbers (e.g., 1025 in Table 5.5) as they encode the length of the offset in inefficient unary code. δ CODES   δ *codes* differ from γ codes in that they encode the first part of the code (*length*) in γ code instead of unary code. The encoding of *offset* is the same. For example, the δ code of 7 is 10,0,11 (again, we add commas for readability). 10,0 is the γ code for *length* (2 in this case) and the encoding of *offset* (11) is unchanged. (i) Compute the δ codes for the other numbers in Table 5.5. For what range of numbers is the δ code shorter than the γ code? (ii) γ code beats variable byte code in Table 5.6 because the index contains stop words and thus many small gaps. Show that variable byte code is more compact if larger gaps dominate. (iii) Compare the compression ratios of δ code and variable byte code for a distribution of gaps dominated by large gaps.

Exercise 5.10 [⋆] We have defined unary codes as being "10": sequences of 1s terminated by a 0. Interchanging the roles of 0s and 1s yields an equivalent "01" unary code. When this 01 unary code is used, the construction of a γ code can be stated as follows: (1) Write G down in binary using $b = \lfloor \log_2 j \rfloor + 1$ bits. (2) Prepend $(b - 1)$ 0s. (i) Encode the numbers in Table 5.5 in this alternative γ code. (ii) Show that this method produces a well-defined alternative γ code in the sense that it has the same length and can be uniquely decoded.

Exercise 5.11 [⋆ ⋆ ⋆] Unary code is not a universal code in the sense defined above. However, there exists a distribution over gaps for which unary code is optimal. Which distribution is this?

Exercise 5.12 Give some examples of terms that violate the assumption that gaps all have the same size (which we made when estimating the space requirements of a γ-encoded index). What are general characteristics of these terms?

Exercise 5.13 Consider a term whose postings list has size n, say, $n = 10{,}000$. Compare the size of the γ-compressed gap-encoded postings list if the distribution of the term is uniform (i.e., all gaps have the same size) versus its

Table 5.7 Two gap sequences to be merged in blocked sort-based indexing

γ encoded gap sequence of run 1	1110110111111001011111111110100011111001
γ encoded gap sequence of run 2	11111010000111111000100011111110010000011111010101

size when the distribution is not uniform. Which compressed postings list is smaller?

Exercise 5.14 Work out the sum in Equation (5.7) and show it adds up to about 251 MB. Use the numbers in Table 4.2, but do not round Lc, c, and the number of vocabulary blocks.

Exercise 5.15 Go through the above calculation of index size and explicitly state all the approximations that were made to arrive at Equation 5.6.

Exercise 5.16 For a collection of your choosing, determine the number of documents and terms and the average length of a document. (i) How large is the inverted index predicted to be by Equation (5.6)? (ii) Implement an indexer that creates a γ-compressed inverted index for the collection. How large is the actual index? (iii) Implement an indexer that uses variable byte encoding. How large is the variable byte encoded index?

Exercise 5.17 To be able to hold as many postings as possible in main memory, it is a good idea to compress intermediate index files during index construction. (i) This makes merging runs in blocked sort-based indexing more complicated. As an example, work out the γ-encoded merged sequence of the gaps in Table 5.7. (ii) Index construction is more space efficient when using compression. Would you also expect it to be faster?

Exercise 5.18 (i) Show that the size of the vocabulary is finite according to Zipf's law and infinite according to Heaps' law. (ii) Can we derive Heaps' law from Zipf's law?

5.4 References and further reading

Heaps' law was discovered by Heaps (1978). See also Baeza-Yates and Ribeiro-Neto (1999). A detailed study of vocabulary growth in large collections is (Williams and Zobel 2005). Zipf's law is due to Zipf (1949). Witten and Bell (1990) investigate the quality of the fit obtained by the law. Other term distribution models, including K mixture and two-poisson model, are discussed by Manning and Schütze (1999, Chapter 15). Carmel et al. (2001), Büttcher and Clarke (2006), Blanco and Barreiro (2007), and Ntoulas and Cho (2007) show that lossy compression can achieve good compression with no or no significant decrease in retrieval effectiveness.

Dictionary compression is covered in detail by Witten et al. (1999, Chapter 4), which is recommended as additional reading.

Subsection 5.3.1 is based on (Scholer et al. 2002). The authors find that variable byte codes process queries two times faster than either bit-level compressed indexes or uncompressed indexes with a 30% penalty in compression ratio compared with the best bit-level compression method. They also show that compressed indexes can be superior to uncompressed indexes not only in disk usage, but also in query processing speed. Compared with VB codes, "variable nibble" codes showed 5% to 10% better compression and up to one third worse effectiveness in one experiment (Anh and Moffat 2005). Trotman (2003) also recommends using VB codes unless disk space is at a premium. In recent work, Anh and Moffat (2005, 2006a) and Zukowski et al. (2006) have constructed word-aligned binary codes that are both faster in decompression and at least as efficient as VB codes. Zhang et al. (2007) investigate the increased effectiveness of caching when a number of different compression techniques for postings lists are used on modern hardware.

δ codes (Exercise 5.9) and γ codes were introduced by Elias (1975), who proved that both codes are universal. In addition, δ codes are asymptotically optimal for $H(P) \to \infty$. δ codes perform better than γ codes if large numbers (greater than 15) dominate. A good introduction to information theory, including the concept of entropy, is (Cover and Thomas 1991). While Elias codes are only asymptotically optimal, arithmetic codes (Witten et al. 1999, Section 2.4) can be constructed to be arbitrarily close to the optimum $H(P)$ for any P.

Several additional index compression techniques are covered by Witten et al. (1999; Sections 3.3 and 3.4 and Chapter 5). They recommend using PARAMETERIZED *parameterized codes* for index compression, codes that explicitly model the CODE probability distribution of gaps for each term. For example, they show that GOLOMB *Golomb codes* achieve better compression ratios than γ codes for large col- CODES lections. Moffat and Zobel (1992) compare several parameterized methods, including LLRUN (Fraenkel and Klein 1985).

The distribution of gaps in a postings list depends on the assignment of docIDs to documents. A number of researchers have looked into assigning docIDs in a way that is conducive to the efficient compression of gap sequences (Moffat and Stuiver 1996; Blandford and Blelloch 2002; Silvestri et al. 2004; Blanco and Barreiro 2006; Silvestri 2007). These techniques assign docIDs in a small range to documents in a cluster where a cluster can consist of all documents in a given time period, on a particular web site, or sharing another property. As a result, when a sequence of documents from a cluster occurs in a postings list, their gaps are small and can be more effectively compressed.

Different considerations apply to the compression of term frequencies and word positions than to the compression of docIDs in postings lists. See Scholer et al. (2002) and Zobel and Moffat (2006). Zobel and Moffat (2006) is recommended in general as an in-depth and up-to-date tutorial on inverted indexes, including index compression.

This chapter only looks at index compression for Boolean retrieval. For ranked retrieval (Chapter 6), it is advantageous to order postings according to term frequency instead of docID. During query processing, the scanning of many postings lists can then be terminated early because smaller weights do not change the ranking of the highest ranked k documents found so far. It is not a good idea to precompute and store weights in the index (as opposed to frequencies) because they cannot be compressed as well as integers (see Section 7.1.5, page 129).

Document compression can also be important in an efficient information retrieval system. De Moura et al. (2000) and Brisaboa et al. (2007) describe compression schemes that allow direct searching of terms and phrases in the compressed text, which is infeasible with standard text compression utilities like gzip and compress.

6 *Scoring, term weighting, and the vector space model*

Thus far, we have dealt with indexes that support Boolean queries: A document either matches or does not match a query. In the case of large document collections, the resulting number of matching documents can far exceed the number a human user could possibly sift through. Accordingly, it is essential for a search engine to rank-order the documents matching a query. To do this, the search engine computes, for each matching document, a score with respect to the query at hand. In this chapter, we initiate the study of assigning a score to a (query, document) pair. This chapter consists of three main ideas.

1. We introduce parametric and zone indexes in Section 6.1, which serve two purposes. First, they allow us to index and retrieve documents by metadata, such as the language in which a document is written. Second, they give us a simple means for scoring (and thereby ranking) documents in response to a query.
2. Next, in Section 6.2 we develop the idea of weighting the importance of a term in a document, based on the statistics of occurrence of the term.
3. In Section 6.3, we show that by viewing each document as a vector of such weights, we can compute a score between a query and each document. This view is known as vector space scoring.

Section 6.4 develops several variants of term-weighting for the vector space model. Chapter 7 develops computational aspects of vector space scoring and related topics.

As we develop these ideas, the notion of a query assumes multiple nuances. In Section 6.1, we consider queries in which specific query terms occur in specified regions of a matching document. Beginning with Section 6.2, we in fact relax the requirement of matching specific regions of a document; instead, we look at so-called free text queries that simply consist of query terms with no specification on their relative order, importance, or where in a document they should be found. The bulk of our study of scoring is in this latter notion of a query being such a set of terms.

100

Bibliographic Search

Search category	Value
Author	*Example:* Widom, J *or* Garcia-Molina
Title	Also a part of the title possible
Date of publication	*Example:* 1997 *or* <1997 *or* >1997 limits the search to the documents appeared in, before and after 1997 respectively
Language	Language the document was written in English ▾
Project	ANY ▾
Type	ANY ▾
Subject group	ANY ▾
Sorted by	Date of publication ▾
	[Start bibliographic search]

[Find document via ID]

Figure 6.1 Parametric search. In this example, we have a collection with fields allowing us to select publications by zones such as Author and fields such as Language.

6.1 Parametric and zone indexes

METADATA

FIELD

We have thus far viewed a document as a sequence of terms. In fact, most documents have additional structure. Digital documents generally encode, in machine-recognizable form, certain *metadata* associated with each document. By metadata, we mean specific forms of data about a document, such as its author(s), title, and date of publication. These metadata would generally include *fields*, such as the date of creation and the format of the document, as well the author and possibly the title of the document. The possible values of a field should be thought of as finite – for instance, the set of all dates of authorship.

PARAMETRIC
INDEX

Consider queries of the form "find documents authored by William Shakespeare in 1601, containing the phrase alas poor Yorick." Query processing then consists as usual of postings intersections, except that we may merge postings from standard inverted as well as *parametric indexes*. There is one parametric index for each field (say, date of creation); it allows us to select only the documents matching a date specified in the query. Figure 6.1 illustrates the user's view of such a parametric search. Some of the fields may assume ordered values, such as dates; in the example query above, the year 1601 is one such field value. The search engine may support querying ranges on such ordered values; to this end, a structure like a B-tree may be used for the field's dictionary.

ZONE

Zones are similar to fields, except the contents of a zone can be arbitrary free text. Whereas a field may take on a relatively small set of values, a zone

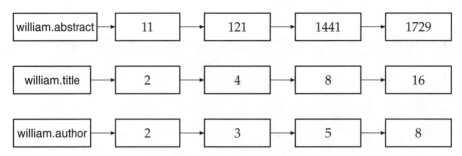

Figure 6.2 Basic zone index; zones are encoded as extensions of dictionary entries.

can be thought of as an arbitrary, unbounded amount of text. For instance, document titles and abstracts are generally treated as zones. We may build a separate inverted index for each zone of a document, to support queries such as "find documents with merchant in the title and william in the author list and the phrase gentle rain in the body." This has the effect of building an index that looks like Figure 6.2. Whereas the dictionary for a parametric index comes from a fixed vocabulary (the set of languages, or the set of dates), the dictionary for a zone index must structure whatever vocabulary stems from the text of that zone.

In fact, we can reduce the size of the dictionary by encoding the zone in which a term occurs in the postings. In Figure 6.3 for instance, we show how occurrences of william in the title and author zones of various documents are encoded. Such an encoding is useful when the size of the dictionary is a concern (because we require the dictionary to fit in main memory). But there is another important reason why the encoding of Figure 6.3 is useful:
WEIGHTED   the efficient computation of scores using a technique we call *weighted zone*
ZONE   *scoring*.
SCORING

6.1.1 Weighted zone scoring

Thus far in Section 6.1 we have focused on retrieving documents based on Boolean queries on fields and zones. We now turn to a second application of zones and fields.

Given a Boolean query q and a document d, weighted zone scoring assigns to the pair (q, d) a score in the interval $[0, 1]$, by computing a linear combination of *zone scores*, where each zone of the document contributes a Boolean value. More specifically, consider a set of documents, each of which

Figure 6.3 Zone index in which the zone is encoded in the postings rather than the dictionary.

has ℓ zones. Let $g_1, \ldots, g_\ell \in [0, 1]$ such that $\sum_{i=1}^{\ell} g_i = 1$. For $1 \le i \le \ell$, let s_i be the Boolean score denoting a match (or absence thereof) between q and the ith zone. For instance, the Boolean score from a zone could be 1 if all the query term(s) occur in that zone, and zero otherwise; indeed, it could be any Boolean function that maps the presence of query terms in a zone to $\{0, 1\}$. Then, the weighted zone score is defined to be

(6.1)
$$\sum_{i=1}^{\ell} g_i s_i.$$

RANKED Weighted zone scoring is sometimes referred to also as *ranked Boolean re-*
BOOLEAN *trieval.*
RETRIEVAL

Example 6.1: Consider the query shakespeare in a collection in which each document has three zones: *author, title,* and *body.* The Boolean score function for a zone takes on the value 1 if the query term shakespeare is present in the zone, and 0 otherwise. Weighted zone scoring in such a collection requires three weights $g_1, g_2,$ and $g_3,$ respectively corresponding to the *author, title,* and *body* zones. Suppose we set $g_1 = 0.2, g_2 = 0.3,$ and $g_3 = 0.5$ (so that the three weights add up to 1); this corresponds to an application in which a match in the *author* zone is least important to the overall score, the *title* zone somewhat more, and the *body* contributes even more.

Thus, if the term shakespeare were to appear in the *title* and *body* zones but not the *author* zone of a document, the score of this document would be 0.8.

How do we implement the computation of weighted zone scores? A simple approach is to compute the score for each document in turn, adding in all the contributions from the various zones. However, we now show how we may compute weighted zone scores directly from inverted indexes. The algorithm in Figure 6.4 treats the case when the query q is a two-term query consisting of query terms q_1 and $q_2,$ and the Boolean function is AND: 1 if both query terms are present in a zone and 0 otherwise. After the description of the algorithm, we describe the extension to more complex queries and Boolean functions.

The reader may have noticed the close similarity between this algorithm and that in Figure 1.6. Indeed, they represent the same postings traversal, except that, instead of merely adding a document to the set of results for a Boolean AND query, we now compute a score for each such document. Some
ACCUMULATOR literature refers to the array scores[] above as a set of *accumulators.* The reason for this will be clear as we consider more complex Boolean functions than the AND; thus, we may assign a nonzero score to a document even if it does not contain all query terms.

ZoneScore(q_1, q_2)

```
1   float scores[N] = [0]
2   constant g[ℓ]
3   p₁ ← postings(q₁)
4   p₂ ← postings(q₂)
5   // scores[] is an array with a score entry for each document, initialized to zero.
6   //p₁ and p₂ are initialized to point to the beginning of their respective postings.
7   //Assume g[] is initialized to the respective zone weights.
8   while p₁ ≠ NIL and p₂ ≠ NIL
9   do if docI D(p₁) = docI D(p₂)
10      then scores[docI D(p₁)] ← WeightedZone(p₁, p₂, g)
11           p₁ ← next(p₁)
12           p₂ ← next(p₂)
13      else  if docI D(p₁) < docI D(p₂)
14           then p₁ ← next(p₁)
15           else  p₂ ← next(p₂)
16  return scores
```

Figure 6.4 Algorithm for computing the weighted zone score from two postings lists. Function WeightedZone (not shown here) is assumed to compute the inner loop of Equation 6.1.

6.1.2 *Learning weights*

How do we determine the weights g_i for weighted zone scoring? These weights could be specified by an expert (or, in principle, the user); but increasingly, these weights are "learned" using training examples that have been judged editorially. This methodology falls under a general class of ap-

MACHINE- proaches to scoring and ranking in information retrieval known as *machine-*
LEARNED *learned relevance*. We provide a brief introduction to this topic here because
RELEVANCE weighted zone scoring presents a clean setting for introducing it; a complete development demands an understanding of machine learning and is deferred to Chapter 15.

1. We are provided with a set of *training examples*, each of which is a tuple consisting of a query q and a document d, together with a relevance judgment for d on q. In the simplest form, each relevance judgment is either *relevant* or *nonrelevant*. More sophisticated implementations of the methodology make use of more nuanced judgments.

2. The weights g_i are then "learned" from these examples, in order that the learned scores approximate the relevance judgments in the training examples.

For weighted zone scoring, the process may be viewed as learning a linear function of the Boolean match scores contributed by the various zones. The expensive component of this methodology is the labor-intensive assembly of user-generated relevance judgments from which to learn the weights,

Example	DocID	Query	s_T	s_B	Judgment
Φ_1	37	linux	1	1	Relevant
Φ_2	37	penguin	0	1	Nonrelevant
Φ_3	238	system	0	1	Relevant
Φ_4	238	penguin	0	0	Nonrelevant
Φ_5	1741	kernel	1	1	Relevant
Φ_6	2094	driver	0	1	Relevant
Φ_7	3191	driver	1	0	Nonrelevant

Figure 6.5 An illustration of training examples.

especially in a collection that changes frequently (such as the Web). We now detail a simple example that illustrates how we can reduce the problem of learning the weights g_i to a simple optimization problem.

We now consider a simple case of weighted zone scoring, where each document has a *title* zone and a *body* zone. Given a query q and a document d, we use the given Boolean match function to compute Boolean variables $s_T(d, q)$ and $s_B(d, q)$, depending on whether the title (respectively, body) zone of d matches query q. For instance, the algorithm in Figure 6.4 uses an AND of the query terms for this Boolean function. We will compute a score between 0 and 1 for each (document, query) pair using $s_T(d, q)$ and $s_B(d, q)$ by using a constant $g \in [0, 1]$, as follows:

$$(6.2) \qquad score\,(d, q) = g \cdot s_T(d, q) + (1 - g)s_B(d, q).$$

We now describe how to determine the constant g from a set of *training examples*, each of which is a triple of the form $\Phi_j = (d_j, q_j, r(d_j, q_j))$. In each training example, a given training document d_j and a given training query q_j are assessed by a human editor who delivers a relevance judgment $r(d_j, q_j)$ that is either *relevant* or *nonrelevant*. This is illustrated in Figure 6.5, where seven training examples are shown.

For each training example Φ_j we have Boolean values $s_T(d_j, q_j)$ and $s_B(d_j, q_j)$ that we use to compute a score from (6.2)

$$(6.3) \qquad score\,(d_j, q_j) = g \cdot s_T(d_j, q_j) + (1 - g)s_B(d_j, q_j).$$

We now compare this computed score with the human relevance judgment for the same document–query pair (d_j, q_j); to this end, we quantize each *relevant* judgment as a 1 and each *nonrelevant* judgment as a 0. Suppose that we define the error of the scoring function with weight g as

$$\varepsilon(g, \Phi_j) = (r(d_j, q_j) - score\,(d_j, q_j))^2,$$

where we have quantized the editorial relevance judgment $r(d_j, q_j)$ to 0 or 1. Then, the total error of a set of training examples is given by

$$(6.4) \qquad \sum_j \varepsilon(g, \Phi_j).$$

s_T	s_B	Score
0	0	0
0	1	$1 - g$
1	0	g
1	1	1

Figure 6.6   The four possible combinations of s_T and s_B.

The problem of learning the constant g from the given training examples then reduces to picking the value of g that minimizes the total error in (6.4).

Picking the best value of g in (6.4) in the formulation of Section 6.1.3 reduces to the problem of minimizing a quadratic function of g over the interval $[0, 1]$. This reduction is detailed in Section 6.1.3.

6.1.3 The optimal weight g

We begin by noting that for any training example Φ_j for which $s_T(d_j, q_j) = 0$ and $s_B(d_j, q_j) = 1$, the score computed by Equation (6.2) is $1 - g$. In similar fashion, we may write down the score computed by Equation (6.2) for the three other possible combinations of $s_T(d_j, q_j)$ and $s_B(d_j, q_j)$; this is summarized in Figure 6.6.

Let n_{01r} (respectively, n_{01n}) denote the number of training examples for which $s_T(d_j, q_j) = 0$ and $s_B(d_j, q_j) = 1$ and the editorial judgment is *relevant* (respectively, *nonrelevant*). Then the contribution to the total error in Equation (6.4) from training examples for which $s_T(d_j, q_j) = 0$ and $s_B(d_j, q_j) = 1$ is

$$[1 - (1 - g)]^2 n_{01r} + [0 - (1 - g)]^2 n_{01n}.$$

By writing in similar fashion the error contributions from training examples of the other three combinations of values for $s_T(d_j, q_j)$ and $s_B(d_j, q_j)$ (and extending the notation in the obvious manner), the total error corresponding to Equation (6.4) is

$$(6.5) \qquad (n_{01r} + n_{10n})g^2 + (n_{10r} + n_{01n})(1 - g)^2 + n_{00r} + n_{11n}.$$

By differentiating Equation (6.5) with respect to g and setting the result to 0, it follows that the optimal value of g is

$$(6.6) \qquad \frac{n_{10r} + n_{01n}}{n_{10r} + n_{10n} + n_{01r} + n_{01n}}.$$

Exercise 6.1 When using weighted zone scoring, is it necessary for all zones to use the same Boolean match function?

Exercise 6.2 In Example 6.1 above with weights $g_1 = 0.2$, $g_2 = 0.31$ and $g_3 = 0.49$, what are all the distinct score values a document may get?

Exercise 6.3 Rewrite the algorithm in Figure 6.4 to the case of more than two query terms.

Exercise 6.4 Write pseudocode for the function WeightedZone for the case of two postings lists in Figure 6.4.

Exercise 6.5 Apply Equation 6.6 to the sample training set in Figure 6.5 to estimate the best value of g for this sample.

Exercise 6.6 For the value of g estimated in Exercise 6.5, compute the weighted zone score for each (query, document) example. How do these scores relate to the relevance judgments in Figure 6.5 (quantized to $0/1$)?

Exercise 6.7 Why does the expression for g in (6.6) not involve training examples in which $s_T(d_t, q_t)$ and $s_B(d_t, q_t)$ have the same value?

6.2 Term frequency and weighting

Thus far, scoring has hinged on whether or not a query term is present in a zone within a document. We take the next logical step: a document or zone that mentions a query term more often has more to do with that query and therefore should receive a higher score. To motivate this, we recall the notion of a free text query introduced in Section 1.4: a query in which the terms of the query are typed freeform into the search interface, without any connecting search operators (such as Boolean operators). This query style, which is extremely popular on the web, views the query as simply a set of words. A plausible scoring mechanism then is to compute a score that is the sum, over the query terms, of the match scores between each query term and the document.

Toward this end, we assign to each term in a document a *weight* for that term that depends on the number of occurrences of the term in the document. We would like to compute a score between a query term t and a document d, based on the weight of t in d. The simplest approach is to assign the weight to be equal to the number of occurrences of term t in document TERM d. This weighting scheme is referred to as *term frequency* and is denoted $\mathrm{tf}_{t,d}$, FREQUENCY with the subscripts denoting the term and the document in order.

For a document d, the set of weights determined by the tf weights above (or indeed any weighting function that maps the number of occurrences of t in d to a positive real value) may be viewed as a quantitative digest of that BAG OF WORDS document. In this view of a document, known in the literature as the *bag of words model*, the exact ordering of the terms in a document is ignored but the number of occurrences of each term is material (in contrast with Boolean retrieval). We only retain information on the number of occurrences of each term. Thus, the document *Mary is quicker than John* is, in this view, identical to the document *John is quicker than Mary*. Nevertheless, it seems intuitive that two documents with similar bag of words representations are similar in content. We will develop this intuition further in Section 6.3.

Word	cf	df
try	10422	8760
insurance	10440	3997

Figure 6.7 Collection frequency (cf) and document frequency (df) behave differently, as in this example from the Reuters-RCV1 collection.

Before doing so we first study this question: Are all words in a document equally important? Clearly not; in Section 2.2.2 (page 25) we looked at the idea of *stop words* – words that we decide not to index at all, and therefore do not contribute in any way to retrieval and scoring.

6.2.1 Inverse document frequency

Raw term frequency as above suffers from a critical problem: All terms are considered equally important when it comes to assessing relevancy on a query. In fact, certain terms have little or no discriminating power in determining relevance. For instance, a collection of documents on the auto industry is likely to have the term auto in almost every document. To this end, we introduce a mechanism for attenuating the effect of terms that occur too often in the collection to be meaningful for relevance determination. An immediate idea is to scale down the term weights of terms with high *collection frequency*, defined to be the total number of occurrences of a term in the collection. The idea is to reduce the tf weight of a term by a factor that grows with its collection frequency.

DOCUMENT   Instead, it is more commonplace to use for this purpose the *document fre-*
FREQUENCY *quency* df_t, defined to be the number of documents in the collection that contain a term t. This is because in trying to discriminate between documents for the purpose of scoring, it is better to use a document-level statistic (such as the number of documents containing a term) than to use a collection-wide statistic for the term. The reason to prefer df to cf is illustrated in Figure 6.7, where a simple example shows that collection frequency (cf) and document frequency (df) can behave rather differently. In particular, the cf values for both try and insurance are roughly equal, but their df values differ significantly. Intuitively, we want the few documents that contain insurance to get a higher boost for a query on insurance than the many documents containing try get from a query on try.

How is the document frequency df of a term used to scale its weight? Denoting as usual the total number of documents in a collection by N, we define
INVERSE the *inverse document frequency* (idf) of a term t as follows:
DOCUMENT
FREQUENCY

(6.7)
$$\mathrm{idf}_t = \log \frac{N}{\mathrm{df}_t}.$$

term	df_t	idf_t
car	18,165	1.65
auto	6723	2.08
insurance	19,241	1.62
best	25,235	1.5

Figure 6.8 Example of idf values. Here we give the idf's of terms with various frequencies in the Reuters collection of 806,791 documents.

Thus the idf of a rare term is high, whereas the idf of a frequent term is likely to be low. Figure 6.8 gives an example of idf's in the Reuters-RCV1 collection of 806,791 documents; in this example, logarithms are to the base 10. In fact, as we will see in Exercise 6.12, the precise base of the logarithm is not material to ranking. We will give on page 209 a justification of the particular form in Equation (6.7).

6.2.2 Tf–idf weighting

We now combine the definitions of term frequency and inverse document frequency to produce a composite weight for each term in each document.

TF–IDF The *tf–idf* weighting scheme assigns to term t a weight in document d given by

$$(6.8) \qquad \text{tf-idf}_{t,d} = \text{tf}_{t,d} \times \text{idf}_t.$$

In other words, tf–idf$_{t,d}$ assigns to term t a weight in document d that is

1. highest when t occurs many times within a small number of documents (thus lending high discriminating power to those documents);
2. lower when the term occurs fewer times in a document, or occurs in many documents (thus offering a less pronounced relevance signal);
3. lowest when the term occurs in virtually all documents.

DOCUMENT At this point, we may view each document as a *vector* with one component
VECTOR corresponding to each term in the dictionary, together with a weight for each component that is given by (6.8). For dictionary terms that do not occur in a document, this weight is zero. This vector form will prove to be crucial to scoring and ranking; we will develop these ideas in Section 6.3. As a first step, we introduce the *overlap score measure*: The score of a document d is the sum, over all query terms, of the number of times each of the query terms occurs in d. We can refine this idea so that we add up not the number of occurrences of each query term t in d, but instead the tf–idf weight of each term in d.

$$(6.9) \qquad \text{Score}(q, d) = \sum_{t \in q} \text{tf-idf}_{t,d}.$$

	Doc1	Doc2	Doc3
car	27	4	24
auto	3	33	0
insurance	0	33	29
best	14	0	17

Figure 6.9 Table of tf values for Exercise 6.10.

In Section 6.3, we will develop a more rigorous form of Equation (6.9).

?

Exercise 6.8 Why is the idf of a term always finite?

Exercise 6.9 What is the idf of a term that occurs in every document? Compare this with the use of stop word lists.

Exercise 6.10 Consider the table of term frequencies for 3 documents denoted Doc1, Doc2, Doc3 in Figure 6.9. Compute the tf–idf weights for the terms car, auto, insurance, and best, for each document, using the idf values from Figure 6.8.

Exercise 6.11 Can the tf–idf weight of a term in a document exceed 1?

Exercise 6.12 How does the base of the logarithm in (6.7) affect the score calculation in (6.9)? How does the base of the logarithm affect the relative scores of two documents on a given query?

Exercise 6.13 If the logarithm in (6.7) is computed base 2, suggest a simple approximation to the idf of a term.

6.3 The vector space model for scoring

In Section 6.2 (page 107) we developed the notion of a document vector that captures the relative importance of the terms in a document. The representation of a set of documents as vectors in a common vector space is known VECTOR SPACE as the *vector space model* and is fundamental to a host of information retrieval MODEL (IR) operations including scoring documents on a query, document classification, and document clustering. We first develop the basic ideas underlying vector space scoring; a pivotal step in this development is the view (Section 6.3.2) of queries as vectors in the same vector space as the document collection.

6.3.1 Dot products

We denote by $\vec{V}(d)$ the vector derived from document d, with one component in the vector for each dictionary term. Unless otherwise specified, the reader may assume that the components are computed using the tf–idf weighting

	Doc1	Doc2	Doc3
car	0.88	0.09	0.58
auto	0.10	0.71	0
insurance	0	0.71	0.70
best	0.46	0	0.41

Figure 6.10 Euclidean normalized tf values for documents in Figure 6.9.

scheme, although the particular weighting scheme is immaterial to the discussion that follows. The set of documents in a collection then may be viewed as a set of vectors in a vector space, in which there is one axis for each term. This representation loses the relative ordering of the terms in each document; recall our example from Section 6.2 (page 107), where we pointed out that the documents *Mary is quicker than John* and *John is quicker than Mary* are identical in such a *bag of words* representation.

How do we quantify the similarity between two documents in this vector space? A first attempt might consider the magnitude of the vector difference between two document vectors. This measure suffers from a drawback: Two documents with very similar content can have a significant vector difference simply because one is much longer than the other. Thus, the relative distributions of terms may be identical in the two documents, but the absolute term frequencies of one may be far larger.

To compensate for the effect of document length, the standard way of quantifying the similarity between two documents d_1 and d_2 is to compute the *cosine similarity* of their vector representations $\vec{V}(d_1)$ and $\vec{V}(d_2)$

COSINE
SIMILARITY

$$(6.10) \qquad \text{sim}(d_1, d_2) = \frac{\vec{V}(d_1) \cdot \vec{V}(d_2)}{|\vec{V}(d_1)||\vec{V}(d_2)|},$$

DOT PRODUCT where the numerator represents the *dot product* (also known as the *inner product*) of the vectors $\vec{V}(d_1)$ and $\vec{V}(d_2)$, and the denominator is the product of EUCLIDEAN their *Euclidean lengths*. The dot product $\vec{x} \cdot \vec{y}$ of two vectors is defined as LENGTH $\sum_{i=1}^{M} x_i y_i$. Let $\vec{V}(d)$ denote the document vector for d, with M components $\vec{V}_1(d) \ldots \vec{V}_M(d)$. The Euclidean length of d is defined as $\sqrt{\sum_{i=1}^{M} \vec{V}_i^2(d)}$.

LENGTH- The effect of the denominator of Equation (6.10) is thus to *length-normalize*
NORMALIZATION the vectors $\vec{V}(d_1)$ and $\vec{V}(d_2)$ to unit vectors $\vec{v}(d_1) = \vec{V}(d_1)/|\vec{V}(d_1)|$ and $\vec{v}(d_2) = \vec{V}(d_2)/|\vec{V}(d_2)|$. We can then rewrite (6.10) as

$$(6.11) \qquad \text{sim}(d_1, d_2) = \vec{v}(d_1) \cdot \vec{v}(d_2).$$

Example 6.2: Consider the documents in Figure 6.9. We now apply Euclidean normalization to the tf values from the table, for each of the three documents in the table. The quantity $\sqrt{\sum_{i=1}^{M} \vec{V}_i^2(d)}$ has the values 30.56, 46.84, and 41.30 respectively for Doc1, Doc2, and Doc3. The resulting Euclidean normalized tf values for these documents are shown in Figure 6.10.

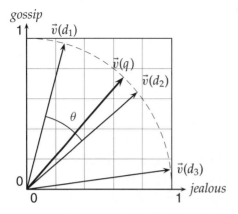

Figure 6.11 Cosine similarity illustrated: $\mathrm{sim}(d_1, d_2) = \cos\theta$.

Thus, (6.11) can be viewed as the dot product of the normalized versions of the two document vectors. This measure is the cosine of the angle θ between the two vectors, shown in Figure 6.11. What use is the similarity measure $\mathrm{sim}(d_1, d_2)$? Given a document d (potentially one of the d_i in the collection), consider searching for the documents in the collection most similar to d. Such a search is useful in a system where a user may identify a document and seek others like it – a feature available in the results lists of search engines as a *more like this* feature. We reduce the problem of finding the document(s) most similar to d to that of finding the d_i with the highest dot products (sim values) $\vec{v}(d) \cdot \vec{v}(d_i)$. We could do this by computing the dot products between $\vec{v}(d)$ and each of $\vec{v}(d_1), \ldots, \vec{v}(d_N)$, then picking off the highest resulting sim values.

 Example 6.3: Figure 6.12 shows the number of occurrences of three terms (affection, jealous, and gossip) in each of the following three novels: Jane Austen's *Sense and Sensibility* (SaS) and *Pride and Prejudice* (PaP) and Emily Brontë's *Wuthering Heights* (WH). Of course, there are many other terms occurring in each of these novels. In this example, we represent each of these novels as a unit vector in three dimensions, corresponding to these three terms (only); we use raw term frequencies here, with no idf multiplier. The resulting weights are as shown in Figure 6.13.

Now consider the cosine similarities between pairs of the resulting three-dimensional vectors. A simple computation shows that $\mathrm{sim}(\vec{v}(\mathrm{SAS}),$

term	SaS	PaP	WH
affection	115	58	20
jealous	10	7	11
gossip	2	0	6

Figure 6.12 Term frequencies in three novels. The novels are Austen's *Sense and Sensibility*, and *Pride and Prejudice*, and Brontë's *Wuthering Heights*.

term	SaS	PaP	WH
affection	0.996	0.993	0.847
jealous	0.087	0.120	0.466
gossip	0.017	0	0.254

Figure 6.13 Term vectors for the three novels of Figure 6.12. These are based on raw term frequency only and are normalized as if these were the only terms in the collection. (Because affection and jealous occur in all three documents, their tf–idf weight is 0 in most formulations.)

$\vec{v}$(PAP)) is 0.999, whereas sim($\vec{v}$(SAS), $\vec{v}$(WH)) is 0.888; thus, the two books authored by Austen (SaS and PaP) are considerably closer to each other than to Brontë's *Wuthering Heights*. In fact, the similarity between the first two is almost perfect (when restricted to the three terms we consider). Here we have considered tf weights, but we could of course use other term weight functions.

Viewing a collection of N documents as a collection of vectors leads to a natural view of a collection as a *term–document matrix*: this is an $M \times N$ matrix whose rows represent the M terms (dimensions) of the N columns, each of which corresponds to a document. As always, the terms being indexed could be stemmed before indexing; for instance, jealous and jealousy would, under stemming, be considered as a single dimension. This matrix view will prove to be useful in Chapter 18.

TERM–DOCUMENT MATRIX

6.3.2 Queries as vectors

There is a far more compelling reason to represent documents as vectors: we can also view a *query* as a vector. Consider the query q = jealous gossip. This query turns into the unit vector $\vec{v}(q) = (0, 0.707, 0.707)$ on the three co-ordinates of Figures 6.12 and 6.13. The key idea now is to assign to each document d a score equal to the dot product

$$\vec{v}(q) \cdot \vec{v}(d).$$

In the example of Figure 6.13, *Wuthering Heights* is the top-scoring document for this query with a score of 0.509, with *Pride and Prejudice* a distant second with a score of 0.085, and *Sense and Sensibility* last with a score of 0.074. This simple example is somewhat misleading: the number of dimensions in practice is far larger than three; it equals the vocabulary size M.

To summarize, by viewing a query as a "bag of words," we are able to treat it as a very short document. As a consequence, we can use the cosine similarity between the query vector and a document vector as a measure of the score of the document for that query. The resulting scores can then be used to select the top-scoring documents for a query. Thus, we have

(6.12)
$$\text{score}(q, d) = \frac{\vec{V}(q) \cdot \vec{V}(d)}{|\vec{V}(q)||\vec{V}(d)|}.$$

A document may have a high cosine score for a query, even if it does not contain all query terms. Note that the preceding discussion does not hinge on any specific weighting of terms in the document vector, although for the present we may think of them as either tf or tf–idf weights. In fact, a number of weighting schemes are possible for query as well as document vectors, as illustrated in Example 6.4 and developed further in Section 6.4.

Computing the cosine similarities between the query vector and each document vector in the collection, sorting the resulting scores and selecting the top K documents can be expensive – a single similarity computation can entail a dot product in tens of thousands of dimensions, demanding tens of thousands of arithmetic operations. In Section 7.1 we study how to use an inverted index for this purpose, followed by a series of heuristics for improving on this.

Example 6.4: We now consider the query best car insurance on a fictitious collection with $N = 1,000,000$ documents where the document frequencies of auto, best, car and insurance are respectively 5000, 50000, 10000, and 1000.

term	query				document			product
	tf	df	idf	$w_{t,q}$	tf	wf	$w_{t,d}$	
auto	0	5000	2.3	0	1	1	0.41	0
best	1	50000	1.3	1.3	0	0	0	0
car	1	10000	2.0	2.0	1	1	0.41	0.82
insurance	1	1000	3.0	3.0	2	2	0.82	2.46

In this example, the weight of a term in the query is simply the idf (and 0 for a term not in the query, such as auto); this is reflected in the column header $w_{t,q}$ (the entry for auto is 0 because the query does not contain the term auto). For documents, we use tf weighting with no use of idf but with Euclidean normalization. The former is shown under the column headed wf, and the latter is shown under the column headed $w_{t,d}$. Invoking (6.12) now gives a net score of $0 + 0 + 0.82 + 2.46 = 3.28$.

6.3.3 *Computing vector scores*

In a typical setting, we have a collection of documents each represented by a vector, a free text query represented by a vector, and a positive integer K. We seek the K documents of the collection with the highest vector space scores on the given query. We now initiate the study of determining the K documents with the highest vector space scores for a query. Typically,

CosineScore(q)

1 float $Scores[N] = 0$
2 Initialize $Length[N]$
3 **for each** query term t
4 **do** calculate $w_{t,q}$ and fetch postings list for t
5   **for each** pair(d, $\text{tf}_{t,d}$) in postings list
6   **do** $Scores[d] += \text{wf}_{t,d} \times w_{t,q}$
7 Read the array $Length[d]$
8 **for each** d
9 **do** $Scores[d] = Scores[d]/Length[d]$
10 **return** Top K components of $Scores[]$

Figure 6.14 The basic algorithm for computing vector space scores.

we seek these K top documents ordered by decreasing score; for instance, many search engines use $K = 10$ to retrieve and rank-order the first page of the ten best results. Here we give the basic algorithm for this computation; we develop a fuller treatment of efficient techniques and approximations in Chapter 7.

Figure 6.14 gives the basic algorithm for computing vector space scores. The array Length holds the lengths (normalization factors) for each of the N documents, whereas the array Scores holds the scores for each of the documents. When the scores are finally computed in Step 9, all that remains in Step 10 is to pick off the K documents with the highest scores.

The outermost loop beginning Step 3 repeats the updating of Scores, iterating over each query term t in turn. In Step 5, we calculate the weight in the query vector for term t. Steps 6 to 8 update the score of each document by adding in the contribution from term t. This process of adding in contributions one query term at a time is sometimes known as *term-at-a-time* scoring or accumulation, and the N elements of the array *Scores* are therefore known as *accumulators*. For this purpose, it seems necessary to store, with each postings entry, the weight $\text{wf}_{t,d}$ of term t in document d (we have thus far used either tf or tf–idf for this weight, but leave open the possibility of other functions to be developed in Section 6.4). In fact this is wasteful, because storing this weight may require a floating point number. Two ideas help to alleviate this space problem. First, if we are using inverse document frequency, we need not precompute idf_t; it suffices to store N/df_t at the head of the postings for t. Second, we store the term frequency $\text{tf}_{t,d}$ for each postings entry. Finally, Step 12 extracts the top K scores – this requires a priority queue data structure, often implemented using a heap. Such a heap takes no more than $2N$ comparisons to construct, following which each of the K top scores can be extracted from the heap at a cost of $O(\log N)$ comparisons.

Note that the general algorithm of Figure 6.14 does not prescribe a specific implementation of how we traverse the postings lists of the various query terms; we may traverse them one term at a time as in the loop beginning at

TERM-AT-A-TIME

ACCUMULATOR

Step 3, or we could in fact traverse them concurrently as in Figure 1.6. In such a concurrent postings traversal, we compute the scores of one document at a time, so that it is sometimes called *document-at-a-time* scoring. We will say more about this in Section 7.1.5.

DOCUMENT-
AT-A-TIME

? **Exercise 6.14** If we were to stem jealous and jealousy to a common stem before setting up the vector space, detail how the definitions of tf and idf should be modified.

Exercise 6.15 Recall the tf–idf weights computed in Exercise 6.10. Compute the Euclidean normalized document vectors for each of the documents, where each vector has four components, one for each of the four terms.

Exercise 6.16 Verify that the sum of the squares of the components of each of the document vectors in Exercise 6.15 is 1 (to within rounding error). Why is this the case?

Exercise 6.17 With term weights as computed in Exercise 6.15, rank the three documents by computed score for the query car insurance for each of the following cases of term weighting in the query:

1. The weight of a term is 1 if present in the query, 0 otherwise.
2. Euclidean normalized idf.

6.4 Variant tf–idf functions

For assigning a weight for each term in each document, a number of alternatives to tf and tf–idf have been considered. We discuss some of the principal ones here; a more complete development is deferred to Chapter 11. We will summarize these alternatives in Section 6.4.3 (page 118).

6.4.1 Sublinear tf scaling

It seems unlikely that twenty occurrences of a term in a document truly carry twenty times the significance of a single occurrence. Accordingly, there has been considerable research into variants of term frequency that go beyond counting the number of occurrences of a term. A common modification is to use instead the logarithm of the term frequency, which assigns a weight given by

$$(6.13) \qquad \mathrm{wf}_{t,d} = \begin{cases} 1 + \log \mathrm{tf}_{t,d} & \text{if } \mathrm{tf}_{t,d} > 0 \\ 0 & \text{otherwise} \end{cases}.$$

In this form, we may replace tf by some other function wf as in (6.13), to obtain:

(6.14) $$\text{wf–idf}_{t,d} = \text{wf}_{t,d} \times \text{idf}_t.$$

Equation (6.9) can then be modified by replacing tf–idf by wf–idf as defined in Equation (6.14).

6.4.2 *Maximum tf normalization*

One well-studied technique is to normalize the tf weights of all terms occurring in a document by the maximum tf in that document. For each document d, let $\text{tf}_{\max}(d) = \max_{\tau \in d} \text{tf}_{\tau,d}$, where τ ranges over all terms in d. Then, we compute a normalized term frequency for each term t in document d by

(6.15) $$\text{ntf}_{t,d} = a + (1-a)\frac{\text{tf}_{t,d}}{\text{tf}_{\max}(d)},$$

SMOOTHING where a is a value between 0 and 1 and is generally set to 0.4, although some early work used the value 0.5. The term a in (6.15) is a *smoothing* term whose role is to damp the contribution of the second term, which may be viewed as a scaling down of tf by the largest tf value in d. We encounter smoothing further in Chapter 13 when discussing classification; the basic idea is to avoid a large swing in $\text{ntf}_{t,d}$ from modest changes in $\text{tf}_{t,d}$ (say from 1 to 2). The main idea of maximum tf normalization is to mitigate the following anomaly: We observe higher term frequencies in longer documents, merely because longer documents tend to repeat the same words over and over again. To appreciate this, consider the following extreme example: Suppose we were to take a document d and create a new document d' by simply appending a copy of d to itself. Although d' should be no more relevant to any query than d is, the use of (6.9) assigns it twice as high a score as d. Replacing tf–idf$_{t,d}$ in (6.9) by ntf–idf$_{t,d}$ eliminates the anomaly in this example. Maximum tf normalization does suffer from the following issues:

1. The method is unstable in the following sense: A change in the stop word list can dramatically alter term weightings (and therefore ranking). Thus, it is hard to tune.
2. A document may contain an outlier term with an unusually large number of occurrences of that term, not representative of the content of that document.
3. More generally, a document in which the most frequent term appears roughly as often as many other terms should be treated differently from one with a more skewed distribution.

term frequency		document frequency		normalization	
n (natural)	$\text{tf}_{t,d}$	n (no)	1	n (none)	1
l (logarithm)	$1+\log(\text{tf}_{t,d})$	t (idf)	$\log\frac{N}{\text{df}_t}$	c (cosine)	$\frac{1}{\sqrt{w_1^2+w_2^2+...+w_M^2}}$
a (augmented)	$0.5+\frac{0.5\times\text{tf}_{t,d}}{\max_t(\text{tf}_{t,d})}$	p (prob idf)	$\max\{0,\log\frac{N-\text{df}_t}{\text{df}_t}\}$	u (pivoted unique)	$1/u$ (Section 17.4.4)
b (boolean)	$\begin{cases}1 \text{ if } \text{tf}_{t,d}>0\\0 \text{ otherwise}\end{cases}$			b (byte size)	$1/CharLength^{\alpha}$, $\alpha<1$
L (log ave)	$\frac{1+\log(\text{tf}_{t,d})}{1+\log(\text{ave}_{t\in d}(\text{tf}_{t,d}))}$				

Figure 6.15 SMART notation for tf–idf variants. Here *Char Length* is the number of characters in the document.

6.4.3 Document and query weighting schemes

Equation (6.12) is fundamental to IR systems that use any form of vector space scoring. Variations from one vector space scoring method to another hinge on the specific choices of weights in the vectors $\vec{V}(d)$ and $\vec{V}(q)$. Figure 6.15 lists some of the principal weighting schemes in use for each of $\vec{V}(d)$ and $\vec{V}(q)$, together with a mnemonic for representing a specific combination of weights; this system of mnemonics is sometimes called SMART notation, following the authors of an early text retrieval system. The mnemonic for representing a combination of weights takes the form *ddd.qqq*, where the first triplet gives the term weighting of the document vector and the second triplet gives the weighting in the query vector. The first letter in each triplet specifies the term frequency component of the weighting, the second the document frequency component, and the third the form of normalization used. It is quite common to apply different normalization functions to $\vec{V}(d)$ and $\vec{V}(q)$. For example, a very standard weighting scheme is *lnc.ltc*, where the document vector has log-weighted term frequency, no idf (for both effectiveness and efficiency reasons), and cosine normalization, while the query vector uses log-weighted term frequency, idf weighting, and cosine normalization.

6.4.4 Pivoted normalized document length

In Section 6.3.1 we normalized each document vector by the Euclidean length of the vector, so that all document vectors turned into unit vectors. In doing so, we eliminated all information on the length of the original document; this masks some subtleties about longer documents. First, longer documents will – as a result of containing more terms – have higher tf values. Second, longer documents contain more distinct terms. These factors can conspire to raise the scores of longer documents, which (at least for some information needs) is unnatural. Longer documents can broadly be lumped into two categories: (1) *verbose* documents that essentially repeat the same content – in these, the length of the document does not alter the relative weights of different terms; (2) documents covering multiple different topics, in which the

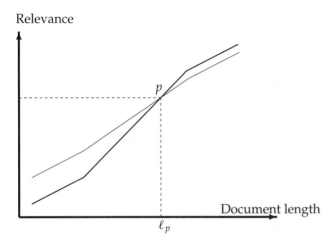

Figure 6.16   Pivoted document length normalization.

search terms probably match small segments of the document but not all of it – in this case, the relative weights of terms are quite different from a single short document that matches the query terms. Compensating for this phenomenon is a form of document length normalization that is independent of term and document frequencies. To this end, we introduce a form of normalizing the vector representations of documents in the collection, so that the resulting "normalized" documents are not necessarily of unit length. Then, when we compute the dot product score between a (unit) query vector and such a normalized document, the score is skewed to account for the effect of document length on relevance. This form of compensation for document length is known as *pivoted document length normalization.*

PIVOTED
DOCUMENT
LENGTH
ORMALIZATION

Consider a document collection together with an ensemble of queries for that collection. Suppose that we were given, for each query q and for each document d, a Boolean judgment of whether or not d is relevant to the query q; in Chapter 8 we will see how to procure such a set of relevance judgments for a query ensemble and a document collection. Given this set of relevance judgments, we may compute a *probability of relevance* as a function of document length, averaged over all queries in the ensemble. The resulting plot may look like the curve drawn in thick lines in Figure 6.16. To compute this curve, we bucket documents by length and compute the fraction of relevant documents in each bucket, then plot this fraction against the median document length of each bucket. (Thus, even though the "curve" in Figure 6.16 appears to be continuous, it is in fact a histogram of discrete buckets of document length.)

On the other hand, the curve in thin lines shows what might happen with the same documents and query ensemble if we were to use relevance as prescribed by cosine normalization Equation (6.12) – thus, cosine normalization has a tendency to distort the computed relevance vis-à-vis the true relevance, at the expense of longer documents. The thin and thick curves crossover at a point p corresponding to document length ℓ_p, which we refer to as the *pivot length*; dashed lines mark this point on the x- and y- axes. The idea of pivoted document length normalization would then be to "rotate" the cosine normalization curve counterclockwise about p so that it more closely matches thick line representing the relevance versus document length curve. As mentioned at the beginning of this section, we do so by using in Equation (6.12) a normalization factor for each document vector $\vec{V}(d)$ that is not the Euclidean length of that vector, but instead one that is larger than the Euclidean length for documents of length less than ℓ_p, and smaller for longer documents.

To this end, we first note that the normalizing term for $\vec{V}(d)$ in the denominator of Equation (6.12) is its Euclidean length, denoted $|\vec{V}(d)|$. In the simplest implementation of pivoted document length normalization, we use a normalization factor in the denominator that is linear in $|\vec{V}(d)|$, but one of slope < 1 as in Figure 6.17. In this figure, the x- axis represents $|\vec{V}(d)|$, and the y-axis represents possible normalization factors we can use. The thin line $y = x$ depicts the use of cosine normalization. Notice the following aspects of the thick line representing pivoted length normalization:

1. It is linear in the document length and has the form

(6.16)
$$a|\vec{V}(d)| + (1 - a)\mathrm{piv},$$

   where piv is the cosine normalization value at which the two curves intersect.
2. Its slope is $a < 1$.
3. It crosses the $y = x$ line at piv.

It has been argued that in practice, Equation (6.16) is well approximated by

$$a\,u_d + (1 - a)\mathrm{piv},$$

where u_d is the number of unique terms in document d.

Of course, pivoted document length normalization is not appropriate for all applications. For instance, in a collection of answers to frequently asked questions (say, at a customer service website), relevance may have little to do with document length. In other cases, the dependency may be more complex than can be accounted for by a simple linear pivoted normalization. In such cases, document length can be used as a feature in the machine learning based scoring approach of Section 6.1.2.

Pivoted normalization

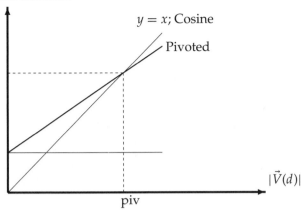

Figure 6.17 Implementing pivoted document length normalization by linear scaling.

Exercise 6.18 One measure of the similarity of two vectors is the *Euclidean distance* (or L_2 distance) between them:

EUCLIDEAN
DISTANCE

$$|\vec{x} - \vec{y}| = \sqrt{\sum_{i=1}^{M}(x_i - y_i)^2}$$

Given a query q and documents $d_1, d_2, \ldots$, we may rank the documents d_i in order of increasing Euclidean distance from q. Show that if q and the d_i are all normalized to unit vectors, then the rank ordering produced by Euclidean distance is identical to that produced by cosine similarities.

Exercise 6.19 Compute the vector space similarity between the query "digital cameras" and the document "digital cameras and video cameras" by filling out the empty columns in Table 6.1 Assume $N = 10,000,000$, logarithmic term weighting (wf columns) for query and document, idf weighting for the query only and cosine normalization for the document only. Treat and as a stop word. Enter term counts in the tf columns. What is the final similarity score?

Table 6.1 Cosine computation for Exercise 6.19.

			query				document		
word	tf	wf	df	idf	q_i = wf-idf	tf	wf	d_i = normalized wf	$q_i \cdot d_i$
digital			10,000						
video			100,000						
cameras			50,000						

Exercise 6.20 Show that, for the query affection, the relative ordering of the scores of the three documents in Figure 6.13 is the reverse of the ordering of the scores for the query jealous gossip.

Exercise 6.21 In turning a query into a unit vector in Figure 6.13, we assigned equal weights to each of the query terms. What other principled approaches are plausible?

Exercise 6.22 Consider the case of a query term that is not in the set of M indexed terms; thus, our standard construction of the query vector results in $\vec{V}(q)$ not being in the vector space created from the collection. How would one adapt the vector space representation to handle this case?

Exercise 6.23 Refer to the tf and idf values for four terms and three documents in Exercise 6.10. Compute the two top-scoring documents on the query best car insurance for each of the following weighing schemes: (i) nnn.atc and (ii) ntc.atc.

Exercise 6.24 Suppose that the word coyote does not occur in the collection used in Exercises 6.10 and 6.23. How would one compute ntc.atc scores for the query coyote insurance?

6.5 References and further reading

Chapter 7 develops the computational aspects of vector space scoring. Luhn (1957, 1958) describes some of the earliest reported applications of term weighting. His paper dwells on the importance of medium frequency terms (terms that are neither too commonplace nor too rare) and may be thought of as anticipating tf–idf and related weighting schemes. Spärck Jones (1972) builds on this intuition through detailed experiments showing the use of inverse document frequency in term weighting. A series of extensions and theoretical justifications of idf are due to Salton and Buckley (1987), Robertson and Jones (1976), Croft and Harper (1979), and Papineni (2001). Robertson maintains a web page (www.soi.city.ac.uk/˜ser/idf.html) containing the history of idf, including soft copies of early papers that predated electronic versions of journal articles. Singhal et al. (1996a) develop pivoted document length normalization. Probabilistic language models (Chapter 11) develop weighting techniques that are more nuanced than tf–idf; the reader will find this development in Section 11.4.3.

We observed that by assigning a weight for each term in a document, a document may be viewed as a vector of term weights, one for each term in the collection. The SMART information retrieval system at Cornell (Salton 1971b) due to Salton and colleagues was perhaps the first to view a document as a vector of weights. The basic computation of cosine scores as described in Section 6.3.3 is due to Zobel and Moffat (2006). The two query evaluation strategies term-at-a-time and document-at-a-time are discussed by Turtle and Flood (1995).

The SMART notation for tf–idf term weighting schemes in Figure 6.15 is presented in (Salton and Buckley 1988; Singhal et al. 1995, 1996b). Not all versions of the notation are consistent; we most closely follow (Singhal et al. 1996b). A more detailed and exhaustive notation was developed in Moffat and Zobel (1998), considering a larger palette of schemes for term and document frequency weighting. Beyond the notation, Moffat and Zobel (1998) sought to set up a space of feasible weighting functions through which hill-climbing approaches could be used to begin with weighting schemes that performed well, then make local improvements to identify the best combinations. However, they report that such hill-climbing methods failed to lead to any conclusions on the best weighting schemes.

7 Computing scores in a complete search system

Chapter 6 developed the theory underlying term weighting in documents for the purposes of scoring, leading up to vector space models and the basic cosine scoring algorithm of Section 6.3.3 (page 114). In this chapter, we begin in Section 7.1 with heuristics for speeding up this computation; many of these heuristics achieve their speed at the risk of not finding quite the top K documents matching the query. Some of these heuristics generalize beyond cosine scoring. With Section 7.1 in place, we have essentially all the components needed for a complete search engine. We therefore take a step back from cosine scoring, to the more general problem of computing scores in a search engine. In Section 7.2, we outline a complete search engine, including indexes and structures to support not only cosine scoring, but also more general ranking factors such as query term proximity. We describe how all of the various pieces fit together in Section 7.2.4. We conclude this chapter with Section 7.3, where we discuss how the vector space model for free text queries interacts with common query operators.

7.1 Efficient scoring and ranking

We begin by recapping the algorithm of Figure 6.14. For a query such as $q =$ jealous gossip, two observations are immediate:

1. The unit vector $\vec{v}(q)$ has only two nonzero components.
2. In the absence of any weighting for query terms, these nonzero components are equal – in this case, both equal 0.707.

For the purpose of ranking the documents matching this query, we are really interested in the relative (rather than absolute) scores of the documents in the collection. To this end, it suffices to compute the cosine similarity from each document unit vector $\vec{v}(d)$ to $\vec{V}(q)$ (in which all nonzero components of the query vector are set to 1), rather than to the unit vector $\vec{v}(q)$. For any two

FASTCOSINESCORE(q)

1   float $Scores[N] = 0$
2   **for** each d
3   **do** Initialize $Length[d]$ to the length of doc d
4   **for** each query term t
5   **do** fetch postings list for t
6   **for** each pair(d, tf$_{t,d}$) in postings list
7   **do** add wf$_{t,d}$ to $Scores[d]$
8   Read the array $Length[d]$
9   **for** each d
10   **do** Divide $Scores[d]$ by $Length[d]$
11   **return** Top K components of $Scores[]$

Figure 7.1 A faster algorithm for vector space scores.

documents d_1, d_2

(7.1) $$\vec{V}(q) \cdot \vec{v}(d_1) > \vec{V}(q) \cdot \vec{v}(d_2) \Leftrightarrow \vec{v}(q) \cdot \vec{v}(d_1) > \vec{v}(q) \cdot \vec{v}(d_2).$$

For any document d, the cosine similarity $\vec{V}(q) \cdot \vec{v}(d)$ is the weighted sum, over all terms in the query q, of the weights of those terms in d. This in turn can be computed by a postings intersection exactly as in the algorithm of Figure 6.14, with line 7 altered because we take $w_{t,q}$ to be 1 so that the multiply-add in that step becomes just an addition; the result is shown in Figure 7.1. We walk through the postings in the inverted index for the terms in q, accumulating the total score for each document – very much as in processing a Boolean query, except we assign a positive score to each document that appears in any of the postings being traversed. As mentioned in Section 6.3.3, we maintain an idf value for each dictionary term and a tf value for each postings entry. This scheme computes a score for every document in the postings of any of the query terms; the total number of such documents may be considerably smaller than N.

Given these scores, the final step before presenting results to a user is to pick out the K highest-scoring documents. Although one could sort the complete set of scores, a better approach is to use a heap to retrieve only the top K documents in order. Where J is the number of documents with nonzero cosine scores, constructing such a heap can be performed in $2J$ comparison steps, following which each of the K highest scoring documents can be "read off" the heap with log J comparison steps.

7.1.1 Inexact top K document retrieval

Thus far, we have focused on retrieving precisely the K highest-scoring documents for a query. We now consider schemes by which we produce K documents that are *likely* to be among the K highest scoring documents for a query. In doing so, we hope to dramatically lower the cost of computing the K documents we output, without materially altering the user's perceived relevance of the top K results. Consequently, in most applications it suffices to retrieve K documents whose scores are very close to those of the K best. In the sections that follow, we detail schemes that retrieve K such documents while potentially avoiding computing scores for most of the N documents in the collection.

Such inexact top K retrieval is not necessarily, from the user's perspective, a bad thing. The top K documents by the cosine measure are in any case not necessarily the K best for the query: cosine similarity is only a proxy for the user's perceived relevance. In Sections 7.1.2 through 7.1.6, we give heuristics, using which we are likely to retrieve K documents with cosine scores close to those of the top K documents. The principal cost in computing the output stems from computing cosine similarities between the query and a large number of documents. Having a large number of documents in contention also increases the selection cost in the final stage of culling the top K documents from a heap. We now consider a series of ideas designed to eliminate a large number of documents without computing their cosine scores. The heuristics have the following two-step scheme:

1. Find a set A of documents that are contenders, where $K < |A| \ll N$. A does not necessarily contain the K top-scoring documents for the query, but is likely to have many documents with scores near those of the top K.
2. Return the K top-scoring documents in A.

From the descriptions of these ideas, it will be clear that many of them require parameters to be tuned to the collection and application at hand; pointers to experience in setting these parameters may be found at the end of this chapter. It should also be noted that most of these heuristics are well-suited to free text queries, but not for Boolean or phrase queries.

7.1.2 Index elimination

For a multiterm query q, it is clear we only consider documents containing at least one of the query terms. We can take this a step further using additional heuristics:

1. We only consider documents containing terms whose idf exceeds a preset threshold. Thus, in the postings traversal, we only traverse the postings for terms with high idf. This has a fairly significant benefit: The postings lists of low-idf terms are generally long; with these removed from contention, the set of documents for which we compute cosines is greatly reduced. One way of viewing this heuristic: Low-idf terms are treated as stop words and do not contribute to scoring. For instance, on the query

catcher in the rye, we only traverse the postings for catcher and rye. The cutoff threshold can of course be adapted in a query-dependent manner.

2. We only consider documents that contain many (and as a special case, all) of the query terms. This can be accomplished during the postings traversal; we only compute scores for documents containing all (or many) of the query terms. A danger of this scheme is that by requiring all (or even many) query terms to be present in a document before considering it for cosine computation, we may end up with fewer than K candidate documents in the output. This issue is discussed further in Section 7.2.1.

7.1.3 Champion lists

The idea of *champion lists* (sometimes also called *fancy lists* or *top docs*) is to precompute, for each term t in the dictionary, the set of the r documents with the highest weights for t; the value of r is chosen in advance. For tf–idf weighting, these are the r documents with the highest tf values for term t. We call this set of r documents the *champion list* for term t.

Now, given a query q we create a set A as follows: We take the union of the champion lists for each of the terms comprising q. We now restrict cosine computation to only the documents in A. A critical parameter in this scheme is the value r, which is highly application dependent. Intuitively, r should be large compared with K, especially if we use any form of the index elimination described in Section 7.1.2. One issue here is that the value r is set at the time of index construction, whereas K is application dependent and may not be available until the query is received; as a result, we may (as in the case of index elimination) find ourselves with a set A that has fewer than K documents. There is no reason to have the same value of r for all terms in the dictionary; it could for instance be set to be higher for rarer terms.

7.1.4 Static quality scores and ordering

We now further develop the idea of champion lists, in the somewhat more general setting of *static quality scores*. In many search engines, we have available a measure of quality $g(d)$ for each document d that is query independent and thus *static*. This quality measure may be viewed as a number between 0 and 1. For instance, in the context of news stories on the web, $g(d)$ may be derived from the number of favorable reviews of the story by web surfers. Section 4.6 (page 73) provides further discussion on this topic, as does Chapter 21 in the context of web search.

STATIC QUALITY SCORES

The net score for a document d is some combination of $g(d)$ together with the query-dependent score induced (say) by (6.12). The precise combination may be determined by the learning methods of Section 6.1.2, to be developed

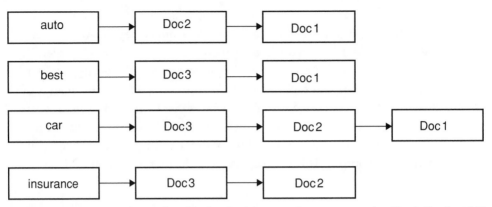

Figure 7.2 A static quality-ordered index. In this example we assume that Doc1, Doc2 and Doc3 respectively have static quality scores $g(1) = 0.25, g(2) = 0.5, g(3) = 1$.

further in Section 15.4.1; but for the purposes of our exposition here, let us consider a simple sum:

$$(7.2) \qquad \text{net-score}(q, d) = g(d) + \frac{\vec{V}(q) \cdot \vec{V}(d)}{|\vec{V}(q)||\vec{V}(d)|}.$$

In this simple form, the static quality $g(d)$ and the query-dependent score from (6.10) have equal contributions, assuming each is between 0 and 1. Other relative weightings are possible; the effectiveness of our heuristics depends on the specific relative weighting.

First, consider ordering the documents in the postings list for each term by decreasing value of $g(d)$. This allows us to perform the postings intersection algorithm of Figure 1.6. To perform the intersection by a single pass through the postings of each query term, the algorithm of Figure 1.6 relied on the postings being ordered by document IDs. But, in fact, we only required that all postings be ordered by a single common ordering; here, we rely on the $g(d)$ values to provide this common ordering. This is illustrated in Figure 7.2, where the postings are ordered in decreasing order of $g(d)$.

The next idea is a direct extension of champion lists: For a well-chosen value r, we maintain for each term t a *global champion list* of the r documents with the highest values for $g(d) + \text{tf-idf}_{t,d}$. The list itself is, like all the postings lists considered so far, sorted by a common order (either by document IDs or by static quality). Then at query time, we only compute the net scores (7.2) for documents in the union of these global champion lists. Intuitively, this has the effect of focusing on documents likely to have large net scores.

We conclude the discussion of global champion lists with one further idea. We maintain for each term t two postings lists consisting of disjoint sets of documents, each sorted by $g(d)$ values. The first list, which we call *high*, contains the m documents with the highest tf values for t. The second list, which we call *low*, contains all other documents containing t. When processing a query, we first scan only the high lists of the query terms, computing net scores for any document on the high lists of all (or more than a certain number of) query terms. If we obtain scores for K documents in the process, we terminate. If not, we continue the scanning into the low lists, scoring documents in these postings lists. This idea is developed further in Section 7.2.1.

7.1.5 Impact ordering

In all the postings lists described thus far, we order the documents consistently by some common ordering: typically by document ID but in Section 7.1.4 by static quality scores. As noted at the end of Section 6.3.3, such a common ordering supports the concurrent traversal of all of the query terms' postings lists, computing the score for each document as we encounter it. Computing scores in this manner is sometimes referred to as *document-at-a-time scoring*. We now introduce a technique for inexact top K retrieval in which the postings are not all ordered by a common ordering, thereby precluding such a concurrent traversal. We therefore require scores to be "accumulated" one term at a time as in the scheme of Figure 6.14, so that we have term-at-a-time scoring.

The idea is to order the documents d in the postings list of term t by decreasing order of $\text{tf}_{t,d}$. Thus, the ordering of documents varies from one postings list to another, and we cannot compute scores by a concurrent traversal of the postings lists of all query terms. Given postings lists ordered by decreasing order of $\text{tf}_{t,d}$, two ideas have been found to significantly lower the number of documents for which we accumulate scores: (1) when traversing the postings list for a query term t, we stop after considering a prefix of the postings list – either after a fixed number of documents r have been seen, or after the value of $\text{tf}_{t,d}$ has dropped below a threshold; (2) when accumulating scores in the outer loop of Figure 6.14, we consider the query terms in decreasing order of idf, so that the query terms likely to contribute the most to the final scores are considered first. This latter idea can be adaptive at the time of processing a query: As we get to query terms with lower idf, we can determine whether to proceed based on the changes in document scores from processing the previous query term. If these changes are minimal, we may omit accumulation from the remaining query terms, or alternatively process shorter prefixes of their postings lists.

These ideas form a common generalization of the methods introduced in Sections 7.1.2 through 7.1.4. We may also implement a version of static ordering in which each postings list is ordered by an additive combination of static and query-dependent scores. We again lose the consistency of ordering across postings, and therefore have to process query terms one at time, accumulating scores for all documents as we go along. Depending on the particular scoring function, the postings list for a document may be ordered by other quantities than term frequency; under this more general setting, this idea is known as *impact ordering*.

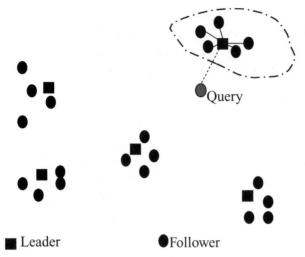

Figure 7.3   Cluster pruning.

7.1.6 Cluster pruning

In *cluster pruning*, we have a preprocessing step during which we cluster the document vectors. Then, at query time, we consider only documents in a small number of clusters as candidates for which we compute cosine scores. Specifically, the preprocessing step is as follows:

1. Pick $\sqrt{N}$ documents at random from the collection. Call these *leaders*.
2. For each document that is not a leader, we compute its nearest leader.

We refer to documents that are not leaders as *followers*. Intuitively, in the partition of the followers induced by the use of $\sqrt{N}$ randomly chosen leaders, the expected number of followers for each leader is $\approx N/\sqrt{N} = \sqrt{N}$. Next, query processing proceeds as follows:

1. Given a query q, find the leader L that is closest to q. This entails computing cosine similarities from q to each of the $\sqrt{N}$ leaders.
2. The candidate set A consists of L together with its followers. We compute the cosine scores for all documents in this candidate set.

The use of randomly chosen leaders for clustering is fast and likely to reflect the distribution of the document vectors in the vector space: A region of the vector space that is dense in documents is likely to produce multiple leaders and thus a finer partition into subregions. This illustrated in Figure 7.3.

Variations of cluster pruning introduce additional parameters b_1 and b_2, both of which are positive integers. In the preprocessing step, we attach each follower to its b_1 closest leaders, rather than a single closest leader. At query time we consider the b_2 leaders closest to the query q. Clearly, this basic scheme corresponds to the case $b_1 = b_2 = 1$. Further, increasing b_1 or b_2 increases the likelihood of finding K documents that are more likely to be in the set of true top-scoring K documents, at the expense of more computation. We reiterate this approach when describing clustering in Chapter 16 (page 325).

Exercise 7.1 We suggested (Figure 7.2) that the postings for static quality ordering be in decreasing order of $g(d)$. Why do we use the decreasing rather than the increasing order?

Exercise 7.2 When discussing champion lists, we simply used the r documents with the largest tf values to create the champion list for t. But, when considering global champion lists, we used idf as well, identifying documents with the largest values of $g(d) + \text{tf-idf}_{t,d}$. Why do we differentiate between these two cases?

Exercise 7.3 If we were to only have one-term queries, explain why the use of global champion lists with $r = K$ suffices for identifying the K highest scoring documents. What is a simple modification to this idea if we were to only have s-term queries for any fixed integer $s > 1$?

Exercise 7.4 Explain how the common global ordering by $g(d)$ values in all high and low lists helps to make the score computation efficient.

Exercise 7.5 Consider again the data of Exercise 6.23 with `nnn.atc` for query-dependent scoring. Suppose that we were given static quality scores of 1 for Doc1 and 2 for Doc2. Determine under Equation (7.2) what ranges of static quality score for Doc3 result in it being the first, second, or third result for the query best car insurance.

Exercise 7.6 Sketch the frequency-ordered postings for the data in Figure 6.9.

Exercise 7.7 Let the static quality scores for Doc1, Doc2, and Doc3 in Figure 6.10 be respectively 0.25, 0.5, and 1. Sketch the postings for impact ordering when each postings list is ordered by the sum of the static quality score and the Euclidean normalized tf values in Figure 6.10.

Exercise 7.8 The nearest neighbor problem in the plane is the following: Given a set of N data points on the plane, we preprocess them into some data structure such that, given a query point Q, we seek the point in N that is closest to Q in Euclidean distance. Clearly, cluster pruning can be used as an approach to the nearest neighbor problem in the plane, if we wished to avoid computing the distance from Q to every one of the query points. Devise a simple example on the plane so that with two leaders, the answer returned by cluster pruning is incorrect (it is not the data point closest to Q).

7.2 Components of an information retrieval system

In this section, we combine the ideas developed so far to describe a rudimentary search system that retrieves and scores documents. We first develop further ideas for scoring, beyond vector spaces. After this, we put together all of these elements to outline a complete system. Because we consider a complete system, we do not restrict ourselves to vector space retrieval in this section. Indeed, our complete system has provisions for vector space as well as other query operators and forms of retrieval. In Section 7.3, we return to how vector space queries interact with other query operators.

7.2.1 Tiered indexes

We mentioned in Section 7.1.2 that, when using heuristics such as index elimination for inexact top-K retrieval, we may occasionally find ourselves with a set A of contenders that has fewer than K documents. A common solution TIERED to this issue is the use of *tiered indexes*, which may be viewed as a generINDEXES alization of champion lists. We illustrate this idea in Figure 7.4, where we represent the documents and terms of Figure 6.9. In this example, we set a tf threshold of 20 for tier 1 and 10 for tier 2, meaning that the tier 1 index only has postings entries with tf values exceeding 20, and the tier 2 index only has postings entries with tf values exceeding 10. In this example, we have chosen to order the postings entries within a tier by document ID.

7.2.2 Query term proximity

Especially for free text queries on the web (Chapter 19), users prefer a document in which most or all of the query terms appear close to each other, because this is evidence that the document has text focused on their query intent. Consider a query with two or more query terms, $t_1, t_2, \ldots, t_k$. Let ω be the width of the smallest window in a document d that contains all the query terms, measured in the number of words in the window. For instance, if the document were to simply consist of the sentence The quality of mercy is not strained, the smallest window for the query strained mercy is 4. Intuitively, the smaller that ω is, the better that d matches the query. In cases where the document does not contain all of the query terms, we can set ω to be some enormous number. We could also consider variants in which only words that are not stop words are considered in computing ω. Such proximity-weighted scoring functions are a departure from pure cosine similarity and closer to the "soft conjunctive" semantics that Google and other web search engines evidently use.

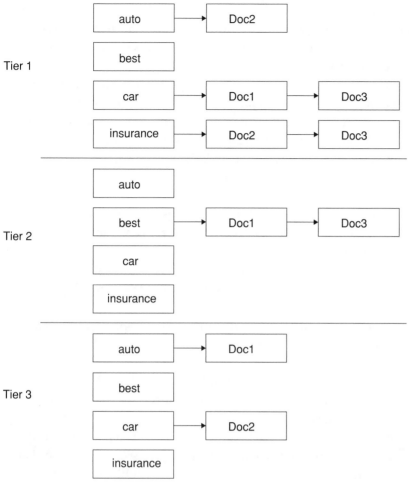

Figure 7.4 Tiered indexes. If we fail to get K results from tier 1, query processing "falls back" to tier 2, and so on. Within each tier, postings are ordered by document ID.

PROXIMITY   How can we design such a *proximity-weighted* scoring function to depend WEIGHTING on ω? The simplest answer relies on a "hand coding" technique we introduce in Section 7.2.3. A more scalable approach goes back to Section 6.1.2 – we treat the integer ω as yet another feature in the scoring function, whose importance is assigned by machine learning, as will be developed further in Section 15.4.1.

7.2.3 Designing parsing and scoring functions

Common search interfaces, particularly for consumer-facing search applications on the web, tend to mask query operators from the end user. The intent is to hide the complexity of these operators from the largely nontechnical audience for such applications, inviting *free text queries*. Given such interfaces, how should a search equipped with indexes for various retrieval operators treat a query such as rising interest rates? More generally, given the various factors we have studied that could affect the score of a document, how should we combine these features?

The answer of course depends on the user population, the query distribution, and the collection of documents. Typically, a *query parser* is used to translate the user-specified keywords into a query with various operators that is executed against the underlying indexes. Sometimes, this execution can entail multiple queries against the underlying indexes; for example, the query parser may issue a stream of queries:

1. Run the user-generated query string as a phrase query. Rank the results by vector space scoring using as query the vector consisting of the three terms rising interest rates.
2. If fewer than ten documents contain the phrase rising interest rates, run the two 2-term phrase queries rising interest and interest rates; rank these using vector space scoring, as well.
3. If we still have fewer than ten results, run the vector space query consisting of the three individual query terms.

Each of these steps (if invoked) may yield a list of scored documents, for each of which we compute a score. This score must combine contributions from vector space scoring, static quality, proximity weighting, and, potentially, other factors – particularly because a document may appear in the lists from multiple steps. This demands an aggregate scoring function that EVIDENCE *accumulates evidence* of a document's relevance from multiple sources. How ACCUMULATION do we devise a query parser and how do we devise the aggregate scoring function?

The answer depends on the setting. In many enterprise settings, we have application builders who make use of a toolkit of available scoring operators, along with a query parsing layer, with which to manually configure the scoring function as well as the query parser. Such application builders make use of the available zones, metadata, and knowledge of typical documents and queries to tune the parsing and scoring. In collections whose characteristics change infrequently (in an enterprise application, significant changes in collection and query characteristics typically happen with infrequent events such as the introduction of new document formats or document management systems, or a merger with another company). Web search, on the other hand, is faced with a constantly changing document collection with new characteristics being introduced all the time. It is also a setting in which the number of scoring factors can run into the hundreds, making hand-tuned scoring a difficult exercise. To address this, it is becoming increasingly common to use machine-learned scoring, extending the ideas we introduced in Section 6.1.2, as will be discussed further in Section 15.4.1.

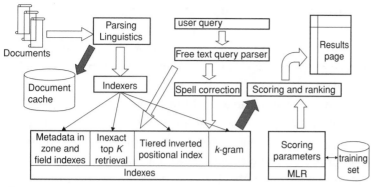

Figure 7.5 A complete search system. Data paths are shown primarily for a free text query.

7.2.4 Putting it all together

We have now studied all the components necessary for a basic search system that supports free text queries as well as Boolean, zone, and field queries. We briefly review how the various pieces fit together into an overall system; this is depicted in Figure 7.5.

In this figure, documents stream in from the left for parsing and linguistic processing (language and format detection, tokenization, and stemming). The resulting stream of tokens feeds into two modules. First, we retain a copy of each parsed document in a document cache. This enables us to generate results snippets: snippets of text accompanying each document in the results list for a query. This snippet tries to give a succinct explanation to the user of why the document matches the query. The automatic generation of such snippets is the subject of Section 8.7. A second copy of the tokens is fed to a bank of indexers that create a bank of indexes, including zone and field indexes that store the metadata for each document, (tiered) positional indexes, indexes for spelling correction and other tolerant retrieval, and structures for accelerating inexact top K retrieval. A free text user query (top center) is sent down to the indexes both directly and through a module for generating spelling-correction candidates. As noted in Chapter 3, the latter may optionally be invoked only when the original query fails to retrieve enough results. Retrieved documents (dark arrow) are passed to a scoring module that computes scores based on machine-learned ranking (MLR), a technique that builds on Section 6.1.2 (to be further developed in Section 15.4.1) for scoring and ranking documents. Finally, these ranked documents are rendered as a results page.

? **Exercise 7.9** Explain how the postings intersection algorithm first introduced in Section 1.3 can be adapted to find the smallest integer ω that contains all query terms.

Exercise 7.10 Adapt this procedure to work when not all query terms are present in a document.

7.3 Vector space scoring and query operator interaction

We introduced the vector space model as a paradigm for free text queries. We conclude this chapter by discussing how the vector space scoring model relates to the query operators we have studied in earlier chapters. The relationship should be viewed at two levels: in terms of the expressiveness of queries that a sophisticated user may pose, and in terms of the index that supports the evaluation of the various retrieval methods. In building a search engine, we may opt to support multiple query operators for an end user. In doing so, we need to understand what components of the index can be shared for executing various query operators, as well as how to handle user queries that mix various query operators.

Vector space scoring supports so-called free text retrieval, in which a query is specified as a set of words without any query operators connecting them. It allows documents matching the query to be scored and thus ranked, unlike the Boolean, wildcard, and phrase queries studied earlier. Classically, the interpretation of such free text queries was that at least one of the query terms be present in any retrieved document. However, more recently, web search engines such as Google have popularized the notion that a set of terms typed into their query boxes (thus on the face of it, a free text query) carries the semantics of a conjunctive query that only retrieves documents containing all or most query terms.

Boolean retrieval

Clearly, a vector space index can be used to answer Boolean queries, as long as the weight of a term t in the document vector for d is nonzero whenever t occurs in d. The reverse is not true; a Boolean index does not by default maintain term weight information. There is no easy way of combining vector space and Boolean queries from a user's standpoint: Vector space queries are fundamentally a form of *evidence accumulation*, where the presence of more query terms in a document adds to the score of a document. Boolean retrieval, on the other hand, requires a user to specify a formula for *selecting* documents through the presence (or absence) of specific combinations of keywords, without inducing any relative ordering among them. Mathematically, it is in fact possible to invoke so-called p-norms to combine Boolean and vector space queries, but we know of no system that makes use of this fact.

Wildcard queries

Wildcard and vector space queries require different indexes, except at the basic level, that both can be implemented using postings and a dictionary (e.g., a dictionary of trigrams for wildcard queries). If a search engine allows a user to specify a wildcard operator as part of a free text query (for instance, the query rom* restaurant), we may interpret the wildcard component of the query as spawning multiple terms in the vector space (in this example, rome and roman are two such terms), all of which are added to the query vector. The vector space query is then executed as usual, with matching documents being scored and ranked; thus, a document containing both rome and roma is likely to be scored higher than another containing only one of them. The exact score ordering, of course, depends on the relative weights of each term in matching documents.

Phrase queries

The representation of documents as vectors is fundamentally lossy: The relative order of terms in a document is lost in the encoding of a document as a vector. Even if we were to try and somehow treat every biword as a term (and thus an axis in the vector space), the weights on different axes are not independent: For instance, the phrase German shepherd gets encoded in the axis german shepherd, but immediately has a nonzero weight on the axes german and shepherd. Further, notions such as idf would have to be extended to such biwords. Thus, an index built for vector space retrieval cannot, in general, be used for phrase queries. Moreover, there is no way of demanding a vector space score for a phrase query – we only know the relative weights of each term in a document.

For the query german shepherd, we could use vector space retrieval to identify documents heavy in these two terms, with no way of prescribing that they occur consecutively. Phrase retrieval, on the other hand, tells us of the existence of the phrase german shepherd in a document, without any indication of the relative frequency or weight of this phrase. Although these two retrieval paradigms (phrase and vector space) consequently have different implementations in terms of indexes and retrieval algorithms, they can in some cases be combined usefully, as in the three-step example of query parsing in Section 7.2.3.

7.4 References and further reading

Heuristics for fast query processing with early termination are described by Anh et al. (2001), Garcia et al. (2004), Anh and Moffat (2006b), Persin et al. (1996). Cluster pruning is investigated by Singitham et al. (2004) and by Chierichetti et al. (2007); see also Section 16.6 (page 343). Champion lists are described in Persin (1994) and (under the name *top docs*) in TOP DOCS Brown (1995), and further developed in Brin and Page (1998), Long and Suel (2003). Although these heuristics are well-suited to free text queries that can be viewed as vectors, they complicate phrase queries; see Anh and Moffat (2006c) for an index structure that supports both weighted and Boolean/phrase searches. Carmel et al. (2001), Clarke et al. (2000), and Song et al. (2005) treat the use of query term proximity in assessing relevance. Pioneering work on learning of ranking functions was done by Fuhr (1989), Fuhr and Pfeifer (1994), Cooper et al. (1994), Bartell (1994), Bartell et al. (1998), and Cohen et al. (1998).

8 Evaluation in information retrieval

We have seen in the preceding chapters many alternatives in designing an information retrieval (IR) system. How do we know which of these techniques are effective in which applications? Should we use stop lists? Should we stem? Should we use inverse document frequency weighting? IR has developed as a highly empirical discipline, requiring careful and thorough evaluation to demonstrate the superior performance of novel techniques on representative document collections.

In this chapter, we begin with a discussion of measuring the effectiveness of IR systems (Section 8.1) and the test collections that are most often used for this purpose (Section 8.2). We then present the straightforward notion of relevant and nonrelevant documents and the formal evaluation methodology that has been developed for evaluating unranked retrieval results (Section 8.3). This includes explaining the kinds of evaluation measures that are standardly used for document retrieval and related tasks like text classification and why they are appropriate. We then extend these notions and develop further measures for evaluating ranked retrieval results (Section 8.4) and discuss developing reliable and informative test collections (Section 8.5).

We then step back to introduce the notion of user utility, and how it is approximated by the use of document relevance (Section 8.6). The key utility measure is user happiness. Speed of response and the size of the index are factors in user happiness. It seems reasonable to assume that relevance of results is the most important factor: blindingly fast, useless answers do not make a user happy. However, user perceptions do not always coincide with system designers' notions of quality. For example, user happiness commonly depends very strongly on user interface design issues, including the layout, clarity, and responsiveness of the user interface, which are independent of the quality of the results returned. We touch on other measures of the quality of a system, in particular the generation of high-quality result summary snippets, which strongly influence user utility, but are not measured in the basic relevance ranking paradigm (Section 8.7).

8.1 Information retrieval system evaluation

To measure ad hoc IR effectiveness in the standard way, we need a test collection consisting of three things:

1. A document collection
2. A test suite of information needs, expressible as queries
3. A set of relevance judgments, standardly a binary assessment of either *relevant* or *nonrelevant* for each query–document pair.

RELEVANCE

GOLD
STANDARD
GROUND
TRUTH

The standard approach to IR system evaluation revolves around the notion of *relevant* and *nonrelevant* documents. With respect to a user information need, a document in the test collection is given a binary classification as either relevant or nonrelevant. This decision is referred to as the *gold standard* or *ground truth* judgment of relevance. The test document collection and suite of information needs have to be of a reasonable size: You need to average performance over fairly large test sets because results are highly variable over different documents and information needs. As a rule of thumb, fifty information needs has usually been found to be a sufficient minimum.

INFORMATION
NEED

Relevance is assessed relative to an information need, *not* a query. For example, an information need might be:

Information on whether drinking red wine is more effective at reducing your risk of heart attacks than drinking white wine.

This might be translated into a query such as:

wine AND red AND white AND heart AND attack AND effective

A document is relevant if it addresses the stated information need, not because it just happens to contain all the words in the query. This distinction is often misunderstood in practice, because the information need is not overt. But, nevertheless, an information need is present. If a user types python into a web search engine, they might be wanting to know where they can purchase a pet python. Or they might be wanting information on the programming language Python. From a one-word query, it is very difficult for a system to know what the information need is. But, nevertheless, the user has one, and can judge the returned results on the basis of their relevance to it. To evaluate a system, we require an overt expression of an information need, which can be used for judging returned documents as relevant or nonrelevant. At this point, we make a simplification: Relevance can reasonably be thought of as a scale, with some documents highly relevant and others marginally so. But, for the moment, we use just a binary decision of relevance. We discuss the reasons for using binary relevance judgments and alternatives in Section 8.5.1.

Many systems contain various weights (often known as parameters) that can be adjusted to tune system performance. It is wrong to report results on a test collection that were obtained by tuning these parameters to maximize performance on that collection. That is because such tuning overstates the expected performance of the system, because the weights will be set to maximize performance on one particular set of queries rather than for a random sample of queries. In such cases, the correct procedure is to have one or more DEVELOPMENT *development test collections*, and to tune the parameters on the development TEST test collection. The tester then runs the system with those weights on the test COLLECTION collection and reports the results on that collection as an unbiased estimate of performance.

8.2 Standard test collections

Here is a list of the most standard test collections and evaluation series. We focus particularly on test collections for ad hoc information retrieval system evaluation, but also mention a couple of similar test collections for text classification.

CRANFIELD   The *Cranfield* collection. This was the pioneering test collection in allowing precise quantitative measures of information retrieval effectiveness, but is nowadays too small for anything but the most elementary pilot experiments. Collected in the United Kingdom starting in the late 1950s, it contains 1,398 abstracts of aerodynamics journal articles, a set of 225 queries, and exhaustive relevance judgments of all (query, document) pairs.

TREC   *Text Retrieval Conference (TREC)*. The U.S. National Institute of Standards and Technology (NIST) has run a large IR test bed evaluation series since 1992. Within this framework, there have been many tracks over a range of different test collections, but the best known test collections are the ones used for the TREC Ad Hoc track during the first eight TREC evaluations between 1992 and 1999. In total, these test collections comprise six CDs containing 1.89 million documents (mainly, but not exclusively, newswire articles) and relevance judgments for 450 information needs, which are called *topics* and specified in detailed text passages. Individual test collections are defined over different subsets of this data. The early TRECs each consisted of fifty information needs, evaluated over different but overlapping sets of documents. TRECs 6 through 8 provide 150 information needs over about 528,000 newswire and Foreign Broadcast Information Service articles. This is probably the best subcollection to use in future work, because it is the largest and the topics are more consistent. Because the test document collections are so large, there are no exhaustive relevance judgments. Rather, NIST assessors' relevance judgments are available only for the documents that were among the top k returned for some system that was entered in the TREC evaluation for which the information need was developed.

GOV2

In more recent years, NIST has done evaluations on larger document collections, including the 25-million page *GOV2* web page collection. From the beginning, the NIST test document collections were orders of magnitude larger than anything available to researchers previously and GOV2 is now the largest Web collection easily available for research purposes. Nevertheless, the size of GOV2 is still more than two orders of magnitude smaller than the current size of the document collections indexed by the large web search companies.

NTCIR

CROSS-LANGUAGE
INFORMATION
RETRIEVAL

NII Test Collections for IR Systems (*NTCIR*). The NTCIR project has built various test collections of similar sizes to the TREC collections, focusing on East Asian language and *cross-language information retrieval*, where queries are made in one language over a document collection containing documents in one or more other languages. See: http://research.nii.ac.jp/ntcir/data/data-en.html

CLEF

Cross Language Evaluation Forum (*CLEF*). This evaluation series has concentrated on European languages and cross-language information retrieval. See: www.clef-campaign.org/

REUTERS

Reuters-21578 and Reuters-RCV1. For text classification, the most used test collection has been the Reuters-21578 collection of 21,578 newswire articles (see Chapter 13, page 258). More recently, Reuters released the much larger Reuters Corpus Volume 1 (RCV1), consisting of 806,791 documents (see Chapter 4, page 63). Its scale and rich annotation makes it a better basis for future research.

20
NEWSGROUPS

20 Newsgroups. This is another widely used text classification collection, collected by Ken Lang. It consists of 1,000 articles from each of twenty Usenet newsgroups (the newsgroup name being regarded as the category). After the removal of duplicate articles, as it is usually used, it contains 18,941 articles.

8.3 Evaluation of unranked retrieval sets

Given these ingredients, how is system effectiveness measured? The two most frequent and basic measures for information retrieval effectiveness are precision and recall. These are first defined for the simple case where an IR system returns a set of documents for a query. We will see later how to extend these notions to ranked retrieval situations.

PRECISION

Precision (P) is the fraction of retrieved documents that are relevant

(8.1)
$$\text{Precision} = \frac{\#(\text{relevant items retrieved})}{\#(\text{retrieved items})} = P(\text{relevant|retrieved}).$$

Recall (R) is the fraction of relevant documents that are retrieved

(8.2) $$\text{Recall} = \frac{\#(\text{relevant items retrieved})}{\#(\text{relevant items})} = P(\text{retrieved}|\text{relevant}).$$

These notions can be made clear by examining the following contingency table:

(8.3)

	relevant	nonrelevant
retrieved	true positives (tp)	false positives (fp)
not retrieved	false negatives (fn)	true negatives (tn)

Then:

(8.4)
$$P = tp/(tp + fp)$$
$$R = tp/(tp + fn).$$

An obvious alternative that may occur to the reader is to judge an infor-
ACCURACY mation retrieval system by its *accuracy*, that is, the fraction of its classifica-
tions that are correct. In terms of the contingency table above, accuracy =
$(tp + tn)/(tp + fp + fn + tn)$. This seems plausible, because there are two actual classes, relevant and nonrelevant, and an IR system can be thought of as
a two-class classifier that attempts to label them as such (it retrieves the subset of documents it believes to be relevant). This is precisely the effectiveness
measure often used for evaluating machine-learning classification problems.

There is a good reason why accuracy is not an appropriate measure for
IR problems. In almost all circumstances, the data are extremely skewed;
normally, over 99.9% of the documents are in the nonrelevant category. A
system tuned to maximize accuracy can appear to perform well by simply
deeming all documents nonrelevant to all queries. Even if the system is quite
good, trying to label some documents as relevant almost always leads to a
high rate of false positives. However, labeling all documents as nonrelevant
is completely unsatisfying to an IR system user. Users are always going to
want to see some documents, and can be assumed to have a certain tolerance
for seeing some false positives providing that they get some useful information. The measures of precision and recall concentrate the evaluation on the
return of true positives, asking what percentage of the relevant documents
have been found and how many false positives have also been returned.

The advantage of having the two numbers for precision and recall is that
one is more important than the other in many circumstances. Typical web
surfers would like every result on the first page to be relevant (high precision), but have not the slightest interest in knowing let alone looking at every
document that is relevant. In contrast, various professional searchers such as
paralegals and intelligence analysts are very concerned with trying to get as
high recall as possible, and will tolerate fairly low precision results to get it.
Individuals searching their hard disks are also often interested in high recall

searches. Nevertheless, the two quantities clearly trade off against one another: You can always get a recall of 1 (but very low precision) by retrieving all documents for all queries! Recall is a nondecreasing function of the number of documents retrieved. On the other hand, in a good system, precision usually decreases as the number of documents retrieved is increased. In general, we want to get some amount of recall while tolerating only a certain percentage of false positives.

F MEASURE   A single measure that trades off precision versus recall is the *F measure*, which is the weighted harmonic mean of precision and recall:

$$(8.5) \qquad F = \frac{1}{\alpha \frac{1}{P} + (1 - \alpha)\frac{1}{R}} = \frac{(\beta^2 + 1)PR}{\beta^2 P + R} \quad \text{where} \quad \beta^2 = \frac{1 - \alpha}{\alpha}$$

where $\alpha \in [0, 1]$ and thus $\beta^2 \in [0, \infty]$. The default *balanced F measure* equally weights precision and recall, which means making $\alpha = 1/2$ or $\beta = 1$. It is commonly written as F_1, which is short for $F_{\beta=1}$, even though the formulation in terms of α more transparently exhibits the F measure as a weighted harmonic mean. When using $\beta = 1$, the formula on the right simplifies to:

$$(8.6) \qquad F_{\beta=1} = \frac{2PR}{P + R}.$$

However, using an even weighting is not the only choice. Values of $\beta < 1$ emphasize precision, whereas values of $\beta > 1$ emphasize recall. For example, a value of $\beta = 3$ or $\beta = 5$ might be used if recall is to be emphasized. Recall, precision, and the F measure are inherently measures between 0 and 1, but they are also very commonly written as percentages, on a scale between 0 and 100.

Why do we use a harmonic mean rather than the simpler average (arithmetic mean)? Recall that we can always get 100% recall by just returning all documents, and therefore we can always get a 50% arithmetic mean by the same process. This strongly suggests that the arithmetic mean is an unsuitable measure to use. In contrast, if we assume that 1 document in 10,000 is relevant to the query, the harmonic mean score of this strategy is 0.02%. The harmonic mean is always less than or equal to the arithmetic mean and the geometric mean. When the values of two numbers differ greatly, the harmonic mean is closer to their minimum than to their arithmetic mean (Figure 8.1).

?   **Exercise 8.1** [⋆] An IR system returns eight relevant documents and ten non-relevant documents. There are a total of twenty relevant documents in the collection. What is the precision of the system on this search, and what is its recall?

Exercise 8.2 [⋆] The balanced F measure (a.k.a. F_1) is defined as the harmonic mean of precision and recall. What is the advantage of using the harmonic mean rather than "averaging" (using the arithmetic mean)?

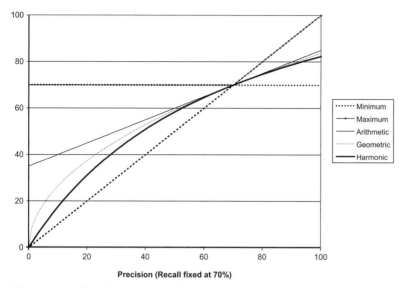

Precision (Recall fixed at 70%)

Figure 8.1 Graph comparing the harmonic mean to other means. The graph shows a slice through the calculation of various means of precision and recall for the fixed recall value of 70%. The harmonic mean is always less than either the arithmetic or geometric mean, and often quite close to the minimum of the two numbers. When the precision is also 70%, all the measures coincide.

Exercise 8.3 [⋆⋆] Derive the equivalence between the two formulas for F measure shown in Equation (8.5), given that $\alpha = 1/(\beta^2 + 1)$.

8.4 Evaluation of ranked retrieval results

Precision, recall, and the F measure are set-based measures. They are computed using unordered sets of documents. We need to extend these measures (or to define new measures) if we are to evaluate the ranked retrieval results that are now standard with search engines. In a ranked retrieval context, appropriate sets of retrieved documents are naturally given by the top k retrieved documents. For each such set, precision and recall values can be PRECISION– plotted to give a *precision–recall curve*, such as the one shown in Figure 8.2. RECALL Precision–recall curves have a distinctive sawtooth shape: if the $(k + 1)^{\text{th}}$ doc-CURVE ument retrieved is nonrelevant, then recall is the same as for the top k documents, but precision has dropped. If it is relevant, then both precision and recall increase, and the curve jags up and to the right. It is often useful to remove these jiggles and the standard way to do this is with an interpolated INTERPOLATED precision: the *interpolated precision* (p_{interp}) at a certain recall level r is defined PRECISION as the highest precision found for any recall level $r' \geq r$:

$$(8.7) \qquad p_{interp}(r) = \max_{r' \geq r} p(r').$$

The justification is that almost anyone would be prepared to look at a few more documents if it would increase the percentage of the viewed set that

Table 8.1 Calculation of eleven-point interpolated average precision. This is for the precision–recall curve shown in Figure 8.2.

recall	interp. precision
0.0	1.00
0.1	0.67
0.2	0.63
0.3	0.55
0.4	0.45
0.5	0.41
0.6	0.36
0.7	0.29
0.8	0.13
0.9	0.10
1.0	0.08

were relevant (i.e., if the precision of the larger set is higher). Interpolated precision is shown by a thinner line in Figure 8.2. With this definition, the interpolated precision at a recall of 0 is well-defined (Exercise 8.4).

Examining the entire precision–recall curve is very informative, but there is often a desire to boil this information down to a few numbers, or perhaps even a single number. The traditional way of doing this (used for instance in the first eight TREC Ad Hoc evaluations) is the *eleven-point interpolated average precision*. For each information need, the interpolated precision is measured at the 11 recall levels of 0.0, 0.1, 0.2, ..., 1.0. For the precision–recall curve in Figure 8.2, these eleven values are shown in Table 8.1. For each recall level, we then calculate the arithmetic mean of the interpolated precision at that recall level for each information need in the test collection. A composite precision–recall curve showing eleven points can then be graphed. Figure 8.3

ELEVEN-POINT
INTERPOLATED
AVERAGE
PRECISION

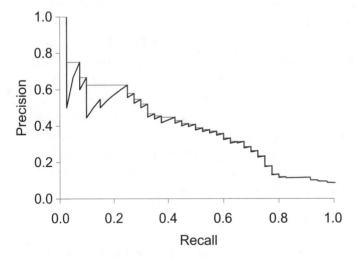

Figure 8.2 Precision–recall graph.

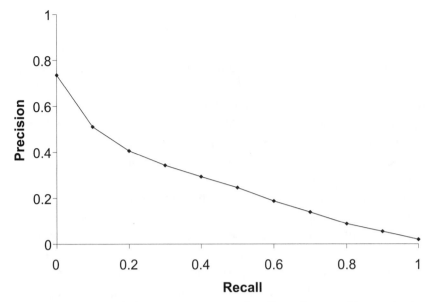

Figure 8.3   Averaged eleven-point precision/recall graph across fifty queries for a representative TREC system. The MAP for this system is 0.2553.

shows an example graph of such results from a representative good system at TREC 8.

In recent years, other measures have become more common. Most stan- MEAN dard among the TREC community is *mean average precision* (MAP), which AVERAGE provides a single-figure measure of quality across recall levels. Among eval- PRECISION uation measures, MAP has been shown to have especially good discrimination and stability. For a single information need, average precision is the average of the precision value obtained for the set of top k documents existing after each relevant document is retrieved, and this value is then averaged over information needs. That is, if the set of relevant documents for an information need $q_j \in Q$ is $\{d_1, \ldots d_{m_j}\}$ and R_{jk} is the set of ranked retrieval results from the top result until you get to document d_k, then

(8.8)
$$\text{MAP}(Q) = \frac{1}{|Q|} \sum_{j=1}^{|Q|} \frac{1}{m_j} \sum_{k=1}^{m_j} \text{Precision}(R_{jk}).$$

When a relevant document is not retrieved at all,[1] the precision value in the above equation is taken to be 0. For a single information need, the average precision approximates the area under the uninterpolated precision–recall curve, and so the MAP is roughly the average area under the precision–recall curve for a set of queries.

Using MAP, fixed recall levels are not chosen, and there is no interpolation. The MAP value for a test collection is the arithmetic mean of average preci-

---

[1] A system may not fully order all documents in the collection in response to a query or, at any rate, an evaluation exercise may be based on submitting only the top k results for each information need.

sion values for individual information needs. (This has the effect of weighting each information need equally in the final reported number, even if many documents are relevant to some queries and very few are relevant to other queries.) Calculated MAP scores normally vary widely across information needs when measured within a single system, for instance, between 0.1 and 0.7. Indeed, there is normally more agreement in MAP for an individual information need across systems than for MAP scores for different information needs for the same system. This means that a set of test information needs must be large and diverse enough to be representative of system effectiveness across different queries.

The above measures factor in precision at all recall levels. For many prominent applications, particularly web search, this may not be germane to users. What matters is rather how many good results there are on the first page or the first three pages. This leads to measuring precision at fixed low levels of retrieved results, such as ten or thirty documents. This is referred to as PRECISION AT k *precision at k*, for example "Precision at 10." It has the advantage of not requiring any estimate of the size of the set of relevant documents; the disadvantages that it is the least stable of the commonly used evaluation measures and that it does not average well because the total number of relevant documents for a query has a strong influence on precision at k.

R-PRECISION   An alternative, which alleviates this problem, is *R-precision*. It requires having a set of known relevant documents *Rel*, from which we calculate the precision of the top *Rel* documents returned. (The set *Rel* may be incomplete, such as when *Rel* is formed by creating relevance judgments for the pooled top k results of particular systems in a set of experiments.) R-precision adjusts for the size of the set of relevant documents: A perfect system could score 1 on this metric for each query, whereas, even a perfect system could only achieve a precision at twenty of 0.4 if there were only eight documents in the collection relevant to an information need. Averaging this measure across queries thus makes more sense. This measure is harder to explain to naive users than precision at k but easier to explain than MAP. If there are $|Rel|$ relevant documents for a query, we examine the top $|Rel|$ results of a system, and find that r are relevant, then by definition, not only is the precision (and hence R-precision) $r/|Rel|$, but the recall of this result set is also BREAK-EVEN $r/|Rel|$. Thus, R-precision turns out to be identical to the *break-even point*, anPOINT other measure that is sometimes used, defined in terms of this equality relationship holding. Like precision at k, R-precision describes only one point on the precision–recall curve, rather than attempting to summarize effectiveness across the curve, and it is somewhat unclear why you should be interested in the break-even point rather than either the best point on the curve (the point with maximal F-measure) or a retrieval level of interest to a particular application (precision at k). Nevertheless, R-precision turns out to be highly correlated with MAP empirically, despite measuring only a single point on the curve.

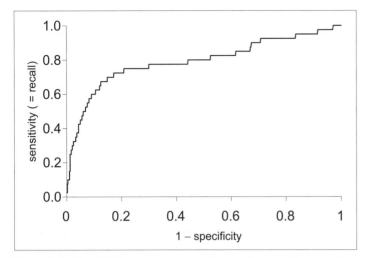

Figure 8.4 The ROC curve corresponding to the precision–recall curve in Figure 8.2.

ROC CURVE   Another concept sometimes used in evaluation is an *ROC curve*. (*ROC* stands for *receiver operating characteristics*, but knowing that doesn't help most people.) An ROC curve plots the true positive rate or sensitivity against the SENSITIVITY false-positive rate or $(1 - \text{specificity})$. Here, *sensitivity* is just another term for recall. The false-positive rate is given by $fp/(fp + tn)$. Figure 8.4 shows the ROC curve corresponding to the precision–recall curve in Figure 8.2. An ROC curve always goes from the bottom left to the top right of the graph. For a good system, the graph climbs steeply on the left side. For unranked result SPECIFICITY sets, *specificity*, given by $tn/(fp + tn)$, was not seen as a very useful notion. Because the set of true negatives is always so large, its value would be almost 1 for all information needs (and, correspondingly, the value of the false-positive rate would be almost 0). That is, the "interesting" part of Figure 8.2 is $0 < \text{recall} < 0.4$, a part that is compressed to a small corner of Figure 8.4. But an ROC curve could make sense when looking over the full retrieval spectrum, and it provides another way of looking at the data. In many fields, a common aggregate measure is to report the area under the ROC curve, which is the ROC analog of MAP. Precision–recall curves are sometimes loosely referred to as ROC curves. This is understandable, but not accurate.

A final approach that has seen increasing adoption, especially when employed with machine learning approaches to ranking (see Section 15.4, CUMULATIVE page 314) is measures of *cumulative gain*, and in particular *normalized dis-* GAIN *counted cumulative gain* (*NDCG*). NDCG is designed for situations of nonbi- NORMALIZED nary notions of relevance (cf. Section 8.5.1). Like precision at k, it is evaluated DISCOUNTED CUMULATIVE over some number k of top search results. Let $R(j, d)$ be the relevance score GAIN assessors gave to document d for query j. Then, (NDCG)

(8.9)
$$\text{NDCG}(Q, k) = \frac{1}{|Q|} \sum_{j=1}^{|Q|} Z_k \sum_{m=1}^{k} \frac{2^{R(j,m)} - 1}{\log(1 + m)},$$

where Z_k is a normalization factor calculated to make it so that a perfect ranking's NDCG at k is 1. For queries for which $k' < k$ documents are retrieved, the last summation is done up to k'.

Exercise 8.4 [$\star$] What are the possible values for interpolated precision at a recall level of 0?

Exercise 8.5 [$\star\star$] Must there always be a break-even point between precision and recall? Either show there must be or give a counterexample.

Exercise 8.6 [$\star\star$] What is the relationship between the value of F_1 and the break-even point?

DICE **Exercise 8.7** [$\star\star$] The *Dice coefficient* of two sets is a measure of their intersec-
COEFFICIENT tion scaled by their size (giving a value in the range 0 to 1):

$$\mathrm{Dice}(X, Y) = \frac{2|X \cap Y|}{|X| + |Y|}.$$

Show that the balanced F-measure (F_1) is equal to the Dice coefficient of the retrieved and relevant document sets.

Exercise 8.8 [$\star$] Consider an information need for which there are four relevant documents in the collection. Contrast two systems run on this collection. Their top ten results are judged for relevance as follows (the leftmost item is the top ranked search result):

System 1   R N R N N   N N N R R

System 2   N R N N R   R R N N N

a. What is the MAP of each system? Which has a higher MAP?
b. Does this result intuitively make sense? What does it say about what is important in getting a good MAP score?
c. What is the R-precision of each system? (Does it rank the systems the same as MAP?)

Exercise 8.9 [$\star\star$] The following list of Rs and Ns represents relevant (R) and nonrelevant (N) returned documents in a ranked list of twenty documents retrieved in response to a query from a collection of 10,000 documents. The top of the ranked list (the document the system thinks is most likely to be relevant) is on the left of the list. This list shows six relevant documents. Assume that there are eight relevant documents in total in the collection.

R R N N N   N N N R N   R N N N R   N N N N R

a. What is the precision of the system on the top twenty?
b. What is the F_1 on the top twenty?
c. What is the uninterpolated precision of the system at 25% recall?
d. What is the interpolated precision at 33% recall?

e. Assume that these twenty documents are the complete result set of the system. What is the MAP for the query?

Assume, now, instead, that the system returned the entire 10,000 documents in a ranked list, and these are the first twenty results returned.

f. What is the largest possible MAP that this system could have?

g. What is the smallest possible MAP that this system could have?

h. In a set of experiments, only the top twenty results are evaluated by hand. The result in (e) is used to approximate the range (f) to (g). For this example, how large (in absolute terms) can the error for the MAP be by calculating (e) instead of (f) and (g) for this query?

8.5 Assessing relevance

To properly evaluate a system, your test information needs must be germane to the documents in the test document collection, and appropriate for predicted usage of the system. These information needs are best designed by domain experts. Using random combinations of query terms as an information need is generally not a good idea because typically they will not resemble the actual distribution of information needs.

Given information needs and documents, you need to collect relevance assessments. This is a time-consuming and expensive process involving human beings. For tiny collections like Cranfield, exhaustive judgments of relevance for each query and document pair were obtained. For large modern collections, it is usual for relevance to be assessed only for a subset POOLING of the documents for each query. The most standard approach is *pooling*, where relevance is assessed over a subset of the collection that is formed from the top k documents returned by a number of different IR systems (usually the ones to be evaluated), and perhaps other sources such as the results of Boolean keyword searches or documents found by expert searchers in an interactive process.

A human is not a device that reliably reports a gold standard judgment of relevance of a document to a query. Rather, humans and their relevance judgments are quite idiosyncratic and variable. But this is not a problem to be solved: In the final analysis, the success of an IR system depends on how good it is at satisfying the needs of these idiosyncratic humans, one information need at a time.

Nevertheless, it is interesting to consider and measure how much agreement between judges there is on relevance judgments. In the social sciences, KAPPA a common measure for agreement between judges is the *kappa statistic*. It is STATISTIC designed for categorical judgments and corrects a simple agreement rate for the rate of chance agreement.

(8.10)
$$kappa = \frac{P(A) - P(E)}{1 - P(E)}$$

Table 8.2 Calculating the kappa statistic.

		judge 2 relevance		
		yes	no	total
judge 1	yes	300	20	320
relevance	no	10	70	80
	total	310	90	400

Observed proportion of the times the judges agreed
$P(A) = (300 + 70)/400 = 370/400 = 0.925$
Pooled marginals
$P(nonrelevant) = (80 + 90)/(400 + 400) = 170/800 = 0.2125$
$P(relevant) = (320 + 310)/(400 + 400) = 630/800 = 0.7878$
Probability that the two judges agreed by chance
$P(E) = P(nonrelevant)^2 + P(relevant)^2 = 0.2125^2 + 0.7878^2 = 0.665$
Kappa statistic
$\kappa = (P(A) - P(E))/(1 - P(E)) = (0.925 - 0.665)/(1 - 0.665) = 0.776$

where $P(A)$ is the proportion of the times the judges agreed, and $P(E)$ is the proportion of the times they would be expected to agree by chance. There are choices in how the latter is estimated: If we simply say we are making a two-class decision and assume nothing more, then the expected chance agreement rate is 0.5. However, normally the class distribution assigned is MARGINAL skewed, and it is usual to use *marginal* statistics to calculate expected agreement.[2] There are still two ways to do it depending on whether one pools the marginal distribution across judges or uses the marginals for each judge separately; both forms have been used, but we present the pooled version because it is more conservative in the presence of systematic differences in assessments across judges. The calculations are shown in Table 8.2. The kappa value is 1 if two judges always agree, 0 if they agree only at the rate given by chance, and negative if they are worse than random. If there are more than two judges, it is normal to calculate an average pairwise kappa value. As a rule of thumb, a kappa value above 0.8 is taken as good agreement, a kappa value between 0.67 and 0.8 is taken as fair agreement, and agreement below 0.67 is seen as data providing a dubious basis for an evaluation, although the precise cutoffs depend on the purposes for which the data will be used.

Interjudge agreement of relevance has been measured within the TREC evaluations and for medical IR collections. Using the above rules of thumb, the level of agreement normally falls in the range of "fair" (0.67–0.8). The fact that human agreement on a binary relevance judgment is quite modest is one reason for not requiring more fine-grained relevance labeling from the test set creator. To answer the question of whether IR evaluation results are valid despite the variation of individual assessors' judgments, people have

---

[2] For a contingency table, as in Table 8.2, a marginal statistic is formed by summing a row or column. The marginal $a_{i.k} = \sum_j a_{ijk}$.

experimented with evaluations taking one or the other of two judges' opinions as the gold standard. The choice can make a considerable *absolute* difference to reported scores, but has in general been found to have little impact on the *relative* effectiveness ranking of either different systems or variants of a single system that are being compared for effectiveness.

8.5.1 Critiques and justifications of the concept of relevance

The advantage of system evaluation, as enabled by the standard model of relevant and nonrelevant documents, is that we have a fixed setting in which we can vary IR systems and system parameters to carry out comparative experiments. Such formal testing is much less expensive and allows clearer diagnosis of the effect of changing system parameters than doing user studies of retrieval effectiveness. Indeed, once we have a formal measure that we have confidence in, we can proceed to optimize effectiveness by machine-learning methods, rather than tuning parameters by hand. Of course, if the formal measure poorly describes what users actually want, doing this will not be effective in improving user satisfaction. Our perspective is that, in practice, the standard formal measures for IR evaluation, although a simplification, are good enough, and recent work in optimizing formal evaluation measures in IR has succeeded brilliantly. There are numerous examples of techniques developed in formal evaluation settings that improve effectiveness in operational settings, such as the development of document length normalization methods within the context of TREC (Sections 6.4.4 and 11.4.3) and machine learning methods for adjusting parameter weights in scoring (Section 6.1.2).

That is not to say that there are not problems latent within the abstractions used. The relevance of one document is treated as independent of the relevance of other documents in the collection. (This assumption is actually built into most retrieval systems – documents are scored against queries, not against each other – as well as being assumed in the evaluation methods.) Assessments are binary: There aren't any nuanced assessments of relevance. Relevance of a document to an information need is treated as an absolute, objective decision. But judgments of relevance are subjective, varying across people, as we discussed. In practice, human assessors are also imperfect measuring instruments, susceptible to failures of understanding and attention. We also have to assume that users' information needs do not change as they start looking at retrieval results. Any results based on one collection are heavily skewed by the choice of collection, queries, and relevance judgment set; the results may not translate from one domain to another or to a different user population.

Some of these problems may be fixable. A number of recent evaluations, including INEX, some TREC tracks, and NTCIR have adopted an ordinal notion of relevance with documents divided into three or four classes, distinguishing slightly relevant documents from highly relevant documents. See

Section 10.4 (page 192) for a detailed discussion of how this is implemented in the INEX evaluations.

One clear problem with the relevance-based assessment that we have pre- MARGINAL sented is the distinction between relevance and *marginal relevance*: whether RELEVANCE a document still has distinctive usefulness after the user has looked at cer- tain other documents (Carbonell and Goldstein 1998). Even if a document is highly relevant, its information can be completely redundant with other documents that have already been examined. The most extreme case of this is documents that are duplicates – a phenomenon that is actually very common on the World Wide Web – but it can also easily occur when several documents provide a similar precis of an event. In such circumstances, marginal rele- vance is clearly a better measure of utility to the user. Maximizing marginal relevance requires returning documents that exhibit diversity and novelty. One way to approach measuring this is by using distinct facts or entities as evaluation units. This perhaps more directly measures true utility to the user but doing this makes it harder to create a test collection.

> **Exercise 8.10** [**] Below is a table showing how two human judges rated the relevance of a set of twelve documents to a particular information need (0 = nonrelevant, 1 = relevant). Let us assume that you've written an IR system that for this query returns the set of documents {4, 5, 6, 7, 8}.
>
> | docID | Judge 1 | Judge 2 |
> |-------|---------|---------|
> | 1 | 0 | 0 |
> | 2 | 0 | 0 |
> | 3 | 1 | 1 |
> | 4 | 1 | 1 |
> | 5 | 1 | 0 |
> | 6 | 1 | 0 |
> | 7 | 1 | 0 |
> | 8 | 1 | 0 |
> | 9 | 0 | 1 |
> | 10 | 0 | 1 |
> | 11 | 0 | 1 |
> | 12 | 0 | 1 |
>
> a. Calculate the kappa measure between the two judges.
> b. Calculate precision, recall, and F_1 of your system if a document is considered relevant only if the two judges agree.
> c. Calculate precision, recall, and F_1 of your system if a document is considered relevant if either judge thinks it is relevant.

8.6 A broader perspective: System quality and user utility

Formal evaluation measures are at some distance from our ultimate interest in measures of human utility: How satisfied is each user with the results the system gives for each information need that they pose? The standard way to measure human satisfaction is by various kinds of user studies. These might include quantitative measures, both objective, such as time to complete a task, as well as subjective, such as a score for satisfaction with the search engine, and qualitative measures, such as user comments on the search interface. In this section, we touch on other system aspects that allow quantitative evaluation and the issue of user utility.

8.6.1 System issues

There are many practical benchmarks on which to rate an IR system beyond its retrieval quality. These include:

- How fast does it index; that is, how many documents per hour does it index for a certain distribution over document lengths? (Cf. Chapter 4.)
- How fast does it search; that is, what is its latency as a function of index size?
- How expressive is its query language? How fast is it on complex queries?
- How large is its document collection, in terms of the number of documents or the collection having information distributed across a broad range of topics?

All these criteria, apart from query language expressiveness, are straightforwardly *measurable*: We can quantify the speed or size. Various kinds of feature checklists can make query language expressiveness semiprecise.

8.6.2 User utility

What we would really like is a way of quantifying aggregate user happiness, based on the relevance, speed, and user interface of a system. One part of this is understanding the distribution of people we wish to make happy, and this depends entirely on the setting. For a web search engine, happy search users are those who find what they want. One indirect measure of such users is that they tend to return to the same engine. Measuring the rate of return of users is thus an effective metric, which would of course be more effective if you could also measure how much these users used other search engines. But advertisers are also users of modern web search engines. They are happy if customers click through to their sites and then make purchases. On an eCommerce web site, a user is likely to be wanting to purchase something. Thus, we can measure the time to purchase, or the fraction of searchers who become buyers. On a shopfront web site, perhaps both the user's and the store owner's needs are satisfied if a purchase is made. Nevertheless, in general, we need to decide whether it is the end user's or the eCommerce site owner's happiness that we are trying to optimize. Usually, it is the store owner who is paying us.

For an "enterprise" (company, government, or academic) intranet search engine, the relevant metric is more likely to be user productivity: How much time do users spend looking for information that they need? There are also many other practical criteria concerning such matters as information security, which we mentioned in Section 4.6 (page 73).

User happiness is elusive to measure, and this is part of why the standard methodology uses the proxy of relevance of search results. The standard direct way to get at user satisfaction is to run user studies, where people engage in tasks, and usually various metrics are measured, the participants are observed, and ethnographic interview techniques are used to get qualitative information on satisfaction. User studies are very useful in system design, but they are time consuming and expensive. They are also difficult to do well, and expertise is required to design the studies and to interpret the results. We will not discuss the details of human usability testing here.

8.6.3 *Refining a deployed system*

If an IR system has been built and is being used by a large number of users, the system's builders can evaluate possible changes by deploying variant versions of the system and recording measures that are indicative of user satisfaction with one variant versus others as they are being used. This method is frequently used by web search engines.

A/B TEST   The most common version of this is *A/B testing*, a term borrowed from the advertising industry. For such a test, precisely one thing is changed between the current system and a proposed system, and a small proportion of traffic (say, 1%–10% of users) is randomly directed to the variant system, while most users use the current system. For example, if we wish to investigate a change to the ranking algorithm, we redirect a random sample of users to a variant system and evaluate measures such as the frequency with which people click on the top result, or any result on the first page. (This particular

CLICKTHROUGH analysis method is referred to as *clickthrough log analysis* or *clickstream min-*
LOG ANALYSIS *ing*. It is further discussed as a method of implicit feedback in Section 9.1.7
CLICKSTREAM (page 172).)
MINING   The basis of A/B testing is running a bunch of single variable tests (either in sequence or in parallel): For each test, only one parameter is varied from the control (the current live system). It is therefore easy to see whether varying each parameter has a positive or negative effect. Such testing of a live system can easily and cheaply gauge the effect of a change on users, and, with a large enough user base, it is practical to measure even very small positive and negative effects. In principle, more analytic power can be achieved by varying multiple things at once in an uncorrelated (random) way, and doing standard multivariate statistical analysis, such as multiple linear regression. In practice, though, A/B testing is widely used, because A/B tests are easy to deploy, easy to understand, and easy to explain to management.

8.7 Results snippets

Having chosen or ranked the documents matching a query, we wish to present a results list that will be informative to the user. In many cases the user will not want to examine all the returned documents and so we want to make the results list informative enough that the user can do a final ranking of the documents for themselves based on relevance to their information SNIPPET need.[3] The standard way of doing this is to provide a *snippet*, a short summary of the document, which is designed so as to allow the user to decide its relevance. Typically, the snippet consists of the document title and a short summary, which is automatically extracted. The question is how to design the summary so as to maximize its usefulness to the user.

STATIC The two basic kinds of summaries are *static*, which are always the same
SUMMARY regardless of the query, and *dynamic* (or query dependent), which are cus-
DYNAMIC tomized according to the user's information need as deduced from a query.
SUMMARY Dynamic summaries attempt to explain why a particular document was retrieved for the query at hand.

A static summary is generally composed of either or both a subset of the document and metadata associated with the document. The simplest form of summary takes the first two sentences or fifty words of a document, or extracts particular zones of a document, such as the title and author. Instead of zones of a document, the summary can instead use metadata associated with the document. This may be an alternative way to provide an author or date, or may include elements which are designed to give a summary, such as the `description` metadata that can appear in the `meta` element of a web HTML page. This summary is typically extracted and cached at indexing time, in such a way that it can be retrieved and presented quickly when displaying search results, whereas having to access the actual document content might be a relatively expensive operation.

There has been extensive work within natural language processing (NLP)
TEXT SUMMA- on better ways to do *text summarization*. Most such work still aims only to
RIZATION choose sentences from the original document to present and concentrates on how to select good sentences. The models typically combine positional factors, favoring the first and last paragraphs of documents and the first and last sentences of paragraphs, with content factors, emphasizing sentences with key terms, which have low document frequency in the collection as a whole, but high frequency and good distribution across the particular document being returned. In sophisticated NLP approaches, the system synthesizes sentences for a summary, either by doing full text generation or by editing and perhaps combining sentences used in the document. For example, it might delete a relative clause or replace a pronoun with the noun phrase that it

---

[3] There are exceptions, in domains where recall is emphasized. For instance, in many legal disclosure cases, a legal associate will review *every* document that matches a keyword search.

*... **In recent years, Papua New Guinea has faced severe economic difficulties and** economic growth has slowed*, partly as a result of weak governance and civil war, and partly as a result of external factors such as the Bougainville civil war which led to the closure in 1989 of the Panguna mine (at that time the most important foreign exchange earner and contributor to Government finances), the Asian financial crisis, a decline in the prices of gold and copper, and a fall in the production of oil. ***PNG's economic development record over the past few years is evidence that*** governance issues underlly many of the country's problems. Good governance, which may be defined as the transparent and accountable management of human, natural, economic and financial resources for the purposes of equitable and sustainable development, flows from proper public sector management, efficient fiscal and accounting mechanisms, and a willingness to make service delivery a priority in practice. ...

Figure 8.5   An example of selecting text for a dynamic snippet. This snippet was generated for a document in response to the query new guinea economic development. The figure shows in bold italic where the selected snippet text occurred in the original document.

refers to. This last class of methods remains in the realm of research and is seldom used for search results: It is easier, safer, and often even better to just use sentences from the original document.

Dynamic summaries display one or more "windows" on the document, aiming to present the pieces that have the most utility to the user in evaluating the document with respect to their information need. Usually these windows contain one or several of the query terms, and so are often re-

KEYWORD-IN-   ferred to as *keyword-in-context* (KWIC) snippets, although sometimes they
CONTEXT   may still be pieces of the text, such as the title, that are selected for their query-independent information value just as in the case of static summarization (Figure 8.5). Dynamic summaries are generated in conjunction with scoring. If the query is found as a phrase, occurrences of the phrase in the document will be shown as the summary. If not, windows within the document that contain multiple query terms will be selected. Commonly, these windows may just stretch some number of words to the left and right of the query terms. This is a place where NLP techniques can usefully be employed: Users prefer snippets that read well because they contain complete phrases.

Dynamic summaries are generally regarded as greatly improving the usability of IR systems, but they present a complication for IR system design. A dynamic summary cannot be precomputed, but, on the other hand, if a system has only a positional index, then it cannot easily reconstruct the context surrounding search engine hits to generate such a dynamic summary. This is one reason for using static summaries. The standard solution to this in a world of large and cheap disk drives is to locally cache all the documents at index time (notwithstanding that this approach raises various legal, information security, and control issues that are far from resolved) as shown in Figure 7.5 (page 135). Then, a system can simply scan a document that is about to appear in a displayed results list to find snippets containing the query

words. Beyond simply access to the text, producing a good KWIC snippet requires some care. Given a variety of keyword occurrences in a document, the goal is to choose fragments that are (i) maximally informative about the discussion of those terms in the document, (ii) self-contained enough to be easy to read, and (iii) short enough to fit within the normally strict constraints on the space available for summaries.

Generating snippets must be fast because the system is typically generating many snippets for each query that it handles. Rather than caching an entire document, it is common to cache only a generous but fixed size prefix of the document, such as perhaps 10,000 characters. For most common, short documents, the entire document is thus cached, but huge amounts of local storage will not be wasted on potentially vast documents. Summaries of documents whose length exceeds the prefix size will be based on material in the prefix only, which is in general a useful zone in which to look for a document summary anyway.

If a document has been updated since it was last processed by a crawler and indexer, these changes will be neither in the cache nor in the index. In these circumstances, neither the index nor the summary will accurately reflect the current contents of the document, but it is the differences between the summary and the actual document content that will be more glaringly obvious to the end user.

8.8 References and further reading

Definition and implementation of the notion of relevance to a query got off to a rocky start in 1953. Swanson (1988) reports that in an evaluation in that year between two teams, they agreed that 1,390 documents were variously relevant to a set of ninety-eight questions, but disagreed on a further 1,577 documents, and the disagreements were never resolved.

Rigorous formal testing of IR systems was first completed in the Cranfield experiments, beginning in the late 1950s. A retrospective discussion of the Cranfield test collection and experimentation with it can be found in (Cleverdon 1991). The other seminal series of early IR experiments were those on the SMART system by Gerard Salton and colleagues (Salton 1971b, 1991). The TREC evaluations are described in detail by Voorhees and Harman (2005). Online information is available at http://trec.nist.gov/. Initially, few researchers computed the statistical significance of their experimental results, but the IR community increasingly demands this (Hull 1993). User studies of IR system effectiveness began more recently (Saracevic and Kantor 1988, 1996).

The notions of recall and precision were first used by Kent et al. (1955), F MEASURE although the term *precision* did not appear until later. The F measure (or, rather its complement $E = 1 - F$) was introduced by van Rijsbergen (1979). He provides an extensive theoretical discussion, which shows how adopting a principle of decreasing marginal relevance (at some point a user will be unwilling to sacrifice a unit of precision for an added unit of recall) leads to the harmonic mean being the appropriate method for combining precision and recall (and hence to its adoption rather than the minimum or geometric mean).

Buckley and Voorhees (2000) compare several evaluation measures, including precision at k, MAP, and R-precision, and evaluate the error rate of R-PRECISION each measure. R-precision was adopted as the official evaluation metric in the TREC HARD track (Allan 2005). Aslam and Yilmaz (2005) examine its surprisingly close correlation to MAP, which had been noted in earlier studies (Tague-Sutcliffe and Blustein 1995; Buckley and Voorhees 2000). A standard program for evaluating IR systems that computes many measures of ranked retrieval effectiveness is Chris Buckley's `trec_eval` program used in the TREC evaluations. It can be downloaded from: http://trec.nist.gov/trec_eval/.

Kekäläinen and Järvelin (2002) argue for the superiority of graded relevance judgments when dealing with very large document collections, and Järvelin and Kekäläinen (2002) introduce cumulated gain-based methods for IR system evaluation in this context. Sakai (2007) does a study of the stability and sensitivity of evaluation measures based on graded relevance judgments from NTCIR tasks, and concludes that NDCG is best for evaluating document ranking.

Schamber et al. (1990) examine the concept of relevance, stressing its multidimensional and context-specific nature, but also arguing that it can be measured effectively. (Voorhees 2000) is the standard article for examining variation in relevance judgments and their effects on retrieval system scores and ranking for the TREC Ad Hoc task. Voorhees concludes that, although the numbers change, the rankings are quite stable. Hersh et al. (1994) present similar analysis for a medical IR collection. In contrast, Kekäläinen (2005) analyzes some of the later TRECs, exploring a four-way relevance judgment and the notion of cumulative gain, arguing that the relevance measure used does substantially affect system rankings. See also Harter (1998). Zobel (1998) studies whether the pooling method used by TREC to collect a subset of documents that will be evaluated for relevance is reliable and fair, and concludes that it is.

KAPPA   The kappa statistic and its use for language-related purposes is discussed STATISTIC by Carletta (1996). Many standard sources (e.g., Siegel and Castellan 1988) present pooled calculation of the expected agreement, but Di Eugenio and Glass (2004) argue for preferring the unpooled agreement (although perhaps presenting multiple measures). For further discussion of alternative measures of agreement, which may in fact be better, see Lombard et al. (2002) and Krippendorff (2003).

Text summarization has been actively explored for many years. Modern work on sentence selection was initiated by Kupiec et al. (1995). More recent work includes (Barzilay and Elhadad 1997) and (Jing 2000), together with a broad selection of work appearing at the yearly DUC conferences and at other NLP venues. Tombros and Sanderson (1998) demonstrate the advantages of dynamic summaries in the IR context. Turpin et al. (2007) address how to generate snippets efficiently.

Clickthrough log analysis is studied in (Joachims 2002b; Joachims et al. 2005).

In a series of papers, Hersh, Turpin and colleagues show how improvements in formal retrieval effectiveness, as evaluated in batch experiments, do not always translate into an improved system for users (Hersh et al. 2000a, 2000b, 2001; Turpin and Hersh 2001, 2002).

User interfaces for IR and human factors such as models of human information seeking and usability testing are outside the scope of what we cover in this book. More information on these topics can be found in other textbooks, including (Baeza-Yates and Ribeiro-Neto 1999, Chapter 10) and (Korfhage 1997), and collections focused on cognitive aspects (Spink and Cole 2005).

9 *Relevance feedback and query expansion*

In most collections, the same concept may be referred to using different words. This issue, known as *synonymy*, has an impact on the recall of most information retrieval (IR) systems. For example, you would want a search for aircraft to match plane (but only for references to an *airplane*, not a woodworking plane), and for a search on thermodynamics to match references to heat in appropriate discussions. Users often attempt to address this problem themselves by manually refining a query, as was discussed in Section 1.4; in this chapter, we discuss ways in which a system can help with query refinement, either fully automatically or with the user in the loop.

SYNONYMY

The methods for tackling this problem split into two major classes: global methods and local methods. Global methods are techniques for expanding or reformulating query terms independent of the query and results returned from it, so that changes in the query wording will cause the new query to match other semantically similar terms. Global methods include:

- Query expansion/reformulation with a thesaurus or WordNet (Section 9.2.2)
- Query expansion via automatic thesaurus generation (Section 9.2.3)
- Techniques like spelling correction (discussed in Chapter 3)

Local methods adjust a query relative to the documents that initially appear to match the query. The basic methods here are:

- Relevance feedback (Section 9.1)
- Pseudorelevance feedback, also known as *blind relevance feedback* (Section 9.1.6)
- (Global) Indirect relevance feedback (Section 9.1.7)

In this chapter, we mention all of these approaches, but concentrate on relevance feedback, which is one of the most used and most successful approaches.

162

9.1 Relevance feedback and pseudo relevance feedback

RELEVANCE FEEDBACK The idea of *relevance feedback* (RF) is to involve the user in the IR process so as to improve the final result set. In particular, the user gives feedback on the relevance of documents in an initial set of results. The basic procedure is:

- The user issues a (short, simple) query.
- The system returns an initial set of retrieval results.
- The user marks some returned documents as relevant or nonrelevant.
- The system computes a better representation of the information need based on the user feedback.
- The system displays a revised set of retrieval results.

RF can go through one or more iterations of this sort. The process exploits the idea that it may be difficult to formulate a good query when you don't know the collection well, but it is easy to judge particular documents, and so it makes sense to engage in iterative query refinement of this sort. In such a scenario, RF can also be effective in tracking a user's evolving information need: Seeing some documents may lead users to refine their understanding of the information they are seeking.

Image search provides a good example of RF. Not only is it easy to see the results at work, but this is a domain where a user can easily have difficulty formulating what they want in words, but can easily indicate relevant or nonrelevant images. After the user enters an initial query for bike on the demonstration system at:

http://nayana.ece.ucsb.edu/imsearch/imsearch.html

the initial results (in this case, images) are returned. In Figure 9.1 (a), the user has selected some of them as relevant. These will be used to refine the query, while other displayed results have no effect on the reformulation. Figure 9.1 (b) then shows the new top-ranked results calculated after this round of relevance feedback.

Figure 9.2 shows a textual IR example where the user wishes to find out about new applications of space satellites.

9.1.1 The Rocchio algorithm for relevance feedback

The Rocchio algorithm is the classic algorithm for implementing RF. It models a way of incorporating relevance feedback information into the vector space model of Section 6.3.

The underlying theory. We want to find a query vector, denoted as $\vec{q}$, that maximizes similarity with relevant documents while minimizing similarity with nonrelevant documents. If C_r is the set of relevant documents and C_{nr}

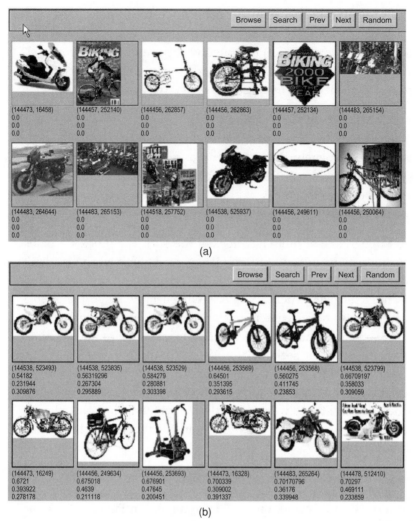

Figure 9.1 RF searching over images. (a) The user views the initial query results for a query of bike, selects the first, third, and fourth results in the top row and the fourth result in the bottom row as relevant, and submits this feedback. (b) The user sees the revised result set. Precision is greatly improved. From http://nayana.ece.ucsb.edu/imsearch/imsearch.html (Newsam et al. 2001).

is the set of nonrelevant documents, then we wish to find[1]:

$$(9.1) \qquad \vec{q}_{opt} = \arg\max_{\vec{q}}[\text{sim}(\vec{q}, C_r) - \text{sim}(\vec{q}, C_{nr})],$$

where sim is defined as in Equation (6.10). Under cosine similarity, the optimal query vector $\vec{q}_{opt}$ for separating the relevant and nonrelevant documents is:

$$(9.2) \qquad \vec{q}_{opt} = \frac{1}{|C_r|} \sum_{\vec{d}_j \in C_r} \vec{d}_j - \frac{1}{|C_{nr}|} \sum_{\vec{d}_j \in C_{nr}} \vec{d}_j.$$

---

[1] In the equation, $\arg\max_x f(x)$ returns a value of x, which maximizes the value of the function $f(x)$. Similarly, $\arg\min_x f(x)$ returns a value of x, which minimizes the value of the function $f(x)$.

(a)   Query: New space satellite applications

(b)   +   1. 0.539, 08/13/91, NASA Hasn't Scrapped Imaging Spectrometer
          +   2. 0.533, 07/09/91, NASA Scratches Environment Gear From Satellite Plan
               3. 0.528, 04/04/90, Science Panel Backs NASA Satellite Plan, But Urges
               Launches of Smaller Probes
               4. 0.526, 09/09/91, A NASA Satellite Project Accomplishes Incredible Feat:
               Staying Within Budget
               5. 0.525, 07/24/90, Scientist Who Exposed Global Warming Proposes
               Satellites for Climate Research
               6. 0.524, 08/22/90, Report Provides Support for the Critics Of Using Big
               Satellites to Study Climate
               7. 0.516, 04/13/87, Arianespace Receives Satellite Launch Pact From Telesat
               Canada
          +   8. 0.509, 12/02/87, Telecommunications Tale of Two Companies

(c)   2.074 new   15.106 space
               30.816 satellite   5.660 application
               5.991 nasa   5.196 eos
               4.196 launch   3.972 aster
               3.516 instrument   3.446 arianespace
               3.004 bundespost   2.806 ss
               2.790 rocket   2.053 scientist
               2.003 broadcast   1.172 earth
               0.836 oil   0.646 measure

(d)   *   1. 0.513, 07/09/91, NASA Scratches Environment Gear From Satellite Plan
          *   2. 0.500, 08/13/91, NASA Hasn't Scrapped Imaging Spectrometer
               3. 0.493, 08/07/89, When the Pentagon Launches a Secret Satellite, Space
               Sleuths Do Some Spy Work of Their Own
               4. 0.493, 07/31/89, NASA Uses 'Warm' Superconductors For Fast Circuit
          *   5. 0.492, 12/02/87, Telecommunications Tale of Two Companies
               6. 0.491, 07/09/91, Soviets May Adapt Parts of SS-20 Missile For Commercial
               Use
               7. 0.490, 07/12/88, Gaping Gap: Pentagon Lags in Race To Match the Soviets
               In Rocket Launchers
               8. 0.490, 06/14/90, Rescue of Satellite By Space Agency To Cost $90 Million

Figure 9.2 Example of relevance feedback on a text collection. (a) The initial query. (b) The user marks some relevant documents (shown with a plus sign). (c) The query is then expanded by 18 terms with weights as shown. (d) The revised top results are then shown. A * marks the documents which were judged relevant in the relevance feedback phase.

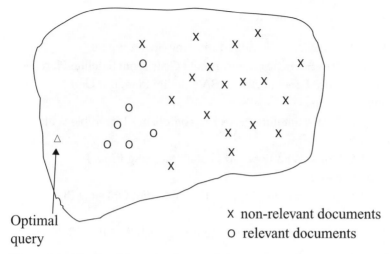

Optimal
query

x non-relevant documents
o relevant documents

Figure 9.3   The Rocchio optimal query for separating relevant and nonrelevant documents.

That is, the optimal query is the vector difference between the centroids of the relevant and nonrelevant documents (Figure 9.3). However, this observation is not terribly useful, precisely because the full set of relevant documents is not known; it is what we want to find.

ROCCHIO **The Rocchio (1971) algorithm.** This was the relevance feedback mechanism
ALGORITHM introduced in and popularized by Salton's SMART system around 1970. In a real IR query context, we have a user query and partial knowledge of known relevant and nonrelevant documents. The algorithm proposes using the modified query $\vec{q}_m$:

$$(9.3) \qquad \vec{q}_m = \alpha \vec{q}_0 + \beta \frac{1}{|D_r|} \sum_{\vec{d}_j \in D_r} \vec{d}_j - \gamma \frac{1}{|D_{nr}|} \sum_{\vec{d}_j \in D_{nr}} \vec{d}_j$$

where q_0 is the original query vector; D_r and D_{nr} are the set of known relevant and nonrelevant documents, respectively; and α, β, and γ are weights attached to each term. These control the balance between trusting the judged document set versus the query: If we have a lot of judged documents, we would like a higher β and γ. Starting from q_0, the new query moves you some distance toward the centroid of the relevant documents and some distance away from the centroid of the nonrelevant documents. This new query can be used for retrieval in the standard vector space model (see Section 6.3). We can easily leave the positive quadrant of the vector space by subtracting off a nonrelevant document's vector. In the Rocchio algorithm, negative term weights are ignored. That is, the term weight is set to 0. Figure 9.4 shows the effect of applying relevance feedback.

Relevance feedback can improve both recall and precision. But, in practice, it has been shown to be most useful for increasing recall in situations where recall is important. This is partly because the technique expands the

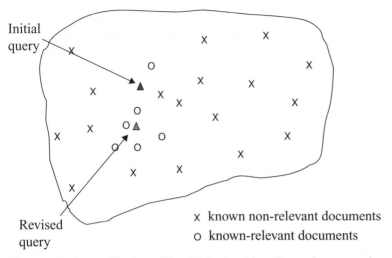

Figure 9.4   An application of Rocchio's algorithm. Some documents have been labeled as relevant and nonrelevant and the initial query vector is moved in response to this feedback.

query, but it is also partly an effect of the use case: When they want high recall, users can be expected to take time to review results and to iterate on the search. Positive feedback also turns out to be much more valuable than negative feedback, and so most IR systems set $\gamma < \beta$. Reasonable values might be $\alpha = 1$, $\beta = 0.75$, and $\gamma = 0.15$. In fact, many systems, such as the image search system in Figure 9.1, allow only positive feedback, which is equivalent to setting $\gamma = 0$. Another alternative is to use only the marked nonrelevant document that received the highest ranking from the IR system as negative feedback (here, $|D_{nr}| = 1$ in Equation (9.3)). Although many of the experimental results comparing various relevance feedback variants are

IDE DEC-HI   rather inconclusive, some studies have suggested that this variant, called *Ide dec-hi* is the most effective or at least the most consistent performer.

?   **Exercise 9.1** Under what conditions would the modified query q_m in Equation (9.3) be the same as the original query q_0? In all other cases, is q_m closer than q_0 to the centroid of the relevant documents?

Exercise 9.2 Why is positive feedback likely to be more useful than negative feedback to an IR system? Why might only using one nonrelevant document be more effective than using several?

Exercise 9.3 Suppose that a user's initial query is cheap CDs cheap DVDs extremely cheap CDs. The user examines two documents, d_1 and d_2. She judges d_1, with the content *CDs cheap software cheap CDs* relevant and d_2 with content *cheap thrills DVDs* nonrelevant. Assume that we are using direct term frequency (with no scaling and no document frequency). There is no need to length-normalize vectors. Using Rocchio relevance feedback as in Equation (9.3), what would the revised query vector be after relevance feedback? Assume $\alpha = 1$, $\beta = 0.75$, $\gamma = 0.25$.

Exercise 9.4 [⋆] Omar has implemented an RF web search system, where he
is going to do RF based only on words in the title text returned for a page
(for efficiency). The user is going to rank three results. The first user, Jinxing, queries for:

banana slug

and the top three titles returned are:

banana slug Ariolimax columbianus
Santa Cruz mountains banana slug
Santa Cruz Campus Mascot

Jinxing judges the first two documents relevant, and the third nonrelevant.
Assume that Omar's search engine uses term frequency but no length
normalization or IDF. Assume that he is using the Rocchio RF mecha-
nism, with $\alpha = \beta = \gamma = 1$. Show the final revised query that would be run.
(Please list the vector elements in alphabetical order.)

9.1.2 Probabilistic relevance feedback

Rather than reweighting the query in a vector space, if a user has told us
some relevant and nonrelevant documents, then we can proceed to build a
classifier. One way of doing this is with a Naive Bayes probabilistic model.
If R is a Boolean indicator variable expressing the relevance of a document,
then we can estimate $P(x_t = 1)$, the probability of a term t appearing in a
document, depending on whether it is relevant or not, as:

(9.4)
$$\hat{P}(x_t = 1 | R = 1) = |VR_t|/|VR|$$
$$\hat{P}(x_t = 0 | R = 0) = (df_t - |VR_t|)/(N - |VR|)$$

where N is the total number of documents, df_t is the number that contain t,
VR is the set of known relevant documents, and VR_t is the subset of this set
containing t. Even though the set of known relevant documents is a perhaps
small subset of the true set of relevant documents, if we assume that the set of
relevant documents is a small subset of the set of all documents, then the estimates given above will be reasonable. This gives a basis for another way of
changing the query term weights. We discuss such probabilistic approaches
more in Chapters 11 and 13, and in particular outline the application to relevance feedback in Section 11.3.4 (page 209). For the moment, observe that
using just Equation (9.4) as a basis for term weighting is likely insufficient.
The equations use only collection statistics and information about the term
distribution within the documents judged relevant. They preserve no memory of the original query.

9.1.3 When does relevance feedback work?

The success of RF depends on certain assumptions. First, the user has to have sufficient knowledge to be able to make an initial query that is at least somewhere close to the documents they desire. This is needed anyhow for successful IR in the basic case, but it is important to see the kinds of problems that relevance feedback cannot solve alone. Cases where RF alone is not sufficient include:

- Misspellings. If the user spells a term in a different way to the way it is spelled in any document in the collection, then RF is unlikely to be effective. This can be addressed by the spelling correction techniques of Chapter 3.
- Cross-language IR. Documents in another language are not nearby in a vector space that is based on term distribution. Rather, documents in the same language cluster more closely together.
- Mismatch of searcher's vocabulary versus collection vocabulary. If the user searches for laptop but all the documents use the term notebook computer, then the query will fail, and relevance feedback is again most likely ineffective.

Second, the RF approach requires relevant documents to be similar to each other. That is, they should cluster. Ideally, the term distribution in all relevant documents will be similar to that in the documents marked by the users, and the term distribution in all nonrelevant documents will be different from those in relevant documents. Things will work well if all relevant documents are tightly clustered around a single prototype, or, at least, if there are different prototypes, if the relevant documents have significant vocabulary overlap, and similarities between relevant and nonrelevant documents are small. Implicitly, the Rocchio RF model treats relevant documents as a single *cluster*, which it models via the centroid of the cluster. This approach does not work as well if the relevant documents are a multimodal class, that is, they consist of several clusters of documents within the vector space. This can happen with:

- Subsets of the documents using different vocabulary, such as Burma versus Myanmar.
- A query for which the answer set is inherently disjunctive, such as Pop stars who once worked at Burger King
- Instances of a general concept, which often appear as a disjunction of more specific concepts, for example, felines.

Good editorial content in the collection can often provide a solution to this problem. For example, an article on the attitudes of different groups to the situation in Burma could introduce the terminology used by different parties, thus linking the document clusters.

Relevance feedback is not necessarily popular with users. Users are often reluctant to provide explicit feedback, or in general do not wish to prolong the search interaction. Furthermore, it is often harder to understand why a particular document was retrieved after relevance feedback is applied.

Relevance feedback can also have practical problems. The long queries that are generated by straightforward application of RF techniques are inefficient for a typical IR system. This results in a high computing cost for the retrieval and potentially long response times for the user. A partial solution to this is to only reweight certain prominent terms in the relevant documents, such as perhaps the top twenty terms by term frequency. Some experimental results have also suggested that using a limited number of terms like this may give better results (Harman 1992), although other work has suggested that using more terms is better in terms of retrieved document quality (Buckley et al. 1994b).

9.1.4 Relevance feedback on the web

Some web search engines offer a similar/related pages feature: The user indicates a document in the results set as exemplary from the standpoint of meeting his information need and requests more documents like it. This can be viewed as a particular simple form of RF. However, in general, RF has been little used in web search. One exception was the Excite web search engine, which initially provided full RF. However, the feature was in time dropped, owing to lack of use. On the web, few people use advanced search interfaces and most would like to complete their search in a single interaction. But the lack of uptake also probably reflects two other factors: RF is hard to explain to the average user, and RF is mainly a recall enhancing strategy, and web search users are only rarely concerned with getting sufficient recall.

Spink et al. (2000) present results from the use of RF in the Excite search engine. Only about 4% of user query sessions used the RF option, and these were usually exploiting the "More like this" link next to each result. About 70% of users only looked at the first page of results and did not pursue things any further. For people who used RF, results were improved about two thirds of the time.

An important more recent thread of work is the use of clickstream data (what links a user clicks on) to provide indirect RF. Use of this data is studied in detail in (Joachims 2002b; Joachims et al. 2005). The very successful use of web link structure (see Chapter 21) can also be viewed as implicit feedback, but provided by page authors rather than readers (although in practice most authors are also readers).

9.1.5 Evaluation of relevance feedback strategies

Interactive RF can give very substantial gains in retrieval performance. Empirically, one round of RF is often very useful. Two rounds is sometimes marginally more useful. Successful use of RF requires enough judged documents, otherwise the process is unstable in that it may drift away from the user's information need. Accordingly, having at least five judged documents is recommended.

There is some subtlety to evaluating the effectiveness of RF in a sound and enlightening way. The obvious first strategy is to start with an initial query q_0 and to compute a precision–recall graph. After one round of feedback from the user, we compute the modified query q_m and again compute a precision–recall graph. Here, in both rounds we assess performance over all documents in the collection, which makes comparisons straightforward. If we do this, we find spectacular gains from RF: Gains on the order of 50% in mean average precision. But, unfortunately, it is cheating. The gains are partly due to the fact that known relevant documents (judged by the user) are now ranked higher. Fairness demands that we should only evaluate with respect to documents not seen by the user.

A second idea is to use documents in the *residual collection* (the set of documents minus those assessed relevant) for the second round of evaluation. This seems like a more realistic evaluation. Unfortunately, the measured performance can then often be lower than for the original query. This is particularly the case if there are few relevant documents, and so a fair proportion of them have been judged by the user in the first round. The relative performance of variant relevance feedback methods can be validly compared, but it is difficult to validly compare performance with and without RF because the collection size and the number of relevant documents changes from before the feedback to after it.

Thus, neither of these methods is fully satisfactory. A third method is to have two collections, one that is used for the initial query and relevance judgments, and the second that is then used for comparative evaluation. The performance of both q_0 and q_m can be validly compared on the second collection.

Perhaps the best evaluation of the utility of RF is to do user studies of its effectiveness, in particular by doing a time-based comparison: How fast does a user find relevant documents with RF versus another strategy (such as query reformulation), or alternatively, how many relevant documents does a user find in a certain amount of time. Such notions of user utility are fairest and closest to real system usage.

9.1.6 Pseudo relevance feedback

PSEUDO RELEVANCE FEEDBACK
BLIND RELEVANCE FEEDBACK

Pseudo relevance feedback, also known as *blind relevance feedback*, provides a method for automatic local analysis. It automates the manual part of RF, so that the user gets improved retrieval performance without an extended interaction. The method is to do normal retrieval to find an initial set of most

Precision at $k = 50$

Term weighting	no RF	pseudo RF
lnc.ltc	64.2%	72.7%
Lnu.ltu	74.2%	87.0%

Figure 9.5 Results showing pseudorelevance feedback greatly improving performance. These results are taken from the Cornell SMART system at TREC 4 (Buckley et al. 1995), and also contrast the use of two different length normalization schemes (L vs. l; cf. Figure 6.15 (page 118)). Pseudorelevance feedback consisted of adding twenty terms to each query.

relevant documents, to then *assume* that the top k ranked documents are relevant, and finally to do RF as before under this assumption.

This automatic technique mostly works. Evidence suggests that it tends to work better than global analysis (Section 9.2). It has been found to improve performance in the TREC ad hoc task. See, for example, the results in Figure 9.5. But it is not without the dangers of an automatic process. For example, if the query is about copper mines and the top several documents are all about mines in Chile, then there may be query drift in the direction of documents on Chile.

9.1.7 *Indirect relevance feedback*

We can also use indirect sources of evidence rather than explicit feedback on IMPLICIT relevance as the basis for relevance feedback. This is often called *implicit (rel-* RELEVANCE *evance) feedback*. Implicit feedback is less reliable than explicit feedback, but is FEEDBACK more useful than pseudo RF, which contains no evidence of user judgments. Moreover, although users are often reluctant to provide explicit feedback, it is easy to collect implicit feedback in large quantities for a high-volume system, such as a web search engine.

On the web, DirectHit introduced the idea of ranking more highly documents that users chose to look at more often. In other words, clicks on links were assumed to indicate that the page was likely relevant to the query. This approach makes various assumptions, such as that the document summaries displayed in results lists (on whose basis users choose which documents to click on) are indicative of the relevance of these documents. In the original DirectHit search engine, the data about the click rates on pages was gathered globally, rather than being user or query specific. This is one form of the gen-CLICKSTREAM eral area of *clickstream mining*. Today, a closely related approach is used in MINING ranking the advertisements that match a web search query (Chapter 19).

9.1.8 *Summary*

RF has been shown to be very effective at improving relevance of results. Its successful use requires queries for which the set of relevant documents is medium to large. Full RF is often onerous for the user, and its implementation is not very efficient in most IR systems. In many cases, other types of interactive retrieval may improve relevance by about as much with less work.

Beyond the core ad hoc retrieval scenario, other uses of RF include:

- Following a changing information need (e.g., names of car models of interest change over time).
- Maintaining an information filter (e.g., for a news feed). Such filters are discussed further in Chapter 13.
- Active learning (deciding which examples it is most useful to know the class of to reduce annotation costs).

?

Exercise 9.5 In Rocchio's algorithm, what weight setting for $\alpha/\beta/\gamma$ does a "Find pages like this one" search correspond to?

Exercise 9.6 [$\star$] Give three reasons why RF has been little used in web searches.

9.2 Global methods for query reformulation

In this section, we more briefly discuss three global methods for expanding a query: By simply aiding the user in doing so, by using a manual thesaurus, and through building a thesaurus automatically.

9.2.1 *Vocabulary tools for query reformulation*

Various user supports in the search process can help the user to see how their searches are or are not working. This includes information about words that were omitted from the query because they were on stop lists, what words were stemmed to, the number of hits on each term or phrase, and whether words were dynamically turned into phrases. The IR system might also suggest search terms by means of a thesaurus or a controlled vocabulary. A user can also be allowed to browse lists of the terms that are in the inverted index, and thus find good terms that appear in the collection.

9.2.2 *Query expansion*

In RF, users give additional input on documents (by marking documents in the results set as relevant or not), and this input is used to reweight the terms QUERY in the query for documents. In *query expansion*, on the other hand, users give EXPANSION additional input on query words or phrases, possibly suggesting additional query terms. Some search engines (especially on the web) suggest related

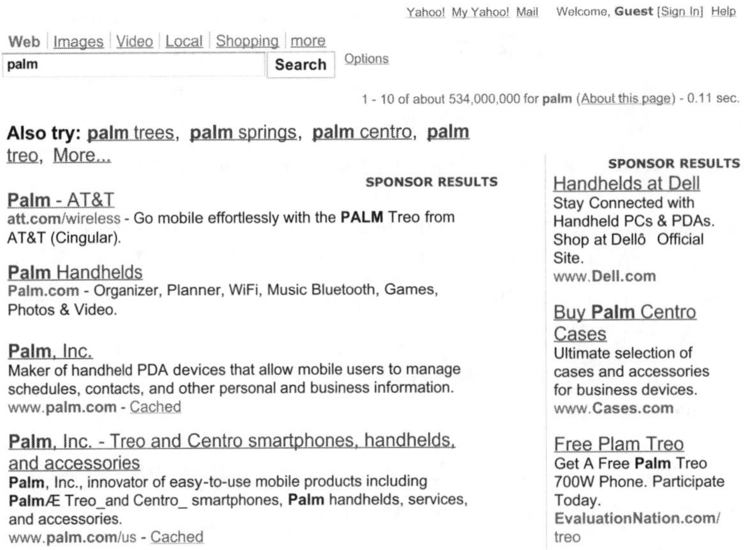

Yahoo! My Yahoo! Mail   Welcome, **Guest** [Sign In] Help

Web | Images | Video | Local | Shopping | more

palm   [Search]   Options

1 - 10 of about 534,000,000 for **palm** (About this page) - 0.11 sec.

Also try: palm trees, **palm** springs, **palm** centro, **palm**
treo, More...

SPONSOR RESULTS

Palm - AT&T
att.com/wireless - Go mobile effortlessly with the **PALM** Treo from
AT&T (Cingular).

Palm Handhelds
Palm.com - Organizer, Planner, WiFi, Music Bluetooth, Games,
Photos & Video.

Palm, Inc.
Maker of handheld PDA devices that allow mobile users to manage
schedules, contacts, and other personal and business information.
www.**palm**.com - Cached

Palm, Inc. - Treo and Centro smartphones, handhelds,
and accessories
Palm, Inc., innovator of easy-to-use mobile products including
Palm Æ Treo_and Centro_ smartphones, **Palm** handhelds, services,
and accessories.
www.**palm**.com/us - Cached

SPONSOR RESULTS
Handhelds at Dell
Stay Connected with
Handheld PCs & PDAs.
Shop at Dellô Official
Site.
www.**Dell**.com

Buy **Palm** Centro
Cases
Ultimate selection of
cases and accessories
for business devices.
www.**Cases**.com

Free Plam Treo
Get A Free **Palm** Treo
700W Phone. Participate
Today.
EvaluationNation.com/
treo

Figure 9.6 An example of query expansion in the interface of the Yahoo! web search engine in 2008. The expanded query suggestions appear just below the "Search Results" bar.

queries in response to a query; the users then opt to use one of these alternative query suggestions. Figure 9.6 shows an example of query suggestion options being presented in the Yahoo! web search engine. The central question in this form of query expansion is how to generate alternative or expanded queries for the user. The most common form of query expansion is global analysis, using some form of thesaurus. For each term t in a query, the query can be automatically expanded with synonyms and related words of t from the thesaurus. Use of a thesaurus can be combined with ideas of term weighting; for instance, one might weight added terms less than original query terms.

Methods for building a thesaurus for query expansion include the following.

- Use of a controlled vocabulary that is maintained by human editors. Here, there is a canonical term for each concept. The subject headings of traditional library subject indexes, such as the Library of Congress Subject Headings or the Dewey Decimal system, are examples of a controlled vocabulary. Use of a controlled vocabulary is quite common for well-resourced domains. A well-known example is the Unified Medical Language System (UMLS) used with Medline for querying the biomedical research literature. For example, in Figure 9.7, neoplasms was added to a search for cancer. This Medline query expansion also contrasts with the Yahoo! example. The Yahoo! interface is a case of interactive query expansion, whereas PubMed does automatic query expansion. Unless the user chooses to examine the submitted query, they may not even realize that query expansion has occurred.

- User query: `cancer`
- PubMed query: ("neoplasms"[TIAB] NOT Medline[SB]) OR "neoplasms"[MeSH Terms] OR cancer[Text Word]
- User query: `skin itch`
- PubMed query: ("skin"[MeSH Terms] OR ("integumentary system"[TIAB] NOT Medline[SB]) OR "integumentary system"[MeSH Terms] OR skin[Text Word]) AND (("pruritus"[TIAB] NOT Medline[SB]) OR "pruritus"[MeSH Terms] OR itch[Text Word])

Figure 9.7 Examples of query expansion via the PubMed thesaurus. When a user issues a query on the PubMed interface to Medline at www.ncbi.nlm.nih.gov/entrez/, their query is mapped on to the Medline vocabulary as shown.

- A manual thesaurus. Here, human editors have built up sets of synony-mous names for concepts, without designating a canonical term. The UMLS metathesaurus is one example of a thesaurus. Statistics Canada maintains a thesaurus of preferred terms, synonyms, broader terms, and narrower terms for matters on which the government collects statistics, such as goods and services. This thesaurus is also bilingual (English and French).
- An automatically derived thesaurus. Here, word co-occurrence statistics over a collection of documents in a domain are used to automatically in-duce a thesaurus (see Section 9.2.3).
- Query reformulations based on query log mining. Here, we exploit the manual query reformulations of other users to make suggestions to a new user. This requires a huge query volume, and is thus particularly appro-priate to web search.

Thesaurus-based query expansion has the advantage of not requiring any user input. Use of query expansion generally increases recall and is widely used in many science and engineering fields. As well as such global analysis techniques, it is also possible to do query expansion by local analysis, for instance, by analyzing the documents in the result set. User input is now usually required, but a distinction remains as to whether the user is giving feedback on documents or on query terms.

9.2.3 Automatic thesaurus generation

As an alternative to the cost of a manual thesaurus, we could attempt to generate a thesaurus automatically by analyzing a collection of documents. There are two main approaches. One is simply to exploit word cooccurrence. We say that words co-occurring in a document or paragraph are likely to be in some sense similar or related in meaning, and simply count text statistics to find the most similar words. The other approach is to use a shallow gram-matical analysis of the text and to exploit grammatical relations or grammat-ical dependencies. For example, we say that entities that are grown, cooked,

word	nearest neighbors
absolutely	absurd, whatsoever, totally, exactly, nothing
bottomed	dip, copper, drops, topped, slide, trimmed
captivating	shimmer, stunningly, superbly, plucky, witty
doghouse	dog, porch, crawling, beside, downstairs
makeup	repellent, lotion, glossy, sunscreen, skin, gel
mediating	reconciliation, negotiate, case, conciliation
keeping	hoping, bring, wiping, could, some, would
lithographs	drawings, Picasso, Dali, sculptures, Gauguin
pathogens	toxins, bacteria, organisms, bacterial, parasite
senses	grasp, psyche, truly, clumsy, naive, innate

Figure 9.8 An example of an automatically generated thesaurus. This example is based on the work in Schütze (1998), which employs latent semantic indexing (see Chapter 18).

eaten, and digested are more likely to be food items. Simply using word co-occurrence is more robust (it cannot be misled by parser errors), but using grammatical relations is more accurate.

The simplest way to compute a co-occurrence thesaurus is based on term-term similarities. We begin with a term–document matrix A, where each cell $A_{t,d}$ is a weighted count $w_{t,d}$ for term t and document d, with weighting so A has length-normalized rows. If we then calculate $C = AA^T$, then $C_{u,v}$ is a similarity score between terms u and v, with a larger number being better. Figure 9.8 shows an example of a thesaurus derived in basically this manner, but with an extra step of dimensionality reduction via Latent Semantic Indexing, which we discuss in Chapter 18. Although some of the thesaurus terms are good or at least suggestive, others are marginal or bad. The quality of the associations is typically a problem. Term ambiguity easily introduces irrelevant statistically correlated terms. For example, a query for Apple computer may expand to Apple red fruit computer. In general these thesauri suffer from both false positives and false negatives. Moreover, because the terms in the automatic thesaurus are highly correlated in documents anyway (and often the collection used to derive the thesaurus is the same as the one being indexed), this form of query expansion may not retrieve many additional documents.

Query expansion is often effective in increasing recall. However, there is a high cost to manually producing a thesaurus and then updating it for scientific and terminological developments within a field. In general a domain-specific thesaurus is required: General thesauri and dictionaries give far too little coverage of the rich, domain-particular vocabularies of most scientific fields. However, query expansion may also significantly decrease precision, particularly when the query contains ambiguous terms. For example, if the user searches for interest rate, expanding the query to interest rate fascinate evaluate is unlikely to be useful. Overall, query expansion is less successful than RF, although it may be as good as pseudo RF. It does, however, have the advantage of being much more understandable to the system user.

? **Exercise 9.7** If *A* is simply a Boolean cooccurrence matrix, then what do you get as the entries in *C*?

9.3 References and further reading

Work in IR quickly confronted the problem of variant expression, which meant that the words in a query might not appear in a document, despite it being relevant to the query. An early experiment about 1960 cited by Swanson (1988) found that only eleven out of twenty-three documents properly indexed under the subject *toxicity* had any use of a word containing the stem *toxi*. There is also the issue of translation, of users knowing what terms a document will use. Blair and Maron (1985) conclude that "it is impossibly difficult for users to predict the exact words, word combinations, and phrases that are used by all (or most) relevant documents and only (or primarily) by those documents."

The main initial papers on relevance feedback using vector space models all appear in Salton (1971b), including the presentation of the Rocchio algorithm (Rocchio 1971) and the Ide dec-hi variant along with evaluation of several variants (Ide 1971). Another variant is to regard *all* documents in the collection apart from those judged relevant as nonrelevant, rather than only ones that are explicitly judged nonrelevant. However, Schütze et al. (1995) and Singhal et al. (1997) show that better results are obtained for routing by using only documents close to the query of interest rather than all documents. Other later work includes Salton and Buckley (1990), Riezler et al. (2007) (a statistical NLP approach to RF), and the recent survey paper Ruthven and Lalmas (2003).

The effectiveness of interactive RF systems is discussed in (Salton 1989; Harman 1992; Buckley et al. 1994b). Koenemann and Belkin (1996) do user studies of the effectiveness of relevance feedback.

Traditionally, *Roget's Thesaurus* has been the best known English language thesaurus (Roget 1946). In recent computational work, people almost always use WordNet (Fellbaum 1998), not only because it is free, but also because of its rich link structure. It is available at: http://wordnet.princeton.edu.

Qiu and Frei (1993) and Schütze (1998) discuss automatic thesaurus generation. Xu and Croft (1996) explore using both local and global query expansion.

10 *XML retrieval*

Information retrieval (IR) systems are often contrasted with relational databases. Traditionally, IR systems have retrieved information from *unstructured text* – by which we mean "raw" text without markup. Databases are designed for querying *relational data*, sets of records that have values for predefined attributes such as employee number, title, and salary. There are fundamental differences between IR and database systems in terms of retrieval model, data structures, and query language as shown in Table 10.1.[1]

Some highly structured text search problems are most efficiently handled by a relational database; for example, if the employee table contains an attribute for short textual job descriptions and you want to find all employees who are involved with invoicing. In this case, the SQL query:

```
select lastname from employees where job_desc like 'invoic%';
```

may be sufficient to satisfy your information need with high precision and recall.

However, many structured data sources containing text are best modeled as structured documents rather than relational data. We call the search over STRUCTURED such structured documents *structured retrieval*. Queries in structured retrieval RETRIEVAL can be either structured or unstructured, but we assume in this chapter that the collection consists only of structured documents. Applications of structured retrieval include digital libraries, patent databases, blogs, text in which entities like persons and locations have been tagged (in a process called *named entity tagging*), and output from office suites like OpenOffice that save documents as marked up text. In all of these applications, we want to be able to run queries that combine textual criteria with structural criteria. Examples of such queries are give me a full-length article on fast fourier transforms (digital libraries), give me patents whose claims mention RSA public key encryption and

---

[1] In most modern database systems, one can enable full-text search for text columns. This usually means that an inverted index is created and Boolean or vector space search enabled, effectively combining core database with IR technologies.

Table 10.1 Relational database (RDB) search, unstructured IR, and structured IR. There is no consensus yet as to which methods work best for structured retrieval, although many researchers believe that XQuery (page 197) will become the standard for structured queries.

	RDB search	unstructured retrieval	structured retrieval
objects	records	unstructured documents	trees with text at leaves
model	relational model	vector space & others	?
main data structure	table	inverted index	?
queries	SQL	free text queries	?

that cite US patent 4,405,829 (patents), or give me articles about sightseeing tours of the Vatican and the Coliseum (entity-tagged text). These three queries are structured queries that cannot be answered well by an unranked retrieval system. As we argued in Example 1.1 (page 14), unranked retrieval models like the Boolean model suffer from low recall. For instance, an unranked system would return a potentially large number of articles that mention the Vatican, the Coliseum, and sightseeing tours without ranking the ones that are most relevant for the query first. Most users are also notoriously bad at precisely stating structural constraints. For instance, users may not know for which structured elements the search system supports search. In our example, the user may be unsure whether to issue the query as sightseeing AND COUNTRY:Vatican AND LANDMARK:Coliseum, as sightseeing AND STATE:Vatican AND BUILDING:Coliseum or in some other form. Users may also be completely unfamiliar with structured search and advanced search interfaces or unwilling to use them. In this chapter, we look at how ranked retrieval methods can be adapted to structured documents to address these problems.

XML   We will only look at one standard for encoding structured documents: *Extensible markup language* or *XML*, which is currently the most widely used such standard. We will not cover the specifics that distinguish XML from other types of markup such as HTML and SGML. But most of what we say in this chapter is applicable to markup languages in general.

In the context of IR, we are only interested in XML as a language for encoding text and documents. A perhaps more widespread use of XML is to encode nontext data. For example, we may want to export data in XML format from an enterprise resource planning system and then read them into an analytics program to produce graphs for a presentation. This type of application of DATA-CENTRIC XML is called *data-centric* because numerical and nontext attribute-value data XML dominate and text is usually a small fraction of the overall data. Most datacentric XML is stored in databases – in contrast to the inverted index-based methods for text-centric XML that we present in this chapter.

We call XML retrieval *structured retrieval* in this chapter. Some researchers SEMISTRUCTURED prefer the term *semistructured retrieval* to distinguish XML retrieval from RETRIEVAL database querying. We have adopted the terminology that is widespread in

```
<play>
<author>Shakespeare</author>
<title>Macbeth</title>
<act number="I">
<scene number="vii">
<title>Macbeth's castle</title>
<verse>Will I with wine and wassail ...</verse>
</scene>
</act>
</play>
```

Figure 10.1 An XML document.

the XML retrieval community. For instance, the standard way of referring to XML queries is *structured queries*, not *semistructured queries*. The term *structured retrieval* is rarely used for database querying and it always refers to XML retrieval in this book.

There is a second type of IR problem that is intermediate between unstructured retrieval and querying a relational database: parametric and zone search, which we discussed in Section 6.1 (page 101). In the data model of parametric and zone search, there are parametric fields (relational attributes like *date* or *file-size*) and zones – text attributes that each take a chunk of unstructured text as value, for example, *author* and *title* in Figure 6.1 (page 101). The data model is flat; that is, there is no nesting of attributes. The number of attributes is small. In contrast, XML documents have the more complex tree structure that we see in Figure 10.2, in which attributes are nested. The number of attributes and nodes is greater than in parametric and zone search.

After presenting the basic concepts of XML in Section 10.1, this chapter first discusses the challenges we face in XML retrieval (Section 10.2). Next we describe a vector space model for XML retrieval (Section 10.3). Section 10.4 presents INEX, a shared task evaluation that has been held for a number of years and currently is the most important venue for XML retrieval research. We discuss the differences between data-centric and text-centric approaches to XML in Section 10.5.

10.1 Basic XML concepts

An XML document is an ordered, labeled tree. Each node of the tree is an XML ELEMENT *XML element* and is written with an opening and closing *tag*. An element can XML have one or more *XML attributes*. In the XML document in Figure 10.1, the ATTRIBUTE *scene* element is enclosed by the two tags <scene ...> and </scene>. It has an attribute *number* with value *vii* and two child elements, *title* and *verse*.

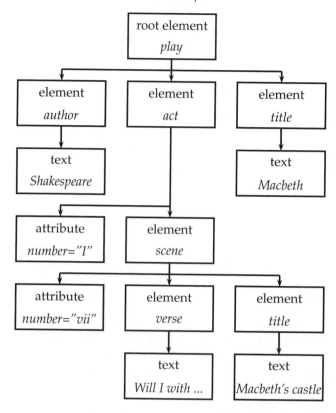

Figure 10.2 The XML document in Figure 10.1 as a simplified DOM object.

Figure 10.2 shows Figure 10.1 as a tree. The *leaf nodes* of the tree consist of text, for example, Shakespeare, Macbeth, and Macbeth's castle. The tree's *internal nodes* encode either the structure of the document (*title, act,* and *scene*) or metadata functions (*author*).

XML DOM The standard for accessing and processing XML documents is the XML document object model or *DOM*. The DOM represents elements, attributes, and text within elements as nodes in a tree. Figure 10.2 is a simplified DOM representation of the XML document in Figure 10.1.[2] With a DOM API, we can process an XML document by starting at the root element and then descending down the tree from parents to children.

XPath *XPath* is a standard for enumerating paths in an XML document collection.
XML CONTEXT We will also refer to paths as *XML contexts* or simply *contexts* in this chapter. Only a small subset of XPath is needed for our purposes. The XPath expression `node` selects all nodes of that name. Successive elements of a path are separated by slashes, so `act/scene` selects all *scene* elements whose parent is an *act* element. Double slashes indicate that an arbitrary number of elements can intervene on a path: `play//scene` selects all *scene* elements occurring in a *play* element. In Figure 10.2, this set consists of a single *scene* element, which

---

[2] The representation is simplified in a number of respects. For example, we do not show the *root* node and text is not embedded in *text* nodes. See www.w3.org/DOM/.

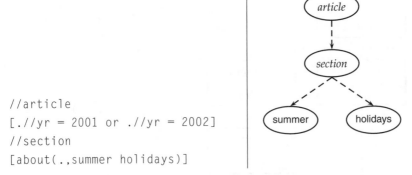

```
//article
[.//yr = 2001 or .//yr = 2002]
//section
[about(.,summer holidays)]
```

Figure 10.3 An XML query in NEXI format and its partial representation as a tree.

is accessible via the path *play, act, scene* from the top. An initial slash starts the path at the root element. /play/title selects the play's title in Figure 10.1, /play//title selects a set with two members (the play's title and the scene's title), and /scene/title selects no elements. For notational convenience, we allow the final element of a path to be a vocabulary term and separate it from the element path by the symbol #, even though this does not conform to the XPath standard. For example, title#"Macbeth" selects all titles containing the term Macbeth.

SCHEMA   We also need the concept of *schema* in this chapter. A schema puts constraints on the structure of allowable XML documents for a particular application. A schema for Shakespeare's plays may stipulate that scenes can only occur as children of acts and that only acts and scenes have the *num-*
XML DTD *ber* attribute. Two standards for schemas for XML documents are *XML DTD*
XML SCHEMA (document type definition) and *XML schema*. Users can only write structured queries for an XML retrieval system if they have some minimal knowledge about the schema of the collection.

NEXI   A common format for XML queries is *NEXI* (Narrowed Extended XPath I). We give an example in Figure 10.3. We display the query on four lines for typographical convenience, but it is intended to be read as one unit without line breaks. In particular, //section is embedded under //article.

The query in Figure 10.3 specifies a search for sections about the summer holidays that are part of articles from 2001 or 2002. As in XPath, double slashes indicate that an arbitrary number of elements can intervene on a path. The dot in a clause in square brackets refers to the element the clause modifies. The clause [.//yr = 2001 or .//yr = 2002] modifies //article. Thus, the dot refers to //article in this case. Similarly, the dot in [about(., summer holidays)] refers to the section that the clause modifies.

The two yr conditions are relational attribute constraints. Only articles whose yr attribute is 2001 or 2002 (or that contain an element whose yr attribute is 2001 or 2002) are to be considered. The about clause is a ranking

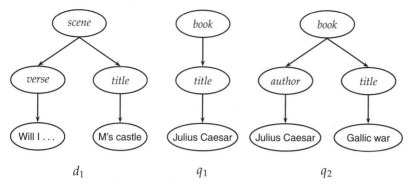

Figure 10.4 Tree representation of XML documents and queries.

constraint: Sections that occur in the right type of article are to be ranked according to how relevant they are to the topic summer holidays.

We usually handle relational attribute constraints by prefiltering or post-filtering: We simply exclude all elements from the result set that do not meet the relational attribute constraints. In this chapter, we will not address how to do this efficiently and instead focus on the core information retrieval problem in XML retrieval, namely, how to rank documents according to the relevance criteria expressed in the about conditions of the NEXI query.

If we discard relational attributes, we can represent documents as trees with only one type of node: element nodes. In other words, we remove all attribute nodes from the XML document, such as, the *number* attribute in Figure 10.1. Figure 10.4 shows a subtree of the document in Figure 10.1 as an element–node tree (labeled d_1).

We can represent queries as trees in the same way. This is a query-by-example approach to query language design because users pose queries by creating objects that satisfy the same formal description as documents. In Figure 10.4, q_1 is a search for books whose titles score highly for the keywords Julius Caesar. q_2 is a search for books whose author elements score highly for Julius Caesar and whose title elements score highly for Gallic war.[3]

10.2 Challenges in XML retrieval

In this section, we discuss a number of challenges that make structured retrieval more difficult than unstructured retrieval. Recall from page 178 the basic setting we assume in structured retrieval: The collection consists of structured documents and queries are either structured (as in Figure 10.3) or unstructured (e.g., summer holidays).

---

[3] To represent the semantics of NEXI queries fully, we would also need to designate one node in the tree as a "target node," for example, the *section* in the tree in Figure 10.3. Without the designation of a target node, the tree in Figure 10.3 is not a search for sections embedded in articles (as specified by NEXI), but a search for articles that contain sections.

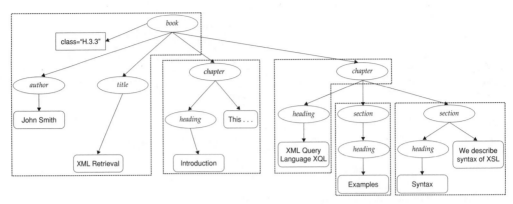

Figure 10.5 Partitioning an XML document into nonoverlapping indexing units.

The first challenge in structured retrieval is that users want us to return parts of documents (i.e., XML elements), not entire documents as IR systems usually do in unstructured retrieval. If we query Shakespeare's plays for Macbeth's castle, should we return the scene, the act, or the entire play in Figure 10.2? In this case, the user is probably looking for the scene. On the other hand, an otherwise unspecified search for Macbeth should return the play of this name, not a subunit.

One criterion for selecting the most appropriate part of a document is the STRUCTURED *structured document retrieval principle*:
DOCUMENT
RETRIEVAL   **Structured document retrieval principle.** A system should always retrieve
PRINCIPLE   the most specific part of a document answering the query.

This principle motivates a retrieval strategy that returns the smallest unit that contains the information sought, but does not go below this level. However, it can be hard to implement this principle algorithmically. Consider the query title#"Macbeth" applied to Figure 10.2. The title of the tragedy, *Macbeth*, and the title of Act I, Scene vii, *Macbeth's castle*, are both good hits because they contain the matching term Macbeth. But in this case, the title of the tragedy, the higher node, is preferred. Deciding which level of the tree is right for answering a query is difficult.

Parallel to the issue of which parts of a document to return to the user is the issue of which parts of a document to index. In Section 2.1.2 (page 20), we INDEXING UNIT discussed the need for a document unit or *indexing unit* in indexing and retrieval. In unstructured retrieval, it is usually clear what the right document unit is: files on your desktop, email messages, Web pages on the Web, and so on. In structured retrieval, there are a number of different approaches to defining the indexing unit.

One approach is to group nodes into nonoverlapping pseudodocuments as shown in Figure 10.5. In the example, books, chapters, and sections have been designated to be indexing units, but without overlap. For example, the left-most dashed indexing unit contains only those parts of the tree dominated by *book* that are not already part of other indexing units. The disadvantage of this approach is that pseudodocuments may not make sense to the user because they are not coherent units. For instance, the left most indexing unit in Figure 10.5 merges three disparate elements, the *class*, *author*, and *title* elements.

We can also use one of the largest elements as the indexing unit, for example, the *book* element in a collection of books or the *play* element for Shakespeare's works. We can then postprocess search results to find for each book or play the subelement that is the best hit. For example, the query Macbeth's castle may return the play *Macbeth*, which we can then postprocess to identify act I, scene vii as the best matching subelement. Unfortunately, this two-stage retrieval process fails to return the best subelement for many queries because the relevance of a whole book is often not a good predictor of the relevance of small subelements within it.

Instead of retrieving large units and identifying subelements (top down), we can also search all leaves, select the most relevant ones, and extend them to larger units in postprocessing (bottom up). For the query Macbeth's castle in Figure 10.1, we would retrieve the title *Macbeth's castle* in the first pass and then decide in a postprocessing step whether to return the title, the scene, the act, or the play. This approach has a similar problem as the last one: The relevance of a leaf element is often not a good predictor of the relevance of elements in which it is contained.

The least restrictive approach is to index all elements. This is also problematic. Many XML elements are not meaningful search results, for example, typographical elements like `<b>definitely</b>` or an ISBN number, which cannot be interpreted without context. Also, indexing all elements means that search results will be highly redundant. For the query Macbeth's castle and the document in Figure 10.1, we would return all of the *play*, *act*, *scene*, and *title* elements on the path between the root node and Macbeth's castle. The leaf node would then occur four times in the result set, once directly and three times as part of other elements. We call elements that are contained NESTED within each other *nested*. Returning redundant nested elements in a list of ELEMENTS returned hits is not very user friendly.

Because of the redundancy caused by nested elements, it is common to restrict the set of elements that are eligible to be returned. Restriction strategies include:

- Discard all small elements
- Discard all element types that users do not look at (this requires a working XML retrieval system that logs this information)
- Discard all element types that assessors generally do not judge to be relevant (if relevance assessments are available)
- Only keep element types that a system designer or librarian has deemed to be useful search results

In most of these approaches, result sets still contain nested elements. Thus, we may want to remove some elements in a postprocessing step to reduce redundancy. Alternatively, we can collapse several nested elements in the results list and use *highlighting* of query terms to draw the user's attention to the relevant passages. If query terms are highlighted, then scanning a medium-sized element (e.g., a section) takes little more time than scanning a small subelement (e.g., a paragraph). Thus, if the section and the paragraph both occur in the results list, it is sufficient to show the section. An additional advantage of this approach is that the paragraph is presented together with its context (i.e., the embedding section). This context may be helpful in interpreting the paragraph (e.g., the source of the information reported) even if the paragraph on its own satisfies the query.

If the user knows the schema of the collection and is able to specify the desired type of element, then the problem of redundancy is alleviated because few nested elements have the same type. But as we discussed in the introduction, users often do not know what the name of an element in the collection is (Is the Vatican a *country* or a *city*?) or they may not know how to compose structured queries at all.

A challenge in XML retrieval related to nesting is that we may need to distinguish different contexts of a term when we compute term statistics for ranking, in particular inverse document frequency (idf) statistics as defined in Section 6.2.1 (page 108). For example, the term Gates under the node *author* is unrelated to an occurrence under a content node like *section* if used to refer to the plural of gate. It makes little sense to compute a single document frequency for Gates in this example.

One solution is to compute idf for XML-context/term pairs, for example, to compute different idf weights for author#"Gates" and section#"Gates". Unfortunately, this scheme runs into sparse data problems – that is, many XML–context pairs occur too rarely to reliably estimate document frequency (see Section 13.2, page 240, for a discussion of sparseness). A compromise is only to consider the parent node x of the term and not the rest of the path from the root to x to distinguish contexts. There are still conflations of contexts that are harmful in this scheme. For instance, we do not distinguish names of authors and names of corporations if both have the parent node *name*. But most important distinctions, like the example contrast author#"Gates" versus section#"Gates", will be respected.

In many cases, several different XML schemas occur in a collection because the XML documents in an IR application often come from more SCHEMA than one source. This phenomenon is called *schema heterogeneity* or *schema* HETEROGENEITY *diversity* and presents yet another challenge. As illustrated in Figure 10.6, comparable elements may have different names: *creator* in d_2 vs. *author* in d_3. In other cases, the structural organization of the schemas may be different: Author names are direct descendants of the node *author* in q_3, but there are the intervening nodes *firstname* and *lastname* in d_3. If we employ strict

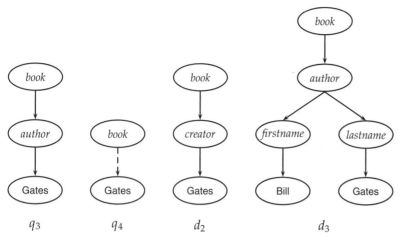

q_3 q_4 d_2 d_3

Figure 10.6 Schema heterogeneity: intervening nodes and mismatched names.

matching of trees, then q_3 will retrieve neither d_2 nor d_3, although both documents are relevant. Some form of approximate matching of element names in combination with semiautomatic matching of different document structures can help here. Human editing of correspondences of elements in different schemas will usually do better than automatic methods.

Schema heterogeneity is one reason for query–document mismatches like q_3/d_2 and q_3/d_3. Another reason is that users often are not familiar with the element names and the structure of the schemas of collections they search, as mentioned. This poses a challenge for interface design in XML retrieval. Ideally, the user interface should expose the tree structure of the collection and allow users to specify the elements they are querying. If we take this approach, then designing the query interface in structured retrieval is more complex than a search box for keyword queries in unstructured retrieval.

We can also support the user by interpreting all parent–child relationships in queries as descendant relationships with any number of intervening nodes EXTENDED allowed. We call such queries *extended queries*. The tree in Figure 10.3 and q_4 QUERY in Figure 10.6 are examples of extended queries. We show edges that are interpreted as descendant relationships as dashed arrows. In q_4, a dashed arrow connects *book* and Gates. As a pseudo-XPath notation for q_4, we adopt book//#"Gates": a book that somewhere in its structure contains the word Gates where the path from the *book* node to Gates can be arbitrarily long. The pseudo-XPath notation for the extended query that in addition specifies that Gates occurs in a *section* of the *book* is book//section//#"Gates". It is convenient for users to be able to issue such extended queries without having to specify the exact structural configuration in which a query term should occur – either because they do not care about the exact configuration or because they do not know enough about the schema of the collection to be able to specify it.

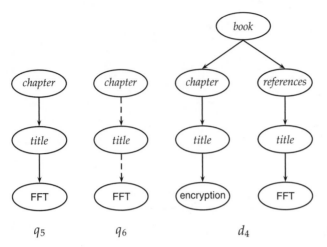

Figure 10.7 A structural mismatch between two queries and a document.

In Figure 10.7, the user is looking for a chapter entitled FFT (q_5). Suppose there is no such chapter in the collection, but that there are references to books on FFT (d_4). A reference to a book on FFT is not exactly what the user is looking for, but it is better than returning nothing. Extended queries do not help here. The extended query q_6 also returns nothing. This is a case where we may want to interpret the structural constraints specified in the query as hints as opposed to as strict conditions. As we will discuss in Section 10.4, users prefer a relaxed interpretation of structural constraints: Elements that do not meet structural constraints perfectly should be ranked lower, but they should not be omitted from search results.

10.3 A vector space model for XML retrieval

In this section, we present a simple vector space model for XML retrieval. It is not intended to be a complete description of a state-of-the-art system. Instead, we want to give the reader a flavor of how documents can be represented and retrieved in XML retrieval.

To take account of structure in retrieval in Figure 10.4, we want a book entitled *Julius Caesar* to be a match for q_1 and no match (or a lower weighted match) for q_2. In unstructured retrieval, there would be a single dimension of the vector space for Caesar. In XML retrieval, we must separate the title word Caesar from the author name Caesar. One way of doing this is to have each dimension of the vector space encode a word together with its position within the XML tree.

Figure 10.8 illustrates this representation. We first take each text node (which in our setup is always a leaf) and break it into multiple nodes, one for each word. So the leaf node Bill Gates is split into two leaves, Bill and Gates. Next we define the dimensions of the vector space to be *lexicalized subtrees*

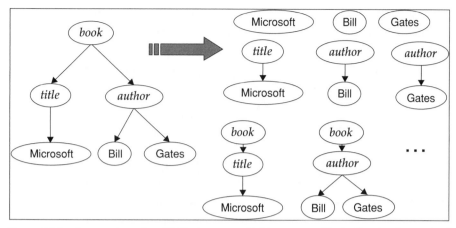

Figure 10.8 A mapping of an XML document (left) to a set of lexicalized subtrees (right).

of documents – subtrees that contain at least one vocabulary term. A subset of these possible lexicalized subtrees is shown in the figure, but there are others – for example, the subtree corresponding to the whole document with the leaf node Gates removed. We can now represent queries and documents as vectors in this space of lexicalized subtrees and compute matches between them. This means that we can use the vector space formalism from Chapter 6 for XML retrieval. The main difference is that the dimensions of vector space in unstructured retrieval are vocabulary terms, whereas they are lexicalized subtrees in XML retrieval.

There is a tradeoff between the dimensionality of the space and accuracy of query results. If we trivially restrict dimensions to vocabulary terms, then we have a standard vector space retrieval system that will retrieve many documents that do not match the structure of the query (e.g., Gates in the title as opposed to the author element). If we create a separate dimension for each lexicalized subtree occurring in the collection, the dimensionality of the space becomes too large. A compromise is to index all paths that end in a single vocabulary term, in other words, all XML-context/term pairs. We STRUCTURAL call such an XML-context/term pair a *structural term* and denote it by $\langle c, t \rangle$: TERM a pair of XML-context c and vocabulary term t. The document in Figure 10.8 has nine structural terms. Seven are shown (e.g., `"Bill"` and `Author#"Bill"`) and two are not shown: `/Book/Author#"Bill"` and `/Book/Author#"Gates"`. The tree with the leaves Bill and Gates is a lexicalized subtree that is not a structural term. We use the previously introduced pseudo-XPath notation for structural terms.

As we discussed in the last section, users are bad at remembering details about the schema and at constructing queries that comply with the schema. We will therefore interpret all queries as extended queries – that is, there can be an arbitrary number of intervening nodes in the document for any parent–child node pair in the query. For example, we interpret q_5 in Figure 10.7 as q_6.

But we still prefer documents that match the query structure closely by inserting fewer additional nodes. We ensure that retrieval results respect this preference by computing a weight for each match. A simple measure of the similarity of a path c_q in a query and a path c_d in a document is the following **CONTEXT** *context resemblance* function CR:

RESEMBLANCE

$$(10.1) \qquad \text{Cr}(c_q, c_d) = \begin{cases} \frac{1+|c_q|}{1+|c_d|} & \text{if } c_q \text{ matches } c_d \\ 0 & \text{if } c_q \text{ does not match } c_d \end{cases}$$

where $|c_q|$ and $|c_d|$ are the number of nodes in the query path and document path, respectively, and c_q matches c_d iff we can transform c_q into c_d by inserting additional nodes. Two examples from Figure 10.6 are $\text{Cr}(c_{q_4}, c_{d_2}) = 3/4 = 0.75$ and $\text{Cr}(c_{q_4}, c_{d_3}) = 3/5 = 0.6$ where c_{q_4}, c_{d_2}, and c_{d_3} are the relevant paths from top to leaf node in q_4, d_2, and d_3, respectively. The value of $\text{Cr}(c_q, c_d)$ is 1.0 if q and d are identical.

The final score for a document is computed as a variant of the cosine measure (Equation (6.10), page 111), which we call SimNoMerge for reasons that will become clear shortly. SimNoMerge is defined as follows:

SimNoMerge(q, d)

$$(10.2) \qquad = \sum_{c_k \in B} \sum_{c_l \in B} \text{Cr}(c_k, c_l) \sum_{t \in V} \text{weight}(q, t, c_k) \frac{\text{weight}(d, t, c_l)}{\sqrt{\sum_{c \in B, t \in V} \text{weight}^2(d, t, c)}}$$

where V is the vocabulary of nonstructural terms; B is the set of all XML contexts; and weight(q, t, c) and weight(d, t, c) are the weights of term t in XML context c in query q and document d, respectively. We compute the weights using one of the weightings from Chapter 6, such as, $\text{idf}_t \cdot \text{wf}_{t,d}$. The inverse document frequency idf_t depends on which elements we use to compute df_t, as discussed in Section 10.2. The similarity measure SimNoMerge(q, d) is not a true cosine measure because its value can be larger than 1.0 (Exercise 10.11). We divide by $\sqrt{\sum_{c \in B, t \in V} \text{weight}^2(d, t, c)}$ to normalize for document length (Section 6.3.1, page 111). We have omitted query length normalization to simplify the formula. It has no effect on ranking; for a given query, the normalizer $\sqrt{\sum_{c \in B, t \in V} \text{weight}^2(q, t, c)}$ is the same for all documents.

The algorithm for computing SimNoMerge for all documents in the collection is shown in Figure 10.9. The array *normalizer* in Figure 10.9 contains $\sqrt{\sum_{c \in B, t \in V} \text{weight}^2(d, t, c)}$ from Equation (10.2) for each document.

We give an example of how SimNoMerge computes query–document similarities in Figure 10.10. $\langle c_1, t \rangle$ is one of the structural terms in the query. We successively retrieve all postings lists for structural terms $\langle c', t \rangle$ with the same vocabulary term t. Three example postings lists are shown. For the first one, we have $\text{Cr}(c_1, c_1) = 1.0$ because the two contexts are identical. The next context has no context resemblance with c_1: $\text{Cr}(c_1, c_2) = 0$ and the corresponding postings list is ignored. The context match of c_1 with c_3 is 0.63 > 0, and it will be processed. In this example, the highest ranking document is d_9 with a

SCOREDOCUMENTSWITHSIMNOMERGE(q, B, V, N, $normalizer$)
```
 1  for n ← 1 to N
 2  do score[n] ← 0
 3  for each ⟨c_q, t⟩ ∈ q
 4  do w_q ← WEIGHT(q, t, c_q)
 5     for each c ∈ B
 6     do if CR(c_q, c) > 0
 7           then postings ← GETPOSTINGS(⟨c, t⟩)
 8                for each posting ∈ postings
 9                do x ← CR(c_q, c) * w_q * weight(posting)
10                     score[docID(posting)] += x
11  for n ← 1 to N
12  do score[n] ← score[n]/normalizer[n]
13  return score
```

Figure 10.9 The algorithm for scoring documents with SIMNOMERGE.

similarity of $1.0 \times 0.2 + 0.63 \times 0.6 = 0.578$. To simplify the figure, the query weight of $\langle c_1, t\rangle$ is assumed to be 1.0.

The query–document similarity function in Figure 10.9 is called SIM-NOMERGE because different XML contexts are kept separate for the purpose of weighting. An alternative similarity function is SIMMERGE, which relaxes the matching conditions of query and document further in the following three ways.

- We collect the statistics used for computing weight(q, t, c) and weight(d, t, c) from *all* contexts that have a nonzero resemblance to c (as opposed to just from c as in SIMNOMERGE). For instance, for computing the document frequency of the structural term `atl#"recognition"`, we also count occurrences of recognition in XML contexts `fm/atl`, `article//atl` etc.

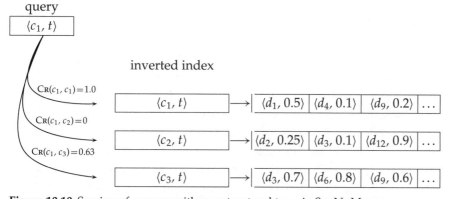

Figure 10.10 Scoring of a query with one structural term in SIMNOMERGE.

- We modify Equation (10.2) by merging all structural terms in the document that have a nonzero context resemblance to a given query structural term. For example, the contexts `/play/act/scene/title` and `/play/title` in the document will be merged when matching against the query term `/play/title#"Macbeth"`.
- The context resemblance function is further relaxed: Contexts have a nonzero resemblance in many cases where the definition of CR in Equation (10.1) returns 0.

See the references in Section 10.6 for details.

These three changes alleviate the problem of sparse term statistics discussed in Section 10.2 and increase the robustness of the matching function against poorly posed structural queries. The evaluation of SIMNOMERGE and SIMMERGE in the next section shows that the relaxed matching conditions of SIMMERGE increase the effectiveness of XML retrieval.

? **Exercise 10.1** Consider computing the document frequency for a structural term as the number of times that the structural term occurs under a particular parent node. Assume the following: The structural term $\langle c, t \rangle$ = `author#"Herbert"` occurs once as the child of the node *squib*; there are ten *squib* nodes in the collection; $\langle c, t \rangle$ occurs 1,000 times as the child of *article*; there are 1,000,000 *article* nodes in the collection. The idf weight of $\langle c, t \rangle$ then is $\log_2 10/1 \approx 3.3$ when occurring as the child of *squib* and $\log_2 1{,}000{,}000/1000 \approx 10.0$ when occurring as the child of *article*. (i) Explain why this is not an appropriate weighting for $\langle c, t \rangle$. Why should $\langle c, t \rangle$ not receive a weight that is three times higher in articles than in squibs? (ii) Suggest a better way of computing idf.

Exercise 10.2 Write down all the structural terms occurring in the XML document in Figure 10.8.

Exercise 10.3 How many structural terms does the document in Figure 10.1 yield?

10.4 Evaluation of XML retrieval

INEX   The premier venue for research on XML retrieval is the *INEX* (**IN***itiative for the* **E***valuation of* **X***ML retrieval*) program, a collaborative effort that has produced reference collections, sets of queries, and relevance judgments. A yearly INEX meeting is held to present and discuss research results. The INEX 2002 collection consisted of about 12,000 articles from IEEE journals. We give collection statistics in Table 10.2 and show part of the schema of the collection in Figure 10.11. The IEEE journal collection was expanded in 2005. Since 2006, INEX uses the much larger English Wikipedia as a test collection.

Table 10.2 INEX 2002 collection statistics.

12,107	number of documents
494 MB	size
1995–2002	time of publication of articles
1,532	average number of XML nodes per document
6.9	average depth of a node
30	number of CAS topics
30	number of CO topics

The relevance of documents is judged by human assessors using the methodology introduced in Section 8.1 (page 140), appropriately modified for structured documents as we will discuss shortly.

Two types of information needs or topics in INEX are content-only (CO) topics and content-and-structure (CAS) topics. *CO topics* are regular keyword queries as in unstructured information retrieval. *CAS topics* have structural constraints in addition to keywords. We already encountered an example of a CAS topic in Figure 10.3. The keywords in this case are summer and holidays, and the structural constraints specify that the keywords occur in a section that in turn is part of an article and that this article has an embedded year attribute with value 2001 or 2002.

CO TOPICS

CAS TOPICS

Because CAS queries have both structural and content criteria, relevance assessments are more complicated than in unstructured retrieval. INEX 2002 defined component coverage and topical relevance as orthogonal dimensions of relevance. The *component coverage* dimension evaluates whether the

COMPONENT
COVERAGE

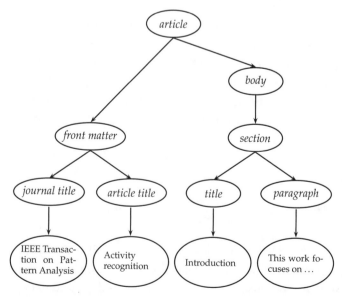

Figure 10.11 Simplified schema of the documents in the INEX collection.

element retrieved is "structurally" correct, that is, neither too low nor too high in the tree. We distinguish four cases:

- Exact coverage (E). The information sought is the main topic of the component and the component is a meaningful unit of information.
- Too small (S). The information sought is the main topic of the component, but the component is not a meaningful (self-contained) unit of information.
- Too large (L). The information sought is present in the component, but is not the main topic.
- No coverage (N). The information sought is not a topic of the component.

TOPICAL   The *topical relevance* dimension also has four levels: highly relevant (3),
RELEVANCE   fairly relevant (2), marginally relevant (1), and nonrelevant (0). Components are judged on both dimensions and the judgments are then combined into a digit–letter code. 2S is a fairly relevant component that is too small and 3E is a highly relevant component that has exact coverage. In theory, there are sixteen combinations of coverage and relevance, but many cannot occur. For example, a nonrelevant component cannot have exact coverage, so the combination 3N is not possible.

The relevance–coverage combinations are quantized as follows:

$$\mathbf{Q}(rel, cov) = \begin{cases} 1.00 & \text{if} \quad (rel, cov) = 3\text{E} \\ 0.75 & \text{if} \quad (rel, cov) \in \{2\text{E}, 3\text{L}\} \\ 0.50 & \text{if} \quad (rel, cov) \in \{1\text{E}, 2\text{L}, 2\text{S}\} \\ 0.25 & \text{if} \quad (rel, cov) \in \{1\text{S}, 1\text{L}\} \\ 0.00 & \text{if} \quad (rel, cov) = 0\text{N} \end{cases}$$

This evaluation scheme takes account of the fact that binary relevance judgments, which are standard in unstructured information retrieval (Section 8.5.1, page 153), are not appropriate for XML retrieval. A 2S component provides incomplete information and may be difficult to interpret without more context, but it does answer the query partially. The quantization function $\mathbf{Q}$ does not impose a binary choice relevant/nonrelevant and instead allows us to grade the component as partially relevant.

The number of relevant components in a retrieved set A of components can then be computed as:

$$\#(\text{relevant items retrieved}) = \sum_{c \in A} \mathbf{Q}(rel(c), cov(c)).$$

As an approximation, the standard definitions of precision, recall and F from Chapter 8 can be applied to this modified definition of relevant items retrieved, with some subtleties because we sum graded as opposed to binary relevance assessments. See the references on focused retrieval in Section 10.6 for further discussion.

Table 10.3 INEX 2002 results of the vector space model in Section 10.3 for CAS queries and the quantization function **Q**.

algorithm	average precision
SIMNOMERGE	0.242
SIMMERGE	0.271

One flaw of measuring relevance this way is that overlap is not accounted for. We discussed the concept of marginal relevance in the context of unstructured retrieval in Section 8.5.1 (page 153). This problem is worse in XML retrieval because of the problem of multiple nested elements occurring in a search result as we discussed on page 185. Much of the recent focus at INEX has been on developing algorithms and evaluation measures that return nonredundant results lists and evaluate them properly. See the references in Section 10.6.

Table 10.3 shows two INEX 2002 runs of the vector space system we described in Section 10.3. The better run is the SIMMERGE run, which incorporates few structural constraints and mostly relies on keyword matching. SIMMERGE's median average precision (where the median is with respect to average precision numbers over topics) is only 0.147. Effectiveness in XML retrieval is often lower than in unstructured retrieval because XML retrieval is harder. Instead of just finding a document, we have to find the subpart of a document that is most relevant to the query. Also, XML retrieval effectiveness – when evaluated as described here – can be lower than unstructured retrieval effectiveness on a standard evaluation because graded judgments lower measured performance. Consider a system that returns a document with graded relevance 0.6 and binary relevance 1 at the top of the retrieved list. Then, interpolated precision at 0.00 recall (cf. page 145) is 1.0 on a binary evaluation, but can be as low as 0.6 on a graded evaluation.

Table 10.3 gives us a sense of the typical performance of XML retrieval, but it does not compare structured with unstructured retrieval. Table 10.4 directly shows the effect of using structure in retrieval. The results are for a language-model–based system (cf. Chapter 12) that is evaluated on a subset of CAS topics from INEX 2003 and 2004. The evaluation metric is precision

Table 10.4 A comparison of content-only and full-structure search in INEX 2003/2004.

	content only	full structure	improvement
precision at 5	0.2000	0.3265	63.3%
precision at 10	0.1820	0.2531	39.1%
precision at 20	0.1700	0.1796	5.6%
precision at 30	0.1527	0.1531	0.3%

at k as defined in Chapter 8 (page 148). The discretization function used for the evaluation maps highly relevant elements (roughly corresponding to the 3E elements defined for **Q**) to 1 and all other elements to 0. The content-only system treats queries and documents as unstructured bags of words. The full-structure model ranks elements that satisfy structural constraints higher than elements that do not. For instance, for the query in Figure 10.3 an element that contains the phrase summer holidays in a *section* will be rated higher than one that contains it in an *abstract*.

The table shows that structure helps to increase precision at the top of the results list. There is a large increase of precision at $k = 5$ and at $k = 10$. There is almost no improvement at $k = 30$. These results demonstrate the benefits of structured retrieval. Structured retrieval imposes additional constraints on what to return and documents that pass the structural filter are more likely to be relevant. Recall may suffer because some relevant documents will be filtered out, but for precision-oriented tasks structured retrieval is superior.

10.5 Text-centric versus data-centric XML retrieval

TEXT-CENTRIC XML

DATA-CENTRIC XML

In the type of structured retrieval we cover in this chapter, XML structure serves as a framework within which we match the text of the query with the text of the XML documents. This exemplifies a system that is optimized for *text-centric XML*. Although both text and structure are important, we give higher priority to text. We do this by adapting unstructured retrieval methods to handling additional structural constraints. The premise of our approach is that XML document retrieval is characterized by (i) long text fields (e.g., sections of a document), (ii) inexact matching, and (iii) relevance-ranked results. Relational databases do not deal well with this use case.

In contrast, *data-centric XML* mainly encodes numerical and nontext attribute-value data. When querying data-centric XML, we want to impose exact match conditions in most cases. This puts the emphasis on the structural aspects of XML documents and queries. An example is:

Find employees whose salary is the same this month as it was 12 months ago.

This query requires no ranking. It is purely structural and an exact matching of the salaries in the two time periods is probably sufficient to meet the user's information need.

Text-centric approaches are appropriate for data that are essentially text documents, marked up as XML to capture document structure. This is becoming a de facto standard for publishing text databases because most text documents have some form of interesting structure – paragraphs, sections, footnotes, and so on. Examples include assembly manuals, issues of journals, Shakespeare's collected works, and newswire articles.

Data-centric approaches are commonly used for data collections with complex structures that mainly contain nontext data. A text-centric retrieval engine will have a hard time with proteomic data in bioinformatics or with the representation of a city map that (together with street names and other textual descriptions) forms a navigational database.

Two other types of queries that are difficult to handle in a text-centric structured retrieval model are joins and ordering constraints. The query for employees with unchanged salary requires a join. The following query imposes an ordering constraint:

> Retrieve the chapter of the book *Introduction to algorithms* that follows the chapter *Binomial heaps*.

This query relies on the ordering of elements in XML – in this case the ordering of chapter elements underneath the book node. There are powerful query languages for XML that can handle numerical attributes, joins, and ordering constraints. The best known of these is XQuery, a language proposed for standardization by the W3C. It is designed to be broadly applicable in all areas where XML is used. Due to its complexity, it is challenging to implement an XQuery-based ranked retrieval system with the performance characteristics that users have come to expect in information retrieval. This is currently one of the most active areas of research in XML retrieval.

Relational databases are better equipped to handle many structural constraints, particularly joins (but ordering is also difficult in a database framework – the tuples of a relation in the relational calculus are not ordered). For this reason, most data-centric XML retrieval systems are extensions of relational databases (see the references in Section 10.6). If text fields are short, exact matching meets user needs and retrieval results in form of unordered sets are acceptable, then using a relational database for XML retrieval is appropriate.

? **Exercise 10.4** Find a reasonably sized XML document collection (or a collection using a markup language different from XML like HTML) on the web and download it. Jon Bosak's XML edition of Shakespeare and of various religious works at www.ibiblio.org/bosak/ or the first 10,000 documents of the Wikipedia are good choices. Create three CAS topics of the type shown in Figure 10.3 that you would expect to do better than analogous CO topics. Explain why an XML retrieval system would be able to exploit the XML structure of the documents to achieve better retrieval results on the topics than an unstructured retrieval system.

Exercise 10.5 For the collection and the topics in Exercise 10.4, (i) are there pairs of elements e_1 and e_2, with e_2 a subelement of e_1 such that both answer one of the topics? Find one case each where (ii) e_1 (iii) e_2 is the better answer to the query.

Exercise 10.6 Implement the (i) SIMMERGE (ii) SIMNOMERGE algorithm in Section 10.3 and run it for the collection and the topics in Exercise 10.4. (iii) Evaluate the results by assigning binary relevance judgments to the first five documents of the three retrieved lists for each algorithm. Which algorithm performs better?

Exercise 10.7 Are all of the elements in Exercise 10.4 appropriate to be returned as hits to a user or are there elements (as in the example `<b>definitely</b>` on page 185) that you would exclude?

Exercise 10.8 We discussed the tradeoff between accuracy of results and dimensionality of the vector space on page 189. Give an example of an information need that we can answer correctly if we index all lexicalized subtrees, but can not answer if we only index structural terms.

Exercise 10.9 If we index all structural terms, what is the size of the index as a function of text size?

Exercise 10.10 If we index all lexicalized subtrees, what is the size of the index as a function of text size?

Exercise 10.11 Give an example of a query–document pair for which SIMNOMERGE(q, d) is larger than 1.0.

10.6 References and further reading

There are many good introductions to XML, including (Harold and Means 2004). Table 10.1 is inspired by a similar table in (van Rijsbergen 1979). Section 10.4 follows the overview of INEX 2002 by Gövert and Kazai (2003), published in the proceedings of the meeting (Fuhr et al. 2003a). The proceedings of the four following INEX meetings were published as Fuhr et al. (2003b), Fuhr et al. (2005), Fuhr et al. (2006), and Fuhr et al. (2007). An up-to-date overview article is Fuhr and Lalmas (2007). The results in Table 10.4 are from (Kamps et al. 2006). Chu-Carroll et al. (2006) also present evidence that XML queries increase precision compared with unstructured queries. Instead of coverage and relevance, INEX now evaluates on the related but different dimensions of exhaustivity and specificity (Lalmas and Tombros 2007). Trotman et al. (2006) relate the tasks investigated at INEX to real-world uses of structured retrieval such as structured book search on Internet bookstore sites.

The structured document retrieval principle is due to Chiaramella et al. (1996). Figure 10.5 is from (Fuhr and Großjohann 2004). Rahm and Bernstein (2001) give a survey of automatic schema matching that is applicable to XML.

The vector-space–based XML retrieval method in Section 10.3 is essentially IBM Haifa's JuruXML system as presented by Mass et al. (2003) and Carmel et al. (2003). Schlieder and Meuss (2002) and Grabs and Schek (2002) describe XML similar approaches. Carmel et al. (2003) represent queries as *XML fragments*. FRAGMENT The trees that represent XML queries in this chapter are all XML fragments, but XML fragments also permit the operators $+$, $-$, and *phrase* on content nodes.

We chose to present the vector space model for XML retrieval because it is simple and a natural extension of the unstructured vector space model in Chapter 6. But many other unstructured retrieval methods have been applied to XML retrieval with at least as much success as the vector space model. These methods include language models (cf. Chapter 12; e.g., Kamps et al. (2004), List et al. (2005), Ogilvie and Callan (2005)), systems that use a relational database as a backend (Mihajlović et al. 2005; Theobald et al. 2005, 2008), probabilistic weighting (Lu et al. 2007), and fusion (Larson 2005). There is currently no consensus as to what the best approach to XML retrieval is.

Most early work on XML retrieval accomplished relevance ranking by focusing on individual terms, including their structural contexts, in query and document. As in unstructured IR, there is a trend in more recent work to model relevance ranking as combining evidence from disparate measurements about the query, the document, and their match. The combination function can be tuned manually (Arvola et al. 2005; Sigurbjörnsson et al. 2004) or trained using machine learning methods (Vittaut and Gallinari (2006), cf. Section 15.4.1, page 314).

FOCUSED An active area of XML retrieval research is *focused retrieval* (Trotman et al. RETRIEVAL 2007), which aims to avoid returning nested elements that share one or more common subelements (cf. discussion in Section 10.2, page 185). There is evidence that users dislike redundancy caused by nested elements (Betsi et al. 2006). Focused retrieval requires evaluation measures that penalize redundant results lists (Kazai and Lalmas 2006; Lalmas et al. 2007). Trotman and PASSAGE Geva (2006) argue that XML retrieval is a form of *passage retrieval*. In passage RETRIEVAL retrieval (Salton et al. 1993; Hearst and Plaunt 1993; Zobel et al. 1995; Hearst 1997; Kaszkiel and Zobel 1997), the retrieval system returns short passages instead of documents in response to a user query. Although element boundaries in XML documents are cues for identifying good segment boundaries between passages, the most relevant passage often does not coincide with an XML element.

In the last several years, the query format at INEX has been the NEXI standard proposed by Trotman and Sigurbjörnsson (2004). Figure 10.3 is from their paper. O'Keefe and Trotman (2004) give evidence that users cannot reliably distinguish the child and descendant axes. This justifies only permitting descendant axes in NEXI (and XML fragments). These structural constraints were only treated as "hints" in recent INEXes. Assessors can judge an element highly relevant, even though it violates one of the structural constraints specified in a NEXI query.

An alternative to structured query languages like NEXI is a more sophisticated user interface for query formulation (Tannier and Geva 2005; van Zwol et al. 2006; Woodley and Geva 2006).

A broad overview of XML retrieval that covers database as well as IR approaches is given by Amer-Yahia and Lalmas (2006) and an extensive reference list on the topic can be found in (Amer-Yahia et al. 2005). Chapter 6 of Grossman and Frieder 2004 is a good introduction to structured text retrieval from a database perspective. The proposed standard for XQuery is available at www.w3.org/TR/xquery/ including an extension for full-text queries (Amer-Yahia et al. 2006): www.w3.org/TR/xquery-full-text/. Work that has looked at combining the relational database and the unstructured information retrieval approaches includes (Fuhr and Rölleke 1997); (Navarro and Baeza-Yates 1997); (Cohen 1998); and (Chaudhuri et al. 2006).

11 *Probabilistic information retrieval*

During the discussion of relevance feedback in Section 9.1.2, we observed that if we have some known relevant and nonrelevant documents, then we can straightforwardly start to estimate the probability of a term t appearing in a relevant document $P(t|R = 1)$, and that this could be the basis of a classifier that decides whether documents are relevant or not. In this chapter, we more systematically introduce this probabilistic approach to information retrieval (IR), which provides a different formal basis for a retrieval model and results in different techniques for setting term weights.

Users start with *information needs*, which they translate into *query representations*. Similarly, there are *documents*, which are converted into *document representations* (the latter differing at least by how text is tokenized, but perhaps containing fundamentally less information, as when a nonpositional index is used). Based on these two representations, a system tries to determine how well documents satisfy information needs. In the Boolean or vector space models of IR, matching is done in a formally defined but semantically imprecise calculus of index terms. Given only a query, an IR system has an uncertain understanding of the information need. Given the query and document representations, a system has an uncertain guess of whether a document has content relevant to the information need. Probability theory provides a principled foundation for such reasoning under uncertainty. This chapter provides one answer as to how to exploit this foundation to estimate how likely it is that a document is relevant to an information need.

There is more than one possible retrieval model with a probabilistic basis. Here, we will introduce probability theory and the probability ranking principle (Sections 11.1–11.2), and then concentrate on the *binary independence model* (Section 11.3), which is the original and still most influential probabilistic retrieval model. Finally, we will introduce related but extended methods that use term counts, including the empirically successful Okapi BM25 weighting scheme, and Bayesian network models for IR (Section 11.4). In Chapter 12, we then present the alternative probabilistic language modeling approach to IR, which has been developed with considerable success in recent years.

11.1 Review of basic probability theory

We hope that the reader has seen a little basic probability theory previously. We will give a very quick review; some references for further reading appear at the end of the chapter. A variable A represents an event (a subset of the space of possible outcomes). Equivalently, we can represent the subset via a RANDOM *random variable*, which is a function from outcomes to real numbers; the sub-VARIABLE set is the domain over which the random variable A has a particular value. Often we will not know with certainty whether an event is true in the world. We can ask the probability of the event $0 \leq P(A) \leq 1$. For two events A and B, the joint event of both events occurring is described by the joint probability $P(A, B)$. The conditional probability $P(A|B)$ expresses the probability of event A given that event B occurred. The fundamental relationship between CHAIN RULE joint and conditional probabilities is given by the *chain rule*:

$$(11.1) \qquad P(A, B) = P(A \cap B) = P(A|B)P(B) = P(B|A)P(A)$$

Without making any assumptions, the probability of a joint event equals the probability of one of the events multiplied by the probability of the other event conditioned on knowing the first event happened.

Writing $P(\overline{A})$ for the complement of an event, we similarly have:

$$(11.2) \qquad P(\overline{A}, B) = P(B|\overline{A})P(\overline{A}).$$

PARTITION Probability theory also has a *partition rule*, which says that if an event B can RULE be divided into an exhaustive set of disjoint subcases, then the probability of B is the sum of the probabilities of the subcases. A special case of this rule gives that:

$$(11.3) \qquad P(B) = P(A, B) + P(\overline{A}, B).$$

BAYES' RULE   From these we can derive *Bayes' rule* for inverting conditional probabilities:

$$(11.4) \qquad P(A|B) = \frac{P(B|A)P(A)}{P(B)} = \left[\frac{P(B|A)}{\sum_{X \in \{A, \overline{A}\}} P(B|X)P(X)} \right] P(A).$$

This equation can also be thought of as a way of updating probabilities. We start off with an initial estimate of how likely the event A is when we do PRIOR not have any other information; this is the *prior probability* $P(A)$. Bayes' rule PROBABILITY lets us derive a *posterior probability* $P(A|B)$ after having seen the evidence B, POSTERIOR based on the *likelihood* of B occurring in the two cases that A does or does not PROBABILITY hold.[1]

---

[1] The term *likelihood* is just a synonym for *probability*. It is the probability of an event or data according to a model. The term is usually used when people are thinking of holding the data fixed, while varying the model.

ODDS   Finally, it is often useful to talk about the *odds* of an event, which provide a kind of multiplier for how probabilities change:

(11.5) $$\text{Odds:} \quad O(A) = \frac{P(A)}{P(\overline{A})} = \frac{P(A)}{1 - P(A)}.$$

11.2 The probability ranking principle

11.2.1 The 1/0 loss case

We assume a ranked retrieval setup as in Section 6.3, where there is a collection of documents, the user issues a query, and an ordered list of documents is returned. We also assume a binary notion of relevance as in Chapter 8. For a query q and a document d in the collection, let $R_{d,q}$ be an indicator random variable that says whether d is relevant with respect to a given query q. That is, it takes on a value of 1 when the document is relevant and 0 otherwise. In context we will often write just R for $R_{d,q}$.

Using a probabilistic model, the obvious order in which to present documents to the user is to rank documents by their estimated probability of relevance with respect to the information need: $P(R = 1|d, q)$. This is the basis of the *probability ranking principle* (PRP) (van Rijsbergen 1979, 113–114):

PROBABILITY RANKING PRINCIPLE

If a reference retrieval system's response to each request is a ranking of the documents in the collection in order of decreasing probability of relevance to the user who submitted the request, where the probabilities are estimated as accurately as possible on the basis of whatever data have been made available to the system for this purpose, the overall effectiveness of the system to its user will be the best that is obtainable on the basis of those data.

In the simplest case of the PRP, there are no retrieval costs or other utility concerns that would differentially weight actions or errors. You lose a point for either returning a nonrelevant document or failing to return a relevant document (such a binary situation where you are evaluated on your *accuracy* is called *1/0 loss*). The goal is to return the best possible results as the top k documents, for any value of k the user chooses to examine. The PRP then says to simply rank all documents in decreasing order of $P(R = 1|d, q)$. If a set of retrieval results is to be returned, rather than an ordering, the *Bayes optimal decision rule*, the decision that minimizes the risk of loss, is to simply return documents that are more likely relevant than nonrelevant:

1/0 LOSS

BAYES OPTIMAL DECISION RULE

(11.6) $$d \text{ is relevant iff } P(R = 1|d, q) > P(R = 0|d, q).$$

Theorem 11.1. *The PRP is optimal, in the sense that it minimizes the expected* BAYES RISK *loss (also known as the* Bayes *risk) under 1/0 loss.*

The proof can be found in Ripley (1996). However, it requires that all probabilities be known correctly. This is never the case in practice. Nevertheless, the PRP still provides a very useful foundation for developing models of IR.

11.2.2 *The probability ranking principle with retrieval costs*

Suppose, instead, that we assume a model of retrieval costs. Let C_1 be the cost of not retrieving a relevant document and C_0 the cost of retrieval of a nonrelevant document. Then the PRP says that if for a specific document d and for all documents d' not yet retrieved

(11.7) $$C_0 \cdot P(R = 0|d) - C_1 \cdot P(R = 1|d) \leq C_0 \cdot P(R = 0|d') - C_1 \cdot P(R = 1|d')$$

then d is the next document to be retrieved. Such a model gives a formal framework where we can model differential costs of false positives and false negatives and even system performance issues at the modeling stage, rather than simply at the evaluation stage, as we did in Section 8.6 (page 154). However, we will not further consider loss/utility models in this chapter.

11.3 The binary independence model

BINARY
INDEPENDENCE
MODEL
The *binary independence model* (BIM) we present in this section is the model that has traditionally been used with the PRP. It introduces some simple assumptions, which make estimating the probability function $P(R|d, q)$ practical. Here, "binary" is equivalent to Boolean: Documents and queries are both represented as binary term incidence vectors. That is, a document d is represented by the vector $\vec{x} = (x_1, \ldots, x_M)$ where $x_t = 1$ if term t is present in document d and $x_t = 0$ if t is not present in d. With this representation, many possible documents have the same vector representation. Similarly, we represent q by the incidence vector $\vec{q}$ (the distinction between q and $\vec{q}$ is less central because commonly q is in the form of a set of words). "Independence" means that terms are modeled as occurring in documents independently. The model recognizes no association between terms. This assumption is far from correct, but it nevertheless often gives satisfactory results in practice; it is the "naive" assumption of Naive Bayes models, discussed further in Section 13.4 (page 245). Indeed, the BIM is exactly the same as the multivariate Bernoulli Naive Bayes model presented in Section 13.3 (page 243). In a sense, this assumption is equivalent to an assumption of the vector space model, where each term is a dimension that is orthogonal to all other terms.

We will first present a model that assumes that the user has a single-step information need. As discussed in Chapter 9, seeing a range of results might let the user refine their information need. Fortunately, as mentioned there, it is straightforward to extend the BIM so as to provide a framework for relevance feedback, and we present this model in Section 11.3.4.

To make a probabilistic retrieval strategy precise, we need to estimate how terms in documents contribute to relevance; specifically, we wish to know how term frequency, document frequency, document length, and other statistics that we can compute influence judgments about document relevance, and how they can be reasonably combined to estimate the probability of document relevance. We then order documents by decreasing estimated probability of relevance.

We assume here that the relevance of each document is independent of the relevance of other documents. As we noted in Section 8.5.1 (page 153), this is incorrect; the assumption is especially harmful in practice if it allows a system to return duplicate or near duplicate documents. Under the BIM, we model the probability $P(R|d, q)$ that a document is relevant via the probability in terms of term incidence vectors $P(R|\vec{x}, \vec{q})$. Then, using Bayes rule, we have:

$$(11.8) \qquad P(R = 1|\vec{x}, \vec{q}) = \frac{P(\vec{x}|R = 1, \vec{q})P(R = 1|\vec{q})}{P(\vec{x}|\vec{q})}$$

$$P(R = 0|\vec{x}, \vec{q}) = \frac{P(\vec{x}|R = 0, \vec{q})P(R = 0|\vec{q})}{P(\vec{x}|\vec{q})}.$$

Here, $P(\vec{x}|R = 1, \vec{q})$ and $P(\vec{x}|R = 0, \vec{q})$ are the probability that if a relevant or nonrelevant, respectively, document is retrieved, then that document's representation is $\vec{x}$. You should think of this quantity as defined with respect to a space of possible documents in a domain. How do we compute all these probabilities? We never know the exact probabilities, and so we have to use estimates: Statistics about the actual document collection are used to estimate these probabilities. $P(R = 1|\vec{q})$ and $P(R = 0|\vec{q})$ indicate the prior probability of retrieving a relevant or nonrelevant document, respectively, for a query $\vec{q}$. Again, if we knew the percentage of relevant documents in the collection, then we could use this number to estimate $P(R = 1|\vec{q})$ and $P(R = 0|\vec{q})$. Because a document is either relevant or nonrelevant to a query, we must have that:

$$(11.9) \qquad P(R = 1|\vec{x}, \vec{q}) + P(R = 0|\vec{x}, \vec{q}) = 1.$$

11.3.1 Deriving a ranking function for query terms

Given a query q, we wish to order returned documents by descending $P(R = 1|d, q)$. Under the BIM, this is modeled as ordering by $P(R = 1|\vec{x}, \vec{q})$. Rather than estimating this probability directly, because we are interested only in the ranking of documents, we work with some other quantities which are easier to compute and which give the same ordering of documents. In particular, we can rank documents by their odds of relevance (because the odds of relevance is monotonic with the probability of relevance). This makes things easier, because we can ignore the common denominator in (11.8), giving:

(11.10) $\quad O(R|\vec{x}, \vec{q}) = \dfrac{P(R = 1|\vec{x}, \vec{q})}{P(R = 0|\vec{x}, \vec{q})} = \dfrac{\frac{P(R=1|\vec{q})P(\vec{x}|R=1,\vec{q})}{P(\vec{x}|\vec{q})}}{\frac{P(R=0|\vec{q})P(\vec{x}|R=0,\vec{q})}{P(\vec{x}|\vec{q})}} = \dfrac{P(R = 1|\vec{q})}{P(R = 0|\vec{q})} \cdot \dfrac{P(\vec{x}|R = 1, \vec{q})}{P(\vec{x}|R = 0, \vec{q})}.$

The left term in the rightmost expression of Equation (11.10) is a constant for a given query. Because we are only ranking documents, there is thus no need for us to estimate it. The right-hand term does, however, require estimation, and this initially appears to be difficult: How can we accurately estimate the probability of an entire term incidence vector occurring? It is at this point that NAIVE BAYES we make the *Naive Bayes conditional independence assumption* that the presence ASSUMPTION or absence of a word in a document is independent of the presence or absence of any other word (given the query):

(11.11) $$\frac{P(\vec{x}|R = 1, \vec{q})}{P(\vec{x}|R = 0, \vec{q})} = \prod_{t=1}^{M} \frac{P(x_t|R = 1, \vec{q})}{P(x_t|R = 0, \vec{q})}.$$

So:

(11.12) $$O(R|\vec{x}, \vec{q}) = O(R|\vec{q}) \cdot \prod_{t=1}^{M} \frac{P(x_t|R = 1, \vec{q})}{P(x_t|R = 0, \vec{q})}.$$

Because each x_t is either 0 or 1, we can separate the terms to give:

(11.13) $\quad O(R|\vec{x}, \vec{q}) = O(R|\vec{q}) \cdot \displaystyle\prod_{t:x_t=1} \frac{P(x_t = 1|R = 1, \vec{q})}{P(x_t = 1|R = 0, \vec{q})} \cdot \prod_{t:x_t=0} \frac{P(x_t = 0|R = 1, \vec{q})}{P(x_t = 0|R = 0, \vec{q})}.$

Henceforth, let $p_t = P(x_t = 1|R = 1, \vec{q})$ be the probability of a term appearing in a document relevant to the query, and $u_t = P(x_t = 1|R = 0, \vec{q})$ be the probability of a term appearing in a nonrelevant document. These quantities can be visualized in the following contingency table where the columns add to 1:

(11.14)

document		relevant ($R = 1$)	nonrelevant ($R = 0$)
term present	$x_t = 1$	p_t	u_t
term absent	$x_t = 0$	$1 - p_t$	$1 - u_t$

Let us make an additional simplifying assumption that terms not occurring in the query are equally likely to occur in relevant and nonrelevant documents; that is, if $q_t = 0$ then $p_t = u_t$. (This assumption can be changed, as when doing relevance feedback in Section 11.3.4.) Then we need only consider terms in the products that appear in the query, and so,

(11.15) $$O(R|\vec{q}, \vec{x}) = O(R|\vec{q}) \cdot \prod_{t:x_t=q_t=1} \frac{p_t}{u_t} \cdot \prod_{t:x_t=0,q_t=1} \frac{1 - p_t}{1 - u_t}.$$

The left product is over query terms found in the document and the right product is over query terms not found in the document.

We can manipulate this expression by including the query terms found in the document into the right product, but simultaneously dividing through by them in the left product, so the value is unchanged. Then we have:

$$(11.16) \qquad O(R|\vec{q}, \vec{x}) = O(R|\vec{q}) \cdot \prod_{t:x_t=q_t=1} \frac{p_t(1 - u_t)}{u_t(1 - p_t)} \cdot \prod_{t:q_t=1} \frac{1 - p_t}{1 - u_t}.$$

The left product is still over query terms found in the document, but the right product is now over all query terms. That means that this right product is a constant for a particular query, just like the odds $O(R|\vec{q})$. So the only quantity that needs to be estimated to rank documents for relevance to a query is the left product. We can equally rank documents by the logarithm of this term, since log is a monotonic function. The resulting quantity used for ranking is called the *retrieval status value* (RSV) in this model:

RETRIEVAL
STATUS VALUE

$$(11.17) \qquad RSV_d = \log \prod_{t:x_t=q_t=1} \frac{p_t(1 - u_t)}{u_t(1 - p_t)} = \sum_{t:x_t=q_t=1} \log \frac{p_t(1 - u_t)}{u_t(1 - p_t)}.$$

So everything comes down to computing the RSV. Define c_t:

$$(11.18) \qquad c_t = \log \frac{p_t(1 - u_t)}{u_t(1 - p_t)} = \log \frac{p_t}{(1 - p_t)} + \log \frac{1 - u_t}{u_t}.$$

The c_t terms are log odds ratios for the terms in the query. We have the odds of the term appearing if the document is relevant ($p_t/(1 - p_t)$) and the odds ODDS RATIO of the term appearing if the document is nonrelevant ($u_t/(1 - u_t)$). The *odds ratio* is the ratio of two such odds, and then we finally take the log of that quantity. The value will be 0 if a term has equal odds of appearing in relevant and nonrelevant documents, and positive if it is more likely to appear in relevant documents. The c_t quantities function as term weights in the model, and the document score for a query is $RSV_d = \sum_{x_t=q_t=1} c_t$. Operationally, we sum them in accumulators for query terms appearing in documents, just as for the vector space model calculations discussed in Section 7.1 (page 124). We now turn to how we estimate these c_t quantities for a particular collection and query.

11.3.2 Probability estimates in theory

For each term t, what would these c_t numbers look like for the whole collection? Equation (11.19) gives a contingency table of counts of documents in the collection, where df$_t$ is the number of documents that contain term t:

(11.19)

documents		relevant	nonrelevant	total
term present	$x_t = 1$	s	$\mathrm{df}_t - s$	df_t
term absent	$x_t = 0$	$S - s$	$(N - \mathrm{df}_t) - (S - s)$	$N - \mathrm{df}_t$
	total	S	$N - S$	N

Using this, $p_t = s/S$ and $u_t = (\mathrm{df}_t - s)/(N - S)$ and

(11.20)
$$c_t = K(N, \mathrm{df}_t, S, s) = \log \frac{s/(S - s)}{(\mathrm{df}_t - s)/((N - \mathrm{df}_t) - (S - s))}.$$

To avoid the possibility of zeroes (such as if every or no relevant document has a particular term) it is fairly standard to add $\frac{1}{2}$ to each of the quantities in the center four terms of (11.19), and then to adjust the marginal counts (the totals) accordingly (so, the bottom right cell totals $N + 2$). Then we have:

(11.21)
$$\hat{c}_t = K(N, \mathrm{df}_t, S, s) = \log \frac{(s + \frac{1}{2})/(S - s + \frac{1}{2})}{(\mathrm{df}_t - s + \frac{1}{2})/(N - \mathrm{df}_t - S + s + \frac{1}{2})}.$$

Adding $\frac{1}{2}$ in this way is a simple form of smoothing. For trials with categorical outcomes (such as noting the presence or absence of a term), one way to estimate the probability of an event from data is simply to count the number of times an event occurred divided by the total number of trials. RELATIVE This is referred to as the *relative frequency* of the event. Estimating the probFREQUENCY ability as the relative frequency is the *maximum likelihood estimate* (or *MLE*), MAXIMUM because this value makes the observed data maximally likely. However, if LIKELIHOOD we simply use the MLE, then the probability given to events we happened ESTIMATE to see is usually too high, whereas other events may be completely unseen (MLE) and giving them as a probability estimate their relative frequency of 0 is both an underestimate and normally breaks our models; anything multiplied by 0 is 0. Simultaneously decreasing the estimated probability of seen events SMOOTHING and increasing the probability of unseen events is referred to as *smoothing*. One simple way of smoothing is to add a number α to each of the observed PSEUDOCOUNTS counts. These *pseudocounts* correspond to the use of a uniform distribution BAYESIAN over the vocabulary as a *Bayesian prior*, following Equation (11.4). We initially PRIOR assume a uniform distribution over events, where the size of α denotes the strength of our belief in uniformity, and we then update the probability based on observed events. Because our belief in uniformity is weak, we use $\alpha = \frac{1}{2}$. MAXIMUM A This is a form of *maximum a posteriori* (*MAP*) estimation, where we choose POSTERIORI the most likely point value for probabilities based on the prior and the ob(MAP) served evidence, following Equation (11.4). We will further discuss methods of smoothing estimated counts to give probability models in Section 12.2.2 (page 224); the simple method of adding $\frac{1}{2}$ to each observed count will do for now.

11.3.3 Probability estimates in practice

Under the assumption that relevant documents are a very small percentage of the collection, it is plausible to approximate statistics for nonrelevant documents by statistics from the whole collection. Under this assumption, u_t (the probability of term occurrence in nonrelevant documents for a query) is df_t/N and

(11.22) $$\log[(1 - u_t)/u_t] = \log[(N - df_t)/df_t] \approx \log N/df_t$$

In other words, we can provide a theoretical justification for the most frequently used form of idf weighting, which we saw in Section 6.2.1.

The approximation technique in Equation (11.22) cannot easily be extended to relevant documents. The quantity p_t can be estimated in various ways:

1. We can use the frequency of term occurrence in known relevant documents (if we know some). This is the basis of probabilistic approaches to relevance feedback weighting in a feedback loop, discussed in the next subsection.

2. Croft and Harper (1979) proposed using a constant in their combination match model. For instance, we might assume that p_t is constant over all terms x_t in the query and that $p_t = 0.5$. This means that each term has even odds of appearing in a relevant document, and so the p_t and $(1 - p_t)$ factors cancel out in the expression for RSV. Such an estimate is weak, but doesn't disagree violently with our hopes for the search terms appearing in many but not all relevant documents. Combining this method with our earlier approximation for u_t, the document ranking is determined simply by which query terms occur in documents scaled by their idf weighting. For short documents (titles or abstracts) in situations in which iterative searching is undesirable, using this weighting term alone can be quite satisfactory, although in many other circumstances we would like to do better.

3. Greiff (1998) argues that the constant estimate of p_t in the Croft and Harper (1979) model is theoretically problematic and not observed empirically: as might be expected, p_t is shown to rise with df_t. Based on his data analysis, a plausible proposal would be to use the estimate $p_t = \frac{1}{3} + \frac{2}{3}df_t/N$.

Iterative methods of estimation, which combine some of the above ideas, are discussed in the next subsection.

11.3.4 Probabilistic approaches to relevance feedback

We can use (pseudo) relevance feedback (RF), perhaps in an iterative process of estimation, to get a more accurate estimate of p_t. The probabilistic approach to RF works as follows.

1. Guess initial estimates of p_t and u_t. This can be done using the probability estimates of the previous section. For instance, we can assume that p_t is constant over all x_t in the query, in particular, perhaps taking $p_t = \frac{1}{2}$.
2. Use the current estimates of p_t and u_t to determine a best guess at the set of relevant documents $R = \{d : R_{d,q} = 1\}$. Use this model to retrieve a set of candidate relevant documents, which we present to the user.
3. We interact with the user to refine the model of R. We do this by learning from the user relevance judgments for some subset of documents V. Based on relevance judgments, V is partitioned into two subsets: $VR = \{d \in V, R_{d,q} = 1\} \subset R$ and $VNR = \{d \in V, R_{d,q} = 0\}$, which is disjoint from R.
4. We reestimate p_t and u_t on the basis of known relevant and nonrelevant documents. If the sets VR and VNR are large enough, we may be able to estimate these quantities directly from these documents as maximum likelihood estimates:

(11.23)
$$p_t = |VR_t|/|VR|$$

where VR_t is the set of documents in VR containing x_t. In practice, we usually need to smooth these estimates. We can do this by adding $\frac{1}{2}$ to both the count $|VR_t|$ and to the number of relevant documents not containing the term, giving:

(11.24)
$$p_t = \frac{|VR_t| + \frac{1}{2}}{|VR| + 1}.$$

However, the set of documents judged by the user (V) is usually very small, and so the resulting statistical estimate is quite unreliable (noisy), even if the estimate is smoothed. So it is often better to combine the new information with the original guess in a process of Bayesian updating. In this case we have:

(11.25)
$$p_t^{(k+1)} = \frac{|VR_t| + \kappa p_t^{(k)}}{|VR| + \kappa}.$$

Here $p_t^{(k)}$ is the kth estimate for p_t in an iterative updating process and is used as a Bayesian prior in the next iteration with a weighting of κ. Relating this equation back to Equation (11.4) requires a bit more probability theory than we have presented here (we need to use a beta distribution prior, conjugate to the Bernoulli random variable X_t). But the form of the resulting equation is quite straightforward: Rather than uniformly distributing pseudocounts, we now distribute a total of κ pseudocounts according to the previous estimate, which acts as the prior distribution. In the absence of other evidence (and assuming that the user is perhaps indicating roughly five relevant or nonrelevant documents) then a value of around $\kappa = 5$ is perhaps appropriate. That is, the prior is strongly weighted so that the estimate does not change too much from the evidence provided by a very small number of documents.

5. Repeat the above process from Step 2, generating a succession of approximations to R and hence p_t, until the user is satisfied.

It is also straightforward to derive a pseudo RF version of this algorithm, where we simply pretend that $VR = V$. More briefly:

1. Assume initial estimates for p_t and u_t as above.
2. Determine a guess for the size of the relevant document set. If unsure, a conservative (too small) guess is likely to be best. This motivates use of a fixed size set V of highest ranked documents.
3. Improve our guesses for p_t and u_t. We choose from the methods of Equations (11.23) and (11.25) for reestimating p_t, except now based on the set V instead of VR. If we let V_t be the subset of documents in V containing x_t and use add $\frac{1}{2}$ smoothing, we get:

$$(11.26) \qquad p_t = \frac{|V_t| + \frac{1}{2}}{|V| + 1}$$

and if we assume that documents that are non retrieved are nonrelevant then we can update our u_t estimates as:

$$(11.27) \qquad u_t = \frac{\mathrm{df}_t - |V_t| + \frac{1}{2}}{N - |V| + 1}.$$

4. Go to Step 2 until the ranking of the returned results converges.

Once we have a real estimate for p_t, then the c_t weights used in the RSV value look almost like a tf–idf value. For instance, using Equation (11.18), Equation (11.22), and Equation (11.26), we have:

$$(11.28) \qquad c_t = \log\left[\frac{p_t}{1 - p_t} \cdot \frac{1 - u_t}{u_t}\right] \approx \log\left[\frac{|V_t| + \frac{1}{2}}{|V| - |V_t| + 1} \cdot \frac{N}{\mathrm{df}_t}\right].$$

But things aren't quite the same: $p_t/(1 - p_t)$ measures the (estimated) proportion of relevant documents that the term t occurs in, not term frequency. Moreover, if we apply log identities:

$$(11.29) \qquad c_t = \log\frac{|V_t| + \frac{1}{2}}{|V| - |V_t| + 1} + \log\frac{N}{\mathrm{df}_t}$$

we see that we are now *adding* the two log-scaled components rather than multiplying them.

?

Exercise 11.1 Work through the derivation of Equation (11.20) from Equations (11.18) and (11.19).

Exercise 11.2 What are the differences between standard vector space tf–idf weighting and the BIM probabilistic retrieval model (in the case where no document relevance information is available)?

Exercise 11.3 [★★] Let X_t be a random variable indicating whether the term t appears in a document. Suppose we have $|R|$ relevant documents in the document collection and that $X_t = 1$ in s of the documents. Take the observed data to be just these observations of X_t for each document in R. Show that the MLE for the parameter $p_t = P(X_t = 1 | R = 1, \vec{q})$, that is, the value for p_t which maximizes the probability of the observed data, is $p_t = s/|R|$.

Exercise 11.4 Describe the differences between vector space relevance feedback and probabilistic relevance feedback.

11.4 An appraisal and some extensions

11.4.1 An appraisal of probabilistic models

Probabilistic methods are one of the oldest formal models in IR. Already in the 1970s they were held out as an opportunity to place IR on a firmer theoretical footing, and with the resurgence of probabilistic methods in computational linguistics in the 1990s, that hope has returned, and probabilistic methods are again one of the currently hottest topics in IR. Traditionally, probabilistic IR has had neat ideas but the methods have never won on performance. Getting reasonable approximations of the needed probabilities for a probabilistic IR model is possible, but it requires some major assumptions. In the BIM these are:

- a Boolean representation of documents/queries/relevance
- term independence
- terms not in the query don't affect the outcome
- document relevance values are independent

It is perhaps the severity of the modeling assumptions that makes achieving good performance difficult. A general problem seems to be that probabilistic models either require partial relevance information or else only allow for deriving apparently inferior term weighting models.

Things started to change in the 1990s when the BM25 weighting scheme, which we discuss later in this section, showed very good performance, and started to be adopted as a term weighting scheme by many groups. The difference between "vector space" and "probabilistic" IR systems is not that great; in either case, you build an information retrieval scheme in the exact same way that we discussed in Chapter 7. For a probabilistic IR system, it's just that, at the end, you score queries not by cosine similarity and tf–idf in a vector space, but by a slightly different formula motivated by probability theory. Indeed, sometimes people have changed an existing vector-space IR system into an effectively probabilistic system simply by adopted term weighting formulas from probabilistic models. In this section, we briefly present three extensions of the traditional probabilistic model, and in the next

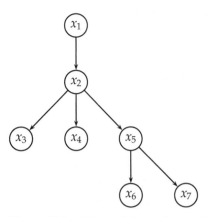

Figure 11.1 A tree of dependencies between terms. In this graphical model representation, a term x_i is directly dependent on a term x_k if there is an arrow $x_k \rightarrow x_i$.

chapter, we look at the somewhat different probabilistic language modeling approach to IR.

11.4.2 Tree-structured dependencies between terms

Some of the assumptions of the BIM can be removed. For example, we can remove the assumption that terms are independent. This assumption is very far from true in practice. A case that particularly violates this assumption is term pairs like Hong and Kong, which are strongly dependent. But dependencies can occur in various complex configurations, such as between the set of terms New, York, England, City, Stock, Exchange, and University. van Rijsbergen (1979) proposed a simple, plausible model that allowed a tree structure of term dependencies, as in Figure 11.1. In this model, each term can be directly dependent on only one other term, giving a tree structure of dependencies. When it was invented in the 1970s, estimation problems held back the practical success of this model, but the idea was reinvented as the tree-augmented Naive Bayes model by Friedman and Goldszmidt (1996), who used it with some success on various machine learning data sets.

11.4.3 Okapi BM25: A nonbinary model

The BIM was originally designed for short catalog records and abstracts of fairly consistent length, and it works reasonably in these contexts, but for modern full-text search collections, it seems clear that a model should pay BM25 WEIGHTS attention to term frequency and document length, as in Chapter 6. The *BM25* OKAPI *weighting scheme*, often called *Okapi weighting*, after the system in which it was WEIGHTING first implemented, was developed as a way of building a probabilistic model sensitive to these quantities while not introducing too many additional parameters into the model (Spärck Jones et al. 2000). We will not develop the full theory behind the model here, but just present a series of forms that build up to the standard form now used for document scoring. The simplest score for document d is just idf weighting of the query terms present, as in Equation (11.22):

$$(11.30) \qquad RSV_d = \sum_{t \in q} \log \frac{N}{\mathrm{df}_t}.$$

Sometimes, an alternative version of idf is used. If we start with the formula in Equation (11.21) but in the absence of relevance feedback information we estimate that $S = s = 0$, then we get an alternative idf formulation as follows:

$$(11.31) \qquad RSV_d = \sum_{t \in q} \log \frac{N - \mathrm{df}_t + \frac{1}{2}}{\mathrm{df}_t + \frac{1}{2}}.$$

This variant behaves slightly strangely: If a term occurs in over half the documents in the collection, then this model gives a negative term weight, which is presumably undesirable. But, assuming the use of a stop list, this normally doesn't happen, and the value for each summand can be given a floor of 0.

We can improve on Equation (11.30) by factoring in the frequency of each term and document length:

$$(11.32) \qquad RSV_d = \sum_{t \in q} \log \left[\frac{N}{\mathrm{df}_t} \right] \cdot \frac{(k_1 + 1)\mathrm{tf}_{td}}{k_1((1 - b) + b \times (L_d / L_{\mathrm{ave}})) + \mathrm{tf}_{td}}.$$

Here, tf_{td} is the frequency of term t in document d, and L_d and L_{ave} are the length of document d and the average document length for the whole collection. The variable k_1 is a positive tuning parameter that calibrates the document term frequency scaling. A k_1 value of 0 corresponds to a binary model (no term frequency), and a large value corresponds to using raw term frequency. b is another tuning parameter ($0 \leq b \leq 1$) that determines the scaling by document length: $b = 1$ corresponds to fully scaling the term weight by the document length, whereas $b = 0$ corresponds to no length normalization.

If the query is long, then we might also use similar weighting for query terms. This is appropriate if the queries are paragraph-long information needs, but unnecessary for short queries.

$$(11.33) \qquad RSV_d = \sum_{t \in q} \left[\log \frac{N}{\mathrm{df}_t} \right] \cdot \frac{(k_1 + 1)\mathrm{tf}_{td}}{k_1((1 - b) + b \times (L_d / L_{\mathrm{ave}})) + \mathrm{tf}_{td}} \cdot \frac{(k_3 + 1)\mathrm{tf}_{tq}}{k_3 + \mathrm{tf}_{tq}}$$

with tf_{tq} being the frequency of term t in the query q, and k_3 being another positive tuning parameter that this time calibrates term frequency scaling of the query. In the equation presented, there is no length normalization of queries (it is as if $b = 0$ here). Length normalization of the query is unnecessary because retrieval is being done with respect to a single fixed query. The tuning parameters of these formulas should ideally be set to optimize performance on a development test collection (see page 141). That is, we can search for values of these parameters that maximize performance on a separate development test collection (either manually or with optimization methods, such as grid search or something more advanced), and then use these parameters on the actual test collection. In the absence of such optimization, experiments have shown reasonable values are to set k_1 and k_3 to a value between 1.2 and 2 and $b = 0.75$.

If we have relevance judgments available, then we can use the full form of (11.21) in place of the approximation $\log(N/\mathrm{df}_t)$ introduced in (11.22):

(11.34)
$$
RSV_d = \sum_{t \in q} \left[\log \left[\frac{(|VR_t| + \frac{1}{2})/(|VNR_t| + \frac{1}{2})}{(\mathrm{df}_t - |VR_t| + \frac{1}{2})/(N - \mathrm{df}_t - |VR| + |VR_t| + \frac{1}{2})} \right] \right.
$$
$$
\left. \times \frac{(k_1 + 1)\mathrm{tf}_{td}}{k_1((1 - b) + b(L_d/L_{\mathrm{ave}})) + \mathrm{tf}_{td}} \times \frac{(k_3 + 1)\mathrm{tf}_{tq}}{k_3 + \mathrm{tf}_{tq}} \right].
$$

Here, VR_t, NVR_t, and VR are used as in Section 11.3.4. The first part of the expression reflects relevance feedback (or just idf weighting if no relevance information is available), the second implements document term frequency and document length scaling, and the third considers term frequency in the query.

Rather than just providing a term weighting method for terms in a user's query, relevance feedback can also involve augmenting the query (automatically or with manual review) with some (say, ten to twenty) of the top terms in the known-relevant documents as ordered by the relevance factor $\hat{c}_t$ from Equation (11.21), and the above formula can then be used with such an augmented query q.

The BM25 term weighting formulas have been used quite widely and quite successfully across a range of collections and search tasks. Especially in the TREC evaluations, they performed well and were widely adopted by many groups. See Spärck Jones et al. (2000) for extensive motivation and discussion of experimental results.

11.4.4 Bayesian network approaches to information retrieval

Turtle and Croft (1989, 1991) introduced into information retrieval the use BAYESIAN of *Bayesian networks* (Jensen and Jensen 2001), a form of probabilistic graph-NETWORKS ical model. We skip the details because fully introducing the formalism of Bayesian networks would require much too much space, but conceptually, Bayesian networks use directed graphs to show probabilistic dependencies between variables, as in Figure 11.1, and have led to the development of sophisticated algorithms for propagating influence so as to allow learning and inference with arbitrary knowledge within arbitrary directed acyclic graphs. Turtle and Croft used a sophisticated network to better model the complex dependencies between a document and a user's information need.

The model decomposes into two parts: a document collection network and a query network. The document collection network is large, but can be pre-computed; it maps from documents to terms to concepts. The concepts are a thesaurus-based expansion of the terms appearing in the document. The query network is relatively small but a new network needs to be built each time a query comes in, and then attached to the document network. The query network maps from query terms, to query subexpressions (built using probabilistic or "noisy" versions of AND and OR operators), to the user's information need.

The result is a flexible probabilistic network that can generalize various simpler Boolean and probabilistic models. Indeed, this is the primary case of a statistical ranked retrieval model that naturally supports structured query operators. The system allowed efficient large-scale retrieval, and was the basis of the InQuery text retrieval system, built at the University of Massachusetts. This system performed very well in TREC evaluations and for a time was sold commercially. On the other hand, the model still used various approximations and independence assumptions to make parameter estimation and computation possible. There has not been much follow-on work along these lines, but we would note that this model was actually built very early on in the modern era of using Bayesian networks, and there have been many subsequent developments in the theory, and the time is perhaps right for a new generation of Bayesian network-based IR systems.

11.5 References and further reading

Longer introductions to probability theory can be found in most introductory probability and statistics books, such as (Grinstead and Snell 1997; Rice 2006; Ross 2006). An introduction to Bayesian utility theory can be found in (Ripley 1996).

The probabilistic approach to IR originated in the United Kingdom in the 1950s. The first major presentation of a probabilistic model is Maron and Kuhns (1960). Robertson and Jones (1976) introduce the main foundations of the BIM and van Rijsbergen (1979) presents in detail the classic BIM probabilistic model. The idea of the PRP is variously attributed to S. E. Robertson, M. E. Maron, and W. S. Cooper (the term *probabilistic ordering principle* is used in Robertson and Jones (1976), but PRP dominates in later work). Fuhr (1992) is a more recent presentation of probabilistic IR, which includes coverage of other approaches such as probabilistic logics and Bayesian networks. Crestani et al. (1998) is another survey. Spärck Jones et al. (2000) is the definitive presentation of probabilistic IR experiments by the "London school," and Robertson (2005) presents a retrospective on the group's participation in TREC evaluations, including detailed discussion of the Okapi

BM25 scoring function and its development. Robertson et al. (2004) extend BM25 to the case of multiple weighted fields.

The open-source Indri search engine, which is distributed with the Lemur toolkit (www.lemurproject.org/) merges ideas from Bayesian inference networks and statistical language modeling approaches (see Chapter 12), in particular preserving the former's support for structured query operators.

12 *Language models for information retrieval*

A common suggestion to users for coming up with good queries is to think of words that would likely appear in a relevant document, and to use those words as the query. The language modeling approach to information retrieval (IR) directly models that idea: A document is a good match to a query if the document model is likely to generate the query, which will in turn happen if the document contains the query words often. This approach thus provides a different realization of some of the basic ideas for document ranking which we saw in Section 6.2 (page 107). Instead of overtly modeling the probability $P(R = 1|q, d)$ of relevance of a document d to a query q, as in the traditional probabilistic approach to IR (Chapter 11), the basic language modeling approach instead builds a probabilistic language model M_d from each document d, and ranks documents based on the probability of the model generating the query: $P(q|M_d)$.

In this chapter, we first introduce the concept of language models (Section 12.1) and then describe the basic and most commonly used language modeling approach to IR, the query likelihood model (Section 12.2). After some comparisons between the language modeling approach and other approaches to IR (Section 12.3), we finish by briefly describing various extensions to the language modeling approach (Section 12.4).

12.1 Language models

12.1.1 Finite automata and language models

What do we mean by a document model generating a query? A traditional GENERATIVE *generative model* of a language, of the kind familiar from formal language MODEL theory, can be used either to recognize or to generate strings. For example, the finite automaton shown in Figure 12.1 can generate strings that include

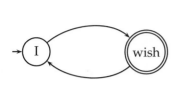

I wish

I wish I wish

I wish I wish I wish

I wish I wish I wish I wish I wish I wish

...

CANNOT GENERATE: wish I wish

Figure 12.1 A simple finite automaton and some of the strings in the language it generates. → shows the start state of the automaton and a double circle indicates a (possible) finishing state.

the examples shown. The full set of strings that can be generated is called the LANGUAGE *language* of the automaton.[1]

If instead each node has a probability distribution over generating different terms, we have a language model. The notion of a language model is LANGUAGE inherently probabilistic. A *language model* is a function that puts a probability MODEL measure over strings drawn from some vocabulary. That is, for a language model M over an alphabet Σ:

(12.1)
$$\sum_{s \in \Sigma^*} P(s) = 1.$$

One simple kind of language model is equivalent to a probabilistic finite automaton consisting of just a single node with a single probability distribution over producing different terms, so that $\sum_{t \in V} P(t) = 1$, as shown in Figure 12.2. After generating each word, we decide whether to stop or to loop around and then produce another word, and so the model also requires a probability of stopping in the finishing state. Such a model places a probability distribution over any sequence of words. By construction, it also provides a model for generating text according to its distribution.

 Example 12.1: To find the probability of a word sequence, we just multiply the probabilities that the model gives to each word in the sequence, together with the probability of continuing or stopping after producing each word. For example,

(12.2) $P(\text{frog said that toad likes frog}) = (0.01 \times 0.03 \times 0.04 \times 0.01 \times 0.02 \times 0.01)$
$$\times (0.8 \times 0.8 \times 0.8 \times 0.8 \times 0.8 \times 0.8 \times 0.2)$$
$$\approx 0.000000000001573$$

As you can see, the probability of a particular string/document is usually a very small number! Here we stopped after generating *frog* the second time. The first line of numbers are the term emission probabilities, and the second line gives the probability of continuing or stopping after generating each word. An explicit stop probability is needed for a finite automaton

---

[1] Finite automata can have outputs attached to either their states or their arcs; we use states here, because that maps directly on to the way probabilistic automata are usually formalized.

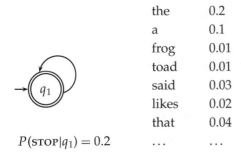

the	0.2
a	0.1
frog	0.01
toad	0.01
said	0.03
likes	0.02
that	0.04

$P(\text{STOP}|q_1) = 0.2$ ... ...

Figure 12.2 A one-state finite automaton that acts as a unigram language model. We show a partial specification of the state emission probabilities.

LIKELIHOOD
RATIO

to be a well-formed language model according to Equation (12.1). Nevertheless, most of the time, we will omit to include STOP and $(1 - \text{STOP})$ probabilities (as do most other authors). To compare two models for a data set, we can calculate their *likelihood ratio*, which results from simply dividing the probability of the data according to one model by the probability of the data according to the other model. Providing that the stop probability is fixed, its inclusion will not alter the likelihood ratio that results from comparing the likelihood of two language models generating a string. Hence, it will not alter the ranking of documents.[2] Nevertheless, formally, the numbers will no longer truly be probabilities, but only proportional to probabilities. See Exercise 12.4.

Example 12.2: Suppose, now, that we have two language models M_1 and M_2, shown partially in Figure 12.3. Each gives a probability estimate to a sequence of terms, as already illustrated in Example 12.1. The language model that gives the higher probability to the sequence of terms is more likely to have generated the term sequence. This time, we will omit STOP probabilities from our calculations. For the sequence shown, we get:

(12.3)

s	frog	said	that	toad	likes	that	dog
M_1	0.01	0.03	0.04	0.01	0.02	0.04	0.005
M_2	0.0002	0.03	0.04	0.0001	0.04	0.04	0.01

$P(s|M_1) = 0.00000000000048$
$P(s|M_2) = 0.000000000000000384$

and we see that $P(s|M_1) > P(s|M_2)$. We present the formulas here in terms of products of probabilities, but, as is common in probabilistic applications, in practice it is usually best to work with sums of log probabilities (cf. page 239).

[2] In the IR context that we are leading up to, taking the stop probability to be fixed across models seems reasonable. This is because we are generating queries, and the length distribution of queries is fixed and independent of the document from which we are generating the language model.

model M_1		model M_2	
the	0.2	the	0.15
a	0.1	a	0.12
frog	0.01	frog	0.0002
toad	0.01	toad	0.0001
said	0.03	said	0.03
likes	0.02	likes	0.04
that	0.04	that	0.04
dog	0.005	dog	0.01
cat	0.003	cat	0.015
monkey	0.001	monkey	0.002
...	...	...	...

Figure 12.3 Partial specification of two unigram language models.

12.1.2 Types of language models

How do we build probabilities over sequences of terms? We can always use the chain rule from Equation (11.1) to decompose the probability of a sequence of events into the probability of each successive event conditioned on earlier events:

(12.4) $$P(t_1t_2t_3t_4) = P(t_1)P(t_2|t_1)P(t_3|t_1t_2)P(t_4|t_1t_2t_3).$$

The simplest form of language model simply throws away all conditioning context, and estimates each term independently. Such a model is called a *unigram language model*:

UNIGRAM
LANGUAGE
MODEL

(12.5) $$P_{\text{uni}}(t_1t_2t_3t_4) = P(t_1)P(t_2)P(t_3)P(t_4).$$

BIGRAM
LANGUAGE
MODEL

There are many more complex kinds of language models, such as *bigram language models*, which condition on the previous term,

(12.6) $$P_{\text{bi}}(t_1t_2t_3t_4) = P(t_1)P(t_2|t_1)P(t_3|t_2)P(t_4|t_3)$$

and even more complex grammar-based language models such as probabilistic context-free grammars. Such models are vital for tasks like speech recognition, spelling correction, and machine translation, where you need the probability of a term conditioned on surrounding context. However, most language-modeling work in IR has used unigram language models. IR is not the place where you most immediately need complex language models, because IR does not directly depend on the structure of sentences to the extent that other tasks like speech recognition do. Unigram models are often sufficient to judge the topic of a text. Moreover, as we shall see, IR language models are frequently estimated from a single document and so it is questionable whether there is enough training data to do more. Losses from data sparseness (see the discussion on page 240) tend to outweigh any gains from richer models. This is an example of the bias-variance tradeoff (cf. Section 14.6, page 284): With limited training data, a more constrained model tends to perform better. In addition, unigram models are more efficient to estimate and apply than higher order models. Nevertheless, the importance of phrase and proximity queries in IR in general suggests that future work should make use of more sophisticated language models, and some has begun to (see Section 12.5, page 232). Indeed, making this move parallels the model of van Rijsbergen in Chapter 11 (page 213).

12.1.3 *Multinomial distributions over words*

Under the unigram language model the order of words is irrelevant, and so such models are often called bag-of-words models, as discussed in Chapter 6 (page 107). Even though there is no conditioning on preceding context, this model nevertheless still gives the probability of a particular ordering of terms. However, any other ordering of this bag of terms will have the same probability. So, really, we have a multinomial distribution over words. So long as we stick to unigram models, the language model name and motivation could be viewed as historical rather than necessary. We could instead just refer to the model as a multinomial model. From this perspective, the equations presented above do not present the multinomial probability of a bag of words, because they do not sum over all possible orderings of those words, as is done by the multinomial coefficient (the first term on the right-hand side) in the standard presentation of a multinomial model:

$$(12.7) \qquad P(d) = \frac{L_d!}{\text{tf}_{t_1,d}!\,\text{tf}_{t_2,d}!\cdots\text{tf}_{t_M,d}!}\, P(t_1)^{\text{tf}_{t_1,d}}\, P(t_2)^{\text{tf}_{t_2,d}} \cdots P(t_M)^{\text{tf}_{t_M,d}}.$$

Here, $L_d = \sum_{1 \le i \le M} \text{tf}_{t_i,d}$ is the length of document d, M is the size of the term vocabulary, and the products are now over the terms in the vocabulary, not the positions in the document. However, just as with STOP probabilities, in practice we can also leave out the multinomial coefficient in our calculations; for a particular bag of words, it will be a constant, and so it has no effect on the likelihood ratio of two different models generating a particular bag of words. Multinomial distributions also appear in Section 13.2 (page 238).

The fundamental problem in designing language models is that we do not know what exactly we should use as the model M_d. However, we do generally have a sample of text that is representative of that model. This problem makes a lot of sense in the original, primary uses of language models. For example, in speech recognition, we have a training sample of (spoken) text. But we have to expect that, in the future, users will use different words and in different sequences, which we have never observed before, and so the model has to generalize beyond the observed data to allow unknown words and sequences. This interpretation is not so clear in the IR case, where a document is finite and usually fixed. The strategy we adopt in IR is as follows. We pretend that the document *d* is only a representative sample of text drawn from a model distribution, treating it like a fine-grained topic. We then estimate a language model from this sample, and use that model to calculate the probability of observing any word sequence, and, finally, we rank documents according to their probability of generating the query.

> **?**
>
> **Exercise 12.1** [⋆] Including STOP probabilities in the calculation, what will the sum of the probability estimates of all strings in the language of length 1 be? Assume that you generate a word and then decide whether to stop or not (i.e., the null string is not part of the language).
>
> **Exercise 12.2** [⋆] If the stop probability is omitted from calculations, what will the sum of the scores assigned to strings in the language of length 1 be?
>
> **Exercise 12.3** [⋆] What is the likelihood ratio of the document according to M_1 and M_2 in Example 12.2?
>
> **Exercise 12.4** [⋆] No explicit STOP probability appeared in Example 12.2. Assuming that the STOP probability of each model is 0.1, does this change the likelihood ratio of a document according to the two models?
>
> **Exercise 12.5** [⋆⋆] How might a language model be used in a spelling correction system? In particular, consider the case of context-sensitive spelling correction, and correcting incorrect usages of words, such as *their* in *Are you their?* (See Section 3.5 (page 59) for pointers to some literature on this topic.)

12.2 The query likelihood model

12.2.1 *Using query likelihood language models in IR*

Language modeling is a quite general formal approach to IR, with many variant realizations. The original and basic method for using language models in IR is the *query likelihood model*. In it, we construct from each document *d* in the collection a language model M_d. Our goal is to rank documents by $P(d|q)$, where the probability of a document is interpreted as the likelihood that it is relevant to the query. Using Bayes rule (as introduced in Section 11.1, page 202), we have:

QUERY LIKELIHOOD MODEL

$$P(d|q) = P(q|d)P(d)/P(q).$$

$P(q)$ is the same for all documents, and so can be ignored. The prior probability of a document $P(d)$ is often treated as uniform across all *d* and so it can also be ignored, but we could implement a genuine prior, which could include criteria like authority, length, genre, newness, and number of previous people who have read the document. But, given these simplifications, we return results ranked by simply $P(q|d)$, the probability of the query q under the language model derived from d. The language modeling approach thus attempts to model the query generation process: Documents are ranked by the probability that a query would be observed as a random sample from the respective document model.

The most common way to do this is to use the multinomial unigram language model, which is equivalent to a multinomial naive Bayes model (page 243), where the documents are the classes, each treated in the estimation as a separate "language." Under this model, we have that:

$$(12.8) \qquad P(q|M_d) = K_q \prod_{t \in V} P(t|M_d)^{\text{tf}_{t,d}}$$

where, again $K_q = L_d!/(\text{tf}_{t_1,d}!\text{tf}_{t_2,d}! \cdots \text{tf}_{t_M,d}!)$ is the multinomial coefficient for the query q, which we henceforth ignore because it is a constant for a particular query.

For retrieval based on a language model (henceforth LM), we treat the generation of queries as a random process. The approach is to

1. Infer a LM for each document.
2. Estimate $P(q|M_{d_i})$, the probability of generating the query according to each of these document models.
3. Rank the documents according to these probabilities.

The intuition of the basic model is that the user has a prototype document in mind and generates a query based on words that appear in this document. Often, users have a reasonable idea of terms that are likely to occur in documents of interest and they will choose query terms that distinguish these documents from others in the collection.[3] Collection statistics are an integral part of the language model, rather than being used heuristically as in many other approaches.

12.2.2 *Estimating the query generation probability*

In this section we describe how to estimate $P(q|M_d)$. The probability of producing the query given the LM M_d of document d using maximum likelihood estimation (MLE) and the unigram assumption is:

$$(12.9) \qquad \hat{P}(q|M_d) = \prod_{t \in q} \hat{P}_{\text{mle}}(t|M_d) = \prod_{t \in q} \frac{\text{tf}_{t,d}}{L_d}$$

where M_d is the LM of document d, $\text{tf}_{t,d}$ is the (raw) term frequency of term t in document d, and L_d is the number of tokens in document d. That is, we

---

[3] Of course, in other cases, they do not. The answer to this within the language modeling approach is translation LMs, as briefly discussed in Section 12.4.

just count up how often each word occurred, and divide through by the total number of words in the document d. This is the same method of calculating an MLE as we saw in Section 11.3.2 (page 207); but now using a mutinomial over word counts.

The classic problem with using LMs is one of estimation (the ^ symbol on the Ps is used above to stress that the model is estimated): Terms appear very sparsely in documents. In particular, some words will not have appeared in the document at all, but are possible words for the information need, which the user may have used in the query. If we estimate $\hat{P}(t|M_d) = 0$ for a term missing from a document d, then we get a strict conjunctive semantics: Documents will only give a query nonzero probability if all of the query terms appear in the document. Zero probabilities are clearly a problem in other uses of LMs, such as when predicting the next word in a speech recognition application, because many words will be sparsely represented in the training data. It may seem rather less clear whether this is problematic in an IR application. This could be thought of as a human–computer interface issue: Vector space systems have generally preferred more lenient matching, although recent web search developments have tended more in the direction of doing searches with such conjunctive semantics. Regardless of the approach here, there is a more general problem of estimation: Occurring words are also poorly estimated; in particular, the probability of words occurring once in the document is normally overestimated, because their one occurrence was partly by chance. The answer to this (as we saw in Section 11.3.2, page 207) is smoothing. But as people have come to understand the LM approach better, it has become apparent that the role of smoothing in this model is not only to avoid zero probabilities. The smoothing of terms actually implements major parts of the term weighting component (Exercise 12.8). It is not just that an unsmoothed model has conjunctive semantics; an unsmoothed model works badly because it lacks parts of the term weighting component.

Thus, we need to smooth probabilities in our document LMs to discount nonzero probabilities and to give some probability mass to unseen words. There's a wide space of approaches to smoothing probability distributions to deal with this problem. In Section 11.3.2 (page 207), we already discussed adding a number $(1, 1/2,$ or a small $\alpha)$ to the observed counts and renormalizing to give a probability distribution.[4] In this section, we mention a couple of other smoothing methods that involve combining observed counts with a more general reference probability distribution. The general approach is that a nonoccurring term should be possible in a query, but its probability should

---

[4] In the context of probability theory, (re)normalization refers to summing numbers that cover an event space and dividing them through by their sum, so that the result is a probability distribution, which sums to 1. This is distinct from both the concept of term normalization in Chapter 2 and the concept of length normalization in Chapter 6, which is done with a L_2 norm.

be somewhat close to but no more likely than would be expected by chance from the whole collection. That is, if $\text{tf}_{t,d} = 0$ then

$$\hat{P}(t|M_d) \leq \text{cf}_t / T$$

where cf_t is the raw count of the term in the collection, and T is the raw size (number of tokens) of the entire collection. A simple idea that works well in practice is to use a mixture between a document-specific multinomial distribution and a multinomial distribution estimated from the entire collection:

(12.10) $$\hat{P}(t|d) = \lambda \hat{P}_{\text{mle}}(t|M_d) + (1 - \lambda) \hat{P}_{\text{mle}}(t|M_c)$$

where $0 < \lambda < 1$ and M_c is a language model built from the entire document collection. This mixes the probability from the document with the general LINEAR INTER- collection frequency of the word. Such a model is referred to as a *linear inter-* POLATION *polation* LM.[5] Correctly setting λ is important to the good performance of this model.

An alternative is to use an LM built from the whole collection as a prior BAYESIAN distribution in a *Bayesian updating process* (rather than a uniform distribution, SMOOTHING as we saw in Section 11.3.2). We then get the following equation:

(12.11) $$\hat{P}(t|d) = \frac{\text{tf}_{t,d} + \alpha \hat{P}(t|M_c)}{L_d + \alpha}.$$

Both of these smoothing methods have been shown to perform well in IR experiments; we stick with the linear interpolation smoothing method for the rest of this section. Although different in detail, they are both conceptually similar; in both cases, the probability estimate for a word present in the document combines a discounted MLE and a fraction of the estimate of its prevalence in the whole collection, whereas for words not present in a document, the estimate is just a fraction of the estimate of the prevalence of the word in the whole collection.

The role of smoothing in LMs for IR is not simply or principally to avoid estimation problems. This was not clear when the models were first proposed, but it is now understood that smoothing is essential to the good properties of the models. The reason for this is explored in Exercise 12.8. The extent of smoothing in these two models is controlled by the λ and α parameters: A small value of λ or a large value of α means more smoothing. This parameter can be tuned to optimize performance using a line search (or, for the linear interpolation model, by other methods, such as the expectation maximization algorithm; see Section 16.5, page 338). The value need not be a constant. One approach is to make the value a function of the query size. This is useful because a small amount of smoothing (a "conjunctive-like" search) is more

---

[5] It is also referred to as *Jelinek-Mercer smoothing*.

suitable for short queries, whereas a lot of smoothing is more suitable for long queries.

To summarize, the retrieval ranking for a query q under the basic LM for IR we have been considering is given by:

$$(12.12) \qquad P(d|q) \propto P(d) \prod_{t \in q} ((1-\lambda)P(t|M_c) + \lambda P(t|M_d)).$$

This equation captures the probability that the document that the user had in mind was in fact d.

Example 12.3: Suppose the document collection contains two documents:

- d_1: Xyzzy reports a profit but revenue is down
- d_2: Quorus narrows quarter loss but revenue decreases further

The model will be MLE unigram models from the documents and collection, mixed with $\lambda = 1/2$.

Suppose the query is *revenue down*. Then:

$$
\begin{aligned}
(12.13) \qquad P(q|d_1) &= [(1/8 + 2/16)/2] \times [(1/8 + 1/16)/2] \\
&= 1/8 \times 3/32 = 3/256 \\
P(q|d_2) &= [(1/8 + 2/16)/2] \times [(0/8 + 1/16)/2] \\
&= 1/8 \times 1/32 = 1/256
\end{aligned}
$$

So, the ranking is $d_1 > d_2$.

12.2.3 Ponte and Croft's experiments

Ponte and Croft (1998) present the first experiments on the language modeling approach to IR. Their basic approach is the model that we have presented until now. However, we have presented an approach where the LM is a mixture of two multinomials, much as in (Miller et al. 1999; Hiemstra 2000) rather than Ponte and Croft's multivariate Bernoulli model. The use of multinomials has been standard in most subsequent work in the LM approach and experimental results in IR, as well as evidence from text classification which we consider in Section 13.3 (page 243), suggests that it is superior. Ponte and Croft argued strongly for the effectiveness of the term weights that come from the language modeling approach over traditional tf–idf weights. We present a subset of their results in Figure 12.4 where they compare tf–idf to language modeling by evaluating TREC topics 202 through 250 over TREC disks 2 and 3. The queries are sentence-length natural language queries. The LM approach yields significantly better results than their baseline tf-idf–based term weighting approach. And, indeed, the gains shown here have been extended in subsequent work.

	precision			
Rec.	tf-idf	LM	%chg	
0.0	0.7439	0.7590	+2.0	
0.1	0.4521	0.4910	+8.6	
0.2	0.3514	0.4045	+15.1	*
0.3	0.2761	0.3342	+21.0	*
0.4	0.2093	0.2572	+22.9	*
0.5	0.1558	0.2061	+32.3	*
0.6	0.1024	0.1405	+37.1	*
0.7	0.0451	0.0760	+68.7	*
0.8	0.0160	0.0432	+169.6	*
0.9	0.0033	0.0063	+89.3	
1.0	0.0028	0.0050	+76.9	
Ave	0.1868	0.2233	+19.55	*

Figure 12.4 Results of a comparison of tf–idf with LM term weighting by Ponte and Croft (1998). The version of tf–idf from the INQUERY IR system includes length normalization of tf. The table gives an evaluation according to eleven-point average precision with significance marked with a * according to a Wilcoxon signed-rank test. The LM approach always does better in these experiments, but note that where the approach shows significant gains is at higher levels of recall.

?

Exercise 12.6 [⋆] Consider making a LM from the following training text:

the martian has landed on the latin pop sensation ricky martin

a. Under a MLE-estimated unigram probability model, what are $P(\text{the})$ and $P(\text{martian})$?

b. Under a MLE-estimated bigram model, what are $P(\text{sensation}|\text{pop})$ and $P(\text{pop}|\text{the})$?

Exercise 12.7 [⋆⋆] Suppose we have a collection that consists of the four documents given in the below table.

docID	document text
1	click go the shears boys click click click
2	click click
3	metal here
4	metal shears click here

Build a query likelihood LM for this document collection. Assume a mixture model between the documents and the collection, with both weighted at 0.5. MLE is used to estimate both as unigram models. Work out the model probabilities of the queries click, shears, and hence click shears for each document, and use those probabilities to rank the documents returned by each query. Fill in these probabilities in the below table:

query	doc 1	doc 2	doc 3	doc 4
click				
shears				
click shears				

What is the final ranking of the documents for the query click shears?

Exercise 12.8 [★★] Using the calculations in Exercise 12.7 as inspiration or as examples where appropriate, write one sentence each describing the treatment that the model in Equation (12.10) gives to each of the following quantities. Include whether it is present in the model or not and whether the effect is raw or scaled.
a. Term frequency in a document
b. Collection frequency of a term
c. Document frequency of a term
d. Length normalization of a term

Exercise 12.9 [★★] In the mixture model approach to the query likelihood model (Equation (12.12)), the probability estimate of a term is based on the term frequency of a word in a document, and the collection frequency of the word. Doing this certainly guarantees that each term of a query (in the vocabulary) has a nonzero chance of being generated by each document. But it has a more subtle but important effect of implementing a form of term weighting, related to what we saw in Chapter 6. Explain how this works. In particular, include in your answer a concrete numeric example showing this term weighting at work.

12.3 Language modeling versus other approaches in information retrieval

The LM approach provides a novel way of looking at the problem of text retrieval, which links it with a lot of recent work in speech and language processing. As Ponte and Croft (1998) emphasize, the LM approach to IR provides a different approach to scoring matches between queries and documents, and the hope is that the probabilistic language modeling foundation improves the weights that are used, and hence the performance of the model. The major issue is estimation of the document model, such as choices of how to smooth it effectively. The model has achieved very good retrieval results. Compared with other probabilistic approaches, such as the BIM from Chapter 11, the main difference initially appears to be that the LM approach does away with explicitly modeling relevance (whereas this is the central variable evaluated in the BIM approach). But this may not be the correct way to think about things, as some of the papers in Section 12.5 further discuss. The LM approach assumes that documents and expressions of information needs are objects of the same type, and assesses their match by importing the tools and methods of language modeling from speech and natural language processing. The resulting model is mathematically precise, conceptually simple, computationally tractable, and intuitively appealing. This seems similar to the situation with XML retrieval (Chapter 10); there, the approaches that assume queries and documents are objects of the same type are also among the most successful.

On the other hand, like all IR models, you can also raise objections to the model. The assumption of equivalence between document and information need representation is unrealistic. Current LM approaches use very simple models of language, usually unigram models. Without an explicit notion of relevance, relevance feedback is difficult to integrate into the model, as are user preferences. It also seems necessary to move beyond a unigram model to accommodate notions of phrase or passage matching or Boolean retrieval operators. Subsequent work in the LM approach has looked at addressing some of these concerns, including putting relevance back into the model and allowing a language mismatch between the query language and the document language.

The model has significant relations to traditional tf–idf models. Term frequency is directly represented in tf–idf models, and much recent work has recognized the importance of document length normalization. The effect of doing a mixture of document generation probability with collection generation probability is a little like idf; terms rare in the general collection but common in some documents will have a greater influence on the ranking of documents. In most concrete realizations, the models share treating terms as if they were independent. On the other hand, the intuitions are probabilistic rather than geometric, the mathematical models are more principled rather than heuristic, and the details of how statistics like term frequency and document length are used differ. If you are concerned mainly with performance numbers, recent work has shown the LM approach to be very effective in retrieval experiments, beating tf–idf and BM25 weights. Nevertheless, there is perhaps still insufficient evidence that its performance so greatly exceeds that of a well-tuned traditional vector space retrieval system as to justify changing an existing implementation.

12.4 Extended language modeling approaches

In this section, we briefly mention some of the work that extends the basic LM approach.

There are other ways to think of using the LM idea in IR settings, and many of them have been tried in subsequent work. Rather than looking at the probability of a document language model M_d generating the query, you

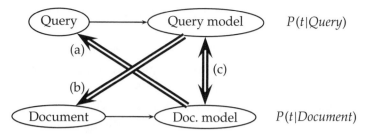

Figure 12.5 Three ways of developing the language modeling approach. (a) Query likelihood. (b) Document likelihood. (c) Model comparison.

can look at the probability of a query language model M_q generating the document. The main reason that doing things in this direction and creating **DOCUMENT** a *document likelihood model* is less appealing is that there is much less text **LIKELIHOOD** available to estimate a LM based on the query text, and so the model will **MODEL** be worse estimated, and will have to depend more on being smoothed with some other language model. On the other hand, it is easy to see how to incorporate relevance feedback into such a model; you can expand the query with terms taken from relevant documents in the usual way and hence update the language model M_q (Zhai and Lafferty 2001a). Indeed, with appropriate modeling choices, this approach leads to the BIM model of Chapter 11. The relevance model of Lavrenko and Croft (2001) is an instance of a document likelihood model, which incorporates pseudo relevance feedback into an LM approach. It achieves very strong empirical results.

Rather than directly generating in either direction, we can make an LM from both the document and query, and then ask how different these two language models are from each other. Lafferty and Zhai (2001) lay out these three ways of thinking about the problem, which we show in Figure 12.5, and develop a general risk minimization approach for document retrieval. For instance, one way to model the risk of returning a document d as relevant to **KULLBACK-** a query q is to use the *Kullback-Leibler (KL) divergence* between their respective **LEIBLER** language models: **DIVERGENCE**

(12.14)

$$R(d;q) = KL(M_d \| M_q) = \sum_{t \in V} P(t|M_q) \log \frac{P(t|M_q)}{P(t|M_d)}.$$

KL divergence is an asymmetric divergence measure originating in information theory, which measures how bad the probability distribution M_q is at modeling M_d (Cover and Thomas 1991; Manning and Schütze 1999). Lafferty and Zhai (2001) present results suggesting that a model comparison approach outperforms both query-likelihood and document-likelihood approaches. One disadvantage of using KL divergence as a ranking function is that scores are not comparable across queries. This does not matter for ad hoc retrieval, but is important in other applications such as topic tracking. Kraaij and Spitters (2003) suggest an alternative proposal which models similarity as a normalized log-likelihood ratio (or, equivalently, as a difference between cross-entropies).

Basic LMs do not address issues of alternate expression, that is, synonymy, or any deviation in use of language between queries and documents. Berger and Lafferty (1999) introduce translation models to bridge this query–document gap. A *translation model* lets you generate query words not in a document by translation to alternate terms with similar meaning. This also provides a basis for performing cross-language IR. We assume that the translation model can be represented by a conditional probability distribution $T(\cdot|\cdot)$ between vocabulary terms. The form of the translation query generation model is then:

TRANSLATION MODEL

(12.15) $$P(q|M_d) = \prod_{t \in q} \sum_{v \in V} P(v|M_d)T(t|v).$$

The term $P(v|M_d)$ is the basic document language model, and the term $T(t|v)$ performs translation. This model is clearly more computationally intensive and we needs to build a translation model. The translation model is usually built using separate resources (such as a traditional thesaurus or bilingual dictionary or a statistical machine translation system's translation dictionary), but can be built using the document collection if there are pieces of text that naturally paraphrase or summarize other pieces of text. Candidate examples are documents and their titles or abstracts, or documents and anchor text pointing to them in a hypertext environment.

Building extended LM approaches remains an active area of research. In general, translation models, relevance feedback models, and model comparison approaches have all been demonstrated to improve performance over the basic query likelihood LM.

12.5 References and further reading

For more details on the basic concepts of probabilistic LMs and techniques for smoothing, see either Manning and Schütze 1999 (1999, Chapter 6) or Jurafsky and Martin (2008, Chapter 4).

The important initial papers that originated the language modeling approach to IR are: (Ponte and Croft 1998; Hiemstra 1998; Berger and Lafferty 1999; Miller et al. 1999). Other relevant papers can be found in the next several years of SIGIR proceedings. (Croft and Lafferty 2003) contains a collection of papers from a workshop on language modeling approaches and Hiemstra and Kraaij (2005) review one prominent thread of work on using LM approaches for TREC tasks. Zhai and Lafferty (2001b) clarify the role of smoothing in LMs for IR and present detailed empirical comparisons of different smoothing methods. Zaragoza et al. (2003) advocate using full Bayesian predictive distributions rather than MAP point estimates, but although they outperform Bayesian smoothing, they fail to outperform a linear interpolation. Zhai and Lafferty (2002) argue that a two-stage smoothing model with first Bayesian smoothing followed by linear interpolation gives a good model of the task, and performs better and more stably than a single form of smoothing. A nice feature of the LM approach is that it provides a convenient and principled way to put various kinds of prior information into the model; Kraaij et al. (2002) demonstrate this by showing the value of link information as a prior in improving web entry page retrieval performance. As briefly discussed in Chapter 16 (page 325), Liu and Croft (2004) show some gains by smoothing a document LM with estimates from a cluster of similar documents; Tao et al. (2006) report larger gains by doing document-similarity based smoothing.

Hiemstra and Kraaij (2005) present TREC results showing a LM approach beating use of BM25 weights. Recent work has achieved some gains by going beyond the unigram model, providing the higher order models are smoothed with lower order models (Gao et al. 2004; Cao et al. 2005), though the gains to date remain modest. Spärck Jones (2004) presents a critical viewpoint on the rationale for the language modeling approach, but Lafferty and Zhai (2003) argue that a unified account can be given of the probabilistic semantics underlying both the LM approach presented in this chapter and the classical probabilistic information retrieval approach of Chapter 11. The Lemur Toolkit (www.lemurproject.org/) provides a flexible open source framework for investigating language modeling approaches to IR.

13 *Text classification and Naive Bayes*

Thus far, this book has mainly discussed the process of *ad hoc retrieval*, where users have transient information needs that they try to address by posing one or more queries to a search engine. However, many users have ongoing information needs. For example, you might need to track developments in *multicore computer chips*. One way of doing this is to issue the query multicore AND computer AND chip against an index of recent newswire articles each morning. In this and the following two chapters we examine the question: How can this repetitive task be automated? To this end, many systems support *standing queries*. A standing query is like any other query except that it is periodically executed on a collection to which new documents are incrementally added over time.

STANDING
QUERY

If your standing query is just multicore AND computer AND chip, you will tend to miss many relevant new articles which use other terms such as *multicore processors*. To achieve good recall, standing queries thus have to be refined over time and can gradually become quite complex. In this example, using a Boolean search engine with stemming, you might end up with a query like (multicore OR multi-core) AND (chip OR processor OR microprocessor).

To capture the generality and scope of the problem space to which standing queries belong, we now introduce the general notion of a *classification* problem. Given a set of *classes*, we seek to determine which class(es) a given object belongs to. In the example, the standing query serves to divide new newswire articles into the two classes: documents about multicore computer chips and documents not about multicore computer chips. We refer to this as *two-class classification*. Classification using standing queries is also called *routing* or *filtering* and will be discussed further in Section 15.3.1 (page 308).

CLASSIFICATION

ROUTING
FILTERING

A class need not be as narrowly focused as the standing query *multicore computer chips*. Often, a class is a more general subject area like *China* or *coffee*. Such more general classes are usually referred to as *topics*, and the classification task is then called *text classification*, *text categorization*, *topic classification*, or *topic spotting*. An example for *China* appears in Figure 13.1. Standing

TEXT
CLASSIFICATION

queries and topics differ in their degree of specificity, but the methods for solving routing, filtering, and text classification are essentially the same. We therefore include routing and filtering under the rubric of text classification in this and the following chapters.

The notion of classification is very general and has many applications within and beyond information retrieval (IR). For instance, in computer vision, a classifier may be used to divide images into classes such as *landscape*, *portrait*, and *neither*. We focus here on examples from information retrieval such as:

- Several of the preprocessing steps necessary for indexing as discussed in Chapter 2: detecting a document's encoding (ASCII, Unicode UTF-8 etc; page 18); word segmentation (Is the white space between two letters a word boundary or not? page 24); truecasing (page 28); and identifying the language of a document (page 43).
- The automatic detection of spam pages (which then are not included in the search engine index).
- The automatic detection of sexually explicit content (which is included in search results only if the user turns an option such as SafeSearch off).

SENTIMENT
DETECTION
- *Sentiment detection* or the automatic classification of a movie or product review as positive or negative. An example application is a user searching for negative reviews before buying a camera to make sure it has no undesirable features or quality problems.

EMAIL
SORTING
- Personal *email sorting*. A user may have folders like *talk announcements*, *electronic bills*, *email from family and friends*, and so on, and may want a classifier to classify each incoming email and automatically move it to the appropriate folder. It is easier to find messages in sorted folders than in a very large inbox. The most common case of this application is a spam folder that holds all suspected spam messages.

VERTICAL
SEARCH
ENGINE
- Topic-specific or *vertical* search. *Vertical search engines* restrict searches to a particular topic. For example, the query computer science on a vertical search engine for the topic *China* will return a list of Chinese computer science departments with higher precision and recall than the query computer science China on a general purpose search engine. This is because the vertical search engine does not include web pages in its index that contain the term china in a different sense (e.g., referring to a hard white ceramic), but does include relevant pages even if they do not explicitly mention the term China.
- Finally, the ranking function in ad hoc information retrieval can also be based on a document classifier as we will explain in Section 15.4 (page 314).

This list shows the general importance of classification in IR. Most retrieval systems today contain multiple components that use some form of classifier.

The classification task we will use as an example in this book is text classification.

A computer is not essential for classification. Many classification tasks have traditionally been solved manually. Books in a library are assigned Library of Congress categories by a librarian. But manual classification is expensive to scale. The *multicore computer chips* example illustrates one alternative approach: classification by the use of standing queries – which can be thought of as *rules* – most commonly written by hand. As in our example (multicore OR multi-core) AND (chip OR processor OR microprocessor), rules are sometimes equivalent to Boolean expressions.

RULES IN TEXT
CLASSIFICATION

A rule captures a certain combination of keywords that indicates a class. Hand-coded rules have good scaling properties, but creating and maintaining them over time is labor intensive. A technically skilled person (e.g., a domain expert who is good at writing regular expressions) can create rule sets that will rival or exceed the accuracy of the automatically generated classifiers we will discuss shortly; however, it can be hard to find someone with this specialized skill.

Apart from manual classification and hand-crafted rules, there is a third approach to text classification, namely, machine learning-based text classification. It is the approach that we focus on in the next several chapters. In machine learning, the set of rules or, more generally, the decision criterion of the text classifier, is learned automatically from training data. This approach is also called *statistical text classification* if the learning method is statistical. In statistical text classification, we require a number of good example documents (or training documents) for each class. The need for manual classification is not eliminated because the training documents come from a person who has labeled them – where *labeling* refers to the process of annotating each document with its class. But labeling is arguably an easier task than writing rules. Almost anybody can look at a document and decide whether or not it is related to China. Sometimes such labeling is already implicitly part of an existing workflow. For instance, you may go through the news articles returned by a standing query each morning and give relevance feedback (cf. Chapter 9) by moving the relevant articles to a special folder like *multicore-processors*.

STATISTICAL
TEXT
CLASSIFICATION

LABELING

We begin this chapter with a general introduction to the text classification problem including a formal definition (Section 13.1); we then cover Naive Bayes, a particularly simple and effective classification method (Sections 13.2–13.4). All of the classification algorithms we study represent documents in high-dimensional spaces. To improve the efficiency of these algorithms, it is generally desirable to reduce the dimensionality of these spaces; to this end, a technique known as *feature selection* is commonly applied in text classification as discussed in Section 13.5. Section 13.6 covers evaluation of text classification. In the following chapters, Chapters 14 and 15, we look at two other families of classification methods, vector space classifiers and support vector machines.

13.1 The text classification problem

In text classification, we are given a description $d \in \mathbb{X}$ of a document, where
DOCUMENT $\mathbb{X}$ is the *document space*; and a fixed set of *classes* $\mathbb{C} = \{c_1, c_2, \ldots, c_J\}$. Classes
SPACE are also called *categories* or *labels*. Typically, the document space $\mathbb{X}$ is some
CLASS type of high-dimensional space, and the classes are human defined for the
needs of an application, as in the examples *China* and *documents that talk about*
TRAINING SET *multicore computer chips* above. We are given a *training set* $\mathbb{D}$ of labeled documents $\langle d, c \rangle$, where $\langle d, c \rangle \in \mathbb{X} \times \mathbb{C}$. For example:

$$\langle d, c \rangle = \langle \text{Beijing joins the World Trade Organization}, \textit{China} \rangle$$

for the one-sentence document *Beijing joins the World Trade Organization* and
the class (or label) *China*.

LEARNING   Using a *learning method* or *learning algorithm*, we then wish to learn a clas-
METHOD sifier or *classification function* γ that maps documents to classes:
CLASSIFIER
(13.1) $\gamma : \mathbb{X} \to \mathbb{C}$

SUPERVISED   This type of learning is called *supervised learning* because a supervisor (the
LEARNING human who defines the classes and labels training documents) serves as a
teacher directing the learning process. We denote the supervised learning
method by Γ and write $\Gamma(\mathbb{D}) = \gamma$. The learning method Γ takes the training
set $\mathbb{D}$ as input and returns the learned classification function γ.

Most names for learning methods Γ are also used for classifiers γ. We talk
about the Naive Bayes (NB) *learning method* Γ when we say that "Naive Bayes
is robust," meaning that it can be applied to many different learning problems and is unlikely to produce classifiers that fail catastrophically. But when
we say that "Naive Bayes had an error rate of 20%," we are describing an experiment in which a particular NB *classifier* γ (which was produced by the
NB learning method) had a 20% error rate in an application.

Figure 13.1 shows an example of text classification from the Reuters-RCV1
collection, introduced in Section 4.2, page 63. There are six classes (*UK, China,*
..., *sports*), each with three training documents. We show a few mnemonic
words for each document's content. The training set provides some typical
examples for each class, so that we can learn the classification function γ.
TEST SET Once we have learned γ, we can apply it to the *test set* (or *test data*), for example, the new document *first private Chinese airline* whose class is unknown.
In Figure 13.1, the classification function assigns the new document to class
$\gamma(d') = China$, which is the correct assignment.

The classes in text classification often have some interesting structure
such as the hierarchy in Figure 13.1. There are two instances each of region

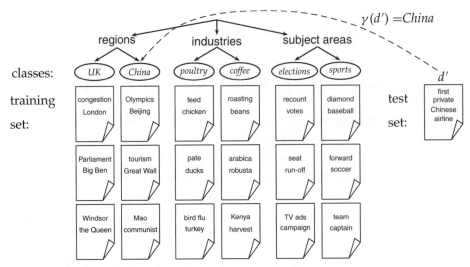

Figure 13.1 Classes, training set, and test set in text classification.

categories, industry categories, and subject area categories. A hierarchy can be an important aid in solving a classification problem; see Section 15.3.2 for further discussion. Until then, we will make the assumption in the text classification chapters that the classes form a set with no subset relationships between them.

Definition (13.1) stipulates that a document is a member of exactly one class. This is not the most appropriate model for the hierarchy in Figure 13.1. For instance, a document about the 2008 Olympics should be a member of two classes: the *China* class and the *sports* class. This type of classification problem is referred to as an *any-of* problem and we will return to it in Section 14.5 (page 281). For the time being, we only consider *one-of* problems where a document is a member of exactly one class.

Our goal in text classification is high accuracy on test data or *new data* – for example, the newswire articles that we will encounter tomorrow morning in the multicore chip example. It is easy to achieve high accuracy on the training set (e.g., we can simply memorize the labels). But high accuracy on the training set in general does not mean that the classifier will work well on new data in an application. When we use the training set to learn a classifier for test data, we make the assumption that training data and test data are similar or from *the same distribution*. We defer a precise definition of this notion to Section 14.6 (page 284).

13.2 Naive Bayes text classification

MULTINOMIAL   The first supervised learning method we introduce is the *multinomial*
NAIVE BAYES   *Naive Bayes* or *multinomial NB* model, a probabilistic learning method. The

probability of a document d being in class c is computed as

(13.2)
$$P(c|d) \propto P(c) \prod_{1 \le k \le n_d} P(t_k|c)$$

where $P(t_k|c)$ is the conditional probability of term t_k occurring in a document of class c.[1] We interpret $P(t_k|c)$ as a measure of how much evidence t_k contributes that c is the correct class. $P(c)$ is the prior probability of a document occurring in class c. If a document's terms do not provide clear evidence for one class versus another, we choose the one that has a higher prior probability. $\langle t_1, t_2, \ldots, t_{n_d} \rangle$ are the tokens in d that are part of the vocabulary we use for classification and n_d is the number of such tokens in d. For example, $\langle t_1, t_2, \ldots, t_{n_d} \rangle$ for the one-sentence document *Beijing and Taipei join the WTO* might be $\langle$Beijing, Taipei, join, WTO$\rangle$, with $n_d = 4$, if we treat the terms *and* and *the* as stop words.

In text classification, our goal is to find the *best* class for the document. The MAXIMUM A best class in NB classification is the most likely or *maximum a posteriori* (MAP) POSTERIORI class c_{map}:
CLASS

(13.3)
$$c_{\text{map}} = \arg\max_{c \in \mathbb{C}} \hat{P}(c|d) = \arg\max_{c \in \mathbb{C}} \hat{P}(c) \prod_{1 \le k \le n_d} \hat{P}(t_k|c).$$

We write $\hat{P}$ for P because we do not know the true values of the parameters $P(c)$ and $P(t_k|c)$, but estimate them from the training set as we will see in a moment.

In Equation (13.3), many conditional probabilities are multiplied, one for each position $1 \le k \le n_d$. This can result in a floating point underflow. It is therefore better to perform the computation by adding logarithms of probabilities instead of multiplying probabilities. The class with the highest log probability score is still the most probable; $\log(xy) = \log(x) + \log(y)$ and the logarithm function is monotonic. Hence, the maximization that is actually done in most implementations of NB is:

(13.4)
$$c_{\text{map}} = \arg\max_{c \in \mathbb{C}} [\log \hat{P}(c) + \sum_{1 \le k \le n_d} \log \hat{P}(t_k|c)].$$

Equation (13.4) has a simple interpretation. Each conditional parameter $\log \hat{P}(t_k|c)$ is a weight that indicates how good an indicator t_k is for c. Similarly, the prior $\log \hat{P}(c)$ is a weight that indicates the relative frequency of c. More frequent classes are more likely to be the correct class than infrequent classes. The sum of log prior and term weights is then a measure of how much evidence there is for the document being in the class, and Equation (13.4) selects the class for which we have the most evidence.

We will initially work with this intuitive interpretation of the multinomial NB model and defer a formal derivation to Section 13.4.

---

[1] We will explain in the next section why $P(c|d)$ is proportional to ($\propto$), not equal to the quantity on the right.

How do we estimate the parameters $\hat{P}(c)$ and $\hat{P}(t_k|c)$? We first try the maximum likelihood estimate (MLE; Section 11.3.2, page 207), which is simply the relative frequency and corresponds to the most likely value of each parameter given the training data. For the priors this estimate is:

$$(13.5) \qquad \hat{P}(c) = \frac{N_c}{N},$$

where N_c is the number of documents in class c and N is the total number of documents.

We estimate the conditional probability $\hat{P}(t|c)$ as the relative frequency of term t in documents belonging to class c:

$$(13.6) \qquad \hat{P}(t|c) = \frac{T_{ct}}{\sum_{t' \in V} T_{ct'}},$$

where T_{ct} is the number of occurrences of t in training documents from class c, including multiple occurrences of a term in a document. We have made the *positional independence assumption* here, which we will discuss in more detail in the next section: T_{ct} is a count of occurrences in all positions k in the documents in the training set. Thus, we do not compute different estimates for different positions and, for example, if a word occurs twice in a document, in positions k_1 and k_2, then $\hat{P}(t_{k_1}|c) = \hat{P}(t_{k_2}|c)$.

The problem with the MLE estimate is that it is zero for a term–class combination that did not occur in the training data. If the term WTO in the training data only occurred in *China* documents, then the MLE estimates for the other classes, for example *UK*, will be zero:

$$\hat{P}(\text{WTO}|UK) = 0.$$

Now, the one-sentence document *Britain is a member of the WTO* will get a conditional probability of zero for *UK* because we are multiplying the conditional probabilities for all terms in Equation (13.2). Clearly, the model should assign a high probability to the *UK* class because the term Britain occurs. The problem is that the zero probability for WTO cannot be "conditioned away," no matter how strong the evidence for the class *UK* from other features. The SPARSENESS estimate is 0 because of *sparseness*: The training data are never large enough to represent the frequency of rare events adequately, for example, the frequency of WTO occurring in *UK* documents.

ADD-ONE   To eliminate zeros, we use *add-one* or *Laplace smoothing*, which simply adds SMOOTHING one to each count (cf. Section 11.3.2):

$$(13.7) \qquad \hat{P}(t|c) = \frac{T_{ct} + 1}{\sum_{t' \in V}(T_{ct'} + 1)} = \frac{T_{ct} + 1}{(\sum_{t' \in V} T_{ct'}) + B},$$

where $B = |V|$ is the number of terms in the vocabulary. Add-one smoothing can be interpreted as a uniform prior (each term occurs once for each class) that is then updated as evidence from the training data comes in. Note that this is a prior probability for the occurrence of a *term* as opposed to the prior

TRAINMULTINOMIALNB($\mathbb{C}$, $\mathbb{D}$)
1   $V \leftarrow$ EXTRACTVOCABULARY($\mathbb{D}$)
2   $N \leftarrow$ COUNTDOCS($\mathbb{D}$)
3   **for each** $c \in \mathbb{C}$
4   **do** $N_c \leftarrow$ COUNTDOCSINCLASS($\mathbb{D}$, c)
5       $prior[c] \leftarrow N_c/N$
6       $text_c \leftarrow$ CONCATENATETEXTOFALLDOCSINCLASS($\mathbb{D}$, c)
7   **for each** $t \in V$
8   **do** $T_{ct} \leftarrow$ COUNTTOKENSOFTERM($text_c$, t)
9   **for each** $t \in V$
10   **do** $condprob[t][c] \leftarrow \frac{T_{ct}+1}{\sum_{t'}(T_{ct'}+1)}$
11 **return** V, $prior$, $condprob$

APPLYMULTINOMIALNB($\mathbb{C}$, V, $prior$, $condprob$, d)
1   $W \leftarrow$ EXTRACTTOKENSFROMDOC(V, d)
2   **for each** $c \in \mathbb{C}$
3   **do** $score[c] \leftarrow \log prior[c]$
4   **for each** $t \in W$
5   **do** $score[c] += \log condprob[t][c]$
6   **return** $\arg\max_{c \in \mathbb{C}} score[c]$

Figure 13.2 Naive Bayes algorithm (multinomial model): Training and testing.

probability of a *class* which we estimate in Equation (13.5) on the document level.

We have now introduced all the elements we need for training and applying an NB classifier. The complete algorithm is described in Figure 13.2.

Example 13.1: For the example in Table 13.1, the multinomial parameters we need to classify the test document are the priors $\hat{P}(c) = 3/4$ and $\hat{P}(\bar{c}) = 1/4$ and the following conditional probabilities:

$$\hat{P}(\text{Chinese}|c) = (5+1)/(8+6) = 6/14 = 3/7$$
$$\hat{P}(\text{Tokyo}|c) = \hat{P}(\text{Japan}|c) = (0+1)/(8+6) = 1/14$$
$$\hat{P}(\text{Chinese}|\bar{c}) = (1+1)/(3+6) = 2/9$$
$$\hat{P}(\text{Tokyo}|\bar{c}) = \hat{P}(\text{Japan}|\bar{c}) = (1+1)/(3+6) = 2/9$$

Table 13.1 Data for parameter estimation examples.

	docID	words in document	in $c = China$?
training set	1	Chinese Beijing Chinese	yes
	2	Chinese Chinese Shanghai	yes
	3	Chinese Macao	yes
	4	Tokyo Japan Chinese	no
test set	5	Chinese Chinese Chinese Tokyo Japan	?

Table 13.2   Training and test times for NB.

mode	time complexity
training	$\Theta(\lvert\mathbb{D}\rvert L_{\mathrm{ave}} + \lvert\mathbb{C}\rvert\lvert V\rvert)$
testing	$\Theta(L_{\mathrm{a}} + \lvert\mathbb{C}\rvert M_{\mathrm{a}}) = \Theta(\lvert\mathbb{C}\rvert M_{\mathrm{a}})$

The denominators are $(8+6)$ and $(3+6)$ because the lengths of $text_c$ and $text_{\bar{c}}$ are 8 and 3, respectively, and because the constant B in Equation (13.7) is 6 as the vocabulary consists of six terms. We then get:

$$\hat{P}(c\lvert d_5) \propto 3/4 \cdot (3/7)^3 \cdot 1/14 \cdot 1/14 \approx 0.0003.$$
$$\hat{P}(\bar{c}\lvert d_5) \propto 1/4 \cdot (2/9)^3 \cdot 2/9 \cdot 2/9 \approx 0.0001.$$

Thus, the classifier assigns the test document to $c = China$. The reason for this classification decision is that the three occurrences of the positive indicator Chinese in d_5 outweigh the occurrences of the two negative indicators Japan and Tokyo.

What is the time complexity of NB? The complexity of computing the parameters is $\Theta(\lvert\mathbb{C}\rvert\lvert V\rvert)$ because the set of parameters consists of $\lvert\mathbb{C}\rvert\lvert V\rvert$ conditional probabilities and $\lvert\mathbb{C}\rvert$ priors. The preprocessing necessary for computing the parameters (extracting the vocabulary, counting terms, etc.) can be done in one pass through the training data. The time complexity of this component is therefore $\Theta(\lvert\mathbb{D}\rvert L_{\mathrm{ave}})$ where $\lvert\mathbb{D}\rvert$ is the number of documents and L_{ave} is the average length of a document.

We use $\Theta(\lvert\mathbb{D}\rvert L_{\mathrm{ave}})$ as a notation for $\Theta(T)$ here, where T is the length of the training collection. This is nonstandard; $\Theta(.)$ is not defined for an average. We prefer expressing the time complexity in terms of $\mathbb{D}$ and L_{ave} because these are the primary statistics used to characterize training collections.

The time complexity of APPLYMULTINOMIALNB in Figure 13.2 is $\Theta(\lvert\mathbb{C}\rvert L_{\mathrm{a}})$. L_{a} and M_{a} are the numbers of tokens and types, respectively, in the test document. APPLYMULTINOMIALNB can be modified to be $\Theta(L_{\mathrm{a}} + \lvert\mathbb{C}\rvert M_{\mathrm{a}})$ (Exercise 13.8). Finally, assuming that the length of test documents is bounded, $\Theta(L_{\mathrm{a}} + \lvert\mathbb{C}\rvert M_{\mathrm{a}}) = \Theta(\lvert\mathbb{C}\rvert M_{\mathrm{a}})$ because $L_{\mathrm{a}} < b\lvert\mathbb{C}\rvert M_{\mathrm{a}}$ for a fixed constant b.[2]

Table 13.2 summarizes the time complexities. In general, we have $\lvert\mathbb{C}\rvert\lvert V\rvert < \lvert\mathbb{D}\rvert L_{\mathrm{ave}}$, so both training and testing complexity are linear in the time it takes to scan the data. Because we have to look at the data at least once, NB can be said to have optimal time complexity. Its efficiency is one reason why NB is a popular text classification method.

13.2.1 Relation to multinomial unigram language model

The multinomial NB model is formally identical to the multinomial unigram language model (Section 12.2.1, page 223). In particular, Equation (13.2) is

---

[2] Our assumption here is that the length of test documents is bounded. L_{a} would exceed $b\lvert\mathbb{C}\rvert M_{\mathrm{a}}$ for extremely long test documents.

a special case of Equation (12.12) from page 224, which we repeat here for $\lambda = 1$:

(13.8)
$$P(d|q) \propto P(d) \prod_{t \in q} P(t|M_d).$$

The document d in text classification (Equation (13.2)) takes the role of the query in language modeling (Equation (13.8)) and the classes c in text classification take the role of the documents d in language modeling. We used Equation (13.8) to rank documents according to the probability that they are relevant to the query q. In NB classification, we are usually only interested in the top-ranked class.

We also used MLE estimates in Section 12.2.2 (page 224) and encountered the problem of zero estimates owing to sparse data (page 225); but instead of add-one smoothing, we used a mixture of two distributions to address the problem there. Add-one smoothing is closely related to add-$\frac{1}{2}$ smoothing in Section 11.3.4 (page 209).

? Exercise 13.1 Why is $|\mathbb{C}||V| < |\mathbb{D}|L_{\text{ave}}$ in Table 13.2 expected to hold for most text collections?

13.3 The Bernoulli model

There are two different ways we can set up an NB classifier. The model we introduced in the previous section is the multinomial model. It generates one term from the vocabulary in each position of the document, where we assume a generative model that will be discussed in more detail in Section 13.4 (see also page 218).

BERNOULLI MODEL
An alternative to the multinomial model is the *multivariate Bernoulli model* or *Bernoulli model*. It is equivalent to the binary independence model of Section 11.3 (page 204), which generates an indicator for each term of the vocabulary, either 1 indicating presence of the term in the document or 0 indicating absence. Figure 13.3 presents training and testing algorithms for the Bernoulli model. The Bernoulli model has the same time complexity as the multinomial model.

The different generation models imply different estimation strategies and different classification rules. The Bernoulli model estimates $\hat{P}(t|c)$ as the *fraction of documents* of class c that contain term t (Figure 13.3, TRAINBERNOULLINB, line 8). In contrast, the multinomial model estimates $\hat{P}(t|c)$ as the *fraction of tokens* or *fraction of positions* in documents of class c that contain term t (Equation (13.7)). When classifying a test document, the Bernoulli model uses binary occurrence information, ignoring the number of occurrences, whereas the multinomial model keeps track of multiple occurrences. As a result, the Bernoulli model typically makes many mistakes when classifying long documents. For example, it may assign an entire book to the class *China* because of a single occurrence of the term China.

TRAINBERNOULLINB($\mathbb{C}$, $\mathbb{D}$)
1 $V \leftarrow$ EXTRACTVOCABULARY($\mathbb{D}$)
2 $N \leftarrow$ COUNTDOCS($\mathbb{D}$)
3 **for each** $c \in \mathbb{C}$
4 **do** $N_c \leftarrow$ COUNTDOCSINCLASS($\mathbb{D}$, c)
5      $prior[c] \leftarrow N_c/N$
6   **for each** $t \in V$
7   **do** $N_{ct} \leftarrow$ COUNTDOCSINCLASSCONTAININGTERM($\mathbb{D}$, c, t)
8          $condprob[t][c] \leftarrow (N_{ct} + 1)/(N_c + 2)$
9 **return** V, $prior$, $condprob$

APPLYBERNOULLINB($\mathbb{C}$, V, $prior$, $condprob$, d)
1 $V_d \leftarrow$ EXTRACTTERMSFROMDOC(V, d)
2 **for each** $c \in \mathbb{C}$
3 **do** $score[c] \leftarrow \log prior[c]$
4   **for each** $t \in V$
5   **do if** $t \in V_d$
6   **then** $score[c] += \log condprob[t][c]$
7   **else** $score[c] += \log(1 - condprob[t][c])$
8 **return** $\arg\max_{c \in \mathbb{C}} score[c]$

Figure 13.3 NB algorithm (Bernoulli model): Training and testing. The add-one smoothing in Line 8 (top) is in analogy to Equation (13.7) with $B = 2$.

The models also differ in how nonoccurring terms are used in classification. They do not affect the classification decision in the multinomial model; but in the Bernoulli model the probability of nonoccurrence is factored in when computing $P(c|d)$ (Figure 13.3, APPLYBERNOULLINB, Line 7). This is because only the Bernoulli NB model models absence of terms explicitly.

 Example 13.2: Applying the Bernoulli model to the example in Table 13.1, we have the same estimates for the priors as before: $\hat{P}(c) = 3/4$, $\hat{P}(\bar{c}) = 1/4$. The conditional probabilities are:

$$\hat{P}(\text{Chinese}|c) = (3 + 1)/(3 + 2) = 4/5$$
$$\hat{P}(\text{Japan}|c) = \hat{P}(\text{Tokyo}|c) = (0 + 1)/(3 + 2) = 1/5$$
$$\hat{P}(\text{Beijing}|c) = \hat{P}(\text{Macao}|c) = \hat{P}(\text{Shanghai}|c) = (1 + 1)/(3 + 2) = 2/5$$
$$\hat{P}(\text{Chinese}|\bar{c}) = (1 + 1)/(1 + 2) = 2/3$$
$$\hat{P}(\text{Japan}|\bar{c}) = \hat{P}(\text{Tokyo}|\bar{c}) = (1 + 1)/(1 + 2) = 2/3$$
$$\hat{P}(\text{Beijing}|\bar{c}) = \hat{P}(\text{Macao}|\bar{c}) = \hat{P}(\text{Shanghai}|\bar{c}) = (0 + 1)/(1 + 2) = 1/3$$

The denominators are $(3 + 2)$ and $(1 + 2)$ because there are three documents in c and one document in $\bar{c}$ and because the constant B in Equation (13.7) is 2 – there are two cases to consider for each term, occurrence and nonoccurrence.

The scores of the test document for the two classes are

$$\hat{P}(c|d_5) \propto \hat{P}(c) \cdot \hat{P}(\text{Chinese}|c) \cdot \hat{P}(\text{Japan}|c) \cdot \hat{P}(\text{Tokyo}|c)$$
$$\cdot (1 - \hat{P}(\text{Beijing}|c)) \cdot (1 - \hat{P}(\text{Shanghai}|c)) \cdot (1 - \hat{P}(\text{Macao}|c))$$
$$= 3/4 \cdot 4/5 \cdot 1/5 \cdot 1/5 \cdot (1-2/5) \cdot (1-2/5) \cdot (1-2/5)$$
$$\approx 0.005$$

and, analogously,

$$\hat{P}(\overline{c}|d_5) \propto 1/4 \cdot 2/3 \cdot 2/3 \cdot 2/3 \cdot (1-1/3) \cdot (1-1/3) \cdot (1-1/3)$$
$$\approx 0.022$$

Thus, the classifier assigns the test document to $\overline{c} = \textit{not-China}$. When looking only at binary occurrence and not at term frequency, Japan and Tokyo are indicators for $\overline{c}$ ($2/3 > 1/5$) and the conditional probabilities of Chinese for c and $\overline{c}$ are not different enough ($4/5$ vs. $2/3$) to affect the classification decision.

13.4 Properties of Naive Bayes

To gain a better understanding of the two models and the assumptions they make, let us go back and examine how we derived their classification rules in Chapters 11 and 12. We decide class membership of a document by assigning it to the class with the maximum a posteriori probability (cf. Section 11.3.2, page 207), which we compute as follows:

$$c_{\text{map}} = \arg\max_{c \in \mathbb{C}} P(c|d)$$

(13.9)
$$= \arg\max_{c \in \mathbb{C}} \frac{P(d|c)P(c)}{P(d)}$$

(13.10)
$$= \arg\max_{c \in \mathbb{C}} P(d|c)P(c),$$

where Bayes' rule (Equation (11.4), page 202) is applied in (13.9) and we drop the denominator in the last step because $P(d)$ is the same for all classes and does not affect the argmax.

We can interpret Equation (13.10) as a description of the generative process we assume in Bayesian text classification. To generate a document, we first choose class c with probability $P(c)$ (top nodes in Figures 13.4 and 13.5). The two models differ in the formalization of the second step, the generation of the document given the class, corresponding to the conditional distribution $P(d|c)$:

(13.11)   **Multinomial** $P(d|c) = P(\langle t_1, \ldots, t_k, \ldots, t_{n_d} \rangle|c)$

(13.12)   **Bernoulli** $P(d|c) = P(\langle e_1, \ldots, e_i, \ldots, e_M \rangle|c),$

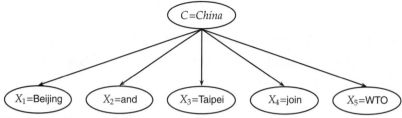

Figure 13.4 The multinomial NB model.

where $\langle t_1, \ldots, t_{n_d} \rangle$ is the sequence of terms as it occurs in d (minus terms that were excluded from the vocabulary) and $\langle e_1, \ldots, e_i, \ldots, e_M \rangle$ is a binary vector of dimensionality M that indicates for each term whether it occurs in d or not.

It should now be clearer why we introduced the document space $\mathbb{X}$ in Equation (13.1) when we defined the classification problem. A critical step in solving a text classification problem is to choose the document representation. $\langle t_1, \ldots, t_{n_d} \rangle$ and $\langle e_1, \ldots, e_M \rangle$ are two different document representations. In the first case, $\mathbb{X}$ is the set of all term sequences (or, more precisely, sequences of term tokens). In the second case, $\mathbb{X}$ is $\{0, 1\}^M$.

We cannot use Equations (13.11) and (13.12) for text classification directly. For the Bernoulli model, we would have to estimate $2^M |\mathbb{C}|$ different parameters, one for each possible combination of M values e_i and a class. The number of parameters in the multinomial case has the same order of magnitude.[3] This being a very large quantity, estimating these parameters reliably is infeasible.

CONDITIONAL
INDEPENDENCE
ASSUMPTION
To reduce the number of parameters, we make the Naive Bayes *conditional independence assumption*. We assume that attribute values are independent of each other given the class:

(13.13) **Multinomial** $\quad P(d|c) = P(\langle t_1, \ldots, t_{n_d} \rangle | c) = \displaystyle\prod_{1 \le k \le n_d} P(X_k = t_k | c)$

(13.14) **Bernoulli** $\quad P(d|c) = P(\langle e_1, \ldots, e_M \rangle | c) = \displaystyle\prod_{1 \le i \le M} P(U_i = e_i | c).$

RANDOM
VARIABLE X
RANDOM
VARIABLE U
We have introduced two random variables here to make the two different generative models explicit. X_k is the random variable for position k in the document and takes as values terms from the vocabulary. $P(X_k = t | c)$ is the probability that in a document of class c the term t will occur in position k. U_i is the random variable for vocabulary term i and takes as values 0 (absence) and 1 (presence). $\hat{P}(U_i = 1 | c)$ is the probability that in a document of class c the term t_i will occur – in any position and possibly multiple times.

We illustrate the conditional independence assumption in Figures 13.4 and 13.5. The class *China* generates values for each of the five term attributes

---

[3] In fact, if the length of documents is not bounded, the number of parameters in the multinomial case is infinite.

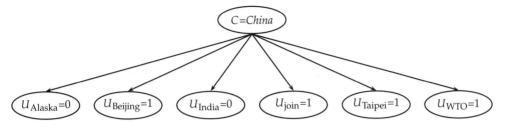

Figure 13.5 The Bernoulli NB model.

(multinomial) or six binary attributes (Bernoulli) with a certain probability, independent of the values of the other attributes. The fact that a document in the class *China* contains the term Taipei does not make it more likely or less likely that it also contains Beijing.

In reality, the conditional independence assumption does not hold for text data. Terms *are* conditionally dependent on each other. But as we will discuss shortly, NB models perform well despite the conditional independence assumption.

Even when assuming conditional independence, we still have too many parameters for the multinomial model if we assume a different probability distribution for each position k in the document. The position of a term in a document by itself does not carry information about the class. Although there is a difference between *China sues France* and *France sues China*, the occurrence of China in position 1 versus position 3 of the document is not useful in NB classification because we look at each term separately. The conditional independence assumption commits us to this way of processing the evidence.

Also, if we assumed different term distributions for each position k, we would have to estimate a different set of parameters for each k. The probability of bean appearing as the first term of a *coffee* document could be different from it appearing as the second term, and so on. This again causes problems in estimation owing to data sparseness.

For these reasons, we make a second independence assumption for the POSITIONAL multinomial model, *positional independence*: The conditional probabilities for INDEPENDENCE a term are the same independent of position in the document.

$$P(X_{k_1} = t|c) = P(X_{k_2} = t|c)$$

for all positions k_1, k_2, terms t and classes c. Thus, we have a single distribution of terms that is valid for all positions k_i and we can use X as its symbol.[4] Positional independence is equivalent to adopting the bag of words model, which we introduced in the context of ad hoc retrieval in Chapter 6 (page 107).

---

[4] Our terminology is nonstandard. The random variable X is a categorical variable, not a multinomial variable, and the corresponding NB model should perhaps be called a *sequence model*. We have chosen to present this sequence model and the multinomial model in Section 13.4.1 as the same model because they are computationally identical.

Table 13.3 Multinomial versus Bernoulli model.

	multinomial model	Bernoulli model
event model	generation of token	generation of document
random variable(s)	$X = t$ iff t occurs at given pos	$U_t = 1$ iff t occurs in doc
document representation	$d = \langle t_1, \ldots, t_k, \ldots, t_{n_d} \rangle, t_k \in V$	$d = \langle e_1, \ldots, e_i, \ldots, e_M \rangle,$ $e_i \in \{0, 1\}$
parameter estimation	$\hat{P}(X = t\|c)$	$\hat{P}(U_i = e\|c)$
decision rule: maximize	$\hat{P}(c) \prod_{1 \leq k \leq n_d} \hat{P}(X = t_k\|c)$	$\hat{P}(c) \prod_{t_i \in V} \hat{P}(U_i = e_i\|c)$
multiple occurrences	taken into account	ignored
length of docs	can handle longer docs	works best for short docs
# features	can handle more	works best with fewer
estimate for term the	$\hat{P}(X = \text{the}\|c) \approx 0.05$	$\hat{P}(U_{\text{the}} = 1\|c) \approx 1.0$

With conditional and positional independence assumptions, we only need to estimate $\Theta(M|\mathbb{C}|)$ parameters $P(t_k|c)$ (multinomial model) or $P(e_i|c)$ (Bernoulli model), one for each term–class combination, rather than a number that is at least exponential in M, the size of the vocabulary. The independence assumptions reduce the number of parameters to be estimated by several orders of magnitude.

To summarize, we generate a document in the multinomial model (Figure 13.4) by first picking a class $C = c$ with $P(c)$ where C is a random variable RANDOM taking values from $\mathbb{C}$ as values. Next we generate term t_k in position k with VARIABLE C $P(X_k = t_k|c)$ for each of the n_d positions of the document. The X_k all have the same distribution over terms for a given c. In the example in Figure 13.4, we show the generation of $\langle t_1, t_2, t_3, t_4, t_5 \rangle = \langle$Beijing, and, Taipei, join, WTO$\rangle$, corresponding to the one-sentence document *Beijing and Taipei join WTO*.

For a completely specified document generation model, we would also have to define a distribution $P(n_d|c)$ over lengths. Without it, the multinomial model is a token generation model rather than a document generation model.

We generate a document in the Bernoulli model (Figure 13.5) by first picking a class $C = c$ with $P(c)$ and then generating a binary indicator e_i for each term t_i of the vocabulary ($1 \leq i \leq M$). In the example in Figure 13.5, we show the generation of $\langle e_1, e_2, e_3, e_4, e_5, e_6 \rangle = \langle 0, 1, 0, 1, 1, 1 \rangle$, corresponding, again, to the one-sentence document *Beijing and Taipei join WTO* where we have assumed that and is a stop word.

We compare the two models in Table 13.3, including estimation equations and decision rules.

Naive Bayes is so called because the independence assumptions we have just made are indeed very naive for a model of natural language. The conditional independence assumption states that features are independent of each other given the class. This is hardly ever true for terms in documents. In many cases, the opposite is true. The pairs hong and kong or london and english in Figure 13.7 are examples of highly dependent terms. In addition, the

Table 13.4 Correct estimation implies accurate prediction, but accurate prediction does not imply correct estimation.

	c_1	c_2	class selected
true probability $P(c\|d)$	0.6	0.4	c_1
$\hat{P}(c)\prod_{1\leq k\leq n_d}\hat{P}(t_k\|c)$ (Equation (13.13))	0.00099	0.00001	
NB estimate $\hat{P}(c\|d)$	0.99	0.01	c_1

multinomial model makes an assumption of positional independence. The Bernoulli model ignores positions in documents altogether because it only cares about absence or presence. This bag-of-words model discards all information that is communicated by the order of words in natural language sentences. How can NB be a good text classifier when its model of natural language is so oversimplified?

The answer is that even though the *probability estimates* of NB are of low quality, its *classification decisions* are surprisingly good. Consider a document d with true probabilities $P(c_1|d) = 0.6$ and $P(c_2|d) = 0.4$ as shown in Table 13.4. Assume that d contains many terms that are positive indicators for c_1 and many terms that are negative indicators for c_2. Thus, when using the multinomial model in Equation (13.13), $\hat{P}(c_1)\prod_{1\leq k\leq n_d}\hat{P}(t_k|c_1)$ will be much larger than $\hat{P}(c_2)\prod_{1\leq k\leq n_d}\hat{P}(t_k|c_2)$ (0.00099 vs. 0.00001 in the table). After division by 0.001 to get well-formed probabilities for $P(c|d)$, we end up with one estimate that is close to 1.0 and one that is close to 0.0. This is common: The winning class in NB classification usually has a much larger probability than the other classes and the estimates diverge very significantly from the true probabilities. But the classification decision is based on which class gets the highest score. It does not matter how accurate the estimates are. Despite the bad estimates, NB estimates a higher probability for c_1 and therefore assigns d to the correct class in Table 13.4. *Correct estimation implies accurate prediction, but accurate prediction does not imply correct estimation.* NB classifiers estimate badly, but often classify well.

Even if it is not the method with the highest accuracy for text, NB has many virtues that make it a strong contender for text classification. It excels if there are many equally important features that jointly contribute to the classification decision. It is also somewhat robust to noise features (as defined in CONCEPT DRIFT the next section) and *concept drift* – the gradual change over time of the concept underlying a class like *US president* from Bill Clinton to George W. Bush (see Section 13.7). Classifiers like kNN (Section 14.3, page 273) can be carefully tuned to idiosyncratic properties of a particular time period. This will then hurt them when documents in the following time period have slightly different properties.

The Bernoulli model is particularly robust with respect to concept drift. We will see in Figure 13.8 that it can have decent performance when using fewer than a dozen terms. The most important indicators for a class are less likely

Table 13.5 A set of documents for which the NB independence assumptions are problematic.

(1)	He moved from London, Ontario, to London, England.
(2)	He moved from London, England, to London, Ontario.
(3)	He moved from England to London, Ontario.

to change. Thus, a model that only relies on these features is more likely to maintain a certain level of accuracy in concept drift.

NB's main strength is its efficiency: Training and classification can be accomplished with one pass over the data. Because it combines efficiency with good accuracy it is often used as a baseline in text classification research. It is often the method of choice if (i) squeezing out a few extra percentage points of accuracy is not worth the trouble in a text classification application, (ii) a very large amount of training data is available and there is more to be gained from training on a lot of data than using a better classifier on a smaller training set, or (iii) if its robustness to concept drift can be exploited.

In this book, we discuss NB as a classifier for text. The independence assumptions do not hold for text. However, it can be shown that NB is an OPTIMAL *optimal classifier* (in the sense of minimal error rate on new data) for data CLASSIFIER where the independence assumptions do hold.

13.4.1 A variant of the multinomial model

An alternative formalization of the multinomial model represents each document d as an M-dimensional vector of counts $\langle \text{tf}_{t_1,d}, \ldots, \text{tf}_{t_M,d} \rangle$ where $\text{tf}_{t_i,d}$ is the term frequency of t_i in d. $P(d|c)$ is then computed as follows (cf. Equation (12.8), page 224);

$$(13.15) \qquad P(d|c) = P(\langle \text{tf}_{t_1,d}, \ldots, \text{tf}_{t_M,d} \rangle | c) \propto \prod_{1 \leq i \leq M} P(X = t_i | c)^{\text{tf}_{t_i,d}}$$

Note that we have omitted the multinomial factor. See Equation (12.8) (page 224).

Equation (13.15) is equivalent to the sequence model in Equation (13.2) as $P(X = t_i|c)^{\text{tf}_{t_i,d}} = 1$ for terms that do not occur in d ($\text{tf}_{t_i,d} = 0$) and a term that occurs $\text{tf}_{t_i,d} \geq 1$ times will contribute $\text{tf}_{t_i,d}$ factors both in Equation (13.2) and in Equation (13.15).

? **Exercise 13.2** [$\star$] Which of the documents in Table 13.5 have identical and different bag of words representations for (i) the Bernoulli model (ii) the multinomial model? If there are differences, describe them.

Exercise 13.3 The rationale for the positional independence assumption is that there is no useful information in the fact that a term occurs in position k of a document. Find exceptions. Consider formulaic documents with a fixed document structure.

SELECTFEATURES($\mathbb{D}, c, k$)
1 $V \leftarrow$ EXTRACTVOCABULARY($\mathbb{D}$)
2 $L \leftarrow []$
3 **for each** $t \in V$
4 **do** $A(t, c) \leftarrow$ COMPUTEFEATUREUTILITY($\mathbb{D}, t, c$)
5   APPEND($L, \langle A(t, c), t \rangle$)
6 **return** FEATURESWITHLARGESTVALUES(L, k)

Figure 13.6 Basic feature selection algorithm for selecting the k best features.

> **Exercise 13.4** Table 13.3 gives Bernoulli and multinomial estimates for the word the. Explain the difference.

13.5 Feature selection

FEATURE *Feature selection* is the process of selecting a subset of the terms occurring in
SELECTION the training set and using only this subset as features in text classification.
Feature selection serves two main purposes. First, it makes training and applying a classifier more efficient by decreasing the size of the effective vocabulary. This is of particular importance for classifiers that, unlike NB, are expensive to train. Second, feature selection often increases classification ac-
NOISE FEATURE curacy by eliminating noise features. A *noise feature* is one that, when added to the document representation, increases the classification error on new data. Suppose a rare term, say arachnocentric, has no information about a class, say *China*, but all instances of arachnocentric happen to occur in *China* documents in our training set. Then the learning method might produce a classifier that misassigns test documents containing arachnocentric to *China*. Such an incorrect generalization from an accidental property of the training
OVERFITTING set is called *overfitting*.

We can view feature selection as a method for replacing a complex classifier (using all features) with a simpler one (using a subset of the features). It may appear counterintuitive at first that a seemingly weaker classifier is advantageous in statistical text classification, but when discussing the bias-variance tradeoff in Section 14.6 (page 284), we will see that weaker models are often preferable when limited training data are available.

The basic feature selection algorithm is shown in Figure 13.6. For a given class c, we compute a utility measure $A(t, c)$ for each term of the vocabulary and select the k terms that have the highest values of $A(t, c)$. All other terms are discarded and not used in classification. We will introduce three different utility measures in this section: mutual information, $A(t, c) = I(U_t; C_c)$; the χ^2 test, $A(t, c) = X^2(t, c)$; and frequency, $A(t, c) = N(t, c)$.

Of the two NB models, the Bernoulli model is particularly sensitive to noise features. A Bernoulli NB classifier requires some form of feature selection or else its accuracy will be low.

This section mainly addresses feature selection for two-class classification tasks like *China* versus *not-China*. Section 13.5.5 briefly discusses optimizations for systems with more than two classes.

13.5.1 Mutual information

MUTUAL
INFORMATION

A common feature selection method is to compute $A(t, c)$ as the expected *mutual information* (MI) of term t and class c.[5] MI measures how much information the presence/absence of a term contributes to making the correct classification decision on c. Formally:

(13.16)
$$I(U;C) = \sum_{e_t \in \{1,0\}} \sum_{e_c \in \{1,0\}} P(U = e_t, C = e_c) \log_2 \frac{P(U = e_t, C = e_c)}{P(U = e_t)P(C = e_c)},$$

where U is a random variable that takes values $e_t = 1$ (the document contains term t) and $e_t = 0$ (the document does not contain t), as defined on page 246, and C is a random variable that takes values $e_c = 1$ (the document is in class c) and $e_c = 0$ (the document is not in class c). We write U_t and C_c if it is not clear from context which term t and class c we are referring to.

For MLEs of the probabilities, Equation (13.16) is equivalent to Equation (13.17):

(13.17)
$$I(U;C) = \frac{N_{11}}{N} \log_2 \frac{NN_{11}}{N_{1.}N_{.1}} + \frac{N_{01}}{N} \log_2 \frac{NN_{01}}{N_{0.}N_{.1}}$$
$$+ \frac{N_{10}}{N} \log_2 \frac{NN_{10}}{N_{1.}N_{.0}} + \frac{N_{00}}{N} \log_2 \frac{NN_{00}}{N_{0.}N_{.0}}$$

where the Ns are counts of documents that have the values of e_t and e_c that are indicated by the two subscripts. For example, N_{10} is the number of documents that contain t ($e_t = 1$) and are not in c ($e_c = 0$). $N_{1.} = N_{10} + N_{11}$ is the number of documents that contain t ($e_t = 1$) and we count documents independent of class membership ($e_c \in \{0, 1\}$). $N = N_{00} + N_{01} + N_{10} + N_{11}$ is the total number of documents. An example of one of the MLE estimates that transform Equation (13.16) into Equation (13.17) is $P(U = 1, C = 1) = N_{11}/N$.

Example 13.3: Consider the class *poultry* and the term export in Reuters-RCV1. The counts of the number of documents with the four possible combinations of indicator values are as follows:

	$e_c = e_{poultry} = 1$	$e_c = e_{poultry} = 0$
$e_t = e_{export} = 1$	$N_{11} = 49$	$N_{10} = 27{,}652$
$e_t = e_{export} = 0$	$N_{01} = 141$	$N_{00} = 774{,}106$

---

[5] Take care not to confuse expected mutual information with *pointwise mutual information*, which is defined as $\log N_{11}/E_{11}$ where N_{11} and E_{11} are defined as in Equation (13.18). The two measures have different properties. See Section 13.7.

After plugging these values into Equation (13.17) we get:

$$I(U;C) = \frac{49}{801,948} \log_2 \frac{801,948 \cdot 49}{(49+27,652)(49+141)}$$

$$+ \frac{141}{801,948} \log_2 \frac{801,948 \cdot 141}{(141+774,106)(49+141)}$$

$$+ \frac{27,652}{801,948} \log_2 \frac{801,948 \cdot 27,652}{(49+27,652)(27,652+774,106)}$$

$$+ \frac{774,106}{801,948} \log_2 \frac{801,948 \cdot 774,106}{(141+774,106)(27,652+774,106)}$$

$$\approx 0.0001105$$

To select k terms $t_1, \ldots, t_k$ for a given class, we use the feature selection algorithm in Figure 13.6: We compute the utility measure as $A(t, c) = I(U_t, C_c)$ and select the k terms with the largest values.

Mutual information measures how much information – in the information-theoretic sense – a term contains about the class. If a term's distribution is the same in the class as it is in the collection as a whole, then $I(U;C) = 0$. MI reaches its maximum value if the term is a perfect indicator for class membership, that is, if the term is present in a document if and only if the document is in the class.

Figure 13.7 shows terms with high mutual information scores for the six classes in Figure 13.1.[6] The selected terms (e.g., london, uk, british for the class *UK*) are of obvious utility for making classification decisions for their respective classes. At the bottom of the list for *UK* we find terms like peripherals and tonight (not shown in the figure) that are clearly not helpful in deciding whether the document is in the class. As you might expect, keeping the informative terms and eliminating the non-informative ones tends to reduce noise and improve the classifier's accuracy.

Such an accuracy increase can be observed in Figure 13.8, which shows F_1 as a function of vocabulary size after feature selection for Reuters-RCV1.[7] Comparing F_1 at 132,776 features (corresponding to selection of all features) and at 10–100 features, we see that MI feature selection increases F_1 by about 0.1 for the multinomial model and by more than 0.2 for the Bernoulli model. For the Bernoulli model, F_1 peaks early, at ten features selected. At that point, the Bernoulli model is better than the multinomial model. When basing a classification decision on only a few features, it is more robust to consider binary occurrence only. For the multinomial model (MI feature selection), the peak occurs later, at 100 features, and its effectiveness recovers somewhat at the end when we use all features. The reason is that the multinomial takes

---

[6] Feature scores were computed on the first 100,000 documents, except for *poultry*, a rare class, for which 800,000 documents were used. We have omitted numbers and other special words from the top ten lists.

[7] We trained the classifiers on the first 100,000 documents and computed F_1 on the next 100,000. The graphs are averages over five classes.

UK	
london	0.1925
uk	0.0755
british	0.0596
stg	0.0555
britain	0.0469
plc	0.0357
england	0.0238
pence	0.0212
pounds	0.0149
english	0.0126

China	
china	0.0997
chinese	0.0523
beijing	0.0444
yuan	0.0344
shanghai	0.0292
hong	0.0198
kong	0.0195
xinhua	0.0155
province	0.0117
taiwan	0.0108

poultry	
poultry	0.0013
meat	0.0008
chicken	0.0006
agriculture	0.0005
avian	0.0004
broiler	0.0003
veterinary	0.0003
birds	0.0003
inspection	0.0003
pathogenic	0.0003

coffee	
coffee	0.0111
bags	0.0042
growers	0.0025
kg	0.0019
colombia	0.0018
brazil	0.0016
export	0.0014
exporters	0.0013
exports	0.0013
crop	0.0012

elections	
election	0.0519
elections	0.0342
polls	0.0339
voters	0.0315
party	0.0303
vote	0.0299
poll	0.0225
candidate	0.0202
campaign	0.0202
democratic	0.0198

sports	
soccer	0.0681
cup	0.0515
match	0.0441
matches	0.0408
played	0.0388
league	0.0386
beat	0.0301
game	0.0299
games	0.0284
team	0.0264

Figure 13.7 Features with high mutual information scores for six Reuters-RCV1 classes.

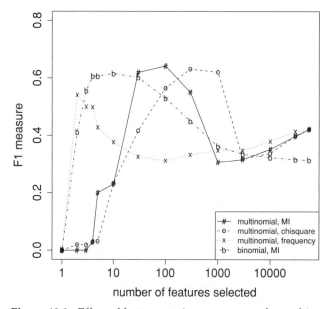

Figure 13.8 Effect of feature set size on accuracy for multinomial and Bernoulli models.

the number of occurrences into account in parameter estimation and classification and therefore better exploits a larger number of features than the Bernoulli model. Regardless of the differences between the two methods, using a carefully selected subset of the features results in better effectiveness than using all features.

13.5.2 χ^2 Feature selection

χ^2 FEATURE
SELECTION

INDEPENDENCE

Another popular feature selection method is χ^2. In statistics, the χ^2 test is applied to test the independence of two events, where two events A and B are defined to be *independent* if $P(AB) = P(A)P(B)$ or, equivalently, $P(A|B) = P(A)$ and $P(B|A) = P(B)$. In feature selection, the two events are occurrence of the term and occurrence of the class. We then rank terms with respect to the following quantity:

(13.18)
$$X^2(\mathbb{D}, t, c) = \sum_{e_t \in \{0,1\}} \sum_{e_c \in \{0,1\}} \frac{(N_{e_t e_c} - E_{e_t e_c})^2}{E_{e_t e_c}}$$

where e_t and e_c are defined as in Equation (13.16). N is the *observed* frequency in $\mathbb{D}$ and E the *expected* frequency. For example, E_{11} is the expected frequency of t and c occurring together in a document assuming that term and class are independent.

Example 13.4: We first compute E_{11} for the data in Example 13.3:

$$E_{11} = N \times P(t) \times P(c) = N \times \frac{N_{11} + N_{10}}{N} \times \frac{N_{11} + N_{01}}{N}$$

$$= N \times \frac{49 + 141}{N} \times \frac{49 + 27652}{N} \approx 6.6$$

where N is the total number of documents as before.

We compute the other $E_{e_t e_c}$ in the same way:

	$e_{poultry} = 1$		$e_{poultry} = 0$	
$e_{export} = 1$	$N_{11} = 49$	$E_{11} \approx 6.6$	$N_{10} = 27{,}652$	$E_{10} \approx 27{,}694.4$
$e_{export} = 0$	$N_{01} = 141$	$E_{01} \approx 183.4$	$N_{00} = 774{,}106$	$E_{00} \approx 774{,}063.6$

Plugging these values into Equation (13.18), we get a X^2 value of 284:

$$X^2(\mathbb{D}, t, c) = \sum_{e_t \in \{0,1\}} \sum_{e_c \in \{0,1\}} \frac{(N_{e_t e_c} - E_{e_t e_c})^2}{E_{e_t e_c}} \approx 284$$

X^2 is a measure of how much expected counts E and observed counts N deviate from each other. A high value of X^2 indicates that the hypothesis of independence, which implies that expected and observed counts are similar, is incorrect. In our example, $X^2 \approx 284 > 10.83$. Based on Table 13.6, we can reject the hypothesis that *poultry* and export are independent with

Table 13.6 Critical values of the χ^2 distribution with one degree of freedom. For example, if the two events are independent, then $P(X^2 > 6.63) < 0.01$. So for $X^2 > 6.63$ the assumption of independence can be rejected with 99% confidence.

p	χ^2 critical value
0.1	2.71
0.05	3.84
0.01	6.63
0.005	7.88
0.001	10.83

only a 0.001 chance of being wrong.[8] Equivalently, we say that the outcome
STATISTICAL $X^2 \approx 284 > 10.83$ is *statistically significant* at the 0.001 level. If the two events
SIGNIFICANCE are dependent, then the occurrence of the term makes the occurrence of the
class more likely (or less likely), so it should be helpful as a feature. This is
the rationale of χ^2 feature selection.

An arithmetically simpler way of computing X^2 is the following:

$$(13.19) \qquad X^2(\mathbb{D}, t, c) = \frac{(N_{11} + N_{10} + N_{01} + N_{00}) \times (N_{11} N_{00} - N_{10} N_{01})^2}{(N_{11} + N_{01}) \times (N_{11} + N_{10}) \times (N_{10} + N_{00}) \times (N_{01} + N_{00})}$$

This is equivalent to Equation (13.18) (Exercise 13.14).

Assessing χ^2 as a feature selection method

From a statistical point of view, χ^2 feature selection is problematic. For a test
with one degree of freedom, the so-called Yates correction should be used
(see Section 13.7), which makes it harder to reach statistical significance.
Also, whenever a statistical test is used multiple times, then the probability of getting at least one error increases. If 1,000 hypotheses are rejected,
each with 0.05 error probability, then $0.05 \times 1000 = 50$ calls of the test will be
wrong on average. However, in text classification it rarely matters whether a
few additional terms are added to the feature set or removed from it. Rather,
the *relative* importance of features is important. As long as χ^2 feature selection only ranks features with respect to their usefulness and is not used to
make statements about statistical dependence or independence of variables,
we need not be overly concerned that it does not adhere strictly to statistical
theory.

---

[8] We can make this inference because, if the two events are independent, then $X^2 \sim \chi^2$, where χ^2 is the χ^2 distribution. See, for example, Rice (2006).

13.5.3 Frequency-based feature selection

A third feature selection method is *frequency-based feature selection*, that is, selecting the terms that are most common in the class. Frequency can be either defined as document frequency (the number of documents in the class c that contain the term t) or as collection frequency (the number of tokens of t that occur in documents in c). Document frequency is more appropriate for the Bernoulli model, collection frequency for the multinomial model.

Frequency-based feature selection selects some frequent terms that have no specific information about the class, for example, the days of the week (Monday, Tuesday, ...), which are frequent across classes in newswire text. When many thousands of features are selected, then frequency-based feature selection often does well. Thus, if somewhat suboptimal accuracy is acceptable, then frequency-based feature selection can be a good alternative to more complex methods. However, Figure 13.8 is a case where frequency-based feature selection performs a lot worse than MI and χ^2 and should not be used.

13.5.4 Feature selection for multiple classifiers

In an operational system with a large number of classifiers, it is desirable to select a single set of features instead of a different one for each classifier. One way of doing this is to compute the X^2 statistic for an $n \times 2$ table where the columns are occurrence and nonoccurrence of the term and each row corresponds to one of the classes. We can then select the k terms with the highest X^2 statistic as before.

More commonly, feature selection statistics are first computed separately for each class on the two-class classification task c versus $\bar{c}$ and then combined. One combination method computes a single figure of merit for each feature, for example, by averaging the values $A(t, c)$ for feature t, and then selects the k features with highest figures of merit. Another frequently used combination method selects the top k/n features for each of n classifiers and then combines these n sets into one global feature set.

Classification accuracy often decreases when selecting k common features for a system with n classifiers as opposed to n different sets of size k. But even if it does, the gain in efficiency owing to a common document representation may be worth the loss in accuracy.

13.5.5 Comparison of feature selection methods

Mutual information and χ^2 represent rather different feature selection methods. The independence of term t and class c can sometimes be rejected with high confidence even if t carries little information about membership of a document in c. This is particularly true for rare terms. If a term occurs once in a large collection and that one occurrence is in the *poultry* class, then this is statistically significant. But a single occurrence is not very informative according to the information-theoretic definition of information. Because its criterion is significance, χ^2 selects more rare terms (which are often less reliable indicators) than mutual information. But the selection criterion of mutual information also does not necessarily select the terms that maximize classification accuracy.

Despite the differences between the two methods, the classification accuracy of feature sets selected with χ^2 and MI does not seem to differ systematically. In most text classification problems, there are a few strong indicators and many weak indicators. As long as all strong indicators and a large number of weak indicators are selected, accuracy is expected to be good. Both methods do this.

Figure 13.8 compares MI and χ^2 feature selection for the multinomial model. Peak effectiveness is virtually the same for both methods. χ^2 reaches this peak later, at 300 features, probably because the rare, but highly significant features it selects initially do not cover all documents in the class. However, features selected later (in the range of 100–300) are of better quality than those selected by MI.

GREEDY   All three methods – MI, χ^2 and frequency based – are *greedy* methods.
FEATURE   They may select features that contribute no incremental information over
SELECTION previously selected features. In Figure 13.7, kong is selected as the seventh term even though it is highly correlated with previously selected hong and therefore redundant. Although such redundancy can negatively impact accuracy, non-greedy methods (see Section 13.7 for references) are rarely used in text classification due to their computational cost.

? **Exercise 13.5** Consider the following frequencies for the class *coffee* for four terms in the first 100,000 documents of Reuters-RCV1:

term	N_{00}	N_{01}	N_{10}	N_{11}
brazil	98,012	102	1835	51
council	96,322	133	3525	20
producers	98,524	119	1118	34
roasted	99,824	143	23	10

Select two of these four terms based on (i) χ^2, (ii) mutual information, (iii) frequency.

13.6 Evaluation of text classification

Historically, the classic Reuters-21578 collection was the main benchmark for text classification evaluation. This is a collection of 21,578 newswire articles, originally collected and labeled by Carnegie Group, Inc. and Reuters,

Table 13.7 The ten largest classes in the Reuters-21578 collection with number of documents in training and test sets.

class	# train	# test	class	# train	# test
earn	2877	1087	*trade*	369	119
acquisitions	1650	179	*interest*	347	131
money-fx	538	179	*ship*	197	89
grain	433	149	*wheat*	212	71
crude	389	189	*corn*	182	56

Ltd. in the course of developing the CONSTRUE text classification system. It is much smaller than and predates the Reuters-RCV1 collection discussed in Chapter 4 (page 63). The articles are assigned classes from a set of 118 topic categories. A document may be assigned several classes or none, but the commonest case is single assignment (documents with at least one class received an average of 1.24 classes). The standard approach to this *any-of* problem (Chapter 14, page 282) is to learn 118 two-class classifiers, one for TWO-CLASS each class, where the *two-class classifier* for class c is the classifier for the two CLASSIFIER classes c and its complement $\bar{c}$.

For each of these classifiers, we can measure recall, precision, and accu-
MODAPTE racy. In recent work, people almost invariably use the *ModApte split*, which
SPLIT includes only documents that were viewed and assessed by a human indexer, and comprises 9,603 training documents and 3,299 test documents. The distribution of documents in classes is very uneven, and some work evaluates systems on only documents in the ten largest classes. They are listed in Table 13.7. A typical document with topics is shown in Figure 13.9.

In Section 13.1, we stated as our goal in text classification the minimization of classification error on test data. Classification error is 1.0 minus classification accuracy, the proportion of correct decisions, a measure we introduced in Section 8.3 (page 143). This measure is appropriate if the percentage of documents in the class is high, perhaps 10% to 20% and higher. But as we discussed in Section 8.3, accuracy is not a good measure for "small" classes because always saying no, a strategy that defeats the purpose of building a classifier, will achieve high accuracy. The always-no classifier is 99% accurate for a class with relative frequency 1%. For small classes, precision, recall and F_1 are better measures.

EFFECTIVENESS We will use *effectiveness* as a generic term for measures that evaluate the quality of classification decisions, including precision, recall, F_1, and accu-
PERFORMANCE racy. *Performance* refers to the computational efficiency of classification and
EFFICIENCY IR systems in this book. However, many researchers mean effectiveness, not efficiency of text classification when they use the term performance.

When we process a collection with several two-class classifiers (such as Reuters-21578 with its 118 classes), we often want to compute a single aggregate measure that combines the measures for individual classifiers. There
ACROAVERAGING are two methods for doing this. *Macroaveraging* computes a simple average
ICROAVERAGING over classes. *Microaveraging* pools per-document decisions across classes, and

```
<REUTERS TOPICS="YES" LEWISSPLIT="TRAIN"
CGISPLIT="TRAINING-SET" OLDID="12981" NEWID="798">
<DATE> 2-MAR-1987 16:51:43.42</DATE>
<TOPICS><D>livestock</D><D>hog</D></TOPICS>
<TITLE>AMERICAN PORK CONGRESS KICKS OFF TOMORROW</TITLE>
<DATELINE> CHICAGO, March 2 - </DATELINE><BODY>The American Pork
Congress kicks off tomorrow, March 3, in Indianapolis with 160
of the nations pork producers from 44 member states determining
industry positions on a number of issues, according to the
National Pork Producers Council, NPPC.
Delegates to the three day Congress will be considering 26
resolutions concerning various issues, including the future
direction of farm policy and the tax law as it applies to the
agriculture sector. The delegates will also debate whether to
endorse concepts of a national PRV (pseudorabies virus) control
and eradication program, the NPPC said. A large
trade show, in conjunction with the congress, will feature
the latest in technology in all areas of the industry, the NPPC
added. Reuter
&#3;</BODY></TEXT></REUTERS>
```

Figure 13.9 A sample document from the Reuters-21578 collection.

then computes an effectiveness measure on the pooled contingency table. Table 13.8 gives an example.

The differences between the two methods can be large. Macroaveraging gives equal weight to each class, whereas microaveraging gives equal weight to each per-document classification decision. Because the F_1 measure ignores true negatives and its magnitude is mostly determined by the number of true positives, large classes dominate small classes in microaveraging. In the example, microaveraged precision (0.83) is much closer to the precision of c_2 (0.9) than to the precision of c_1 (0.5) because c_2 is five times larger than c_1. Microaveraged results are therefore really a measure of effectiveness on the large classes in a test collection. To get a sense of effectiveness on small classes, you should compute macroaveraged results.

Table 13.8 Macro- and microaveraging. "Truth" is the true class and "call" the decision of the classifier. In this example, macroaveraged precision is $[10/(10+10)+90/(10+90)]/2 = (0.5+0.9)/2 = 0.7$. Microaveraged precision is $100/(100+20) \approx 0.83$.

	class 1			class 2			pooled table	
	truth: yes	truth: no		truth: yes	truth: no		truth: yes	truth: no
call: yes	10	10	call: yes	90	10	call: yes	100	20
call: no	10	970	call: no	10	890	call: no	20	1860

Table 13.9 Text classification effectiveness numbers on Reuters-21578 for F_1 (in percent). Results from Li and Yang (2003) (a), Joachims (1998) (b: kNN) and Dumais et al. (1998) (b: NB, Rocchio, trees, SVM).

(a)	NB	Rocchio	kNN		SVM
micro-avg-L (90 classes)	80	85	86		89
macro-avg (90 classes)	47	59	60		60

(b)	NB	Rocchio	kNN	trees	SVM
earn	96	93	97	98	98
acq	88	65	92	90	94
money-fx	57	47	78	66	75
grain	79	68	82	85	95
crude	80	70	86	85	89
trade	64	65	77	73	76
interest	65	63	74	67	78
ship	85	49	79	74	86
wheat	70	69	77	93	92
corn	65	48	78	92	90
micro-avg (top 10)	82	65	82	88	92
micro-avg-D (118 classes)	75	62	n/a	n/a	87

In one-of classification (Section 14.5, page 281), microaveraged F_1 is the same as accuracy (Exercise 13.6).

Table 13.9 gives microaveraged and macroaveraged effectiveness of Naive Bayes for the ModApte split of Reuters-21578. To give a sense of the relative effectiveness of NB, we compare it with linear SVMs (rightmost column; see Chapter 15), one of the most effective classifiers, but also one that is more expensive to train than NB. NB has a microaveraged F_1 of 80%, which is 9% less than the SVM (89%), a 10% relative decrease (row "micro-avg-L (90 classes)"). So there is a surprisingly small effectiveness penalty for its simplicity and efficiency. However, on small classes, some of which only have on the order of ten positive examples in the training set, NB does much worse. Its macroaveraged F_1 is 13% below the SVM, a 22% relative decrease (row "macro-avg (90 classes)").

The table also compares NB with the other classifiers we cover in this book: DECISION Rocchio and kNN. In addition, we give numbers for *decision trees*, an im-TREES portant classification method we do not cover. The bottom part of the table shows that there is considerable variation from class to class. For instance, NB beats kNN on *ship*, but is much worse on *money-fx*.

Comparing parts (a) and (b) of the table, one is struck by the degree to which the cited papers' results differ. This is partly due to the fact that the numbers in (b) are break-even scores (cf. page 148) averaged over 118 classes, whereas the numbers in (a) are true F_1 scores (computed without any knowledge of the test set) averaged over ninety classes. This is unfortunately typical of what happens when comparing different results in text classification: There are often differences in the experimental setup or the evaluation that complicate the interpretation of the results.

These and other results have shown that the average effectiveness of NB is uncompetitive with classifiers like SVMs when trained and tested on *independent and identically distributed (i.i.d.)* data, that is, uniform data with all the good properties of statistical sampling. However, these differences may often be invisible or even reverse themselves when working in the real world where, usually, the training sample is drawn from a subset of the data to which the classifier will be applied, the nature of the data drifts over time rather than being stationary (the problem of concept drift we mentioned on page 249), and there may well be errors in the data (among other problems). Many practitioners have had the experience of being unable to build a fancy classifier for a certain problem that consistently performs better than NB.

Our conclusion from the results in Table 13.9 is that, although most researchers believe that an SVM is better than kNN and kNN better than NB, the ranking of classifiers ultimately depends on the class, the document collection, and the experimental setup. In text classification, there is always more to know than simply which machine learning algorithm was used, as we further discuss in Section 15.3 (page 307).

When performing evaluations like the one in Table 13.9, it is important to maintain a strict separation between the training set and the test set. We can easily make correct classification decisions on the test set by using information we have gleaned from the test set, such as the fact that a particular term is a good predictor in the test set (even though this is not the case in the training set). A more subtle example of using knowledge about the test set is to try a large number of values of a parameter (e.g., the number of selected features) and select the value that is best for the test set. As a rule, accuracy on new data – the type of data we will encounter when we use the classifier in an application – will be much lower than accuracy on a test set that the classifier has been tuned for. We discussed the same problem in ad hoc retrieval in Section 8.1 (page 141).

In a clean statistical text classification experiment, you should never run any program on or even look at the test set while developing a text classifica- DEVELOPMENT tion system. Instead, set aside a *development set* for testing while you develop SET your method. When such a set serves the primary purpose of finding a good value for a parameter, for example, the number of selected features, then it HELD-OUT is also called *held-out data*. Train the classifier on the rest of the training set DATA with different parameter values, and then select the value that gives best results on the held-out part of the training set. Ideally, at the very end, when all parameters have been set and the method is fully specified, you run one final experiment on the test set and publish the results. Because no information about the test set was used in developing the classifier, the results of this experiment should be indicative of actual performance in practice.

This ideal often cannot be met; researchers tend to evaluate several systems on the same test set over a period of several years. But it is nevertheless highly important to not look at the test data and to run systems on it as sparingly as possible. Beginners often violate this rule, and their results lose

Table 13.10 Data for parameter estimation exercise.

	docID	words in document	in $c = China$?
training set	1	Taipei Taiwan	yes
	2	Macao Taiwan Shanghai	yes
	3	Japan Sapporo	no
	4	Sapporo Osaka Taiwan	no
test set	5	Taiwan Taiwan Sapporo	?

validity because they have implicitly tuned their system to the test data simply by running many variant systems and keeping the tweaks to the system that worked best on the test set.

Exercise 13.6 [★★] Assume a situation where every document in the test collection has been assigned exactly one class, and that a classifier also assigns exactly one class to each document. This setup is called one-of classification (Section 14.5, page 281). Show that in one-of classification (i) the total number of false positive decisions equals the total number of false negative decisions and (ii) microaveraged F_1 and accuracy are identical.

Exercise 13.7 The class priors in Figure 13.2 are computed as the fraction of *documents* in the class as opposed to the fraction of *tokens* in the class. Why?

Exercise 13.8 The function APPLYMULTINOMIALNB in Figure 13.2 has time complexity $\Theta(L_a + |\mathbb{C}|L_a)$. How would you modify the function so that its time complexity is $\Theta(L_a + |\mathbb{C}|M_a)$?

Exercise 13.9 Based on the data in Table 13.10, (i) estimate a multinomial Naive Bayes classifier, (ii) apply the classifier to the test document, (iii) estimate a Bernoulli NB classifier, (iv) apply the classifier to the test document. You need not estimate parameters that you don't need for classifying the test document.

Exercise 13.10 Your task is to classify words as English or not English. Words are generated by a source with the following distribution:

event	word	English?	probability
1	ozb	no	4/9
2	uzu	no	4/9
3	zoo	yes	1/18
4	bun	yes	1/18

(i) Compute the parameters (priors and conditionals) of a multinomial NB classifier that uses the letters b, n, o, u, and z as features. Assume a training set that reflects the probability distribution of the source perfectly. Make the same independence assumptions that are usually made for a multinomial classifier that uses terms as features for text classification. Compute parameters using smoothing, in which computed-zero probabilities are smoothed into probability 0.01, and computed-nonzero probabilities are untouched. (This simplistic smoothing may cause $P(A) + P(\overline{A}) > 1$. Solutions are not required to correct this.) (ii) How does the classifier classify the word zoo? (iii) Classify the word zoo using a multinomial classifier as in part (i), but do not make the assumption of positional independence. That is, estimate separate parameters for each position in a word. You only need to compute the parameters you need for classifying zoo.

Exercise 13.11 What are the values of $I(U_t; C_c)$ and $X^2(\mathbb{D}, t, c)$ if term and class are completely independent? What are the values if they are completely dependent?

Exercise 13.12 The feature selection method in Equation (13.16) is most appropriate for the Bernoulli model. Why? How could one modify it for the multinomial model?

INFORMATION **Exercise 13.13** Features can also be selected according to *information gain*
GAIN (IG), which is defined as:

$$\text{IG}(\mathbb{D}, t, c) = H(p_{\mathbb{D}}) - \sum_{x \in \{\mathbb{D}_{t+}, \mathbb{D}_{t-}\}} \frac{|x|}{|\mathbb{D}|} H(p_x)$$

where H is entropy, $\mathbb{D}$ is the training set, and $\mathbb{D}_{t+}$, and $\mathbb{D}_{t-}$ are the subset of $\mathbb{D}$ with term t, and the subset of $\mathbb{D}$ without term t, respectively. p_A is the class distribution in (sub)collection A, e.g., $p_A(c) = 0.25$, $p_A(\overline{c}) = 0.75$ if a quarter of the documents in A are in class c.

Show that mutual information and information gain are equivalent.

Exercise 13.14 Show that the two X^2 formulas (Equations (13.18) and (13.19)) are equivalent.

Exercise 13.15 In the χ^2 example on page 255 we have $|N_{11} - E_{11}| = |N_{10} - E_{10}| = |N_{01} - E_{01}| = |N_{00} - E_{00}|$. Show that this holds in general.

Exercise 13.16 χ^2 and mutual information do not distinguish between positively and negatively correlated features. Because most good text classification features are positively correlated (i.e., they occur more often in c than in $\overline{c}$), one may want to explicitly rule out the selection of negative indicators. How would you do this?

13.7 References and further reading

General introductions to statistical classification and machine learning can be found in (Hastie et al. 2001), (Mitchell 1997), and (Duda et al. 2000), including many important methods (e.g., decision trees and boosting) that we do not cover. A comprehensive review of text classification methods and results is (Sebastiani 2002). Manning and Schütze (1999, Chapter 16) give an accessible introduction to text classification with coverage of decision trees, perceptrons and maximum entropy models. More information on the superlinear time complexity of learning methods that are more accurate than Naive Bayes can be found in (Perkins et al. 2003) and (Joachims 2006a).

Maron and Kuhns (1960) described one of the first NB text classifiers. Lewis (1998) focuses on the history of NB classification. Bernoulli and multinomial models and their accuracy for different collections are discussed by McCallum and Nigam (1998). Eyheramendy et al. (2003) present additional NB models. Domingos and Pazzani (1997), Friedman (1997), and Hand and Yu (2001) analyze why NB performs well although its probability estimates are poor. The first paper also discusses NB's optimality when the independence assumptions are true of the data. Pavlov et al. (2004) propose a modified document representation that partially addresses the inappropriateness of the independence assumptions. Bennett (2000) attributes the tendency of NB probability estimates to be close to either 0 or 1 to the effect of document length. Ng and Jordan (2001) show that NB is sometimes (although rarely) superior to discriminative methods because it more quickly reaches its optimal error rate. The basic NB model presented in this chapter can be tuned for better effectiveness (Rennie et al. 2003; Kołcz and Yih 2007). The problem of concept drift and other reasons why state-of-the-art classifiers do not always excel in practice are discussed by Forman (2006) and Hand (2006).

Early uses of mutual information and χ^2 for feature selection in text classification are Lewis and Ringuette (1994) and Schütze et al. (1995), respectively. Yang and Pedersen (1997) review feature selection methods and their POINTWISE impact on classification effectiveness. They find that *pointwise mutual infor-* MUTUAL *mation* is not competitive with other methods. Yang and Pedersen refer to INFORMATION expected mutual information (Equation (13.16)) as information gain (see Exercise 13.13, page 264). (Snedecor and Cochran 1989) is a good reference for the χ^2 test in statistics, including the Yates' correction for continuity for 2×2 tables. Dunning (1993) discusses problems of the χ^2 test when counts are small. Nongreedy feature selection techniques are described by Hastie et al. (2001). Cohen (1995) discusses the pitfalls of using multiple significance tests and methods to avoid them. Forman (2004) evaluates different methods for feature selection for multiple classifiers.

David D. Lewis defines the ModApte split at www.daviddlewis.com/ resources/testcollections/reuters21578/readme.txt based on Apté et al. (1994). UTILITY Lewis (1995) describes *utility measures* for the evaluation of text classifica- MEASURE tion systems. Yang and Liu (1999) employ significance tests in the evaluation of text classification methods.

Lewis et al. (2004) find that SVMs (Chapter 15) perform better on Reuters-RCV1 than kNN and Rocchio (Chapter 14).

14 *Vector space classification*

The document representation in Naive Bayes is a sequence of terms or a binary vector $\langle e_1, \ldots, e_M \rangle \in \{0, 1\}^{|V|}$. In this chapter, we adopt a different representation for text classification, the vector space model, developed in Chapter 6. It represents each document as a vector with one real-valued component, usually a tf–idf weight, for each term. Thus, the document space $\mathbb{X}$, the domain of the classification function γ, is $\mathbb{R}^{|V|}$. This chapter introduces a number of classification methods that operate on real-valued vectors.

The basic hypothesis in using the vector space model for classification is CONTIGUITY the *contiguity hypothesis*.
HYPOTHESIS

> **Contiguity hypothesis.** Documents in the same class form a contiguous region and regions of different classes do not overlap.

There are many classification tasks, in particular the type of text classification that we encountered in Chapter 13, where classes can be distinguished by word patterns. For example, documents in the class *China* tend to have high values on dimensions like Chinese, Beijing, and Mao, whereas documents in the class *UK* tend to have high values for London, British, and Queen. Documents of the two classes therefore form distinct contiguous regions as shown in Figure 14.1 and we can draw boundaries that separate them and classify new documents. How exactly this is done is the topic of this chapter.

Whether or not a set of documents is mapped into a contiguous region depends on the particular choices we make for the document representation: type of weighting, stop list, and so on. To see that the document representation is crucial, consider the two classes *written by a group* versus *written by a single person*. Frequent occurrence of the first person pronoun I is evidence for the single-person class. But that information is likely deleted from the document representation if we use a stop list. If the document representation chosen is unfavorable, the contiguity hypothesis will not hold and successful vector space classification is not possible.

266

The same considerations that led us to prefer weighted representations, in particular length-normalized tf–idf representations, in Chapters 6 and 7 also apply here. For example, a term with five occurrences in a document should get a higher weight than a term with one occurrence, but a weight five times larger would give too much emphasis to the term. Unweighted and unnormalized counts should not be used in vector space classification.

We introduce two vector space classification methods in this chapter, Rocchio and kNN. Rocchio classification (Section 14.2) divides the vector space PROTOTYPE　into regions centered on centroids or *prototypes*, one for each class, computed as the center of mass of all documents in the class. Rocchio classification is simple and efficient, but inaccurate if classes are not approximately spheres with similar radii.

kNN or k nearest neighbor classification (Section 14.3) assigns the majority class of the k nearest neighbors to a test document. kNN requires no explicit training and can use the unprocessed training set directly in classification. It is less efficient than other classification methods in classifying documents. If the training set is large, then kNN can handle nonspherical and other complex classes better than Rocchio.

A large number of text classifiers can be viewed as linear classifiers – classifiers that classify based on a simple linear combination of the features (Section 14.4). Such classifiers partition the space of features into regions separated by linear *decision hyperplanes*, in a manner to be detailed below. Because of the bias-variance tradeoff (Section 14.6) more complex nonlinear models are not systematically better than linear models. Nonlinear models have more parameters to fit on a limited amount of training data and are more likely to make mistakes for small and noisy data sets.

When applying two-class classifiers to problems with more than two classes, there are *one-of* tasks – a document must be assigned to exactly one of several mutually exclusive classes – and *any-of* tasks – a document can be assigned to any number of classes as we will explain in Section 14.5. Two-class classifiers solve any-of problems and can be combined to solve one-of problems.

14.1 Document representations and measures of relatedness in vector spaces

As in Chapter 6, we represent documents as vectors in $\mathbb{R}^{|V|}$ in this chapter. To illustrate properties of document vectors in vector classification, we will render these vectors as points in a plane as in the example in Figure 14.1. In reality, document vectors are length-normalized unit vectors that point to the surface of a hypersphere. We can view the two-dimensional (2D) planes in our figures as projections onto a plane of the surface of a (hyper-)sphere

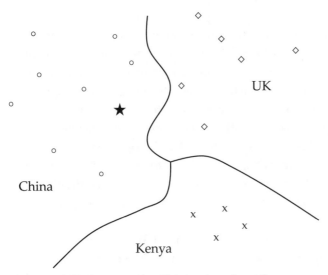

Figure 14.1 Vector space classification into three classes.

as shown in Figure 14.2. Distances on the surface of the sphere and on the projection plane are approximately the same as long as we restrict ourselves to small areas of the surface and choose an appropriate projection (Exercise 14.1).

Decisions of many vector space classifiers are based on a notion of distance, such as when computing the nearest neighbors in kNN classification. We will use Euclidean distance in this chapter as the underlying distance measure. We observed earlier (Exercise 6.18, page 121) that there is a direct correspondence between cosine similarity and Euclidean distance for length-normalized vectors. In vector space classification, it rarely matters whether the relatedness of two documents is expressed in terms of similarity or distance.

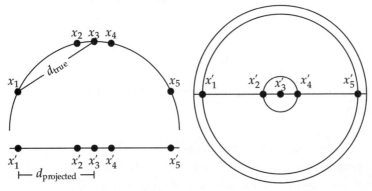

Figure 14.2 Projections of small areas of the unit sphere preserve distances. *Left:* A projection of the 2D semicircle to 1D. For the points x_1, x_2, x_3, x_4, x_5 at x coordinates -0.9, -0.2, 0, 0.2, 0.9 the distance $|x_2x_3| \approx 0.201$ only differs by 0.5% from $|x_2'x_3'| = 0.2$; but $|x_1x_3|/|x_1'x_3'| = d_{\text{true}}/d_{\text{projected}} \approx 1.06/0.9 \approx 1.18$ is an example of a large distortion (18%) when projecting a large area. *Right:* The corresponding projection of the 3D hemisphere to 2D.

However, in addition to documents, centroids or averages of vectors also play an important role in vector space classification. Centroids are not length normalized. For unnormalized vectors, dot product, cosine similarity, and Euclidean distance all have different behaviors in general (Exercise 14.6). We are mostly concerned with small local regions when computing the similarity between a document and a centroid, and the smaller the region the more similar the behavior of the three measures is.

?

Exercise 14.1 For small areas, distances on the surface of the hypersphere are approximated well by distances on its projection (Figure 14.2) because $\alpha \approx \sin \alpha$ for small angles. For what size angle is the distortion $\alpha / \sin(\alpha)$ (i) 1.01, (ii) 1.05 and (iii) 1.1?

14.2 Rocchio classification

Figure 14.1 shows three classes, *China*, *UK*, and *Kenya*, in a 2D space. Documents are shown as circles, diamonds, and Xs. The boundaries in the figure, which we call *decision boundaries*, are chosen to separate the three classes, but are otherwise arbitrary. To classify a new document, depicted as a star in the figure, we determine the region it occurs in and assign it the class of that region – *China* in this case. Our task in vector space classification is to devise algorithms that compute good boundaries where "good" means high classification accuracy on data unseen during training.

DECISION
BOUNDARY

The main work we must do in vector space classification is to define the boundaries between classes because they determine the classification decision. Perhaps the best-known way of doing this is *Rocchio classification*, which uses *centroids* to define the boundaries. The centroid of a class c is computed as the vector average or center of mass of its members:

ROCCHIO
LASSIFICATION
CENTROID

(14.1)
$$\vec{\mu}(c) = \frac{1}{|D_c|} \sum_{d \in D_c} \vec{v}(d),$$

where D_c is the set of documents in $\mathbb{D}$ whose class is c: $D_c = \{d : \langle d, c \rangle \in \mathbb{D}\}$. We denote the normalized vector of d by $\vec{v}(d)$ (Equation (6.11), page 111). Three example centroids are shown as solid circles in Figure 14.3.

The boundary between two classes in Rocchio classification is the set of points with equal distance from the two centroids. For example, $|a_1| = |a_2|$, $|b_1| = |b_2|$, and $|c_1| = |c_2|$ in the figure. This set of points is always a line. The generalization of a line in M-dimensional space is a hyperplane, which we define as the set of points $\vec{x}$ that satisfy:

(14.2)
$$\vec{w}^T \vec{x} = b$$

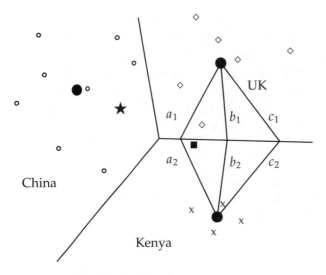

Figure 14.3 Rocchio classification.

NORMAL
VECTOR where $\vec{w}$ is the M-dimensional *normal vector*[1] of the hyperplane and b is a constant. This definition of hyperplanes includes lines (any line in 2D can be defined by $w_1 x_1 + w_2 x_2 = b$) and 2-dimensional planes (any plane in three dimensions (3D) can be defined by $w_1 x_1 + w_2 x_2 + w_3 x_3 = b$). A line divides a plane in two, a plane divides 3D space in two, and hyperplanes divide higher-dimensional spaces in two.

Thus, the boundaries of class regions in Rocchio classification are hyperplanes. The classification rule in Rocchio is to classify a point in accordance with the region it falls into. Equivalently, we determine the centroid $\vec{\mu}(c)$ that the point is closest to and then assign it to c. As an example, consider the star in Figure 14.3. It is located in the *China* region of the space and Rocchio therefore assigns it to *China*. We show the Rocchio algorithm in pseudocode in Figure 14.4.

Example 14.1: Table 14.1 shows the tf–idf vector representations of the five documents in Table 13.1 (page 241), using the formula $(1 + \log_{10} \mathrm{tf}_{t,d}) \log_{10}(4/\mathrm{df}_t)$ if $\mathrm{tf}_{t,d} > 0$ (Equation (6.14), page 117). The two class centroids are $\mu_c = 1/3 \cdot (\vec{d}_1 + \vec{d}_2 + \vec{d}_3)$ and $\mu_{\bar{c}} = 1/1 \cdot (\vec{d}_4)$. The distances of the test document from the centroids are $|\mu_c - \vec{d}_5| \approx 1.15$ and $|\mu_{\bar{c}} - \vec{d}_5| = 0.0$. Thus, Rocchio assigns d_5 to $\bar{c}$.

The separating hyperplane in this case has the following parameters:

$$\vec{w} \approx (0 \ -0.71 \ -0.71 \ 1/3 \ 1/3 \ 1/3)^T$$

$$b = -1/3$$

See Exercise 14.15 for how to compute $\vec{w}$ and b. We can easily verify that this hyperplane separates the documents as desired:

---

[1] Recall from basic linear algebra that $\vec{v} \cdot \vec{w} = \vec{v}^T \vec{w}$, that is, the dot product of $\vec{v}$ and $\vec{w}$ equals the product by matrix multiplication of the transpose of $\vec{v}$ and $\vec{w}$.

TRAINROCCHIO($\mathbb{C}, \mathbb{D}$)

1 **for each** $c_j \in \mathbb{C}$
2   **do** $D_j \leftarrow \{d : \langle d, c_j \rangle \in \mathbb{D}\}$
3     $\vec{\mu}_j \leftarrow \frac{1}{|D_j|} \sum_{d \in D_j} \vec{v}(d)$
4 **return** $\{\vec{\mu}_1, \ldots, \vec{\mu}_J\}$

APPLYROCCHIO($\{\vec{\mu}_1, \ldots, \vec{\mu}_J\}, d$)

1 **return** $\arg \min_j |\vec{\mu}_j - \vec{v}(d)|$

Figure 14.4 Rocchio classification: Training and testing.

$$\vec{w}^T \vec{d}_1 \approx 0 \cdot 0 + -0.71 \cdot 0 + -0.71 \cdot 0 + 1/3 \cdot 0 + 1/3 \cdot 1.0 + 1/3 \cdot 0 = 1/3 > b$$

(and, similarly, $\vec{w}^T \vec{d}_i > b$ for $2 \leq i \leq 3$) and $\vec{w}^T \vec{d}_4 = -1 < b$. Thus, documents in c are above the hyperplane ($\vec{w}^T \vec{d} > b$) and documents in $\bar{c}$ are below the hyperplane ($\vec{w}^T \vec{d} < b$).

The assignment criterion in Figure 14.4 is Euclidean distance. An alternative is cosine similarity:

$$\text{Assign } d \text{ to class } c = \arg \max_{c'} \cos(\vec{\mu}(c'), \vec{v}(d)).$$

As discussed in Section 14.1, the two assignment criteria will sometimes make different classification decisions. We present the Euclidean distance variant of Rocchio classification here because it emphasizes Rocchio's close correspondence to K-means clustering (Section 16.4, page 331).

Rocchio classification is a form of Rocchio relevance feedback (Section 9.1.1, page 163). The average of the relevant documents, corresponding to the most important component of the Rocchio vector in relevance feedback (Equation (9.3), page 166), is the centroid of the "class" of relevant documents. We omit the query component of the Rocchio formula in Rocchio classification because there is no query in text classification. Rocchio classification can be applied to $J > 2$ classes, whereas Rocchio relevance feedback is designed to distinguish only two classes, relevant and nonrelevant.

Table 14.1 Vectors and class centroids for the data in Table 13.1.

vector	term weights					
	Chinese	Japan	Tokyo	Macao	Beijing	Shanghai
$\vec{d}_1$	0	0	0	0	1.0	0
$\vec{d}_2$	0	0	0	0	0	1.0
$\vec{d}_3$	0	0	0	1.0	0	0
$\vec{d}_4$	0	0.71	0.71	0	0	0
$\vec{d}_5$	0	0.71	0.71	0	0	0
$\vec{\mu}_c$	0	0	0	0.33	0.33	0.33
$\vec{\mu}_{\bar{c}}$	0	0.71	0.71	0	0	0

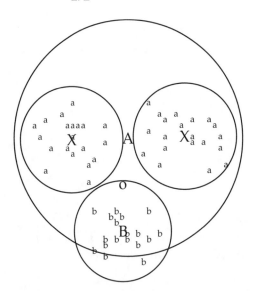

Figure 14.5 The multimodal class "a" consists of two different clusters (small upper circles centered on Xs). Rocchio classification will misclassify "o" as "a" because it is closer to the centroid A of the "a" class than to the centroid B of the "b" class.

In addition to respecting contiguity, the classes in Rocchio classification must be approximate spheres with similar radii. In Figure 14.3, the solid square just below the boundary between *UK* and *Kenya* is a better fit for the class *UK* because *UK* is more scattered than *Kenya*. But Rocchio assigns it to *Kenya* because it ignores details of the distribution of points in a class and only uses distance from the centroid for classification.

The assumption of sphericity also does not hold in Figure 14.5. We cannot represent the "a" class well with a single prototype because it has two MULTIMODAL clusters. Rocchio often misclassifies this type of *multimodal class*. A text clas- CLASS sification example for multimodality is a country like Burma, which changed its name to Myanmar in 1989. The two clusters before and after the name change need not be close to each other in space. We also encountered the problem of multimodality in relevance feedback (Section 9.1.2, page 169).

Two-class classification is another case where classes are rarely distributed like spheres with similar radii. Most two-class classifiers distinguish between a class like *China* that occupies a small region of the space and its widely scattered complement. Assuming equal radii will result in a large number of false positives. Most two-class classification problems therefore require a modified decision rule of the form:

$$\text{Assign } d \text{ to class } c \text{ iff } |\vec{\mu}(c) - \vec{v}(d)| < |\vec{\mu}(\bar{c}) - \vec{v}(d)| - b$$

for a positive constant b. As in Rocchio relevance feedback, the centroid of the negative documents is often not used at all, so that the decision criterion simplifies to $|\vec{\mu}(c) - \vec{v}(d)| < b'$ for a positive constant b'.

Table 14.2 Training and test times for Rocchio classification. L_{ave} is the average number of tokens per document. L_a and M_a are the numbers of tokens and types, respectively, in the test document. Computing Euclidean distance between the class centroids and a document is $\Theta(|\mathbb{C}|M_a)$.

mode	time complexity
training	$\Theta(|\mathbb{D}|L_{ave} + |\mathbb{C}||V|)$
testing	$\Theta(L_a + |\mathbb{C}|M_a) = \Theta(|\mathbb{C}|M_a)$

Table 14.2 gives the time complexity of Rocchio classification.[2] Adding all documents to their respective vector sum is $\Theta(|\mathbb{D}|L_{ave})$ (as opposed to $\Theta(|\mathbb{D}||V|)$) because we need only consider nonzero entries. Dividing each vector sum by the size of its class to compute the centroid is $\Theta(|V|)$. Overall, training time is linear in the size of the collection (cf. Exercise 13.1). Thus, Rocchio classification and Naive Bayes have the same linear training time complexity.

In the next section, we will introduce another vector space classification method, kNN, that deals better with classes that have non-spherical, disconnected or other irregular shapes.

? **Exercise 14.2** [⋆] Show that Rocchio classification can assign a label to a document that is different from its training set label.

14.3 *k* nearest neighbor

k NEAREST NEIGHBOR CLASSIFICATION Unlike Rocchio, *k nearest neighbor* or *kNN classification* determines the decision boundary locally. For 1NN we assign each document to the class of its closest neighbor. For kNN we assign each document to the majority class of its *k* closest neighbors where *k* is a parameter. The rationale of kNN classification is that, based on the contiguity hypothesis, we expect a test document *d* to have the same label as the training documents located in the local region surrounding *d*.

VORONOI TESSELLATION Decision boundaries in 1NN are concatenated segments of the *Voronoi tessellation* as shown in Figure 14.6. The Voronoi tessellation of a set of objects decomposes space into Voronoi cells, where each object's cell consists of all points that are closer to the object than to other objects. In our case, the objects are documents. The Voronoi tessellation then partitions the plane into $|\mathbb{D}|$ convex polygons, each containing its corresponding document (and no other) as shown in Figure 14.6, where a convex polygon is a convex region in 2D space bounded by lines.

---

[2] We write $\Theta(|\mathbb{D}|L_{ave})$ for $\Theta(T)$ and assume that the length of test documents is bounded as we did on page 242.

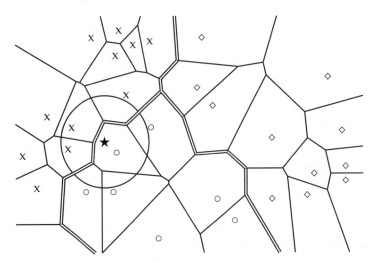

Figure 14.6 Voronoi tessellation and decision boundaries (double lines) in 1NN classification. The three classes are: X, circle and diamond.

For general $k \in \mathbb{N}$ in kNN, consider the region in the space for which the set of k nearest neighbors is the same. This again is a convex polygon and the space is partitioned into convex polygons, within each of which the set of k nearest neighbors is invariant (Exercise 14.11).[3]

1NN is not very robust. The classification decision of each test document relies on the class of a single training document, which may be incorrectly labeled or atypical. kNN for $k > 1$ is more robust. It assigns documents to the majority class of their k closest neighbors, with ties broken randomly.

There is a probabilistic version of this kNN classification algorithm. We can estimate the probability of membership in class c as the proportion of the k nearest neighbors in c. Figure 14.6 gives an example for $k = 3$. Probability estimates for class membership of the star are $\hat{P}(\text{circle class|star}) = 1/3$, $\hat{P}(\text{X class|star}) = 2/3$, and $\hat{P}(\text{diamond class|star}) = 0$. The 3NN estimate ($\hat{P}_1(\text{circle class|star}) = 1/3$) and the 1NN estimate ($\hat{P}_1(\text{circle class|star}) = 1$) differ with 3NN preferring the X class and 1NN preferring the circle class.

The parameter k in kNN is often chosen based on experience or knowledge about the classification problem at hand. It is desirable for k to be odd to make ties less likely. $k = 3$ and $k = 5$ are common choices, but much larger values, between 50 and 100, are also used. An alternative way of setting the parameter is to select the k that gives best results on a held-out portion of the training set.

---

[3] The generalization of a polygon to higher dimensions is a polytope. A *polytope* is a region in M-dimensional space bounded by $(M-1)$-dimensional hyperplanes. In M dimensions, the decision boundaries for kNN consist of segments of $(M-1)$-dimensional hyperplanes that form the Voronoi tessellation into convex polytopes for the training set of documents. The decision criterion of assigning a document to the majority class of its k nearest neighbors applies equally to $M = 2$ (tessellation into polygons) and $M > 2$ (tessellation into polytopes).

Train-kNN($\mathbb{C}, \mathbb{D}$)
1   $\mathbb{D}' \leftarrow$ Preprocess($\mathbb{D}$)
2   $k \leftarrow$ Select-k($\mathbb{C}, \mathbb{D}'$)
3   **return** $\mathbb{D}', k$

Apply-kNN($\mathbb{C}, \mathbb{D}', k, d$)
1   $S_k \leftarrow$ ComputeNearestNeighbors($\mathbb{D}', k, d$)
2   **for each** $c_j \in \mathbb{C}$
3   **do** $p_j \leftarrow |S_k \cap c_j|/k$
4   **return** $\arg\max_j p_j$

Figure 14.7   kNN training (with preprocessing) and testing. p_j is an estimate for $P(c_j|S_k) = P(c_j|d)$. c_j denotes the set of all documents in the class c_j.

We can also weight the "votes" of the k nearest neighbors by their cosine similarity. In this scheme, a class's score is computed as:

$$\text{score}(c, d) = \sum_{d' \in S_k} I_c(d') \cos(\vec{v}(d'), \vec{v}(d))$$

where S_k is the set of d's k nearest neighbors and $I_c(d') = 1$ iff d' is in class c and 0 otherwise. We then assign the document to the class with the highest score. Weighting by similarities is often more accurate than simple voting. For example, if two classes have the same number of neighbors in the top k, the class with the more similar neighbors wins.

Figure 14.7 summarizes the kNN algorithm.

Example 14.2:   The distances of the test document from the four training documents in Table 14.1 are $|\vec{d}_1 - \vec{d}_5| = |\vec{d}_2 - \vec{d}_5| = |\vec{d}_3 - \vec{d}_5| \approx 1.41$ and $|\vec{d}_4 - \vec{d}_5| = 0.0$. d_5's nearest neighbor is therefore d_4 and 1NN assigns d_5 to d_4's class, $\bar{c}$.

14.3.1 Time complexity and optimality of k nearest neighbor

Table 14.3 gives the time complexity of kNN. kNN has properties that are quite different from most other classification algorithms. Training a kNN classifier simply consists of determining k and preprocessing documents. In fact, if we preselect a value for k and do not preprocess, then kNN requires no training at all. In practice, we have to perform preprocessing steps like tokenization. It makes more sense to preprocess training documents once as part of the training phase rather than repeatedly every time we classify a new test document.

Test time is $\Theta(|\mathbb{D}|M_{ave}M_a)$ for kNN. It is linear in the size of the training set; we need to compute the distance of each training document from the

Table 14.3 Training and test times for kNN classification. M_{ave} is the average size of the vocabulary of documents in the collection.

kNN with preprocessing of training set	
training	$\Theta(|\mathbb{D}|L_{ave})$
testing	$\Theta(L_a + |\mathbb{D}|M_{ave}M_a) = \Theta(|\mathbb{D}|M_{ave}M_a)$
kNN without preprocessing of training set	
training	$\Theta(1)$
testing	$\Theta(L_a + |\mathbb{D}|L_{ave}M_a) = \Theta(|\mathbb{D}|L_{ave}M_a)$

test document. Test time is independent of the number of classes J. kNN therefore has a potential advantage for problems with large J.

In kNN classification, we do not perform any estimation of parameters as we do in Rocchio classification (centroids) or in Naive Bayes (priors and conditional probabilities). kNN simply memorizes all examples in the training set and then compares the test document to them. For this reason, kNN is also MEMORY- called *memory-based learning* or *instance-based learning*. It is usually desirable BASED to have as much training data as possible in machine learning. But in kNN, LEARNING large training sets come with a severe efficiency penalty in classification.

Can kNN testing be made more efficient than $\Theta(|\mathbb{D}|M_{ave}M_a)$ or, ignoring the length of documents, more efficient than $\Theta(|\mathbb{D}|)$? There are fast kNN algorithms for small dimensionality M (Exercise 14.12). There are also approximations for large M that give error bounds for specific efficiency gains (see Section 14.7). These approximations have not been extensively tested for text classification applications, so it is not clear whether they can achieve much better efficiency than $\Theta(|\mathbb{D}|)$ without a significant loss of accuracy.

The reader may have noticed the similarity between the problem of finding nearest neighbors of a test document and ad hoc retrieval, where we search for the documents with the highest similarity to the query (Section 6.3.2, page 113). In fact, the two problems are both k nearest neighbor problems and only differ in the relative density of (the vector of) the test document in kNN (10s or 100s of non-zero entries) versus the sparseness of (the vector of) the query in ad hoc retrieval (usually fewer than ten nonzero entries). We introduced the inverted index for efficient ad hoc retrieval in Section 1.1 (page 5). Is the inverted index also the solution for efficient kNN?

An inverted index restricts a search to those documents that have at least one term in common with the query. Thus, in the context of kNN, the inverted index will be efficient if the test document has no term overlap with a large number of training documents. Whether this is the case depends on the classification problem. If documents are long and no stop list is used, then less time will be saved. But with short documents and a large stop list, an inverted index may well cut the average test time by a factor of 10 or more.

The search time in an inverted index is a function of the length of the postings lists of the terms in the query. Postings lists grow sublinearly with the length of the collection since the vocabulary increases according to Heaps' law – if the probability of occurrence of some terms increases, then the probability of occurrence of others must decrease. However, most new terms are infrequent. We therefore take the complexity of inverted index search to be $\Theta(T)$ (as discussed in Section 2.4.2, page 38) and, assuming average document length does not change over time, $\Theta(T) = \Theta(|\mathbb{D}|)$.

As we will see in Chapter 15, kNN's effectiveness is close to that of the most accurate learning methods in text classification (Table 15.2, page 307). A BAYES ERROR measure of the quality of a learning method is its *Bayes error rate*, the average RATE error rate of classifiers learned by it for a particular problem. kNN is not optimal for problems with a nonzero Bayes error rate, that is, for problems where even the best possible classifier has a nonzero classification error. The error of 1NN is asymptotically (as the training set increases) bounded by twice the Bayes error rate. That is, if the optimal classifier has an error rate of x, then 1NN has an asymptotic error rate of $2x$. This is due to the effect of noise – we already saw one example of noise in the form of noisy features in Section 13.5 (page 251), but noise can also take other forms as we will discuss in the next section. Noise affects two components of kNN: the test document and the closest training document. The two sources of noise are additive, so the overall error of 1NN is twice the optimal error rate. For problems with Bayes error rate 0, the error rate of 1NN will approach 0 as the size of the training set increases.

?
Exercise 14.3 Explain why kNN handles multimodal classes better than Rocchio.

14.4 Linear versus nonlinear classifiers

In this section, we show that the two learning methods – Naive Bayes and Rocchio – are instances of linear classifiers, the perhaps most important group of text classifiers, and contrast them with nonlinear classifiers. To simplify the discussion, we will only consider two-class classifiers in this section LINEAR and define a *linear classifier* as a two-class classifier that decides class mem-CLASSIFIER bership by comparing a linear combination of the features to a threshold.

In two dimensions, a linear classifier is a line. Five examples are shown in Figure 14.8. These lines have the functional form $w_1x_1 + w_2x_2 = b$. The classification rule of a linear classifier is to assign a document to c if $w_1x_1 + w_2x_2 > b$ and to $\bar{c}$ if $w_1x_1 + w_2x_2 \leq b$. Here, $(x_1, x_2)^T$ is the 2D vector representation of the document and $(w_1, w_2)^T$ is the parameter vector that defines (together with b) the decision boundary. An alternative geometric interpretation of a linear classifier is provided in Figure 15.7 (page 316).

We can generalize this 2D linear classifier to higher dimensions by defining a hyperplane as we did in Equation (14.2), repeated here as Equation (14.3):

$$\vec{w}^T\vec{x} = b.$$

(14.3)

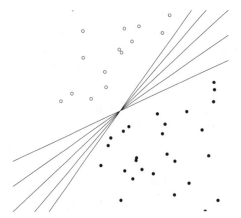

Figure 14.8 There are an infinite number of hyperplanes that separate two linearly separable classes.

The assignment criterion then is: assign to c if $\vec{w}^T\vec{x} > b$ and to $\bar{c}$ if $\vec{w}^T\vec{x} \leq b$.

DECISION   We call a hyperplane that we use as a linear classifier a *decision hyperplane*.

HYPERPLANE   The corresponding algorithm for linear classification in M dimensions is shown in Figure 14.9. Linear classification at first seems trivial given the simplicity of this algorithm. However, the difficulty is in training the linear classifier, that is, in determining the parameters $\vec{w}$ and b based on the training set. In general, some learning methods compute much better parameters than others where our criterion for evaluating the quality of a learning method is the effectiveness of the learned linear classifier on new data.

We now show that Rocchio and Naive Bayes are linear classifiers. To see this for Rocchio, observe that a vector $\vec{x}$ is on the decision boundary if it has equal distance to the two class centroids:

(14.4)
$$|\vec{\mu}(c_1) - \vec{x}| = |\vec{\mu}(c_2) - \vec{x}|.$$

Some basic arithmetic shows that this corresponds to a linear classifier with normal vector $\vec{w} = \vec{\mu}(c_1) - \vec{\mu}(c_2)$ and $b = 0.5 * (|\vec{\mu}(c_1)|^2 - |\vec{\mu}(c_2)|^2)$ (Exercise 14.15).

We can derive the linearity of Naive Bayes from its decision rule, which chooses the category c with the largest $\hat{P}(c|d)$ (Figure 13.2, page 241) where:

$$\hat{P}(c|d) \propto \hat{P}(c) \prod_{1 \leq k \leq n_d} \hat{P}(t_k|c)$$

APPLYLINEARCLASSIFIER($\vec{w}, b, \vec{x}$)
1    $score \leftarrow \sum_{i=1}^{M} w_i x_i$
2   **if** $score > b$
3   **then return** 1
4   **else return** 0

Figure 14.9 Linear classification algorithm.

Table 14.4 A linear classifier. The dimensions t_i and parameters w_i of a linear classifier for the class *interest* (as in interest rate) in Reuters-21578. The threshold is $b = 0$. Terms like dlr and world have negative weights because they are indicators for the competing class *currency*.

t_i	w_i	d_{1i}	d_{2i}	t_i	w_i	d_{1i}	d_{2i}
prime	0.70	0	1	dlrs	-0.71	1	1
rate	0.67	1	0	world	-0.35	1	0
interest	0.63	0	0	sees	-0.33	0	0
rates	0.60	0	0	year	-0.25	0	0
discount	0.46	1	0	group	-0.24	0	0
bundesbank	0.43	0	0	dlr	-0.24	0	0

and n_d is the number of tokens in the document that are part of the vocabulary. Denoting the complement category as $\bar{c}$, we obtain for the log odds:

(14.5)
$$\log \frac{\hat{P}(c|d)}{\hat{P}(\bar{c}|d)} = \log \frac{\hat{P}(c)}{\hat{P}(\bar{c})} + \sum_{1 \le k \le n_d} \log \frac{\hat{P}(t_k|c)}{\hat{P}(t_k|\bar{c})}.$$

We choose class c if the odds are greater than 1 or, equivalently, if the log odds are greater than 0. It is easy to see that Equation (14.5) is an instance of Equation (14.3) for $w_i = \log[\hat{P}(t_i|c)/\hat{P}(t_i|\bar{c})]$, $x_i = $ number of occurrences of t_i in d, and $b = -\log[\hat{P}(c)/\hat{P}(\bar{c})]$. Here, the index i, $1 \le i \le M$, refers to terms of the vocabulary (not to positions in d as k does, cf. Section 13.4.1, page 250) and $\vec{x}$ and $\vec{w}$ are M-dimensional vectors. So in log space, Naive Bayes is a linear classifier.

Example 14.3: Table 14.4 defines a linear classifier for the category *interest* in Reuters-21578 (see Section 13.6, page 258). We assign document $\vec{d}_1$ "rate discount dlrs world" to *interest* since $\vec{w}^T \vec{d}_1 = 0.67 \cdot 1 + 0.46 \cdot 1 + (-0.71) \cdot 1 + (-0.35) \cdot 1 = 0.07 > 0 = b$. We assign $\vec{d}_2$ "prime dlrs" to the complement class (not in *interest*) because $\vec{w}^T \vec{d}_2 = -0.01 \le b$. For simplicity, we assume a simple binary vector representation in this example: 1 for occurring terms, 0 for nonoccurring terms.

Figure 14.10 is a graphical example of a *linear problem*, which we define to mean that the underlying distributions $P(d|c)$ and $P(d|\bar{c})$ of the two classes CLASS are separated by a line. We call this separating line the *class boundary*. It BOUNDARY is the "true" boundary of the two classes and we distinguish it from the decision boundary that the learning method computes to approximate the class boundary.

NOISE As is typical in text classification, there are some *noise documents* in Fig-DOCUMENT ure 14.10 (marked with arrows) that do not fit well into the overall distribution of the classes. In Section 13.5 (page 251), we defined a noise feature as a misleading feature that, when included in the document representation, on average increases the classification error. Analogously, a noise document is a document that, when included in the training set, misleads the learning

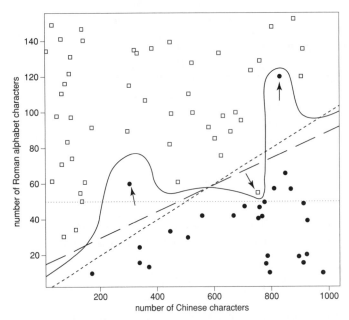

Figure 14.10 A linear problem with noise. In this hypothetical web page classification scenario, Chinese–only web pages are solid circles and mixed Chinese–English web pages are squares. The two classes are separated by a linear class boundary (*dashed line, short dashes*), except for three noise documents (*marked with arrows*).

method and increases classification error. Intuitively, the underlying distribution partitions the representation space into areas with mostly homogeneous class assignments. A document that does not conform with the dominant class in its area is a noise document.

Noise documents are one reason why training a linear classifier is hard. If we pay too much attention to noise documents when choosing the decision hyperplane of the classifier, then it will be inaccurate on new data. More fundamentally, it is usually difficult to determine which documents are noise documents and therefore potentially misleading.

If there exists a hyperplane that perfectly separates the two classes, then we LINEAR call the two classes *linearly separable*. In fact, if linear separability holds, then SEPARABILITY there is an infinite number of linear separators (Exercise 14.4) as illustrated by Figure 14.8, where the number of possible separating hyperplanes is infinite.

Figure 14.8 illustrates another challenge in training a linear classifier. If we are dealing with a linearly separable problem, then we need a criterion for selecting among all decision hyperplanes that perfectly separate the training data. In general, some of these hyperplanes will do well on new data, some will not.

NONLINEAR   An example of a *nonlinear classifier* is kNN. The nonlinearity of kNN is CLASSIFIER intuitively clear when looking at examples like Figure 14.6. The decision boundary of kNN consists of locally linear segments, but in general has a complex shape that is not equivalent to a line in 2D or a hyperplane in higher dimensions.

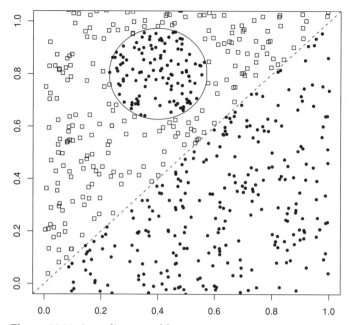

Figure 14.11 A nonlinear problem.

Figure 14.11 is another example of a nonlinear problem: There is no good linear separator between the distributions $P(d|c)$ and $P(d|\bar{c})$ because of the circular "enclave" in the upper left part of the graph. Linear classifiers misclassify the enclave, whereas a nonlinear classifier like kNN will be highly accurate for this type of problem if the training set is large enough.

If a problem is nonlinear and its class boundaries cannot be approximated well with linear hyperplanes, then nonlinear classifiers are often more accurate than linear classifiers. If a problem is linear, it is best to use a simpler linear classifier.

? **Exercise 14.4** Prove that the number of linear separators of two classes is either infinite or zero.

14.5 Classification with more than two classes

We can extend two-class linear classifiers to $J > 2$ classes. The method to use depends on whether the classes are mutually exclusive or not.

ANY-OF   Classification for classes that are not mutually exclusive is called *any-of*,
CLASSIFICATION *multilabel*, or *multivalue classification*. In this case, a document can belong to several classes simultaneously, or to a single class, or to none of the classes. A decision on one class leaves all options open for the others. It is sometimes said that the classes are *independent* of each other, but this is misleading; the classes are rarely statistically independent in the sense defined on page 255. In terms of the formal definition of the classification problem in

Equation (13.1) (page 237), we learn J different classifiers γ_j in any-of classification, each returning either c_j or $\bar{c}_j$: $\gamma_j(d) \in \{c_j, \bar{c}_j\}$.

Solving an any-of classification task with linear classifiers is straightforward:

1. Build a classifier for each class, where the training set consists of the set of documents in the class (positive labels) and its complement (negative labels).
2. Given the test document, apply each classifier separately. The decision of one classifier has no influence on the decisions of the other classifiers.

ONE-OF CLAS-   The second type of classification with more than two classes is *one-of clas-*
SIFICATION *sification*. Here, the classes are mutually exclusive. Each document must belong to exactly one of the classes. One-of classification is also called *multinomial, polytomous,*[4] *multiclass*, or *single-label classification*. Formally, there is a single classification function γ in one-of classification whose range is $\mathbb{C}$, i.e., $\gamma(d) \in \{c_1, \ldots, c_J\}$. kNN is a (nonlinear) one-of classifier.

True one-of problems are less common in text classification than any-of problems. With classes like *UK, China, poultry*, or *coffee*, a document can be relevant to many topics simultaneously – as when the prime minister of the UK visits China to talk about the coffee and poultry trade.

Nevertheless, we will often make a one-of assumption, as we did in Figure 14.1, even if classes are not really mutually exclusive. For the classification problem of identifying the language of a document, the one-of assumption is a good approximation as most text is written in only one language. In such cases, imposing a one-of constraint can increase the classifier's effectiveness because errors that are due to the fact that the any-of classifiers assigned a document to either no class or more than one class are eliminated.

J hyperplanes do not divide $\mathbb{R}^{|V|}$ into J distinct regions as illustrated in Figure 14.12. Thus, we must use a combination method when using two-class linear classifiers for one-of classification. The simplest method is to rank classes and then select the top-ranked class. Geometrically, the ranking can be with respect to the distances from the J linear separators. Documents close to a class's separator are more likely to be misclassified, so the greater the distance from the separator, the more plausible it is that a positive classification decision is correct. Alternatively, we can use a direct measure of confidence to rank classes, for example, probability of class membership. We can state this algorithm for one-of classification with linear classifiers as follows:

1. Build a classifier for each class, where the training set consists of the set of documents in the class (positive labels) and its complement (negative labels).
2. Given the test document, apply each classifier separately.

---

[4] A synonym of polytomous is polychotomous.

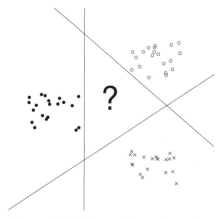

Figure 14.12 J hyperplanes do not divide space into J disjoint regions.

3. Assign the document to the class with
  - the maximum score,
  - the maximum confidence value,
  - or the maximum probability.

An important tool for analyzing the performance of a classifier for $J > 2$
CONFUSION classes is the *confusion matrix*. The confusion matrix shows for each pair of
MATRIX classes $\langle c_1, c_2 \rangle$, how many documents from c_1 were incorrectly assigned to c_2.
In Table 14.5, the classifier manages to distinguish the three financial classes
money-fx, *trade*, and *interest* from the three agricultural classes *wheat*, *corn*,
and *grain*, but makes many errors within these two groups. The confusion
matrix can help pinpoint opportunities for improving the accuracy of the
system. For example, to address the second largest error in Table 14.5, one
could attempt to introduce features that distinguish *wheat* documents from
grain documents.

? **Exercise 14.5** Create a training set of 300 documents, 100 each from three
different languages (e.g., English, French, and Spanish). Create a test set by
the same procedure, but also add 100 documents from a fourth language.
Train (i) a one-of classifier and (ii) an any-of classifier on this training set
and evaluate it on the test set. (iii) Are there any interesting differences in
how the two classifiers behave on this task?

Table 14.5 A confusion matrix for Reuters-21578. For example, fourteen documents
from *grain* were incorrectly assigned to *wheat*. Adapted from Picca et al. (2006).

true class	assigned class	*money-fx*	*trade*	*interest*	*wheat*	*corn*	*grain*
money-fx		95	0	10	0	0	0
trade		1	1	90	0	1	0
interest		13	0	0	0	0	0
wheat		0	0	1	34	3	7
corn		1	0	2	13	26	5
grain		0	0	2	14	5	10

14.6 The bias–variance tradeoff

Nonlinear classifiers are more powerful than linear classifiers. For some problems, there exists a nonlinear classifier with zero classification error, but no such linear classifier. Does that mean that we should always use nonlinear classifiers for optimal effectiveness in statistical text classification?

To answer this question, we introduce the bias–variance tradeoff in this section, one of the most important concepts in machine learning. The tradeoff helps to explain why there is no universally optimal learning method. Selecting an appropriate learning method is therefore an unavoidable part of solving a text classification problem.

Throughout this section, we use linear and nonlinear classifiers as prototypical examples of "less powerful" and "more powerful" learning, respectively. This is a simplification for a number of reasons. First, many nonlinear models subsume linear models as a special case. For instance, a nonlinear learning method like kNN will in some cases produce a linear classifier. Second, there are nonlinear models that are less complex than linear models. For instance, a quadratic polynomial with two parameters is less powerful than a 10,000-dimensional linear classifier. Third, the complexity of learning is not really a property of the classifier because there are many aspects of learning (such as feature selection, cf. Section 13.5, page 251 regularization, and constraints such as margin maximization in Chapter 15) that make a learning method either more powerful or less powerful without affecting the type of classifier that is the final result of learning-regardless of whether that classifier is linear or nonlinear. We refer the reader to the publications listed in Section 14.7 for a treatment of the bias–variance tradeoff that takes into account these complexities. In this section, linear and nonlinear classifiers will simply serve as proxies for weaker and stronger learning methods in text classification.

We first need to state our objective in text classification more precisely. In Section 13.1 (page 237), we said that we want to minimize classification error on the test set. The implicit assumption was that training documents and test documents are generated according to the same underlying distribution. We will denote this distribution by $P(\langle d, c \rangle)$ where d is the document and c its label or class. Figures 13.4 and 13.5 were examples of generative models that decompose $P(\langle d, c \rangle)$ into the product of $P(c)$ and $P(d|c)$. Figures 14.10 and 14.11 depict generative models for $\langle d, c \rangle$ with $d \in \mathbb{R}^2$ and $c \in \{\text{square, solid circle}\}$.

In this section, instead of using the number of correctly classified test documents (or, equivalently, the error rate on test documents) as evaluation measure, we adopt an evaluation measure that addresses the inherent uncertainty of labeling. In many text classification problems, a given document representation can arise from documents belonging to different classes. This is because documents from different classes can be mapped to the same document representation. For example, the one-sentence documents *China sues France* and *France sues China* are mapped to the same document representation $d' = \{$China, France, sues$\}$ in a bag-of-words model. But only the latter document is relevant to the class $c' = $ *legal actions brought by France* (which might be defined, for example, as a standing query by an international trade lawyer).

To simplify the calculations in this section, we do not count the number of errors on the test set when evaluating a classifier, but instead look at how well the classifier estimates the conditional probability $P(c|d)$ of a document being in a class. In the above example, we might have $P(c'|d') = 0.5$.

Our goal in text classification then is to find a classifier γ such that, averaged over documents d, $\gamma(d)$ is as close as possible to the true probability $P(c|d)$. We measure this using mean squared error:

(14.6)
$$\text{MSE}(\gamma) = E_d[\gamma(d) - P(c|d)]^2$$

where E_d is the expectation with respect to $P(d)$. The mean squared error term gives partial credit for decisions by γ that are close if not completely right.

OPTIMAL
CLASSIFIER
We define a classifier γ to be *optimal* for a distribution $P(\langle d, c \rangle)$ if it minimizes $\text{MSE}(\gamma)$.

Minimizing MSE is a desideratum for *classifiers*. We also need a criterion for *learning methods*. Recall that we defined a learning method Γ as a function that takes a labeled training set $\mathbb{D}$ as input and returns a classifier γ.

For learning methods, we adopt as our goal to find a Γ that, averaged over training sets, learns classifiers γ with minimal MSE. We can formalize this as minimizing *learning error*:

LEARNING
ERROR

(14.7)
$$\text{learning-error}(\Gamma) = E_{\mathbb{D}}[\text{MSE}(\Gamma(\mathbb{D}))]$$

where $E_{\mathbb{D}}$ is the expectation over labeled training sets. To keep things simple, we can assume that training sets have a fixed size – the distribution $P(\langle d, c \rangle)$ then defines a distribution $P(\mathbb{D})$ over training sets.

We can use learning error as a criterion for selecting a learning method in statistical text classification. A learning method Γ is *optimal* for a distribution $P(\mathbb{D})$ if it minimizes the learning error.

OPTIMAL
LEARNING
METHOD

Writing $\Gamma_{\mathbb{D}}$ for $\Gamma(\mathbb{D})$ for better readability, we can transform Equation (14.7) as follows:

$$\text{learning-error}(\Gamma) = E_{\mathbb{D}}[\text{MSE}(\Gamma_{\mathbb{D}})]$$

(14.10)
$$= E_{\mathbb{D}} E_d[\Gamma_{\mathbb{D}}(d) - P(c|d)]^2$$

(14.11)
$$= E_d[\text{bias}(\Gamma, d) + \text{variance}(\Gamma, d)]$$

(14.12)
$$\text{bias}(\Gamma, d) = [P(c|d) - E_{\mathbb{D}}\Gamma_{\mathbb{D}}(d)]^2$$

(14.13)
$$\text{variance}(\Gamma, d) = E_{\mathbb{D}}[\Gamma_{\mathbb{D}}(d) - E_{\mathbb{D}}\Gamma_{\mathbb{D}}(d)]^2$$

(14.8)
$$E[x - \alpha]^2 = Ex^2 - 2Ex\alpha + \alpha^2$$
$$= (Ex)^2 - 2Ex\alpha + \alpha^2$$
$$+ Ex^2 - 2(Ex)^2 + (Ex)^2$$
$$= [Ex - \alpha]^2$$
$$+ Ex^2 - E2x(Ex) + E(Ex)^2$$
$$= [Ex - \alpha]^2 + E[x - Ex]^2$$

(14.9)
$$E_\mathbb{D} E_d [\Gamma_\mathbb{D}(d) - P(c|d)]^2 = E_d E_\mathbb{D} [\Gamma_\mathbb{D}(d) - P(c|d)]^2$$
$$= E_d [\ [E_\mathbb{D} \Gamma_\mathbb{D}(d) - P(c|d)]^2$$
$$+ E_\mathbb{D} [\Gamma_\mathbb{D}(d) - E_\mathbb{D} \Gamma_\mathbb{D}(d)]^2 \ ]$$

Figure 14.13 Arithmetic transformations for the bias–variance decomposition. For the derivation of Equation (14.9), we set $\alpha = P(c|d)$ and $x = \Gamma_\mathbb{D}(d)$ in Equation (14.8).

where the equivalence between Equations (14.10) and (14.11) is shown in Equation (14.9) in Figure 14.13. Note that d and $\mathbb{D}$ are independent of each other. In general, for a random document d and a random training set $\mathbb{D}$, $\mathbb{D}$ does not contain a labeled instance of d.

BIAS   *Bias* is the squared difference between $P(c|d)$, the true conditional probability of d being in c, and $\Gamma_\mathbb{D}(d)$, the prediction of the learned classifier, averaged over training sets. Bias is large if the learning method produces classifiers that are consistently wrong. Bias is small if (i) the classifiers are consistently right or (ii) different training sets cause errors on different documents or (iii) different training sets cause positive and negative errors on the same documents, but that average out to close to 0. If one of these three conditions holds, then $E_\mathbb{D} \Gamma_\mathbb{D}(d)$, the expectation over all training sets, is close to $P(c|d)$.

Linear methods like Rocchio and Naive Bayes have a high bias for nonlinear problems because they can only model one type of class boundary, a linear hyperplane. If the generative model $P(\langle d, c \rangle)$ has a complex nonlinear class boundary, the bias term in Equation (14.11) will be high because a large number of points will be consistently misclassified. For example, the circular enclave in Figure 14.11 does not fit a linear model and will be misclassified consistently by linear classifiers.

We can think of bias as resulting from our domain knowledge (or lack thereof) that we build into the classifier. If we know that the true boundary between the two classes is linear, then a learning method that produces linear classifiers is more likely to succeed than a nonlinear method. But if the true class boundary is not linear and we incorrectly bias the classifier to be linear, then classification accuracy will be low on average.

Nonlinear methods like kNN have low bias. We can see in Figure 14.6 that the decision boundaries of kNN are variable – depending on the distribution of documents in the training set, learned decision boundaries can vary greatly. As a result, each document has a chance of being classified correctly for some training sets. The average prediction $E_{\mathbb{D}}\Gamma_{\mathbb{D}}(d)$ is therefore closer to $P(c|d)$ and bias is smaller than for a linear learning method.

VARIANCE   *Variance* is the variation of the prediction of learned classifiers: the average squared difference between $\Gamma_{\mathbb{D}}(d)$ and its average $E_{\mathbb{D}}\Gamma_{\mathbb{D}}(d)$. Variance is large if different training sets $\mathbb{D}$ give rise to very different classifiers $\Gamma_{\mathbb{D}}$. It is small if the training set has a minor effect on the classification decisions $\Gamma_{\mathbb{D}}$ makes, be they correct or incorrect. Variance measures how inconsistent the decisions are, not whether they are correct or incorrect.

Linear learning methods have low variance because most randomly drawn training sets produce similar decision hyperplanes. The decision lines produced by linear learning methods in Figures 14.10 and 14.11 will deviate slightly from the main class boundaries, depending on the training set, but the class assignment for the vast majority of documents (with the exception of those close to the main boundary) will not be affected. The circular enclave in Figure 14.11 will be consistently misclassified.

Nonlinear methods like kNN have high variance. It is apparent from Figure 14.6 that kNN can model very complex boundaries between two classes. It is therefore sensitive to noise documents of the sort depicted in Figure 14.10. As a result the variance term in Equation (14.11) is large for kNN: Test documents are sometimes misclassified – if they happen to be close to a noise document in the training set – and sometimes correctly classified – if there are no noise documents in the training set near them. This results in high variation from training set to training set.

OVERFITTING   High-variance learning methods are prone to *overfitting* the training data. The goal in classification is to fit the training data to the extent that we capture true properties of the underlying distribution $P(\langle d, c \rangle)$. In overfitting, the learning method also learns from noise. Overfitting increases MSE and frequently is a problem for high-variance learning methods.

MEMORY   We can also think of variance as the *model complexity* or, equivalently, *mem-*
CAPACITY   *ory capacity* of the learning method – how detailed a characterization of the training set it can remember and then apply to new data. This capacity corresponds to the number of independent parameters available to fit the training set. Each kNN neighborhood S_k makes an independent classification decision. The parameter in this case is the estimate $\hat{P}(c|S_k)$ from Figure 14.7. Thus, kNN's capacity is only limited by the size of the training set. It can memorize arbitrarily large training sets. In contrast, the number of parameters of Rocchio is fixed – J parameters per dimension, one for each centroid – and independent of the size of the training set. The Rocchio classifier (in form of the centroids defining it) cannot "remember" fine-grained details of the distribution of the documents in the training set.

According to Equation (14.7), our goal in selecting a learning method is to minimize learning error. The fundamental insight captured by

Equation (14.11), which we can succinctly state as: learning error = bias + variance, is that the learning error has two components, bias and variance, which in general cannot be minimized simultaneously. When comparing two learning methods Γ_1 and Γ_2, in most cases the comparison comes down to one method having higher bias and lower variance and the other lower bias and higher variance. The decision for one learning method versus another is then not simply a matter of selecting the one that reliably produces good classifiers across training sets (small variance) or the one that can learn classification problems with very difficult decision boundaries (small bias). Instead, we have to weigh the respective merits of bias and variance in our application and choose accordingly. This tradeoff is called the *bias–variance tradeoff*.

BIAS–
VARIANCE
TRADEOFF

Figure 14.10 provides an illustration, which is somewhat contrived, but will be useful as an example for the tradeoff. Some Chinese text contains English words written in the Roman alphabet like CPU, ONLINE, and GPS. Consider the task of distinguishing Chinese–only web pages from mixed Chinese–English web pages. A search engine might offer Chinese users without knowledge of English (but who understand loanwords like CPU) the option of filtering out mixed pages. We use two features for this classification task: number of Roman alphabet characters and number of Chinese characters on the web page. As stated earlier, the distribution $P(\langle d, c \rangle)$ of the generative model generates most mixed (respectively, Chinese) documents above (respectively, below) the short-dashed line, but there are a few noise documents. In Figure 14.10, we see three classifiers.

- **One-feature classifier.** Shown as a dotted horizontal line. This classifier uses only one feature, the number of Roman alphabet characters. Assuming a learning method that minimizes the number of misclassifications in the training set, the position of the horizontal decision boundary is not greatly affected by differences in the training set (e.g., noise documents). So a learning method producing this type of classifier has low variance, but its bias is high because it will consistently misclassify squares in the lower left corner and "solid circle" documents with more than fifty Roman characters.
- **Linear classifier.** Shown as a dashed line with long dashes. Learning linear classifiers has less bias; only noise documents and possibly a few documents close to the boundary between the two classes are misclassified. The variance is higher than for the one-feature classifiers, but still small: The dashed line with long dashes deviates only slightly from the true boundary between the two classes, and so will almost all linear decision boundaries learned from training sets. Thus, very few documents (documents close to the class boundary) will be inconsistently classified.
- **"Fit-training-set-perfectly" classifier.** Shown as a solid line. Here, the learning method constructs a decision boundary that perfectly separates

the classes in the training set. This method has the lowest bias because there is no document that is consistently misclassified – the classifiers sometimes even get noise documents in the test set right. But the variance of this learning method is high. Because noise documents can move the decision boundary arbitrarily, test documents close to noise documents in the training set will be misclassified – something that a linear learning method is unlikely to do.

It is perhaps surprising that so many of the best-known text classification algorithms are linear. Some of these methods, in particular linear SVMs, regularized logistic regression and regularized linear regression, are among the most effective known methods. The bias–variance tradeoff provides insight into their success. Typical classes in text classification are complex and seem unlikely to be modeled well linearly. However, this intuition is misleading for the high-dimensional spaces that we typically encounter in text applications. With increased dimensionality, the likelihood of linear separability increases rapidly (Exercise 14.17). Thus, linear models in high-dimensional spaces are quite powerful despite their linearity. Even more powerful nonlinear learning methods can model decision boundaries that are more complex than a hyperplane, but they are also more sensitive to noise in the training data. Nonlinear learning methods sometimes perform better if the training set is large, but by no means in all cases.

?

Exercise 14.6 In Figure 14.14, which of the three vectors $\vec{a}$, $\vec{b}$, and $\vec{c}$ is (i) most similar to $\vec{x}$ according to dot product similarity, (ii) most similar to $\vec{x}$ according to cosine similarity, (iii) closest to $\vec{x}$ according to Euclidean distance?

Exercise 14.7 Download Reuters-21578 and train and test Rocchio and kNN classifiers for the classes *acquisitions, corn, crude, earn, grain, interest, money-fx, ship, trade,* and *wheat.* Use the ModApte split. You may want to use one of a number of software packages that implement Rocchio classification and kNN classification, for example, the Bow toolkit (McCallum 1996).

Exercise 14.8 Download 20 Newgroups (page 142) and train and test Rocchio and kNN classifiers for its twenty classes.

Exercise 14.9 Show that the decision boundaries in Rocchio classification are, as in kNN, given by the Voronoi tessellation.

Exercise 14.10 [⋆] Computing the distance between a dense centroid and a sparse vector is $\Theta(M)$ for a naive implementation that iterates over all M dimensions. Based on the equality $\sum(x_i - \mu_i)^2 = 1.0 + \sum \mu_i^2 - 2 \sum x_i \mu_i$ and assuming that $\sum \mu_i^2$ has been precomputed, write down an algorithm that is $\Theta(M_a)$ instead, where M_a is the number of distinct terms in the test document.

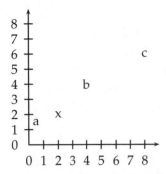

Figure 14.14 Example for differences between Euclidean distance, dot product similarity and cosine similarity. The vectors are $\vec{a} = (0.5\ 1.5)^T$, $\vec{x} = (2\ 2)^T$, $\vec{b} = (4\ 4)^T$, and $\vec{c} = (8\ 6)^T$.

Exercise 14.11 [$\star\star\star$] Prove that the region of the plane consisting of all points with the same k nearest neighbors is a convex polygon.

Exercise 14.12 Design an algorithm that performs an efficient 1NN search in one dimension (where efficiency is with respect to the number of documents N). What is the time complexity of the algorithm?

Exercise 14.13 [$\star\star\star$] Design an algorithm that performs an efficient 1NN search in two dimensions with at most polynomial (in N) preprocessing time.

Exercise 14.14 [$\star\star\star$] Can one design an exact efficient algorithm for 1NN for very large M along the ideas you used to solve the last exercise?

Exercise 14.15 Show that Equation (14.4) defines a hyperplane with $\vec{w} = \vec{\mu}(c_1) - \vec{\mu}(c_2)$ and $b = 0.5 * (|\vec{\mu}(c_1)|^2 - |\vec{\mu}(c_2)|^2)$.

Exercise 14.16 We can easily construct nonseparable data sets in high dimensions by embedding a nonseparable set like the one shown in Figure 14.15. Consider embedding Figure 14.15 in 3D and then perturbing the four points slightly (i.e., moving them a small distance in a random direction). Why would you expect the resulting configuration to be linearly separable? How likely is then a non-separable set of $m \ll M$ points in M-dimensional space?

Exercise 14.17 Assuming two classes, show that the percentage of nonseparable assignments of the vertices of a hypercube decreases with dimensionality M for $M > 1$. For example, for $M = 1$ the proportion of nonseparable

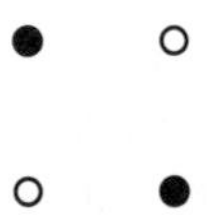

Figure 14.15 A simple nonseparable set of points.

assignments is 0, for $M = 2$, it is 2/16. One of the two nonseparable cases for $M = 2$ is shown in Figure 14.15, the other is its mirror image. Solve the exercise either analytically or by simulation.

Exercise 14.18 Although we point out the similarities of Naive Bayes with linear vector space classifiers, it does not make sense to represent count vectors (the document representations in NB) in a continuous vector space. There is however a formalization of NB that is analogous to Rocchio. Show that NB assigns a document to the class (represented as a parameter vector) whose Kullback-Leibler (KL) divergence (Section 12.4, page 231) to the document (represented as a count vector as in Section 13.4.1 (page 250), normalized to sum to 1) is smallest.

14.7 References and further reading

As discussed in Chapter 9, Rocchio relevance feedback is due to Rocchio (1971). Joachims (1997) presents a probabilistic analysis of the method. Rocchio classification was widely used as a classification method in TREC in the 1990s (Buckley et al. 1994a,b; Voorhees and Harman 2005). Initially, it ROUTING was used as a form of *routing*. Routing merely ranks documents according to relevance to a class without assigning them. Early work on *filtering*, FILTERING a true classification approach that makes an assignment decision on each document, was published by Ittner et al. (1995) and Schapire et al. (1998). The definition of routing we use here should not be confused with another sense. *Routing* can also refer to the electronic distribution of documents to subscribers, the so-called *push model* of document distribution. In a PUSH MODEL *pull model*, each transfer of a document to the user is initiated by the user, for PULL MODEL example, by means of search or by selecting it from a list of documents on a news aggregation website.

Some authors restrict the name *Rocchio classification* to two-class problems CENTROID- and use the terms *cluster-based* (Iwayama and Tokunaga 1995) and *centroid-BASED based classification* (Han and Karypis 2000; Tan and Cheng 2007) for Rocchio CLASSIFICATION classification with $J > 2$.

A more detailed treatment of kNN can be found in (Hastie et al. 2001), including methods for tuning the parameter k. An example of an approximate fast kNN algorithm is locality-based hashing (Andoni et al. 2006). Kleinberg (1997) presents an approximate $\Theta((M \log^2 M)(M + \log N))$ kNN algorithm (where M is the dimensionality of the space and N the number of data points), but at the cost of exponential storage requirements: $\Theta((N \log M)^{2M})$. Indyk (2004) surveys nearest neighbor methods in high-dimensional spaces. Early work on kNN in text classification was motivated by the availability of massively parallel hardware architectures (Creecy et al. 1992). Yang (1994) uses an inverted index to speed up kNN classification. The optimality result for 1NN (twice the Bayes error rate asymptotically) is due to Cover and Hart (1967).

The effectiveness of Rocchio classification and kNN is highly dependent on careful parameter tuning (in particular, the parameters b' for Rocchio on page 272 and k for kNN), feature engineering (Section 15.3, page 307) and feature selection (Section 13.5, page 251). Buckley and Salton (1995), Schapire et al. (1998), Yang and Kisiel (2003), and Moschitti (2003) address these issues for Rocchio and Yang (2001) and Ault and Yang (2002) for kNN. Zavrel et al. (2000) compare feature selection methods for kNN.

The bias–variance tradeoff was introduced by Geman et al. (1992). The derivation in Section 14.6 is for $MSE(\gamma)$, but the tradeoff applies to many loss functions (cf. Friedman (1997), Domingos (2000)). Schütze et al. (1995) and Lewis et al. (1996) discuss linear classifiers for text and Hastie et al. (2001) linear classifiers in general. Readers interested in the algorithms mentioned, but not described in this chapter, may wish to consult Bishop (2006) for neural networks, Hastie et al. (2001) for linear and logistic regression, and Minsky and Papert (1988) for the perceptron algorithm. Anagnostopoulos et al. (2006) show that an inverted index can be used for highly efficient document classification with any linear classifier, provided that the classifier is still effective when trained on a modest number of features via feature selection.

We have only presented the simplest method for combining two-class classifiers into a one-of classifier. Another important method is the use of error-correcting codes, where a vector of decisions of different two-class classifiers is constructed for each document. A test document's decision vector is then "corrected" based on the distribution of decision vectors in the training set, a procedure that incorporates information from all two-class classifiers and their correlations into the final classification decision (Dietterich and Bakiri 1995). Ghamrawi and McCallum (2005) also exploit dependencies between classes in any-of classification. Allwein et al. (2000) propose a general framework for combining two-class classifiers.

15 *Support vector machines and machine learning on documents*

Improving classifier effectiveness has been an area of intensive machine-learning research over the last two decades, and this work has led to a new generation of state-of-the-art classifiers, such as support vector machines, boosted decision trees, regularized logistic regression, neural networks, and random forests. Many of these methods, including support vector machines (SVMs), the main topic of this chapter, have been applied with success to information retrieval problems, particularly text classification. An SVM is a kind of large-margin classifier: It is a vector-space–based machine-learning method where the goal is to find a decision boundary between two classes that is maximally far from any point in the training data (possibly discounting some points as outliers or noise).

We will initially motivate and develop SVMs for the case of two-class data sets that are separable by a linear classifier (Section 15.1), and then extend the model in Section 15.2 to nonseparable data, multiclass problems, and nonlinear models, and also present some additional discussion of SVM performance. The chapter then moves to consider the practical deployment of text classifiers in Section 15.3: What sorts of classifiers are appropriate when, and how can you exploit domain-specific text features in classification? Finally, we will consider how the machine-learning technology that we have been building for text classification can be applied back to the problem of learning how to rank documents in ad hoc retrieval (Section 15.4). Although several machine learning methods have been applied to this task, use of SVMs has been prominent. SVMs are not necessarily better than other machine-learning methods (except perhaps in situations with few training data), but they perform at the state-of-the-art level and have much current theoretical and empirical appeal.

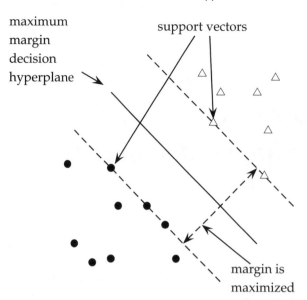

Figure 15.1 The support vectors are the five points right up against the margin of the classifier.

15.1 Support vector machines: The linearly separable case

For two-class, separable training data sets, such as the one in Figure 14.8 (page 278), there are lots of possible linear separators. Intuitively, a decision boundary drawn in the middle of the void between data items of the two classes seems better than one which approaches very close to examples of one or both classes. Although some learning methods such as the perceptron algorithm (see references in Section 14.7, page 291) find just any linear separator, others, like Naive Bayes, search for the best linear separator according to some criterion. The SVM in particular defines the criterion to be looking for a decision surface that is maximally far away from any data point. This distance from the decision surface to the closest data point determines the MARGIN *margin* of the classifier. This method of construction necessarily means that the decision function for an SVM is fully specified by a (usually small) subset of the data that defines the position of the separator. These points are SUPPORT referred to as the *support vectors* (in a vector space, a point can be thought of VECTOR as a vector between the origin and that point). Figure 15.1 shows the margin and support vectors for a sample problem. Other data points play no part in determining the decision surface that is chosen.

Maximizing the margin seems good because points near the decision surface represent very uncertain classification decisions; there is almost a 50% chance of the classifier deciding either way. A classifier with a large margin makes no low-certainty classification decisions. This gives you a classification safety margin: A slight error in measurement or a slight document variation will not cause a misclassification. Another intuition motivating SVMs

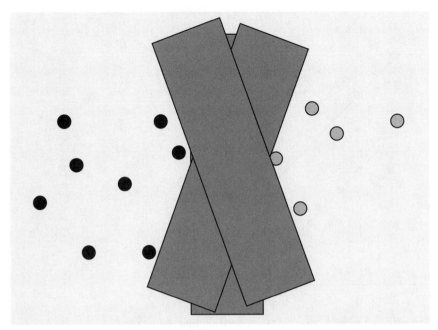

Figure 15.2 An intuition for large-margin classification. Insisting on a large margin reduces the capacity of the model: The range of angles at which the fat decision surface can be placed is smaller than for a decision hyperplane (cf. Figure 14.8, page 278).

is shown in Figure 15.2. By construction, an SVM classifier insists on a large margin around the decision boundary. Compared with a decision hyperplane, if you have to place a fat separator between classes, you have fewer choices of where it can be put. As a result of this, the memory capacity of the model has been decreased, and hence we expect that its ability to correctly generalize to test data is increased (cf. the discussion of the bias-variance tradeoff in Chapter 14, page 288).

Let us formalize an SVM with algebra. A decision hyperplane (page 278) can be defined by an intercept term b and a decision hyperplane normal vector $\vec{w}$, which is perpendicular to the hyperplane. This vector is commonly WEIGHT referred to in the machine learning literature as the *weight vector*. To choose VECTOR among all the hyperplanes that are perpendicular to the normal vector, we specify the intercept term b. Because the hyperplane is perpendicular to the normal vector, all points $\vec{x}$ on the hyperplane satisfy $\vec{w}^\mathsf{T}\vec{x} = -b$. Now suppose that we have a set of training data points $\mathbb{D} = \{(\vec{x}_i, y_i)\}$, where each member is a pair of a point $\vec{x}_i$ and a class label y_i corresponding to it.[1] For SVMs, the two data classes are always named $+1$ and -1 (rather than 1 and 0), and the intercept term is always explicitly represented as b (rather than being folded into the weight vector $\vec{w}$ by adding an extra always-on feature). The math works out much more cleanly if you do things this way, as

---

[1] As discussed in Section 14.1 (page 267), we present the general case of points in a vector space, but if the points are length-normalized document vectors, then all the action is taking place on the surface of a unit sphere, and the decision surface intersects the sphere's surface.

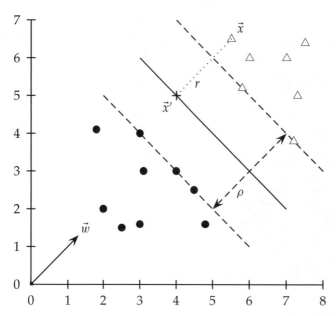

Figure 15.3 The geometric margin of a point (r) and a decision boundary (ρ).

we will see almost immediately in the definition of functional margin. The linear classifier is then:

(15.1) $$f(\vec{x}) = \text{sign}(\vec{w}^\mathsf{T}\vec{x} + b).$$

A value of -1 indicates one class, and a value of $+1$ the other class.

We are confident in the classification of a point if it is far away from the decision boundary. For a given data set and decision hyperplane, we define FUNCTIONAL the *functional margin* of the ith example $\vec{x}_i$ with respect to a hyperplane $\langle \vec{w}, b \rangle$ MARGIN as the quantity $y_i(\vec{w}^\mathsf{T}\vec{x}_i + b)$. The functional margin of a data set with respect to a decision surface is then twice the functional margin of any of the points in the data set with minimal functional margin (the factor of 2 comes from measuring across the whole width of the margin, as in Figure 15.3). However, there is a problem with using this definition as is: The value is undercon- strained, because we can always make the functional margin as big as we wish by simply scaling up $\vec{w}$ and b. For example, if we replace $\vec{w}$ by $5\vec{w}$ and b by $5b$, then the functional margin $y_i(5\vec{w}^\mathsf{T}\vec{x}_i + 5b)$ is five times as large. This suggests that we need to place some constraint on the size of the $\vec{w}$ vector. To get a sense of how to do that, let us look at the actual geometry.

What is the Euclidean distance from a point $\vec{x}$ to the decision boundary? In Figure 15.3, we denote by r this distance. We know that the shortest distance between a point and a hyperplane is perpendicular to the plane, and hence, parallel to $\vec{w}$. A unit vector in this direction is $\vec{w}/|\vec{w}|$. The dotted line in the diagram is then a translation of the vector $r\vec{w}/|\vec{w}|$. Let us label the point on the hyperplane closest to $\vec{x}$ as $\vec{x}'$. Then:

(15.2)
$$\vec{x}' = \vec{x} - yr\frac{\vec{w}}{|\vec{w}|},$$

where multiplying by y just changes the sign for the two cases of $\vec{x}$ being on either side of the decision surface. Moreover, $\vec{x}'$ lies on the decision boundary and so satisfies $\vec{w}^{\mathrm{T}}\vec{x}' + b = 0$. Hence:

(15.3)
$$\vec{w}^{\mathrm{T}}\left(\vec{x} - yr\frac{\vec{w}}{|\vec{w}|}\right) + b = 0.$$

Solving for r gives[2]:

(15.4)
$$r = y\frac{\vec{w}^{\mathrm{T}}\vec{x} + b}{|\vec{w}|}.$$

Again, the points closest to the separating hyperplane are support vectors. GEOMETRIC The *geometric margin* of the classifier is the maximum width of the band that MARGIN can be drawn separating the support vectors of the two classes. That is, it is twice the minimum value over data points for r given in Equation (15.4), or, equivalently, the maximal width of one of the fat separators shown in Figure 15.2. The geometric margin is clearly invariant to scaling of parameters: if we replace $\vec{w}$ by $5\vec{w}$ and b by $5b$, then the geometric margin is the same, because it is inherently normalized by the length of $\vec{w}$. This means that we can impose any scaling constraint we wish on $\vec{w}$ without affecting the geometric margin. Among other choices, we could use unit vectors, as in Chapter 6, by requiring that $|\vec{w}| = 1$. This would have the effect of making the geometric margin the same as the functional margin.

Because we can scale the functional margin as we please, for convenience in solving large SVMs, let us choose to require that the functional margin of all data points is at least 1 and that it is equal to 1 for at least one data vector. That is, for all items in the data:

(15.5)
$$y_i(\vec{w}^{\mathrm{T}}\vec{x}_i + b) \geq 1$$

and there exist support vectors for which the inequality is an equality. Because each example's distance from the hyperplane is $r_i = y_i(\vec{w}^{\mathrm{T}}\vec{x}_i + b)/|\vec{w}|$, the geometric margin is $\rho = 2/|\vec{w}|$. Our desire is still to maximize this geometric margin. That is, we want to find $\vec{w}$ and b such that:

- $\rho = 2/|\vec{w}|$ is maximized
- For all $(\vec{x}_i, y_i) \in \mathbb{D}$, $y_i(\vec{w}^{\mathrm{T}}\vec{x}_i + b) \geq 1$

Maximizing $2/|\vec{w}|$ is the same as minimizing $|\vec{w}|/2$. This gives the final standard formulation of an SVM as a minimization problem:

[2] Recall that $|\vec{w}| = \sqrt{\vec{w}^{\mathrm{T}}\vec{w}}$.

(15.6)   Find $\vec{w}$ and b such that:

- $\frac{1}{2}\vec{w}^{\mathsf{T}}\vec{w}$ is minimized, and
- for all $\{(\vec{x}_i, y_i)\}$, $y_i(\vec{w}^{\mathsf{T}}\vec{x}_i + b) \geq 1$

We are now optimizing a quadratic function subject to linear constraints. QUADRATIC *Quadratic optimization* problems are a standard, well-known class of mathe- PROGRAMMING matical optimization problems, and many algorithms exist for solving them. We could in principle build our SVM using standard quadratic programming (QP) libraries, but there has been much recent research in this area aiming to exploit the structure of the kind of QP that emerges from an SVM. As a result, there are more intricate but much faster and more scalable libraries available especially for building SVMs, which almost everyone uses to build models. We will not present the details of such algorithms here.

However, it will be helpful in what follows to understand the shape of the solution of such an optimization problem. The solution involves constructing a dual problem where a Lagrange multiplier α_i is associated with each constraint $y_i(\vec{w}^{\mathsf{T}}\vec{x}_i + b) \geq 1$ in the primal problem:

(15.7)   Find $\alpha_1, \ldots \alpha_N$ such that $\sum \alpha_i - \frac{1}{2}\sum_i \sum_j \alpha_i \alpha_j y_i y_j \vec{x}_i^{\mathsf{T}}\vec{x}_j$ is maximized, and

- $\sum_i \alpha_i y_i = 0$
- $\alpha_i \geq 0$ for all $1 \leq i \leq N$

The solution is then of the form:

(15.8) $\vec{w} = \sum \alpha_i y_i \vec{x}_i$
$b = y_k - \vec{w}^{\mathsf{T}}\vec{x}_k$ for any $\vec{x}_k$ such that $\alpha_k \neq 0$

In the solution, most of the α_i are zero. Each nonzero α_i indicates that the corresponding $\vec{x}_i$ is a support vector. The classification function is then:

(15.9)
$$f(\vec{x}) = \text{sign}\left(\sum_i \alpha_i y_i \vec{x}_i^{\mathsf{T}}\vec{x} + b\right).$$

Both the term to be maximized in the dual problem and the classifying function involve a *dot product* between pairs of points ($\vec{x}$ and $\vec{x}_i$ or $\vec{x}_i$ and $\vec{x}_j$), and that is the only way the data are used – we will return to the significance of this later.

To recap, we start with a training data set. The data set uniquely defines the best separating hyperplane, and we feed the data through a quadratic optimization procedure to find this plane. Given a new point $\vec{x}$ to classify, the classification function $f(\vec{x})$ in either Equation (15.1) or Equation (15.9) is computing the projection of the point onto the hyperplane normal. The sign of this function determines the class to assign to the point. If the point is within the margin of the classifier (or another confidence threshold t that we might have determined to minimize classification mistakes) then the classifier can return "don't know" rather than one of the two classes. The value of $f(\vec{x})$ may also be transformed into a probability of classification; fitting a sigmoid to transform the values is standard (Platt 2000). Also, because the

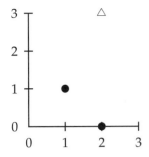

Figure 15.4 A tiny-three-data point training set for an SVM.

margin is constant, if the model includes dimensions from various sources, careful rescaling of some dimensions may be required. However, this is not a problem if our documents (points) are on the unit hypersphere.

Example 15.1: Consider building an SVM over the (very little) data set shown in Figure 15.4. Working geometrically, for an example like this, the maximum margin weight vector will be parallel to the shortest line connecting points of the two classes, that is, the line between $(1, 1)$ and $(2, 3)$, giving a weight vector of $(1, 2)$. The optimal decision surface is orthogonal to that line and intersects it at the halfway point. Therefore, it passes through $(1.5, 2)$. So, the SVM decision boundary is:

$$y = x_1 + 2x_2 - 5.5.$$

Working algebraically, with the standard constraint that $\text{sign}(y_i(\vec{w}^T\vec{x}_i + b)) \geq 1$, we seek to minimize $|\vec{w}|$. This happens when this constraint is satisfied with equality by the two support vectors. Further we know that the solution is $\vec{w} = (a, 2a)$ for some a. So we have that:

$$a + 2a + b = -1$$
$$2a + 6a + b = 1.$$

Therefore, $a = 2/5$ and $b = -11/5$. So the optimal hyperplane is given by $\vec{w} = (2/5, 4/5)$ and $b = -11/5$.

The margin ρ is $2/|\vec{w}| = 2/\sqrt{4/25 + 16/25} = 2/(2\sqrt{5}/5) = \sqrt{5}$. This answer can be confirmed geometrically by examining Figure 15.4.

Exercise 15.1 [$\star$] What is the minimum number of support vectors that there can be for a data set (which contains instances of each class)?

Exercise 15.2 [$\star\star$] The basis of being able to use kernels in SVMs (see Section 15.2.3) is that the classification function can be written in the form of Equation (15.9) (where, for large problems, most α_i are 0). Show explicitly how the classification function could be written in this form for the data set from Example 15.1. That is, write f as a function where the data points appear and the only variable is $\vec{x}$.

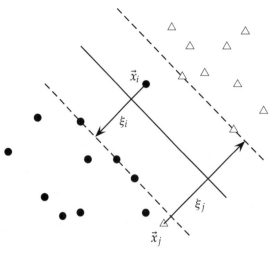

Figure 15.5 Large margin classification with slack variables.

Exercise 15.3 [★★] Install an SVM package such as SVMlight (http://svmlight. joachims.org/), and build an SVM for the data set discussed in Example 15.1. Confirm that the program gives the same solution as the text. For SVM-light, or another package that accepts the same training data format, the training file would be:

```
+1 1:2 2:3
−1 1:2 2:0
−1 1:1 2:1
```

The training command for SVMlight is then:

```
svm_learn -c 1 -a alphas.dat train.dat model.dat
```

The -c 1 option is needed to turn off use of the slack variables that we discuss in Section 15.2.1. Check that the norm of the weight vector agrees with what we found in Example 15.1. Examine the file alphas.dat which contains the α_i values, and check that they agree with your answers in Exercise 15.2.

15.2 Extensions to the support vector machine model

15.2.1 Soft margin classification

For the very high dimensional problems common in text classification, some-times the data are linearly separable. But in the general case they are not, and even if they are, we might prefer a solution that better separates the bulk of the data while ignoring a few weird noise documents.

If the training set $\mathbb{D}$ is not linearly separable, the standard approach is to allow the fat decision margin to make a few mistakes (some points – outliers or noisy examples – are inside or on the wrong side of the margin). We then pay a cost for each misclassified example, which depends on how far it is from meeting the margin requirement given in Equation (15.5). To implement SLACK this, we introduce *slack variables* ξ_i. A nonzero value for ξ_i allows $\vec{x}_i$ to not VARIABLES meet the margin requirement at a cost proportional to the value of ξ_i. See Figure 15.5.

The formulation of the SVM optimization problem with slack variables is:

(15.10)   Find $\vec{w}$, b, and $\xi_i \geq 0$ such that:

- $\frac{1}{2}\vec{w}^\mathrm{T}\vec{w} + C\sum_i \xi_i$ is minimized
- and for all $\{(\vec{x}_i, y_i)\}$, $y_i(\vec{w}^\mathrm{T}\vec{x}_i + b) \geq 1 - \xi_i$

The optimization problem is then trading off how fat it can make the margin versus how many points have to be moved around to allow this margin. The margin can be less than 1 for a point $\vec{x}_i$ by setting $\xi_i > 0$, but then one pays a penalty of $C\xi_i$ in the minimization for having done that. The sum of the ξ_i gives an upper bound on the number of training errors. Soft-margin SVMs minimize training error traded off against margin. The parameter C GULARIZATION is a *regularization* term, which provides a way to control overfitting: As C becomes large, it is unattractive to not respect the data at the cost of reducing the geometric margin; when it is small, it is easy to account for some data points with the use of slack variables and to have a fat margin placed so it models the bulk of the data.

The dual problem for soft margin classification becomes:

(15.11)   Find $\alpha_1, \ldots \alpha_N$ such that $\sum \alpha_i - \frac{1}{2}\sum_i \sum_j \alpha_i \alpha_j y_i y_j \vec{x}_i^\mathrm{T}\vec{x}_j$ is maximized, and

- $\sum_i \alpha_i y_i = 0$
- $0 \leq \alpha_i \leq C$ for all $1 \leq i \leq N$

Neither the slack variables ξ_i nor Lagrange multipliers for them appear in the dual problem. All we are left with is the constant C bounding the possible size of the Lagrange multipliers for the support vector data points. As before, the $\vec{x}_i$ with nonzero α_i will be the support vectors. The solution of the dual problem is of the form:

(15.12) $\vec{w} = \sum \alpha y_i \vec{x}_i$
$b = y_k(1 - \xi_k) - \vec{w}^\mathrm{T}\vec{x}_k$ for $k = \arg\max_k \alpha_k$

Again, $\vec{w}$ is not needed explicitly for classification, which can be done in terms of dot products with data points, as in Equation (15.9).

Typically, the support vectors will be a small proportion of the training data. However, if the problem is nonseparable or with small margin, then every data point that is misclassified or within the margin will have a nonzero α_i. If this set of points becomes large, then, for the nonlinear case which we turn to in Section 15.2.3, this can be a major slowdown for using SVMs at test time.

Table 15.1 Training and testing complexity of various classifiers including SVMs. Training is the time the learning method takes to learn a classifier over $\mathbb{D}$, whereas testing is the time it takes a classifier to classify one document. For SVMs, multiclass classification is assumed to be done by a set of $|\mathbb{C}|$ one-versus-rest classifiers. L_{ave} is the average number of tokens per document, and M_{ave} is the average vocabulary (number of nonzero features) of a document. L_a and M_a are the numbers of tokens and types, respectively, in the test document.

classifier	mode	method	time complexity
NB	training		$\Theta(|\mathbb{D}|L_{ave} + |\mathbb{C}||V|)$
NB	testing		$\Theta(|\mathbb{C}|M_a)$
Rocchio	training		$\Theta(|\mathbb{D}|L_{ave} + |\mathbb{C}||V|)$
Rocchio	testing		$\Theta(|\mathbb{C}|M_a)$
kNN	training	preprocessing	$\Theta(|\mathbb{D}|L_{ave})$
kNN	testing	preprocessing	$\Theta(|\mathbb{D}|M_{ave}M_a)$
kNN	training	no preprocessing	$\Theta(1)$
kNN	testing	no preprocessing	$\Theta(|\mathbb{D}|L_{ave}M_a)$
SVM	training	conventional	$O(|\mathbb{C}||\mathbb{D}|^3 M_{ave})$; $\approx O(|\mathbb{C}||\mathbb{D}|^{1.7}M_{ave})$, empirically
SVM	training	cutting planes	$O(|\mathbb{C}||\mathbb{D}|M_{ave})$
SVM	testing		$O(|\mathbb{C}|M_a)$

The complexity of training and testing with linear SVMs is shown in Table 15.1.[3] The time for training an SVM is dominated by the time for solving the underlying QP, and so the theoretical and empirical complexity varies depending on the method used to solve it. The standard result for solving QPs is that it takes time cubic in the size of the data set (Kozlov et al. 1979). All the recent work on SVM training has worked to reduce that complexity, often by being satisfied with approximate solutions. Standardly, empirical complexity is about $O(|\mathbb{D}|^{1.7})$ (Joachims 2006a). Nevertheless, the superlinear training time of traditional SVM algorithms makes them difficult or impossible to use on very large training data sets. Alternative traditional SVM solution algorithms which are linear in the number of training examples scale badly with a large number of features, which is another standard attribute of text problems. However, a new training algorithm based on cutting plane techniques gives a promising answer to this issue by having running time linear in the number of training examples and the number of nonzero features in examples (Joachims 2006a). Nevertheless, the actual speed of doing quadratic optimization remains much slower than simply counting terms as is done in a Naive Bayes model. Extending SVM algorithms to nonlinear SVMs, as in the next section, standardly increases training complexity by a factor of $|\mathbb{D}|$ (because dot products between examples need to be calculated), making

---

[3] We write $\Theta(|\mathbb{D}|L_{ave})$ for $\Theta(T)$ (page 242) and assume that the length of test documents is bounded as we did on page 242.

them impractical. In practice it can often be cheaper to materialize the higher order features and to train a linear SVM.[4]

15.2.2 Multiclass support vector machines

SVMs are inherently two-class classifiers. The traditional way to do multi-class classification with SVMs is to use one of the methods discussed in Section 14.5 (page 281). In particular, the most common technique in practice has been to build $|\mathbb{C}|$ one-versus-rest classifiers (commonly referred to as "one-versus-all" or OVA classification), and to choose the class that classifies the test datum with greatest margin. Another strategy is to build a set of one-versus-one classifiers, and to choose the class that is selected by the most classifiers. Although this involves building $|\mathbb{C}|(|\mathbb{C}| - 1)/2$ classifiers, the time for training classifiers may actually decrease, because the training data set for each classifier is much smaller.

However, these are not very elegant approaches to solving multiclass problems. A better alternative is provided by the construction of multiclass SVMs, where we build a two-class classifier over a feature vector $\Phi(\vec{x}, y)$ derived from the pair consisting of the input features and the class of the datum. At test time, the classifier chooses the class $y = \arg\max_{y'} \vec{w}^\mathrm{T} \Phi(\vec{x}, y')$. The margin during training is the gap between this value for the correct class and for the nearest other class, and so the quadratic program formulation will require that $\forall i \; \forall y \neq y_i \; \vec{w}^\mathrm{T} \Phi(\vec{x}_i, y_i) - \vec{w}^\mathrm{T} \Phi(\vec{x}_i, y) \geq 1 - \xi_i$. This general method can be extended to give a multiclass formulation of various kinds of linear classifiers. It is also a simple instance of a generalization of classification where the classes are not just a set of independent, categorical labels, but may be arbitrary structured objects with relationships defined between them. In the STRUCTURAL SVM world, such work comes under the label of *structural SVMs*. We mention them again in Section 15.4.2.

15.2.3 Nonlinear support vector machines

With what we have presented so far, data sets that are linearly separable (perhaps with a few exceptions or some noise) are well-handled. But what are we going to do if the data set just doesn't allow classification by a linear classifier? Let us look at a one-dimensional case. The top data set in Figure 15.6 is straightforwardly classified by a linear classifier but the middle data set is not. We instead need to be able to pick out an interval. One way to solve this problem is to map the data onto a higher dimensional space and then to use a linear classifier in the higher dimensional space. For example, the bottom

---

[4] Materializing the features refers to directly calculating higher order and interaction terms and then putting them into a linear model.

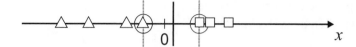

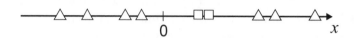

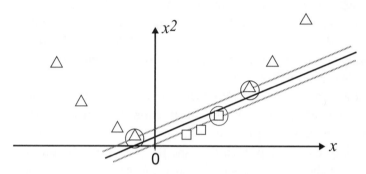

Figure 15.6 Projecting data that is not linearly separable into a higher dimensional space can make it linearly separable.

part of the figure shows that a linear separator can easily classify the data if we use a quadratic function to map the data into two dimensions (a polar coordinates projection would be another possibility). The general idea is to map the original feature space to some higher dimensional feature space where the training set is separable. Of course, we would want to do so in ways that preserve relevant dimensions of relatedness between data points, so that the resultant classifier should still generalize well.

SVMs, and also a number of other linear classifiers, provide an easy and efficient way of doing this mapping to a higher dimensional space, which is KERNEL TRICK referred to as the *kernel trick*. It's not really a trick; it just exploits the math that we have seen. The SVM linear classifier relies on a dot product between data point vectors. Let $K(\vec{x}_i, \vec{x}_j) = \vec{x}_i^{\mathrm{T}}\vec{x}_j$. Then the classifier we have seen so far is:

$$(15.13) \qquad f(\vec{x}) = \mathrm{sign}\left(\sum_i \alpha_i y_i K(\vec{x}_i, \vec{x}) + b\right).$$

Now suppose we decide to map every data point into a higher dimensional space via some transformation $\Phi: \vec{x} \mapsto \phi(\vec{x})$. Then the dot product becomes $\phi(\vec{x}_i)^{\mathrm{T}}\phi(\vec{x}_j)$. If it turned out that this dot product (which is just a real number) could be computed simply and efficiently in terms of the original data points, then we wouldn't have to actually map from $\vec{x} \mapsto \phi(\vec{x})$. Rather, we could simply compute the quantity $K(\vec{x}_i, \vec{x}_j) = \phi(\vec{x}_i)^{\mathrm{T}}\phi(\vec{x}_j)$, and then use the

KERNEL function's value in Equation (15.13). A *kernel function K* is such a function
FUNCTION that corresponds to a dot product in some expanded feature space.

 Example 15.2: The quadratic kernel in two dimensions. For two-dimensional vectors $\vec{u} = (u_1 \ u_2)$, $\vec{v} = (v_1 \ v_2)$, consider $K(\vec{u}, \vec{v}) = (1 + \vec{u}^T\vec{v})^2$. We wish to show that this is a kernel, namely, that $K(\vec{u}, \vec{v}) = \phi(\vec{u})^T\phi(\vec{v})$ for some ϕ. Consider $\phi(\vec{u}) = (1 \ u_1^2 \ \sqrt{2}u_1u_2 \ u_2^2 \ \sqrt{2}u_1 \ \sqrt{2}u_2)$. Then:

(15.14) $\quad K(\vec{u}, \vec{v}) = (1 + \vec{u}^T\vec{v})^2$

$\qquad = 1 + u_1^2v_1^2 + 2u_1v_1u_2v_2 + u_2^2v_2^2 + 2u_1v_1 + 2u_2v_2$

$\qquad = (1 \ u_1^2 \ \sqrt{2}u_1u_2 \ u_2^2 \ \sqrt{2}u_1 \ \sqrt{2}u_2)^T(1 \ v_1^2 \ \sqrt{2}v_1v_2 \ v_2^2 \ \sqrt{2}v_1 \ \sqrt{2}v_2)$

$\qquad = \phi(\vec{u})^T\phi(\vec{v}).$

In the language of functional analysis, what kinds of functions are valid
KERNEL *kernel functions*? Kernel functions are sometimes more precisely referred to
MERCER as *Mercer kernels*, because they must satisfy Mercer's condition: For any $g(\vec{x})$
KERNEL such that $\int g(\vec{x})^2 d\vec{x}$ is finite, we must have that:

(15.15) $$\int K(\vec{x}, \vec{z})g(\vec{x})g(\vec{z})d\vec{x}d\vec{z} \geq 0.$$

A kernel function K must be continuous, symmetric, and have a positive definite gram matrix. Such a K means that there exists a mapping to a reproducing kernel Hilbert space (a Hilbert space is a vector space closed under dot products) such that the dot product there gives the same value as the function K. If a kernel does not satisfy Mercer's condition, then the corresponding QP may have no solution. If you would like to better understand these issues, you should consult the books on SVMs mentioned in Section 15.5. Otherwise, you can content yourself with knowing that 90% of work with kernels uses one of two straightforward families of functions of two vectors, which we define below, and which define valid kernels.

The two commonly used families of kernels are polynomial kernels and radial basis functions. Polynomial kernels are of the form $K(\vec{x}, \vec{z}) = (1 + \vec{x}^T\vec{z})^d$. The case of $d = 1$ is a linear kernel, which is what we had before the start of this section (the constant 1 just changing the threshold). The case of $d = 2$ gives a quadratic kernel, and is very commonly used. We illustrated the quadratic kernel in Example 15.2.

The most common form of radial basis function is a Gaussian distribution, calculated as:

(15.16) $$K(\vec{x}, \vec{z}) = e^{-(\vec{x}-\vec{z})^2/(2\sigma^2)}.$$

A radial basis function (rbf) is equivalent to mapping the data into an infinite dimensional Hilbert space, and so we cannot illustrate the radial basis function concretely, as we did a quadratic kernel. Beyond these two families, there has been interesting work developing other kernels, some of which is promising for text applications. In particular, there has been investigation of string kernels (see Section 15.5).

The world of SVMs comes with its own language, which is rather different from the language otherwise used in machine learning. The terminology does have deep roots in mathematics, but it is important not to be too awed by that terminology. Really, we are talking about some quite simple things. A polynomial kernel allows us to model feature conjunctions (up to the order of the polynomial). That is, if we want to be able to model occurrences of pairs of words, which give distinctive information about topic classification, not given by the individual words alone, like perhaps *operating* AND *system* or *ethnic* AND *cleansing*, then we need to use a quadratic kernel. If occurrences of triples of words give distinctive information, then we need to use a cubic kernel. Simultaneously you also get the powers of the basic features – for most text applications, that probably is not useful, but just comes along with the math and hopefully does not do harm. A radial basis function allows you to have features that pick out circles (hyperspheres), although the decision boundaries become much more complex as multiple such features interact. A string kernel lets you have features that are character subsequences of terms. All of these are straightforward notions which have also been used in many other places under different names.

15.2.4 Experimental results

We presented results in Section 13.6 showing that an SVM is a very effective text classifier. The results of Dumais et al. (1998) given in Table 13.9 show SVMs clearly performing the best. This was one of several pieces of work from this time that established the strong reputation of SVMs for text classification. Another pioneering work on scaling and evaluating SVMs for text classification was (Joachims 1998). We present some of his results from (Joachims 2002a) in Table 15.2.[5] Joachims used a large number of term features, in contrast with Dumais et al. (1998), who used MI feature selection (Section 13.5.1, page 252) to build classifiers with a much more limited number of features. The success of the linear SVM mirrors the results discussed in Section 14.6 (page 284) on other linear approaches like Naive Bayes. It seems that working with simple term features can get one a long way. It

---

[5] These results are in terms of the break-even F_1 (see Section 8.4). Many researchers disprefer this measure for text classification evaluation; its calculation may involve interpolation rather than an actual parameter setting of the system and it is not clear why this value should be reported rather than maximal F_1 or another point on the precision/recall curve motivated by the task at hand. Whereas earlier results in (Joachims 1998) suggested notable gains on this task from the use of higher order polynomial or rbf kernels, this was with hard-margin SVMs. With soft-margin SVMs, a simple linear SVM with the default $C = 1$ performs best.

Table 15.2 SVM classifier break-even F_1 from (Joachims 2002a, p. 114). Results are shown for the ten largest categories and for microaveraged performance over all ninety categories on the Reuters-21578 data set.

	NB	Rocchio	dec. Trees	kNN	linear SVM $C = 0.5$	linear SVM $C = 1.0$	rbf-SVM $\sigma \approx 7$
earn	96.0	96.1	96.1	97.8	98.0	98.2	98.1
acq	90.7	92.1	85.3	91.8	95.5	95.6	94.7
money-fx	59.6	67.6	69.4	75.4	78.8	78.5	74.3
grain	69.8	79.5	89.1	82.6	91.9	93.1	93.4
crude	81.2	81.5	75.5	85.8	89.4	89.4	88.7
trade	52.2	77.4	59.2	77.9	79.2	79.2	76.6
interest	57.6	72.5	49.1	76.7	75.6	74.8	69.1
ship	80.9	83.1	80.9	79.8	87.4	86.5	85.8
wheat	63.4	79.4	85.5	72.9	86.6	86.8	82.4
corn	45.2	62.2	87.7	71.4	87.5	87.8	84.6
microavg.	72.3	79.9	79.4	82.6	86.7	87.5	86.4

is again noticeable the extent to which different papers' results for the same machine learning methods differ. In particular, based on replications by other researchers, the Naive Bayes results of (Joachims 1998) appear too weak, and the results in Table 13.9 should be taken as representative.

15.3 Issues in the classification of text documents

There are lots of applications of text classification in the commercial world; email spam filtering is perhaps now the most ubiquitous. Jackson and Moulinier (2002) write: "There is no question concerning the commercial value of being able to classify documents automatically by content. There are myriad potential applications of such a capability for corporate Intranets, government departments, and Internet publishers."

Most of our discussion of classification has focused on introducing various machine-learning methods rather than discussing particular features of text documents relevant to classification. This bias is appropriate for a textbook, but is misplaced for an application developer. It is frequently the case that greater performance gains can be achieved from exploiting domain-specific text features than from changing from one machine learning method to another. Jackson and Moulinier (2002) suggest that "Understanding the data is one of the keys to successful categorization, yet this is an area in which most categorization tool vendors are extremely weak. Many of the 'one size fits all' tools on the market have not been tested on a wide range of content types." In this section, we wish to step back a little and consider the applications of text classification, the space of possible solutions, and the utility of application-specific heuristics.

15.3.1 Choosing what kind of classifier to use

When confronted with a need to build a text classifier, the first question to ask is how much training data is there currently available? None? Very little? Quite a lot? Or a huge amount, growing every day? Often one of the biggest practical challenges in fielding a machine-learning classifier in real applications is creating or obtaining enough training data. For many problems and algorithms, hundreds or thousands of examples from each class are required to produce a high-performance classifier and many real-world contexts involve large sets of categories. We will initially assume that the classifier is needed as soon as possible; if a lot of time is available for implementation, much of it might be spent on assembling data resources.

If you have no labeled training data, and especially if there are existing staff knowledgeable about the domain of the data, then you should never forget the solution of using hand-written rules. That is, you write standing queries, as we touched on at the beginning of Chapter 13. For example:

IF (wheat OR grain) AND NOT (whole OR bread) THEN c = grain

In practice, rules get a lot bigger than this, and can be phrased using more sophisticated query languages than just Boolean expressions, including the use of numeric scores. With careful crafting (i.e., by humans tuning the rules on development data), the accuracy of such rules can become very high. Jacobs and Rau (1990) report identifying articles about takeovers with 92% precision and 88.5% recall, and Hayes and Weinstein (1990) report 94% recall and 84% precision over 675 categories on Reuters newswire documents. Nevertheless, the amount of work to create such well-tuned rules is very large. A reasonable estimate is two days per class, and extra time has to go into maintenance of rules, as the content of documents in classes drifts over time (cf. page 249).

If you have fairly little data and you are going to train a supervised classifier, then machine-learning theory says you should stick to a classifier with high bias, as we discussed in Section 14.6 (page 284). For example, there are theoretical and empirical results that Naive Bayes does well in such circumstances (Ng and Jordan 2001; Forman and Cohen 2004), although this effect is not necessarily observed in practice with regularized models over textual data (Klein and Manning 2002). At any rate, a very low bias model like a nearest neighbor model is probably contraindicated. Regardless, the quality of the model will be adversely affected by the limited training data.

SEMISUPERVISED   Here, the theoretically interesting answer is to try to apply *semisuper-*
LEARNING   *vised training methods*. This includes methods such as bootstrapping or the expectation-maximization (EM) algorithm, which we will introduce in Section 16.5 (page 338). In these methods, the system gets some labeled documents, and a further large supply of unlabeled documents over which it can attempt to learn. One of the big advantages of Naive Bayes is that it can be

straightforwardly extended to be a semisupervised learning algorithm, but for SVMs, there is also semi supervised learning work which goes under the title of *transductive SVMs*. See the references for pointers.

TRANSDUCTIVE
SVMs

Often, the practical answer is to work out how to get more labeled data as quickly as you can. The best way to do this is to insert yourself into a process where humans will be willing to label data for you as part of their natural tasks. For example, in many cases humans will sort or route email for their own purposes, and these actions give information about classes. The alternative of getting human labelers expressly for the task of training classifiers is often difficult to organize, and the labeling is often of lower quality, because the labels are not embedded in a realistic task context. Rather than getting people to label all or a random sample of documents, there has also been considerable research on *active learning*, where a system that decides which documents a human should label is built. Usually these are the ones on which a classifier is uncertain of the correct classification. This can be effective in reducing annotation costs by a factor of 2 to 4, but has the problem that the good documents to label to train one type of classifier often are not the good documents to label to train a different type of classifier.

ACTIVE
LEARNING

If there is a reasonable amount of labeled data, then you are in the perfect position to use everything that we have presented about text classification. For instance, you may wish to use an SVM. However, if you are deploying a linear classifier such as an SVM, you should probably design an application that overlays a Boolean rule-based classifier over the machine-learning classifier. Users frequently like to adjust things that do not come out quite right, and if management gets on the phone and wants the classification of a particular document fixed right now, then this is much easier to do by hand-writing a rule than by working out how to adjust the weights of an SVM without destroying the overall classification accuracy. This is one reason why machine-learning models like decision trees, which produce user-interpretable Boolean-like models, retain considerable popularity.

If a huge amount of data are available, then the choice of classifier probably has little effect on your results and the best choice may be unclear (cf. Banko and Brill 2001). It may be best to choose a classifier based on the scalability of training or even runtime efficiency. To get to this point, you need to have huge amounts of data. The general rule of thumb is that each doubling of the training data size produces a linear increase in classifier performance, but with very large amounts of data, the improvement becomes sublinear.

15.3.2 *Improving classifier performance*

For any particular application, there is usually significant room for improving classifier effectiveness through exploiting features specific to the domain or document collection. Often documents will contain zones that are especially useful for classification. Often there will be particular subvocabularies which demand special treatment for optimal classification effectiveness.

Large and difficult category taxonomies

If a text classification problem consists of a small number of well-separated categories, then many classification algorithms are likely to work well. But many real classification problems consist of a very large number of often very similar categories. The reader might think of examples like web directories (the Yahoo! Directory or the Open Directory Project), library classification schemes (Dewey Decimal or Library of Congress), or the classification schemes used in legal or medical applications. For instance, the Yahoo! Directory consists of over 200,000 categories in a deep hierarchy. Accurate classification over large sets of closely related classes is inherently difficult.

HIERARCHICAL   Most large sets of categories have a hierarchical structure, and attempting
CLASSIFICATION   to exploit the hierarchy by doing *hierarchical classification* is a promising approach. However, at present the effectiveness gains from doing this rather than just working with the classes that are the leaves of the hierarchy remain modest.[6] But the technique can be very useful simply to improve the scalability of building classifiers over large hierarchies. Another simple way to improve the scalability of classifiers over large hierarchies is the use of aggressive feature selection. We provide references to some work on hierarchical classification in Section 15.5.

A general result in machine learning is that you can always get a small boost in classification accuracy by combining multiple classifiers, provided only that the mistakes that they make are at least somewhat independent. There is now a large literature on techniques such as voting, bagging, and boosting multiple classifiers. Again, there are some pointers in the references. Nevertheless, ultimately a hybrid automatic/manual solution may be needed to achieve sufficient classification accuracy. A common approach in such situations is to run a classifier first, and to accept all its high-confidence decisions, but to put low confidence decisions in a queue for manual review. Such a process also automatically leads to the production of new training data that can be used in future versions of the machine learning classifier. However, note that this is a case in point where the resulting training data is clearly *not* randomly sampled from the space of documents.

Features for text

The default in both ad hoc retrieval and text classification is to use terms as features. However, for text classification, a great deal of mileage can be

---

[6] Using the small hierarchy in Figure 13.1 (page 238) as an example, the leaf classes are ones like *poultry* and *coffee*, as opposed to higher-up classes like *industries*.

achieved by designing additional features suited to a specific problem. Unlike the case of IR query languages, because these features are internal to the classifier, there is no problem of communicating these features to an end

FEATURE user. This process is generally referred to as *feature engineering*. At present,
ENGINEERING feature engineering remains a human craft, rather than something done by machine learning. Good feature engineering can often markedly improve the performance of a text classifier. It is especially beneficial in some of the most important applications of text classification, like spam and pornography filtering.

Classification problems will often contain large numbers of terms that can be conveniently grouped and have a similar vote in text classification problems. Typical examples might be year mentions or strings of exclamation marks. Or they may be more specialized tokens like ISBNs or chemical formulas. Often, using them directly in a classifier would greatly increase the vocabulary without providing classificatory power beyond knowing that, say, a chemical formula is present. In such cases, the number of features and feature sparseness can be reduced by matching such items with regular expressions and converting them into distinguished tokens. Consequently, effectiveness and classifier speed are normally enhanced. Sometimes all numbers are converted into a single feature, but often some value can be had by distinguishing different kinds of numbers, such as four-digit numbers (which are usually years) versus other cardinal numbers versus real numbers with a decimal point. Similar techniques can be applied to dates, ISBN numbers, sports game scores, and so on.

Going in the other direction, it is often useful to increase the number of features by matching parts of words, and by matching selected multiword patterns that are particularly discriminative. Parts of words are often matched by character k-gram features. Such features can be particularly good at providing classification clues for otherwise unknown words when the classifier is deployed. For instance, an unknown word ending in *-rase* is likely to be an enzyme, even if it wasn't seen in the training data. Good multiword patterns are often found by looking for distinctively common word pairs (perhaps using a mutual information criterion between words, in a similar way to its use in Section 13.5.1 (page 252) for feature selection) and then using feature selection methods evaluated against classes. They are useful when the components of a compound would themselves be misleading as classification cues. For instance, this would be the case if the keyword *ethnic* was most indicative of the categories *food* and *arts*, the keyword *cleansing* was most indicative of the category *home*, but the collocation *ethnic cleansing* instead indicates the category *world news*. Some text classifiers also make use of features from named entity recognizers (cf. page 178).

Do techniques like stemming and lowercasing (Section 2.2, page 21) help for text classification? As always, the ultimate test is empirical evaluations conducted on an appropriate test collection. But it is nevertheless useful to note that such techniques have a more restricted chance of being useful for classification. For IR, you often need to collapse forms of a word like *oxygenate* and *oxygenation*, because the appearance of either in a document is a good clue that the document will be relevant to a query about oxygenation. Given copious training data, stemming necessarily delivers no value for text classification. If several forms that stem together have a similar signal, the parameters estimated for all of them will have similar weights. Techniques like stemming help only in compensating for data sparseness. This can be a useful role (as noted at the start of this section), but often different forms of a word can convey significantly different cues about the correct document classification. Overly aggressive stemming can easily degrade classification performance.

Document zones in text classification

As discussed in Section 6.1, documents usually have zones, such as mail message headers like the subject and author, or the title and keywords of a research article. Text classifiers can usually gain from making use of these zones during training and classification.

Upweighting document zones. In text classification problems, you can frequently get a nice boost to effectiveness by differentially weighting contributions from different document zones. Often, upweighting title words is particularly effective (Cohen and Singer 1999, p. 163). As a rule of thumb, it is often effective to double the weight of title words in text classification problems. You can also get value from upweighting words from pieces of text that are not so much clearly defined zones, but where nevertheless evidence from document structure or content suggests that they are important. Murata et al. (2000) suggest that you can also get value (in an ad hoc retrieval context) from upweighting the first sentence of a (newswire) document.

Separate feature spaces for document zones. There are two strategies that can be used for document zones. Above we upweighted words that appear in certain zones. This means that we are using the same features (that is, parameters are "tied" across different zones), but we pay more attention to the occurrence of terms in particular zones. An alternative strategy is to have a completely separate set of features and corresponding parameters for words occurring in different zones. This is in principle more powerful: A word could usually indicate the topic *Middle East* when in the title but *Commodities* when in the body of a document. But, in practice, tying parameters is usually more successful. Having separate feature sets means having two or more times as many parameters, many of which will be much more sparsely seen in the training data, and hence with worse estimates, whereas upweighting has no adverse effects of this sort. Moreover, it is quite uncommon for words

PARAMETER
TYING

to have different preferences when appearing in different zones; it is mainly the strength of their vote that should be adjusted. Nevertheless, ultimately this is a contingent result, depending on the nature and quantity of the training data.

Connections to text summarization. In Section 8.7, we mentioned the field of text summarization, and how most work in that field has adopted the limited goal of extracting and assembling pieces of the original text that are judged to be central based on features of sentences that consider the sentence's position and content. Much of this work can be used to suggest zones that may be distinctively useful for text classification. For example, Kołcz et al. (2000) consider a form of feature selection where you classify documents based only on words in certain zones. Based on text summarization research, they consider using (i) only the title, (ii) only the first paragraph, (iii) only the paragraph with the most title words or keywords, (iv) the first two paragraphs or the first and last paragraphs, or (v) all sentences with a minimum number of title words or keywords. In general, these positional feature selection methods produced as good results as mutual information (Section 13.5.1), and resulted in quite competitive classifiers. Ko et al. (2004) also took inspiration from text summarization research to upweight sentences with either words from the title or words that are central to the document's content, leading to classification accuracy gains of almost 1%. This presumably works because most such sentences are somehow more central to the concerns of the document.

?

Exercise 15.4 [⋆⋆] Spam email often makes use of various cloaking techniques to try to get through. One method is to pad or substitute characters so as to defeat word-based text classifiers. For example, you see terms like the following in spam email:

Rep1icaRolex	bonmus	Viiiaaaagra	pi11z
PHARlbdMACY	[LEV]i[IT]l[RA]	se∧xual	ClAfLlS

Discuss how you could engineer features that would largely defeat this strategy.

Exercise 15.5 [⋆⋆] Another strategy often used by purveyors of email spam is to follow the message they wish to send (such as buying a cheap stock or whatever) with a paragraph of text from another innocuous source (such as a news article). Why might this strategy be effective? How might it be addressed by a text classifier?

Exercise 15.6 [⋆] What other kinds of features appear as if they would be useful in an email spam classifier?

15.4 Machine-learning methods in ad hoc information retrieval

Rather than coming up with term and document weighting functions by hand, as we primarily did in Chapter 6, we can view different sources of relevance signal (cosine score, title match, etc.) as features in a learning problem. A classifier that has been fed examples of relevant and nonrelevant documents for each of a set of queries can then figure out the relative weights of these signals. If we configure the problem so that there are pairs of a document and a query that are assigned a relevance judgment of *relevant* or *nonrelevant*, then we can think of this problem too as a text classification problem. Taking such a classification approach is not necessarily best, and we present an alternative in Section 15.4.2. Nevertheless, given the material we have covered, the simplest place to start is to approach this problem as a classification problem, by ordering the documents according to the confidence of a two-class classifier in its relevance decision. And this move is not purely pedagogical; exactly this approach is sometimes used in practice.

15.4.1 A simple example of machine-learned scoring

In this section, we generalize the methodology of Section 6.1.2 (page 104) to *machine learning* of the scoring function. In Section 6.1.2, we considered a case where we had to combine Boolean indicators of relevance; here we consider more general factors to further develop the notion of machine-learned relevance. In particular, the factors we now consider go beyond Boolean functions of query term presence in document zones, as in Section 6.1.2.

We develop the ideas in a setting where the scoring function is a linear combination of two factors: (i) the vector space cosine similarity between query and document and (ii) the minimum window width ω within which the query terms lie. As we noted in Section 7.2.2 (page 132), query term proximity is often very indicative of a document being on topic, especially with longer documents and on the web. Among other things, this quantity gives us an implementation of implicit phrases. Thus, we have one factor that depends on the statistics of query terms in the document as a bag of words, and another that depends on proximity weighting. We consider only two features in the development of the ideas because a two-feature exposition remains simple enough to visualize. The technique can be generalized to many more features.

As in Section 6.1.2, we are provided with a set of *training examples*, each of which is a pair consisting of a query and a document, together with a relevance judgment for that document on that query that is either *relevant* or *nonrelevant*. For each such example we can compute the vector space cosine similarity, as well as the window width ω. The result is a training set as shown in Table 15.3, which resembles Figure 6.5 (page 105) from Section 6.1.2.

Table 15.3   Training examples for machine-learned scoring.

example	docID	query	cosine score	ω	judgment
Φ_1	37	linux operating system	0.032	3	*relevant*
Φ_2	37	penguin logo	0.02	4	*nonrelevant*
Φ_3	238	operating system	0.043	2	*relevant*
Φ_4	238	runtime environment	0.004	2	*nonrelevant*
Φ_5	1741	kernel layer	0.022	3	*relevant*
Φ_6	2094	device driver	0.03	2	*relevant*
Φ_7	3191	device driver	0.027	5	*nonrelevant*
$\ldots$	$\ldots$	$\ldots$	$\ldots$	$\ldots$	$\ldots$

Here, the two features (cosine score denoted α and window width ω) are real-valued predictors. If we once again quantify the judgment *relevant* as 1 and *nonrelevant* as 0, we seek a scoring function that combines the values of the features to generate a value that is (close to) 0 or 1. We wish this function to be in agreement with our set of training examples as far as possible. Without loss of generality, a linear classifier will use a linear combination of features of the form

$$(15.17) \qquad Score(d, q) = Score(\alpha, \omega) = a\alpha + b\omega + c,$$

with the coefficients a, b, c to be learned from the training data. Although it is possible to formulate this as an error minimization problem as we did in Section 6.1.2, it is instructive to visualize the geometry of Equation (15.17). The examples in Table 15.3 can be plotted on a two-dimensional plane with axes corresponding to the cosine score α and the window width ω. This is depicted in Figure 15.7.

In this setting, the function $Score(\alpha, \omega)$ from Equation (15.17) represents a plane "hanging above" Figure 15.7. Ideally, this plane (in the direction perpendicular to the page containing Figure 15.7) assumes values close to 1 above the points marked R, and values close to 0 above the points marked N. Because a plane is unlikely to assume only values close to 0 or 1 above the training sample points, we make use of *thresholding*: Given any query and document for which we wish to determine relevance, we pick a value θ and if $Score(\alpha, \omega) > \theta$ we declare the document to be *relevant*, else we declare the document to be *nonrelevant*. As we know from Figure 14.8 (page 278), all points that satisfy $Score(\alpha, \omega) = \theta$ form a line (shown as a dashed line in Figure 15.7) and we thus have a linear classifier that separates relevant from nonrelevant instances. Geometrically, we can find the separating line as follows. Consider the line passing through the plane $Score(\alpha, \omega)$ whose height is θ above the page containing Figure 15.7. Project this line down onto Figure 15.7; this will be the dashed line in Figure 15.7. Then, any subsequent query–document pair that falls below the dashed line in Figure 15.7 is deemed *nonrelevant*; above the dashed line, *relevant*.

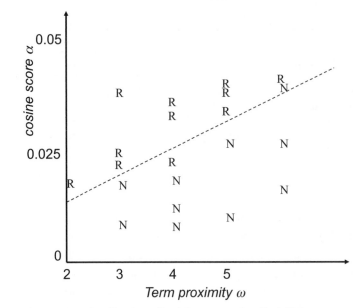

Figure 15.7   A collection of training examples. Each R denotes a training example labeled *relevant* and each N is a training example labeled *nonrelevant*.

Thus, the problem of making a binary *relevant/nonrelevant* judgment given training examples as above turns into one of learning the dashed line in Figure 15.7 separating *relevant* training examples from the *nonrelevant* ones. Being in the α–ω plane, this line can be written as a linear equation involving α and ω, with two parameters (slope and intercept). The methods of linear classification that we have already looked at in Chapters 13 through 15 provide methods for choosing this line. Provided we can build a sufficiently rich collection of training samples, we can thus altogether avoid hand-tuning score functions as in Section 7.2.3 (page 133). The bottleneck of course is the ability to maintain a suitably representative set of training examples, whose relevance assessments must be made by experts.

15.4.2 *Result ranking by machine learning*

These ideas can be readily generalized to functions of many more than two variables. There are lots of other scores that are indicative of the relevance of a document to a query, including static quality (PageRank-style measures, discussed in Chapter 21), document age, zone contributions, document length, and so on. Providing that these measures can be calculated for a training document collection with relevance judgments, any number of such measures can be used to train a machine-learning classifier. For instance, we could train an SVM over binary relevance judgments, and order documents based on their probability of relevance, which is monotonic with the documents' signed distance from the decision boundary.

However, approaching IR result ranking like this is not necessarily the right way to think about the problem. Statisticians normally first divide problems into classification problems (where a categorical variable is predicted) REGRESSION versus *regression* problems (where a real number is predicted). In between is ORDINAL the specialized field of *ordinal regression* where a ranking is predicted. Machine learning for ad hoc retrieval is most properly thought of as an ordinal regression problem, where the goal is to rank a set of documents for a query, given training data of the same sort. This formulation gives some additional power, because documents can be evaluated relative to other candidate documents for the same query, rather than having to be mapped to a global scale of goodness, while also weakening the problem space; just a ranking is required rather than an absolute measure of relevance. Issues of ranking are especially germane for web searches, where the ranking at the very top of the results list is exceedingly important, whereas decisions of relevance of a document to a query may be much less important. Such work can and has been pursued using the structural SVM framework that we mentioned in Section 15.2.2, where the class being predicted is a ranking of results for a query, but here we will present the slightly simpler ranking SVM.

RANKING SVM The construction of a *ranking SVM* proceeds as follows. We begin with a set of judged queries. For each training query q, we have a set of documents returned in response to the query, which have been totally ordered by a person for relevance to the query. We construct a vector of features $\psi_j = \psi(d_j, q)$ for each document–query pair, using features such as those discussed in Section 15.4.1, and many more. For two documents d_i and d_j, we then form the vector of feature differences:

$$(15.18) \qquad \Phi(d_i, d_j, q) = \psi(d_i, q) - \psi(d_j, q).$$

By hypothesis, one of d_i and d_j has been judged more relevant. If d_i is judged more relevant than d_j, denoted $d_i \prec d_j$ (d_i should precede d_j in the results ordering), then we will assign the vector $\Phi(d_i, d_j, q)$ the class $y_{ijq} = +1$; otherwise -1. The goal then is to build a classifier, which will return

$$(15.19) \qquad \vec{w}^\mathsf{T} \Phi(d_i, d_j, q) > 0 \quad \text{iff} \quad d_i \prec d_j.$$

This SVM learning task is formalized in a manner much like the other examples that we saw before:

(15.20)   Find $\vec{w}$, and $\xi_{i,j} \geq 0$ such that:

- $\frac{1}{2}\vec{w}^\mathsf{T}\vec{w} + C \sum_{i,j} \xi_{i,j}$ is minimized
- and for all $\{\Phi(d_i, d_j, q) : d_i \prec d_j\}$, $\vec{w}^\mathsf{T}\Phi(d_i, d_j, q) \geq 1 - \xi_{i,j}$

We can leave out y_{ijq} in the statement of the constraint; we only need to consider the constraint for document pairs ordered in one direction because $\prec$ is antisymmetric. These constraints are then solved, as before, to give a linear classifier that can rank pairs of documents. This approach has been used to build ranking functions which outperform standard hand-built ranking functions in IR evaluations on standard data sets; see the references for papers that present such results.

Both of the methods that we have just looked at use a linear weighting of document features that are indicators of relevance, as has most work in this area. It is therefore perhaps interesting to note that much of traditional IR weighting involves *nonlinear* scaling of basic measurements (such as log-weighting of term frequency, or idf). At the present time, machine learning is very good at producing optimal weights for features in a linear combination (or other similar restricted model classes), but it is not good at coming up with good nonlinear scalings of basic measurements. This area remains the domain of human feature engineering.

The idea of learning ranking functions has been around for a number of years, but it is only very recently that sufficient machine-learning knowledge, training document collections, and computational power have come together to make this method practical and exciting. It is thus too early to write something definitive on machine-learning approaches to ranking in IR, but there is every reason to expect the use and importance of machine-learned ranking approaches to grow over time. Although skilled humans can do a very good job at defining ranking functions by hand, hand tuning is difficult, and it has to be done again for each new document collection and class of users.

? **Exercise 15.7** Plot the first seven rows of Table 15.3 in the α–ω plane to produce a figure like that in Figure 15.7.

Exercise 15.8 Write down the equation of a line in the α–ω plane separating the Rs from the Ns.

Exercise 15.9 Give a training example (consisting of values for α, ω and the relevance judgment) that when added to the training set makes it impossible to separate the Rs from the Ns using a line in the α–ω plane.

15.5 References and further reading

The somewhat quirky name *support vector machine* originates in the neural networks literature, where learning algorithms were thought of as architectures, and often referred to as "machines." The distinctive element of this model is that the decision boundary to use is completely decided ("supported") by a few training data points, the support vectors.

For a more detailed presentation of SVMs, a good, well-known article-length introduction is (Burges 1998). Chen et al. (2005) introduce the more recent ν-SVM, which provides an alternative parameterization for dealing with inseparable problems, whereby rather than specifying a penalty C, you specify a parameter ν that bounds the number of examples that can appear on the wrong side of the decision surface. There are now also several books dedicated to SVMs, large margin learning, and kernels: (Cristianini and Shawe-Taylor 2000) and (Schölkopf and Smola 2001) are more mathematically oriented, whereas (Shawe-Taylor and Cristianini 2004) aims to be more practical. For the foundations by their originator, see (Vapnik 1998). Some recent, more general books on statistical learning, such as (Hastie et al. 2001) also give thorough coverage of SVMs.

The construction of *multiclass SVMs* is discussed in (Weston and Watkins 1999), (Crammer and Singer 2001), and (Tsochantaridis et al. 2005). The last reference provides an introduction to the general framework of structural SVMs.

The kernel trick was first presented in (Aizerman et al. 1964). For more about string kernels and other kernels for structured data, see (Lodhi et al. 2002) and (Gaertner et al. 2002). The Advances in Neural Information Processing (NIPS) conferences have become the premier venue for theoretical machine learning work, such as on SVMs. Other venues such as SIGIR are much stronger on experimental methodology and using text-specific features to improve classifier effectiveness.

A recent comparison of most current machine learning classifiers (though on problems rather different from typical text problems) can be found in (Caruana and Niculescu-Mizil 2006). (Li and Yang 2003), discussed in Section 13.6, is the most recent comparative evaluation of machine learning classifiers on text classification. Older examinations of classifiers on text problems can be found in (Yang 1999; Yang and Liu 1999; Dumais et al. 1998). Joachims (2002a) presents his work on SVMs applied to text problems in detail. Zhang and Oles (2001) present an insightful comparison of Naive Bayes, regularized logistic regression and SVM classifiers.

Joachims (1999) discusses methods of making SVM learning practical over large text data sets. Joachims (2006a) improves on this work.

A number of approaches to hierarchical classification have been developed to deal with the common situation where the classes to be assigned have a natural hierarchical organization (Koller and Sahami 1997; McCallum et al. 1998; Weigend et al. 1999; Dumais and Chen 2000). In a recent large study on scaling SVMs to the entire Yahoo! directory, Liu et al. (2005) conclude that hierarchical classification noticeably if still modestly outperforms flat classification. Classifier effectiveness remains limited by the very small number of training documents for many classes. For a more general approach that can be applied to modeling relations between classes, which may be arbitrary rather than simply the case of a hierarchy, see Tsochantaridis et al. (2005).

Moschitti and Basili (2004) investigate the use of complex nominals, proper nouns and word senses as features in text classification.

Dieterich (2002) overviews ensemble methods for classifier combination, while Schapire (2003) focuses particularly on boosting, which is applied to text classification in (Schapire and Singer 2000).

Chapelle et al. (2006) present an introduction to work in semi-supervised methods, including in particular chapters on using EM for semi-supervised text classification (Nigam et al. 2006) and on transductive SVMs (Joachims 2006b). Sindhwani and Keerthi (2006) present a more efficient implementation of a transductive SVM for large data sets.

Tong and Koller (2001) explore active learning with SVMs for text classification; Baldridge and Osborne (2004) point out that examples selected for annotation with one classifier in an active learning context may be no better than random examples when used with another classifier.

Machine learning approaches to ranking for ad hoc retrieval were pioneered in (Wong et al. 1988), (Fuhr 1992), and (Gey 1994). But limited training data and poor machine learning techniques meant that these pieces of work achieved only middling results, and hence they only had limited impact at the time.

Taylor et al. (2006) study using machine learning to tune the parameters of the BM25 family of ranking functions (Section 11.4.3, page 213) so as to maximize NDCG (Section 8.4, page 149). Machine learning approaches to ordinal regression appear in (Herbrich et al. 2000) and (Burges et al. 2005), and are applied to clickstream data in (Joachims 2002b). Cao et al. (2006) study how to make this approach effective in IR, and Qin et al. (2007) suggest an extension involving using multiple hyperplanes. Yue et al. (2007) study how to do ranking with a structural SVM approach, and in particular show how this construction can be effectively used to directly optimize for MAP (Section 8.4, page 145), rather than using surrogate measures like accuracy or area under the ROC curve. Geng et al. (2007) study feature selection for the ranking problem.

Other approaches to learning to rank have also been shown to be effective for web search, such as (Burges et al. 2005; Richardson et al. 2006).

16 *Flat clustering*

CLUSTER   Clustering algorithms group a set of documents into subsets or *clusters*. The algorithms' goal is to create clusters that are coherent internally, but clearly different from each other. In other words, documents within a cluster should be as similar as possible; and documents in one cluster should be as dissimilar as possible from documents in other clusters.

UNSUPERVISED   Clustering is the most common form of *unsupervised learning*. No super-
LEARNING   vision means that there is no human expert who has assigned documents to classes. In clustering, it is the distribution and makeup of the data that will determine cluster membership. A simple example is Figure 16.1. It is visually clear that there are three distinct clusters of points. This chapter and Chapter 17 introduce algorithms that find such clusters in an unsupervised fashion.

The difference between clustering and classification may not seem great at first. After all, in both cases we have a partition of a set of documents into groups. But as we will see the two problems are fundamentally different. Classification is a form of supervised learning (Chapter 13, page 237): Our goal is to replicate a categorical distinction that a human supervisor imposes on the data. In unsupervised learning, of which clustering is the most important example, we have no such teacher to guide us.

The key input to a clustering algorithm is the distance measure. In Figure 16.1, the distance measure is distance in the two-dimensional (2D) plane. This measure suggests three different clusters in the figure. In document clustering, the distance measure is often Euclidean distance. Different distance measures give rise to different clusterings. Thus, the distance measure is an important means by which we can influence the outcome of clustering.

FLAT   *Flat clustering* creates a flat set of clusters without any explicit structure that
CLUSTERING   would relate clusters to each other. *Hierarchical clustering* creates a hierarchy of clusters and will be covered in Chapter 17. Chapter 17 also addresses the difficult problem of labeling clusters automatically.

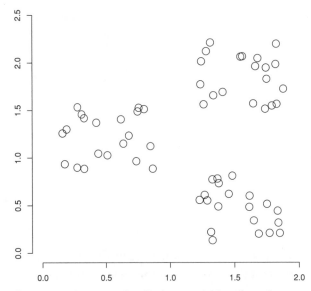

Figure 16.1 An example of a data set with a clear cluster structure.

A second important distinction can be made between hard and soft clus-
HARD tering algorithms. *Hard clustering* computes a *hard assignment* – each docu-
CLUSTERING ment is a member of exactly one cluster. The assignment of *soft clustering*
SOFT *algorithms* is *soft* – a document's assignment is a distribution over all clusters.
CLUSTERING In a soft assignment, a document has fractional membership in several clus-
ters. Latent semantic indexing, a form of dimensionality reduction, is a soft
clustering algorithm (Chapter 18, page 382).

This chapter motivates the use of clustering in information retrieval by introducing a number of applications (Section 16.1), defines the problem we
are trying to solve in clustering (Section 16.2), and discusses measures for
evaluating cluster quality (Section 16.3). It then describes two flat clustering
algorithms, K-means (Section 16.4), a hard clustering algorithm, and the expectation maximization (or EM) algorithm (Section 16.5), a soft clustering algorithm. K-means is perhaps the most widely used flat clustering algorithm
because of its simplicity and efficiency. The EM algorithm is a generalization
of K-means and can be applied to a large variety of document representations and distributions.

16.1 Clustering in information retrieval

CLUSTER The *cluster hypothesis* states the fundamental assumption we make when us-
HYPOTHESIS ing clustering in information retrieval (IR).

Cluster hypothesis. Documents in the same cluster behave similarly with
respect to relevance to information needs.

Table 16.1   Some applications of clustering in IR.

application	What is clustered?	benefit	example
search result clustering	search results	more effective information presentation to user	Figure 16.2
scatter-gather	(subsets of) collection	alternative user interface: "search without typing"	Figure 16.3
collection clustering	collection	effective information presentation for exploratory browsing	McKeown et al. (2002), http://news.google.com
language modeling	collection	increased precision and/or recall	Liu and Croft (2004)
cluster-based retrieval	collection	higher efficiency: faster search	Salton (1971a)

The hypothesis states that if there is a document from a cluster that is relevant to a search request, then it is likely that other documents from the same cluster are also relevant. This is because clustering puts together documents that share many terms. The cluster hypothesis essentially is the contiguity hypothesis in Chapter 14 (page 266). In both cases, we posit that similar documents behave similarly with respect to relevance.

Table 16.1 shows some of the main applications of clustering in IR. They differ in the set of documents that they cluster – search results, collection, or subsets of the collection – and the aspect of an IR system they try to improve – user experience, user interface, effectiveness or efficiency of the search system. But they are all based on the basic assumption stated by the cluster hypothesis.

SEARCH RESULT CLUSTERING   The first application mentioned in Table 16.1 is *search result clustering* where by search results we mean the documents that were returned in response to a query. The default presentation of search results in IR is a simple list. Users scan the list from top to bottom until they have found the information they are looking for. Instead, search result clustering clusters the search results, so that similar documents appear together. It is often easier to scan a few coherent groups than many individual documents. This is particularly useful if a search term has different word senses. The example in Figure 16.2 is jaguar. Three frequent senses on the web refer to the car, the animal, and an Apple operating system. The *Clustered Results* panel returned by the Vivísimo search engine (http://vivisimo.com) can be a more effective user interface for understanding what is in the search results than a simple list of documents.

SCATTER-GATHER   A better user interface is also the goal of *scatter-gather*, the second application in Table 16.1. Scatter-gather clusters the whole collection to get groups of documents that the user can select or *gather*. The selected groups are merged and the resulting set is again clustered. This process is repeated until a cluster of interest is found. An example is shown in Figure 16.3.

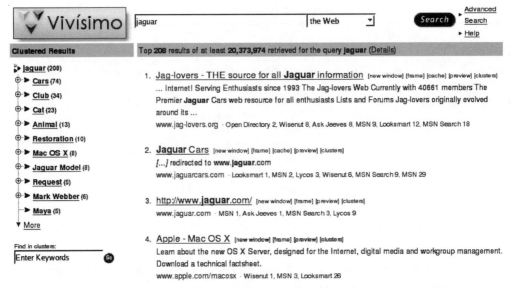

Figure 16.2 Clustering of search results to improve recall. None of the top hits cover the animal sense of jaguar, but users can easily access it by clicking on the *Cat* cluster in the *Clustered Results* panel on the left (third arrow from the top).

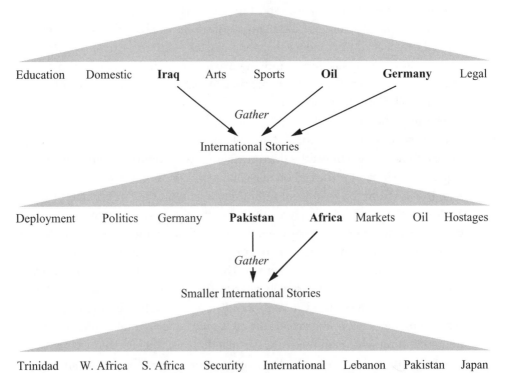

Figure 16.3 An example of a user session in scatter-gather. A collection of *New York Times* news stories is clustered ("scattered") into eight clusters (*top row*). The user manually *gathers* three of these into a smaller collection *International Stories* and performs another scattering operation. This process repeats until a small cluster with *relevant* documents is found (e.g., *Trinidad*).

Automatically generated clusters like those in Figure 16.3 are not as neatly organized as a manually constructed hierarchical tree like the Open Directory at http://dmoz.org. Also, finding descriptive labels for clusters automatically is a difficult problem (Section 17.7, page 363). But cluster-based navigation is an interesting alternative to keyword searching, the standard IR paradigm. This is especially true in scenarios where users prefer browsing over searching because they are unsure about which search terms to use.

As an alternative to the user-mediated iterative clustering in scatter-gather, we can also compute a static hierarchical clustering of a collection that is not influenced by user interactions ("Collection clustering" in Table 16.1). Google News and its precursor, the Columbia NewsBlaster system, are examples of this approach. In the case of news, we need to frequently recompute the clustering to make sure that users can access the latest breaking stories. Clustering is well suited for access to a collection of news stories because news reading is not really search, but rather a process of selecting a subset of stories about recent events.

The fourth application of clustering exploits the cluster hypothesis directly for improving search results, based on a clustering of the entire collection. We use a standard inverted index to identify an initial set of documents that match the query, but we then add other documents from the same clusters even if they have low similarity to the query. For example, if the query is car and several car documents are taken from a cluster of automobile documents, then we can add documents from this cluster that use terms other than car (automobile, vehicle, etc.). This can increase recall; a group of documents with high mutual similarity is often relevant as a whole.

More recently, this idea has been used for language modeling. Equation (12.10), page 226, showed that to avoid sparse data problems in the language modeling approach to IR, the model of document d can be interpolated with a collection model. But the collection contains many documents with terms untypical of d. By replacing the collection model with a model derived from d's cluster, we get more accurate estimates of the occurrence probabilities of terms in d.

Clustering can also speed up search. As we saw in Section 6.3.2 (page 113), search in the vector space model amounts to finding the nearest neighbors to the query. The inverted index supports fast nearest-neighbor search for the standard IR setting. However, sometimes we may not be able to use an inverted index efficiently, for example, in latent semantic indexing (Chapter 18). In such cases, we could compute the similarity of the query to every document, but this is slow. The cluster hypothesis offers an alternative: Find the clusters that are closest to the query and only consider documents from these clusters. Within this much smaller set, we can compute similarities exhaustively and rank documents in the usual way. Because there are many fewer clusters than documents, finding the closest cluster is fast, and because the documents matching a query are all similar to each other, they tend to be in the same clusters. Although this algorithm is inexact, the expected decrease in search quality is small. This is essentially the application of clustering that was covered in Section 7.1.6 (page 130).

? **Exercise 16.1** Define two documents as similar if they have at least two proper names like Clinton or Sarkozy in common. Give an example of an information need and two documents, for which the cluster hypothesis does *not* hold for this notion of similarity.

Exercise 16.2 Make up a simple, one-dimensional example (i.e., points on a line) with two clusters where the inexactness of cluster-based retrieval shows up. In your example, retrieving clusters close to the query should do worse than direct nearest neighbor search.

16.2 Problem statement

We can define the goal in hard flat clustering as follows. Given (i) a set of documents $D = \{d_1, \ldots, d_N\}$, (ii) a desired number of clusters K, and (iii) an OBJECTIVE *objective function* that evaluates the quality of a clustering, we want to com-FUNCTION pute an assignment $\gamma : D \to \{1, \ldots, K\}$ that minimizes (or, in other cases, maximizes) the objective function. In most cases, we also demand that γ is surjective, that is, that none of the K clusters is empty.

The objective function is often defined in terms of similarity or distance between documents. Below, we will see that the objective in K-means clustering is to minimize the average distance between documents and their centroids or, equivalently, to maximize the similarity between documents and their centroids. The discussion of similarity measures and distance metrics in Chapter 14 (page 267) also applies to this chapter. As in Chapter 14, we use both similarity and distance to talk about relatedness between documents.

For documents, the type of similarity we want is usually topic similarity or high values on the same dimensions in the vector space model. For example, documents about China have high values on dimensions like Chinese, Beijing, and Mao whereas documents about the UK tend to have high values for London, Britain, and Queen. We approximate topic similarity with cosine similarity or Euclidean distance in vector space (Chapter 6). If we intend to capture similarity of a type other than topic, for example, similarity of language, then a different representation may be appropriate. When computing topic similarity, stop words can be safely ignored, but they are important cues for separating clusters of English (in which the occurs frequently and la infrequently) and French documents (in which the occurs infrequently and la frequently).

PARTITIONAL **A note on terminology.** An alternative definition of hard clustering is that CLUSTERING a document can be a full member of more than one cluster. *Partitional* *clustering* always refers to a clustering where each document belongs to exactly one cluster. (But in a partitional hierarchical clustering (Chapter 17), all members of a cluster are of course also members of its parent.) On the definition of hard clustering that permits multiple membership, the difference between soft clustering and hard clustering is that membership values in hard clustering are either 0 or 1, whereas they can take on any non-negative value in soft clustering.

EXHAUSTIVE Some researchers distinguish between *exhaustive* clusterings that assign each document to a cluster and nonexhaustive clusterings, in which some documents will be assigned to no cluster. Nonexhaustive clusterings, in which each document is a member of either no cluster or one cluster, are called *exclusive*. We define clustering to be exhaustive in this book.

16.2.1 Cardinality – The number of clusters

CARDINALITY A difficult issue in clustering is determining the number of clusters or *cardinality* of a clustering, which we denote by K. Often K is nothing more than a good guess based on experience or domain knowledge. But for K-means, we will also introduce a heuristic method for choosing K and an attempt to incorporate the selection of K into the objective function. Sometimes the application puts constraints on the range of K. For example, the scatter-gather interface in Figure 16.3 could not display more than about $K = 10$ clusters per layer because of the size and resolution of computer monitors in the early 1990s.

Because our goal is to optimize an objective function, clustering is essentially a search problem. The brute force solution would be to enumerate all possible clusterings and pick the best. However, there are exponentially many partitions, so this approach is not feasible.[1] For this reason, most flat clustering algorithms refine an initial partitioning iteratively. If the search starts at an unfavorable initial point, we may miss the global optimum. Finding a good starting point is therefore another important problem we have to solve in flat clustering.

16.3 Evaluation of clustering

Typical objective functions in clustering formalize the goal of attaining high intracluster similarity (documents within a cluster are similar) and low intercluster similarity (documents from different clusters are dissimilar). This is INTERNAL an *internal criterion* for the quality of a clustering. But good scores on an CRITERION internal criterion do not necessarily translate into good effectiveness in an OF QUALITY

---

[1] An upper bound on the number of clusterings is $K^N/K!$. The exact number of different partitions of N documents into K clusters is the Stirling number of the second kind. See http://mathworld.wolfram.com/StirlingNumberoftheSecondKind.html or Comtet (1974).

application. An alternative to internal criteria is direct evaluation in the application of interest. For search result clustering, we may want to measure the time it takes users to find an answer with different clustering algorithms. This is the most direct evaluation, but it is expensive, especially if large user studies are necessary.

As a surrogate for user judgments, we can use a set of classes in an evaluation benchmark or gold standard (see Section 8.5, page 151, and Section 13.6, page 258). The gold standard is ideally produced by human judges with a good level of inter-judge agreement (see Chapter 8, page 140). We can then

EXTERNAL CRITERION OF QUALITY compute an *external criterion* that evaluates how well the clustering matches the gold standard classes. For example, we may want to say that the optimal clustering of the search results for jaguar in Figure 16.2 consists of three classes corresponding to the three senses *car*, *animal*, and *operating system*. In this type of evaluation, we only use the partition provided by the gold standard, not the class labels.

This section introduces four external criteria of clustering quality. *Purity* is a simple and transparent evaluation measure. *Normalized mutual information* can be information-theoretically interpreted. The *Rand index* penalizes both false-positive and false-negative decisions during clustering. The *F measure* in addition supports differential weighting of these two types of errors.

PURITY To compute *purity*, each cluster is assigned to the class which is most frequent in the cluster, and then the accuracy of this assignment is measured by counting the number of correctly assigned documents and dividing by N. Formally:

(16.1)
$$\text{purity}(\Omega, \mathbb{C}) = \frac{1}{N} \sum_k \max_j |\omega_k \cap c_j|$$

where $\Omega = \{\omega_1, \omega_2, \ldots, \omega_K\}$ is the set of clusters and $\mathbb{C} = \{c_1, c_2, \ldots, c_J\}$ is the set of classes. We interpret ω_k as the set of documents in ω_k and c_j as the set of documents in c_j in Equation (16.1).

We present an example of how to compute purity in Figure 16.4.[2] Bad clusterings have purity values close to 0, a perfect clustering has a purity of 1. Purity is compared with the other three measures discussed in this chapter in Table 16.2.

High purity is easy to achieve when the number of clusters is large – in particular, purity is 1 if each document gets its own cluster. Thus, we cannot use purity to trade off the quality of the clustering against the number of clusters.

---

[2] Recall our note of caution from Figure 14.2 (page 268) when looking at this and other 2D figures in this and the following chapter: these illustrations can be misleading because 2D projections of length-normalized vectors distort similarities and distances between points.

Table 16.2 The four external evaluation measures applied to the clustering in Figure 16.4.

	purity	NMI	RI	F_5
lower bound	0.0	0.0	0.0	0.0
maximum	1.0	1.0	1.0	1.0
value for Figure 16.4	0.71	0.36	0.68	0.46

NORMALIZED
MUTUAL
INFORMATION

A measure that allows us to make this tradeoff is *normalized mutual information* or *NMI*:

$$(16.2) \qquad \text{NMI}(\Omega, \mathbb{C}) = \frac{I(\Omega; \mathbb{C})}{[H(\Omega) + H(\mathbb{C})]/2}.$$

I is mutual information (cf. Chapter 13, page 252):

$$(16.3) \qquad I(\Omega; \mathbb{C}) = \sum_k \sum_j P(\omega_k \cap c_j) \log \frac{P(\omega_k \cap c_j)}{P(\omega_k)P(c_j)}$$

$$(16.4) \qquad = \sum_k \sum_j \frac{|\omega_k \cap c_j|}{N} \log \frac{N|\omega_k \cap c_j|}{|\omega_k||c_j|}$$

where $P(\omega_k)$, $P(c_j)$, and $P(\omega_k \cap c_j)$ are the probabilities of a document being in cluster ω_k, class c_j, and in the intersection of ω_k and c_j, respectively. Equation (16.4) is equivalent to Equation (16.3) for maximum likelihood estimates (MLE) of the probabilities (i.e., the estimate of each probability is the corresponding relative frequency).

H is entropy as defined in Chapter 5 (page 91):

$$(16.5) \qquad H(\Omega) = -\sum_k P(\omega_k) \log P(\omega_k)$$

$$(16.6) \qquad = -\sum_k \frac{|\omega_k|}{N} \log \frac{|\omega_k|}{N}$$

where, again, the second equation is based on MLEs of the probabilities.

$I(\Omega; \mathbb{C})$ in Equation (16.3) measures the amount of information by which our knowledge about the classes increases when we are told what the clusters

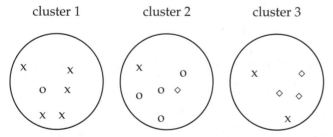

Figure 16.4 Purity as an external evaluation criterion for cluster quality. Majority class and number of members of the majority class for the three clusters are: x, 5 (cluster 1); o, 4 (cluster 2); and ⋄, 3 (cluster 3). Purity is $(1/17) \times (5 + 4 + 3) \approx 0.71$.

are. The minimum of $I(\Omega; \mathbb{C})$ is 0 if the clustering is random with respect to class membership. In that case, knowing that a document is in a particular cluster does not give us any new information about what its class might be. Maximum mutual information is reached for a clustering Ω_{exact} that perfectly recreates the classes – but also if clusters in Ω_{exact} are further subdivided into smaller clusters (Exercise 16.7). In particular, a clustering with $K = N$ one-document clusters has maximum MI. So MI has the same problem as purity: It does not penalize large cardinalities and thus does not formalize our bias that, other things being equal, fewer clusters are better.

The normalization by the denominator $[H(\Omega) + H(\mathbb{C})]/2$ in Equation (16.2) fixes this problem; entropy tends to increase with the number of clusters. For example, $H(\Omega)$ reaches its maximum of $\log N$ for $K = N$, which ensures that NMI is low for $K = N$. Because NMI is normalized, we can use it to compare clusterings with different numbers of clusters. The particular form of the denominator is chosen because $[H(\Omega) + H(\mathbb{C})]/2$ is a tight upper bound on $I(\Omega; \mathbb{C})$ (Exercise 16.8). Thus, NMI is always a number between 0 and 1.

An alternative to this information-theoretic interpretation of clustering is to view it as a series of decisions, one for each of the $N(N-1)/2$ pairs of documents in the collection. We want to assign two documents to the same cluster if and only if they are similar. A true-positive (TP) decision assigns two similar documents to the same cluster, a true-negative (TN) decision assigns two dissimilar documents to different clusters. There are two types of errors we can commit. A false-positive (FP) decision assigns two dissimilar documents to the same cluster. A false-negative (FN) decision assigns two RAND INDEX similar documents to different clusters. The *Rand index (RI)* measures the RI (RI) percentage of decisions that are correct. That is, it is simply accuracy (Section 8.3, page 143).

$$\text{RI} = \frac{\text{TP} + \text{TN}}{\text{TP} + \text{FP} + \text{FN} + \text{TN}}$$

As an example, we compute RI for Figure 16.4. We first compute TP + FP. The three clusters contain six, six, and five points, respectively, so the total number of "positives" or pairs of documents that are in the same cluster is:

$$\text{TP} + \text{FP} = \binom{6}{2} + \binom{6}{2} + \binom{5}{2} = 40.$$

Of these, the x pairs in cluster 1, the o pairs in cluster 2, the ◇ pairs in cluster 3, and the x pair in cluster 3 are true positives:

$$\text{TP} = \binom{5}{2} + \binom{4}{2} + \binom{3}{2} + \binom{2}{2} = 20.$$

Thus, FP $= 40 - 20 = 20$.

FN and TN are computed similarly, resulting in the following contingency table:

	same cluster	different clusters
same class	TP = 20	FN = 24
different classes	FP = 20	TN = 72

RI is then $(20 + 72)/(20 + 20 + 24 + 72) \approx 0.68$.

The RI gives equal weight to FPs and FNs. Separating similar documents is sometimes worse than putting pairs of dissimilar documents in the same F MEASURE cluster. We can use the *F measure* (Section 8.3, page 142) to penalize FNs more strongly than FPs by selecting a value $\beta > 1$, thus giving more weight to recall.

$$P = \frac{\text{TP}}{\text{TP} + \text{FP}} \qquad R = \frac{\text{TP}}{\text{TP} + \text{FN}} \qquad F_\beta = \frac{(\beta^2 + 1)PR}{\beta^2 P + R}.$$

Based on the numbers in the contingency table, $P = 20/40 = 0.5$ and $R = 20/44 \approx 0.455$. This gives us $F_1 \approx 0.48$ for $\beta = 1$ and $F_5 \approx 0.456$ for $\beta = 5$. In IR, evaluating clustering with F has the advantage that the measure is already familiar to the research community.

? **Exercise 16.3** Replace every point d in Figure 16.4 with two identical copies of d in the same class. (i) Is it less difficult, equally difficult or more difficult to cluster this set of thirty-four points as opposed to the seventeen points in Figure 16.4? (ii) Compute purity, NMI, RI, and F_5 for the clustering with thirty-four points. Which measures increase and which stay the same after doubling the number of points? (iii) Given your assessment in (i) and the results in (ii), which measures are best suited to compare the quality of the two clusterings?

16.4 *K*-means

K-means is the most important flat clustering algorithm. Its objective is to minimize the average squared Euclidean distance (Chapter 6, page 121) of documents from their cluster centers where a cluster center is defined as the CENTROID mean or *centroid* $\vec{\mu}$ of the documents in a cluster ω:

$$\vec{\mu}(\omega) = \frac{1}{|\omega|} \sum_{\vec{x} \in \omega} \vec{x}.$$

The definition assumes that documents are represented as length-normalized vectors in a real-valued space in the familiar way. We used centroids for Rocchio classification in Chapter 14 (page 269). They play a similar role here. The ideal cluster in *K*-means is a sphere with the centroid as its center of gravity. Ideally, the clusters should not overlap. Our desiderata for classes in Rocchio classification were the same. The difference is that we have no labeled training set in clustering for which we know which documents should be in the same cluster.

K-MEANS($\{\vec{x}_1, \ldots, \vec{x}_N\}, K$)

1 $(\vec{s}_1, \vec{s}_2, \ldots, \vec{s}_K) \leftarrow$ SELECTRANDOMSEEDS($\{\vec{x}_1, \ldots, \vec{x}_N\}, K$)
2 **for** $k \leftarrow 1$ **to** K
3 **do** $\vec{\mu}_k \leftarrow \vec{s}_k$
4 **while** stopping criterion has not been met
5 **do for** $k \leftarrow 1$ **to** K
6   **do** $\omega_k \leftarrow \{\}$
7   **for** $n \leftarrow 1$ **to** N
8   **do** $j \leftarrow \arg\min_{j'} |\vec{\mu}_{j'} - \vec{x}_n|$
9          $\omega_j \leftarrow \omega_j \cup \{\vec{x}_n\}$ *(reassignment of vectors)*
10   **for** $k \leftarrow 1$ **to** K
11   **do** $\vec{\mu}_k \leftarrow \frac{1}{|\omega_k|} \sum_{\vec{x} \in \omega_k} \vec{x}$ *(recomputation of centroids)*
12 **return** $\{\vec{\mu}_1, \ldots, \vec{\mu}_K\}$

Figure 16.5 The K-means algorithm. For most IR applications, the vectors $\vec{x}_n \in \mathbb{R}^M$ should be length normalized. Alternative methods of seed selection and initialization are discussed on page 334.

A measure of how well the centroids represent the members of their clus-
RESIDUAL SUM   ters is the *residual sum of squares* or *RSS*, the squared distance of each vector
OF SQUARES   from its centroid summed over all vectors:

$$\text{RSS}_k = \sum_{\vec{x} \in \omega_k} |\vec{x} - \vec{\mu}(\omega_k)|^2$$

(16.7)
$$\text{RSS} = \sum_{k=1}^{K} \text{RSS}_k$$

RSS is the objective function in K-means and our goal is to minimize it. Because N is fixed, minimizing RSS is equivalent to minimizing the average squared distance, a measure of how well centroids represent their documents.

The first step of K-means is to select as initial cluster centers K randomly
SEED   selected documents, the *seeds*. The algorithm then moves the cluster centers around in space to minimize RSS. As shown in Figure 16.5, this is done iteratively by repeating two steps until a stopping criterion is met: Reassigning documents to the cluster with the closest centroid and recomputing each centroid based on the current members of its cluster. Figure 16.6 shows snapshots from nine iterations of the K-means algorithm for a set of points. The "centroid" column of Table 17.2 (page 364) shows examples of centroids.

We can apply one of the following termination conditions.

- A fixed number of iterations I has been completed. This condition limits the runtime of the clustering algorithm, but in some cases the quality of the clustering will be poor because of an insufficient number of iterations.

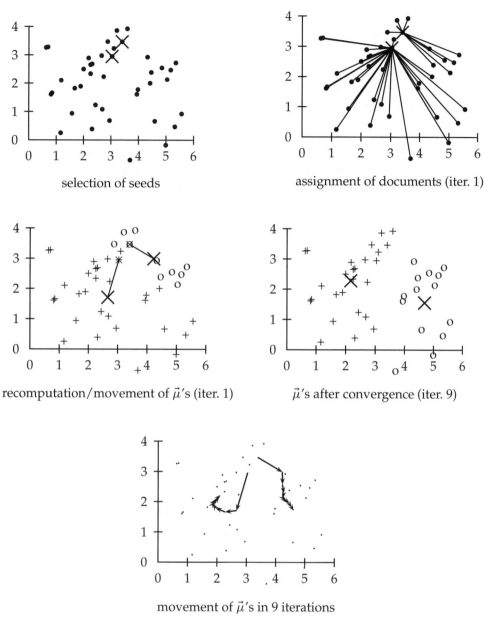

selection of seeds

assignment of documents (iter. 1)

recomputation/movement of $\vec{\mu}$'s (iter. 1)

$\vec{\mu}$'s after convergence (iter. 9)

movement of $\vec{\mu}$'s in 9 iterations

Figure 16.6 A *K*-means example for $K = 2$ in $\mathbb{R}^2$. The position of the two centroids ($\vec{\mu}$'s shown as X's in the top four panels) converges after nine iterations.

- Assignment of documents to clusters (the partitioning function γ) does not change between iterations. Except for cases with a bad local minimum, this produces a good clustering, but runtime may be unacceptably long.
- Centroids $\vec{\mu}_k$ do not change between iterations. This is equivalent to γ not changing (Exercise 16.5).

- Terminate when RSS falls below a threshold. This criterion ensures that the clustering is of a desired quality after termination. In practice, we need to combine it with a bound on the number of iterations to guarantee termination.

- Terminate when the decrease in RSS falls below a threshold θ. For small θ, this indicates that we are close to convergence. Again, we need to combine it with a bound on the number of iterations to prevent very long runtimes.

We now show that K-means converges by proving that RSS monotonically decreases in each iteration. We will use *decrease* in the meaning *decrease or does not change* in this section. First, RSS decreases in the reassignment step; each vector is assigned to the closest centroid, so the distance it contributes to RSS decreases. Second, it decreases in the recomputation step because the new centroid is the vector $\vec{v}$ for which RSS_k reaches its minimum.

$$(16.8) \qquad \text{RSS}_k(\vec{v}) = \sum_{\vec{x} \in \omega_k} |\vec{v} - \vec{x}|^2 = \sum_{\vec{x} \in \omega_k} \sum_{m=1}^{M} (v_m - x_m)^2$$

$$(16.9) \qquad \frac{\partial \text{RSS}_k(\vec{v})}{\partial v_m} = \sum_{\vec{x} \in \omega_k} 2(v_m - x_m)$$

where x_m and v_m are the mth components of their respective vectors. Setting the partial derivative to zero, we get:

$$(16.10) \qquad v_m = \frac{1}{|\omega_k|} \sum_{\vec{x} \in \omega_k} x_m$$

which is the componentwise definition of the centroid. Thus, we minimize RSS_k when the old centroid is replaced with the new centroid. RSS, the sum of the RSS_k, must then also decrease during recomputation.

Because there is only a finite set of possible clusterings, a monotonically decreasing algorithm will eventually arrive at a (local) minimum. Take care, however, to break ties consistently, for example, by assigning a document to the cluster with the lowest index if there are several equidistant centroids. Otherwise, the algorithm can cycle forever in a loop of clusterings that have the same cost.

Although this proves the convergence of K-means, there is unfortunately no guarantee that a *global minimum* in the objective function will be reached. OUTLIER This is a particular problem if a document set contains many *outliers*, documents that are far from any other documents and therefore do not fit well into any cluster. Frequently, if an outlier is chosen as an initial seed, then no other vector is assigned to it during subsequent iterations. Thus, we end up SINGLETON with a *singleton cluster* (a cluster with only one document) even though there CLUSTER is probably a clustering with lower RSS. Figure 16.7 shows an example of a suboptimal clustering resulting from a bad choice of initial seeds.

Another type of suboptimal clustering that frequently occurs is one with empty clusters (Exercise 16.11).

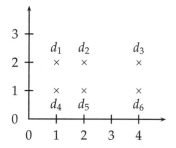

Figure 16.7 The outcome of clustering in K-means depends on the initial seeds. For seeds d_2 and d_5, K-means converges to $\{\{d_1, d_2, d_3\}, \{d_4, d_5, d_6\}\}$, a suboptimal clustering. For seeds d_2 and d_3, it converges to $\{\{d_1, d_2, d_4, d_5\}, \{d_3, d_6\}\}$, the global optimum for $K = 2$.

Effective heuristics for seed selection include (i) excluding outliers from the seed set; (ii) trying out multiple starting points and choosing the clustering with lowest cost; and (iii) obtaining seeds from another method such as hierarchical clustering. Because deterministic hierarchical clustering methods are more predictable than K-means, a hierarchical clustering of a small random sample of size iK (e.g., for $i = 5$ or $i = 10$) often provides good seeds (see the description of the Buckshot algorithm, Chapter 17, page 366).

Other initialization methods compute seeds that are not selected from the vectors to be clustered. A robust method that works well for a large variety of document distributions is to select i (e.g., $i = 10$) random vectors for each cluster and use their centroid as the seed for this cluster. See Section 16.6 for more sophisticated initializations.

What is the time complexity of K-means? Most of the time is spent on computing vector distances. One such operation costs $\Theta(M)$. The reassignment step computes KN distances, so its overall complexity is $\Theta(KNM)$. In the recomputation step, each vector gets added to a centroid once, so the complexity of this step is $\Theta(NM)$. For a fixed number of iterations I, the overall complexity is therefore $\Theta(IKNM)$. Thus, K-means is linear in all relevant factors: iterations, number of clusters, number of vectors, and dimensionality of the space. This means that K-means is more efficient than the hierarchical algorithms in Chapter 17. We had to fix the number of iterations I, which can be tricky in practice. But in most cases, K-means quickly reaches either complete convergence or a clustering that is close to convergence. In the latter case, a few documents would switch membership if further iterations were computed, but this has a small effect on the overall quality of the clustering.

There is one subtlety in the preceding argument. Even a linear algorithm can be quite slow if one of the arguments of $\Theta(\ldots)$ is large, and M usually is large. High dimensionality is not a problem for computing the distance of two documents. Their vectors are sparse, so that only a small fraction of the theoretically possible M componentwise differences need to be computed. Centroids, however, are dense; they pool all terms that occur in any of the documents of their clusters. As a result, distance computations are time consuming in a naive implementation of K-means. But there are simple and effective heuristics for making centroid–document similarities as fast to compute as document–document similarities. Truncating centroids to the most significant k terms (e.g., $k = 1,000$) hardly decreases cluster quality while achieving a significant speedup of the reassignment step (see references in Section 16.6).

K-MEDOIDS   The same efficiency problem is addressed by *K-medoids*, a variant of K-means that computes medoids instead of centroids as cluster centers. We
MEDOID   define the *medoid* of a cluster as the document vector that is closest to the centroid. Since medoids are sparse document vectors, distance computations are fast.

16.4.1 Cluster cardinality in K-means

We stated in Section 16.2 that the number of clusters K is an input to most flat clustering algorithms. What do we do if we cannot come up with a plausible guess for K?

A naive approach would be to select the optimal value of K according to the objective function, namely, the value of K that minimizes RSS. Defining $\text{RSS}_{\min}(K)$ as the minimal RSS of all clusterings with K clusters, we observe that $\text{RSS}_{\min}(K)$ is a monotonically decreasing function in K (Exercise 16.13), which reaches its minimum 0 for $K = N$ where N is the number of documents. We would end up with each document being in its own cluster. Clearly, this is not an optimal clustering.

A heuristic method that gets around this problem is to estimate $\text{RSS}_{\min}(K)$ as follows. We first perform i (e.g., $i = 10$) clusterings with K clusters (each with a different initialization) and compute the RSS of each. Then we take the minimum of the i RSS values. We denote this minimum by $\widehat{\text{RSS}}_{\min}(K)$. Now we can inspect the values $\widehat{\text{RSS}}_{\min}(K)$ as K increases and find the "knee" in the curve – the point where successive decreases in $\widehat{\text{RSS}}_{\min}$ become noticeably smaller. There are two such points in Figure 16.8, one at $K = 4$, where the gradient flattens slightly, and a clearer flattening at $K = 9$. This is typical: There is seldom a single best number of clusters. We still need to employ an external constraint to choose from a number of possible values of K (four and nine in this case).

A second type of criterion for cluster cardinality imposes a penalty for each new cluster – where conceptually we start with a single cluster containing all documents and then search for the optimal number of clusters K by successively increasing K. To determine the cluster cardinality in this way, we create a generalized objective function that combines two elements:
DISTORTION   *distortion*, a measure of how much documents deviate from the prototype
MODEL   of their clusters (e.g., RSS for K-means); and a measure of *model complexity*.
COMPLEXITY   We interpret a clustering here as a model of the data. Model complexity in clustering is usually the number of clusters or a function thereof. For

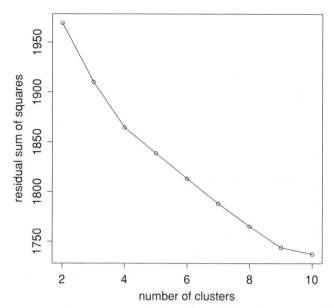

Figure 16.8 Estimated minimal residual sum of squares ($\widehat{\text{RSS}}_{\text{min}}$) as a function of the number of clusters in K-means. In this clustering of 1203 Reuters-RCV1 documents, there are two points where the $\widehat{\text{RSS}}_{\text{min}}$ curve flattens: at four clusters and at nine clusters. The documents were selected from the categories *China, Germany, Russia,* and *Sports,* so the $K = 4$ clustering is closest to the RCV1-Reuters classification.

K-means, we then get this selection criterion for K:

$$(16.11) \qquad K = \arg\min_{K}[\text{RSS}_{\text{min}}(K) + \lambda K]$$

where λ is a weighting factor. A large value of λ favors solutions with few clusters. For $\lambda = 0$, there is no penalty for more clusters and $K = N$ is the best solution.

The obvious difficulty with Equation (16.11) is that we need to determine λ. Unless this is easier than determining K directly, then we are back to square one. In some cases, we can choose values of λ that have worked well for similar data sets in the past. For example, if we periodically cluster news stories from a newswire, there is likely to be a fixed value of λ that gives us the right K in each successive clustering. In this application, we would not be able to determine K based on past experience because K changes.

AKAIKE INFORMATION CRITERION A theoretical justification for Equation (16.11) is the *Akaike information criterion* or AIC, an information-theoretic measure that trades off distortion against model complexity. The general form of AIC is:

$$(16.12) \qquad \textbf{AIC:} \quad K = \arg\min_{K}[-2L(K) + 2q(K)]$$

where $-L(K)$, the negative maximum log-likelihood of the data for K clusters, is a measure of distortion and $q(K)$, the number of parameters of a model with K clusters, is a measure of model complexity. We will not attempt to derive the AIC here, but it is easy to understand intuitively. The first property of a good model of the data is that each data point is modeled well by the model. This is the goal of low distortion. But models should also be small (i.e., have low model complexity); a model that merely describes the data (and therefore has zero distortion) is worthless. AIC provides a theoretical justification for one particular way of weighting these two factors, distortion and model complexity, when selecting a model.

For K-means, the AIC can be stated as follows:

(16.13) $$\textbf{AIC:}\quad K = \arg\min_K[\text{RSS}_{\min}(K) + 2MK]$$

Equation (16.13) is a special case of Equation (16.11) for $\lambda = 2M$.

To derive Equation (16.13) from Equation (16.12), observe that $q(K) = KM$ in K-means because each element of the K centroids is a parameter that can be varied independently; and that $L(K) = -(1/2)\text{RSS}_{\min}(K)$ (modulo a constant) if we view the model underlying K-means as a Gaussian mixture with hard assignment, uniform cluster priors and identical spherical covariance matrices (see Exercise 16.19).

The derivation of AIC is based on a number of assumptions, for example, that the data are independent and identically distributed. These assumptions are only approximately true for data sets in information retrieval. As a consequence, the AIC can rarely be applied without modification in text clustering. In Figure 16.8, the dimensionality of the vector space is $M \approx 50{,}000$. Thus, $2MK > 50{,}000$ dominates the smaller RSS-based term ($\widehat{\text{RSS}}_{\min}(1) < 5000$, not shown in the figure) and the minimum of the expression is reached for $K = 1$. But as we know, $K = 4$ (corresponding to the four classes *China*, *Germany*, *Russia*, and *Sports*) is a better choice than $K = 1$. In practice, Equation (16.11) is often more useful than Equation (16.13) – with the caveat that we need to come up with an estimate for λ.

? Exercise 16.4 Why are documents that do not use the same term for the concept *car* likely to end up in the same cluster in K-means clustering?

Exercise 16.5 Two of the possible termination conditions for K-means were (i) assignment does not change, (ii) centroids do not change (page 332). Do these two conditions imply each other?

 ## 16.5 Model-based clustering

In this section, we describe a generalization of K-means, the EM algorithm. It can be applied to a larger variety of document representations and distributions than K-means.

In K-means, we attempt to find centroids that are good representatives. We can view the set of K centroids as a model that generates the data. Generating a document in this model consists of first picking a centroid at random and then adding some noise. If the noise is normally distributed and covariance is spherical, this procedure will result in clusters of spherical shape.

MODEL-BASED
CLUSTERING

Model-based clustering assumes that the data were generated by a model and tries to recover the original model from the data. The model that we recover from the data then defines clusters and an assignment of documents to clusters.

A commonly used criterion for estimating the model parameters is maximum likelihood. In K-means, the quantity $\exp(-\text{RSS})$ is proportional to the likelihood that a particular model (i.e., a set of centroids) generated the data. For K-means, maximum likelihood and minimal RSS are equivalent criteria. We denote the model parameters by Θ. In K-means, $\Theta = \{\vec{\mu}_1, \ldots, \vec{\mu}_K\}$.

More generally, the maximum likelihood criterion is to select the parameters Θ that maximize the log-likelihood of generating the data D:

$$\Theta = \arg\max_\Theta L(D|\Theta) = \arg\max_\Theta \log \prod_{n=1}^N P(d_n|\Theta) = \arg\max_\Theta \sum_{n=1}^N \log P(d_n|\Theta).$$

$L(D|\Theta)$ is the objective function that measures the goodness of the clustering. Given two clusterings with the same number of clusters, we prefer the one with higher $L(D|\Theta)$.

This is the same approach taken in Chapter 12 (page 218) for language modeling and in Section 13.1 (page 245) for text classification. In text classification, we chose the class that maximizes the likelihood of generating a particular document. Here, we choose the clustering Θ that maximizes the likelihood of generating a given set of documents. Once we have Θ, we can compute an assignment probability $P(d|\omega_k; \Theta)$ for each document–cluster pair. This set of assignment probabilities defines a soft clustering.

An example of a soft assignment is that a document about Chinese cars may have a fractional membership of 0.5 in each of the two clusters *China* and *automobiles*, reflecting the fact that both topics are pertinent. A hard clustering like K-means cannot model this simultaneous relevance to two topics.

Model-based clustering provides a framework for incorporating our knowledge about a domain. K-means and the hierarchical algorithms in Chapter 17 make fairly rigid assumptions about the data. For example, clusters in K-means are assumed to be spheres. Model-based clustering offers more flexibility. The clustering model can be adapted to what we know about the underlying distribution of the data, be it Bernoulli (as in the example in Table 16.3), Gaussian with nonspherical variance (another model that is important in document clustering) or a member of a different family.

EXPECTATION-
MAXIMIZATION
ALGORITHM

A commonly used algorithm for model-based clustering is the *expectation-maximization algorithm* or *EM algorithm*. EM clustering is an iterative algorithm that maximizes $L(D|\Theta)$. EM can be applied to many different types of probabilistic modeling. We will work with a mixture of multivariate Bernoulli distributions here, the distribution we know from Section 11.3 (page 204) and Section 13.3 (page 243):

(16.14)
$$P(d|\omega_k; \Theta) = \left(\prod_{t_m \in d} q_{mk}\right) \left(\prod_{t_m \notin d} (1 - q_{mk})\right)$$

where $\Theta = \{\Theta_1, \ldots, \Theta_K\}$, $\Theta_k = (\alpha_k, q_{1k}, \ldots, q_{Mk})$, and $q_{mk} = P(U_m = 1|\omega_k)$ are the parameters of the model.[3] $P(U_m = 1|\omega_k)$ is the probability that a document from cluster k contains term t_m. The probability α_k is the prior of cluster ω_k: the probability that a document d is in ω_k if we have no information about d.

The mixture model then is:

$$(16.15) \qquad P(d|\Theta) = \sum_{k=1}^{K} \alpha_k \left(\prod_{t_m \in d} q_{mk} \right) \left(\prod_{t_m \notin d} (1 - q_{mk}) \right).$$

In this model, we generate a document by first picking a cluster ω_k with probability α_k and then generating the terms of the document according to the parameters q_{mk}. Recall that the document representation of the multivariate Bernoulli is a vector of M Boolean values (and not a real-valued vector).

How do we use EM to infer the parameters of the clustering from the data? That is, how do we choose parameters Θ that maximize $L(D|\Theta)$? EM is similar to K-means in that it alternates between an *expectation step*, corresponding to reassignment, and a *maximization step*, corresponding to recomputation of the parameters of the model. The parameters of K-means are the centroids, the parameters of the instance of EM in this section are the α_k and q_{mk}.

The maximization step recomputes the conditional parameters q_{mk} and the priors α_k as follows:

$$(16.16) \qquad \textbf{Maximization step:} \quad q_{mk} = \frac{\sum_{n=1}^{N} r_{nk} I(t_m \in d_n)}{\sum_{n=1}^{N} r_{nk}} \quad \alpha_k = \frac{\sum_{n=1}^{N} r_{nk}}{N}$$

where $I(t_m \in d_n) = 1$ if $t_m \in d_n$ and 0 otherwise and r_{nk} is the soft assignment of document d_n to cluster k as computed in the preceding iteration. (We'll address the issue of initialization in a moment.) These are the maximum likelihood estimates for the parameters of the multivariate Bernoulli from Table 13.3 (page 248) except that documents are assigned fractionally to clusters here. These maximum likelihood estimates maximize the likelihood of the data given the model.

The expectation step computes the soft assignment of documents to clusters given the current parameters q_{mk} and α_k:

$$(16.17) \qquad \textbf{Expectation step:} \quad r_{nk} = \frac{\alpha_k (\prod_{t_m \in d_n} q_{mk})(\prod_{t_m \notin d_n} (1 - q_{mk}))}{\sum_{k=1}^{K} \alpha_k (\prod_{t_m \in d_n} q_{mk})(\prod_{t_m \notin d_n} (1 - q_{mk}))}.$$

This expectation step applies Equations (16.14) and (16.15) to computing the likelihood that ω_k generated document d_n. It is the classification procedure

---

[3] U_m is the random variable we defined in Section 13.3 (page 246) for the Bernoulli Naive Bayes model. It takes the values 1 (term t_m is present in the document) and 0 (term t_m is absent in the document).

Table 16.3 The EM clustering algorithm. The table shows a set of documents (a) and parameter values for selected iterations during EM clustering (b). Parameters shown are prior α_1, soft assignment scores $r_{n,1}$ (both omitted for cluster 2), and lexical parameters $q_{m,k}$ for a few terms. The authors initially assigned document 6 to cluster 1 and document 7 to cluster 2 (iteration 0). EM converges after 25 iterations. For smoothing, the r_{nk} in Equation (16.16) were replaced with $r_{nk} + \epsilon$ where $\epsilon = 0.0001$.

(a)

docID	document text	docID	document text
1	hot chocolate cocoa beans	7	sweet sugar
2	cocoa ghana africa	8	sugar cane brazil
3	beans harvest ghana	9	sweet sugar beet
4	cocoa butter	10	sweet cake icing
5	butter truffles	11	cake black forest
6	sweet chocolate		

(b)

				iteration of clustering				
parameter	0	1	2	3	4	5	15	25
α_1		0.50	0.45	0.53	0.57	0.58	0.54	0.45
$r_{1,1}$		1.00	1.00	1.00	1.00	1.00	1.00	1.00
$r_{2,1}$		0.50	0.79	0.99	1.00	1.00	1.00	1.00
$r_{3,1}$		0.50	0.84	1.00	1.00	1.00	1.00	1.00
$r_{4,1}$		0.50	0.75	0.94	1.00	1.00	1.00	1.00
$r_{5,1}$		0.50	0.52	0.66	0.91	1.00	1.00	1.00
$r_{6,1}$	1.00	1.00	1.00	1.00	1.00	1.00	0.83	0.00
$r_{7,1}$	0.00	0.00	0.00	0.00	0.00	0.00	0.00	0.00
$r_{8,1}$		0.00	0.00	0.00	0.00	0.00	0.00	0.00
$r_{9,1}$		0.00	0.00	0.00	0.00	0.00	0.00	0.00
$r_{10,1}$		0.50	0.40	0.14	0.01	0.00	0.00	0.00
$r_{11,1}$		0.50	0.57	0.58	0.41	0.07	0.00	0.00
$q_{\text{africa},1}$		0.000	0.100	0.134	0.158	0.158	0.169	0.200
$q_{\text{africa},2}$		0.000	0.083	0.042	0.001	0.000	0.000	0.000
$q_{\text{brazil},1}$		0.000	0.000	0.000	0.000	0.000	0.000	0.000
$q_{\text{brazil},2}$		0.000	0.167	0.195	0.213	0.214	0.196	0.167
$q_{\text{cocoa},1}$		0.000	0.400	0.432	0.465	0.474	0.508	0.600
$q_{\text{cocoa},2}$		0.000	0.167	0.090	0.014	0.001	0.000	0.000
$q_{\text{sugar},1}$		0.000	0.000	0.000	0.000	0.000	0.000	0.000
$q_{\text{sugar},2}$		1.000	0.500	0.585	0.640	0.642	0.589	0.500
$q_{\text{sweet},1}$		1.000	0.300	0.238	0.180	0.159	0.153	0.000
$q_{\text{sweet},2}$		1.000	0.417	0.507	0.610	0.640	0.608	0.667

for the multivariate Bernoulli in Table 13.3. Thus, the expectation step is nothing else but Bernoulli Naive Bayes classification (including normalization, i.e. dividing by the denominator, to get a probability distribution over clusters).

We clustered a set of eleven documents into two clusters using EM in Table 16.3. After convergence in iteration 25, the first five documents are assigned to cluster 1 ($r_{i,1} = 1.00$) and the last six to cluster 2 ($r_{i,1} = 0.00$). Somewhat atypically, the final assignment is a hard assignment here. EM usually converges to a soft assignment. In iteration 25, the prior α_1 for cluster 1 is $5/11 \approx 0.45$ because five of the eleven documents are in cluster 1. Some terms are quickly associated with one cluster because the initial assignment can "spread" to them unambiguously. For example, membership in cluster 2 spreads from document 7 to document 8 in the first iteration because they share *sugar*. ($r_{8,1} = 0$ in iteration 1.) For parameters of terms occurring in ambiguous contexts, convergence takes longer. Seed documents 6 and 7 both contain *sweet*. As a result, it takes 25 iterations for the term to be unambiguously associated with cluster 2 ($q_{\text{sweet},1} = 0$ in iteration 25).

Finding good seeds is even more critical for EM than for K-means. EM is prone to get stuck in local optima if the seeds are not chosen well. This is a general problem that also occurs in other applications of EM.[4] Therefore, as with K-means, the initial assignment of documents to clusters is often computed by a different algorithm. For example, a hard K-means clustering may provide the initial assignment, which EM can then "soften up."

? **Exercise 16.6** We saw above that the time complexity of K-means is $\Theta(IKNM)$. What is the time complexity of EM?

Exercise 16.7 Let Ω be a clustering that exactly reproduces a class structure $\mathbb{C}$ and Ω' a clustering that further subdivides some clusters in Ω. Show that $I(\Omega; \mathbb{C}) = I(\Omega'; \mathbb{C})$.

Exercise 16.8 Show that $I(\Omega; \mathbb{C}) \leq [H(\Omega) + H(\mathbb{C})]/2$.

Exercise 16.9 Mutual information is symmetric in the sense that its value does not change if the roles of clusters and classes are switched: $I(\Omega; \mathbb{C}) = I(\mathbb{C}; \Omega)$. Which of the other three evaluation measures are symmetric in this sense?

Exercise 16.10 Compute RSS for the two clusterings in Figure 16.7.

Exercise 16.11 (i) Give an example of a set of points and three initial centroids (which need not be members of the set of points) for which 3-means converges to a clustering with an empty cluster. (ii) Can a clustering with an empty cluster be the global optimum with respect to RSS?

Exercise 16.12 Download Reuters-21578. Discard documents that do not occur in one of the ten classes *acquisitions, corn, crude, earn, grain, interest, money-fx, ship, trade,* and *wheat*. Discard documents that occur in two of these ten classes. (i) Compute a K-means clustering of this subset into ten clusters. There are a number of software packages that implement K-means, such as, WEKA (Witten and Frank 2005) and R (R Development Core Team 2005). (ii) Compute purity, normalized mutual information, F_1

---

[4] For example, this problem is common when EM is used to estimate parameters of hidden Markov models, probabilistic grammars, and machine translation models in natural language processing (Manning and Schütze 1999).

and RI for the clustering with respect to the ten classes. (iii) Compile a confusion matrix (Table 14.5, page 283) for the ten classes and ten clusters. Identify classes that give rise to FPs and FNs.

Exercise 16.13 Prove that $\text{RSS}_{\min}(K)$ is monotonically decreasing in K.

Exercise 16.14 There is a soft version of K-means that computes the fractional membership of a document in a cluster as a monotonically decreasing function of the distance Δ from its centroid, for example, as $e^{-\Delta}$. Modify reassignment and recomputation steps of hard K-means for this soft version.

Exercise 16.15 In the last iteration in Table 16.3, document 6 is in cluster 2 even though it was the initial seed for cluster 1. Why does the document change membership?

Exercise 16.16 The values of the parameters q_{mk} in iteration 25 in Table 16.3 are rounded. What are the exact values that EM will converge to?

Exercise 16.17 Perform a K-means clustering for the documents in Table 16.3. After how many iterations does K-means converge? Compare the result with the EM clustering in Table 16.3 and discuss the differences.

Exercise 16.18 [⋆ ⋆ ⋆] Modify the expectation and maximization steps of EM for a Gaussian mixture. The maximization step computes the maximum likelihood parameter estimates α_k, $\vec{\mu}_k$, and Σ_k for each of the clusters. The expectation step computes for each vector a soft assignment to clusters (Gaussians) based on their current parameters. Write down the equations for Gaussian mixtures corresponding to Equations (16.16) and (16.17).

Exercise 16.19 [⋆ ⋆ ⋆] Show that K-means can be viewed as the limiting case of EM for Gaussian mixtures if variance is very small and all covariances are 0.

WITHIN-POINT **Exercise 16.20** [⋆ ⋆ ⋆] The *within-point scatter* of a clustering is defined as
SCATTER $\sum_k \frac{1}{2} \sum_{\vec{x}_i \in \omega_k} \sum_{\vec{x}_j \in \omega_k} |\vec{x}_i - \vec{x}_j|^2$. Show that minimizing RSS and minimizing within-point scatter are equivalent.

Exercise 16.21 [⋆ ⋆ ⋆] Derive an AIC criterion for the multivariate Bernoulli mixture model from Equation (16.12).

16.6 References and further reading

Berkhin (2006b) gives a general up-to-date survey of clustering methods with special attention to scalability. The classic reference for clustering in pattern recognition, covering both K-means and EM, is (Duda et al. 2000).

Rasmussen (1992) introduces clustering from an information retrieval perspective. Anderberg (1973) provides a general introduction to clustering for applications. In addition to Euclidean distance and cosine similarity, Kullback-Leibler divergence is often used in clustering as a measure of how (dis)similar documents and clusters are (Xu and Croft 1999; Muresan and Harper 2004; Kurland and Lee 2004).

The cluster hypothesis is due to Jardine and van Rijsbergen (1971) who state it as follows: *Associations between documents convey information about the relevance of documents to requests.* Salton (1971a, 1975), Croft (1978), Voorhees (1985a), Can and Ozkarahan (1990), Cacheda et al. (2003), Can et al. (2004), Singitham et al. (2004), and Altingövde et al. (2008) investigate the efficiency and effectiveness of cluster-based retrieval. Although some of these studies show improvements in effectiveness, efficiency, or both, there is no consensus that cluster-based retrieval works well consistently across scenarios. Cluster-based language modeling was pioneered by Liu and Croft (2004).

There is good evidence that clustering of search results improves user experience and search result quality (Hearst and Pedersen 1996; Zamir and Etzioni 1999; Tombros et al. 2002; Käki 2005; Toda and Kataoka 2005); although not as much as search result structuring based on carefully edited category hierarchies (Hearst 2006). The scatter-gather interface for browsing collections was presented by Cutting et al. (1992). A theoretical framework for analyzing the properties of scatter-gather and other information seeking user interfaces is presented by Pirolli (2007). Schütze and Silverstein (1997) evaluate LSI (Chapter 18) and truncated representations of centroids for efficient K-means clustering.

The Columbia NewsBlaster system (McKeown et al. 2002), a forerunner to the now much more famous and refined Google News (http://news.google.com), used hierarchical clustering (Chapter 17) to give two levels of news topic granularity. See Hatzivassiloglou et al. (2000) for details, and Chen and Lin (2000) and Radev et al. (2001) for related systems. Other applications of clustering in information retrieval are duplicate detection (Yang and Callan (2006), Section 19.6, page 400), novelty detection (see references in Section 17.9, page 367) and metadata discovery on the semantic web (Alonso et al. 2006).

The discussion of external evaluation measures is partially based on Strehl (2002). Dom (2002) proposes a measure Q_0 that is better motivated theoretically than NMI. Q_0 is the number of bits needed to transmit class memberships assuming cluster memberships are known. The Rand index is due to ADJUSTED Rand (1971). Hubert and Arabie (1985) propose an *adjusted Rand index* that RAND INDEX ranges between -1 and 1 and is 0 if there is only chance agreement between clusters and classes (similar to κ in Chapter 8, page 152). Basu et al. (2004) argue that the three evaluation measures NMI, Rand index, and F measure give very similar results. Stein et al. (2003) propose *expected edge density* as an internal measure and give evidence that it is a good predictor of the quality of a clustering. Kleinberg (2002) and Meilă (2005) present axiomatic frameworks for comparing clusterings.

Authors that are often credited with the invention of the K-means algorithm include Lloyd (1982) (first distributed in 1957), Ball (1965), MacQueen (1967), and Hartigan and Wong (1979). Arthur and Vassilvitskii (2006) investigate the worst-case complexity of K-means. Bradley and Fayyad (1998), Pelleg and Moore (1999), and Davidson and Satyanarayana (2003) investigate the convergence properties of K-means empirically and how it depends on initial seed selection. Dhillon and Modha (2001) compare K-means clusters with SVD-based clusters (Chapter 18). The K-medoid algorithm was presented by Kaufman and Rousseeuw (1990). The EM algorithm was originally introduced by Dempster et al. (1977). An in-depth treatment of EM is (McLachlan and Krishnan 1996). See Section 18.5 (page 383) for publications on latent analysis, which can also be viewed as soft clustering.

AIC is due to Akaike (1974) (see also Burnham and Anderson (2002)). An alternative to AIC is BIC, which can be motivated as a Bayesian model selection procedure (Schwarz 1978). Fraley and Raftery (1998) show how to choose an optimal number of clusters based on BIC. An application of BIC to K-means is (Pelleg and Moore 2000). Hamerly and Elkan (2003) propose an alternative to BIC that performs better in their experiments. Another influential Bayesian approach for determining the number of clusters (simultaneously with cluster assignment) is described by Cheeseman and Stutz (1996). Two methods for determining cardinality without external criteria are presented by Tibshirani et al. (2001).

We only have space here for classical completely unsupervised clustering. An important current topic of research is how to use prior knowledge to guide clustering (e.g., Ji and Xu (2006)) and how to incorporate interactive feedback during clustering (e.g., Huang and Mitchell (2006)). Fayyad et al. (1998) propose an initialization for EM clustering. For algorithms that can cluster very large data sets in one scan through the data see Bradley et al. (1998).

The applications in Table 16.1 all cluster documents. Other information retrieval applications cluster words (e.g., Crouch 1988), contexts of words (e.g., Schütze and Pedersen 1995) or words and documents simultaneously (e.g., Tishby and Slonim 2000, Dhillon 2001, Zha et al. 2001). Simultaneous clustering of words and documents is an example of *co-clustering* or *biclustering*.

CO-CLUSTERING

17 *Hierarchical clustering*

Flat clustering is efficient and conceptually simple, but as we saw in Chapter 16 it has a number of drawbacks. The algorithms introduced in Chapter 16 return a flat unstructured set of clusters, require a prespecified number

HIERARCHICAL of clusters as input and are nondeterministic. *Hierarchical clustering* (or *hi-*

CLUSTERING *erarchic clustering*) outputs a *hierarchy*, a structure that is more informative than the unstructured set of clusters returned by flat clustering.[1] Hierarchical clustering does not require us to prespecify the number of clusters and most hierarchical algorithms that have been used in information retrieval (IR) are deterministic. These advantages of hierarchical clustering come at the cost of lower efficiency. The most common hierarchical clustering algorithms have a complexity that is at least quadratic in the number of documents compared to the linear complexity of K-means and EM (cf. Section 16.4, page 335).

This chapter first introduces *agglomerative* hierarchical clustering (Section 17.1) and presents four different agglomerative algorithms, in Sections 17.2 through 17.4, which differ in the similarity measures they employ: single-link, complete-link, group-average, and centroid similarity. We then discuss the optimality conditions of hierarchical clustering in Section 17.5. Section 17.6 introduces top-down (or *divisive*) hierarchical clustering. Section 17.7 looks at labeling clusters automatically, a problem that must be solved whenever humans interact with the output of clustering. We discuss implementation issues in Section 17.8. Section 17.9 provides pointers to further reading, including references to soft hierarchical clustering, which we do not cover in this book.

There are few differences between the applications of flat and hierarchical clustering in information retrieval. In particular, hierarchical clustering is appropriate for any of the applications shown in Table 16.1 (page 323; see also Section 16.6, page 343). In fact, the example we gave for collection

---

[1] In this chapter, we only consider hierarchies that are binary trees as the one shown in Figure 17.1 – but hierarchical clustering can be easily extended to other types of trees.

clustering is hierarchical. In general, we select flat clustering when efficiency is important and hierarchical clustering when one of the potential problems of flat clustering (not enough structure, predetermined number of clusters, nondeterminism) is a concern. In addition, many researchers believe that hierarchical clustering produces better clusters than flat clustering. However, there is no consensus on this issue (see references in Section 17.9).

17.1 Hierarchical agglomerative clustering

Hierarchical clustering algorithms are either top-down or bottom-up. Bottom-up algorithms treat each document as a singleton cluster at the outset and then successively merge (or *agglomerate*) pairs of clusters until all clusters have been merged into a single cluster that contains all documents. HIERARCHICAL Bottom-up hierarchical clustering is therefore called *hierarchical agglomera-* AGGLOMERATIVE *tive clustering* or *HAC*. Top-down clustering requires a method for splitting CLUSTERING a cluster. It proceeds by splitting clusters recursively until individual docu- (HAC) ments are reached. See Section 17.6. HAC is more frequently used in IR than top-down clustering and is the main subject of this chapter.

Before looking at specific similarity measures used in HAC in Sections 17.2 through 17.4, we first introduce a method for depicting hierarchical clusterings graphically, discuss a few key properties of HACs and present a simple algorithm for computing an HAC.

DENDROGRAM An HAC clustering is typically visualized as a *dendrogram* as shown in Figure 17.1. Each merge is represented by a horizontal line. The *y*-coordinate of the horizontal line is the similarity of the two clusters that were merged, where documents are viewed as singleton clusters. We call this similarity the COMBINATION *combination similarity* of the merged cluster. For example, the combination SIMILARITY similarity of the cluster consisting of *Lloyd's CEO questioned* and *Lloyd's chief / U.S. grilling* in Figure 17.1 is ≈ 0.56. We define the combination similarity of a singleton cluster as its document's self-similarity (which is 1.0 for cosine similarity).

By moving up from the bottom layer to the top node, a dendrogram allows us to reconstruct the history of merges that resulted in the depicted clustering. For example, we see that the two documents entitled *War hero Colin Powell* were merged first in Figure 17.1 and that the last merge added *Ag trade reform* to a cluster consisting of the other twenty-nine documents.

MONOTONICITY A fundamental assumption in HAC is that the merge operation is *monotonic*. Monotonic means that if $s_1, s_2, \ldots, s_{K-1}$ are the combination similarities of the successive merges of an HAC, then $s_1 \geq s_2 \geq \ldots \geq s_{K-1}$ holds. A non-INVERSION monotonic hierarchical clustering contains at least one *inversion* $s_i < s_{i+1}$ and contradicts the fundamental assumption that we chose the best merge available at each step. We will see an example of an inversion in Figure 17.12.

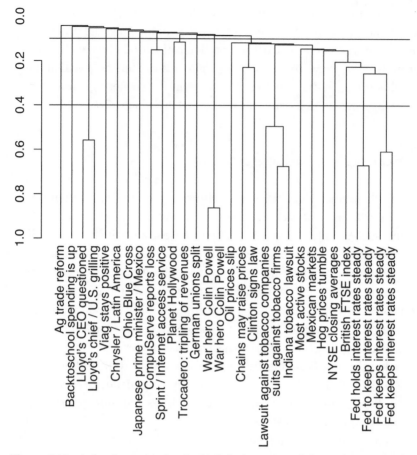

Figure 17.1 A dendrogram of a single-link clustering of thirty documents from Reuters-RCV1. Two possible cuts of the dendrogram are shown: at 0.4 into twenty-four clusters and at 0.1 into twelve clusters.

Hierarchical clustering does not require a prespecified number of clusters. However, in some applications we want a partition of disjoint clusters just as in flat clustering. In those cases, the hierarchy needs to be cut at some point. A number of criteria can be used to determine the cutting point:

- Cut at a prespecified level of similarity. For example, we cut the dendrogram at 0.4 if we want clusters with a minimum combination similarity of 0.4. In Figure 17.1, cutting the diagram at $y = 0.4$ yields twenty-four clusters (grouping only documents with high similarity together) and cutting it at $y = 0.1$ yields twelve clusters (one large financial news cluster and eleven smaller clusters).

- Cut the dendrogram where the gap between two successive combination similarities is largest. Such large gaps arguably indicate "natural" clusterings. Adding one more cluster decreases the quality of the clustering significantly, so cutting before this steep decrease occurs is desirable. This strategy is analogous to looking for the knee in the K-means graph in Figure 16.8 (page 337).

SIMPLEHAC($d_1, \ldots, d_N$)
1 **for** $n \leftarrow 1$ **to** N
2 **do for** $i \leftarrow 1$ **to** N
3   **do** $C[n][i] \leftarrow$ SIM(d_n, d_i)
4       $I[n] \leftarrow 1$ *(keeps track of active clusters)*
5 $A \leftarrow []$ *(assembles clustering as a sequence of merges)*
6 **for** $k \leftarrow 1$ **to** $N - 1$
7 **do** $\langle i, m \rangle \leftarrow \arg\max_{\{\langle i,m \rangle : i \neq m \wedge I[i]=1 \wedge I[m]=1\}} C[i][m]$
8   A.APPEND($\langle i, m \rangle$) *(store merge)*
9   **for** $j \leftarrow 1$ **to** N
10   **do** $C[i][j] \leftarrow$ SIM(i, m, j)
11          $C[j][i] \leftarrow$ SIM(i, m, j)
12      $I[m] \leftarrow 0$ *(deactivate cluster)*
13 **return** A

Figure 17.2 A simple, but inefficient HAC algorithm.

- Apply Equation (16.11) (page 337):

$$K = \arg\min_{K'}[\text{RSS}(K') + \lambda K']$$

  where K' refers to the cut of the hierarchy that results in K' clusters, RSS is the residual sum of squares and λ is a penalty for each additional cluster. Instead of RSS, another measure of distortion can be used.
- As in flat clustering, we can also prespecify the number of clusters K and select the cutting point that produces K clusters.

A simple, naive HAC algorithm is shown in Figure 17.2. We first compute the $N \times N$ similarity matrix C. The algorithm then executes $N - 1$ steps of merging the currently most similar clusters. In each iteration, the two most similar clusters are merged and the rows and columns of the merged cluster i in C are updated.[2] The clustering is stored as a list of merges in A. I indicates which clusters are still available to be merged. The function SIM(i, m, j) computes the similarity of cluster j with the merge of clusters i and m. For some HAC algorithms, SIM(i, m, j) is simply a function of $C[j][i]$ and $C[j][m]$, for example, the maximum of these two values for single link.

We will now refine this algorithm for the different similarity measures of single-link and complete-link clustering (Section 17.2) and group-average and centroid clustering (Sections 17.3 and 17.4). The merge criteria of these four variants of HAC are shown in Figure 17.3.

---

[2] We assume that we use a deterministic method for breaking ties, such as always choose the merge that is the first cluster with respect to a total ordering of the subsets of the document set D.

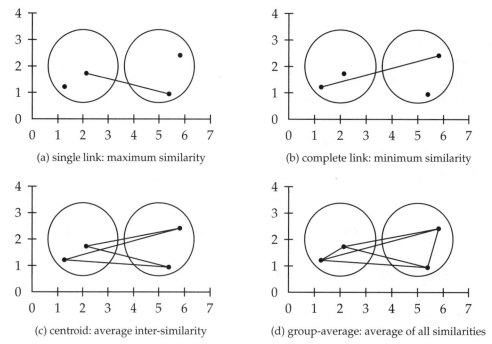

(a) single link: maximum similarity

(b) complete link: minimum similarity

(c) centroid: average inter-similarity

(d) group-average: average of all similarities

Figure 17.3 The different notions of cluster similarity used by the four HAC algorithms. An *inter-similarity* is a similarity between two documents from different clusters.

17.2 Single-link and complete-link clustering

SINGLE-LINK   In *single-link clustering* or *single-linkage clustering*, the similarity of two clus-
CLUSTERING   ters is the similarity of their *most similar* members (see Figure 17.3, (a)).[3] This
single-link merge criterion is *local*. We pay attention solely to the area where
the two clusters come closest to each other. Other, more distant parts of the
cluster and the clusters' overall structure are not taken into account.

COMPLETE-   In *complete-link clustering* or *complete-linkage clustering*, the similarity of two
LINK   clusters is the similarity of their *most dissimilar* members (see Figure 17.3, (b)).
CLUSTERING   This is equivalent to choosing the cluster pair whose merge has the smallest
diameter. This complete-link merge criterion is nonlocal; the entire structure
of the clustering can influence merge decisions. This results in a preference
for compact clusters with small diameters over long, straggly clusters, but
also causes sensitivity to outliers. A single document far from the center can
increase diameters of candidate merge clusters dramatically and completely
change the final clustering.

Figure 17.4 depicts a single-link and a complete-link clustering of eight
documents. The first four steps, each producing a cluster consisting of
a pair of two documents, are identical. Then single-link clustering joins
the upper two pairs (and after that the lower two pairs) because on the

---

[3] Throughout this chapter, we equate similarity with proximity in 2D depictions of clustering.

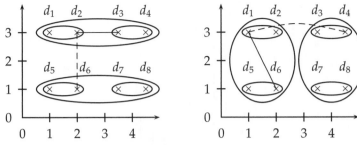

Figure 17.4 A single-link (*left*) and complete-link (*right*) clustering of eight documents. The ellipses correspond to successive clustering stages. *Left*: The single-link similarity of the two upper two-point clusters is the similarity of d_2 and d_3 (*solid line*), which is greater than the single-link similarity of the two left two-point clusters (*dashed line*). *Right*: The complete-link similarity of the two upper two-point clusters is the similarity of d_1 and d_4 (*dashed line*), which is smaller than the complete-link similarity of *the two left* two-point clusters (*solid line*).

maximum-similarity definition of cluster similarity, those two clusters are closest. Complete-link clustering joins the left two pairs (and then the right two pairs) because those are the closest pairs according to the minimum-similarity definition of cluster similarity.[4]

Figure 17.1 is an example of a single-link clustering of a set of documents and Figure 17.5 is the complete-link clustering of the same set. When cutting the last merge in Figure 17.5, we obtain two clusters of similar size (documents 1–16, from *NYSE closing averages* to *Lloyd's chief / U.S. grilling*, and documents 17–30, from *Ohio Blue Cross* to *Clinton signs law*). There is no cut of the dendrogram in Figure 17.1 that would give us an equally balanced clustering.

Both single-link and complete-link clustering have graph-theoretic interpretations. Define s_k to be the combination similarity of the two clusters merged in step k, and $G(s_k)$ the graph that links all data points with a similarity of at least s_k. Then the clusters after step k in single-link clustering are the connected components of $G(s_k)$ and the clusters after step k in complete-link clustering are maximal cliques of $G(s_k)$. A *connected component* is a maximal set of connected points such that there is a path connecting each pair. A *clique* is a set of points that are completely linked with each other.

CONNECTED COMPONENT

CLIQUE

These graph-theoretic interpretations motivate the terms single-link and complete-link clustering. Single-link clusters at step k are maximal sets of points that are linked via at least one link (a single link) of similarity $s \geq s_k$; complete-link clusters at step k are maximal sets of points that are completely linked with each other via links of similarity $s \geq s_k$.

Single-link and complete-link clustering reduce the assessment of cluster quality to a single similarity between a pair of documents: the two most similar documents in single-link clustering and the two most dissimilar

---

[4] If you are bothered by the possibility of ties, assume that d_1 has coordinates $(1 + \epsilon, 3 - \epsilon)$ and that all other points have integer coordinates.

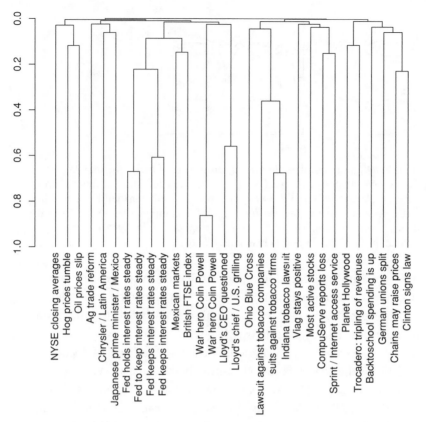

Figure 17.5 A dendrogram of a complete-link clustering. The same thirty documents were clustered with single-link clustering in Figure 17.1.

documents in complete-link clustering. A measurement based on one pair cannot fully reflect the distribution of documents in a cluster. It is therefore not surprising that both algorithms often produce undesirable clusters. Single-link clustering can produce straggling clusters as shown in Figure 17.6. Because the merge criterion is strictly local, a chain of points can be extended for long distances without regard to the overall shape of the emerging cluster. This effect is called *chaining*.

CHAINING

The chaining effect is also apparent in Figure 17.1. The last eleven merges of the single-link clustering (those above the 0.1 line) add on single

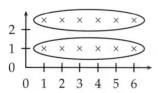

Figure 17.6 Chaining in single-link clustering. The local criterion in single-link clustering can cause undesirable elongated clusters.

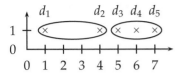

Figure 17.7 Outliers in complete-link clustering. The five documents have the x-coordinates $1 + 2\epsilon$, 4, $5 + 2\epsilon$, 6 and $7 - \epsilon$. Complete-link clustering creates the two clusters shown as ellipses. The most intuitive two-cluster clustering is $\{\{d_1\}, \{d_2, d_3, d_4, d_5\}\}$, but in complete-link clustering, the outlier d_1 splits $\{d_2, d_3, d_4, d_5\}$ as shown.

documents or pairs of documents, corresponding to a chain. The complete-link clustering in Figure 17.5 avoids this problem. Documents are split into two groups of roughly equal size when we cut the dendrogram at the last merge. In general, this is a more useful organization of the data than a clustering with chains.

However, complete-link clustering has a different problem. It pays too much attention to outliers, points that do not fit well into the global structure of the cluster. In the example in Figure 17.7 the four documents d_2, d_3, d_4, d_5 are split because of the outlier d_1 at the left edge (Exercise 17.1). Complete-link clustering does not find the most intuitive cluster structure in this example.

17.2.1 Time complexity

The complexity of the naive HAC algorithm in Figure 17.2 is $\Theta(N^3)$ because we exhaustively search the $N \times N$ matrix C for the largest similarity in each of $N - 1$ iterations.

For the four HAC methods discussed in this chapter, a more efficient algorithm is the priority-queue algorithm shown in Figure 17.8. Its time complexity is $\Theta(N^2 \log N)$. The rows $C[k]$ of the $N \times N$ similarity matrix C are sorted in decreasing order of similarity in the priority queues P. $P[k].\textsc{max}()$ then returns the cluster in $P[k]$ that currently has the highest similarity with ω_k, where we use ω_k to denote the kth cluster as in Chapter 16. After creating the merged cluster of ω_{k_1} and ω_{k_2}, ω_{k_1} is used as its representative. The function $\textsc{sim}$ computes the similarity function for potential merge pairs: largest similarity for single-link, smallest similarity for complete-link, average similarity for GAAC (Section 17.3), and centroid similarity for centroid clustering (Section 17.4). We give an example of how a row of C is processed (Figure 17.8, bottom panel). Both high-level loops (lines 1–7 and 9–21) are $\Theta(N^2 \log N)$ for an implementation of priority queues that supports deletion and insertion in $\Theta(\log N)$. The overall complexity of the algorithm is therefore $\Theta(N^2 \log N)$. In the definition of the function $\textsc{sim}$, $\vec{v}_m$ and $\vec{v}_i$ are the vector sums of $\omega_{k_1} \cup \omega_{k_2}$ and ω_i, respectively, and N_m and N_i are the number of documents in $\omega_{k_1} \cup \omega_{k_2}$ and ω_i, respectively.

EfficientHAC($\vec{d}_1, \ldots, \vec{d}_N$)

```
 1  for n ← 1 to N
 2  do for i ← 1 to N
 3     do C[n][i].sim ← d_n · d_i
 4        C[n][i].index ← i
 5     I[n] ← 1
 6     P[n] ← priority queue for C[n] sorted on sim
 7     P[n].Delete(C[n][n])  (don't want self-similarities)
 8  A ← []
 9  for k ← 1 to N − 1
10  do k_1 ← arg max_{k:I[k]=1} P[k].Max().sim
11     k_2 ← P[k_1].Max().index
12     A.Append(⟨k_1, k_2⟩)
13     I[k_2] ← 0
14     P[k_1] ← []
15     for each i with I[i] = 1 ∧ i ≠ k_1
16     do P[i].Delete(C[i][k_1])
17        P[i].Delete(C[i][k_2])
18        C[i][k_1].sim ← Sim(i, k_1, k_2)
19        P[i].Insert(C[i][k_1])
20        C[k_1][i].sim ← Sim(i, k_1, k_2)
21        P[k_1].Insert(C[k_1][i])
22  return A
```

clustering algorithm	$\text{sim}(i, k_1, k_2)$
single-link	$\max(\text{sim}(i, k_1), \text{sim}(i, k_2))$
complete-link	$\min(\text{sim}(i, k_1), \text{sim}(i, k_2))$
centroid	$(\frac{1}{N_m}\vec{v}_m) \cdot (\frac{1}{N_i}\vec{v}_i)$
group-average	$\frac{1}{(N_m+N_i)(N_m+N_i-1)}[(\vec{v}_m + \vec{v}_i)^2 - (N_m + N_i)]$

compute $C[5]$	1	2	3	4	5
	0.2	0.8	0.6	0.4	1.0

create $P[5]$ (by sorting)	2	3	4	1
	0.8	0.6	0.4	0.2

merge 2 and 3, update similarity of 2, delete 3	2	4	1
	0.3	0.4	0.2

delete and reinsert 2	4	2	1
	0.4	0.3	0.2

Figure 17.8 The priority-queue algorithm for HAC. *Top*: The algorithm. *Center*: Four different similarity measures. *Bottom*: An example for processing steps 6 and 16–19. This is a made up example showing $P[5]$ for a 5×5 matrix C.

SINGLELINKCLUSTERING($d_1, \ldots, d_N$)

```
 1  for n ← 1 to N
 2  do for i ← 1 to N
 3      do C[n][i].sim ← SIM(d_n, d_i)
 4         C[n][i].index ← i
 5      I[n] ← n
 6      NBM[n] ← arg max_{X∈{C[n][i]:n≠i}} X.sim
 7  A ← []
 8  for n ← 1 to N − 1
 9  do i_1 ← arg max_{{i:I[i]=i}} NBM[i].sim
10     i_2 ← I[NBM[i_1].index]
11     A.APPEND(⟨i_1, i_2⟩)
12     for i ← 1 to N
13     do if I[i] = i ∧ i ≠ i_1 ∧ i ≠ i_2
14        then C[i_1][i].sim ← C[i][i_1].sim ← max(C[i_1][i].sim, C[i_2][i].sim)
15        if I[i] = i_2
16           then I[i] ← i_1
17     NBM[i_1] ← arg max_{X∈{C[i_1][i]:I[i]=i∧i≠i_1}} X.sim
18  return A
```

Figure 17.9 Single-link clustering algorithm using an NBM array. After merging two clusters i_1 and i_2, the first one (i_1) represents the merged cluster. If $I[i] = i$, then i is the representative of its current cluster. If $I[i] \neq i$, then i has been merged into the cluster represented by $I[i]$ and will therefore be ignored when updating $NBM[i_1]$.

The argument of EFFICIENTHAC in Figure 17.8 is a set of vectors (as opposed to a set of generic documents) because group-average agglomerative clustering and centroid clustering (Sections 17.3 and 17.4) require vectors as input. The complete-link version of EFFICIENTHAC can also be applied to documents that are not represented as vectors.

For single link, we can introduce a next-best-merge array (NBM) as a further optimization as shown in Figure 17.9. NBM keeps track of what the best merge is for each cluster. Each of the two top level for-loops in Figure 17.9 are $\Theta(N^2)$, thus the overall complexity of single-link clustering is $\Theta(N^2)$.

Can we also speed up the other three HAC algorithms with an NBM array? BEST-MERGE We cannot because only single-link clustering is *best-merge persistent*. Sup-PERSISTENCE pose that the best merge cluster for ω_k is ω_j in single-link clustering. Then after merging ω_j with a third cluster $\omega_i \neq \omega_k$, the merge of ω_i and ω_j will be ω_k's best merge cluster (Exercise 17.6). In other words, the best-merge candidate for the merged cluster is one of the two best-merge candidates of its components in single-link clustering. This means that C can be updated in $\Theta(N)$ in each iteration by taking a simple max of two values on Line 14 in Figure 17.9 for each of the remaining $\leq N$ clusters.

Figure 17.10 demonstrates that best-merge persistence does not hold for complete-link clustering, which means that we cannot use an NBM array to

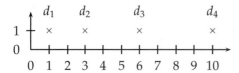

Figure 17.10 Complete-link clustering is not best-merge persistent. At first, d_2 is the best-merge cluster for d_3. But after merging d_1 and d_2, d_4 becomes d_3's best-merge candidate. In a best-merge persistent algorithm like single-link, d_3's best-merge cluster would be $\{d_1, d_2\}$.

speed up clustering. After merging d_3's best merge candidate d_2 with cluster d_1, an unrelated cluster d_4 becomes the best merge candidate for d_3. This is because the complete-link merge criterion is nonlocal and can be affected by points at a great distance from the area where two merge candidates meet.

In practice, the efficiency penalty of the $\Theta(N^2 \log N)$ algorithm is small compared with the $\Theta(N^2)$ single-link algorithm because computing the similarity between two documents (e.g., as a dot product) is an order of magnitude slower than a comparison of two values in sorting. All four HAC algorithms in this chapter are $\Theta(N^2)$ with respect to similarity computations. So the difference in complexity is rarely a concern in practice when choosing one of the algorithms.

? **Exercise 17.1** Show that complete-link clustering creates the two-cluster clustering depicted in Figure 17.7.

17.3 Group-average agglomerative clustering

GROUP-AVERAGE AGGLOMERA-TIVE CLUSTERING   *Group-average agglomerative clustering* or *GAAC* (see Figure 17.3, (d)) evaluates cluster quality based on *all* similarities between documents, thus avoiding the pitfalls of the single-link and complete-link criteria, which equate cluster similarity with the similarity of a single pair of documents. GAAC is also called *group-average clustering* and *average-link clustering*. GAAC computes the average similarity SIM-GA of all pairs of documents, including pairs from the same cluster. But self-similarities are not included in the average:

$$(17.1) \quad \text{SIM-GA}(\omega_i, \omega_j) = \frac{1}{(N_i + N_j)(N_i + N_j - 1)} \sum_{d_m \in \omega_i \cup \omega_j} \sum_{d_n \in \omega_i \cup \omega_j, d_n \neq d_m} \vec{d}_m \cdot \vec{d}_n$$

where $\vec{d}$ is the length-normalized vector of document d, $\cdot$ denotes the dot product, and N_i and N_j are the number of documents in ω_i and ω_j, respectively.

The motivation for GAAC is that our goal in selecting two clusters ω_i and ω_j as the next merge in HAC is that the resulting merge cluster $\omega_k = \omega_i \cup \omega_j$ should be coherent. To judge the coherence of ω_k, we need to look at all document–document similarities within ω_k, including those that occur within ω_i and those that occur within ω_j.

We can compute the measure SIM-GA efficiently because the sum of individual vector similarities is equal to the similarities of their sums:

(17.2)
$$\sum_{d_m \in \omega_i} \sum_{d_n \in \omega_j} (\vec{d}_m \cdot \vec{d}_n) = \left(\sum_{d_m \in \omega_i} \vec{d}_m \right) \cdot \left(\sum_{d_n \in \omega_j} \vec{d}_n \right).$$

With (17.2), we have:

(17.3) $\text{SIM-GA}(\omega_i, \omega_j) = \dfrac{1}{(N_i + N_j)(N_i + N_j - 1)} \left[\left(\displaystyle\sum_{d_m \in \omega_i \cup \omega_j} \vec{d}_m \right)^2 - (N_i + N_j) \right].$

The term $(N_i + N_j)$ on the right is the sum of $N_i + N_j$ self-similarities of value 1.0. With this trick we can compute cluster similarity in constant time (assuming we have available the two vector sums $\sum_{d_m \in \omega_i} \vec{d}_m$ and $\sum_{d_m \in \omega_j} \vec{d}_m$) instead of in $\Theta(N_i N_j)$. This is important because we need to be able to compute the function SIM on lines 18 and 20 in EFFICIENTHAC (Figure 17.8) in constant time for efficient implementations of GAAC. Note that for two singleton clusters equation (17.3) is equivalent to the dot product.

Equation (17.2) relies on the distributivity of the dot product with respect to vector addition. Because this is crucial for the efficient computation of a GAAC clustering, the method cannot be easily applied to representations of documents that are not real-valued vectors. Also, Equation (17.2) only holds for the dot product. Although many algorithms introduced in this book have near-equivalent descriptions in terms of dot product, cosine similarity, and Euclidean distance (cf. Section 14.1, page 267), Equation (17.2) can only be expressed using the dot product. This is a fundamental difference between single-link/complete-link clustering and GAAC. The first two only require a square matrix of similarities as input and do not care how these similarities were computed.

To summarize, GAAC requires (i) documents represented as vectors, (ii) length normalization of vectors, so that self-similarities are 1.0, and (iii) the dot product for computing the similarity between vectors and sums of vectors.

The merge algorithms for GAAC and complete-link clustering are the same except that we use Equation (17.3) as similarity function in Figure 17.8. So the overall time complexity of GAAC is the same as for complete-link clustering: $\Theta(N^2 \log N)$. Like complete-link clustering, GAAC is not best-merge persistent (Exercise 17.6). This means that there is no $\Theta(N^2)$ algorithm for GAAC that would be analogous to the $\Theta(N^2)$ algorithm for single-link in Figure 17.9.

We can also define group-average similarity as including self-similarities:

(17.4) $\text{SIM-GA}'(\omega_i, \omega_j) = \dfrac{1}{(N_i + N_j)^2} \left(\displaystyle\sum_{d_m \in \omega_i \cup \omega_j} \vec{d}_m \right)^2 = \dfrac{1}{N_i + N_j} \displaystyle\sum_{d_m \in \omega_i \cup \omega_j} [\vec{d}_m \cdot \vec{\mu}(\omega_i \cup \omega_j)]$

where the centroid $\vec{\mu}(\omega)$ is defined as in Equation (14.1) (page 269). This definition is equivalent to the intuitive definition of cluster quality as average similarity of documents $\vec{d}_m$ to the cluster's centroid $\vec{\mu}$.

Self-similarities are always equal to 1.0, the maximum possible value for length-normalized vectors. The proportion of self-similarities in Equation (17.4) is $i/i^2 = 1/i$ for a cluster of size i. This gives an unfair advantage to small clusters; they will have proportionally more self-similarities. For two documents d_1, d_2 with a similarity s, we have $\text{SIM-GA}'(d_1, d_2) = (1 + s)/2$. In contrast, $\text{SIM-GA}(d_1, d_2) = s \leq (1 + s)/2$. This similarity $\text{SIM-GA}(d_1, d_2)$ of two documents is the same as in single-link, complete-link, and centroid clustering. We prefer the definition in Equation (17.3), which excludes self-similarities from the average, because we do not want to penalize large clusters for their smaller proportion of self-similarities and because we want a consistent similarity value s for document pairs in all four HAC algorithms.

? **Exercise 17.2** Apply group-average clustering to the points in Figures 17.6 and 17.7. Map them onto the surface of the unit sphere in a threedimensional space to get length-normalized vectors. Is the group-average clustering different from the single-link and complete-link clusterings?

17.4 Centroid clustering

In centroid clustering, the similarity of two clusters is defined as the similarity of their centroids:

(17.5)
$$\text{SIM-CENT}(\omega_i, \omega_j) = \vec{\mu}(\omega_i) \cdot \vec{\mu}(\omega_j)$$

$$= \left(\frac{1}{N_i} \sum_{d_m \in \omega_i} \vec{d}_m \right) \cdot \left(\frac{1}{N_j} \sum_{d_n \in \omega_j} \vec{d}_n \right)$$

(17.6)
$$= \frac{1}{N_i N_j} \sum_{d_m \in \omega_i} \sum_{d_n \in \omega_j} \vec{d}_m \cdot \vec{d}_n$$

Equation (17.5) is centroid similarity. Equation (17.6) shows that centroid similarity is equivalent to average similarity of all pairs of documents from *different* clusters. Thus, the difference between GAAC and centroid clustering is that GAAC considers all pairs of documents in computing average pairwise similarity (Figure 17.3, (d)) whereas centroid clustering excludes pairs from the same cluster (Figure 17.3, (c)).

Figure 17.11 shows the first three steps of a centroid clustering. The first two iterations form the clusters $\{d_5, d_6\}$ with centroid μ_1 and $\{d_1, d_2\}$ with centroid μ_2 because the pairs $\langle d_5, d_6 \rangle$ and $\langle d_1, d_2 \rangle$ have the highest centroid similarities. In the third iteration, the highest centroid similarity is between μ_1 and d_4 producing the cluster $\{d_4, d_5, d_6\}$ with centroid μ_3.

Like GAAC, centroid clustering is not best-merge persistent and therefore $\Theta(N^2 \log N)$ (Exercise 17.6).

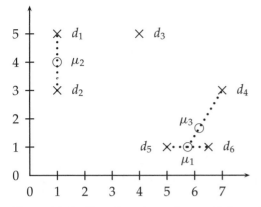

Figure 17.11 Three iterations of centroid clustering. Each iteration merges the two clusters whose centroids are closest.

In contrast to the other three HAC algorithms, centroid clustering is not
INVERSION monotonic. So-called *inversions* can occur: Similarity can increase during
clustering as in the example in Figure 17.12, where we define similarity as
negative distance. In the first merge, the similarity of d_1 and d_2 is $-(4 - \epsilon)$. In
the second merge, the similarity of the centroid of d_1 and d_2 (the circle) and
d_3 is $\approx -\cos(\pi/6) \times 4 = -\sqrt{3}/2 \times 4 \approx -3.46 > -(4 - \epsilon)$. This is an example
of an inversion: Similarity *increases* in this sequence of two clustering steps.
In a monotonic HAC algorithm, similarity is monotonically *decreasing* from
iteration to iteration.

Increasing similarity in a series of HAC clustering steps contradicts the
fundamental assumption that small clusters are more coherent than large
clusters. An inversion in a dendrogram shows up as a horizontal merge line
that is *lower* than the previous merge line. All merge lines in Figures 17.1
and 17.5 are higher than their predecessors because single-link and complete-
link clustering are monotonic clustering algorithms.

Despite its nonmonotonicity, centroid clustering is often used because its
similarity measure – the similarity of two centroids – is conceptually simpler
than the average of all pairwise similarities in GAAC. Figure 17.11 is all one
needs to understand centroid clustering. There is no equally simple graph
that would explain how GAAC works.

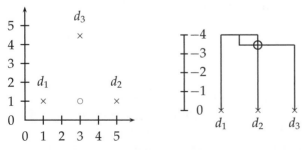

Figure 17.12 Centroid clustering is not monotonic. The documents d_1 at $(1 + \epsilon, 1)$, d_2 at $(5, 1)$, and
d_3 at $(3, 1 + 2\sqrt{3})$ are almost equidistant, with d_1 and d_2 closer to each other than to d_3. The non-
monotonic inversion in the hierarchical clustering of the three points appears as an intersecting
merge line in the dendrogram. The intersection is circled.

Exercise 17.3 For a fixed set of N documents there are up to N^2 distinct similarities between clusters in single-link and complete-link clustering. How many distinct cluster similarities are there in GAAC and centroid clustering?

17.5 Optimality of hierarchical agglomerative clustering

To state the optimality conditions of hierarchical clustering precisely, we first define the combination similarity COMB-SIM of a clustering $\Omega = \{\omega_1, \ldots, \omega_K\}$ as the smallest combination similarity of any of its K clusters:

$$\text{COMB-SIM}(\{\omega_1, \ldots, \omega_K\}) = \min_k \text{COMB-SIM}(\omega_k).$$

Recall that the combination similarity of a cluster ω that was created as the merge of ω_1 and ω_2 is the similarity of ω_1 and ω_2 (page 347).

OPTIMAL   We then define $\Omega = \{\omega_1, \ldots, \omega_K\}$ to be *optimal* if all clusterings Ω' with k
CLUSTERING clusters, $k \le K$, have lower combination similarities:

$$|\Omega'| \le |\Omega| \Rightarrow \text{COMB-SIM}(\Omega') \le \text{COMB-SIM}(\Omega).$$

Figure 17.12 shows that centroid clustering is not optimal. The clustering $\{\{d_1, d_2\}, \{d_3\}\}$ (for $K = 2$) has combination similarity $-(4 - \epsilon)$ and $\{\{d_1, d_2, d_3\}\}$ (for $K = 1$) has combination similarity -3.46. So the clustering $\{\{d_1, d_2\}, \{d_3\}\}$ produced in the first merge is not optimal because there is a clustering with fewer clusters ($\{\{d_1, d_2, d_3\}\}$) that has higher combination similarity. Centroid clustering is not optimal because inversions can occur.

The above definition of optimality would be of limited use if it was only applicable to a clustering together with its merge history. However, we can
COMBINATION show (Exercise 17.4) that *combination similarity* for the three non-inversion al-
SIMILARITY gorithms can be read off from the cluster without knowing its history. These direct definitions of combination similarity are as follows.

single-link The combination similarity of a cluster ω is the smallest similarity of any bipartition of the cluster, where the similarity of a bipartition is the largest similarity between any two documents from the two parts:

$$\text{COMB-SIM}(\omega) = \min_{\{\omega':\omega'\subset\omega\}} \max_{d_i \in \omega'} \max_{d_j \in \omega-\omega'} \text{SIM}(d_i, d_j)$$

where each $\langle \omega', \omega - \omega' \rangle$ is a possible bipartition of ω.

complete link The combination similarity of a cluster ω is the smallest similarity of any two points in ω: $\min_{d_i \in \omega} \min_{d_j \in \omega} \text{SIM}(d_i, d_j)$.

GAAC The combination similarity of a cluster ω is the average of all pairwise similarities in ω (where self-similarities are not included in the average): Equation (17.3).

If we use these definitions of combination similarity, then optimality is a property of a set of clusters and not of a process that produces a set of clusters.

We can now prove the optimality of single-link clustering by induction on the number of clusters K. We will give a proof for the case where no two pairs of documents have the same similarity, but it can easily be extended to the case with ties.

The inductive basis of the proof is that a clustering with $K = N$ clusters has combination similarity 1.0, which is the largest value possible. The induction hypothesis is that a single-link clustering Ω_K with K clusters is optimal: COMB-SIM$(\Omega_K) >$ COMB-SIM(Ω'_K) for all Ω'_K. Assume for contradiction that the clustering Ω_{K-1} we obtain by merging the two most similar clusters in Ω_K is not optimal and that instead a different sequence of merges Ω'_K, Ω'_{K-1} leads to the optimal clustering with $K-1$ clusters. We can write the assumption that Ω'_{K-1} is optimal and that Ω_{K-1} is not as COMB-SIM$(\Omega'_{K-1}) >$ COMB-SIM(Ω_{K-1}).

Case 1: The two documents linked by $s =$ COMB-SIM(Ω'_{K-1}) are in the same cluster in Ω_K. They can only be in the same cluster if a merge with similarity smaller than s has occurred in the merge sequence producing Ω_K. This implies $s >$ COMB-SIM(Ω_K). Thus, COMB-SIM$(\Omega'_{K-1}) = s >$ COMB-SIM$(\Omega_K) >$ COMB-SIM$(\Omega'_K) >$ COMB-SIM(Ω'_{K-1}). Contradiction.

Case 2: The two documents linked by $s =$ COMB-SIM(Ω'_{K-1}) are not in the same cluster in Ω_K. But $s =$ COMB-SIM$(\Omega'_{K-1}) >$ COMB-SIM(Ω_{K-1}), so the single-link merging rule should have merged these two clusters when processing Ω_K. Contradiction.

Thus, Ω_{K-1} is optimal.

In contrast to single-link clustering, complete-link clustering and GAAC are not optimal as this example shows:

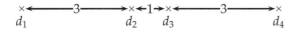

Both algorithms merge the two points with distance 1 (d_2 and d_3) first and thus cannot find the two-cluster clustering $\{\{d_1, d_2\}, \{d_3, d_4\}\}$. But $\{\{d_1, d_2\}, \{d_3, d_4\}\}$ is optimal on the optimality criteria of complete-link clustering and GAAC.

However, the merge criteria of complete-link clustering and GAAC approximate the desideratum of approximate sphericity better than the merge criterion of single-link clustering. In many applications, we want spherical clusters. Thus, even though single-link clustering may seem preferable at first because of its optimality, it is optimal with respect to the wrong criterion in many document clustering applications.

Table 17.1 summarizes the properties of the four HAC algorithms introduced in this chapter. We recommend GAAC for document clustering

Table 17.1 Comparison of HAC algorithms.

method	combination similarity	time compl.	optimal?	comment
single link	max inter-similarity of any 2 docs	$\Theta(N^2)$	yes	chaining effect
complete link	min inter-similarity of any 2 docs	$\Theta(N^2 \log N)$	no	sensitive to outliers
group average	average of all sims	$\Theta(N^2 \log N)$	no	best choice for most applications
centroid	average inter-similarity	$\Theta(N^2 \log N)$	no	inversions can occur

because it is generally the method that produces the clustering with the best properties for applications. It does not suffer from chaining, from sensitivity to outliers and from inversions.

There are two exceptions to this recommendation. First, for nonvector representations, GAAC is not applicable and clustering should typically be performed with the complete-link method.

Second, in some applications the purpose of clustering is not to create a complete hierarchy or exhaustive partition of the entire document set. For FIRST STORY instance, *first story detection* or *novelty detection* is the task of detecting the first DETECTION occurrence of an event in a stream of news stories. One approach to this task is to find a tight cluster within the documents that were sent across the wire in a short period of time and are dissimilar from all previous documents. For example, the documents sent over the wire in the minutes after the World Trade Center attack on September 11, 2001, form such a cluster. Variations of single-link clustering can do well on this task since it is the structure of small parts of the vector space – and not global structure – that is important in this case.

Similarly, we will describe an approach to duplicate detection on the web in Section 19.6 (page 403) where single-link clustering is used in the guise of the union-find algorithm. Again, the decision whether a group of documents are duplicates of each other is not influenced by documents that are located far away and single-link clustering is a good choice for duplicate detection.

? **Exercise 17.4** Show the equivalence of the two definitions of combination similarity: the process definition on page 347 and the static definition on page 360.

17.6 Divisive clustering

So far we have only looked at agglomerative clustering, but a cluster hierarchy can also be generated top-down. This variant of hierarchical clustering TOP-DOWN is called *top-down clustering* or *divisive clustering*. We start at the top with all CLUSTERING documents in one cluster. The cluster is split using a flat clustering algorithm.

This procedure is applied recursively until each document is in its own singleton cluster.

Top-down clustering is conceptually more complex than bottom-up clustering; we need a second, flat clustering algorithm as a "subroutine." It has the advantage of being more efficient if we do not generate a complete hierarchy all the way down to individual document leaves. For a fixed number of top levels, using an efficient flat algorithm like K-means, top-down algorithms are linear in the number of documents and clusters. So they run much faster than HAC algorithms, which are at least quadratic.

There is evidence that divisive algorithms produce more accurate hierarchies than bottom-up algorithms in some circumstances. See the references on bisecting K-means in Section 17.9. Bottom-up methods make clustering decisions based on local patterns without initially taking into account the global distribution. These early decisions cannot be undone. Top-down clustering benefits from complete information about the global distribution when making top-level partitioning decisions.

17.7 Cluster labeling

In many applications of flat clustering and hierarchical clustering, particularly in analysis tasks and in user interfaces (see applications in Table 16.1, page 323), human users interact with clusters. In such settings, we must label clusters, so that users can see what a cluster is about.

DIFFERENTIAL CLUSTER LABELING *Differential cluster labeling* selects cluster labels by comparing the distribution of terms in one cluster with that of other clusters. The feature selection methods we introduced in Section 13.5 (page 251) can all be used for differential cluster labeling.[5] In particular, mutual information (MI) (Section 13.5.1, page 252) or, equivalently, information gain and the χ^2 test (Section 13.5.2, page 255) will identify cluster labels that characterize one cluster in contrast to other clusters. A combination of a differential test with a penalty for rare terms often gives the best labeling results because rare terms are not necessarily representative of the cluster as a whole.

We apply three labeling methods to a K-means clustering in Table 17.2. In this example, there is almost no difference between MI and χ^2. We therefore omit the latter.

CLUSTER-INTERNAL LABELING *Cluster-internal labeling* computes a label that solely depends on the cluster itself, not on other clusters. Labeling a cluster with the title of the document closest to the centroid is one cluster-internal method. Titles are easier to read than a list of terms. A full title can also contain important context that did not make it into the top ten terms selected by MI. On the web, anchor text

---

[5] Selecting the most frequent terms is a non-differential feature selection technique we discussed in Section 13.5. It can also be used for labeling clusters.

Table 17.2 Automatically computed cluster labels. This is for three of ten clusters (4, 9, and 10) in a *K*-means clustering of the first 10,000 documents in Reuters-RCV1. The last three columns show cluster summaries computed by three labeling methods: most highly weighted terms in centroid (centroid), mutual information, and the title of the document closest to the centroid of the cluster (title). Terms selected by only one of the first two methods are in bold.

		labeling method		
	# docs	centroid	mutual information	title
4	622	oil plant mexico production crude **power 000 refinery** gas bpd	plant oil production **barrels** crude bpd mexico **dolly capacity petroleum**	MEXICO: Hurricane Dolly heads for Mexico coast
9	1017	police security **russian** people military peace killed told **grozny court**	police killed military security peace told **troops forces rebels** people	RUSSIA: Russia's Lebed meets rebel chief in Chechnya
10	1259	00 000 tonnes traders futures wheat prices **cents september** tonne	**delivery** traders futures tonne tonnes **desk** wheat prices 000 00	USA: Export Business - Grain/oilseeds complex

can play a role similar to a title since the anchor text pointing to a page can serve as a concise summary of its contents.

In Table 17.2, the title for cluster 9 suggests that many of its documents are about the Chechnya conflict, a fact the MI terms do not reveal. However, a single document is unlikely to be representative of all documents in a cluster. An example is cluster 4, whose selected title is misleading. The main topic of the cluster is oil. Articles about hurricane Dolly only ended up in this cluster because of its effect on oil prices.

We can also use a list of terms with high weights in the centroid of the cluster as a label. Such highly weighted terms (or, even better, phrases, especially noun phrases) are often more representative of the cluster than a few titles can be, even if they are not filtered for distinctiveness as in the differential methods. However, a list of phrases takes more time to digest for users than a well crafted title.

Cluster-internal methods are efficient, but they fail to distinguish terms that are frequent in the collection as a whole from those that are frequent only in the cluster. Terms like year or Tuesday may be among the most frequent in a cluster, but they are not helpful in understanding the contents of a cluster with a specific topic like oil.

In Table 17.2, the centroid method selects a few more uninformative terms (000, court, cents, september) than MI (forces, desk), but most of the terms selected by either method are good descriptors. We get a good sense of the documents in a cluster from scanning the selected terms.

For hierarchical clustering, additional complications arise in cluster labeling. Not only do we need to distinguish an internal node in the tree from its siblings, but also from its parent and its children. Documents in child nodes are by definition also members of their parent node, so we cannot use a naive differential method to find labels that distinguish the parent from its children. However, more complex criteria, based on a combination of overall collection frequency and prevalence in a given cluster, can determine whether a term is a more informative label for a child node or a parent node (see Section 17.9).

17.8 Implementation notes

Most problems that require the computation of a large number of dot products benefit from an inverted index. This is also the case for HAC clustering. Computational savings due to the inverted index are large if there are many zero similarities – either because many documents do not share any terms or because an aggressive stop list is used.

In low dimensions, more aggressive optimizations are possible that make the computation of most pairwise similarities unnecessary (Exercise 17.10). However, no such algorithms are known in higher dimensions. We encountered the same problem in k nearest neighbor (kNN) classification (see Section 14.7, page 291).

When using GAAC on a large document set in high dimensions, we have to take care to avoid dense centroids. For dense centroids, clustering can take time $\Theta(MN^2 \log N)$ where M is the size of the vocabulary, whereas complete-link clustering is $\Theta(M_{\mathrm{ave}}N^2 \log N)$ where M_{ave} is the average size of the vocabulary of a document. So for large vocabularies complete-link clustering can be more efficient than an unoptimized implementation of GAAC. We discussed this problem in the context of K-means clustering in Chapter 16 (page 336) and suggested two solutions: truncating centroids (keeping only highly weighted terms) and representing clusters by means of sparse medoids instead of dense centroids. These optimizations can also be applied to GAAC and centroid clustering.

Even with these optimizations, HAC algorithms are all $\Theta(N^2)$ or $\Theta(N^2 \log N)$ and therefore infeasible for large sets of 1,000,000 or more documents. For such large sets, HAC can only be used in combination with a flat clustering algorithm like K-means. Recall that K-means requires a set of seeds as initialization (Figure 16.5, page 332). If these seeds are badly chosen, then the resulting clustering will be of poor quality. We can employ an HAC algorithm to compute seeds of high quality. If the HAC algorithm is applied to a document subset of size $\sqrt{N}$, then the overall runtime of K-means cum HAC seed generation is $\Theta(N)$. This is because the application of a quadratic algorithm to a sample of size $\sqrt{N}$ has an overall complexity of $\Theta(N)$. An appropriate adjustment can be made for an $\Theta(N^2 \log N)$ algorithm to guarantee linearity. This algorithm is referred to as the *Buckshot algorithm*. It combines the determinism and higher reliability of HAC with the efficiency of K-means.

BUCKSHOT ALGORITHM

?

MINIMUM SPANNING TREE

Exercise 17.5 A single-link clustering can also be computed from the *minimum spanning tree* of a graph. The minimum spanning tree connects the vertices of a graph at the smallest possible cost, where cost is defined as the sum over all edges of the graph. In our case the cost of an edge is the distance between two documents. Show that if $\Delta_{k-1} > \Delta_k > \ldots > \Delta_1$ are the costs of the edges of a minimum spanning tree, then these edges correspond to the $k - 1$ merges in constructing a single-link clustering.

Exercise 17.6 Show that single-link clustering is best-merge persistent and that GAAC and centroid clustering are not best-merge persistent.

Exercise 17.7
a. Consider running 2-means clustering on a collection with documents from two different languages. What result would you expect?
b. Would you expect the same result when running an HAC algorithm?

Exercise 17.8 Download Reuters-21578. Keep only documents that are in the classes *crude*, *interest*, and *grain*. Discard documents that are members of more than one of these three classes. Compute a (i) single-link, (ii) complete-link, (iii) GAAC, and (iv) centroid clustering of the documents. (v) Cut each dendrogram at the second branch from the top to obtain $K = 3$ clusters. Compute the Rand index for each of the four clusterings. Which clustering method performs best?

Exercise 17.9 Suppose a run of HAC finds the clustering with $K = 7$ to have the highest value on some prechosen goodness measure of clustering. Have we found the highest-value clustering among all clusterings with $K = 7$?

Exercise 17.10 Consider the task of producing a single-link clustering of N points on a line:

Show that we only need to compute a total of about N similarities. What is the overall complexity of single-link clustering for a set of points on a line?

Exercise 17.11 Prove that single-link, complete-link, and group-average clustering are monotonic in the sense defined on page 347.

Exercise 17.12 For N points, there are $\leq N^K$ different flat clusterings into K clusters (Section 16.2, page 327). What is the number of different hierarchical clusterings (or dendrograms) of N documents? Are there more flat clusterings or more hierarchical clusterings for given K and N?

17.9 References and further reading

An excellent general review of clustering is (Jain et al. 1999). Early references for specific HAC algorithms are (King 1967) (single-link), (Sneath and Sokal 1973) (complete-link, GAAC), and (Lance and Williams 1967) (discussing a large variety of hierarchical clustering algorithms). The single-link algorithm KRUSKAL'S in Figure 17.9 is similar to *Kruskal's algorithm* for constructing a minimum ALGORITHM spanning tree. A graph-theoretical proof of the correctness of Kruskal's algorithm (which is analogous to the proof in Section 17.5) is provided by Cormen et al. (1990, Theorem 23.1). See Exercise 17.5 for the connection between minimum spanning trees and single-link clusterings.

It is often claimed that hierarchical clustering algorithms produce better clusterings than flat algorithms (Jain and Dubes (1988, p. 140); Cutting et al. (1992); Larsen and Aone (1999)) although more recently there have been experimental results suggesting the opposite (Zhao and Karypis 2002). Even without a consensus on average behavior, there is no doubt that results of EM and K-means are highly variable since they will often converge to a local optimum of poor quality. The HAC algorithms we have presented here are deterministic and thus more predictable.

The complexity of complete-link, group-average, and centroid clustering is sometimes given as $\Theta(N^2)$ (Day and Edelsbrunner 1984; Voorhees 1985b; Murtagh 1983) because a document similarity computation is an order of magnitude more expensive than a simple comparison, the main operation executed in the merging steps after the $N \times N$ similarity matrix has been computed.

The centroid algorithm described here is due to Voorhees (1985b). Voorhees recommends complete-link and centroid clustering over single-link for a retrieval application. The Buckshot algorithm was originally published by Cutting et al. (1993). Allan et al. (1998) apply single-link clustering to first story detection.

WARD'S An important HAC technique not discussed here is *Ward's method* (Ward METHOD Jr. 1963; El-Hamdouchi and Willett 1986), also called *minimum variance clustering*. In each step, it selects the merge with the smallest RSS (Chapter 16, page 332). The merge criterion in Ward's method (a function of all individual distances from the centroid) is closely related to the merge criterion in GAAC (a function of all individual similarities to the centroid).

Despite its importance for making the results of clustering useful, comparatively little work has been done on labeling clusters. Popescul and Ungar (2000) obtain good results with a combination of χ^2 and collection frequency of a term. Glover et al. (2002b) use information gain for labeling clusters of web pages. Stein and zu Eissen's approach is ontology based (2004). The more complex problem of labeling nodes in a hierarchy (which requires distinguishing more general labels for parents from more specific labels for children) is tackled by Glover et al. (2002a) and Treeratpituk and Callan (2006). Some clustering algorithms attempt to find a set of labels first and then build (often overlapping) clusters around the labels, thereby avoiding the problem of labeling altogether (Zamir and Etzioni 1999; Käki 2005; Osiński and Weiss 2005). We know of no comprehensive study that compares the quality of such "label-based" clustering to the clustering algorithms discussed in this chapter and in Chapter 16. In principle, work on multidocument summarization (McKeown and Radev 1995) is also applicable to cluster labeling, but multidocument summaries are usually longer than the short text fragments needed when labeling clusters (cf. Section 8.7, page 157). Presenting clusters in a way that users can understand is a UI problem. We recommend reading (Baeza-Yates and Ribeiro-Neto 1999, Chapter 10) for an introduction to user interfaces in IR.

An example of an efficient divisive algorithm is bisecting K-means (Steinbach et al. 2000). *Spectral clustering* algorithms (Kannan et al. 2000; Dhillon 2001; Zha et al. 2001; Ng et al. 2001a), including *principal direction divisive partitioning* (PDDP) (whose bisecting decisions are based on SVD, see Chapter 18) (Boley 1998; Savaresi and Boley 2004), are computationally more expensive than bisecting K-means, but have the advantage of being deterministic.

Unlike K-means and EM, most hierarchical clustering algorithms do not have a probabilistic interpretation. Model-based hierarchical clustering (Vaithyanathan and Dom 2000; Kamvar et al. 2002; Castro et al. 2004) is an exception.

The evaluation methodology described in Section 16.3 (page 327) is also applicable to hierarchical clustering. Specialized evaluation measures for hierarchies are discussed by Fowlkes and Mallows (1983), Larsen and Aone (1999), and Sahoo et al. (2006).

The R environment (R Development Core Team 2005) offers good support for hierarchical clustering. The R function `hclust` implements single-link, complete-link, group-average, and centroid clustering, and Ward's method. Another option provided is `median` clustering, which represents each cluster by its medoid (cf. k-medoids in Chapter 16, page 336). Support for clustering vectors in high-dimensional spaces is provided by the software package CLUTO (http://glaros.dtc.umn.edu/gkhome/views/cluto).

18 *Matrix decompositions and latent semantic indexing*

On page 113, we introduced the notion of a *term-document matrix:* an $M \times N$ matrix C, each of whose rows represents a term and each of whose columns represents a document in the collection. Even for a collection of modest size, the term-document matrix C is likely to have several tens of thousands of rows and columns. In Section 18.1.1, we first develop a class of operations from linear algebra, known as *matrix decomposition*. In Section 18.2, we use a special form of matrix decomposition to construct a *low-rank* approximation to the term-document matrix. In Section 18.3 we examine the application of such low-rank approximations to indexing and retrieving documents, a technique referred to as *latent semantic indexing*. Although latent semantic indexing has not been established as a significant force in scoring and ranking for information retrieval (IR), it remains an intriguing approach to clustering in a number of domains including for collections of text documents (Section 16.6, page 343). Understanding its full potential remains an area of active research.

Readers who do not require a refresher on linear algebra may skip Section 18.1, although Example 18.1 is especially recommended as it highlights a property of eigenvalues that we exploit later in the chapter.

18.1 Linear algebra review

We briefly review some necessary background in linear algebra. Let C be an $M \times N$ matrix with real-valued entries; for a term–document matrix, all entries are in fact non-negative. The *rank* of a matrix is the number of linearly independent rows (or columns) in it; thus, $rank(C) \leq \min\{M, N\}$. A square $r \times r$ matrix all of whose off-diagonal entries are zero is called a *diagonal matrix*; its rank is equal to the number of nonzero diagonal entries. If all r diagonal entries of such a diagonal matrix are 1, it is called the identity matrix of dimension r and represented by I_r.

For a square $M \times M$ matrix C and a vector $\vec{x}$ that is not all zeros, the values of λ satisfying

(18.1)
$$C\vec{x} = \lambda\vec{x}$$

EIGENVALUE are called the *eigenvalues* of C. The N-vector $\vec{x}$ satisfying Equation (18.1) for an eigenvalue λ is the corresponding *right eigenvector*. The eigenvector corresponding to the eigenvalue of largest magnitude is called the *principal eigenvector*. In a similar fashion, the *left eigenvectors* of C are the M-vectors y such that

(18.2)
$$\vec{y}^T C = \lambda\vec{y}^T.$$

The number of nonzero eigenvalues of C is at most rank(C).

The eigenvalues of a matrix are found by solving the *characteristic equation*, which is obtained by rewriting Equation (18.1) in the form $(C - \lambda I_M)\vec{x} = 0$. The eigenvalues of C are then the solutions of $|(C - \lambda I_M)| = 0$, where $|S|$ denotes the determinant of a square matrix S. The equation $|(C - \lambda I_M)| = 0$ is an Mth-order polynomial equation in λ and can have at most M roots, which are the eigenvalues of C. These eigenvalues can in general be complex, even if all entries of C are real.

We now examine some further properties of eigenvalues and eigenvectors, to set up the central idea of singular value decompositions in Section 18.2 below. First, we look at the relationship between matrix-vector multiplication and eigenvalues.

Example 18.1: Consider the matrix

$$S = \begin{pmatrix} 30 & 0 & 0 \\ 0 & 20 & 0 \\ 0 & 0 & 1 \end{pmatrix}.$$

Clearly, the matrix has rank 3, and has three nonzero eigenvalues $\lambda_1 = 30$, $\lambda_2 = 20$, and $\lambda_3 = 1$, with the three corresponding eigenvectors

$$\vec{x}_1 = \begin{pmatrix} 1 \\ 0 \\ 0 \end{pmatrix}, \vec{x}_2 = \begin{pmatrix} 0 \\ 1 \\ 0 \end{pmatrix} \text{ and } \vec{x}_3 = \begin{pmatrix} 0 \\ 0 \\ 1 \end{pmatrix}.$$

For each of the eigenvectors, multiplication by S acts as if we were multiplying the eigenvector by a multiple of the identity matrix; the multiple is different for each eigenvector. Now, consider an arbitrary vector, such as $\vec{v} = \begin{pmatrix} 2 \\ 4 \\ 6 \end{pmatrix}$. We can always express $\vec{v}$ as a linear combination of the three eigenvectors of S; in the current example we have

$$\vec{v} = \begin{pmatrix} 2 \\ 4 \\ 6 \end{pmatrix} = 2\vec{x}_1 + 4\vec{x}_2 + 6\vec{x}_3.$$

Suppose we multiply $\vec{v}$ by S:

$$
\begin{aligned}
S\vec{v} &= S(2\vec{x}_1 + 4\vec{x}_2 + 6\vec{x}_3) \\
&= 2S\vec{x}_1 + 4S\vec{x}_2 + 6S\vec{x}_3 \\
&= 2\lambda_1\vec{x}_1 + 4\lambda_2\vec{x}_2 + 6\lambda_3\vec{x}_3 \\
&= 60\vec{x}_1 + 80\vec{x}_2 + 6\vec{x}_3.
\end{aligned}
$$

(18.3)

Example 18.1 shows that even though $\vec{v}$ is an arbitrary vector, the effect of multiplication by S is determined by the eigenvalues and eigenvectors of S. Furthermore, it is intuitively apparent from Equation (18.3) that the product $S\vec{v}$ is relatively unaffected by terms arising from the small eigenvalues of S; in our example, because $\lambda_3 = 1$, the contribution of the third term on the right hand side of Equation (18.3) is small. In fact, if we were to completely ignore the contribution in Equation (18.3) from the third eigenvector corresponding to $\lambda_3 = 1$, then the product $S\vec{v}$ would be computed to be $\begin{pmatrix} 60 \\ 80 \\ 0 \end{pmatrix}$ rather than

the correct product, which is $\begin{pmatrix} 60 \\ 80 \\ 6 \end{pmatrix}$; these two vectors are relatively close to each other by any of various metrics one could apply (such as the length of their vector difference).

This suggests that the effect of small eigenvalues (and their eigenvectors) on a matrix–vector product is small. We will carry forward this intuition when studying matrix decompositions and low-rank approximations in Section 18.2. Before doing so, we examine the eigenvectors and eigenvalues of special forms of matrices that will be of particular interest to us.

For a *symmetric* matrix S, the eigenvectors corresponding to distinct eigenvalues are *orthogonal*. Further, if S is both real and symmetric, the eigenvalues are all real.

Example 18.2: Consider the real, symmetric matrix

(18.4)

$$S = \begin{pmatrix} 2 & 1 \\ 1 & 2 \end{pmatrix}.$$

From the characteristic equation $|S - \lambda I| = 0$, we have the quadratic $(2 - \lambda)^2 - 1 = 0$, whose solutions yield the eigenvalues 3 and 1. The corresponding eigenvectors $\begin{pmatrix} 1 \\ -1 \end{pmatrix}$ and $\begin{pmatrix} 1 \\ 1 \end{pmatrix}$ are orthogonal.

18.1.1 Matrix decompositions

In this section, we examine ways in which a square matrix can be *factored* into the product of matrices derived from its eigenvectors; we refer to this process as *matrix decomposition*. Matrix decompositions similar to the ones in this section forms the basis of our principal text-analysis technique in Section 18.3, where we will look at decompositions of nonsquare term–document matrices. The square decompositions in this section are simpler and can be treated with sufficient mathematical rigor to help the reader to understand how such decompositions work. The detailed mathematical derivation of the more complex decompositions in Section 18.2 are beyond the scope of this book.

MATRIX
DECOMPOSITION

We begin by giving two theorems on the decomposition of a square matrix into the product of three matrices of a special form. The first of these, Theorem 18.1, gives the basic factorization of a square real-valued matrix into three factors. The second, Theorem 18.2, applies to square symmetric matrices and is the basis of the singular value decomposition described in Theorem 18.3.

Theorem 18.1. (Matrix diagonalization theorem) *Let S be a square real-valued $M \times M$ matrix with M linearly independent eigenvectors. Then there exists an eigen decomposition*

EIGEN
DECOMPOSITION

$$(18.5) \qquad S = U \Lambda U^{-1},$$

where the columns of U are the eigenvectors of S and Λ is a diagonal matrix whose diagonal entries are the eigenvalues of S in decreasing order

$$(18.6) \qquad \begin{pmatrix} \lambda_1 & & & \\ & \lambda_2 & & \\ & & \cdots & \\ & & & \lambda_M \end{pmatrix}, \lambda_i \geq \lambda_{i+1}.$$

If the eigenvalues are distinct, then this decomposition is unique.

To understand how Theorem 18.1 works, we note that U has the eigenvectors of S as columns

$$(18.7) \qquad U = (\vec{u}_1 \; \vec{u}_2 \cdots \vec{u}_M).$$

Then we have

$$\begin{aligned} SU &= S(\vec{u}_1 \; \vec{u}_2 \cdots \vec{u}_M) \\ &= (\lambda_1 \vec{u}_1 \; \lambda_2 \vec{u}_2 \cdots \lambda_M \vec{u}_M) \\ &= (\vec{u}_1 \; \vec{u}_2 \cdots \vec{u}_M) \begin{pmatrix} \lambda_1 & & & \\ & \lambda_2 & & \\ & & \cdots & \\ & & & \lambda_M \end{pmatrix}. \end{aligned}$$

Thus, we have $SU = U\Lambda$, or $S = U \Lambda U^{-1}$.

We next state a closely related decomposition of a symmetric square matrix into the product of matrices derived from its eigenvectors. This will pave the way for the development of our main tool for text analysis, the singular value decomposition (Section 18.2).

Theorem 18.2. (Symmetric diagonalization theorem) *Let S be a square, symmetric real-valued M × M matrix with M linearly independent eigenvectors. Then there exists a* symmetric diagonal decomposition

SYMMETRIC
DIAGONAL
DECOMPOSITION

(18.8)
$$S = Q\Lambda Q^T,$$

where the columns of Q are the orthogonal and normalized (unit length, real) eigenvectors of S, and Λ is the diagonal matrix whose entries are the eigenvalues of S. Further, all entries of Q are real and we have $Q^{-1} = Q^T$.

We will build on this symmetric diagonal decomposition to build low-rank approximations to term–document matrices.

? **Exercise 18.1** What is the rank of the 3×3 diagonal matrix below?

$$\begin{pmatrix} 1 & 1 & 0 \\ 0 & 1 & 1 \\ 1 & 2 & 1 \end{pmatrix}$$

Exercise 18.2 Show that $\lambda = 2$ is an eigenvalue of

$$C = \begin{pmatrix} 6 & -2 \\ 4 & 0 \end{pmatrix}.$$

Find the corresponding eigenvector.

Exercise 18.3 Compute the unique eigen decomposition of the 2×2 matrix in (18.4).

18.2 Term–document matrices and singular value decompositions

The decompositions we have been studying thus far apply to square matrices. However, the matrix we are interested in is the $M \times N$ term–document matrix C where (barring a rare coincidence) $M \neq N$; furthermore, C is very unlikely to be symmetric. To this end we first describe an extension of the symmetric diagonal decomposition known as the *singular value decomposition*. We then show in Section 18.3 how this can be used to construct an approximate version of C. It is beyond the scope of this book to develop a full treatment of the mathematics underlying singular value decompositions; following the statement of Theorem 18.3 we relate the singular value

SINGULAR
VALUE
DECOMPOSITION

SYMMETRIC   decomposition to the symmetric diagonal decompositions from Sec-
DIAGONAL   tion 18.1.1. Given C, let U be the $M \times M$ matrix whose columns are the or-
DECOMPOSITION   thogonal eigenvectors of CC^T, and V be the $N \times N$ matrix whose columns
are the orthogonal eigenvectors of $C^T C$. Denote by C^T the transpose of a
matrix C.

Theorem 18.3. *Let r be the rank of the $M \times N$ matrix C. Then, there is a singular-*
SVD   *value decomposition (SVD for short) of C of the form*

(18.9) $$C = U\Sigma V^T,$$

where

1. *The eigenvalues $\lambda_1, \ldots, \lambda_r$ of CC^T are the same as the eigenvalues of $C^T C$;*
2. *For $1 \le i \le r$, let $\sigma_i = \sqrt{\lambda_i}$, with $\lambda_i \ge \lambda_{i+1}$. Then the $M \times N$ matrix Σ is com-*
   posed by setting $\Sigma_{ii} = \sigma_i$ for $1 \le i \le r$, and zero otherwise.

The values σ_i are referred to as the *singular values* of C. It is instructive to
examine the relationship of Theorem 18.3 to Theorem 18.2; we do this rather
than derive the general proof of Theorem 18.3, which is beyond the scope of
this book.

By multiplying Equation (18.9) by its transposed version, we have

(18.10) $$CC^T = U\Sigma V^T \, V\Sigma U^T = U\Sigma^2 U^T.$$

Note now that in Equation (18.10), the left-hand side is a square symmetric
matrix real-valued matrix, and the right-hand side represents its symmetric
diagonal decomposition as in Theorem 18.2. What does the left-hand side
CC^T represent? It is a square matrix with a row and a column corresponding to each of the M terms. The entry (i, j) in the matrix is a measure of the
overlap between the ith and jth terms, based on their co-occurrence in documents. The precise mathematical meaning depends on the manner in which
C is constructed based on term weighting. Consider the case where C is the
term–document incidence matrix of page 3, illustrated in Figure 1.1. Then
the entry (i, j) in CC^T is the number of documents in which both term i and
term j occur.

When writing down the numerical values of the SVD, it is conventional
to represent Σ as an $r \times r$ matrix with the singular values on the diagonals,
because all its entries outside this submatrix are zeros. Accordingly, it is conventional to omit the rightmost $M - r$ columns of U corresponding to these
omitted rows of Σ; likewise the rightmost $N - r$ columns of V are omitted
because they correspond in V^T to the rows that will be multiplied by the
$N - r$ columns of zeros in Σ. This written form of the SVD is sometimes
REDUCED SVD   known as the *reduced SVD* or *truncated SVD* and we will encounter it again
TRUNCATED   in Exercise 18.9. Henceforth, our numerical examples and exercises will use
SVD   this reduced form.

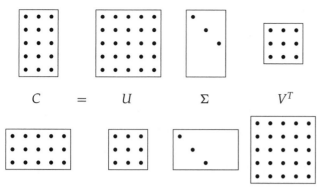

Figure 18.1 Illustration of the SVD. In this schematic illustration of (18.9), we see two cases illustrated. In the top half of the figure, we have a matrix C for which $M > N$. The lower half illustrates the case $M < N$.

Example 18.3: We now illustrate the singular-value decomposition of a 4×2 matrix of rank 2; the singular values are $\Sigma_{11} = 2.236$ and $\Sigma_{22} = 1$.

$$(18.11) \quad C = \begin{pmatrix} 1 & -1 \\ 0 & 1 \\ 1 & 0 \\ -1 & 1 \end{pmatrix} = \begin{pmatrix} -0.632 & 0.000 \\ 0.316 & -0.707 \\ -0.316 & -0.707 \\ 0.632 & 0.000 \end{pmatrix} \begin{pmatrix} 2.236 & 0.000 \\ 0.000 & 1.000 \end{pmatrix} \begin{pmatrix} -0.707 & 0.707 \\ -0.707 & -0.707 \end{pmatrix}.$$

As with the matrix decompositions defined in Section 18.1.1, the singular value decomposition of a matrix can be computed by a variety of algorithms, many of which have been publicly available software implementations; pointers to these are given in Section 18.5.

Exercise 18.4 Let

$$(18.12) \qquad\qquad C = \begin{pmatrix} 1 & 1 \\ 0 & 1 \\ 1 & 0 \end{pmatrix}$$

be the term–document incidence matrix for a collection. Compute the co-occurrence matrix CC^T. What is the interpretation of the diagonal entries of CC^T when C is a term–document incidence matrix?

Exercise 18.5 Verify that the SVD of the matrix in Equation (18.12) is

$$(18.13) \qquad U = \begin{pmatrix} -0.816 & 0.000 \\ -0.408 & -0.707 \\ -0.408 & 0.707 \end{pmatrix}, \Sigma = \begin{pmatrix} 1.732 & 0.000 \\ 0.000 & 1.000 \end{pmatrix} \text{ and } V^T = \begin{pmatrix} -0.707 & -0.707 \\ 0.707 & -0.707 \end{pmatrix},$$

by verifying all of the properties in the statement of Theorem 18.3.

Exercise 18.6 Suppose that C is a term–document incidence matrix. What do the entries of $C^T C$ represent?

Exercise 18.7 Let

$$(18.14) \qquad C = \begin{pmatrix} 0 & 2 & 1 \\ 0 & 3 & 0 \\ 2 & 1 & 0 \end{pmatrix}$$

be a term–document matrix whose entries are term frequencies; thus term 1 occurs twice in document 2 and once in document 3. Compute CC^T; observe that its entries are largest where two terms have their most frequent occurrences together in the same document.

18.3 Low-rank approximations

We next state a matrix approximation problem that at first seems to have little to do with information retrieval. We describe a solution to this matrix problem using SVD, then develop its application to IR.

Given an $M \times N$ matrix C and a positive integer k, we wish to find an FROBENIUS $M \times N$ matrix C_k of rank at most k, so as to minimize the *Frobenius norm* of NORM the matrix difference $X = C - C_k$, defined to be

$$(18.15) \qquad ||X||_F = \sqrt{\sum_{i=1}^{M} \sum_{j=1}^{N} X_{ij}^2}.$$

Thus, the Frobenius norm of X measures the discrepancy between C_k and C; our goal is to find a matrix C_k that minimizes this discrepancy, while constraining C_k to have rank at most k. If r is the rank of C, clearly $C_r = C$ and the Frobenius norm of the discrepancy is zero in this case. When k is far LOW-RANK smaller than r, we refer to C_k as a *low-rank approximation*.

APPROXIMATION   The SVD can be used to solve the low-rank matrix approximation problem. We then derive from it an application to approximating term–document matrices. We invoke the following three-step procedure to this end:

1. Given C, construct its SVD in the form shown in (18.9); thus, $C = U\Sigma V^T$.
2. Derive from Σ the matrix Σ_k formed by replacing by zeros the $r - k$ smallest singular values on the diagonal of Σ.
3. Compute and output $C_k = U\Sigma_k V^T$ as the rank-k approximation to C.

The rank of C_k is at most k: This follows from the fact that Σ_k has at most k nonzero values. Next, we recall the intuition of Example 18.1: The effect of small eigenvalues on matrix products is small. Thus, it seems plausible that replacing these small eigenvalues by zero will not substantially alter the product, leaving it "close" to C. The following theorem due to Eckart and Young tells us that, in fact, this procedure yields the matrix of rank k with the lowest possible Frobenius error.

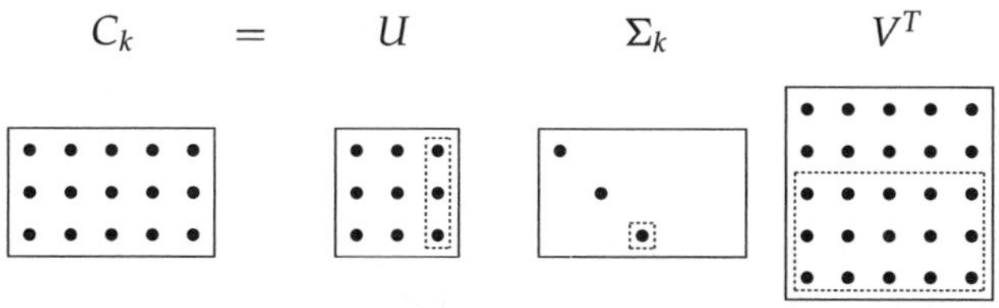

$$C_k \quad = \quad U \qquad \Sigma_k \qquad V^T$$

Figure 18.2 Illustration of low rank approximation using the SVD. The dashed boxes indicate the matrix entries affected by "zeroing out" the smallest singular values.

Theorem 18.4.

(18.16)
$$\min_{Z\mid rank(Z)=k} \|C - Z\|_F = \|C - C_k\|_F = \sqrt{\sum_{i=k+1}^{r} \sigma_i^2}.$$

Recalling that the singular values are in decreasing order $\sigma_1 \geq \sigma_2 \geq \cdots$, we learn from Theorem 18.4 that C_k is the best rank-k approximation to C, incurring an error (measured by the Frobenius norm of $C - C_k$) equal to σ_{k+1}. Thus, the larger k is, the smaller this error (and in particular, for $k = r$, the error is zero since $\Sigma_r = \Sigma$; provided $r < M, N$, then $\sigma_{r+1} = 0$ and thus $C_r = C$).

To derive further insight into why the process of truncating the smallest $r - k$ singular values in Σ helps to generate a rank-k approximation of low error, we examine the form of C_k:

(18.17)
$$C_k = U\Sigma_k V^T$$

(18.18)
$$= U \begin{pmatrix} \sigma_1 & 0 & 0 & 0 & 0 \\ 0 & \cdots & 0 & 0 & 0 \\ 0 & 0 & \sigma_k & 0 & 0 \\ 0 & 0 & 0 & 0 & 0 \\ 0 & 0 & 0 & 0 & \cdots \end{pmatrix} V^T$$

(18.19)
$$= \sum_{i=1}^{k} \sigma_i \vec{u}_i \vec{v}_i^T,$$

where $\vec{u}_i$ and $\vec{v}_i$ are the ith columns of U and V, respectively. Thus, $\vec{u}_i \vec{v}_i^T$ is a rank-1 matrix, so that we have just expressed C_k as the sum of k rank-1 matrices each weighted by a singular value. As i increases, the contribution of the rank-1 matrix $\vec{u}_i \vec{v}_i^T$ is weighted by a sequence of shrinking singular values σ_i.

?

Exercise 18.8 Compute a rank-1 approximation C_1 to the matrix C in Example 18.12, using the SVD as in Exercise 18.13. What is the Frobenius norm of the error of this approximation?

Exercise 18.9 Consider now the computation in Exercise 18.8. Following the schematic in Figure 18.2, notice that for a rank-1 approximation we have

σ_1 being a scalar. Denote by U_1 the first column of U and by V_1 the first column of V. Show that the rank-1 approximation to C can then be written as $U_1 \sigma_1 V_1^T = \sigma_1 U_1 V_1^T$.

Exercise 18.10 Exercise 18.9 can be generalized to rank k approximations: We let U_k' and V_k' denote the "reduced" matrices formed by retaining only the first k columns of U and V, respectively. Thus, U_k' is an $M \times k$ matrix while V'^T_k is a $k \times N$ matrix. Then, we have

(18.20) $$C_k = U_k' \Sigma_k' V'^T_k,$$

where Σ_k' is the square $k \times k$ submatrix of Σ_k with the singular values $\sigma_1, \ldots, \sigma_k$ on the diagonal. The primary advantage of using (18.20) is to eliminate a lot of redundant columns of zeros in U and V, thereby explicitly eliminating multiplication by columns that do not affect the low-rank approximation; this version of the SVD is sometimes known as the reduced SVD or truncated SVD and is a computationally simpler representation from which to compute the low rank approximation.

For the matrix C in Example 18.3, write down both Σ_2 and Σ_2'.

18.4 Latent semantic indexing

We now discuss the approximation of a term-document matrix C by one of lower rank using the SVD. The low-rank approximation to C yields a new representation for each document in the collection. We will cast queries into this low-rank representation as well, enabling us to compute query–document similarity scores in this low-rank representation. This process is known as *latent semantic indexing* (generally abbreviated LSI).

LATENT
SEMANTIC
INDEXING

But first, we motivate such an approximation. Recall the vector space representation of documents and queries introduced in Chapter 6. This vector space representation enjoys a number of advantages including the uniform treatment of queries and documents as vectors, the induced score computation based on cosine similarity, the ability to weight different terms differently, and its extension beyond document retrieval to such applications as clustering and classification. The vector space representation suffers, however, from its inability to cope with two classic problems arising in natural languages: *synonymy* and *polysemy*. *Synonymy* refers to a case where two different words (say, car and automobile) have the same meaning. Because the vector space representation fails to capture the relationship between synonymous terms such as car and automobile – according each a separate dimension in the vector space. Consequently, the computed similarity $\vec{q} \cdot \vec{d}$ between a query $\vec{q}$ (say, car) and a document $\vec{d}$ containing both car and automobile underestimates the true similarity that a user would perceive. *Polysemy* on the other hand refers to the case where a term such as charge has multiple meanings, so that the computed similarity $\vec{q} \cdot \vec{d}$ overestimates the similarity that a user would perceive. Could we use the co-occurrences of terms (whether, for instance, charge occurs in a document containing steed versus in a document containing electron) to capture the latent semantic associations of terms and alleviate these problems?

LSA Even for a collection of modest size, the term–document matrix C is likely to have several tens of thousand of rows and columns, and a rank in the tens of thousands as well. In LSI (sometimes referred to as *latent semantic analysis (LSA)*), we use the SVD to construct a low-rank approximation C_k to the term–document matrix, for a value of k that is far smaller than the original rank of C. In the experimental work cited later in this section, k is generally chosen to be in the low hundreds. We thus map each row/column (respectively corresponding to a term/document) to a k-dimensional space; this space is defined by the k principal eigenvectors (corresponding to the largest eigenvalues) of CC^T and $C^T C$. Note that the matrix C_k is itself still an $M \times N$ matrix, irrespective of k.

Next, we use the new k-dimensional LSI representation as we did the original representation – to compute similarities between vectors. A query vector $\vec{q}$ is mapped into its representation in the LSI space by the transformation

$$(18.21) \qquad \vec{q}_k = \Sigma_k^{-1} U_k^T \vec{q}.$$

Now, we may use cosine similarities as in Chapter 6 to compute the similarity between a query and a document, between two documents, or between two terms. Note especially that Equation (18.21) does not in any way depend on $\vec{q}$ being a query; it is simply a vector in the space of terms. This means that if we have an LSI representation of a collection of documents, a new document not in the collection can be "folded in" to this representation using Equation (18.21). This allows us to incrementally add documents to an LSI representation. Of course, such incremental addition fails to capture the co-occurrences of the newly added documents (and even ignores any new terms they contain). As such, the quality of the LSI representation will degrade as more documents are added and will eventually require a recomputation of the LSI representation.

The fidelity of the approximation of C_k to C leads us to hope that the relative values of cosine similarities are preserved: if a query is close to a document in the original space, it remains relatively close in the k-dimensional space. But this in itself is not sufficiently interesting, especially given that the sparse query vector $\vec{q}$ turns into a dense query vector $\vec{q}_k$ in the low-dimensional space. This has a significant computational cost, when compared with the cost of processing $\vec{q}$ in its native form.

Example 18.4: Consider the term-document matrix $C =$

	d_1	d_2	d_3	d_4	d_5	d_6
ship	1	0	1	0	0	0
boat	0	1	0	0	0	0
ocean	1	1	0	0	0	0
voyage	1	0	0	1	1	0
trip	0	0	0	1	0	1

Its SVD is the product of three matrices as below. First we have U, which in this example is:

	1	2	3	4	5
ship	−0.44	−0.30	0.57	0.58	0.25
boat	−0.13	−0.33	−0.59	0.00	0.73
ocean	−0.48	−0.51	−0.37	0.00	−0.61
voyage	−0.70	0.35	0.15	−0.58	0.16
trip	−0.26	0.65	−0.41	0.58	−0.09

When applying the SVD to a term–document matrix, U is known as the *SVD term matrix*. The singular values are $\Sigma =$

2.16	0.00	0.00	0.00	0.00
0.00	1.59	0.00	0.00	0.00
0.00	0.00	1.28	0.00	0.00
0.00	0.00	0.00	1.00	0.00
0.00	0.00	0.00	0.00	0.39

Finally we have V^T, which in the context of a term-document matrix is known as the *SVD document matrix*:

	d_1	d_2	d_3	d_4	d_5	d_6
1	−0.75	−0.28	−0.20	−0.45	−0.33	−0.12
2	−0.29	−0.53	−0.19	0.63	0.22	0.41
3	0.28	−0.75	0.45	−0.20	0.12	−0.33
4	0.00	0.00	0.58	0.00	−0.58	0.58
5	−0.53	0.29	0.63	0.19	0.41	−0.22

By "zeroing out" all but the two largest singular values of Σ, we obtain $\Sigma_2 =$

2.16	0.00	0.00	0.00	0.00
0.00	1.59	0.00	0.00	0.00
0.00	0.00	0.00	0.00	0.00
0.00	0.00	0.00	0.00	0.00
0.00	0.00	0.00	0.00	0.00

From this, we compute $C_2 =$

	d_1	d_2	d_3	d_4	d_5	d_6
1	−1.62	−0.60	−0.44	−0.97	−0.70	−0.26
2	−0.46	−0.84	−0.30	1.00	0.35	0.65
3	0.00	0.00	0.00	0.00	0.00	0.00
4	0.00	0.00	0.00	0.00	0.00	0.00
5	0.00	0.00	0.00	0.00	0.00	0.00

Notice that the low-rank approximation, unlike the original matrix C, can have negative entries.

Examination of C_2 and Σ_2 in Example 18.4 shows that the last three rows of each of these matrices are populated entirely by zeros. This suggests that the SVD product $U\Sigma V^T$ in Equation (18.18) can be carried out with only two rows in the representations of Σ_2 and V^T; we may then replace these matrices by their truncated versions Σ_2' and $(V')^T$. For instance, the truncated SVD document matrix $(V')^T$ in this example is:

	d_1	d_2	d_3	d_4	d_5	d_6
1	−0.75	−0.28	−0.20	−0.45	−0.33	−0.12
2	−0.29	−0.53	−0.19	0.63	0.22	0.41

Figure 18.3 illustrates the documents in $(V')^T$ in two dimensions. Note also that C_2 is dense relative to C.

We may in general view the low-rank approximation of C by C_k as a *constrained optimization* problem, subject to the constraint that C_k have rank at

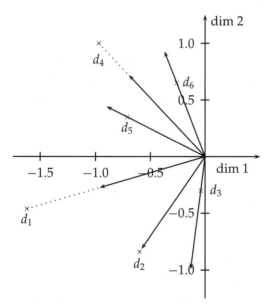

Figure 18.3 The documents of Example 18.4 reduced to two dimensions in $(V')^T$.

most k, we seek a representation of the terms and documents comprising C with low Frobenius norm for the error $C - C_k$. When forced to squeeze the terms/documents down to a k-dimensional space, the SVD should bring together terms with similar co-occurrences. This intuition suggests, then, that not only should retrieval quality not suffer too much from the dimension reduction, but in fact may *improve*.

Dumais (1993) and Dumais (1995) conducted experiments with LSI on TREC documents and tasks, using the commonly used Lanczos algorithm to compute the SVD. At the time of their work in the early 1990s, the LSI computation on tens of thousands of documents took approximately one day on one machine. In these experiments, they achieved precision at or above that of the median TREC participant. In about 20% of TREC topics, their system was the top scorer, and reportedly slightly better on average than standard vector spaces for LSI at about 350 dimensions. Here are some conclusions on LSI first suggested by their work, and subsequently verified by many other experiments.

- The computational cost of the SVD is significant; at the time of this writing, we know of no successful experiment with over one million documents. This has been the biggest obstacle to the widespread adoption to LSI. One approach to this obstacle is to build the LSI representation on a randomly sampled subset of the documents in the collection, following which the remaining documents are "folded in" as detailed with Equation (18.21).
- As we reduce k, recall tends to increase, as expected.
- Most surprisingly, a value of k in the low hundreds can actually *increase* precision on some query benchmarks. This suggests that, for a suitable value of k, LSI addresses some of the challenges of synonymy.
- LSI works best in applications where there is little overlap between queries and documents.

The experiments also documented some modes where LSI failed to match the effectiveness of more traditional indexes and score computations. Most notably (and perhaps obviously), LSI shares two basic drawbacks of vector space retrieval: There is no good way of expressing negations (find documents that contain german but not shepherd), and no way of enforcing Boolean conditions.

SOFT CLUSTERING LSI can be viewed as *soft clustering* by interpreting each dimension of the reduced space as a cluster and the value that a document has on that dimension as its fractional membership in that cluster.

? Exercise 18.11 Assume you have a set of documents each of which is in either English or in Spanish. The collection is given in Figure 18.4.

Figure 18.5 gives a glossary relating the Spanish and English words above for your own information. This glossary is NOT available to the retrieval system:

DocID	document text
1	hello
2	open house
3	mi casa
4	hola Profesor
5	hola y bienvenido
6	hello and welcome

Figure 18.4 Documents for Exercise 18.11.

Spanish	English
mi	my
casa	house
hola	hello
profesor	professor
y	and
bienvenido	welcome

Figure 18.5 Glossary for Exercise 18.11.

1. Construct the appropriate term–document matrix C to use for a collection consisting of these documents. For simplicity, use raw term frequencies rather than normalized tf-idf weights. Make sure to clearly label the dimensions of your matrix.
2. Write down the matrices U_2, Σ_2' and V_2 and from these derive the rank 2 approximation C_2.
3. State succinctly what the (i, j) entry in the matrix $C^T C$ represents.
4. State succinctly what the (i, j) entry in the matrix $C_2^T C_2$ represents, and why it differs from that in $C^T C$.

18.5 References and further reading

Strang (1986) provides an excellent introductory overview of matrix decompositions including the singular value decomposition. Theorem 18.4 is due to Eckart and Young (1936). The connection between IR and low-rank approximations of the term – document matrix was introduced in Deerwester et al. (1990), with a subsequent survey of results in Berry et al. (1995). Dumais (1993) and Dumais (1995) describe experiments on TREC benchmarks giving evidence that at least on some benchmarks, LSI can produce better precision and recall than standard vector-space retrieval. www.cs.utk.edu/~berry/lsi++/ and http://lsi.argreenhouse.com/lsi/LSIpapers.html offer comprehensive pointers to the literature and software of LSI. Schütze and Silverstein (1997) evaluate LSI and truncated representations of centroids for efficient K-means clustering (Section 16.4). Bast and Majumdar (2005) detail the role of the reduced dimension k in LSI and how different pairs of terms get coalesced together at differing values of k. Applications of LSI to *cross-language information retrieval* (where documents in two or more different languages are indexed, and a query posed in one language is expected to retrieve documents in other languages) are developed in Berry and Young (1995) and Littman et al. (1998). LSI (referred to as LSA in more general settings) has been applied to host of other problems in computer science ranging from memory modeling to computer vision.

Hofmann (1999a, 1999b) provides an initial probabilistic extension of the basic LSI technique. A more satisfactory formal basis for a probabilistic latent variable model for dimensionality reduction is the Latent Dirichlet Allocation (LDA) model (Blei et al. 2003), which is generative and assigns probabilities to documents outside of the training set. This model is extended to a hierarchical clustering by Rosen-Zvi et al. (2004). Wei and Croft (2006) present the first large scale evaluation of LDA, finding it to significantly outperform the query likelihood model of Section 12.2 (page 223), but to not perform quite as well as the relevance model mentioned in Section 12.4 (page 230) – but the latter does additional per-query processing unlike LDA. Teh et al. (2006) generalize further by presenting Hierarchical Dirichlet processes, a probabilistic model that allows a group (for us, a document) to be drawn from an infinite mixture of latent topics, while still allowing these topics to be shared across documents.

19 Web search basics

In this and the following two chapters, we consider web search engines. Sections 19.1 through 19.4 provide some background and history to help the reader appreciate the forces that conspire to make the Web chaotic, fast-changing, and (from the standpoint of information retrieval) very different from the "traditional" collections studied thus far in this book. Sections 19.5 through 19.6 deal with estimating the number of documents indexed by web search engines, and the elimination of duplicate documents in web indexes, respectively. These two latter sections serve as background material for the two following chapters.

19.1 Background and history

The Web is unprecedented in many ways: unprecedented in scale, unprecedented in the almost-complete lack of coordination in its creation, and unprecedented in the diversity of backgrounds and motives of its participants. Each of these contributes to making web search different – and generally far harder – than searching "traditional" documents.

The invention of hypertext, envisioned by Vannevar Bush in the 1940s and first realized in working systems in the 1970s, significantly precedes the formation of the World Wide Web (which we will simply refer to as the Web), in the 1990s. Web usage has shown tremendous growth to the point where it now claims a good fraction of humanity as participants, by relying on a simple, open client-server design: (i) the server communicates with the client via a protocol (the *http* or hypertext transfer protocol) that is lightweight and simple, asynchronously carrying a variety of payloads (text, images, and – over time – richer media such as audio and video files) encoded in a simple markup language called *HTML* (for hypertext markup language); (ii) the client – generally a *browser*, an application within a graphical user environment – can ignore what it does not understand. Each of these seemingly

HTTP

HTML

innocuous features has contributed enormously to the growth of the Web, so it is worthwhile to examine them further.

The basic operation is as follows: A client (such as a browser) sends an URL *http request* to a *web server*. The browser specifies a *URL* (for *universal resource locator*) such as `http://www.stanford.edu/home/atoz/contact.html`. In this example URL, the string `http` refers to the protocol to be used for transmitting the data. The string `www.stanford.edu` is known as the *domain* and specifies the root of a hierarchy of web pages (typically mirroring a filesystem hierarchy underlying the web server). In this example, `/home/atoz/contact.html` is a path in this hierarchy with a file `contact.html` that contains the information to be returned by the web server at `www.stanford.edu` in response to this request. The HTML-encoded file `contact.html` holds the hyperlinks and the content (in this instance, contact information for Stanford University), as well as formatting rules for rendering this content in a browser. Such an http request thus allows us to fetch the content of a page, something that will prove to be useful to us for crawling and indexing documents (Chapter 20).

The designers of the first browsers made it easy to view the HTML markup tags on the content of a URL. This simple convenience allowed new users to create their own HTML content without extensive training or experience; rather, they learned from example content that they liked. As they did so, a second feature of browsers supported the rapid proliferation of web content creation and usage: Browsers ignored what they did not understand. This did not, as one might fear, lead to the creation of numerous incompatible dialects of HTML. What it did promote was amateur content creators who could freely experiment with and learn from their newly created web pages without fear that a simple syntax error would "bring the system down." Publishing on the Web became a mass activity that was not limited to a few trained programmers, but rather open to tens and eventually hundreds of millions of individuals. For most users and for most information needs, the Web quickly became the best way to supply and consume information on everything from rare ailments to subway schedules.

The mass publishing of information on the Web is essentially useless unless this wealth of information can be discovered and consumed by other users. Early attempts at making web information "discoverable" fell into two broad categories: (i) full-text index search engines such as Altavista, Excite, and Infoseek and (ii) taxonomies populated with web pages in categories, such as Yahoo! The former presented the user with a keyword search interface supported by inverted indexes and ranking mechanisms building on those introduced in earlier chapters. The latter allowed the user to browse through a hierarchical tree of category labels. Although this is at first blush a convenient and intuitive metaphor for finding web pages, it has a number of drawbacks: First, accurately classifying web pages into taxonomy tree nodes is for the most part a manual editorial process, which is difficult to scale with the size of the Web. Arguably, we only need to have "high-quality" web pages in the taxonomy, with only the best web pages for each category. However, just discovering these and classifying them accurately and consistently into the taxonomy entails significant human effort. Furthermore, for a user to effectively discover web pages classified into the nodes of the taxonomy tree, the user's idea of what subtree(s) to seek for a particular topic should match that of the editors performing the classification. This quickly becomes challenging as the size of the taxonomy grows; the Yahoo! taxonomy tree surpassed 1,000 distinct nodes fairly early on. Given these challenges, the popularity of taxonomies declined over time, even though variants (such as About.com and the Open Directory Project) sprang up with subject matter experts collecting and annotating web pages for each category.

The first generation of web search engines transported classical search techniques such as those in the preceding chapters to the web domain, focusing on the challenge of scale. The earliest web search engines had to contend with indexes containing tens of millions of documents, which was a few orders of magnitude larger than any prior information retrieval (IR) system in the public domain. Indexing, query serving, and ranking at this scale required the harnessing together of tens of machines to create highly available systems, again at scales not witnessed hitherto in a consumer-facing search application. The first generation of web search engines was largely successful at solving these challenges while continually indexing a significant fraction of the Web, all the while serving queries with subsecond response times. However, the quality and relevance of web search results left much to be desired owing to the idiosyncrasies of content creation on the Web that we discuss in Section 19.2. This necessitated the invention of new ranking and spam-fighting techniques to ensure the quality of the search results. Although classical IR techniques (such as those covered earlier in this book) continue to be necessary for web search, they are not by any means sufficient. A key aspect (developed further in Chapter 21) is that whereas classical techniques measure the relevance of a document to a query, there remains a need to gauge the *authoritativeness* of a document based on cues such as which website hosts it.

19.2 Web characteristics

The essential feature that led to the explosive growth of the Web – decentralized content publishing with essentially no central control of authorship – turned out to be the biggest challenge for web search engines in their quest to index and retrieve this content. Web page authors created content in dozens of (natural) languages and thousands of dialects, thus demanding many different forms of stemming and other linguistic operations. Because publishing was now open to tens of millions, web pages exhibited heterogeneity at a daunting scale, in many crucial aspects. First, content creation was no longer the privy of editorially trained writers; although this represented a

Figure 19.1 A dynamically generated web page. The browser sends a request for flight information on flight AA129 to the web application, which fetches the information from back-end databases then creates a dynamic web page that it returns to the browser.

tremendous democratization of content creation, it also resulted in a tremendous variation in grammar and style (and in many cases, no recognizable grammar or style). Indeed, web publishing in a sense unleashed the best and worst of desktop publishing on a planetary scale, so that pages quickly became riddled with wild variations in colors, fonts, and structure. Some web pages, including the professionally created home pages of some large corporations, consisted entirely of images (which, when clicked, led to richer textual content) – and therefore, no indexable text.

What about the substance of the text in web pages? The democratization of content creation on the Web meant a new level of granularity in *opinion* on virtually any subject. This meant that the Web contained truth, lies, contradictions, and suppositions on a grand scale. This gives rise to the question: Which web pages does one trust? In a simplistic approach, one might argue that some publishers are trustworthy and others not – begging the question of how a search engine is to assign such a measure of trust to each website or web page. In Chapter 21, we will examine approaches to understanding this question. More subtly, there may be no universal, user-independent notion of trust; a web page whose contents are trustworthy to one user may not be so to another. In traditional (nonweb) publishing this is not an issue: users self-select sources they find trustworthy. Thus one reader may find the reporting of *The New York Times* to be reliable, whereas another may prefer *The Wall Street Journal*. But when a search engine is the only viable means for a user to become aware of (let alone select) most content, this challenge becomes significant.

Although the question "how big is the Web?" has no easy answer (see Section 19.5), the question "how many web pages are in a search engine's index" is more precise, although, even this question has issues. By the end of 1995, Altavista reported that it had crawled and indexed approximately 30 million *static web pages*. Static web pages are those whose content does not vary STATIC WEB PAGES from one request for that page to the next. For this purpose, a professor who manually updates his home page every week is considered to have a static web page, but an airport's flight status page is considered to be dynamic. *Dynamic pages* are typically mechanically generated by an application server in response to a query to a database, as shown in Figure 19.1. One sign of

Figure 19.2 Two nodes of the web graph joined by a link.

such a page is that the URL has the character "?" in it. Because the number of static web pages was believed to be doubling every few months in 1995, early web search engines such as Altavista had to constantly add hardware and bandwidth for crawling and indexing web pages.

19.2.1 The web graph

We can view the static Web consisting of static HTML pages together with the hyperlinks between them as a directed graph in which each web page is a node and each hyperlink a directed edge.

Figure 19.2 shows two nodes A and B from the web graph, each corresponding to a web page, with a hyperlink from A to B. We refer to the set of all such nodes and directed edges as the web graph. Figure 19.2 also shows that (as is the case with most links on web pages) there is some text surrounding the origin of the hyperlink on page A. This text is generally encapsulated in the href attribute of the <a> (for anchor) tag that encodes the hyperlink ANCHOR TEXT in the HTML code of page A, and is referred to as *anchor text*. As one might suspect, this directed graph is not *strongly connected*: There are pairs of pages such that one cannot proceed from one page of the pair to the other by fol-IN-LINKS lowing hyperlinks. We refer to the hyperlinks into a page as *in-links* and those OUT-LINKS out of a page as *out-links*. The number of in-links to a page (also known as its *in-degree*) has averaged from roughly eight to fifteen, in a range of studies. We similarly define the out-degree of a web page to be the number of links out of it. These notions are represented in Figure 19.3.

There is ample evidence that these links are not randomly distributed; for one thing, the distribution of the number of links into a web page does not follow the Poisson distribution one would expect if every web page were to pick the destinations of its links uniformly at random. Rather, this distribu-POWER LAW tion is widely reported to be a *power law*, in which the total number of web pages with in-degree i is proportional to $1/i^\alpha$; the value of α typically reported by studies is 2.1.[1] Furthermore, several studies have suggested that BOWTIE the directed graph connecting web pages has a *bowtie* shape: there are three major categories of web pages that are sometimes referred to as IN, OUT, and SCC. A web surfer can pass from any page in IN to any page in SCC, by following hyperlinks. Likewise, a surfer can pass from page in SCC to any

---

[1] Cf. Zipf's law of the distribution of words in text in Chapter 5 (page 83), which is a power law with $\alpha = 1$.

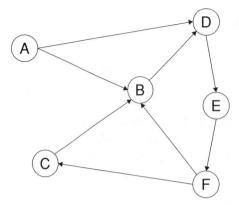

Figure 19.3 A sample small web graph. In this example we have six pages labeled A through F. Page B has in-degree 3 and out-degree 1. This example graph is not strongly connected: There is no path from any of pages B through F to page A.

page in OUT. Finally, the surfer can surf from any page in SCC to any other page in SCC. However, it is not possible to pass from a page in SCC to any page in IN, or from a page in OUT to a page in SCC (or, consequently, IN). Notably, in several studies IN and OUT are roughly equal in size, whereas SCC is somewhat larger; most web pages fall into one of these three sets. The remaining pages form into *tubes* that are small sets of pages outside SCC that lead directly from IN to OUT, and *tendrils* that either lead nowhere from IN, or from nowhere to OUT. Figure 19.4 illustrates this structure of the Web.

19.2.2 Spam

Early in the history of web search, it became clear that web search engines were an important means for connecting advertisers to prospective buyers. A user searching for maui golf real estate is not merely seeking news or entertainment on the subject of housing on golf courses on the island of Maui, but instead likely to be seeking to purchase such a property. Sellers of such

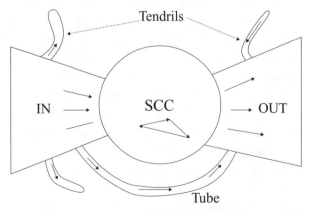

Figure 19.4 The bowtie structure of the Web. Here we show one tube and three tendrils.

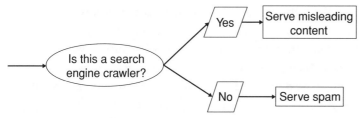

Figure 19.5 Cloaking as used by spammers.

property and their agents, therefore, have a strong incentive to create web pages that rank highly on this query. In a search engine whose scoring was based on term frequencies, a web page with numerous repetitions of maui golf SPAM real estate would rank highly. This led to the first generation of *spam*, which (in the context of web search) is the manipulation of web page content for the purpose of appearing high up in search results for selected keywords. To avoid irritating users with these repetitions, sophisticated *spammers* resorted to such tricks as rendering these repeated terms in the same color as the background. Despite these words being consequently invisible to the human user, a search engine indexer would parse the invisible words out of the HTML representation of the web page and index these words as being present in the page.

At its root, spam stems from the heterogeneity of motives in content creation on the Web. In particular, many web content creators have commercial motives and therefore stand to gain from manipulating search engine results. You might argue that this is no different from a company that uses large fonts to list its phone numbers in the yellow pages; but this generally costs the company more and is thus a fairer mechanism. A more apt analogy, perhaps, is the use of company names beginning with a long string of As to be listed early in a yellow pages category. In fact, the yellow pages' model of companies paying for larger/darker fonts has been replicated in web search: In many search engines, it is possible to pay to have one's web page included PAID in the search engine's index – a model known as *paid inclusion*. Different INCLUSION search engines have different policies on whether to allow paid inclusion, and whether such a payment has any effect on ranking in search results.

Search engines soon became sophisticated enough in their spam detection to screen out a large number of repetitions of particular keywords. Spammers responded with a richer set of spam techniques, the best known of which we now describe. The first of these techniques is *cloaking*, shown in Figure 19.5. Here, the spammer's web server returns different pages depending on whether the http request comes from a web search engine's crawler (the part of the search engine that gathers web pages, to be described in Chapter 20), or from a human user's browser. The former causes the web page to be indexed by the search engine under misleading keywords. When the user searches for these keywords and elects to view the page, he receives a web page that has altogether different content than that indexed by the search engine. Such deception of search indexers is unknown in the traditional world of IR; it stems from the fact that the relationship between page publishers and web search engines is not completely collaborative.

A *doorway page* contains text and metadata carefully chosen to rank highly on selected search keywords. When a browser requests the doorway page, it is redirected to a page containing content of a more commercial nature. More complex spamming techniques involve manipulation of the metadata related to a page including (for reasons we will see in Chapter 21) the links into a web page. Given that spamming is inherently an economically motivated activity, there has sprung around it an industry of *search engine optimizers*, or SEOs, to provide consultancy services for clients who seek to have their web pages rank highly on selected keywords. Web search engines frown on this business of attempting to decipher and adapt to their proprietary ranking techniques and indeed announce policies on forms of SEO behavior they do not tolerate (and have been known to shut down search requests from certain SEOs for violation of these). Inevitably, the parrying between such SEOs (who gradually infer features of each web search engine's ranking methods) and the web search engines (who adapt in response) is an unending struggle; indeed, the research subarea of *adversarial information retrieval* has sprung up around this battle. To combat spammers who manipulate the text of their web pages is the exploitation of the link structure of the Web – a technique known as *link analysis*. The first web search engine known to apply link analysis on a large scale (to be detailed in Chapter 21) was Google, although all web search engines currently make use of it (and correspondingly, spammers now invest considerable effort in subverting it – this is known as *link spam*).

SEARCH ENGINE OPTIMIZERS

ADVERSARIAL INFORMATION RETRIEVAL

LINK SPAM

? **Exercise 19.1** If the number of pages with in-degree i is proportional to $1/i^{2.1}$, what is the probability that a randomly chosen web page has in-degree 1?

Exercise 19.2 If the number of pages with in-degree i is proportional to $1/i^{2.1}$, what is the average in-degree of a web page?

Exercise 19.3 If the number of pages with in-degree i is proportional to $1/i^{2.1}$, then as the largest in-degree goes to infinity, does the fraction of pages with in-degree i grow, stay the same, or diminish? How would your answer change for values of the exponent other than 2.1?

Exercise 19.4 The average in-degree of all nodes in a snapshot of the web graph is 9. What can we say about the average out-degree of all nodes in this snapshot?

19.3 Advertising as the economic model

Early in the history of the Web, companies used graphical banner advertisements on web pages at popular websites (news and entertainment sites such as MSN, America Online, Yahoo!, and CNN). The primary purpose of these advertisements was *branding*: to convey to the viewer a positive feeling about the brand of the company placing the advertisement. Typically these adver-

CPM tisements are priced on a *cost per mil* (*CPM*) basis: the cost to the company of having its banner advertisement displayed 1,000 times. Some websites struck contracts with their advertisers in which an advertisement was priced not by the number of times it is displayed (also known as *impressions*), but rather by the number of times it is *clicked on* by the user. This pricing model is known

CPC as the *cost per click* (*CPC*) model. In such cases, clicking on the advertisement leads the user to a web page set up by the advertiser, where the user is induced to make a purchase. Here, the goal of the advertisement is not so much brand promotion as to induce a transaction. This distinction between brand- and transaction-oriented advertising was already widely recognized in the context of conventional media such as broadcast and print. The interactivity of the web allowed the CPC billing model – clicks could be metered and monitored by the website and billed to the advertiser.

The pioneer in this direction was a company named Goto, which changed its name to Overture before eventual acquisition by Yahoo! Goto was not, in the traditional sense, a search engine; rather, for every query term q it accepted *bids* from companies who wanted their web page shown on the query q. In response to the query q, Goto would return the pages of all advertisers who bid for q, ordered by their bids. Furthermore, when the user clicked on one of the returned results, the corresponding advertiser would make a payment to Goto (in the initial implementation, this payment equaled the advertiser's bid for q).

Several aspects of Goto's model are worth highlighting. First, a user typing the query q into Goto's search interface was actively expressing an interest and intent related to the query q. For instance, a user typing golf clubs is more likely to be imminently purchasing a set than one who is simply browsing news on golf. Second, Goto only got compensated when a user actually expressed interest in an advertisement – as evinced by the user clicking the advertisement. Taken together, these created a powerful mechanism by which to connect advertisers to consumers, quickly raising the annual revenues of Goto/Overture into hundreds of millions of dollars. This style

SPONSORED of search engine came to be known variously as *sponsored search* or *search*
SEARCH *advertising*.
SEARCH Given these two kinds of search engines – the "pure" search engines such
ADVERTISING as Google and Altavista versus the sponsored search engines – the logical next step was to combine them into a single user experience. Current search engines follow precisely this model: They provide pure search results (generally known as *algorithmic search* results) as the primary response

ALGORITHMIC to a user's search, together with sponsored search results displayed sepa-
SEARCH rately and distinctively to the right of the algorithmic results. This is shown in Figure 19.6. Retrieving sponsored search results and ranking them in response to a query has now become considerably more sophisticated than

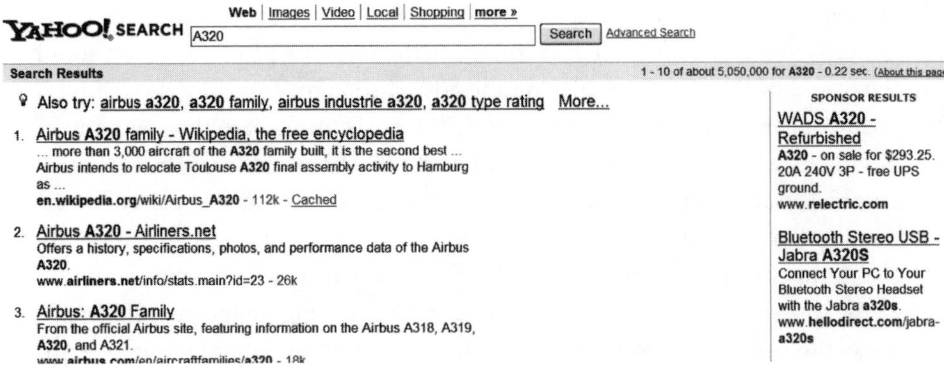

Figure 19.6 Search advertising triggered by query keywords. Here the query A320 returns algorithmic search results about the Airbus aircraft, together with advertisements for various non-aircraft goods numbered A320 that advertisers seek to market to those querying on this query. The lack of advertisements for the aircraft reflects the fact that few marketers attempt to sell A320 aircraft on the web.

the simple Goto scheme; the process entails a blending of ideas from IR and microeconomics, and is beyond the scope of this book. For advertisers, understanding how search engines do this ranking and how to allocate marketing campaign budgets to different keywords and to different sponsored

SEARCH search engines has become a profession known as *search engine marketing*
ENGINE (SEM).
MARKETING

The inherently economic motives underlying sponsored search give rise to attempts by some participants to subvert the system to their advantage.

CLICK SPAM This can take many forms, one of which is known as *click spam*. There is currently no universally accepted definition of click spam. It refers (as the name suggests) to clicks on sponsored search results that are not from bona fide search users. For instance, a devious advertiser may attempt to exhaust the advertising budget of a competitor by clicking repeatedly (through the use of a robotic click generator) on that competitor's sponsored search advertisements. Search engines face the challenge of discerning which of the clicks they observe are part of a pattern of click spam, to avoid charging their advertiser clients for such clicks.

? **Exercise 19.5** The Goto method ranked advertisements matching a query by *bid*: the highest-bidding advertiser got the top position, the second-highest the next, and so on. What can go wrong with this when the highest-bidding advertiser places an advertisement that is irrelevant to the query? Why might an advertiser with an irrelevant advertisement bid high in this manner?

Exercise 19.6 Suppose that, in addition to bids, we had for each advertiser their *click-through rate*, the ratio of the historical number of times users click on their advertisement to the number of times the advertisement was shown. Suggest a modification of the Goto scheme that exploits this data to avoid the problem in Exercise 19.5 above.

19.4 The search user experience

It is crucial that we understand the users of web search as well. This is again a significant change from traditional IR, where users were typically professionals with at least some training in the art of phrasing queries over a well-authored collection whose style and structure they understood well. In contrast, web search users tend to not know (or care) about the heterogeneity of web content, the syntax of query languages, and the art of phrasing queries; indeed, a mainstream tool (as web search has come to become) should not place such onerous demands on billions of people. A range of studies has concluded that the average number of keywords in a web search is somewhere between two and three. Syntax operators (Boolean connectives, wildcards, etc.) are seldom used, again a result of the composition of the audience – "normal" people, not information scientists.

It is clear that the more user traffic a web search engine can attract, the more revenue it stands to earn from sponsored search. How do search engines differentiate themselves and grow their traffic? Here, Google identified two principles that helped it to grow at the expense of its competitors: (i) A focus on relevance, specifically precision rather than recall in the first few results; and (ii) a user experience that is lightweight, meaning that both the search query page and the search results page are uncluttered and almost entirely textual, with very few graphical elements. The effect of the first was simply to save users time in locating the information they sought. The effect of the second is to provide a user experience that is extremely responsive, or at any rate not bottlenecked by the time to load the search query or results page.

19.4.1 User query needs

There appear to be three broad categories into which common web search queries can be grouped: (i) informational, (ii) navigational, and (iii) transactional. We now explain these categories; it should be clear that some queries will fall in more than one of these categories, while others will fall outside them.

INFORMATIONAL QUERIES *Informational queries* seek general information on a broad topic, such as leukemia or Provence. There is typically not a single web page that contains all the information sought; indeed, users with informational queries typically try to assimilate information from multiple web pages.

NAVIGATIONAL QUERIES *Navigational queries* seek the website or home page of a single entity that the user has in mind, say Lufthansa airlines. In such cases, the user's expectation is that the very first search result should be the home page of Lufthansa. The user is not interested in a plethora of documents containing the term Lufthansa; for such a user, the best measure of user satisfaction is precision at 1.

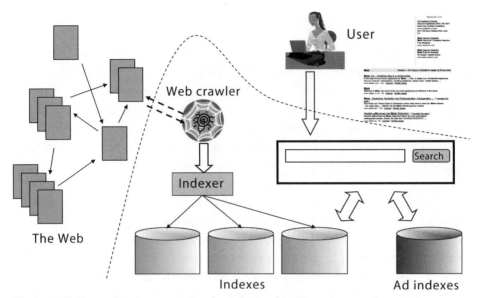

Figure 19.7 The various components of a web search engine.

TRANSACTIONAL   A *transactional query* is one that is a prelude to the user performing a trans-
QUERY   action on the Web – such as purchasing a product, downloading a file, or
making a reservation. In such cases, the search engine should return results
listing services that provide form interfaces for such transactions.

Discerning which of these categories a query falls into can be challenging. The category not only governs the algorithmic search results, but the
suitability of the query for sponsored search results (since the query may reveal an intent to purchase). For navigational queries, some have argued that
the search engine should return only a single result or even the target web
page directly. Nevertheless, web search engines have historically engaged in
a battle of bragging rights over which one indexes more web pages. Does the
user really care? Perhaps not, but the media does highlight estimates (often
statistically indefensible) of the sizes of various search engines. Users are influenced by these reports and thus, search engines do have to pay attention
to how their index sizes compare to competitors'. For informational (and to
a lesser extent, transactional) queries, the user does care about the comprehensiveness of the search engine.

Figure 19.7 shows a composite picture of a web search engine including the
crawler, as well as both the web page and advertisement indexes. The portion
of the figure under the curved dashed line is internal to the search engine.

19.5 Index size and estimation

To a first approximation, comprehensiveness grows with index size, although it does matter which specific pages a search engine indexes – some

pages are more informative than others. It is also difficult to reason about the fraction of the Web indexed by a search engine, because there is an infinite number of dynamic web pages; for instance, `http://www.yahoo.com/any_string` returns a valid HTML page rather than an error, politely informing the user that there is no such page at Yahoo! Such a "soft 404 error" is only one example of many ways in which web servers can generate an infinite number of valid web pages. Indeed, some of these are malicious spider traps devised to cause a search engine's crawler (the component that systematically gathers web pages for the search engine's index, described in Chapter 20) to stay within a spammer's website and index many pages from that site.

We could ask the following better defined question: Given two search engines, what are the relative sizes of their indexes? Even this question turns out to be imprecise, for the following reasons.

1. In response to queries, a search engine can return web pages whose contents it has not (fully or even partially) indexed. For one thing, search engines generally index only the first few thousand words in a web page. In some cases, a search engine is aware of a page p that is *linked to* by pages it has indexed, but has not indexed p itself. As we will see in Chapter 21, it is still possible to meaningfully return p in search results.
2. Search engines generally organize their indexes in various tiers and partitions, not all of which are examined on every search (recall tiered indexes from Section 7.2.1). For instance, a web page deep inside a website may be indexed but not retrieved on general web searches; it is, however, retrieved as a result on a search that a user has explicitly restricted to that website (such site-specific search is offered by most web search engines).

Thus, search engine indexes include multiple classes of indexed pages, so that there is no single measure of index size. These issues notwithstanding, a number of techniques have been devised for crude estimates of the ratio of the index sizes of two search engines, E_1 and E_2. The basic hypothesis underlying these techniques is that each search engine indexes a fraction of the Web chosen independently and uniformly at random. This involves some questionable assumptions: first, that there is a finite size for the Web from which each search engine chooses a subset, and second, that each engine chooses an independent, uniformly chosen subset. As will be clear from the discussion of crawling in Chapter 20, this is far from true. However, if we begin with these assumptions, then we can invoke a classical estimation technique known as the *capture–recapture method*.

CAPTURE–
RECAPTURE
METHOD

Suppose that we could pick a random page from the index of E_1 and test whether it is in E_2's index and symmetrically, test whether a random page from E_2 is in E_1. These experiments give us fractions x and y such that our estimate is that a fraction x of the pages in E_1 are in E_2, while a fraction y

of the pages in E_2 are in E_1. Then, letting $|E_i|$ denote the size of the index of search engine E_i, we have

$$x|E_1| \approx y|E_2|,$$

from which we have the form we will use

(19.1)
$$\frac{|E_1|}{|E_2|} \approx \frac{y}{x}.$$

If our assumption about E_1 and E_2 being independent and uniform random subsets of the Web were true, and our sampling process unbiased, then Equation (19.1) should give us an unbiased estimator for $|E_1|/|E_2|$. We distinguish between two scenarios here. Either the measurement is performed by someone with access to the index of one of the search engines (say an employee of E_1), or the measurement is performed by an independent party with no access to the innards of either search engine. In the former case, we can simply pick a random document from one index. The latter case is more challenging; we pick a random page from one search engine *from outside the search engine*, then verify whether the random page is present in the other search engine.

To implement the sampling phase, we might generate a random page from the entire (idealized, finite) Web and test it for presence in each search engine. Unfortunately, picking a web page uniformly at random is a difficult problem. We briefly outline several attempts to achieve such a sample, pointing out the biases inherent to each; after this we describe in some detail one technique that much research has built on.

1. *Random searches:* Begin with a search log of web searches; send a random search from this log to E_1 and a random page from the results. Because such logs are not widely available outside a search engine, one implementation is to trap all search queries going out of a work group (say scientists in a research center) that agrees to have all its searches logged. This approach has a number of issues, including the bias from the types of searches made by the work group. Further, a random document from the results of such a random search to E_1 is not the same as a random document from E_1.

2. *Random IP addresses:* A second approach is to generate random IP addresses and send a request to a web server residing at the random address, collecting all pages at that server. The biases here include the fact that many hosts might share one IP (due to a practice known as virtual hosting) or not accept http requests from the host where the experiment is conducted. Furthermore, this technique is more likely to hit one of the many sites with few pages, skewing the document probabilities; we may be able to correct for this effect if we understand the distribution of the number of pages on websites.

3. *Random walks:* If the web graph were a strongly connected directed graph, we could run a random walk starting at an arbitrary web page. This

walk would converge to a steady state distribution (see Chapter 21, Section 21.2.1 for more background material on this), from which we could in principle pick a web page with a fixed probability. This method, too, has a number of biases. First, the Web is not strongly connected so that, even with various corrective rules, it is difficult to argue that we can reach a steady-state distribution starting from any page. Second, the time it takes for the random walk to settle into this steady state is unknown and could exceed the length of the experiment.

Clearly, each of these approaches is far from perfect. We now describe a fourth sampling approach, *random queries*. This approach is noteworthy for two reasons: It has been successfully built upon for a series of increasingly refined estimates, and conversely it has turned out to be the approach most likely to be misinterpreted and carelessly implemented, leading to misleading measurements. The idea is to pick a page (almost) uniformly at random from a search engine's index by posing a random query to it. It should be clear that picking a set of random terms from (say) *Webster's Dictionary* is not a good way of implementing this idea. For one thing, not all vocabulary terms occur equally often, so this approach will not result in documents being chosen uniformly at random from the search engine. For another, there are a great many terms in web documents that do not occur in a standard dictionary such as *Webster's*. To address the problem of vocabulary terms not in a standard dictionary, we begin by amassing a sample web dictionary. This could be done by crawling a limited portion of the Web, or by crawling a manually assembled representative subset of the Web such as Yahoo! (as was done in the earliest experiments with this method). Consider a conjunctive query with two or more randomly chosen words from this dictionary.

Operationally, we proceed as follows: We use a random conjunctive query on E_1 and pick from the top 100 returned results a page p at random. We then test p for presence in E_2 by choosing six to eight low-frequency terms in p and using them in a conjunctive query for E_2. We can improve the estimate by repeating the experiment a large number of times. Both the sampling process and the testing process have a number of issues.

1. Our sample is biased toward longer documents.
2. Picking from the top 100 results of E_1 induces a bias from the ranking algorithm of E_1. Picking from all the results of E_1 makes the experiment slower. This is particularly so because most web search engines put up defenses against excessive robotic querying.
3. During the checking phase, a number of additional biases are introduced; for instance, E_2 may not handle eight-word conjunctive queries properly.
4. Either E_1 or E_2 may refuse to respond to the test queries, treating them as robotic spam rather than as bona fide queries.
5. There could be operational problems like connection time outs.

A sequence of research has built on this basic paradigm to eliminate some of these issues; there is no perfect solution yet, but the level of sophistication in statistics for understanding the biases is increasing. The main idea is to address biases by estimating, for each document, the magnitude of the bias. From this, standard statistical sampling methods can generate unbiased samples. In the checking phase, the newer work moves away from conjunctive queries to phrase and other queries that appear to be better-behaved. Finally, newer experiments use other sampling methods besides random queries. The best known of these is *document random walk sampling*, in which a document is chosen by a random walk on a virtual graph derived from documents. In this graph, nodes are documents; two documents are connected by an edge if they share two or more words in common. The graph is never instantiated; rather, a random walk on it can be performed by moving from a document d to another by picking a pair of keywords in d, running a query on a search engine and picking a random document from the results. Details may be found in the references in Section 19.7.

Exercise 19.7 Two web search engines A and B each generate a large number of pages uniformly at random from their indexes. Thirty percent of A's pages are present in B's index, and 50% of B's pages are present in A's index. What is the number of pages in A's index relative to B's?

19.6 Near-duplicates and shingling

One aspect we have ignored in the discussion of index size in Section 19.5 is *duplication*: The Web contains multiple copies of the same content. By some estimates, as many as 40% of the pages on the Web are duplicates of other pages. Many of these are legitimate copies; for instance, certain information repositories are mirrored simply to provide redundancy and access reliability. Search engines try to avoid indexing multiple copies of the same content, to keep down storage and processing overheads.

The simplest approach to detecting duplicates is to compute, for each web page, a *fingerprint* that is a succinct (say 64-bit) digest of the characters on that page. Then, whenever the fingerprints of two web pages are equal, we test whether the pages themselves are equal and if so declare one of them to be a duplicate copy of the other. This simplistic approach fails to capture a crucial and widespread phenomenon on the Web: *near duplication*. In many cases, the contents of one web page are identical to those of another except for a few characters – say, a notation showing the date and time at which the page was last modified. Even in such cases, we want to be able to declare the two pages to be close enough that we only index one copy. Short of exhaustively comparing all pairs of web pages, an infeasible task at the scale of billions of pages, how can we detect and filter out such near duplicates?

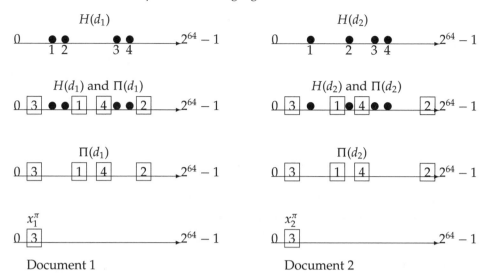

Figure 19.8 Illustration of shingle sketches. We see two documents going through four stages of shingle sketch computation. In the first step (*top row*), we apply a 64-bit hash to each shingle from each document to obtain $H(d_1)$ and $H(d_2)$ (*circles*). Next, we apply a random permutation Π to permute $H(d_1)$ and $H(d_2)$, obtaining $\Pi(d_1)$ and $\Pi(d_2)$ (*squares*). The third row shows only $\Pi(d_1)$ and $\Pi(d_2)$; the bottom row shows the minimum values x_1^{π} and x_2^{π} for each document.

SHINGLING

We now describe a solution to the problem of detecting near-duplicate web pages. The answer lies in a technique known as *shingling* (Figure 19.8). Given a positive integer k and a sequence of terms in a document d, define the k-shingles of d to be the set of all consecutive sequences of k terms in d. As an example, consider the following text: a rose is a rose is a rose. The 4-shingles for this text ($k = 4$ is a typical value used in the detection of near-duplicate web pages) are a rose is a, rose is a rose, and is a rose is. The first two of these shingles each occur twice in the text. Intuitively, two documents are near duplicates if the sets of shingles generated from them are nearly the same. We now make this intuition precise, then develop a method for efficiently computing and comparing the sets of shingles for all web pages.

Let $S(d_j)$ denote the set of shingles of document d_j. Recall the Jaccard coefficient from page 56, which measures the degree of overlap between the sets $S(d_1)$ and $S(d_2)$ as $|S(d_1) \cap S(d_2)|/|S(d_1) \cup S(d_2)|$; denote this by $J(S(d_1), S(d_2))$. Our test for near duplication between d_1 and d_2 is to compute this Jaccard coefficient; if it exceeds a preset threshold (say, 0.9), we declare them near duplicates and eliminate one from indexing. However, this does not appear to have simplified matters: We still have to compute Jaccard coefficients pairwise.

To avoid this, we use a form of hashing. First, we map every shingle into a hash value over a large space, say 64 bits. For $j = 1, 2$, let $H(d_j)$ be the corresponding set of 64-bit hash values derived from $S(d_j)$. We now invoke the following trick to detect document pairs whose sets $H()$ have large Jaccard overlaps. Let π be a random permutation from the 64-bit integers to the

S_{j_1}	S_{j_2}
0	1
1	0
1	1
0	0
1	1
0	1

Figure 19.9 Two sets S_{j_1} and S_{j_2}; their Jaccard coefficient is 2/5.

64-bit integers. Denote by $\Pi(d_j)$ the set of permuted hash values in $H(d_j)$; thus for each $h \in H(d_j)$, there is a corresponding value $\pi(h) \in \Pi(d_j)$.

Let x_j^{π} be the smallest integer in $\Pi(d_j)$. Then

Theorem 19.1.

$$J(S(d_1), S(d_2)) = P(x_1^{\pi} = x_2^{\pi}).$$

Proof: We give the proof in a slightly more general setting: Consider a family of sets whose elements are drawn from a common universe. View the sets as columns of a matrix A, with one row for each element in the universe. The element $a_{ij} = 1$ if element i is present in the set S_j that the jth column represents.

Let Π be a random permutation of the rows of A; denote by $\Pi(S_j)$ the column that results from applying Π to the jth column. Finally, let x_j^{π} be the index of the first row in which the column $\Pi(S_j)$ has a 1. We then prove that for any two columns j_1, j_2,

$$P(x_{j_1}^{\pi} = x_{j_2}^{\pi}) = J(S_{j_1}, S_{j_2}).$$

If we can prove this, the theorem follows.

Consider two columns j_1, j_2 as shown in Figure 19.9. The ordered pairs of entries of S_{j_1} and S_{j_2} partition the rows into four types: Those with 0s in both of these columns, those with a 0 in S_{j_1} and a 1 in S_{j_2}, those with a 1 in S_{j_1} and a 0 in S_{j_2}, and finally those with 1s in both of these columns. Indeed, the first four rows of Figure 19.9 exemplify all of these four types of rows. Denote by C_{00} the number of rows with 0s in both columns, C_{01} the second, C_{10} the third and C_{11} the fourth. Then,

(19.2)
$$J(S_{j_1}, S_{j_2}) = \frac{C_{11}}{C_{01} + C_{10} + C_{11}}.$$

To complete the proof by showing that the right-hand side of Equation (19.2) equals $P(x_{j_1}^{\pi} = x_{j_2}^{\pi})$, consider scanning columns j_1, j_2 in increasing row index until the first nonzero entry is found in either column. Because Π is a random permutation, the probability that this smallest row has a 1 in both columns is exactly the right-hand side of Equation (19.2). $\square$

Thus, our test for the Jaccard coefficient of the shingle sets is probabilistic; we compare the computed values x_i^π from different documents. If a pair coincides, we have candidate near duplicates. Repeat the process independently for 200 random permutations π (a choice suggested in the literature). Call the set of the 200 resulting values of x_i^π the *sketch* $\psi(d_i)$ of d_i. We can then estimate the Jaccard coefficient for any pair of documents d_i, d_j to be $|\psi_i \cap \psi_j|/200$; if this exceeds a preset threshold, we declare that d_i and d_j are similar.

How can we quickly compute $|\psi_i \cap \psi_j|/200$ for all pairs i, j? Indeed, how do we represent all pairs of documents that are similar, without incurring a blowup that is quadratic in the number of documents? First, we use fingerprints to remove all but one copy of *identical* documents. We may also remove common HTML tags and integers from the shingle computation, to eliminate shingles that occur very commonly in documents without telling us anything about duplication. Next we use a *union-find* algorithm to create clusters that contain documents that are similar. To do this, we must accomplish a crucial step: going from the set of sketches to the set of pairs i, j such that d_i and d_j are similar.

To this end, we compute the number of shingles in common for any pair of documents whose sketches have any members in common. We begin with the list $< x_i^\pi, d_i >$ sorted by x_i^π pairs. For each x_i^π, we can now generate all pairs i, j for which x_i^π is present in both their sketches. From these we can compute, for each pair i, j with nonzero sketch overlap, a count of the number of x_i^π values they have in common. By applying a preset threshold, we know which pairs i, j have heavily overlapping sketches. For instance, if the threshold were 80%, we would need the count to be at least 160 for any i, j. As we identify such pairs, we run the union-find to group documents into near-duplicate "syntactic clusters." This is essentially a variant of the single-link clustering algorithm introduced in Section 17.2 (page 350).

One final trick cuts down the space needed in the computation of $|\psi_i \cap \psi_j|/200$ for pairs i, j, which in principle could still demand space quadratic in the number of documents. To remove from consideration those pairs i, j whose sketches have few shingles in common, we preprocess the sketch for each document as follows: Sort the x_i^π in the sketch, then shingle this sorted sequence to generate a set of *super-shingles* for each document. If two documents have a super-shingle in common, we proceed to compute the precise value of $|\psi_i \cap \psi_j|/200$. This again is a heuristic, but can be highly effective in cutting down the number of i, j pairs for which we accumulate the sketch overlap counts.

? Exercise 19.8 Web search engines A and B each crawl a random subset of the same size of the Web. Some of the pages crawled are duplicates – exact textual copies of each other at different URLs. Assume that duplicates are distributed uniformly amongst the pages crawled by A and B. Further, assume that a duplicate is a page that has exactly two copies – no pages have more than two copies. A indexes pages without duplicate elimination, whereas B indexes only one copy of each duplicate page. The two random subsets have the same size before duplicate elimination. If 45% of A's indexed URLs are present in B's index, and 50% of B's indexed URLs are present in A's index, what fraction of the Web consists of pages that do not have a duplicate?

Exercise 19.9 Instead of using the process depicted in Figure 19.8, consider instead the following process for estimating the Jaccard coefficient of the overlap between two sets S_1 and S_2. We pick a random subset of the elements of the universe from which S_1 and S_2 are drawn; this corresponds to picking a random subset of the rows of the matrix A in the proof. We exhaustively compute the Jaccard coefficient of these random subsets. Why is this estimate an unbiased estimator of the Jaccard coefficient for S_1 and S_2?

Exercise 19.10 Explain why this estimator would be very difficult to use in practice.

19.7 References and further reading

Bush (1945) foreshadowed the Web when he described an information management system that he called *memex*. Berners-Lee et al. (1992) describes one of the earliest incarnations of the Web. Kumar et al. (2000) and Broder et al. (2000) provide comprehensive studies of the Web as a graph. The use of anchor text was first described in McBryan (1994). The taxonomy of web queries in Section 19.4 is due to Broder (2002). The observation of the power law with exponent 2.1 in Section 19.2.1 appeared in Kumar et al. (1999). Chakrabarti (2002) is a good reference for many aspects of web search and analysis.

The estimation of web search index sizes has a long history of development covered by Bharat and Broder (1998), Lawrence and Giles (1998), Rusmevichientong et al. (2001), Lawrence and Giles (1999), Henzinger et al. (2000), Bar-Yossef and Gurevich (2006). The state of the art is Bar-Yossef and Gurevich (2006), including several of the bias-removal techniques mentioned at the end of Section 19.5. Shingling was introduced by Broder et al. (1997) and used for detecting websites (rather than simply pages) that are identical by Bharat et al. (2000).

20 *Web crawling and indexes*

20.1 Overview

Web crawling is the process by which we gather pages from the Web to index them and support a search engine. The objective of crawling is to quickly and efficiently gather as many useful web pages as possible, together with the link structure that interconnects them. In Chapter 19, we studied the complexities of the Web stemming from its creation by millions of uncoordinated individuals. In this chapter, we study the resulting difficulties for crawling the Web. The focus of this chapter is the component shown in Figure 19.7 as *web crawler*; it is sometimes referred to as a *spider*.

WEB CRAWLER

SPIDER   The goal of this chapter is not to describe how to build the crawler for a full-scale commercial web search engine. We focus instead on a range of issues that are generic to crawling from the student project scale to substantial research projects. We begin (Section 20.1.1) by listing desiderata for web crawlers, and then discuss in Section 20.2 how each of these issues is addressed. The remainder of this chapter describes the architecture and some implementation details for a distributed web crawler that satisfies these features. Section 20.3 discusses distributing indexes across many machines for a web-scale implementation.

20.1.1 *Features a crawler* **must** *provide*

We list the desiderata for web crawlers in two categories: features that web crawlers *must* provide, followed by features they *should* provide.

> **Robustness:** The Web contains servers that create *spider traps*, which are generators of web pages that mislead crawlers into getting stuck fetching an infinite number of pages in a particular domain. Crawlers must be designed to be resilient to such traps. Not all such traps are malicious; some are the inadvertent side effect of faulty website development.

Politeness: Web servers have both implicit and explicit policies regulating the rate at which a crawler can visit them. These politeness policies must be respected.

20.1.2 *Features a* **crawler** *should* **provide**

Distributed: The crawler should have the ability to execute in a distributed fashion across multiple machines.

Scalable: The crawler architecture should permit scaling up the crawl rate by adding extra machines and bandwidth.

Performance and efficiency: The crawl system should make efficient use of various system resources including processor, storage, and network bandwidth.

Quality: Given that a significant fraction of all web pages are of poor utility for serving user query needs, the crawler should be biased toward fetching "useful" pages first.

Freshness: In many applications, the crawler should operate in continuous mode: It should obtain fresh copies of previously fetched pages. A search engine crawler, for instance, can thus ensure that the search engine's index contains a fairly current representation of each indexed web page. For such continuous crawling, a crawler should be able to crawl a page with a frequency that approximates the rate of change of that page.

Extensible: Crawlers should be designed to be extensible in many ways – to cope with new data formats, new fetch protocols, and so on. This demands that the crawler architecture be modular.

20.2 Crawling

The basic operation of any hypertext crawler (whether for the Web, an intranet, or other hypertext document collection) is as follows. The crawler begins with one or more URLs that constitute a *seed set*. It picks a URL from this seed set, then fetches the web page at that URL. The fetched page is then parsed, to extract both the text and the links from the page (each of which points to another URL). The extracted text is fed to a text indexer (described in Chapters 4 and 5). The extracted links (URLs) are then added to a *URL frontier*, which at all times consists of URLs whose corresponding pages have yet to be fetched by the crawler. Initially, the URL frontier contains the seed set; as pages are fetched, the corresponding URLs are deleted from the URL frontier. The entire process may be viewed as traversing the web graph (see Chapter 19). In continuous crawling, the URL of a fetched page is added back to the frontier for fetching again in the future.

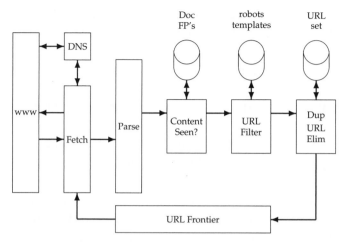

Figure 20.1 Basic crawler architecture.

This, seemingly simple, recursive traversal of the web graph is complicated by the many demands on a practical web crawling system: The crawler
has to be distributed, scalable, efficient, polite, robust, and extensible while
fetching pages of high quality. We examine the effects of each of these issues.
MERCATOR Our treatment follows the design of the *Mercator* crawler that has formed the
basis of a number of research and commercial crawlers. As a reference point,
fetching a billion pages (a small fraction of the static Web at present) in a
month-long crawl requires fetching several hundred pages each second. We
will see how to use a multithreaded design to address several bottlenecks in
the overall crawler system to attain this fetch rate.

Before proceeding to this detailed description, we reiterate for readers who
may attempt to build crawlers of some basic properties any nonprofessional
crawler should satisfy:

1. Only one connection should be open to any given host at a time.
2. A waiting time of a few seconds should occur between successive requests
   to a host.
3. Politeness restrictions detailed in Section 20.2.1 should be obeyed.

20.2.1 Crawler architecture

The simple scheme outlined above for crawling demands several modules
that fit together as shown in Figure 20.1.

1. The URL frontier, containing URLs yet to be fetched in the current crawl
   (in the case of continuous crawling, a URL may have been fetched previously but is back in the frontier for re-fetching). We describe this further
   in Section 20.2.3.

2. A *DNS resolution* module that determines the web server from which to fetch the page specified by a URL. We describe this further in Section 20.2.2.

3. A fetch module that uses the http protocol to retrieve the web page at a URL.

4. A parsing module that extracts the text and set of links from a fetched web page.

5. A duplicate elimination module that determines whether an extracted link is already in the URL frontier or has recently been fetched.

Crawling is performed by anywhere from one to potentially hundreds of threads, each of which loops through the logical cycle in Figure 20.1. These threads may be run in a single process, or be partitioned among multiple processes running at different nodes of a distributed system. We begin by assuming that the URL frontier is in place and nonempty, and defer our description of the implementation of the URL frontier to Section 20.2.3. We follow the progress of a single URL through the cycle of being fetched, passing through various checks and filters, then finally (for continuous crawling) being returned to the URL frontier.

A crawler thread begins by taking a URL from the frontier and fetching the web page at that URL, generally using the http protocol. The fetched page is then written into a temporary store, where a number of operations are performed on it. Next, the page is parsed and the text as well as the links in it are extracted. The text (with any tag information – e.g., terms in boldface) is passed on to the indexer. Link information, including anchor text, is also passed on to the indexer for use in ranking in ways that are described in Chapter 21. In addition, each extracted link goes through a series of tests to determine whether the link should be added to the URL frontier.

First, the thread tests whether a web page with the same content has already been seen at another URL. The simplest implementation for this would use a simple fingerprint such as a checksum (placed in a store labeled "Doc FP's" in Figure 20.1). A more sophisticated test would use shingles instead of fingerprints, as described in Chapter 19.

Next, a *URL filter* is used to determine whether the extracted URL should be excluded from the frontier based on one of several tests. For instance, the crawl may seek to exclude certain domains (say, all .com URLs) – in this case the test would simply filter out the URL if it were from the .com domain. A similar test could be inclusive rather than exclusive. Many hosts on the Web place certain portions of their websites off-limits to crawling, under a ROBOTS standard known as the *robots exclusion protocol*. This is done by placing a file EXCLUSION with the name robots.txt at the root of the URL hierarchy at the site. Here is PROTOCOL an example robots.txt file that specifies that no robot should visit any URL whose position in the file hierarchy starts with /yoursite/temp/, except for the robot called "searchengine."

```
User-agent: *
Disallow: /yoursite/temp/

User-agent: searchengine
Disallow:
```

The robots.txt file must be fetched from a website to test whether the URL under consideration passes the robot restrictions, and can therefore be added to the URL frontier. Rather than fetch it afresh for testing on each URL to be added to the frontier, a cache can be used to obtain a recently fetched copy of the file for the host. This is especially important because many of the links extracted from a page fall within the host from which the page was fetched and therefore can be tested against the host's robots.txt file. Thus, by performing the filtering during the link extraction process, we would have especially high locality in the stream of hosts that we need to test for robots.txt files, leading to high cache hit rates. Unfortunately, this runs afoul of webmasters' politeness expectations. A URL (particularly one referring to a low-quality or rarely changing document) may be in the frontier for days or even weeks. If we were to perform the robots filtering *before* adding such a URL to the frontier, its robots.txt file could have changed by the time the URL is dequeued from the frontier and fetched. We must consequently perform robots-filtering immediately before attempting to fetch a web page. As it turns out, maintaining a cache of robots.txt files is still highly effective; there is sufficient locality even in the stream of URLs dequeued from the URL frontier.

URL   Next, a URL should be *normalized* in the following sense: Often the HTML
NORMALIZATION encoding of a link from a web page p indicates the target of that link relative to the page p. Thus, there is a relative link encoded thus in the HTML of the page en.wikipedia.org/wiki/Main_Page:

<a href="/wiki/Wikipedia:General_disclaimer" title="Wikipedia:General disclaimer">Disclaimers</a>

points to the URL http://en.wikipedia.org/wiki/Wikipedia:General_disclaimer.

Finally, the URL is checked for duplicate elimination: If the URL is already in the frontier or (in the case of a noncontinuous crawl) already crawled, we do not add it to the frontier. When the URL is added to the frontier, it is assigned a priority based on which it is eventually removed from the frontier for fetching. The details of this priority queuing are in Section 20.2.3.

Certain housekeeping tasks are typically performed by a dedicated thread. This thread is generally quiescent except that it wakes up once every few seconds to log crawl progress statistics (URLs crawled, frontier size, etc.), decide whether to terminate the crawl, or (once every few hours of crawling) checkpoint the crawl. In *checkpointing*, a snapshot of the crawler's state (say,

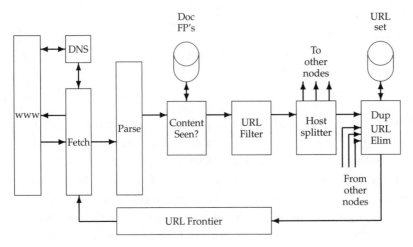

Figure 20.2 Distributing the basic crawl architecture.

the URL frontier) is committed to disk. In the event of a catastrophic crawler failure, the crawl is restarted from the most recent checkpoint.

Distributing the crawler

We have mentioned that the threads in a crawler could run under different processes, each at a different node of a distributed crawling system. Such distribution is essential for scaling; it can also be of use in a geographically distributed crawler system where each node crawls hosts "near" it. Partitioning the hosts being crawled among the crawler nodes can be done by a hash function, or by some more specifically tailored policy. For instance, we may locate a crawler node in Europe to focus on European domains, although this is not dependable for several reasons – the routes that packets take through the Internet do not always reflect geographic proximity, and in any case the domain of a host does not always reflect its physical location.

How do the various nodes of a distributed crawler communicate and share URLs? The idea is to replicate the flow of Figure 20.1 at each node, with one essential difference: Following the URL filter, we use a *host splitter* to dispatch each surviving URL to the crawler node responsible for the URL; thus the set of hosts being crawled is partitioned among the nodes. This modified flow is shown in Figure 20.2. The output of the host splitter goes into the duplicate URL eliminator block of each other node in the distributed system.

The "Content Seen?" module in the distributed architecture of Figure 20.2 is, however, complicated by several factors:

1. Unlike the URL frontier and the duplicate elimination module, document fingerprints/shingles cannot be partitioned based on host name. There is nothing preventing the same (or highly similar) content from appearing on different web servers. Consequently, the set of fingerprints/shingles

must be partitioned across the nodes based on some property of the finger-print/shingle (say by taking the fingerprint modulo the number of nodes). The result of this locality mismatch is that most "Content Seen?" tests result in a remote procedure call (although it is possible to batch lookup requests).

2. There is very little locality in the stream of document fingerprints/ shingles. Thus, caching popular fingerprints does not help (because there are no popular fingerprints).

3. Documents change over time and so, in the context of continuous crawling, we must be able to delete their outdated fingerprints/shingles from the content-seen set(s). To do so, it is necessary to save the fingerprint/ shingle of the document in the URL frontier, along with the URL itself.

20.2.2 DNS resolution

Each web server (and indeed any host connected to the internet) has a
IP ADDRESS unique *IP address*: a sequence of four bytes generally represented as four integers separated by dots; for instance 207.142.131.248 is the numerical IP address associated with the host www.wikipedia.org. Given a URL such as www.wikipedia.org in textual form, translating it to an IP address (in this
DNS case, 207.142.131.248) is a process known as *DNS resolution* or DNS lookup;
RESOLUTION here DNS stands for *domain name service*. During DNS resolution, the program that wishes to perform this translation (in our case, a component of the
DNS SERVER web crawler) contacts a *DNS server* that returns the translated IP address. (In practice, the entire translation may not occur at a single DNS server; rather, the DNS server contacted initially may recursively call upon other DNS servers to complete the translation.) For a more complex URL such as en.wikipedia.org/wiki/Domain_Name_System, the crawler component responsible for DNS resolution extracts the host name – in this case en.wikipedia.org – and looks up the IP address for the host en.wikipedia.org.

DNS resolution is a well-known bottleneck in web crawling. Due to the distributed nature of the domain name service, DNS resolution may entail multiple requests and roundtrips across the Internet, requiring seconds and sometimes even longer. Right away, this puts in jeopardy our goal of fetching several hundred documents a second. A standard remedy is to introduce caching: URLs for which we have recently performed DNS lookups are likely to be found in the DNS cache, avoiding the need to go to the DNS servers on the Internet. However, obeying politeness constraints (see Section 20.2.3) limits the cache hit rate.

There is another important difficulty in DNS resolution; the lookup implementations in standard libraries (likely to be used by anyone developing a crawler) are generally synchronous. This means that once a request is made to the domain name service, other crawler threads at that node are blocked until the first request is completed. To circumvent this, most web crawlers implement their own DNS resolver as a component of the crawler. Thread *i* executing the resolver code sends a message to the DNS server and then performs a timed wait: It resumes either when being signaled by another thread or when a set time quantum expires. A single, separate DNS thread listens on the standard DNS port (port 53) for incoming response packets from the name service. Upon receiving a response, it signals the appropriate crawler thread (in this case, *i*) and hands it the response packet if *i* has not yet resumed because its time quantum has expired. A crawler thread that resumes because its wait time quantum has expired retries for a fixed number of attempts, sending out a new message to the DNS server and performing a timed wait each time; Mercator's designers recommend roughly five attempts. The time quantum of the wait increases exponentially with each of these attempts; Mercator started with one second and ended with roughly 90 seconds, in consideration of the fact that there are host names that take tens of seconds to resolve.

20.2.3 *The URL frontier*

The URL frontier at a node is given a URL by its crawl process (or by the host splitter of another crawl process). It maintains the URLs in the frontier and regurgitates them in some order whenever a crawler thread seeks a URL. Two important considerations govern the order in which URLs are returned by the frontier. First, high-quality pages that change frequently should be prioritized for frequent crawling. Thus, the priority of a page should be a function of both its change rate and its quality (using some reasonable quality estimate). The combination is necessary because a large number of spam pages change completely on every fetch.

The second consideration is politeness: We must avoid repeated fetch requests to a host within a short time span. The likelihood of this is exacerbated because of a form of locality of reference; many URLs link to other URLs at the same host. As a result, a URL frontier implemented as a simple priority queue might result in a burst of fetch requests to a host. This might occur even if we were to constrain the crawler so that at most one thread could fetch from any single host at any time. A common heuristic is to insert a gap between successive fetch requests to a host that is an order of magnitude larger than the time taken for the most recent fetch from that host.

Figure 20.3 shows a polite and prioritizing implementation of a URL frontier. Its goals are to ensure that (i) only one connection is open at a time to any host, (ii) a waiting time of a few seconds occurs between successive requests to a host, and (iii) high-priority pages are crawled preferentially.

The two major submodules are a set of *F front queues* in the upper portion of the figure and a set of *B back queues* in the lower part; all of these are

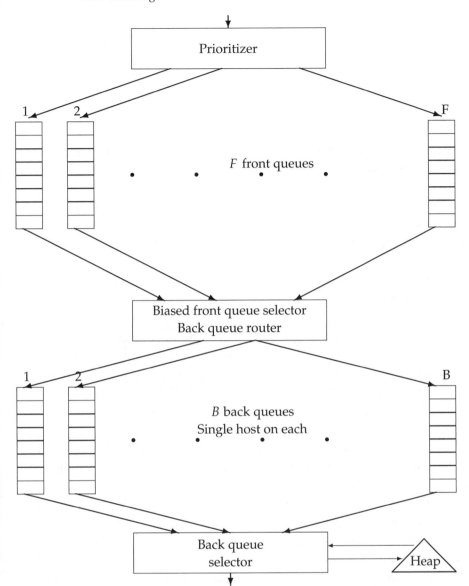

Figure 20.3 The URL frontier. URLs extracted from already crawled pages flow in at the top of the figure. A crawl thread requesting a URL extracts it from the bottom of the figure. En route, a URL flows through one of several *front queues* that manage its priority for crawling, followed by one of several *back queues* that manage the crawler's politeness.

FIFO queues. The front queues implement the prioritization, and the back queues implement politeness. In the flow of a URL added to the frontier as it makes its way through the front and back queues, a *prioritizer* first assigns to the URL an integer priority i between 1 and F based on its fetch history (taking into account the rate at which the web page at this URL has changed between previous crawls). For instance, a document that has exhibited frequent change would be assigned a higher priority. Other heuristics could be application dependent and explicit; for instance, URLs from news services

host	back queue
stanford.edu	23
microsoft.com	47
acm.org	12

Figure 20.4 Example of an auxiliary hosts-to-back queues table.

may always be assigned the highest priority. Now that it has been assigned priority i, the URL is now appended to the ith of the front queues.

Each of the B back queues maintains the following invariants: (i) it is nonempty while the crawl is in progress and (ii) it only contains URLs from a single host.[1] An auxiliary table T (Figure 20.4) is used to maintain the mapping from hosts to back queues. Whenever a back queue is empty and is being refilled from a front queue, table T must be updated accordingly.

In addition, we maintain a heap with one entry for each back queue, the entry being the earliest time t_e at which the host corresponding to that queue can be contacted again.

A crawler thread requesting a URL from the frontier extracts the root of this heap and (if necessary) waits until the corresponding time entry t_e. It then takes the URL u at the head of the back queue j corresponding to the extracted heap root, and proceeds to fetch the URL u. After fetching u, the calling thread checks whether j is empty. If so, it picks a front queue and extracts from its head a URL v. The choice of front queue is biased (usually by a random process) toward queues of higher priority, ensuring that URLs of high priority flow more quickly into the back queues. We examine v to check whether there is already a back queue holding URLs from its host. If so, v is added to that queue and we reach back to the front queues to find another candidate URL for insertion into the now-empty queue j. This process continues until j is nonempty again. In any case, the thread inserts a heap entry for j with a new earliest time t_e based on the properties of the URL in j that was last fetched (such as when its host was last contacted as well as the time taken for the last fetch), then continues with its processing. For instance, the new entry t_e could be the current time plus ten times the last fetch time.

The number of front queues, together with the policy of assigning priorities and picking queues, determines the priority properties we wish to build into the system. The number of back queues governs the extent to which we can keep all crawl threads busy while respecting politeness. The designers of Mercator recommend a rough rule of three times as many back queues as crawler threads.

On a web-scale crawl, the URL frontier may grow to the point where it demands more memory at a node than is available. The solution is to let

---

[1] The number of hosts is assumed to far exceed B.

most of the URL frontier reside on disk. A portion of each queue is kept in memory, with more brought in from disk as it is drained in memory.

?

Exercise 20.1 Why is it better to partition hosts (rather than individual URLs) between the nodes of a distributed crawl system?

Exercise 20.2 Why should the host splitter precede the duplicate URL eliminator?

Exercise 20.3 [$\star\star\star$] In the preceding discussion, we encountered two recommended "hard constants" – the increment on t_e being `ten` times the last fetch time, and the number of back queues being `three` times the number of crawl threads. How are these two constants related?

20.3 Distributing indexes

In Section 4.4 we described distributed indexing. We now consider the distribution of the index across a large computer cluster[2] that supports querying. Two obvious alternative index implementations suggest themselves: *partitioning by terms*, also known as global index organization, and *partitioning by documents*, also known as local index organization. In the former, the dictionary of index terms is partitioned into subsets, each subset residing at a node. Along with the terms at a node, we keep the postings for those terms. A query is routed to the nodes corresponding to its query terms. In principle, this allows greater concurrency because a stream of queries with different query terms would hit different sets of machines.

TERM PARTITIONING

DOCUMENT PARTITIONING

In practice, partitioning indexes by vocabulary terms turns out to be nontrivial. Multiword queries require the sending of long postings lists between sets of nodes for merging, and the cost of this can outweigh the greater concurrency. Load balancing the partition is governed not by an a priori analysis of relative term frequencies, but rather by the distribution of query terms and their co-occurrences, which can drift with time or exhibit sudden bursts. Achieving good partitions is a function of the co-occurrences of query terms and entails the clustering of terms to optimize objectives that are not easy to quantify. Finally, this strategy makes implementation of dynamic indexing more difficult.

A more common implementation is to partition by documents: Each node contains the index for a subset of all documents. Each query is distributed to all nodes, with the results from various nodes being merged before presentation to the user. This strategy trades more local disk seeks for less internode communication. One difficulty in this approach is that global statistics used

---

[2] Please note the different usage of *clusters* elsewhere in this book, in the sense of Chapters 16 and 17.

in scoring – such as idf – must be computed across the entire document collection even though the index at any single node only contains a subset of the documents. These are computed by distributed "background" processes that periodically refresh the node indexes with fresh global statistics.

How do we decide the partition of documents to nodes? Based on our development of the crawler architecture in Section 20.2.1, one simple approach would be to assign all pages from a host to a single node. This partitioning could follow the partitioning of hosts to crawler nodes. A danger of such partitioning is that, on many queries, a preponderance of the results would come from documents at a small number of hosts (and, hence, a small number of index nodes).

A hash of each URL into the space of index nodes results in a more uniform distribution of query time computation across nodes. At query time, the query is broadcast to each of the nodes, with the top k results from each node being merged to find the top k documents for the query. A common implementation heuristic is to partition the document collection into indexes of documents that are more likely to score highly on most queries (using, for instance, techniques in Chapter 21) and low-scoring indexes with the remaining documents. We only search the low-scoring indexes when there are too few matches in the high-scoring indexes, as described in Section 7.2.1.

20.4 Connectivity servers

CONNECTIVITY
SERVER
CONNECTIVITY
QUERIES
For reasons to become clearer in Chapter 21, web search engines require a *connectivity server* that supports fast *connectivity queries* on the web graph. Typical connectivity queries are *which URLs link to a given URL?* and *which URLs does a given URL link to?* To this end, we wish to store mappings in memory from URLs to out-links, and from URLs to in-links. Applications include crawl control, web graph analysis, sophisticated crawl optimization, and *link analysis* (to be covered in Chapter 21).

Suppose that the Web had four billion pages, each with ten links to other pages. In the simplest form, we would require 32 bits or 4 bytes to specify each end (source and destination) of each link, requiring a total of

$$4 \times 10^9 \times 10 \times 8 = 3.2 \times 10^{11}$$

bytes of memory. Some basic properties of the web graph can be exploited to use well under 10% of this memory requirement. At first sight, we appear to have a data compression problem – which is amenable to a variety of standard solutions. However, our goal is not to simply compress the web graph to fit into memory; we must do so in a way that efficiently supports connectivity queries; this challenge is reminiscent of index compression (Chapter 5).

```
1: www.stanford.edu/alchemy
2: www.stanford.edu/biology
3: www.stanford.edu/biology/plant
4: www.stanford.edu/biology/plant/copyright
5: www.stanford.edu/biology/plant/people
6: www.stanford.edu/chemistry
```

Figure 20.5 A lexicographically ordered set of URLs.

We assume that each web page is represented by a unique integer; the specific scheme used to assign these integers is described below. We build an *adjacency table* that resembles an inverted index; it has a row for each web page, with the rows ordered by the corresponding integers. The row for any page p contains a sorted list of integers, each corresponding to a web page that links to p. This table permits us to respond to queries of the form *which pages link to p?* In similar fashion we build a table whose entries are the pages linked to by p.

This table representation cuts the space taken by the naive representation (in which we explicitly represent each link by its two end points, each a 32-bit integer) by 50%. Our description below will focus on the table for the links *from* each page; it should be clear that the techniques apply just as well to the table of links to each page. To further reduce the storage for the table, we exploit several ideas:

1. **Similarity between lists:** Many rows of the table have many entries in common. Thus, if we explicitly represent a prototype row for several similar rows, the remainder can be succinctly expressed in terms of the prototypical row.
2. **Locality:** Many links from a page go to "nearby" pages – pages on the same host, for instance. This suggests that in encoding the destination of a link, we can often use small integers and thereby save space.
3. **We use gap encodings in sorted lists:** Rather than store the destination of each link, we store the offset from the previous entry in the row.

We now develop each of these techniques.

In a *lexicographic* ordering of all URLs, we treat each URL as an alphanumeric string and sort these strings. Figure 20.5 shows a segment of this sorted order. For a true lexicographic sort of web pages, the domain name part of the URL should be inverted, so that www.stanford.edu becomes edu.stanford.www, but this is not necessary here because we are mainly concerned with links local to a single host.

To each URL, we assign its position in this ordering as the unique identifying integer. Figure 20.6 shows an example of such a numbering and the

```
1: 1, 2, 4, 8, 16, 32, 64
2: 1, 4, 9, 16, 25, 36, 49, 64
3: 1, 2, 3, 5, 8, 13, 21, 34, 55, 89, 144
4: 1, 4, 8, 16, 25, 36, 49, 64
```

Figure 20.6 A four-row segment of the table of links.

resulting table. In this example sequence, www.stanford.edu/biology is assigned the integer 2 because it is second in the sequence.

We next exploit a property that stems from the way most websites are structured to get similarity and locality. Most websites have a template with a set of links from each page in the site to a fixed set of pages on the site (such as its copyright notice, terms of use, and so on). In this case, the rows corresponding to pages in a website will have many table entries in common. Moreover, under the lexicographic ordering of URLs, it is very likely that the pages from a website appear as contiguous rows in the table.

We adopt the following strategy: We walk down the table, encoding each table row in terms of the seven preceding rows. In the example of Figure 20.6, we could encode the fourth row as "the same as the row at offset 2 (meaning, two rows earlier in the table), with 9 replaced by 8." This requires the specification of the offset, the integer(s) dropped (in this case 9) and the integer(s) added (in this case 8). The use of only the seven preceding rows has two advantages: (i) the offset can be expressed with only 3 bits; this choice is optimized empirically (the reason for seven and not eight preceding rows is the subject of Exercise 20.4) and (ii) fixing the maximum offset to a small value like seven avoids having to perform an expensive search among many candidate prototypes in terms of which to express the current row.

What if none of the preceding seven rows is a good prototype for expressing the current row? This would happen, for instance, at each boundary between different websites as we walk down the rows of the table. In this case, we simply express the row as starting from the empty set and "adding in" each integer in that row. By using gap encodings to store the gaps (rather than the actual integers) in each row, and encoding these gaps tightly based on the distribution of their values, we obtain further space reduction. In experiments mentioned in Section 20.5, the series of techniques outlined here appears to use as few as 3 bits per link, on average – a dramatic reduction from the 64 required in the naive representation.

Although these ideas give us a representation of sizable web graphs that comfortably fit in memory, we still need to support connectivity queries. What is entailed in retrieving from this representation the set of links from a page? First, we need an index lookup from (a hash of) the URL to its row number in the table. Next, we need to reconstruct these entries, which may be encoded in terms of entries in other rows. This entails following the offsets to reconstruct these other rows – a process that in principle could lead through many levels of indirection. In practice, however, this does not happen very often. A heuristic for controlling this can be introduced into the construction of the table: When examining the preceding seven rows as candidates from which to model the current row, we demand a threshold of similarity between the current row and the candidate prototype. This threshold must be chosen with care. If the threshold is set too high, we seldom use prototypes and express many rows afresh. If the threshold is too low, most rows get expressed in terms of prototypes, so that at query time the reconstruction of a row leads to many levels of indirection through preceding prototypes.

? **Exercise 20.4** We noted that expressing a row in terms of one of seven preceding rows allowed us to use no more than three bits to specify which of the preceding rows we are using as prototype. Why seven and not eight preceding rows? *(Hint: Consider the case when none of the preceding seven rows is a good prototype.)*

Exercise 20.5 We noted that for the scheme in Section 20.4, decoding the links incident on a URL could result in many levels of indirection. Construct an example in which the number of levels of indirection grows linearly with the number of URLs.

20.5 References and further reading

The first web crawler appears to be Matthew Gray's Wanderer, written in the spring of 1993. The Mercator crawler is due to Najork and Heydon (Najork and Heydon 2001, 2002); the treatment in this chapter follows their work. Other classic early descriptions of web crawling include Burner (1997), Brin and Page (1998), Cho et al. (1998), and the creators of the Webbase system at Stanford (Hirai et al. 2000). Cho and Garcia-Molina (2002) give a taxonomy and comparative study of different modes of communication between the nodes of a distributed crawler. The Robots Exclusion Protocol standard is described at www.robotstxt.org/wc/exclusion.html. Boldi et al. (2002) and Shkapenyuk and Suel (2002) provide more recent details of implementing large-scale distributed web crawlers.

Our discussion of DNS resolution (Section 20.2.2) uses the current convention for Internet addresses, known as IPv4 (for Internet Protocol version 4); each IP address is a sequence of four bytes. In the future, the convention for addresses (collectively known as the internet *address space*) is likely to use a new standard known as IPv6 (www.ipv6.org/).

Tomasic and Garcia-Molina (1993) and Jeong and Omiecinski (1995) are key early papers evaluating term partitioning versus document partitioning for distributed indexes. Document partitioning is found to be superior, at least when the distribution of terms is skewed, as it typically is in practice. This result has generally been confirmed in more recent work (MacFarlane et al. 2000). But the outcome depends on the details of the distributed system;

at least one thread of work has reached the opposite conclusion (Ribeiro-Neto and Barbosa 1998; Badue et al. 2001). Sornil (2001) argues for a partitioning scheme that is a hybrid between term and document partitioning. Barroso et al. (2003) describe the distribution methods used at Google. The first implementation of a connectivity server was described by Bharat et al. (1998). The scheme discussed in this chapter, currently believed to be the best published scheme (achieving as few as 3 bits per link for encoding), is described in a series of papers by Boldi and Vigna (2004a, 2004b).

21 *Link analysis*

The analysis of hyperlinks and the graph structure of the Web has been instrumental in the development of web search. In this chapter, we focus on the use of hyperlinks for ranking web search results. Such link analysis is one of many factors considered by web search engines in computing a composite score for a web page on any given query. We begin by reviewing some basics of the Web as a graph in Section 21.1, then proceed to the technical development of the elements of link analysis for ranking.

Link analysis for web search has intellectual antecedents in the field of citation analysis, aspects of which overlap with an area known as bibliometrics. These disciplines seek to quantify the influence of scholarly articles by analyzing the pattern of citations among them. Much as citations represent the conferral of authority from a scholarly article to others, link analysis on the Web treats hyperlinks from a web page to another as a conferral of authority. Clearly, not every citation or hyperlink implies such authority conferral; for this reason, simply measuring the quality of a web page by the number of in-links (citations from other pages) is not robust enough. For instance, one may contrive to set up multiple web pages pointing to a target web page, with the intent of artificially boosting the latter's tally of in-links. This phenomenon is referred to as *link spam*. Nevertheless, the phenomenon of citation is prevalent and dependable enough that it is feasible for web search engines to derive useful signals for ranking from more sophisticated link analysis. Link analysis also proves to be a useful indicator of what page(s) to crawl next while crawling the web; this is done by using link analysis to guide the priority assignment in the front queues of Chapter 20.

Section 21.1 develops the basic ideas underlying the use of the web graph in link analysis. Sections 21.2 and 21.3 then develop two distinct methods for link analysis, PageRank and HITS.

21.1 The Web as a graph

Recall the notion of the web graph from Section 19.2.1 and particularly Figure 19.2. Our study of link analysis builds on two intuitions.

1. The anchor text pointing to page B is a good description of page B.
2. The hyperlink from A to B represents an endorsement of page B, by the creator of page A. This is not always the case; for instance, many links among pages within a single website stem from the user of a common template. For instance, most corporate websites have a pointer from every page to a page containing a copyright notice – this is clearly not an endorsement. Accordingly, implementations of link analysis algorithms typically discount such "internal" links.

21.1.1 Anchor text and the web graph

The following fragment of HTML code from a web page shows a hyperlink pointing to the home page of the Journal of the ACM:

```
<a href="http://www.acm.org/jacm/">Journal of the ACM.</a>
```

In this case, the link points to the page www.acm.org/jacm/ and the anchor text is *Journal of the ACM*. Clearly, in this example the anchor is descriptive of the target page. But then the target page (B = http://www.acm.org/jacm/) itself contains the same description as well as considerable additional information on the journal. So what use is the anchor text?

The Web is full of instances where the page B does not provide an accurate description of itself. In many cases, this is a matter of how the publishers of page B choose to present themselves; this is especially common with corporate web pages, where a web presence is a marketing statement. For example, at the time of the writing of this book the home page of the IBM corporation (www.ibm.com) did not contain the term computer anywhere in its HTML code, despite the fact that IBM is widely viewed as the world's largest computer maker. Similarly, the HTML code for the home page of Yahoo! (www.yahoo.com) does not at this time contain the word portal.

Thus, there is often a gap between the terms in a web page and how web users would describe that web page. Consequently, web searchers need not use the terms in a page to query for it. In addition, many web pages are rich in graphics and images, and/or embed their text in these images; in such cases, the HTML parsing performed when crawling will not extract text that is useful for indexing these pages. The "standard IR" approach to this would be to use the methods outlined in Chapter 9 and Section 12.4. The insight behind anchor text is that such methods can be supplanted by anchor text, thereby tapping the power of the community of web page authors.

The fact that the anchors of many hyperlinks pointing to `www.ibm.com` include the word computer can be exploited by web search engines. For instance, the anchor text terms can be included as terms under which to index the target web page. Thus, the postings for the term computer would include the document `www.ibm.com` and that for the term portal would include the document `www.yahoo.com`, using a special indicator to show that these terms occur as anchor (rather than in-page) text. As with in-page terms, anchor text terms are generally weighted based on frequency, with a penalty for terms that occur very often (the most common terms in anchor text across the Web are Click and here) using methods very similar to idf. The actual weighting of terms is determined by machine-learned scoring, as in Section 15.4.1; current web search engines appear to assign a substantial weighting to anchor text terms.

The use of anchor text has some interesting side effects. Searching for big blue on most web search engines returns the home page of the IBM corporation as the top hit; this is consistent with the popular nickname that many people use to refer to IBM. On the other hand, there have been (and continue to be) many instances where derogatory anchor text such as evil empire leads to somewhat unexpected results on querying for these terms on web search engines. This phenomenon has been exploited in orchestrated campaigns against specific sites. Such orchestrated anchor text may be a form of spamming; a website can create misleading anchor text pointing to itself to boost its ranking on selected query terms. Detecting and combating such systematic abuse of anchor text is another form of spam detection that web search engines perform.

The window of text surrounding anchor text (sometimes referred to as *extended anchor text*) is often usable in the same manner as anchor text itself; consider for instance the fragment of web text `there is good discussion of vedic scripture <a>here</a>`. This has been considered in a number of settings and the useful width of this window has been studied; see Section 21.4 for references.

Exercise 21.1 Is it always possible to follow directed edges (hyperlinks) in the web graph from any node (web page) to any other? Why or why not?

Exercise 21.2 Find an instance of misleading anchor text on the Web.

Exercise 21.3 Given the collection of anchor text phrases for a web page x, suggest a heuristic for choosing one term or phrase from this collection that is most descriptive of x.

Exercise 21.4 Does your heuristic in the previous exercise take into account a single domain D repeating anchor text for x from multiple pages in D?

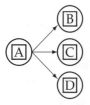

Figure 21.1 The random surfer at node A proceeds with probability 1/3 to each of B, C, and D.

21.2 PageRank

PAGERANK

We now focus on scoring and ranking measures derived from the link structure alone. Our first technique for link analysis assigns to every node in the
web graph a numerical score between 0 and 1, known as its *PageRank*. The
PageRank of a node depends on the link structure of the web graph. Given
a query, a web search engine computes a composite score for each web page
that combines hundreds of features such as cosine similarity (Section 6.3)
and term proximity (Section 7.2.2), together with the PageRank score. This
composite score, developed using the methods of Section 15.4.1, is used to
provide a ranked list of results for the query.

Consider a random surfer who begins at a web page (a node of the web
graph) and executes a random walk on the Web as follows. At each time
step, the surfer proceeds from his current page A to a randomly chosen web
page that A hyperlinks to. Figure 21.1 shows the surfer at a node A, out of
which there are three hyperlinks to nodes B, C, and D; the surfer proceeds at
the next time step to one of these three nodes, with equal probabilities 1/3.

As the surfer proceeds in this random walk from node to node, he visits
some nodes more often than others; intuitively, these are nodes with many
links coming in from other frequently visited nodes. The idea behind Page-
Rank is that pages visited more often in this walk are more important.

What if the current location of the surfer, the node A, has no out-links?
To address this we introduce an additional operation for our random surfer:

TELEPORT

the *teleport* operation. In the teleport operation, the surfer jumps from a node
to any other node in the web graph. This could happen because he types
an address into the URL bar of his browser. The destination of a teleport
operation is modeled as being chosen uniformly at random from all web
pages. In other words, if N is the total number of nodes in the web graph,[1]
the teleport operation takes the surfer to each node with probability $1/N$. The
surfer would also teleport to his present position with probability $1/N$.

In assigning a PageRank score to each node of the web graph, we use the
teleport operation in two ways: (i) When at a node with no out-links, the
surfer invokes the teleport operation. (ii) At any node that has outgoing links,

---

[1] This is consistent with our usage of N for the number of documents in the collection.

the surfer invokes the teleport operation with probability $0 < \alpha < 1$ and the standard random walk (follow an out-link chosen uniformly at random as in Figure 21.1) with probability $1 - \alpha$, where α is a fixed parameter chosen in advance. Typically, α might be 0.1.

In Section 21.2.1, we will use the theory of Markov chains to argue that when the surfer follows this combined process (random walk plus teleport) he visits each node v of the web graph a fixed fraction of the time $\pi(v)$ that depends on (i) the structure of the web graph and (ii) the value of α. We call this value $\pi(v)$ the PageRank of v and will show how to compute this value in Section 21.2.2.

21.2.1 Markov chains

A Markov chain is a *discrete-time stochastic process*, a process that occurs in a series of time steps in each of which a random choice is made. A Markov chain consists of N *states*. Each web page will correspond to a state in the Markov chain we will formulate.

A Markov chain is characterized by an $N \times N$ *transition probability matrix P* each of whose entries is in the interval [0, 1]; the entries in each row of P add up to 1. The Markov chain can be in one of the N states at any given time-step; then, the entry P_{ij} tells us the probability that the state at the next time-step is j, conditioned on the current state being i. Each entry P_{ij} is known as a transition probability and depends only on the current state i; this is known as the Markov property. Thus, by the Markov property,

$$\forall i, j, \ P_{ij} \in [0, 1]$$

and

(21.1)
$$\forall i, \ \sum_{j=1}^{N} P_{ij} = 1.$$

A matrix with non-negative entries that satisfies Equation (21.1) is known
STOCHASTIC as a *stochastic matrix*. A key property of a stochastic matrix is that it has a
MATRIX *principal left eigenvector* corresponding to its largest eigenvalue, which is 1.
PRINCIPAL   In a Markov chain, the probability distribution of next states for a Markov
LEFT chain depends only on the current state, and not on how the Markov chain
EIGENVECTOR arrived at the current state. Figure 21.2 shows a simple Markov chain with three states. From the middle state A, we proceed with (equal) probabilities of 0.5 to either B or C. From either B or C, we proceed with probability 1 to A. The transition probability matrix of this Markov chain is then

$$\begin{pmatrix} 0 & 0.5 & 0.5 \\ 1 & 0 & 0 \\ 1 & 0 & 0 \end{pmatrix}$$

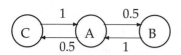

Figure 21.2 A simple Markov chain with three states; the numbers on the links indicate the transition probabilities.

A Markov chain's probability distribution over its states may be viewed as PROBABILITY a *probability vector*, a vector all of whose entries are in the interval [0, 1], and VECTOR the entries add up to 1. An N-dimensional probability vector each of whose components corresponds to one of the N states of a Markov chain can be viewed as a probability distribution over its states. For our simple Markov chain of Figure 21.2, the probability vector would have three components that sum to 1.

We can view a random surfer on the web graph as a Markov chain, with one state for each web page, and each transition probability representing the probability of moving from one web page to another. The teleport operation contributes to these transition probabilities. The adjacency matrix A of the web graph is defined as follows: if there is a hyperlink from page i to page j, then $A_{ij} = 1$, otherwise $A_{ij} = 0$. We can readily derive the transition probability matrix P for our Markov chain from the $N \times N$ matrix A. If a row of A has no 1s, then divide each element by $1/N$. For all other rows proceed as follows:

1. Divide each 1 in A by the number of 1s in its row. Thus, if there is a row with three 1s, then each of them is replaced by 1/3.
2. Multiply the resulting matrix by $1 - \alpha$.
3. Add α/N to every entry of the resulting matrix, to obtain P.

We can depict the probability distribution of the surfer's position at any time by a probability vector $\vec{x}$. At $t = 0$ the surfer may begin at a state whose corresponding entry in $\vec{x}$ is 1 while all others are zero. By definition, the surfer's distribution at $t = 1$ is given by the probability vector $\vec{x}P$; at $t = 2$ by $(\vec{x}P)P = \vec{x}P^2$, and so on. We will detail this process in Section 21.2.2. We can thus compute the surfer's distribution over the states at any time, given only the initial distribution and the transition probability matrix P.

If a Markov chain is allowed to run for many time steps, each state is visited at a (different) frequency that depends on the structure of the Markov chain. In our running analogy, the surfer visits certain web pages (say, popular news home pages) more often than other pages. We now make this intuition precise, establishing conditions under which the visit frequency converges to a fixed, steady-state quantity. Following this, we set the PageRank of each node v to this steady-state visit frequency and show how it can be computed.

Ergodic **Definition:** A Markov chain is said to be *ergodic* if there exists a positive
Markov integer T_0 such that for all pairs of states i, j in the Markov chain, if it is
Chain started at time 0 in state i then for all $t > T_0$, the probability of being in state
j at time t is greater than 0.

For a Markov chain to be ergodic, two technical conditions are required of
its states and the nonzero transition probabilities; these conditions are known
as *irreducibility* and *aperiodicity*. Informally, the first ensures that there is a
sequence of transitions of nonzero probability from any state to any other,
while the latter ensures that the states are not partitioned into sets such that
all state transitions occur cyclically from one set to another.

steady-state **Theorem 21.1.** *For any ergodic Markov chain, there is a unique* steady-state *probability vector $\vec{\pi}$ that is the principal left eigenvector of P, such that if $\eta(i, t)$ is the
number of visits to state i in t steps, then*

$$\lim_{t \to \infty} \frac{\eta(i, t)}{t} = \pi(i),$$

where $\pi(i) > 0$ is the steady-state probability for state i.

It follows from Theorem 21.1 that the random walk with teleporting results
in a unique distribution of steady-state probabilities over the states of the induced Markov chain. This steady-state probability for a state is the PageRank
of the corresponding web page.

21.2.2 The PageRank computation

How do we compute PageRank values? Recall the definition of a left eigenvector from Equation (18.2) the left eigenvectors of the transition probability
matrix P are N-vectors $\vec{\pi}$ such that

(21.2) $$\vec{\pi} P = \lambda \vec{\pi}.$$

The N entries in the principal eigenvector $\vec{\pi}$ are the steady-state probabilities of the random walk with teleporting, and thus the PageRank values
for the corresponding web pages. We may interpret Equation (21.2) as follows: If $\vec{\pi}$ is the probability distribution of the surfer across the web pages,
he remains in the steady-state distribution $\vec{\pi}$. Given that $\vec{\pi}$ is the steady-state
distribution, we have that $\pi P = 1\pi$, so 1 is an eigenvalue of P. Thus, if we
were to compute the principal left eigenvector of the matrix P – the one with
eigenvalue 1 – we would have computed the PageRank values.

There are many algorithms available for computing left eigenvectors; the
references at the end of Chapter 18 and the present chapter are a guide to
these. We give here a rather elementary method, sometimes known as *power
iteration*. If $\vec{x}$ is the initial distribution over the states, then the distribution
at time t is $\vec{x}P^t$. As t grows large, we would expect that the distribution

$\vec{x}_0$	1	0	0
$\vec{x}_1$	1/6	2/3	1/6
$\vec{x}_2$	1/3	1/3	1/3
$\vec{x}_3$	1/4	1/2	1/4
$\vec{x}_4$	7/24	5/12	7/24
...	...	...	...
$\vec{x}$	5/18	4/9	5/18

Figure 21.3 The sequence of probability vectors.

$\vec{x}P^t$ is very similar to the distribution $\vec{x}P^{t+1}$; for large t we would expect the Markov chain to attain its steady state.[2] By Theorem 21.1, this is independent of the initial distribution $\vec{x}$. The power iteration method simulates the surfer's walk: Begin at a state and run the walk for a large number of steps t, keeping track of the visit frequencies for each of the states. After a large number of steps t, these frequencies "settle down" so that the variation in the computed frequencies is below some predetermined threshold. We declare these tabulated frequencies to be the PageRank values.

We consider the web graph in Exercise 21.6 with $\alpha = 0.5$. The transition probability matrix of the surfer's walk with teleportation is then

(21.3)
$$P = \begin{pmatrix} 1/6 & 2/3 & 1/6 \\ 5/12 & 1/6 & 5/12 \\ 1/6 & 2/3 & 1/6 \end{pmatrix}.$$

Imagine that the surfer starts in state 1, corresponding to the initial probability distribution vector $\vec{x}_0 = (1\ 0\ 0)$. Then, after one step the distribution is

(21.4)
$$\vec{x}_0 P = \begin{pmatrix} 1/6 & 2/3 & 1/6 \end{pmatrix} = \vec{x}_1.$$

After two steps it is

(21.5) $\vec{x}_1 P = \begin{pmatrix} 1/6 & 2/3 & 1/6 \end{pmatrix} \begin{pmatrix} 1/6 & 2/3 & 1/6 \\ 5/12 & 1/6 & 5/12 \\ 1/6 & 2/3 & 1/6 \end{pmatrix} = \begin{pmatrix} 1/3 & 1/3 & 1/3 \end{pmatrix} = \vec{x}_2.$

Continuing in this fashion gives a sequence of probability vectors as shown in Figure 21.3.

Continuing for several steps, we see that the distribution converges to the steady state of $\vec{x} = (5/18\ \ 4/9\ \ 5/18)$. In this simple example, we may directly calculate this steady-state probability distribution by observing the symmetry of the Markov chain: States 1 and 3 are symmetric, as evident from the fact that the first and third rows of the transition probability matrix in Equation (21.3) are identical. Postulating, then, that they both have the same

---

[2] Note that P^t represents P raised to the tth power, not the transpose of P, which is denoted P^T.

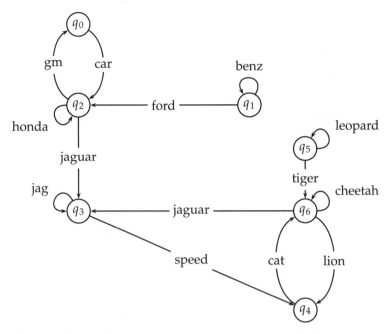

Figure 21.4 A small web graph. Arcs are annotated with the word that occurs in the anchor text of the corresponding link.

steady-state probability and denoting this probability by p, we know that the steady-state distribution is of the form $\vec{\pi} = (p\ 1 - 2p\ p)$. Now, using the identity $\vec{\pi} = \vec{\pi}P$, we solve a simple linear equation to obtain $p = 5/18$ and consequently, $\vec{\pi} = (5/18\ 4/9\ 5/18)$.

The PageRank values of pages (and the implicit ordering among them) are independent of any query a user might pose; PageRank is thus a query-independent measure of the static quality of each web page (recall such static quality measures from Section 7.1.4). On the other hand, the relative ordering of pages should, intuitively, depend on the query being served. For this reason, search engines use static quality measures such as PageRank as just one of many factors in scoring a web page on a query. Indeed, the relative contribution of PageRank to the overall score may again be determined by machine-learned scoring as in Section 15.4.1.

Example 21.1: Consider the graph in Figure 21.4. For a teleportation rate of 0.14 its (stochastic) transition probability matrix is:

0.02	0.02	0.88	0.02	0.02	0.02	0.02
0.02	0.45	0.45	0.02	0.02	0.02	0.02
0.31	0.02	0.31	0.31	0.02	0.02	0.02
0.02	0.02	0.02	0.45	0.45	0.02	0.02
0.02	0.02	0.02	0.02	0.02	0.02	0.88
0.02	0.02	0.02	0.02	0.02	0.45	0.45
0.02	0.02	0.02	0.31	0.31	0.02	0.31

The PageRank vector of this matrix is:

(21.6) $\vec{x} = (0.05 \quad 0.04 \quad 0.11 \quad 0.25 \quad 0.21 \quad 0.04 \quad 0.31)$

Observe that in Figure 21.4, q_2, q_3, q_4 and q_6 are the nodes with at least two in-links. Of these, q_2 has the lowest PageRank since the random walk tends to drift out of the top part of the graph – the walker can only return there through teleportation.

21.2.3 Topic-specific PageRank

Thus far, we have discussed the PageRank computation with a teleport operation in which the surfer jumps to a web page chosen uniformly at random. We now consider teleporting to a random web page chosen *nonuniformly*. In doing so, we are able to derive PageRank values tailored to particular interests. For instance, a sports aficionado might wish that pages on sports be ranked higher than non-sports pages. Suppose that web pages on sports are "near" one another in the web graph. Then, a random surfer who frequently finds himself on random sports pages is likely (in the course of the random walk) to spend most of his time at sports pages, so that the steady-state distribution of sports pages is boosted.

Suppose our random surfer, endowed with a teleport operation as before, teleports to *a random web page on the topic of sports* instead of teleporting to a uniformly chosen random web page. We will not focus on how we collect all web pages on the topic of sports; in fact, we only need a nonzero subset S of sports-related web pages, so that the teleport operation is feasible. This may be obtained, for instance, from a manually built directory of sports pages such as the open directory project (www.dmoz.org/) or that of Yahoo.

Provided the set S of sports-related pages is nonempty, it follows that there is a nonempty set of web pages $Y \supseteq S$ over which the random walk has a steady-state distribution; let us denote this *sports PageRank* distribution by $\vec{\pi}_s$. For web pages not in Y, we set the PageRank values to 0. We call $\vec{\pi}_s$ the
TOPIC-SPECIFIC *topic-specific PageRank* for sports.
PAGERANK   We do not demand that teleporting takes the random surfer to a uniformly chosen sports page; the distribution over teleporting targets S could in fact be arbitrary.

In like manner, we can envision topic-specific PageRank distributions for each of several topics such as science, religion, politics, and so on. Each of these distributions assigns to each web page a PageRank value in the interval $[0, 1)$. For a user interested in only a single topic from among these topics, we may invoke the corresponding PageRank distribution when scoring and ranking search results. This gives us the potential of considering settings in which the search engine knows what topic a user is interested in. This may happen because users either explicitly register their interests, or because the system learns by observing each user's behavior over time.

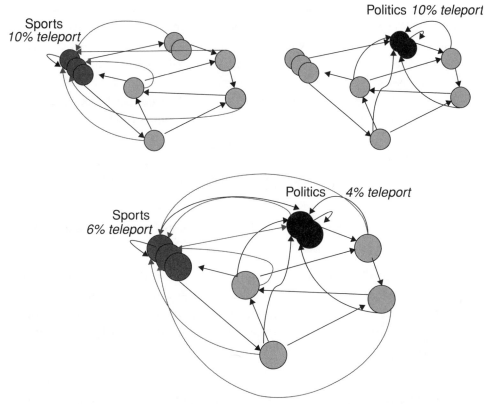

Figure 21.5 Topic-specific PageRank. In this example we consider a user whose interests are 60% sports and 40% politics. If the teleportation probability is 10%, this user is modeled as teleporting 6% to sports pages and 4% to politics pages.

But what if a user is known to have a mixture of interests from multiple topics? For instance, a user may have an interest mixture (or *profile*) that PERSONALIZED is 60% sports and 40% politics; can we compute a *personalized PageRank* for PAGERANK this user? At first glance, this appears daunting; how could we possibly compute a different PageRank distribution for each user profile (with, potentially, infinitely many possible profiles)? We can in fact address this provided we assume that an individual's interests can be well-approximated as a linear combination of a small number of topic page distributions. A user with this mixture of interests could teleport as follows: Determine first whether to teleport to the set S of known sports pages, or to the set of known politics pages. This choice is made at random, choosing sports pages 60% of the time and politics pages 40% of the time (Figure 21.5). Once we choose that a particular teleport step is to (say) a random sports page, we choose a web page in S uniformly at random to teleport to. This in turn leads to an ergodic Markov chain with a steady-state distribution that is personalized to this user's preferences over topics (see Exercise 21.16).

Although this idea has intuitive appeal, its implementation appears cumbersome; it seems to demand that for each user, we compute a transition probability matrix and compute its steady-state distribution. We are rescued by the fact that the evolution of the probability distribution over the states of a Markov chain can be viewed as a linear system. In Exercise 21.16 we will show that it is not necessary to compute a PageRank vector for every distinct combination of user interests over topics; the personalized PageRank vector for any user can be expressed as a linear combination of the underlying topic-specific PageRanks. For instance, the personalized PageRank vector for the user whose interests are 60% sports and 40% politics can be computed as

(21.7)
$$0.6\vec{\pi}_s + 0.4\vec{\pi}_p,$$

where $\vec{\pi}_s$ and $\vec{\pi}_p$ are the topic-specific PageRank vectors for sports and for politics, respectively.

?

Exercise 21.5 Write down the transition probability matrix for the example in Figure 21.2.

Exercise 21.6 Consider a web graph with three nodes 1, 2, and 3. The links are as follows: $1 \rightarrow 2, 3 \rightarrow 2, 2 \rightarrow 1, 2 \rightarrow 3$. Write down the transition probability matrices for the surfer's walk with teleporting, for the following three values of the teleport probability: (i) $\alpha = 0$; (ii) $\alpha = 0.5$; and (iii) $\alpha = 1$.

Exercise 21.7 A user of a browser can, in addition to clicking a hyperlink on the page x he is currently browsing, use the *back button* to go back to the page from which he arrived at x. Can such a user of back buttons be modeled as a Markov chain? How would we model repeated invocations of the back button?

Exercise 21.8 Consider a Markov chain with three states A, B and C, and transition probabilities as follows. From state A, the next state is B with probability 1. From B, the next state is either A with probability p_A, or state C with probability $1 - p_A$. From C the next state is A with probability 1. For what values of $p_A \in [0, 1]$ is this Markov chain ergodic?

Exercise 21.9 Show that for any directed graph, the Markov chain induced by a random walk with the teleport operation is ergodic.

Exercise 21.10 Show that the PageRank of every page is at least α/N. What does this imply about the difference in PageRank values (over the various pages) as α becomes close to 1?

Exercise 21.11 For the data in Example 21.1, write a small routine or use a scientific calculator to compute the PageRank values stated in Equation (21.6).

Exercise 21.12 Suppose that the web graph is stored on disk as an adjacency list, in such a way that you may only query for the out-neighbors of pages in the order in which they are stored. You cannot load the graph in main memory but you may do multiple reads over the full graph. Write the algorithm for computing the PageRank in this setting.

Exercise 21.13 Recall the sets S and Y introduced near the beginning of Section 21.2.3. How does the set Y relate to S?

Exercise 21.14 Is the set Y always the set of all web pages? Why or why not?

Exercise 21.15 [⋆ ⋆ ⋆] Is the sports PageRank of any page in S at least as large as its PageRank?

Exercise 21.16 [⋆ ⋆ ⋆] Consider a setting where we have two topic-specific PageRank values for each web page: a sports PageRank $\vec{\pi}_s$, and a politics PageRank $\vec{\pi}_p$. Let α be the (common) teleportation probability used in computing both sets of topic-specific PageRanks. For $q \in [0, 1]$, consider a user whose interest profile is divided between a fraction q in sports and a fraction $1 - q$ in politics. Show that the user's personalized PageRank is the steady-state distribution of a random walk in which – on a teleport step – the walk teleports to a sports page with probability q and to a politics page with probability $1 - q$.

Exercise 21.17 Show that the Markov chain corresponding to the walk in Exercise 21.16 is ergodic and hence the user's personalized PageRank can be obtained by computing the steady-state distribution of this Markov chain.

Exercise 21.18 Show that in the steady-state distribution of Exercise 21.17, the steady-state probability for any web page i equals $q\pi_s(i) + (1 - q)\pi_p(i)$.

21.3 Hubs and authorities

HUB SCORE
AUTHORITY
SCORE

We now develop a scheme in which, given a query, every web page is assigned *two* scores. One is called its *hub score* and the other its *authority score*. For any query, we compute two ranked lists of results rather than one. The ranking of one list is induced by the hub scores and that of the other by the authority scores.

This approach stems from a particular insight into the creation of web pages, namely, that there are two primary kinds of web pages useful as results for *broad-topic searches*. By a broad topic search we mean an informational query such as "I wish to learn about leukemia." There are authoritative sources of information on the topic; in this case, the National Cancer Institute's page on leukemia would be such a page. We will call such pages *authorities*; in the computation we are about to describe, they are the pages that will emerge with high authority scores.

On the other hand, there are many pages on the Web that are hand-compiled lists of links to authoritative web pages on a specific topic. These *hub* pages are not in themselves authoritative sources of topic-specific information, but rather compilations that someone with an interest in the topic has spent time putting together. The approach we will take, then, is to use these hub pages to discover the authority pages. In the computation we now develop, these hub pages are the pages that will emerge with high hub scores.

A good hub page is one that points to many good authorities; a good authority page is one that is pointed to by many good hub pages. We thus appear to have a circular definition of hubs and authorities; we will turn this into an iterative computation. Suppose that we have a subset of the web containing good hub and authority pages, together with the hyperlinks among them. We will iteratively compute a hub score and an authority score for every web page in this subset, deferring the discussion of how we pick this subset until Section 21.3.1.

For a web page v in our subset of the web, we use $h(v)$ to denote its hub score and $a(v)$ its authority score. Initially, we set $h(v) = a(v) = 1$ for all nodes v. We also denote by $v \mapsto y$ the existence of a hyperlink from v to y. The core of the iterative algorithm is a pair of updates to the hub and authority scores of all pages given by Equation (21.8), which capture the intuitive notions that good hubs point to good authorities and that good authorities are pointed to by good hubs.

$$(21.8) \qquad\qquad h(v) \leftarrow \sum_{v \mapsto y} a(y)$$

$$a(v) \leftarrow \sum_{y \mapsto v} h(y).$$

Thus, the first line of Equation (21.8) sets the hub score of page v to the sum of the authority scores of the pages it links to. In other words, if v links to pages with high authority scores, its hub score increases. The second line plays the reverse role; if page v is linked to by good hubs, its authority score increases.

What happens as we perform these updates iteratively, recomputing hub scores, then new authority scores based on the recomputed hub scores, and so on? Let us recast Equation (21.8) into matrix–vector form. Let $\vec{h}$ and $\vec{a}$ denote the vectors of all hub and all authority scores respectively, for the pages in our subset of the web graph. Let A denote the adjacency matrix of the subset of the web graph that we are dealing with: A is a square matrix with one row and one column for each page in the subset. The entry A_{ij} is 1 if there is a hyperlink from page i to page j, and 0 otherwise. Then, we may write Equation (21.8)

$$(21.9) \qquad\qquad \vec{h} \leftarrow A\vec{a}$$

$$\vec{a} \leftarrow A^T \vec{h},$$

where A^T denotes the transpose of the matrix A. Now the right hand side of each line of Equation (21.9) is a vector that is the left hand side of the other line of Equation (21.9). Substituting these into one another, we may rewrite Equation (21.9) as

(21.10)
$$\vec{h} \leftarrow AA^T\vec{h}$$
$$\vec{a} \leftarrow A^T A\vec{a}.$$

Now, Equation (21.10) bears an uncanny resemblance to a pair of eigenvector equations (Section 18.1); indeed, if we replace the $\leftarrow$ symbols by $=$ symbols and introduce the (unknown) eigenvalue, the first line of Equation (21.10) becomes the equation for the eigenvectors of AA^T, and the second becomes the equation for the eigenvectors of $A^T A$:

(21.11)
$$\vec{h} = (1/\lambda_h)AA^T\vec{h}$$
$$\vec{a} = (1/\lambda_a)A^T A\vec{a}.$$

Here we have used λ_h to denote the eigenvalue of AA^T and λ_a to denote the eigenvalue of $A^T A$.

This leads to some key consequences:

1. The iterative updates in Equation (21.8) (or equivalently, Equation (21.9)), if scaled by the appropriate eigenvalues, are equivalent to the power iteration method for computing the eigenvectors of AA^T and $A^T A$. Provided that the principal eigenvalue of AA^T is unique, the iteratively computed entries of $\vec{h}$ and $\vec{a}$ settle into unique steady-state values determined by the entries of A and hence the link structure of the graph.
2. In computing these eigenvector entries, we are not restricted to using the power iteration method; indeed, we could use any fast method for computing the principal eigenvector of a stochastic matrix.

The resulting computation thus takes the following form:

1. Assemble the target subset of web pages, form the graph induced by their hyperlinks and compute AA^T and $A^T A$.
2. Compute the principal eigenvectors of AA^T and $A^T A$ to form the vector of hub scores $\vec{h}$ and authority scores $\vec{a}$.
3. Output the top-scoring hubs and the top-scoring authorities.

HITS This method of link analysis is known as *HITS*, which is an acronym for *hyperlink-induced topic search*.

Example 21.2: Assuming the query jaguar and double-weighting of links whose anchors contain the query word, the matrix A for Figure 21.4

is as follows:

$$
\begin{matrix}
0 & 0 & 1 & 0 & 0 & 0 & 0 \\
0 & 1 & 1 & 0 & 0 & 0 & 0 \\
1 & 0 & 1 & 2 & 0 & 0 & 0 \\
0 & 0 & 0 & 1 & 1 & 0 & 0 \\
0 & 0 & 0 & 0 & 0 & 0 & 1 \\
0 & 0 & 0 & 0 & 0 & 1 & 1 \\
0 & 0 & 0 & 2 & 1 & 0 & 1
\end{matrix}
$$

The hub and authority vectors are:

$$\vec{h} = (0.03 \quad 0.04 \quad 0.33 \quad 0.18 \quad 0.04 \quad 0.04 \quad 0.35)$$

$$\vec{a} = (0.10 \quad 0.01 \quad 0.12 \quad 0.47 \quad 0.16 \quad 0.01 \quad 0.13)$$

Here, q_3 is the main authority – two hubs (q_2 and q_6) are pointing to it via highly weighted jaguar links.

Because the iterative updates captured the intuition of good hubs and good authorities, the high-scoring pages we output would give us good hubs and authorities from the target subset of web pages. In Section 21.3.1 we describe the remaining detail: How do we gather a target subset of web pages around a topic such as leukemia?

21.3.1 Choosing the subset of the Web

In assembling a subset of web pages around a topic such as leukemia, we must cope with the fact that good authority pages may not contain the specific query term leukemia. This is especially true, as we noted in Section 21.1.1, when an authority page uses its web presence to project a certain marketing image. For instance, many pages on the IBM website are authoritative sources of information on computer hardware, even though these pages may not contain the term computer or hardware. However, a hub compiling computer hardware resources is likely to use these terms and also link to the relevant pages on the IBM website.

Building on these observations, the following procedure has been suggested for compiling the subset of the Web for which to compute hub and authority scores.

1. Given a query (say leukemia), use a text index to get all pages containing leukemia. Call this the *root set* of pages.
2. Build the *base set* of pages, to include the root set as well as any page that either links to a page in the root set, or is linked to by a page in the root set.

We then use the base set for computing hub and authority scores. The base set is constructed in this manner for three reasons:

1. A good authority page may not contain the query text (such as computer hardware).
2. If the text query manages to capture a good hub page v_h in the root set, then the inclusion of all pages linked to by any page in the root set will capture all the good authorities linked to by v_h in the base set.
3. Conversely, if the text query manages to capture a good authority page v_a in the root set, then the inclusion of pages pointing to v_a will bring other good hubs into the base set. In other words, the "expansion" of the root set into the base set enriches the common pool of good hubs and authorities.

Running HITS across a variety of queries reveals some interesting insights about link analysis. Frequently, the documents that emerge as top hubs and authorities include languages other than the language of the query. These pages were presumably drawn into the base set, following the assembly of the root set. Thus, some elements of *cross-language retrieval* (where a query in one language retrieves documents in another) are evident here; interestingly, this cross-language effect resulted purely from link analysis, with no linguistic translation taking place.

We conclude this section with some notes on implementing this algorithm. The root set consists of all pages matching the text query; in fact, implementations (see the references in Section 21.4) suggest that it suffices to use 200 or so web pages for the root set, rather than all pages matching the text query. Any algorithm for computing eigenvectors may be used for computing the hub/authority score vector. In fact, we need not compute the exact values of these scores; it suffices to know the relative values of the scores so that we may identify the top hubs and authorities. To this end, it is possible that a small number of iterations of the power iteration method yields the relative ordering of the top hubs and authorities. Experiments have suggested that in practice, about five iterations of Equation (21.8) yield fairly good results. Moreover, because the link structure of the web graph is fairly sparse (the average web page links to about ten others), we do not perform these as matrix-vector products but rather as additive updates as in Equation (21.8).

Figure 21.6 shows the results of running HITS on the query japan elementary schools. The figure shows the top hubs and authorities; each row lists the `title` tag from the corresponding HTML page. Because the resulting string is not necessarily in Latin characters, the resulting print is (in many cases) a string of gibberish. Each of these corresponds to a web page that does not use Latin characters, in this case very likely pages in Japanese. There also appear to be pages in other non-English languages, which seems surprising given that the query string is in English. In fact, this result is emblematic of the functioning of HITS – following the assembly of the root set, the (English) query string is ignored. The base set is likely to contain

Hubs	Authorities
▪ schools	▪ The American School in Japan
▪ LINK Page-13	▪ The Link Page
▪ °ú–{¡ÌŠw⊏Z	▪ ‰°ª⊏è⊏s—§ª`å°c⊏¬Šw⊏Z*fz*⊏[*f*⊏*fy*⊏[*f*W
▪ ⊏a‰‚⊏¬Šw⊏Z*fz*⊏[*f*⊏*fy*⊏[*f*W	▪ Kids' Space
▪ 100 Schools Home Pages (English)	▪ ˆÀ⊏é⊏s—§ˆÀ⊏é⊏¼•°¬Šw⊏Z
▪ K-12 from Japan 10/...rnet and Education)	▪ «{⊏é«ª'ç'åŠw•⊏'®⊏¬Šw⊏Z
▪ http://www...iglobe.ne.jp/~IKESAN	▪ KEIMEI GAKUEN Home Page (Japanese)
▪ ¸I¸f¸j⊏¬Šw⊏Z¸U'N¸P'g•°Œê	▪ Shiranuma Home Page
▪ ⊏ÒŠ—¸'—¸—§⊏ÒŠ—°ŒE⊏¬Šw⊏Z	▪ fuzoku-es.fukui-u.ac.jp
▪ Koulutus ja oppilaitokset	▪ welcome to Miasa E&J school
▪ TOYODA HOMEPAGE	▪ ⊏_°'Þ⊏ìŒ§⊏E‰‚j•I⊏s—§'†⊏ì⊏¼¬Šw⊏Z¸Ì*fy*
▪ Education	▪ http://www...p/~m_maru/index.html
▪ Cay's Homepage(Japanese)	▪ fukui haruyama-es HomePage
▪ –y'ì⊏¬Šw⊏Z¸Ì*fz*⊏[*f*⊏*fy*⊏[*f*W	▪ Torisu primary school
▪ UNIVERSITY	▪ goo
▪ ‰‚J—ª°¬Šw⊏Z DRAGON97-TOP	▪ Yakumo Elementary,Hokkaido,Japan
▪ ⊏Å‰‚ª°¬Šw⊏Z¸T'N¸P'g*fz*⊏[*f*⊏*fy*⊏[*f*W	▪ FUZOKU Home Page
▪ ¶µ°é¼ÂÅ© ¥å¥Ë¥å¡¼ ¥å¥Ë¥å¡¼	▪ Kamishibun Elementary School...

Figure 21.6 A sample run of HITS on the query japan elementary schools.

pages in other languages, for instance if an English-language hub page links to the Japanese-language home pages of Japanese elementary schools. Because the subsequent computation of the top hubs and authorities is entirely link-based, some of these non-English pages will appear among the top hubs and authorities.

Exercise 21.19 If all the hub and authority scores are initialized to 1, what is the hub/authority score of a node after one iteration?

Exercise 21.20 How would you interpret the entries of the matrices AA^T and $A^T A$? What is the connection to the co-occurrence matrix CC^T in Chapter 18?

Exercise 21.21 What are the principal eigenvalues of AA^T and $A^T A$?

Exercise 21.22 For the web graph in Figure 21.7, compute PageRank, hub and authority scores for each of the three pages. Also give the relative ordering of the three nodes for each of these scores, indicating any ties.

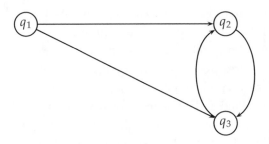

Figure 21.7 Web graph for Exercise 21.22.

PageRank: Assume that at each step of the PageRank random walk, we teleport to a random page with probability 0.1, with a uniform distribution over which particular page we teleport to.

Hubs/authorities: Normalize the hub (authority) scores so that the maximum hub (authority) score is 1.

Hint 1: Using symmetries to simplify and solving with linear equations might be easier than using iterative methods.

Hint 2: Provide the relative ordering (indicating any ties) of the three nodes for each of the three scoring measures.

21.4 References and further reading

Garfield (1955) is seminal in the science of citation analysis. This was built on by Pinski and Narin (1976) to develop a *journal influence weight*, whose definition is remarkably similar to that of the PageRank measure.

The use of anchor text as an aid to searching and ranking stems from the work of McBryan (1994). Extended anchor text was implicit in his work, with systematic experiments reported in Chakrabarti et al. (1998).

Kemeny and Snell (1976) is a classic text on Markov chains. The PageRank measure was developed in Brin and Page (1998) and in Page et al. (1998). A number of methods for the fast computation of PageRank values are surveyed in Berkhin (2005) and in Langville and Meyer (2006); the former also details how the PageRank eigenvector solution may be viewed as solving a linear system, leading to one way of solving Exercise 21.16. The effect of the teleport probability α has been studied by Baeza-Yates et al. (2005) and by Boldi et al. (2005). Topic-specific PageRank and variants were developed in Haveliwala (2002), Haveliwala (2003) and in Jeh and Widom (2003). Berkhin (2006a) develops an alternate view of topic-specific PageRank.

Ng et al. (2001b) suggests that the PageRank score assignment is more robust than HITS in the sense that scores are less sensitive to small changes in graph topology. However, it has also been noted that the teleport operation contributes significantly to PageRank's robustness in this sense. Both Page-Rank and HITS can be "spammed" by the orchestrated insertion of links into LINK FARMS the web graph; indeed, the Web is known to have such *link farms* that collude to increase the score assigned to certain pages by various link analysis algorithms.

The HITS algorithm is due to Kleinberg (1999). Chakrabarti et al. (1998) developed variants that weighted links in the iterative computation based on the presence of query terms in the pages being linked and compared these with results from several web search engines. Bharat and Henzinger (1998) further developed these and other heuristics, showing that certain combinations outperformed the basic HITS algorithm. Borodin et al. (2001) provides a systematic study of several variants of the HITS algorithm. Ng et al. (2001b) introduces a notion of *stability* for link analysis, arguing that small changes to link topology should not lead to significant changes in the ranked list of results for a query. Numerous other variants of HITS have been developed by a number of authors, the best know of which is perhaps SALSA (Lempel and Moran 2000).

Bibliography

We use the following abbreviated journal and conference names in the bibliography:

CACM Communications of the Association for Computing Machinery.
IP&M Information Processing and Management.
IR Information Retrieval.
JACM Journal of the Association for Computing Machinery.
JASIS Journal of the American Society for Information Science.
JASIST Journal of the American Society for Information Science and Technology.
JMLR Journal of Machine Learning Research.
TOIS ACM Transactions on Information Systems.
Proc. ACL Proceedings of the Annual Meeting of the Association for Computational Linguistics. Available from: http://www.aclweb.org/anthology-index/
Proc. CIKM Proceedings of the Conference on Information and Knowledge Management.
Proc. ECIR Proceedings of the European Conference on Information Retrieval.
Proc. ECML Proceedings of the European Conference on Machine Learning.
Proc. ICML Proceedings of the International Conference on Machine Learning.
Proc. IJCAI Proceedings of the International Joint Conference on Artificial Intelligence.
Proc. INEX Proceedings of the Initiative for the Evaluation of XML Retrieval.
Proc. KDD Proceedings of the ACM SIGKDD International Conference on Knowledge Discovery and Data Mining.
Proc. NIPS Proceedings of the Neural Information Processing Systems Conference.
Proc. PODS Proceedings of the ACM Conference on Principles of Database Systems.
Proc. SDAIR Proceedings of the Annual Symposium on Document Analysis and Information Retrieval.
Proc. SIGIR Proceedings of the Annual International ACM/SIGIR Conference on Research and Development in Information Retrieval. Available from: http://www.sigir.org/proceedings/Proc-Browse.html
Proc. SPIRE Proceedings of the Symposium on String Processing and Information Retrieval.
Proc. TREC Proceedings of the Text Retrieval Conference.
Proc. UAI Proceedings of the Conference on Uncertainty in Artificial Intelligence.
Proc. VLDB Proceedings of the Very Large Data Bases Conference.
Proc. WWW Proceedings of the International World Wide Web Conference.

Aberer, Karl. 2001. P-grid: A self-organizing access structure for P2P information systems. In *Proc. International Conference on Cooperative Information Systems*, pp. 179–194. Springer.

Aizerman, Mark A., Emmanuel M. Braverman, and Lev I. Rozonoér. 1964. Theoretical foundations of the potential function method in pattern recognition learning. *Automation and Remote Control* 25:821–837. [319]

Akaike, Hirotugu. 1974. A new look at the statistical model identification. *IEEE Transactions on automatic control* 19(6):716–723. [345]

Allan, James. 2005. HARD track overview in TREC 2005: High accuracy retrieval from documents. In *Proc. TREC.* [160]

Allan, James, Ron Papka, and Victor Lavrenko. 1998. On-line new event detection and tracking. In *Proc. SIGIR*, pp. 37–45. ACM Press. DOI: http://doi.acm.org/10.1145/290941.290954. [367]

Allwein, Erin L., Robert E. Schapire, and Yoram Singer. 2000. Reducing multiclass to binary: A unifying approach for margin classifiers. *JMLR* 1:113–141. URL: www.jmlr.org/papers/volume1/allwein00a/allwein00a.pdf. [292]

Alonso, Omar, Sandeepan Banerjee, and Mark Drake. 2006. GIO: A semantic web application using the information grid framework. In *Proc. WWW*, pp. 857–858. ACM Press. DOI: http://doi.acm.org/10.1145/1135777.1135913. [344]

Altingövde, Ismail Sengör, Engin Demir, Fazli Can, and Özgür Ulusoy. 2008. Incremental cluster-based retrieval using compressed cluster-skipping inverted files. *TOIS.* To appear. 372

Amer-Yahia, Sihem, Chavdar Botev, Jochen Dörre, and Jayavel Shanmugasundaram. 2006. XQuery full-text extensions explained. *IBM Systems Journal* 45(2):335–352. [200]

Amer-Yahia, Sihem, Pat Case, Thomas Rölleke, Jayavel Shanmugasundaram, and Gerhard Weikum. 2005. Report on the DB/IR panel at SIGMOD 2005. *SIGMOD Record* 34(4):71–74. DOI: http://doi.acm.org/10.1145/1107499.1107514. [200]

Amer-Yahia, Sihem, and Mounia Lalmas. 2006. XML search: Languages, INEX and scoring. *SIGMOD Record* 35(4):16–23. DOI: http://doi.acm.org/10.1145/1228268.1228271. [200]

Anagnostopoulos, Aris, Andrei Z. Broder, and Kunal Punera. 2006. Effective and efficient classification on a search-engine model. In *Proc. CIKM*, pp. 208–217. ACM Press. DOI: http://doi.acm.org/10.1145/1183614.1183648. [292]

Anderberg, Michael R. 1973. *Cluster analysis for applications.* Academic Press. [344]

Andoni, Alexandr, Mayur Datar, Nicole Immorlica, Piotr Indyk, and Vahab Mirrokni. 2006. Locality-sensitive hashing using stable distributions. In *Nearest Neighbor Methods in Learning and Vision: Theory and Practice.* MIT Press. [291]

Anh, Vo Ngoc, Owen de Kretser, and Alistair Moffat. 2001. Vector-space ranking with effective early termination. In *Proc. SIGIR*, pp. 35–42. ACM Press. [137]

Anh, Vo Ngoc, and Alistair Moffat. 2005. Inverted index compression using word-aligned binary codes. *IR* 8(1):151–166. DOI: http://dx.doi.org/10.1023/B:INRT.0000048490.99518.5c. [98]

Anh, Vo Ngoc, and Alistair Moffat. 2006a. Improved word-aligned binary compression for text indexing. *IEEE Transactions on Knowledge and Data Engineering* 18(6):857–861. [98]

Anh, Vo Ngoc, and Alistair Moffat. 2006b. Pruned query evaluation using precomputed impacts. In *Proc. SIGIR*, pp. 372–379. ACM Press. DOI: http://doi.acm.org/10.1145/1148170.1148235. [137]

Anh, Vo Ngoc, and Alistair Moffat. 2006c. Structured index organizations for high-throughput text querying. In *Proc. SPIRE*, pp. 304–315. Springer. [138]

Apté, Chidanand, Fred Damerau, and Sholom M. Weiss. 1994. Automated learning of decision rules for text categorization. *TOIS* 12(1):233–251. [265]

Arthur, David, and Sergei Vassilvitskii. 2006. How slow is the k-means method? In *Proc. Symposium on Computational Geometry*, pp. 144–153. [345]

Arvola, Paavo, Marko Junkkari, and Jaana Kekäläinen. 2005. Generalized contextualization method for XML information retrieval. In *Proc. CIKM*, pp. 20–27. ACM Press. [199]

Aslam, Javed A., and Emine Yilmaz. 2005. A geometric interpretation and analysis of R-precision. In *Proc. CIKM*, pp. 664–671. ACM Press. [160]

Ault, Thomas Galen, and Yiming Yang. 2002. Information filtering in TREC-9 and TDT-3: A comparative analysis. *IR* 5(2-3):159–187. [292]

Badue, Claudine Santos, Ricardo A. Baeza-Yates, Berthier Ribeiro-Neto, and Nivio Ziviani. 2001. Distributed query processing using partitioned inverted files. In *Proc. SPIRE*, pp. 10–20. [420]

Baeza-Yates, Ricardo, Paolo Boldi, and Carlos Castillo. 2005. The choice of a damping function for propagating importance in link-based ranking. Technical report, Dipartimento di Scienze dell'Informazione, Università degli Studi di Milano. [439]

Baeza-Yates, Ricardo, and Berthier Ribeiro-Neto. 1999. *Modern Information Retrieval*. Addison-Wesley. [xviii, 76, 97, 161, 368]

Bahle, Dirk, Hugh E. Williams, and Justin Zobel. 2002. Efficient phrase querying with an auxiliary index. In *Proc. SIGIR*, pp. 215–221. ACM Press. [44]

Baldridge, Jason, and Miles Osborne. 2004. Active learning and the total cost of annotation. In *Proc. EMNLP*, pp. 9–16. [320]

Ball, G. H. 1965. Data analysis in the social sciences: What about the details? In *Proc. Fall Joint Computer Conference*, pp. 533–560. Spartan Books. [345]

Banko, Michele, and Eric Brill. 2001. Scaling to very very large corpora for natural language disambiguation. In *Proc. ACL*. [309]

Bar-Ilan, Judit, and Tatyana Gutman. 2005. How do search engines respond to some non-English queries? *Journal of Information Science* 31(1):13–28. [43]

Bar-Yossef, Ziv, and Maxim Gurevich. 2006. Random sampling from a search engine's index. In *Proc. WWW*, pp. 367–376. ACM Press. DOI: http://doi.acm.org/10.1145/1135777.1135833. [404]

Barroso, Luiz André, Jeffrey Dean, and Urs Hölzle. 2003. Web search for a planet: The Google cluster architecture. *IEEE Micro* 23(2):22–28. http://dx.doi.org/10.1109/MM.2003.1196112. [420]

Bartell, Brian Theodore. 1994. *Optimizing ranking functions: A connectionist approach to adaptive information retrieval*. PhD thesis, University of California at San Diego, La Jolla, CA. [138]

Bartell, Brian T., Garrison W. Cottrell, and Richard K. Belew. 1998. Optimizing similarity using multi-query relevance feedback. *JASIS* 49(8):742–761. [138]

Barzilay, Regina, and Michael Elhadad. 1997. Using lexical chains for text summarization. In *Workshop on Intelligent Scalable Text Summarization*, pp. 10–17. [161]

Bast, Holger, and Debapriyo Majumdar. 2005. Why spectral retrieval works. In *Proc. SIGIR*, pp. 11–18. ACM Press. DOI: http://doi.acm.org/10.1145/1076034.1076040. [384]

Basu, Sugato, Arindam Banerjee, and Raymond J. Mooney. 2004. Active semi-supervision for pairwise constrained clustering. In *Proc. SIAM International Conference on Data Mining*, pp. 333–344. [344]

Beesley, Kenneth R. 1998. Language identifier: A computer program for automatic natural-language identification of on-line text. In *Languages at Crossroads: Proceedings of the Annual Conference of the American Translators Association*, pp. 47–54. [43]

Beesley, Kenneth R., and Lauri Karttunen. 2003. *Finite State Morphology*. CSLI Publications. [43]

Bennett, Paul N. 2000. *Assessing the calibration of naive Bayes' posterior estimates*. Technical Report CMU-CS-00-155, School of Computer Science, Carnegie Mellon University. [265]

Berger, Adam, and John Lafferty. 1999. Information retrieval as statistical translation. In *Proc. SIGIR*, pp. 222–229. ACM Press. [232]

Berkhin, Pavel. 2005. A survey on pagerank computing. *Internet Mathematics* 2(1):73–120. [439]

Berkhin, Pavel. 2006a. Bookmark-coloring algorithm for personalized pagerank computing. *Internet Mathematics* 3(1):41–62. [439]

Berkhin, Pavel. 2006b. A survey of clustering data mining techniques. In Jacob Kogan, Charles Nicholas, and Marc Teboulle (eds.), *Grouping Multidimensional Data: Recent Advances in Clustering*, pp. 25–71. Springer. [343]

Berners-Lee, Tim, Robert Cailliau, Jean-Francois Groff, and Bernd Pollermann. 1992. World-Wide Web: The information universe. *Electronic Networking: Research, Applications and Policy* 1(2):74–82. URL: citeseer.ist.psu.edu/article/berners-lee92worldwide.html. [404]

Berry, Michael, and Paul Young. 1995. Using latent semantic indexing for multilanguage information retrieval. *Computers and the Humanities* 29(6):413–429. [384]

Berry, Michael W., Susan T. Dumais, and Gavin W. O'Brien. 1995. Using linear algebra for intelligent information retrieval. *SIAM Review* 37(4):573–595. [383]

Betsi, Stamatina, Mounia Lalmas, Anastasios Tombros, and Theodora Tsikrika. 2006. User expectations from XML element retrieval. In *Proc. SIGIR*, pp. 611–612. ACM Press. [199]

Bharat, Krishna, and Andrei Broder. 1998. A technique for measuring the relative size and overlap of public web search engines. *Computer Networks and ISDN Systems* 30 (1-7):379–388. DOI: http://dx.doi.org/10.1016/S0169-7552(98)00127-5. [404]

Bharat, Krishna, Andrei Broder, Monika Henzinger, Puneet Kumar, and Suresh Venkatasubramanian. 1998. The connectivity server: Fast access to linkage information on the web. In *Proc. WWW*, pp. 469–477. [420]

Bharat, Krishna, Andrei Z. Broder, Jeffrey Dean, and Monika Rauch Henzinger. 2000. A comparison of techniques to find mirrored hosts on the WWW. *JASIS* 51(12): 1114–1122. URL: citeseer.ist.psu.edu/bharat99comparison.html. [404]

Bharat, Krishna, and Monika R. Henzinger. 1998. Improved algorithms for topic distillation in a hyperlinked environment. In *Proc. SIGIR*, pp. 104–111. ACM Press. URL: citeseer.ist.psu.edu/bharat98improved.html. [439]

Bishop, Christopher M. 2006. *Pattern Recognition and Machine Learning*. Springer. [292]

Blair, David C., and M. E. Maron. 1985. An evaluation of retrieval effectiveness for a full-text document-retrieval system. *CACM* 28(3):289–299. [177]

Blanco, Roi, and Alvaro Barreiro. 2006. TSP and cluster-based solutions to the reassignment of document identifiers. *IR* 9(4):499–517. [98]

Blanco, Roi, and Alvaro Barreiro. 2007. Boosting static pruning of inverted files. In *Proc. SIGIR*. ACM Press. [97]

Blandford, Dan, and Guy Blelloch. 2002. Index compression through document reordering. In *Proc. Data Compression Conference*, p. 342. IEEE Computer Society. [98]

Blei, David M., Andrew Y. Ng, and Michael I. Jordan. 2003. Latent Dirichlet allocation. *JMLR* 3:993–1022. [384]

Boldi, Paolo, Bruno Codenotti, Massimo Santini, and Sebastiano Vigna. 2002. Ubicrawler: A scalable fully distributed web crawler. In *Proc. Australian World Wide Web Conference*. URL: citeseer.ist.psu.edu/article/boldi03ubicrawler.html. [419]

Boldi, Paolo, Massimo Santini, and Sebastiano Vigna. 2005. PageRank as a function of the damping factor. In *Proc. WWW*. URL: citeseer.ist.psu.edu/boldi05pagerank.html. [439]

Boldi, Paolo, and Sebastiano Vigna. 2004a. Codes for the World-Wide Web. *Internet Mathematics* 2(4):405–427. [420]

Boldi, Paolo, and Sebastiano Vigna. 2004b. The WebGraph framework I: Compression techniques. In *Proc. WWW*, pp. 595–601. ACM Press. [420]

Boldi, Paolo, and Sebastiano Vigna. 2005. Compressed perfect embedded skip lists for quick inverted-index lookups. In *Proc. SPIRE*. Springer. [44]

Boley, Daniel. 1998. Principal direction divisive partitioning. *Data Mining and Knowledge Discovery* 2(4):325–344. DOI: http://dx.doi.org/10.1023/A:1009740529316. [368]

Borodin, Allan, Gareth O. Roberts, Jeffrey S. Rosenthal, and Panayiotis Tsaparas. 2001. Finding authorities and hubs from link structures on the World Wide Web. In *Proc. WWW*, pp. 415–429. [439]

Bourne, Charles P., and Donald F. Ford. 1961. A study of methods for systematically abbreviating English, words and names. *JACM* 8(4):538–552. DOI: http://doi. acm.org/10.1145/321088.321094. [60]

Bradley, Paul S., and Usama M. Fayyad. 1998. Refining initial points for k-means clustering. In *Proc. ICML*, pp. 91–99. [345]

Bradley, Paul S., Usama M. Fayyad, and Cory Reina. 1998. Scaling clustering algorithms to large databases. In *Proc. KDD*, pp. 9–15. [345]

Brill, Eric, and Robert C. Moore. 2000. An improved error model for noisy channel spelling correction. In *Proc. ACL*, pp. 286–293. [60]

Brin, Sergey, and Lawrence Page. 1998. The anatomy of a large-scale hypertextual web search engine. In *Proc. WWW*, pp. 107–117. [137, 419, 439]

Brisaboa, Nieves R., Antonio Fariña, Gonzalo Navarro, and José R. Paramá. 2007. Lightweight natural language text compression. *IR* 10(1):1–33. [99]

Broder, Andrei. 2002. A taxonomy of web search. *SIGIR Forum* 36(2):3–10. DOI: http://doi.acm.org/10.1145/792550.792552. [404]

Broder, Andrei, S. Ravi Kumar, Farzin Maghoul, Prabhakar Raghavan, Sridhar Rajagopalan, Raymie Stata, Andrew Tomkins, and Janet Wiener. 2000. Graph structure in the web. *Computer Networks* 33(1):309–320. [404]

Broder, Andrei Z., Steven C. Glassman, Mark S. Manasse, and Geoffrey Zweig. 1997. Syntactic clustering of the web. In *Proc. WWW*, pp. 391–404. [404]

Brown, Eric W. 1995. *Execution Performance Issues in Full-Text Information Retrieval*. PhD thesis, University of Massachusets, Amherst. [137]

Buckley, Chris, James Allan, and Gerard Salton. 1994a. Automatic routing and ad-hoc retrieval using SMART: TREC 2. In *Proc. TREC*, pp. 45–55.

Buckley, Chris, and Gerard Salton. 1995. Optimization of relevance feedback weights. In *Proc. SIGIR*, pp. 351–357. ACM Press. DOI: http://doi.acm.org/10.1145/ 215206.215383. [292]

Buckley, Chris, Gerard Salton, and James Allan. 1994b. The effect of adding relevance information in a relevance feedback environment. In *Proc. SIGIR*, pp. 292–300. ACM Press. [170, 177]

Buckley, Chris, Amit Singhal, and Mandar Mitra. 1995. New retrieval approaches using SMART: TREC 4. In *Proc. TREC*. [172]

Buckley, Chris, and Ellen M. Voorhees. 2000. Evaluating evaluation measure stability. In *Proc. SIGIR*, pp. 33–40. [160]

Burges, Chris, Tal Shaked, Erin Renshaw, Ari Lazier, Matt Deeds, Nicole Hamilton, and Greg Hullender. 2005. Learning to rank using gradient descent. In *Proc. ICML*. [320]

Burges, Christopher J. C. 1998. A tutorial on support vector machines for pattern recognition. *Data Mining and Knowledge Discovery* 2(2):121–167. [318]

Burner, Mike. 1997. Crawling towards eternity: Building an archive of the World Wide Web. *Web Techniques Magazine* 2(5). [419]

Burnham, Kenneth P., and David Anderson. 2002. *Model Selection and Multi-Model Inference*. Springer. [345]

Bush, Vannevar. 1945. As we may think. *The Atlantic Monthly*. URL: www.theatlantic. com/doc/194507/bush. [16, 404]

Büttcher, Stefan, and Charles L. A. Clarke. 2005a. Indexing time vs. query time: Tradeoffs in dynamic information retrieval systems. In *Proc. CIKM*, pp. 317–318. ACM Press. DOI: http://doi.acm.org/10.1145/1099554.1099645. [76]

Büttcher, Stefan, and Charles L. A. Clarke. 2005b. A security model for full-text file system search in multi-user environments. In *FAST*. URL: www.usenix.org/events/ fast05/tech/buettcher.html. [77]

Büttcher, Stefan, and Charles L. A. Clarke. 2006. A document-centric approach to static index pruning in text retrieval systems. In *Proc. CIKM*, pp. 182–189. ACM Press. DOI: http://doi.acm.org/10.1145/1183614.1183644. [97]

Büttcher, Stefan, Charles L. A. Clarke, and Brad Lushman. 2006. Hybrid index maintenance for growing text collections. In *Proc. SIGIR*, pp. 356–363. ACM Press. DOI: http://doi.acm.org/10.1145/1148170.1148233. [76]

Cacheda, Fidel, Victor Carneiro, Carmen Guerrero, and Ángel Viña. 2003. Optimization of restricted searches in web directories using hybrid data structures. In *Proc. ECIR*, pp. 436–451. [344]

Callan, Jamie. 2000. Distributed information retrieval. In W. Bruce Croft (ed.), *Advances in information retrieval*, pp. 127–150. Kluwer. [76]

Can, Fazli, Ismail Sengör Altingövde, and Engin Demir. 2004. Efficiency and effectiveness of query processing in cluster-based retrieval. *Information Systems* 29(8): 697–717. DOI: http://dx.doi.org/10.1016/S0306-4379(03)00062-0. [344]

Can, Fazli, and Esen A. Ozkarahan. 1990. Concepts and effectiveness of the cover-coefficient-based clustering methodology for text databases. *ACM Trans. Database Syst.* 15(4):483–517. [344]

Cao, Guihong, Jian-Yun Nie, and Jing Bai. 2005. Integrating word relationships into language models. In *Proc. SIGIR*, pp. 298–305. ACM Press.

Cao, Yunbo, Jun Xu, Tie-Yan Liu, Hang Li, Yalou Huang, and Hsiao-Wuen Hon. 2006. Adapting Ranking SVM to document retrieval. In *Proc. SIGIR*. ACM Press. [320]

Carbonell, Jaime, and Jade Goldstein. 1998. The use of MMR, diversity-based reranking for reordering documents and producing summaries. In *Proc. SIGIR*, pp. 335–336. ACM Press. DOI: http://doi.acm.org/10.1145/290941.291025. [154]

Carletta, Jean. 1996. Assessing agreement on classification tasks: The kappa statistic. *Computational Linguistics* 22:249–254. [160]

Carmel, David, Doron Cohen, Ronald Fagin, Eitan Farchi, Michael Herscovici, Yoelle S. Maarek, and Aya Soffer. 2001. Static index pruning for information retrieval systems. In *Proc. SIGIR*, pp. 43–50. ACM Press. DOI: http://doi.acm.org/10.1145/383952.383958. [97, 138]

Carmel, David, Yoelle S. Maarek, Matan Mandelbrod, Yosi Mass, and Aya Soffer. 2003. Searching XML documents via XML fragments. In *Proc. SIGIR*, pp. 151–158. ACM Press. DOI: http://doi.acm.org/10.1145/860435.860464. [199]

Caruana, Rich, and Alexandru Niculescu-Mizil. 2006. An empirical comparison of supervised learning algorithms. In *Proc. ICML*. [319]

Castro, R. M., M. J. Coates, and R. D. Nowak. 2004. Likelihood based hierarchical clustering. *IEEE Transactions in Signal Processing* 52(8):2308–2321. [368]

Cavnar, William B., and John M. Trenkle. 1994. N-gram-based text categorization. In *Proc. SDAIR*, pp. 161–175. [43]

Chakrabarti, Soumen. 2002. *Mining the Web: Analysis of Hypertext and Semi Structured Data*. Morgan Kaufman. [404]

Chakrabarti, Soumen, Byron Dom, David Gibson, Jon Kleinberg, Prabhakar Raghavan, and Sridhar Rajagopalan. 1998. Automatic resource list compilation by analyzing hyperlink structure and associated text. In *Proc. WWW*. URL: citeseer.ist.psu.edu/chakrabarti98automatic.html. [439]

Chapelle, Olivier, Bernhard Schölkopf, and Alexander Zien (eds.). 2006. *Semi-Supervised Learning*. MIT Press. [319, 459]

Chaudhuri, Surajit, Gautam Das, Vagelis Hristidis, and Gerhard Weikum. 2006. Probabilistic information retrieval approach for ranking of database query results. *ACM Trans. Database Syst.* 31(3):1134–1168. DOI: http://doi.acm.org/10.1145/1166074.1166085. [200]

Cheeseman, Peter, and John Stutz. 1996. Bayesian classification (AutoClass): Theory and results. In *Advances in Knowledge Discovery and Data Mining*, pp. 153–180. MIT Press. [345]

Chen, Hsin-Hsi, and Chuan-Jie Lin. 2000. A multilingual news summarizer. In *Proc. COLING*, pp. 159–165. [344]

Chen, Pai-Hsuen, Chih-Jen Lin, and Bernhard Schölkopf. 2005. A tutorial on v-support vector machines. *Applied Stochastic Models in Business and Industry* 21:111–136. [318]

Chiaramella, Yves, Philippe Mulhem, and Franck Fourel. 1996. A model for multimedia information retrieval. Technical Report 4-96, University of Glasgow. [198]

Chierichetti, Flavio, Alessandro Panconesi, Prabhakar Raghavan, Mauro Sozio, Alessandro Tiberi, and Eli Upfal. 2007. Finding near neighbors through cluster pruning. In *Proc. PODS*. [137]

Cho, Junghoo, and Hector Garcia-Molina. 2002. Parallel crawlers. In *Proc. WWW*, pp. 124–135. ACM Press. DOI: http://doi.acm.org/10.1145/511446.511464. [419]

Cho, Junghoo, Hector Garcia-Molina, and Lawrence Page. 1998. Efficient crawling through URL ordering. In *Proc. WWW*, pp. 161–172. [419]

Chu-Carroll, Jennifer, John Prager, Krzysztof Czuba, David Ferrucci, and Pablo Duboue. 2006. Semantic search via XML fragments: A high-precision approach to IR. In *Proc. SIGIR*, pp. 445–452. ACM Press. DOI: http://doi.acm.org/10.1145/1148170.1148247. [198]

Clarke, Charles L.A., Gordon V. Cormack, and Elizabeth A. Tudhope. 2000. Relevance ranking for one to three term queries. *IP&M* 36:291–311. [138]

Cleverdon, Cyril W. 1991. The significance of the Cranfield tests on index languages. In *Proc. SIGIR*, pp. 3–12. ACM Press. [159]

Coden, Anni R., Eric W. Brown, and Savitha Srinivasan (eds.). 2002. *Information Retrieval Techniques for Speech Applications*. Springer. [xviii]

Cohen, Paul R. 1995. *Empirical Methods for Artificial Intelligence*. MIT Press. [265]

Cohen, William W. 1998. Integration of heterogeneous databases without common domains using queries based on textual similarity. In *Proc. ACM SIGMOD International Conference on Management of Data*, pp. 201–212. ACM Press. [200]

Cohen, William W., Robert E. Schapire, and Yoram Singer. 1998. Learning to order things. In *Proc. NIPS*. The MIT Press. URL: citeseer.ist.psu.edu/article/cohen98learning.html. [138]

Cohen, William W., and Yoram Singer. 1999. Context-sensitive learning methods for text categorization. *TOIS* 17(2):141–173. [312]

Comtet, Louis. 1974. *Advanced Combinatorics*. Reidel. [327]

Cooper, William S., Aitao Chen, and Fredric C. Gey. 1994. Full text retrieval based on probabilistic equations with coefficients fitted by logistic regression. In *Proc. TREC*, pp. 57–66. [138]

Cormen, Thomas H., Charles Eric Leiserson, and Ronald L. Rivest. 1990. *Introduction to Algorithms*. MIT Press. [10, 72, 367]

Cover, Thomas M., and Peter E. Hart. 1967. Nearest neighbor pattern classification. *IEEE Transactions on Information Theory* 13(1):21–27. [292]

Cover, Thomas M., and Joy A. Thomas. 1991. *Elements of Information Theory*. Wiley. [98]

Crammer, Koby, and Yoram Singer. 2001. On the algorithmic implementation of multiclass kernel-based machines. *JMLR* 2:265–292. [319]

Creecy, Robert H., Brij M. Masand, Stephen J. Smith, and David L. Waltz. 1992. Trading MIPS and memory for knowledge engineering. *CACM* 35(8):48–64. DOI: http://doi.acm.org/10.1145/135226.135228. [291]

Crestani, Fabio, Mounia Lalmas, Cornelis J. Van Rijsbergen, and Iain Campbell. 1998. Is this document relevant?... probably: A survey of probabilistic models in information retrieval. *ACM Computing Surveys* 30(4):528–552. DOI: http://doi.acm.org/10.1145/299917.299920. [216]

Cristianini, Nello, and John Shawe-Taylor. 2000. *Introduction to Support Vector Machines and Other Kernel-based Learning Methods*. Cambridge. [319]

Croft, W. Bruce. 1978. A file organization for cluster-based retrieval. In *Proc. SIGIR*, pp. 65–82. ACM Press. [344]

Croft, W. Bruce, and David J. Harper. 1979. Using probabilistic models of document retrieval without relevance information. *Journal of Documentation* 35(4):285–295. [122, 209]

Croft, W. Bruce, and John Lafferty (eds.). 2003. *Language Modeling for Information Retrieval*. Springer. [232]

Crouch, Carolyn J. 1988. A cluster-based approach to thesaurus construction. In *Proc. SIGIR*, pp. 309–320. ACM Press. DOI: http://doi.acm.org/10.1145/62437.62467. [345]

Cucerzan, Silviu, and Eric Brill. 2004. Spelling correction as an iterative process that exploits the collective knowledge of web users. In *Proc. Empirical Methods in Natural Language Processing*. [60]

Cutting, Douglas R., David R. Karger, and Jan O. Pedersen. 1993. Constant interaction-time Scatter/Gather browsing of very large document collections. In *Proc. SIGIR*, pp. 126–134. ACM Press. [367]

Cutting, Douglas R., Jan O. Pedersen, David Karger, and John W. Tukey. 1992. Scatter/Gather: A cluster-based approach to browsing large document collections. In *Proc. SIGIR*, pp. 318–329. ACM Press. [344, 367]

Damerau, Fred J. 1964. A technique for computer detection and correction of spelling errors. *CACM* 7(3):171–176. DOI: http://doi.acm.org/10.1145/363958.363994. [59]

Davidson, Ian, and Ashwin Satyanarayana. 2003. Speeding up k-means clustering by bootstrap averaging. In *ICDM 2003 Workshop on Clustering Large Data Sets*. [345]

Day, William H., and Herbert Edelsbrunner. 1984. Efficient algorithms for agglomerative hierarchical clustering methods. *Journal of Classification* 1:1–24. [367]

de Moura, Edleno Silva, Gonzalo Navarro, Nivio Ziviani, and Ricardo Baeza-Yates. 2000. Fast and flexible word searching on compressed text. *TOIS* 18(2):113–139. DOI: http://doi.acm.org/10.1145/348751.348754. [99]

Dean, Jeffrey, and Sanjay Ghemawat. 2004. MapReduce: Simplified data processing on large clusters. In *Symposium on Operating System Design and Implementation*. [69, 76]

Deerwester, Scott, Susan T. Dumais, George W. Furnas, Thomas K. Landauer, and Richard Harshman. 1990. Indexing by latent semantic analysis. *JASIS* 41(6):391–407. [383]

del Bimbo, Alberto. 1999. *Visual Information Retrieval*. Morgan Kaufmann. [xviii]

Dempster, A.P., N.M. Laird, and D.B. Rubin. 1977. Maximum likelihood from incomplete data via the EM algorithm. *Journal of the Royal Statistical Society Series B* 39: 1–38. [345]

Dhillon, Inderjit S. 2001. Co-clustering documents and words using bipartite spectral graph partitioning. In *Proc. KDD*, pp. 269–274. [345, 368]

Dhillon, Inderjit S., and Dharmendra S. Modha. 2001. Concept decompositions for large sparse text data using clustering. *Machine Learning* 42(1/2):143–175. DOI: http://dx.doi.org/10.1023/A:1007612920971. [345]

Di Eugenio, Barbara, and Michael Glass. 2004. The kappa statistic: A second look. *Computational Linguistics* 30(1):95–101. DOI: http://dx.doi.org/10.1162/089120104773633402. [160]

Dietterich, Thomas G. 2002. Ensemble learning. In Michael A. Arbib (ed.), *The Handbook of Brain Theory and Neural Networks*. 2nd edition. MIT Press. [319]

Dietterich, Thomas G., and Ghulum Bakiri. 1995. Solving multiclass learning problems via error-correcting output codes. *Journal of Artificial Intelligence Research* 2: 263–286. [292]

Dom, Byron E. 2002. An information-theoretic external cluster-validity measure. In *Proc. UAI*. [344]

Domingos, Pedro. 2000. A unified bias-variance decomposition for zero-one and squared loss. In *Proc. National Conference on Artificial Intelligence and Proc. Confer-*

ence Innovative Applications of Artificial Intelligence, pp. 564–569. AAAI Press/The MIT Press. [292]

Domingos, Pedro, and Michael J. Pazzani. 1997. On the optimality of the simple Bayesian classifier under zero-one loss. *Machine Learning* 29(2-3):103–130. URL: citeseer.ist.psu.edu/domingos97optimality.html. [265]

Downie, J. Stephen. 2006. The Music Information Retrieval Evaluation eXchange (MIREX). *D-Lib Magazine* 12(12). [xviii]

Duda, Richard O., Peter E. Hart, and David G. Stork. 2000. *Pattern Classification*, 2nd edition. Wiley-Interscience. [264, 343]

Dumais, Susan, John Platt, David Heckerman, and Mehran Sahami. 1998. Inductive learning algorithms and representations for text categorization. In *Proc. CIKM*, pp. 148–155. ACM Press. DOI: http://doi.acm.org/10.1145/288627.288651. [261, 306, 319]

Dumais, Susan T. 1993. Latent semantic indexing (LSI) and TREC-2. In *Proc. TREC*, pp. 105–115. [382, 383]

Dumais, Susan T. 1995. Latent semantic indexing (LSI): TREC-3 report. In *Proc. TREC*, pp. 219–230. [382, 383]

Dumais, Susan T., and Hao Chen. 2000. Hierarchical classification of Web content. In *Proc. SIGIR*, pp. 256–263. ACM Press. [319]

Dunning, Ted. 1993. Accurate methods for the statistics of surprise and coincidence. *Computational Linguistics* 19(1):61–74. [265]

Dunning, Ted. 1994. *Statistical identification of language*. Technical Report 94-273, Computing Research Laboratory, New Mexico State University. [43]

Eckart, Carl, and Gale Young. 1936. The approximation of a matrix by another of lower rank. *Psychometrika* 1:211–218. [383]

El-Hamdouchi, Abdelmoula, and Peter Willett. 1986. Hierarchic document classification using Ward's clustering method. In *Proc. SIGIR*, pp. 149–156. ACM Press. DOI: http://doi.acm.org/10.1145/253168.253200. [367]

Elias, Peter. 1975. Universal code word sets and representations of the integers. *IEEE Transactions on Information Theory* 21(2):194–203. [98]

Eyheramendy, Susana, David Lewis, and David Madigan. 2003. On the Naive Bayes model for text categorization. In *Proc. International Workshop on Artificial Intelligence and Statistics*. Society for Artificial Intelligence and Statistics. [265]

Fallows, Deborah, 2004. The internet and daily life. URL: www.pewinternet.org/pdfs/PIP_Internet_and_Daily_Life.pdf. Pew/Internet and American Life Project. [xv]

Fayyad, Usama M., Cory Reina, and Paul S. Bradley. 1998. Initialization of iterative refinement clustering algorithms. In *Proc. KDD*, pp. 194–198. [345]

Fellbaum, Christiane D. 1998. *WordNet – An Electronic Lexical Database*. MIT Press. [177]

Ferragina, Paolo, and Rossano Venturini. 2007. Compressed permuterm indexes. In *Proc. SIGIR*. ACM Press. [59]

Forman, George. 2004. A pitfall and solution in multi-class feature selection for text classification. In *Proc. ICML*. [265]

Forman, George. 2006. Tackling concept drift by temporal inductive transfer. In *Proc. SIGIR*, pp. 252–259. ACM Press. DOI: http://doi.acm.org/10.1145/1148170.1148216. [265]

Forman, George, and Ira Cohen. 2004. Learning from little: Comparison of classifiers given little training. In *PKDD*, pp. 161–172. [308]

Fowlkes, Edward B., and Colin L. Mallows. 1983. A method for comparing two hierarchical clusterings. *Journal of the American Statistical Association* 78(383):553–569. URL: www.jstor.org/view/01621459/di985957/98p0926l/0. [368]

Fox, Edward A., and Whay C. Lee. 1991. *FAST-INV: A fast algorithm for building large inverted files*. Technical report, Virginia Polytechnic Institute & State University, Blacksburg, VA, USA. [76]

Fraenkel, Aviezri S., and Shmuel T. Klein. 1985. Novel compression of sparse bit-strings – Preliminary report. In *Combinatorial Algorithms on Words, NATO ASI Series Vol F12*, pp. 169–183. Springer. [98]

Frakes, William B., and Ricardo Baeza-Yates (eds.). 1992. *Information Retrieval: Data Structures and Algorithms*. Prentice-Hall. [451, 461]

Fraley, Chris, and Adrian E. Raftery. 1998. How many clusters? Which clustering method? Answers via model-based cluster analysis. *Computer Journal* 41(8):578–588. [345]

Friedl, Jeffrey E. F. 2006. *Mastering Regular Expressions*, 3rd edition. O'Reilly. [17]

Friedman, Jerome H. 1997. On bias, variance, 0/1–loss, and the curse-of-dimensionality. *Data Mining and Knowledge Discovery* 1(1):55–77. [265, 292]

Friedman, Nir, and Moises Goldszmidt. 1996. Building classifiers using bayesian networks. In *Proc. National Conference on Artificial Intelligence*, pp. 1277–1284. [213]

Fuhr, Norbert. 1989. Optimum polynomial retrieval functions based on the probability ranking principle. *TOIS* 7(3):183–204. [138]

Fuhr, Norbert. 1992. Probabilistic models in information retrieval. *Computer Journal* 35 (3):243–255. [216, 320]

Fuhr, Norbert, Norbert Gövert, Gabriella Kazai, and Mounia Lalmas (eds.). 2003a. *INitiative for the Evaluation of XML Retrieval (INEX). Proc. First INEX Workshop*. ERCIM. [198]

Fuhr, Norbert, and Kai Großjohann. 2004. XIRQL: An XML query language based on information retrieval concepts. *TOIS* 22(2):313–356. URL: http://doi.acm.org/10.1145/984321.984326. [198]

Fuhr, Norbert, and Mounia Lalmas. 2007. Advances in XML retrieval: The INEX initiative. In *Proc. International Workshop on Research Issues in Digital Libraries*. [198]

Fuhr, Norbert, Mounia Lalmas, Saadia Malik, and Gabriella Kazai (eds.). 2006. *Advances in XML Information Retrieval and Evaluation, 4th International Workshop of the Initiative for the Evaluation of XML Retrieval, INEX 2005*. Springer. [198]

Fuhr, Norbert, Mounia Lalmas, Saadia Malik, and Zoltán Szlávik (eds.). 2005. *Advances in XML Information Retrieval, Third International Workshop of the Initiative for the Evaluation of XML Retrieval, INEX 2004*. Springer. [198, 460, 465]

Fuhr, Norbert, Mounia Lalmas, and Andrew Trotman (eds.). 2007. *Comparative Evaluation of XML Information Retrieval Systems, 5th International Workshop of the Initiative for the Evaluation of XML Retrieval, INEX 2006*. Springer. [198, 456, 458]

Fuhr, Norbert, Saadia Malik, and Mounia Lalmas (eds.). 2003b. *INEX 2003 Workshop Proceedings*. URL: http://inex.is.informatik.uni-duisburg.de:2003/proceedings.pdf. [198, 451, 458]

Fuhr, Norbert, and Ulrich Pfeifer. 1994. Probabilistic information retrieval as a combination of abstraction, inductive learning, and probabilistic assumptions. *TOIS* 12 (1):92–115. DOI: http://doi.acm.org/10.1145/174608.174612. [138]

Fuhr, Norbert, and Thomas Rölleke. 1997. A probabilistic relational algebra for the integration of information retrieval and database systems. *TOIS* 15(1):32–66. DOI: http://doi.acm.org/10.1145/239041.239045. [200]

Gaertner, Thomas, John W. Lloyd, and Peter A. Flach. 2002. Kernels for structured data. In *International Conference on Inductive Logic Programming*, pp. 66–83. [319]

Gao, Jianfeng, Mu Li, Chang-Ning Huang, and Andi Wu. 2005. Chinese word segmentation and named entity recognition: A pragmatic approach. *Computational Linguistics* 31(4):531–574. [43]

Gao, Jianfeng, Jian-Yun Nie, Guangyuan Wu, and Guihong Cao. 2004. Dependence language model for information retrieval. In *Proc. SIGIR*, pp. 170–177. ACM Press.

Garcia, Steven, Hugh E. Williams, and Adam Cannane. 2004. Access-ordered indexes. In *Proc. Australasian conference on Computer science*, pp. 7–14. [137]

Garcia-Molina, Hector, Jennifer Widom, and Jeffrey D. Ullman. 1999. *Database System Implementation*. Prentice-Hall. [77]

Garfield, Eugene. 1955. Citation indexes to science: A new dimension in documentation through association of ideas. *Science* 122:108–111. [439]

Garfield, Eugene. 1976. The permuterm subject index: An autobiographic review. *JASIS* 27(5-6):288–291. [59]

Geman, Stuart, Elie Bienenstock, and René Doursat. 1992. Neural networks and the bias/variance dilemma. *Neural Computation* 4(1):1–58. [292]

Geng, Xiubo, Tie-Yan Liu, Tao Qin, and Hang Li. 2007. Feature selection for ranking. In *Proc. SIGIR*, pp. 407–414. ACM Press. [320]

Gerrand, Peter. 2007. Estimating linguistic diversity on the internet: A taxonomy to avoid pitfalls and paradoxes. *Journal of Computer-Mediated Communication* 12(4). URL: http://jcmc.indiana.edu/vol12/issue4/gerrand.html. article 8. [29]

Gey, Fredric C. 1994. Inferring probability of relevance using the method of logistic regression. In *Proc. SIGIR*, pp. 222–231. ACM Press. [320]

Ghamrawi, Nadia, and Andrew McCallum. 2005. Collective multi-label classification. In *Proc. CIKM*, pp. 195–200. ACM Press. DOI: http://doi.acm.org/10.1145/1099554.1099591. [292]

Glover, Eric, David M. Pennock, Steve Lawrence, and Robert Krovetz. 2002a. Inferring hierarchical descriptions. In *Proc. CIKM*, pp. 507–514. ACM Press. DOI: http://doi.acm.org/10.1145/584792.584876. [368]

Glover, Eric J., Kostas Tsioutsiouliklis, Steve Lawrence, David M. Pennock, and Gary W. Flake. 2002b. Using web structure for classifying and describing web pages. In *Proc. WWW*, pp. 562–569. ACM Press. DOI: http://doi.acm.org/10.1145/511446.511520. [367]

Gövert, Norbert, and Gabriella Kazai. 2003. Overview of the INitiative for the Evaluation of XML retrieval (INEX) 2002. In Fuhr et al. (2003b), pp. 1–17. URL: http://inex.is.informatik.uni-duisburg.de:2003/proceedings.pdf. [198]

Grabs, Torsten, and Hans-Jörg Schek. 2002. Generating vector spaces on-the-fly for flexible XML retrieval. In *XML and Information Retrieval Workshop at SIGIR 2002*. [199]

Greiff, Warren R. 1998. A theory of term weighting based on exploratory data analysis. In *Proc. SIGIR*, pp. 11–19. ACM Press. [209]

Grinstead, Charles M., and J. Laurie Snell. 1997. *Introduction to Probability*, 2nd edition. American Mathematical Society. URL: www.dartmouth.edu/~chance/teaching_aids/books_articles/probability_book/amsbook.mac.pdf. [216]

Grossman, David A., and Ophir Frieder. 2004. *Information Retrieval: Algorithms and Heuristics*, 2nd edition. Springer. [xviii, 76, 200]

Gusfield, Dan. 1997. *Algorithms on Strings, Trees and Sequences: Computer Science and Computational Biology*. Cambridge University Press. [60]

Hamerly, Greg, and Charles Elkan. 2003. Learning the k in k-means. In *NIPS*. URL: http://books.nips.cc/papers/files/nips16/NIPS2003_AA36.pdf. [345]

Han, Eui-Hong, and George Karypis. 2000. Centroid-based document classification: Analysis and experimental results. In *PKDD*, pp. 424–431. [291]

Hand, David J. 2006. Classifier technology and the illusion of progress. *Statistical Science* 21:1–14. [265]

Hand, David J., and Keming Yu. 2001. Idiot's Bayes: Not so stupid after all. *International Statistical Review* 69(3):385–398. [265]

Harman, Donna. 1991. How effective is suffixing? *JASIS* 42:7–15. [43]

Harman, Donna. 1992. Relevance feedback revisited. In *Proc. SIGIR*, pp. 1–10. ACM Press. [170, 177]

Harman, Donna, Ricardo Baeza-Yates, Edward Fox, and W. Lee. 1992. Inverted files. In Frakes and Baeza-Yates (1992), pp. 28–43. [76]

Harman, Donna, and Gerald Candela. 1990. Retrieving records from a gigabyte of text on a minicomputer using statistical ranking. *JASIS* 41(8):581–589. [76]

Harold, Elliotte Rusty, and Scott W. Means. 2004. *XML in a Nutshell*, 3rd edition. O'Reilly. [198]

Harter, Stephen P. 1998. Variations in relevance assessments and the measurement of retrieval effectiveness. *JASIS* 47:37–49. [160]

Hartigan, J. A., and M. A. Wong. 1979. A K-means clustering algorithm. *Applied Statistics* 28:100–108. [345]

Hastie, Trevor, Robert Tibshirani, and Jerome H. Friedman. 2001. *The Elements of Statistical Learning: Data Mining, Inference, and Prediction*. Springer. [264, 265, 291, 292, 319]

Hatzivassiloglou, Vasileios, Luis Gravano, and Ankineedu Maganti. 2000. An investigation of linguistic features and clustering algorithms for topical document clustering. In *Proc. SIGIR*, pp. 224–231. ACM Press. DOI: http://doi.acm.org/10.1145/345508.345582. [344]

Haveliwala, Taher. 2003. Topic-sensitive PageRank: A context-sensitive ranking algorithm for web search. *IEEE Transactions on Knowledge and Data Engineering* 15(4): 784–796. URL: citeseer.ist.psu.edu/article/haveliwala03topicsensitive.html. [439]

Haveliwala, Taher H. 2002. Topic-sensitive PageRank. In *Proc. WWW*. URL: citeseer.ist.psu.edu/haveliwala02topicsensitive.html. [439]

Hayes, Philip J., and Steven P. Weinstein. 1990. CONSTRUE/TIS: A system for content-based indexing of a database of news stories. In *Proc. Conference on Innovative Applications of Artificial Intelligence*, pp. 49–66. [308]

Heaps, Harold S. 1978. *Information Retrieval: Computational and Theoretical Aspects*. Academic Press. [97]

Hearst, Marti A. 1997. TextTiling: Segmenting text into multi-paragraph subtopic passages. *Computational Linguistics* 23(1):33–64. [199]

Hearst, Marti A. 2006. Clustering versus faceted categories for information exploration. *CACM* 49(4):59–61. DOI: http://doi.acm.org/10.1145/1121949.1121983. [344]

Hearst, Marti A., and Jan O. Pedersen. 1996. Reexamining the cluster hypothesis. In *Proc. SIGIR*, pp. 76–84. ACM Press. [344]

Hearst, Marti A., and Christian Plaunt. 1993. Subtopic structuring for full-length document access. In *Proc. SIGIR*, pp. 59–68. ACM Press. DOI: http://doi.acm.org/10.1145/160688.160695. [199]

Heinz, Steffen, and Justin Zobel. 2003. Efficient single-pass index construction for text databases. *JASIST* 54(8):713–729. DOI: http://dx.doi.org/10.1002/asi.10268. [76]

Heinz, Steffen, Justin Zobel, and Hugh E. Williams. 2002. Burst tries: A fast, efficient data structure for string keys. *TOIS* 20(2):192–223. DOI: http://doi.acm.org/10.1145/506309.506312. [77]

Henzinger, Monika R., Allan Heydon, Michael Mitzenmacher, and Marc Najork. 2000. On near-uniform URL sampling. In *Proc. WWW*, pp. 295–308. North-Holland. DOI: http://dx.doi.org/10.1016/S1389-1286(00)00055-4. [404]

Herbrich, Ralf, Thore Graepel, and Klaus Obermayer. 2000. Large margin rank boundaries for ordinal regression. In *Advances in Large Margin Classifiers*, pp. 115–132. MIT Press. [320]

Hersh, William, Chris Buckley, T. J. Leone, and David Hickam. 1994. OHSUMED: An interactive retrieval evaluation and new large test collection for research. In *Proc. SIGIR*, pp. 192–201. ACM Press. [160]

Hersh, William R., Andrew Turpin, Susan Price, Benjamin Chan, Dale Kraemer, Lynetta Sacherek, and Daniel Olson. 2000a. Do batch and user evaluation give the same results? In *Proc. SIGIR*, pp. 17–24.

Hersh, William R., Andrew Turpin, Susan Price, Dale Kraemer, Daniel Olson, Benjamin Chan, and Lynetta Sacherek. 2001. Challenging conventional assumptions of automated information retrieval with real users: Boolean searching and batch retrieval evaluations. *IP&M* 37(3):383–402.

Hersh, William R., Andrew Turpin, Lynetta Sacherek, Daniel Olson, Susan Price, Benjamin Chan, and Dale Kraemer. 2000b. Further analysis of whether batch and user evaluations give the same results with a question-answering task. In *Proc. TREC*.

Hiemstra, Djoerd. 1998. A linguistically motivated probabilistic model of information retrieval. In *Proc. ECDL*, pp. 569–584.

Hiemstra, Djoerd. 2000. A probabilistic justification for using tf.idf term weighting in information retrieval. *International Journal on Digital Libraries* 3(2):131–139.

Hiemstra, Djoerd, and Wessel Kraaij. 2005. A language-modeling approach to TREC. In Voorhees and Harman (2005), pp. 373–395. [232, 233]

Hirai, Jun, Sriram Raghavan, Hector Garcia-Molina, and Andreas Paepcke. 2000. WebBase: A repository of web pages. In *Proc. WWW*, pp. 277–293. [419]

Hofmann, Thomas. 1999a. Probabilistic Latent Semantic Indexing. In *UAI*. URL: citeseer.ist.psu.edu/hofmann99probabilistic.html.

Hofmann, Thomas. 1999b. Probabilistic Latent Semantic Indexing. In *Proc. SIGIR*, pp. 50–57. ACM Press. URL: citeseer.ist.psu.edu/article/hofmann99probabilistic.html.

Hollink, Vera, Jaap Kamps, Christof Monz, and Maarten de Rijke. 2004. Monolingual document retrieval for European languages. *IR* 7(1):33–52. [43]

Hopcroft, John E., Rajeev Motwani, and Jeffrey D. Ullman. 2000. *Introduction to Automata Theory, Languages, and Computation*, 2nd edition. Addison Wesley. [17]

Huang, Yifen, and Tom M. Mitchell. 2006. Text clustering with extended user feedback. In *Proc. SIGIR*, pp. 413–420. ACM Press. DOI: http://doi.acm.org/10.1145/1148170.1148242. [345]

Hubert, Lawrence, and Phipps Arabie. 1985. Comparing partitions. *Journal of Classification* 2:193–218. [344]

Hughes, Baden, Timothy Baldwin, Steven Bird, Jeremy Nicholson, and Andrew MacKinlay. 2006. Reconsidering language identification for written language resources. In *International Conference on Language Resources and Evaluation*, pp. 485–488. [43]

Hull, David. 1993. Using statistical testing in the evaluation of retrieval performance. In *Proc. SIGIR*, pp. 329–338. ACM Press. [159]

Hull, David. 1996. Stemming algorithms – A case study for detailed evaluation. *JASIS* 47(1):70–84. [43]

Ide, E. 1971. New experiments in relevance feedback. In Salton (1971b), pp. 337–354. [177]

Indyk, Piotr. 2004. Nearest neighbors in high-dimensional spaces. In J. E. Goodman and J. O'Rourke (eds.), *Handbook of Discrete and Computational Geometry*, 2nd edition. pp. 877–892. Chapman and Hall/CRC Press. [291]

Ingwersen, Peter, and Kalervo Järvelin. 2005. *The Turn: Integration of Information Seeking and Retrieval in Context*. Springer. [xviii]

Ittner, David J., David D. Lewis, and David D. Ahn. 1995. Text categorization of low quality images. In *Proc. Annual Symposium on Document Analysis and Information Retrieval*, pp. 301–315. [291]

Iwayama, Makoto, and Takenobu Tokunaga. 1995. Cluster-based text categorization: A comparison of category search strategies. In *Proc. SIGIR*, pp. 273–280. ACM Press. [291]

Jackson, Peter, and Isabelle Moulinier. 2002. *Natural Language Processing for Online Applications: Text Retrieval, Extraction and Categorization*. John Benjamins. [307]

Jacobs, Paul S., and Lisa F. Rau. 1990. SCISOR: Extracting information from on-line news. *CACM* 33:88–97. [308]

Jain, Anil, M. Narasimha Murty, and Patrick Flynn. 1999. Data clustering: A review. *ACM Computing Surveys* 31(3):264–323. [367]

Jain, Anil K., and Richard C. Dubes. 1988. *Algorithms for Clustering Data*. Prentice-Hall. [367]

Jardine, N., and C. J. van Rijsbergen. 1971. The use of hierarchic clustering in information retrieval. *Information Storage and Retrieval* 7:217–240. [344]

Järvelin, Kalervo, and Jaana Kekäläinen. 2002. Cumulated gain-based evaluation of IR techniques. *TOIS* 20(4):422–446. [160]

Jeh, Glen, and Jennifer Widom. 2003. Scaling personalized web search. In *Proc. WWW*, pp. 271–279. ACM Press. [439]

Jensen, Finn V., and Finn B. Jensen. 2001. *Bayesian Networks and Decision Graphs*. Springer. [215]

Jeong, Byeong-Soo, and Edward Omiecinski. 1995. Inverted file partitioning schemes in multiple disk systems. *IEEE Transactions on Parallel and Distributed Systems* 6(2): 142–153. [419]

Ji, Xiang, and Wei Xu. 2006. Document clustering with prior knowledge. In *Proc. SIGIR*, pp. 405–412. ACM Press. DOI: http://doi.acm.org/10.1145/1148170.1148241. [345]

Jing, Hongyan. 2000. Sentence reduction for automatic text summarization. In *Proc. Conference on applied natural language processing*, pp. 310–315. [161]

Joachims, Thorsten. 1997. A probabilistic analysis of the Rocchio algorithm with tfidf for text categorization. In *Proc. ICML*, pp. 143–151. Morgan Kaufmann. [291]

Joachims, Thorsten. 1998. Text categorization with support vector machines: Learning with many relevant features. In *Proc. ECML*, pp. 137–142. Springer. [261, 306, 307]

Joachims, Thorsten. 1999. Making large-scale SVM learning practical. In B. Schölkopf, C. Burges, and A. Smola (eds.), *Advances in Kernel Methods–Support Vector Learning*. MIT Press. [319]

Joachims, Thorsten. 2002a. *Learning to Classify Text Using Support Vector Machines*. Kluwer. [306, 307, 319]

Joachims, Thorsten. 2002b. Optimizing search engines using clickthrough data. In *Proc. KDD*, pp. 133–142. [161, 170, 320]

Joachims, Thorsten. 2006a. Training linear SVMs in linear time. In *Proc. KDD*, pp. 217–226. ACM Press. DOI: http://doi.acm.org/10.1145/1150402.1150429. [265, 302, 319]

Joachims, Thorsten. 2006b. Transductive support vector machines. In Chapelle et al. (2006), pp. 105–118. [320]

Joachims, Thorsten, Laura Granka, Bing Pan, Helene Hembrooke, and Geri Gay. 2005. Accurately interpreting clickthrough data as implicit feedback. In *Proc. SIGIR*, pp. 154–161. ACM Press. [161, 170]

Johnson, David, Vishv Malhotra, and Peter Vamplew. 2006. More effective web search using bigrams and trigrams. *Webology* 3(4). URL: www.webology.ir/2006/v3n4/a35.html. [44]

Jurafsky, Dan, and James H. Martin. 2008. *Speech and Language Processing: An Introduction to Natural Language Processing, Computational Linguistics and Speech Recognition*, 2nd edition. Prentice-Hall. [xviii]

Käki, Mika. 2005. Findex: Search result categories help users when document ranking fails. In *Proc. SIGCHI Conference on Human Factors in Computing Systems*, pp. 131–140. ACM Press. DOI: http://doi.acm.org/10.1145/1054972.1054991. [344, 368]

Kammenhuber, Nils, Julia Luxenburger, Anja Feldmann, and Gerhard Weikum. 2006. Web search clickstreams. In *ACM SIGCOMM on Internet Measurement*, pp. 245–250. ACM Press. [44]

Kamps, Jaap, Maarten de Rijke, and Börkur Sigurbjörnsson. 2004. Length normalization in XML retrieval. In *Proc. SIGIR*, pp. 80–87. ACM Press. DOI: http://doi.acm.org/10.1145/1008992.1009009. [199]

Kamps, Jaap, Maarten Marx, Maarten de Rijke, and Börkur Sigurbjörnsson. 2006. Articulating information needs in XML query languages. *TOIS* 24(4):407–436. DOI: http://doi.acm.org/10.1145/1185877.1185879. [198]

Kamvar, Sepandar D., Dan Klein, and Christopher D. Manning. 2002. Interpreting and extending classical agglomerative clustering algorithms using a model-based approach. In *Proc. ICML*, pp. 283–290. Morgan Kaufmann. [368]

Kannan, Ravi, Santosh Vempala, and Adrian Vetta. 2000. On clusterings – Good, bad and spectral. In *Proc. Annual Symposium on Foundations of Computer Science*, p. 367. IEEE Computer Society. [368]

Kaszkiel, Marcin, and Justin Zobel. 1997. Passage retrieval revisited. In *Proc. SIGIR*, pp. 178–185. ACM Press. DOI: http://doi.acm.org/10.1145/258525.258561. [199]

Kaufman, Leonard, and Peter J. Rousseeuw. 1990. *Finding groups in data*. Wiley. [345]

Kazai, Gabriella, and Mounia Lalmas. 2006. eXtended cumulated gain measures for the evaluation of content-oriented XML retrieval. *TOIS* 24(4):503–542. DOI: http://doi.acm.org/10.1145/1185883. [199]

Kekäläinen, Jaana. 2005. Binary and graded relevance in IR evaluations – Comparison of the effects on ranking of IR systems. *IP&M* 41:1019–1033. [160]

Kekäläinen, Jaana, and Kalervo Järvelin. 2002. Using graded relevance assessments in IR evaluation. *JASIST* 53(13):1120–1129. [160]

Kemeny, John G., and J. Laurie Snell. 1976. *Finite Markov Chains*. Springer. [439]

Kent, Allen, Madeline M. Berry, Fred U. Luehrs, Jr., and J. W. Perry. 1955. Machine literature searching VIII. Operational criteria for designing information retrieval systems. *American Documentation* 6(2):93–101. [159]

Kernighan, Mark D., Kenneth W. Church, and William A. Gale. 1990. A spelling correction program based on a noisy channel model. In *Proc. ACL*, pp. 205–210. [60]

King, Benjamin. 1967. Step-wise clustering procedures. *Journal of the American Statistical Association* 69:86–101. [367]

Kishida, Kazuaki, Kuang Hua Chen, Sukhoon Lee, Kazuko Kuriyama, Noriko Kando, Hsin-Hsi Chen, and Sung Hyon Myaeng. 2005. Overview of CLIR task at the fifth NTCIR workshop. In *Proc. NTCIR Workshop Meeting on Evaluation of Information Access Technologies: Information Retrieval, Question Answering and Cross-Lingual Information Access*. National Institute of Informatics. [43]

Klein, Dan, and Christopher D. Manning. 2002. Conditional structure versus conditional estimation in NLP models. In *Proc. Empirical Methods in Natural Language Processing*, pp. 9–16. [308]

Kleinberg, Jon M. 1997. Two algorithms for nearest-neighbor search in high dimensions. In *Proc. Annual ACM Symposium on Theory of Computing*, pp. 599–608. ACM Press. DOI: http://doi.acm.org/10.1145/258533.258653. [291]

Kleinberg, Jon M. 1999. Authoritative sources in a hyperlinked environment. *JACM* 46(5):604–632. URL: citeseer.ist.psu.edu/article/kleinberg98authoritative.html. [439]

Kleinberg, Jon M. 2002. An impossibility theorem for clustering. In *Proc. NIPS*. [345]

Knuth, Donald E. 1997. *The Art of Computer Programming, Volume 3: Sorting and Searching*, 3rd edition. Addison-Wesley. [59]

Ko, Youngjoong, Jinwoo Park, and Jungyun Seo. 2004. Improving text categorization using the importance of sentences. *IP&M* 40(1):65–79. [313]

Koenemann, Jürgen, and Nicholas J. Belkin. 1996. A case for interaction: A study of interactive information retrieval behavior and effectiveness. In *Proc. SIGCHI Conference on Human Factors in Computing Systems*, pp. 205–212. ACM Press. DOI: http://doi.acm.org/10.1145/238386.238487. [177]

Kołcz, Aleksander, Vidya Prabakarmurthi, and Jugal Kalita. 2000. Summarization as feature selection for text categorization. In *Proc. CIKM*, pp. 365–370. ACM Press. [313]

Kołcz, Aleksander, and Wen-Tau Yih. 2007. Raising the baseline for high-precision text classifiers. In *Proc. KDD*. [265]

Koller, Daphne, and Mehran Sahami. 1997. Hierarchically classifying documents using very few words. In *Proc. ICML*, pp. 170–178. [319]

Konheim, Alan G. 1981. *Cryptography: A Primer*. John Wiley & Sons. [43]

Korfhage, Robert R. 1997. *Information Storage and Retrieval*. Wiley. [161]

Kozlov, M. K., S. P. Tarasov, and L. G. Khachiyan. 1979. Polynomial solvability of convex quadratic programming. *Soviet Mathematics Doklady* 20:1108–1111. Translated from original in *Doklady Akademiia Nauk SSR*, 228 (1979). [302]

Kraaij, Wessel, and Martijn Spitters. 2003. Language models for topic tracking. In W. B. Croft and J. Lafferty (eds.), *Language Modeling for Information Retrieval*, pp. 95–124. Kluwer. [231]

Kraaij, Wessel, Thijs Westerveld, and Djoerd Hiemstra. 2002. The importance of prior probabilities for entry page search. In *Proc. SIGIR*, pp. 27–34. ACM Press. [233]

Krippendorff, Klaus. 2003. *Content Analysis: An Introduction to its Methodology*. Sage. [160]

Krovetz, Bob. 1995. *Word sense disambiguation for large text databases*. PhD thesis, University of Massachusetts Amherst. [43]

Kukich, Karen. 1992. Techniques for automatically correcting words in text. *ACM Computing Surveys* 24(4):377–439. DOI: http://doi.acm.org/10.1145/146370.146380. [59]

Kumar, Ravi, Prabhakar Raghavan, Sridhar Rajagopalan, and Andrew Tomkins. 1999. Trawling the Web for emerging cyber-communities. *Computer Networks* 31(11–16): 1481–1493. URL: citeseer.ist.psu.edu/kumar99trawling.html. [404]

Kumar, S. Ravi, Prabhakar Raghavan, Sridhar Rajagopalan, Dandapani Sivakumar, Andrew Tomkins, and Eli Upfal. 2000. The Web as a graph. In *Proc. PODS*, pp. 1–10. ACM Press. URL: citeseer.ist.psu.edu/article/kumar00web.html. [404]

Kupiec, Julian, Jan Pedersen, and Francine Chen. 1995. A trainable document summarizer. In *Proc. SIGIR*, pp. 68–73. ACM Press. [160]

Kurland, Oren, and Lillian Lee. 2004. Corpus structure, language models, and ad hoc information retrieval. In *Proc. SIGIR*, pp. 194–201. ACM Press. DOI: http://doi.acm.org/10.1145/1008992.1009027. [344]

Lafferty, John, and Chengxiang Zhai. 2001. Document language models, query models, and risk minimization for information retrieval. In *Proc. SIGIR*, pp. 111–119. ACM Press. [231]

Lafferty, John, and Chengxiang Zhai. 2003. Probabilistic relevance models based on document and query generation. In W. Bruce Croft and John Lafferty (eds.), *Language Modeling and Information Retrieval*. Kluwer. [233]

Lalmas, Mounia, Gabriella Kazai, Jaap Kamps, Jovan Pehcevski, Benjamin Piwowarski, and Stephen E. Robertson. 2007. INEX 2006 evaluation measures. In Fuhr et al. (2007), pp. 20–34. [199]

Lalmas, Mounia, and Anastasios Tombros. 2007. Evaluating XML retrieval effectiveness at INEX. *SIGIR Forum* 41(1):40–57. DOI: http://doi.acm.org/10.1145/1273221.1273225. [198]

Lance, G. N., and W. T. Williams. 1967. A general theory of classificatory sorting strategies 1. Hierarchical systems. *Computer Journal* 9(4):373–380. [367]

Langville, Amy, and Carl Meyer. 2006. *Google's PageRank and Beyond: The Science of Search Engine Rankings*. Princeton University Press. [439]

Larsen, Bjornar, and Chinatsu Aone. 1999. Fast and effective text mining using linear-time document clustering. In *Proc. KDD*, pp. 16–22. ACM Press. DOI: http://doi.acm.org/10.1145/312129.312186. [367, 368]

Larson, Ray R. 2005. A fusion approach to XML structured document retrieval. *IR* 8 (4):601–629. DOI: http://dx.doi.org/10.1007/s10791-005-0749-0. [199]

Lavrenko, Victor, and W. Bruce Croft. 2001. Relevance-based language models. In *Proc. SIGIR*, pp. 120–127. ACM Press. [231]

Lawrence, Steve, and C. Lee Giles. 1998. Searching the World Wide Web. *Science* 280 (5360):98–100. URL: citeseer.ist.psu.edu/lawrence98searching.html. [404]

Lawrence, Steve, and C. Lee Giles. 1999. Accessibility of information on the web. *Nature* 500:107–109. [404]

Lee, Whay C., and Edward A. Fox. 1988. *Experimental comparison of schemes for interpreting Boolean queries*. Technical Report TR-88-27, Computer Science, Virginia Polytechnic Institute and State University. [17]

Lempel, Ronny, and Shlomo Moran. 2000. The stochastic approach for link-structure analysis (SALSA) and the TKC effect. *Computer Networks* 33(1–6):387–401. URL: citeseer.ist.psu.edu/lempel00stochastic.html. [440]

Lesk, Michael. 1988. Grab – Inverted indexes with low storage overhead. *Computing Systems* 1:207–220. [76]

Lesk, Michael. 2004. *Understanding Digital Libraries*, 2nd edition. Morgan Kaufmann. [xviii]

Lester, Nicholas, Alistair Moffat, and Justin Zobel. 2005. Fast on-line index construction by geometric partitioning. In *Proc. CIKM*, pp. 776–783. ACM Press. DOI: http://doi.acm.org/10.1145/1099554.1099739. [76]

Lester, Nicholas, Justin Zobel, and Hugh E. Williams. 2006. Efficient online index maintenance for contiguous inverted lists. *IP&M* 42(4):916–933. DOI: http://dx.doi.org/10.1016/j.ipm.2005.09.005. [76]

Levenshtein, Vladimir I. 1965. Binary codes capable of correcting spurious insertions and deletions of ones. *Problems of Information Transmission* 1:8–17. [59]

Lew, Michael S. 2001. *Principles of Visual Information Retrieval*. Springer. [xviii]

Lewis, David D. 1995. Evaluating and optimizing autonomous text classification systems. In *Proc. SIGIR*. ACM Press. [265]

Lewis, David D. 1998. Naive (Bayes) at forty: The independence assumption in information retrieval. In *ECML*, pp. 4–15. Springer. [265]

Lewis, David D., and Karen Spärck Jones. 1996. Natural language processing for information retrieval. *CACM* 39(1):92–101. DOI: http://doi.acm.org/10.1145/234173.234210. [xviii]

Lewis, David D., and Marc Ringuette. 1994. A comparison of two learning algorithms for text categorization. In *SDAIR*, pp. 81–93. [265]

Lewis, David D., Robert E. Schapire, James P. Callan, and Ron Papka. 1996. Training algorithms for linear text classifiers. In *Proc. SIGIR*, pp. 298–306. ACM Press. DOI: http://doi.acm.org/10.1145/243199.243277. [292]

Lewis, David D., Yiming Yang, Tony G. Rose, and Fan Li. 2004. RCV1: A new benchmark collection for text categorization research. *JMLR* 5:361–397. [77, 265]

Li, Fan, and Yiming Yang. 2003. A loss function analysis for classification methods in text categorization. In *Proc. ICML*, pp. 472–479. [261, 319]

Liddy, Elizabeth D. 2005. Automatic document retrieval. In *Encyclopedia of Language and Linguistics*, 2nd edition. Elsevier.

List, Johan, Vojkan Mihajlovic, Georgina Ramírez, Arjen P. Vries, Djoerd Hiemstra, and Henk Ernst Blok. 2005. TIJAH: Embracing IR methods in XML databases. *IR* 8 (4):547–570. DOI: http://dx.doi.org/10.1007/s10791-005-0747-2. [199]

Lita, Lucian Vlad, Abe Ittycheriah, Salim Roukos, and Nanda Kambhatla. 2003. tRuEcasIng. In *Proc. ACL*, pp. 152–159. [43]

Littman, Michael L., Susan T. Dumais, and Thomas K. Landauer. 1998. Automatic cross-language information retrieval using latent semantic indexing. In Gregory Grefenstette (ed.), *Cross Language Information Retrieval*. Kluwer. URL: citeseer.ist.psu.edu/littman98automatic.html. [384]

Liu, Tie-Yan, Yiming Yang, Hao Wan, Hua-Jun Zeng, Zheng Chen, and Wei-Ying Ma. 2005. Support vector machines classification with very large scale taxonomy. *ACM SIGKDD Explorations* 7(1):36–43. [319]

Liu, Xiaoyong, and W. Bruce Croft. 2004. Cluster-based retrieval using language models. In *Proc. SIGIR*, pp. 186–193. ACM Press. DOI: http://doi.acm.org/10.1145/1008992.1009026. [233, 323, 344]

Lloyd, Stuart P. 1982. Least squares quantization in PCM. *IEEE Transactions on Information Theory* 28(2):129–136. [345]

Lodhi, Huma, Craig Saunders, John Shawe-Taylor, Nello Cristianini, and Chris Watkins. 2002. Text classification using string kernels. *JMLR* 2:419–444. [319]

Lombard, Matthew, Cheryl C. Bracken, and Jennifer Snyder-Duch. 2002. Content analysis in mass communication: Assessment and reporting of intercoder reliability. *Human Communication Research* 28:587–604. [160]

Long, Xiaohui, and Torsten Suel. 2003. Optimized query execution in large search engines with global page ordering. In *Proc. VLDB*. URL: citeseer.ist.psu.edu/long03optimized.html. [137]

Lovins, Julie Beth. 1968. Development of a stemming algorithm. *Translation and Computational Linguistics* 11(1):22–31. [31]

Lu, Wei, Stephen E. Robertson, and Andrew MacFarlane. 2007. CISR at INEX 2006. In Fuhr et al. (2007), pp. 57–63. [199]

Luhn, Hans Peter. 1957. A statistical approach to mechanized encoding and searching of literary information. *IBM Journal of Research and Development* 1(4):309–317. [122]

Luhn, Hans Peter. 1958. The automatic creation of literature abstracts. *IBM Journal of Research and Development* 2(2):159–165, 317. [122]

Luk, Robert W. P., and Kui-Lam Kwok. 2002. A comparison of Chinese document indexing strategies and retrieval models. *ACM Transactions on Asian Language Information Processing* 1(3):225–268. [43]

Lunde, Ken. 1998. *CJKV Information Processing*. O'Reilly. [43]

MacFarlane, A., J.A. McCann, and S.E. Robertson. 2000. Parallel search using partitioned inverted files. In *Proc. SPIRE*, pp. 209–220. [419]

MacQueen, James B. 1967. Some methods for classification and analysis of multivariate observations. In *Proc. Berkeley Symposium on Mathematics, Statistics and Probability*, pp. 281–297. University of California Press. [345]

Manning, Christopher D., and Hinrich Schütze. 1999. *Foundations of Statistical Natural Language Processing*. MIT Press. [xviii, 37, 97, 264, 342]

Maron, M. E., and J. L. Kuhns. 1960. On relevance, probabilistic indexing, and information retrieval. *JACM* 7(3):216–244. [216, 265]

Mass, Yosi, Matan Mandelbrod, Einat Amitay, David Carmel, Yoëlle S. Maarek, and Aya Soffer. 2003. JuruXML – An XML retrieval system at INEX'02. In Fuhr et al. (2003b), pp. 73–80. URL: http://inex.is.informatik.uni-duisburg.de:2003/proceedings.pdf. [199]

McBryan, Oliver A. 1994. GENVL and WWWW: Tools for Taming the Web. In *Proc. WWW*. URL: citeseer.ist.psu.edu/mcbryan94genvl.html. [404, 439]

McCallum, Andrew, and Kamal Nigam. 1998. A comparison of event models for Naive Bayes text classification. In *Working Notes of the 1998 AAAI/ICML Workshop on Learning for Text Categorization*, pp. 41–48. [265]

McCallum, Andrew, Ronald Rosenfeld, Tom M. Mitchell, and Andrew Y. Ng. 1998. Improving text classification by shrinkage in a hierarchy of classes. In *Proc. ICML*, pp. 359–367. Morgan Kaufmann. [319]

McCallum, Andrew Kachites. 1996. Bow: A toolkit for statistical language modeling, text retrieval, classification and clustering. URL: www.cs.cmu.edu/~mccallum/bow. [289]

McKeown, Kathleen, and Dragomir R. Radev. 1995. Generating summaries of multiple news articles. In *Proc. SIGIR*, pp. 74–82. ACM Press. DOI: http://doi.acm.org/10.1145/215206.215334. [368]

McKeown, Kathleen R., Regina Barzilay, David Evans, Vasileios Hatzivassiloglou, Judith L. Klavans, Ani Nenkova, Carl Sable, Barry Schiffman, and Sergey Sigelman. 2002. Tracking and summarizing news on a daily basis with Columbia's Newsblaster. In *Proc. Human Language Technology Conference*. [323, 344]

McLachlan, Geoffrey J., and Thiriyambakam Krishnan. 1996. *The EM Algorithm and Extensions*. John Wiley & Sons. [345]

Meadow, Charles T., Donald H. Kraft, and Bert R. Boyce. 1999. *Text Information Retrieval Systems*. Academic Press.

Meilă, Marina. 2005. Comparing clusterings – An axiomatic view. In *Proc. ICML*. [345]

Melnik, Sergey, Sriram Raghavan, Beverly Yang, and Hector Garcia-Molina. 2001. Building a distributed full-text index for the web. In *Proc. WWW*, pp. 396–406. ACM Press. DOI: http://doi.acm.org/10.1145/371920.372095. [76]

Mihajlović, Vojkan, Henk Ernst Blok, Djoerd Hiemstra, and Peter M. G. Apers. 2005. Score region algebra: Building a transparent XML-R database. In *Proc. CIKM*, pp. 12–19. ACM Press. DOI: http://doi.acm.org/10.1145/1099554.1099560. [199]

Miller, David R. H., Tim Leek, and Richard M. Schwartz. 1999. A hidden Markov model information retrieval system. In *Proc. SIGIR*, pp. 214–221. ACM Press.

Minsky, Marvin Lee, and Seymour Papert (eds.). 1988. *Perceptrons: An Introduction to Computational Geometry*. MIT Press. Expanded edition. [292]

Mitchell, Tom M. 1997. *Machine Learning*. McGraw-Hill. [264]

Moffat, Alistair, and Timothy A. H. Bell. 1995. In situ generation of compressed inverted files. *JASIS* 46(7):537–550. [76]

Moffat, Alistair, and Lang Stuiver. 1996. Exploiting clustering in inverted file compression. In *Proc. Conference on Data Compression*, pp. 82–91. IEEE Computer Society. [98]

Moffat, Alistair, and Justin Zobel. 1992. Parameterised compression for sparse bitmaps. In *Proc. SIGIR*, pp. 274–285. ACM Press. DOI: http://doi.acm.org/10.1145/133160.133210. [98]

Moffat, Alistair, and Justin Zobel. 1996. Self-indexing inverted files for fast text retrieval. *TOIS* 14(4):349–379. [44]

Moffat, Alistair, and Justin Zobel. 1998. Exploring the similarity space. *SIGIR Forum* 32(1). [123]

Mooers, Calvin. 1961. From a point of view of mathematical etc. techniques. In R. A. Fairthorne (ed.), *Towards Information Retrieval*, pp. xvii–xxiii. Butterworths. [17]

Mooers, Calvin E. 1950. Coding, information retrieval, and the rapid selector. *American Documentation* 1(4):225–229. [16]

Moschitti, Alessandro. 2003. A study on optimal parameter tuning for Rocchio text classifier. In *Proc. ECIR*, pp. 420–435. [292]

Moschitti, Alessandro, and Roberto Basili. 2004. Complex linguistic features for text classification: A comprehensive study. In *Proc. ECIR*, pp. 181–196. [319]

Murata, Masaki, Qing Ma, Kiyotaka Uchimoto, Hiromi Ozaku, Masao Utiyama, and Hitoshi Isahara. 2000. Japanese probabilistic information retrieval using location and category information. In *Proc. International Workshop on Information Retrieval With Asian Languages*, pp. 81–88. URL: http://portal.acm.org/citation.cfm?doid=355214.355226. [312]

Muresan, Gheorghe, and David J. Harper. 2004. Topic modeling for mediated access to very large document collections. *JASIST* 55(10):892–910. DOI: http://dx.doi.org/10.1002/asi.20034. [344]

Murtagh, Fionn. 1983. A survey of recent advances in hierarchical clustering algorithms. *Computer Journal* 26(4):354–359. [367]

Najork, Marc, and Allan Heydon. 2001. *High-performance web crawling*. Technical Report 173, Compaq Systems Research Center. [419]

Najork, Marc, and Allan Heydon. 2002. High-performance web crawling. In Panos Pardalos, James Abello and Mauricio Resende (eds.), *Handbook of Massive Data Sets*, chapter 2. Kluwer. [419]

Navarro, Gonzalo, and Ricardo Baeza-Yates. 1997. Proximal nodes: A model to query document databases by content and structure. *TOIS* 15(4):400–435. DOI: http://doi.acm.org/10.1145/263479.263482. [200]

Newsam, Shawn, Sitaram Bhagavathy, and B. S. Manjunath. 2001. Category-based image retrieval. In *IEEE International Conference on Image Processing, Special Session on Multimedia Indexing, Browsing and Retrieval*, pp. 596–599. [164]

Ng, Andrew Y., and Michael I. Jordan. 2001. On discriminative vs. generative classifiers: A comparison of logistic regression and Naive Bayes. In *NIPS*, pp. 841–848. URL: www-2.cs.cmu.edu/Groups/NIPS/NIPS2001/papers/psgz/AA28.ps.gz. [265, 308]

Ng, Andrew Y., Michael I. Jordan, and Yair Weiss. 2001a. On spectral clustering: Analysis and an algorithm. In *Proc. NIPS*, pp. 849–856. [368]

Ng, Andrew Y., Alice X. Zheng, and Michael I. Jordan. 2001b. Link analysis, eigenvectors and stability. In *Proc. IJCAI*, pp. 903–910. URL: citeseer.ist.psu.edu/ng01link.html. [439, 440]

Nigam, Kamal, Andrew McCallum, and Tom Mitchell. 2006. Semi-supervised text classification using EM. In Chapelle et al. (2006), pp. 33–56. [320]

Ntoulas, Alexandros, and Junghoo Cho. 2007. Pruning policies for two-tiered inverted index with correctness guarantee. In *Proc. SIGIR*, pp. 191–198. ACM Press. [97]

Oard, Douglas W., and Bonnie J. Dorr. 1996. *A survey of multilingual text retrieval*. Technical Report UMIACS-TR-96-19, Institute for Advanced Computer Studies, University of Maryland, College Park, MD, USA. [xviii]

Ogilvie, Paul, and Jamie Callan. 2005. Parameter estimation for a simple hierarchical generative model for XML retrieval. In *Proc. INEX*, pp. 211–224. DOI: http://dx.doi.org/10.1007/11766278_16. [199]

O'Keefe, Richard A., and Andrew Trotman. 2004. The simplest query language that could possibly work. In Fuhr et al. (2005), pp. 167–174. [199]

Osiński, Stanisław, and Dawid Weiss. 2005. A concept-driven algorithm for clustering search results. *IEEE Intelligent Systems* 20(3):48–54. [368]

Page, Lawrence, Sergey Brin, Rajeev Motwani, and Terry Winograd. 1998. The PageRank citation ranking: Bringing order to the web. Technical report, Stanford Digital Library Technologies Project. URL: citeseer.ist.psu.edu/page98pagerank.html. [439]

Paice, Chris D. 1990. Another stemmer. *SIGIR Forum* 24(3):56–61. [31]

Papineni, Kishore. 2001. Why inverse document frequency? In *North American Chapter of the Association for Computational Linguistics*, pp. 1–8. [122]

Pavlov, Dmitry, Ramnath Balasubramanyan, Byron Dom, Shyam Kapur, and Jignashu Parikh. 2004. Document preprocessing for naive Bayes classification and clustering with mixture of multinomials. In *Proc. KDD*, pp. 829–834. [265]

Pelleg, Dan, and Andrew Moore. 1999. Accelerating exact k-means algorithms with geometric reasoning. In *Proc. KDD*, pp. 277–281. ACM Press. DOI: http://doi.acm.org/10.1145/312129.312248. [345]

Pelleg, Dan, and Andrew Moore. 2000. X-means: Extending k-means with efficient estimation of the number of clusters. In *Proc. ICML*, pp. 727–734. Morgan Kaufmann. [345]

Perkins, Simon, Kevin Lacker, and James Theiler. 2003. Grafting: Fast, incremental feature selection by gradient descent in function space. *JMLR* 3:1333–1356. [265]

Persin, Michael. 1994. Document filtering for fast ranking. In *Proc. SIGIR*, pp. 339–348. ACM Press. [137]

Persin, Michael, Justin Zobel, and Ron Sacks-Davis. 1996. Filtered document retrieval with frequency-sorted indexes. *JASIS* 47(10):749–764. [137]

Peterson, James L. 1980. Computer programs for detecting and correcting spelling errors. *CACM* 23(12):676–687. DOI: http://doi.acm.org/10.1145/359038.359041. [59]

Picca, Davide, Benoît Curdy, and François Bavaud. 2006. Non-linear correspondence analysis in text retrieval: A kernel view. In *Proc. JADT*. [283]

Pinski, Gabriel, and Francis Narin. 1976. Citation influence for journal aggregates of scientific publications: Theory, with application to the literature of Physics. *IP&M* 12:297–326. [439]

Pirolli, Peter L. T. 2007. *Information Foraging Theory: Adaptive Interaction With Information*. Oxford University Press. [344]

Platt, John. 2000. Probabilistic outputs for support vector machines and comparisons to regularized likelihood methods. In A.J. Smola, P.L. Bartlett, B. Schölkopf, and D. Schuurmans (eds.), *Advances in Large Margin Classifiers*, pp. 61–74. MIT Press. [298]

Ponte, Jay M., and W. Bruce Croft. 1998. A language modeling approach to information retrieval. In *Proc. SIGIR*, pp. 275–281. ACM Press. [227, 228, 229]

Popescul, Alexandrin, and Lyle H. Ungar. 2000. Automatic labeling of document clusters. Unpublished. [367]

Porter, Martin F. 1980. An algorithm for suffix stripping. *Program* 14(3):130–137. [31]

Pugh, William. 1990. Skip lists: A probabilistic alternative to balanced trees. *CACM* 33(6):668–676. [44]

Qin, Tao, Tie-Yan Liu, Wei Lai, Xu-Dong Zhang, De-Sheng Wang, and Hang Li. 2007. Ranking with multiple hyperplanes. In *Proc. SIGIR*. ACM Press. [320]

Qiu, Yonggang, and H.P. Frei. 1993. Concept based query expansion. In *Proc. SIGIR*, pp. 160–169. ACM Press. [177]

R Development Core Team. 2005. *R: A language and environment for statistical computing*. R Foundation for Statistical Computing, Vienna, Austria. URL: www.R-project.org. ISBN 3-900051-07-0. [342, 368]

Radev, Dragomir R., Sasha Blair-Goldensohn, Zhu Zhang, and Revathi Sundara Raghavan. 2001. Interactive, domain-independent identification and summarization of topically related news articles. In *Proc. European Conference on Research and Advanced Technology for Digital Libraries*, pp. 225–238. [344]

Rahm, Erhard, and Philip A. Bernstein. 2001. A survey of approaches to automatic schema matching. *VLDB Journal* 10(4):334–350. URL: citeseer.ist.psu.edu/rahm01survey.html. [198]

Rand, William M. 1971. Objective criteria for the evaluation of clustering methods. *Journal of the American Statistical Association* 66(336):846–850. [344]

Rasmussen, Edie. 1992. Clustering algorithms. In Frakes and Baeza-Yates (1992), pp. 419–442. [344]

Rennie, Jason D., Lawrence Shih, Jaime Teevan, and David R. Karger. 2003. Tackling the poor assumptions of naive Bayes text classifiers. In *Proc. ICML*, pp. 616–623. [265]

Ribeiro-Neto, Berthier, Edleno S. Moura, Marden S. Neubert, and Nivio Ziviani. 1999. Efficient distributed algorithms to build inverted files. In *Proc. SIGIR*, pp. 105–112. ACM Press. DOI: http://doi.acm.org/10.1145/312624.312663. [76]

Ribeiro-Neto, Berthier A., and Ramurti A. Barbosa. 1998. Query performance for tightly coupled distributed digital libraries. In *ACM Conference on Digital Libraries*, pp. 182–190. [420]

Rice, John A. 2006. *Mathematical Statistics and Data Analysis*. Duxbury Press. [91, 216, 256]

Richardson, M., A. Prakash, and E. Brill. 2006. Beyond PageRank: machine learning for static ranking. In *Proc. WWW*, pp. 707–715. [320]

Riezler, Stefan, Alexander Vasserman, Ioannis Tsochantaridis, Vibhu Mittal, and Yi Liu. 2007. Statistical machine translation for query expansion in answer retrieval. In *Proc. ACL*, pp. 464–471. Association for Computational Linguistics. URL: www.aclweb.org/anthology/P/P07/P07-1059. [177]

Ripley, B. D. 1996. *Pattern Recognition and Neural Networks*. Cambridge University Press. [204, 216]

Robertson, Stephen. 2005. How Okapi came to TREC. In Voorhees and Harman (2005), pp. 287–299. [216]

Robertson, Stephen, Hugo Zaragoza, and Michael Taylor. 2004. Simple BM25 extension to multiple weighted fields. In *Proc. CIKM*, pp. 42–49. ACM Press. DOI: http://doi.acm.org/10.1145/1031171.1031181. [217]

Robertson, Stephen E., and Karen Spärck Jones. 1976. Relevance weighting of search terms. *JASIS* 27:129–146. [122, 216]

Rocchio, J. J. 1971. Relevance feedback in information retrieval. In Salton (1971b), pp. 313–323. [166, 177, 291]

Roget, P. M. 1946. *Roget's International Thesaurus*. Thomas Y. Crowell. [177]

Rosen-Zvi, Michal, Thomas Griffiths, Mark Steyvers, and Padhraic Smyth. 2004. The author-topic model for authors and documents. In *Proc. UAI*, pp. 487–494. AUAI Press. [384]

Ross, Sheldon. 2006. *A First Course in Probability*. Pearson Prentice-Hall. [91, 216]

Rusmevichientong, Paat, David M. Pennock, Steve Lawrence, and C. Lee Giles. 2001. Methods for sampling pages uniformly from the world wide web. In *Proc. AAAI Fall Symposium on Using Uncertainty Within Computation*, pp. 121–128. URL: citeseer.ist.psu.edu/rusmevichientong01methods.html. [404]

Ruthven, Ian, and Mounia Lalmas. 2003. A survey on the use of relevance feedback for information access systems. *Knowledge Engineering Review* 18(1). [177]

Sahoo, Nachiketa, Jamie Callan, Ramayya Krishnan, George Duncan, and Rema Padman. 2006. Incremental hierarchical clustering of text documents. In *Proc. CIKM*, pp. 357–366. ACM Press. DOI: http://doi.acm.org/10.1145/1183614.1183667. [368]

Sakai, Tetsuya. 2007. On the reliability of information retrieval metrics based on graded relevance. *IP&M* 43(2):531–548. [160]

Salton, Gerard. 1971a. Cluster search strategies and the optimization of retrieval effectiveness. In *The SMART Retrieval System – Experiments in Automatic Document Processing* Salton (1971b), pp. 223–242. [323, 344]

Salton, Gerard (ed.). 1971b. *The SMART Retrieval System – Experiments in Automatic Document Processing*. Prentice-Hall. [122, 159, 177, 453, 461, 462]

Salton, Gerard. 1975. *Dynamic information and library processing*. Prentice-Hall. [344]

Salton, Gerard. 1989. *Automatic Text Processing: The Transformation, Analysis, and Retrieval of Information by Computer*. Addison Wesley. [43, 177]

Salton, Gerard. 1991. The Smart project in automatic document retrieval. In *Proc. SIGIR*, pp. 356–358. ACM Press. [159]

Salton, Gerard, James Allan, and Chris Buckley. 1993. Approaches to passage retrieval in full text information systems. In *Proc. SIGIR*, pp. 49–58. ACM Press. DOI: http://doi.acm.org/10.1145/160688.160693. [199]

Salton, Gerard, and Chris Buckley. 1987. *Term weighting approaches in automatic text retrieval*. Technical report, Cornell University, Ithaca, NY. [122]

Salton, Gerard, and Christopher Buckley. 1988. Term-weighting approaches in automatic text retrieval. *IP&M* 24(5):513–523. [123]

Salton, Gerard, and Chris Buckley. 1990. Improving retrieval performance by relevance feedback. *JASIS* 41(4):288–297. [177]

Saracevic, Tefko, and Paul Kantor. 1988. A study of information seeking and retrieving. II: Users, questions and effectiveness. *JASIS* 39:177–196. [159]

Saracevic, Tefko, and Paul Kantor. 1996. A study of information seeking and retrieving. III: Searchers, searches, overlap. *JASIS* 39(3):197–216. [159]

Savaresi, Sergio M., and Daniel Boley. 2004. A comparative analysis on the bisecting K-means and the PDDP clustering algorithms. *Intelligent Data Analysis* 8(4):345–362. [368]

Schamber, Linda, Michael Eisenberg, and Michael S. Nilan. 1990. A re-examination of relevance: toward a dynamic, situational definition. *IP&M* 26(6):755–776. [160]

Schapire, Robert E. 2003. The boosting approach to machine learning: An overview. In D. D. Denison, M. H. Hansen, C. Holmes, B. Mallick, and B. Yu (eds.), *Nonlinear Estimation and Classification*. Springer. [319]

Schapire, Robert E., and Yoram Singer. 2000. Boostexter: A boosting-based system for text categorization. *Machine Learning* 39(2/3):135–168. [319]

Schapire, Robert E., Yoram Singer, and Amit Singhal. 1998. Boosting and Rocchio applied to text filtering. In *Proc. SIGIR*, pp. 215–223. ACM Press. [291, 292]

Schlieder, Torsten, and Holger Meuss. 2002. Querying and ranking XML documents. *JASIST* 53(6):489–503. DOI: http://dx.doi.org/10.1002/asi.10060. [199]

Scholer, Falk, Hugh E. Williams, John Yiannis, and Justin Zobel. 2002. Compression of inverted indexes for fast query evaluation. In *Proc. SIGIR*, pp. 222–229. ACM Press. DOI: http://doi.acm.org/10.1145/564376.564416. [98]

Schölkopf, Bernhard, and Alexander J. Smola. 2001. *Learning with Kernels: Support Vector Machines, Regularization, Optimization, and Beyond*. MIT Press. [319]

Schütze, Hinrich. 1998. Automatic word sense discrimination. *Computational Linguistics* 24(1):97–124. [176, 177]

Schütze, Hinrich, David A. Hull, and Jan O. Pedersen. 1995. A comparison of classifiers and document representations for the routing problem. In *Proc. SIGIR*, pp. 229–237. ACM Press. [177, 265, 292]

Schütze, Hinrich, and Jan O. Pedersen. 1995. Information retrieval based on word senses. In *Proc. SDAIR*, pp. 161–175. [345]

Schütze, Hinrich, and Craig Silverstein. 1997. Projections for efficient document clustering. In *Proc. SIGIR*, pp. 74–81. ACM Press. [344, 383]

Schwarz, Gideon. 1978. Estimating the dimension of a model. *Annals of Statistics* 6(2): 461–464. [345]

Sebastiani, Fabrizio. 2002. Machine learning in automated text categorization. *ACM Computing Surveys* 34(1):1–47. [264]

Shawe-Taylor, John, and Nello Cristianini. 2004. *Kernel Methods for Pattern Analysis*. Cambridge University Press. [319]

Shkapenyuk, Vladislav, and Torsten Suel. 2002. Design and implementation of a high-performance distributed web crawler. In *Proc. International Conference on Data Engineering*. URL: citeseer.ist.psu.edu/shkapenyuk02design.html. [419]

Siegel, Sidney, and N. John Castellan, Jr. 1988. *Nonparametric Statistics for the Behavioral Sciences*, 2nd edition. McGraw-Hill. [160]

Sifry, Dave, 2007. The state of the Live Web, April 2007. URL: http://technorati.com/weblog/2007/04/328.html. [29]

Sigurbjörnsson, Börkur, Jaap Kamps, and Maarten de Rijke. 2004. Mixture models, overlap, and structural hints in XML element retrieval. In *Proc. INEX*, pp. 196–210. [199]

Silverstein, Craig, Monika Rauch Henzinger, Hannes Marais, and Michael Moricz. 1999. Analysis of a very large web search engine query log. *SIGIR Forum* 33(1): 6–12. [44]

Silvestri, Fabrizio. 2007. Sorting out the document identifier assignment problem. In *Proc. ECIR*, pp. 101–112. [98]

Silvestri, Fabrizio, Raffaele Perego, and Salvatore Orlando. 2004. Assigning document identifiers to enhance compressibility of web search engines indexes. In *Proc. ACM Symposium on Applied Computing*, pp. 600–605. [98]

Sindhwani, V., and S. S. Keerthi. 2006. Large scale semi-supervised linear SVMs. In *Proc. SIGIR*, pp. 477–484. [320]

Singhal, Amit, Chris Buckley, and Mandar Mitra. 1996a. Pivoted document length normalization. In *Proc. SIGIR*, pp. 21–29. ACM Press. URL: citeseer.ist.psu.edu/singhal96pivoted.html. [122]

Singhal, Amit, Mandar Mitra, and Chris Buckley. 1997. Learning routing queries in a query zone. In *Proc. SIGIR*, pp. 25–32. ACM Press. [177]

Singhal, Amit, Gerard Salton, and Chris Buckley. 1995. *Length normalization in degraded text collections*. Technical report, Cornell University, Ithaca, NY. [123]

Singhal, Amit, Gerard Salton, and Chris Buckley. 1996b. Length normalization in degraded text collections. In *Proc. SDAIR*, pp. 149–162. [123]

Singitham, Pavan Kumar C., Mahathi S. Mahabhashyam, and Prabhakar Raghavan. 2004. Efficiency-quality tradeoffs for vector score aggregation. In *Proc. VLDB*, pp. 624–635. URL: http://www.vldb.org/conf/2004/RS17P1.PDF. [137, 344]

Smeulders, Arnold W. M., Marcel Worring, Simone Santini, Amarnath Gupta, and Ramesh Jain. 2000. Content-based image retrieval at the end of the early years. *IEEE Trans. Pattern Anal. Mach. Intell.* 22(12):1349–1380. DOI: http://dx.doi.org/10.1109/34.895972. [xviii]

Sneath, Peter H.A., and Robert R. Sokal. 1973. *Numerical Taxonomy: The Principles and Practice of Numerical Classification*. W.H. Freeman. [367]

Snedecor, George Waddel, and William G. Cochran. 1989. *Statistical Methods*. Iowa State University Press. [265]

Somogyi, Zoltan. 1990. *The Melbourne University bibliography system*. Technical Report 90/3, Melbourne University, Parkville, Victoria, Australia. [76]

Song, Ruihua, Ji-Rong Wen, and Wei-Ying Ma. 2005. *Viewing term proximity from a different perspective*. Technical Report MSR-TR-2005-69, Microsoft Research. [138]

Sornil, Ohm. 2001. *Parallel Inverted Index for Large-Scale, Dynamic Digital Libraries.* PhD thesis, Virginia Tech. URL: http://scholar.lib.vt.edu/theses/available/etd-02062001-114915/. [420]

Spärck Jones, Karen. 1972. A statistical interpretation of term specificity and its application in retrieval. *Journal of Documentation* 28(1):11–21. [122]

Spärck Jones, Karen. 2004. Language modelling's generative model: Is it rational? MS, Computer Laboratory, University of Cambridge. URL: http://www.cl.cam.ac.uk/~ksj21/langmodnote4.pdf. [233]

Spärck Jones, Karen, S. Walker, and Stephen E. Robertson. 2000. A probabilistic model of information retrieval: Development and comparative experiments. *IP&M* 36(6): 779–808, 809–840. [214, 215, 216]

Spink, Amanda, and Charles Cole (eds.). 2005. *New Directions in Cognitive Information Retrieval.* Springer. [161]

Spink, Amanda, Bernard J. Jansen, and H. Cenk Ozmultu. 2000. Use of query reformulation and relevance feedback by Excite users. *Internet Research: Electronic Networking Applications and Policy* 10(4):317–328. URL: http://ist.psu.edu/faculty_pages/jjansen/academic/pubs/internetresearch2000.pdf. [170]

Sproat, Richard, and Thomas Emerson. 2003. The first international Chinese word segmentation bakeoff. In *SIGHAN Workshop on Chinese Language Processing.* [43]

Sproat, Richard, William Gale, Chilin Shih, and Nancy Chang. 1996. A stochastic finite-state word-segmentation algorithm for Chinese. *Computational Linguistics* 22 (3):377–404. [43]

Sproat, Richard William. 1992. *Morphology and Computation.* MIT Press. [43]

Stein, Benno, and Sven Meyer zu Eissen. 2004. Topic identification: Framework and application. In *Proc. International Conference on Knowledge Management.* [367]

Stein, Benno, Sven Meyer zu Eissen, and Frank Wißbrock. 2003. On cluster validity and the information need of users. In *Proc. Artificial Intelligence and Applications.* [344]

Steinbach, Michael, George Karypis, and Vipin Kumar. 2000. A comparison of document clustering techniques. In *KDD Workshop on Text Mining.* [368]

Strang, Gilbert (ed.). 1986. *Introduction to Applied Mathematics.* Wellesley-Cambridge Press. [383]

Strehl, Alexander. 2002. *Relationship-based Clustering and Cluster Ensembles for High-dimensional Data Mining.* PhD thesis, The University of Texas at Austin. [344]

Strohman, Trevor, and W. Bruce Croft. 2007. Efficient document retrieval in main memory. In *Proc. SIGIR*, pp. 175–182. ACM Press. [44]

Swanson, Don R. 1988. Historical note: Information retrieval and the future of an illusion. *JASIS* 39(2):92–98. [159, 177]

Tague-Sutcliffe, Jean, and James Blustein. 1995. A statistical analysis of the TREC-3 data. In *Proc. TREC*, pp. 385–398. [160]

Tan, Songbo, and Xueqi Cheng. 2007. Using hypothesis margin to boost centroid text classifier. In *Proc. ACM Symposium on Applied Computing*, pp. 398–403. ACM Press. DOI: http://doi.acm.org/10.1145/1244002.1244096. [291]

Tannier, Xavier, and Shlomo Geva. 2005. XML retrieval with a natural language interface. In *Proc. SPIRE*, pp. 29–40. [200]

Tao, Tao, Xuanhui Wang, Qiaozhu Mei, and ChengXiang Zhai. 2006. Language model information retrieval with document expansion. In *Proc. Human Language Technology Conference/North American Chapter of the Association for Computational Linguistics*, pp. 407–414. [233]

Taube, Mortimer, and Harold Wooster (eds.). 1958. *Information Storage and Retrieval: Theory, Systems, and Devices.* Columbia University Press. [16]

Taylor, Michael, Hugo Zaragoza, Nick Craswell, Stephen Robertson, and Chris Burges. 2006. Optimisation methods for ranking functions with multiple parameters. In *Proc. CIKM.* ACM Press. [320]

Teh, Yee Whye, Michael I. Jordan, Matthew J. Beal, and David M. Blei. 2006. Hierarchical Dirichlet processes. *Journal of the American Statistical Association* 101(476): 1566–1581. [384]

Theobald, Martin, Holger Bast, Debapriyo Majumdar, Ralf Schenkel, and Gerhard Weikum. 2008. TopX: Efficient and versatile top-k query processing for semistructured data. *VLDB Journal* 17(1):81–115. [199]

Theobald, Martin, Ralf Schenkel, and Gerhard Weikum. 2005. An efficient and versatile query engine for TopX search. In *Proc. VLDB*, pp. 625–636. VLDB Endowment. [199]

Tibshirani, Robert, Guenther Walther, and Trevor Hastie. 2001. Estimating the number of clusters in a data set via the gap statistic. *Journal of the Royal Statistical Society Series B* 63:411–423. [345]

Tishby, Naftali, and Noam Slonim. 2000. Data clustering by Markovian relaxation and the information bottleneck method. In *Proc. NIPS*, pp. 640–646. [345]

Toda, Hiroyuki, and Ryoji Kataoka. 2005. A search result clustering method using informatively named entities. In *Proc. Annual ACM International Workshop on Web Information and Data Management*, pp. 81–86. ACM Press. DOI: http://doi.acm.org/ 10.1145/1097047.1097063. [344]

Tomasic, Anthony, and Hector Garcia-Molina. 1993. Query processing and inverted indices in shared-nothing document information retrieval systems. *VLDB Journal* 2 (3):243–275. [419]

Tombros, Anastasios, and Mark Sanderson. 1998. Advantages of query biased summaries in information retrieval. In *Proc. SIGIR*, pp. 2–10. ACM Press. DOI: http://doi.acm.org/10.1145/290941.290947. [161]

Tombros, Anastasios, Robert Villa, and C. J. van Rijsbergen. 2002. The effectiveness of query-specific hierarchic clustering in information retrieval. *IP&M* 38(4):559–582. DOI: http://dx.doi.org/10.1016/S0306-4573(01)00048-6. [344]

Tomlinson, Stephen. 2003. Lexical and algorithmic stemming compared for 9 European languages with Hummingbird Searchserver at CLEF 2003. In *Proc. Cross-Language Evaluation Forum*, pp. 286–300. [43]

Tong, Simon, and Daphne Koller. 2001. Support vector machine active learning with applications to text classification. *JMLR* 2:45–66. [320]

Toutanova, Kristina, and Robert C. Moore. 2002. Pronunciation modeling for improved spelling correction. In *Proc. ACL*, pp. 144–151. [60]

Treeratpituk, Pucktada, and Jamie Callan. 2006. An experimental study on automatically labeling hierarchical clusters using statistical features. In *Proc. SIGIR*, pp. 707–708. ACM Press. DOI: http://doi.acm.org/10.1145/1148170.1148328. [368]

Trotman, Andrew. 2003. Compressing inverted files. *IR* 6(1):5–19. DOI: http://dx.doi. org/10.1023/A:1022949613039. [98]

Trotman, Andrew, and Shlomo Geva. 2006. Passage retrieval and other XML-retrieval tasks. In *SIGIR 2006 Workshop on XML Element Retrieval Methodology*, pp. 43–50. [199]

Trotman, Andrew, Shlomo Geva, and Jaap Kamps (eds.). 2007. *Proc. SIGIR 2007 Workshop on Focused Retrieval*. University of Otago, Dunedin, New Zealand. [199]

Trotman, Andrew, Nils Pharo, and Miro Lehtonen. 2006. XML-IR users and use cases. In *Proc. INEX*, pp. 400–412. [198]

Trotman, Andrew, and Börkur Sigurbjörnsson. 2004. Narrowed Extended XPath I (NEXI). In Fuhr et al. (2005), pp. 16–40. DOI: http://dx.doi.org/10.1007/11424550_2. [199]

Tseng, Huihsin, Pichuan Chang, Galen Andrew, Daniel Jurafsky, and Christopher Manning. 2005. A conditional random field word segmenter. In *SIGHAN Workshop on Chinese Language Processing*. [43]

Tsochantaridis, Ioannis, Thorsten Joachims, Thomas Hofmann, and Yasemin Altun. 2005. Large margin methods for structured and interdependent output variables. *JMLR* 6:1453–1484. [319]

Turpin, Andrew, and William R. Hersh. 2001. Why batch and user evaluations do not give the same results. In *Proc. SIGIR*, pp. 225–231.

Turpin, Andrew, and William R. Hersh. 2002. User interface effects in past batch versus user experiments. In *Proc. SIGIR*, pp. 431–432.

Turpin, Andrew, Yohannes Tsegay, David Hawking, and Hugh E. Williams. 2007. Fast generation of result snippets in web search. In *Proc. SIGIR*, pp. 127–134. ACM Press. [161]

Turtle, Howard. 1994. Natural language vs. Boolean query evaluation: A comparison of retrieval performance. In *Proc. SIGIR*, pp. 212–220. ACM Press. [15]

Turtle, Howard, and W. Bruce Croft. 1989. Inference networks for document retrieval. In *Proc. SIGIR*, pp. 1–24. ACM Press. [215]

Turtle, Howard, and W. Bruce Croft. 1991. Evaluation of an inference network-based retrieval model. *TOIS* 9(3):187–222. [215]

Turtle, Howard, and James Flood. 1995. Query evaluation: strategies and optimizations. *IP&M* 31(6):831–850. DOI: http://dx.doi.org/10.1016/0306-4573(95)00020-H. [123]

Vaithyanathan, Shivakumar, and Byron Dom. 2000. Model-based hierarchical clustering. In *Proc. UAI*, pp. 599–608. Morgan Kaufmann. [368]

van Rijsbergen, C. J. 1979. *Information Retrieval*, 2nd edition. Butterworths. [159, 198, 203, 213, 216]

van Rijsbergen, C. J. 1989. Towards an information logic. In *SIGIR*, pp. 77–86. ACM Press. DOI: http://doi.acm.org/10.1145/75334.75344. [xviii]

van Zwol, Roelof, Jeroen Baas, Herre van Oostendorp, and Frans Wiering. 2006. Bricks: The building blocks to tackle query formulation in structured document retrieval. In *Proc. ECIR*, pp. 314–325. [200]

Vapnik, Vladimir N. 1998. *Statistical Learning Theory*. Wiley-Interscience. [319]

Vittaut, Jean-Noël, and Patrick Gallinari. 2006. Machine learning ranking for structured information retrieval. In *Proc. ECIR*, pp. 338–349. [199]

Voorhees, Ellen M. 1985a. The cluster hypothesis revisited. In *Proc. SIGIR*, pp. 188–196. ACM Press. [344]

Voorhees, Ellen M. 1985b. *The effectiveness and efficiency of agglomerative hierarchic clustering in document retrieval*. Technical Report TR 85-705, Cornell. [367]

Voorhees, Ellen M. 2000. Variations in relevance judgments and the measurement of retrieval effectiveness. *IP&M* 36:697–716. [160]

Voorhees, Ellen M., and Donna Harman (eds.). 2005. *TREC: Experiment and Evaluation in Information Retrieval*. MIT Press. [159, 453, 461]

Wagner, Robert A., and Michael J. Fischer. 1974. The string-to-string correction problem. *JACM* 21(1):168–173. DOI: http://doi.acm.org/10.1145/321796.321811. [59]

Ward Jr., J. H. 1963. Hierarchical grouping to optimize an objective function. *Journal of the American Statistical Association* 58:236–244. [367]

Wei, Xing, and W. Bruce Croft. 2006. LDA-based document models for ad-hoc retrieval. In *Proc. SIGIR*, pp. 178–185. ACM Press. DOI: http://doi.acm.org/10.1145/1148170.1148204. [384]

Weigend, Andreas S., Erik D. Wiener, and Jan O. Pedersen. 1999. Exploiting hierarchy in text categorization. *IR* 1(3):193–216. [319]

Weston, Jason, and Chris Watkins. 1999. Support vector machines for multi-class pattern recognition. In *Proc. European Symposium on Artificial Neural Networks*, pp. 219–224. [319]

Williams, Hugh E., and Justin Zobel. 2005. Searchable words on the web. *International Journal on Digital Libraries* 5(2):99–105. DOI: http://dx.doi.org/10.1007/s00799-003-0050-z. [97]

Williams, Hugh E., Justin Zobel, and Dirk Bahle. 2004. Fast phrase querying with combined indexes. *TOIS* 22(4):573–594. [41]

Witten, Ian H., and Timothy C. Bell. 1990. Source models for natural language text. *International Journal Man-Machine Studies* 32(5):545–579. [97]

Witten, Ian H., and Eibe Frank. 2005. *Data Mining: Practical Machine Learning Tools and Techniques*, 2nd edition. Morgan Kaufmann. [342]

Witten, Ian H., Alistair Moffat, and Timothy C. Bell. 1999. *Managing Gigabytes: Compressing and Indexing Documents and Images*, 2nd edition. Morgan Kaufmann. [76, 97, 98]

Wong, S. K. Michael, Yiyu Yao, and Peter Bollmann. 1988. Linear structure in information retrieval. In *Proc. SIGIR*, pp. 219–232. ACM Press. [320]

Woodley, Alan, and Shlomo Geva. 2006. NLPX at INEX 2006. In *Proc. INEX*, pp. 302–311. [200]

Xu, Jinxi, and W. Bruce Croft. 1996. Query expansion using local and global document analysis. In *Proc. SIGIR*, pp. 4–11. ACM Press. [177]

Xu, Jinxi, and W. Bruce Croft. 1999. Cluster-based language models for distributed retrieval. In *Proc. SIGIR*, pp. 254–261. ACM Press. DOI: http://doi.acm.org/10.1145/312624.312687. [344]

Yang, Hui, and Jamie Callan. 2006. Near-duplicate detection by instance-level constrained clustering. In *Proc. SIGIR*, pp. 421–428. ACM Press. DOI: http://doi.acm.org/10.1145/1148170.1148243. [344]

Yang, Yiming. 1994. Expert network: Effective and efficient learning from human decisions in text categorization and retrieval. In *Proc. SIGIR*, pp. 13–22. ACM Press. [291]

Yang, Yiming. 1999. An evaluation of statistical approaches to text categorization. *IR* 1:69–90. [319]

Yang, Yiming. 2001. A study of thresholding strategies for text categorization. In *Proc. SIGIR*, pp. 137–145. ACM Press. DOI: http://doi.acm.org/10.1145/383952.383975. [292]

Yang, Yiming, and Bryan Kisiel. 2003. Margin-based local regression for adaptive filtering. In *Proc. CIKM*, pp. 191–198. ACM Press. DOI: http://doi.acm.org/10.1145/956863.956902. [292]

Yang, Yiming, and Xin Liu. 1999. A re-examination of text categorization methods. In *Proc. SIGIR*, pp. 42–49. ACM Press. [265, 319]

Yang, Yiming, and Jan Pedersen. 1997. Feature selection in statistical learning of text categorization. In *Proc. ICML*. [265]

Yue, Yisong, Thomas Finley, Filip Radlinski, and Thorsten Joachims. 2007. A support vector method for optimizing average precision. In *Proc. SIGIR*. ACM Press. [320]

Zamir, Oren, and Oren Etzioni. 1999. Grouper: A dynamic clustering interface to web search results. In *Proc. WWW*, pp. 1361–1374. Elsevier North-Holland. DOI: http://dx.doi.org/10.1016/S1389-1286(99)00054-7. [344, 368]

Zaragoza, Hugo, Djoerd Hiemstra, Michael Tipping, and Stephen Robertson. 2003. Bayesian extension to the language model for ad hoc information retrieval. In *Proc. SIGIR*, pp. 4–9. ACM Press. [232]

Zavrel, Jakub, Peter Berck, and Willem Lavrijssen. 2000. Information extraction by text classification: Corpus mining for features. In *Proc. Workshop Information Extraction meets Corpus Linguistics*. URL: http://www.cnts.ua.ac.be/Publications/2000/ZBL00. Held in conjunction with LREC-2000. [292]

Zha, Hongyuan, Xiaofeng He, Chris H. Q. Ding, Ming Gu, and Horst D. Simon. 2001. Bipartite graph partitioning and data clustering. In *Proc. CIKM*, pp. 25–32. ACM Press. [345, 368]

Zhai, Chengxiang, and John Lafferty. 2001a. Model-based feedback in the language modeling approach to information retrieval. In *Proc. CIKM*. ACM Press. [231]

Zhai, Chengxiang, and John Lafferty. 2001b. A study of smoothing methods for language models applied to ad hoc information retrieval. In *Proc. SIGIR*, pp. 334–342. ACM Press. [232]

Zhai, ChengXiang, and John Lafferty. 2002. Two-stage language models for information retrieval. In *Proc. SIGIR*, pp. 49–56. ACM Press. DOI: http://doi.acm.org/10.1145/564376.564387. [233]

Zhang, Jiangong, Xiaohui Long, and Torsten Suel. 2007. Performance of compressed inverted list caching in search engines. In *Proc. CIKM*. ACM Press. [98]

Zhang, Tong, and Frank J. Oles. 2001. Text categorization based on regularized linear classification methods. *IR* 4(1):5–31. URL: citeseer.ist.psu.edu/zhang00text.html. [319]

Zhao, Ying, and George Karypis. 2002. Evaluation of hierarchical clustering algorithms for document datasets. In *Proc. CIKM*, pp. 515–524. ACM Press. DOI: http://doi.acm.org/10.1145/584792.584877. [367]

Zipf, George Kingsley. 1949. *Human Behavior and the Principle of Least Effort*. Addison-Wesley. [97]

Zobel, Justin. 1998. How reliable are the results of large-scale information retrieval experiments? In *Proc. SIGIR*, pp. 307–314. [160]

Zobel, Justin, and Philip Dart. 1995. Finding approximate matches in large lexicons. *Software Practice and Experience* 25(3):331–345. URL: citeseer.ifi.unizh.ch/zobel95finding.html. [60]

Zobel, Justin, and Philip Dart. 1996. Phonetic string matching: Lessons from information retrieval. In *Proc. SIGIR*, pp. 166–173. ACM Press. [60]

Zobel, Justin, and Alistair Moffat. 2006. Inverted files for text search engines. *ACM Computing Surveys* 38(2). [17, 76, 98, 122]

Zobel, Justin, Alistair Moffat, Ross Wilkinson, and Ron Sacks-Davis. 1995. Efficient retrieval of partial documents. *IP&M* 31(3):361–377. DOI: http://dx.doi.org/10.1016/0306-4573(94)00052-5. [199]

Zukowski, Marcin, Sandor Heman, Niels Nes, and Peter Boncz. 2006. Super-scalar RAM-CPU cache compression. In *Proc. International Conference on Data Engineering*, p. 59. IEEE Computer Society. DOI: http://dx.doi.org/10.1109/ICDE.2006.150. [98]

Index